RR | AMERICAN INDIANS

AMERICAN INDIANS

Volume I
Abenaki – Hayes, Ira Hamilton

A Magill Book
from the **Editors of Salem Press**

Consulting Editor
Harvey Markowitz
**D'Arcy McNickle Center for the History
of the American Indian, Newberry Library**

Salem Press, Inc.
Pasadena, California   Englewood Cliffs, New Jersey

Editor in Chief: Dawn P. Dawson

Consulting Editor: Harvey Markowitz   *Project Editor:* McCrea Adams
Research Supervisor: Jeff Jensen   *Photograph Editor:* Valerie Krein
Proofreading Supervisor: Yasmine A. Cordoba   *Production Editor:* Janet Long
Layout: James Hutson   *Illustrations:* Craig Attebery
Maps: Moritz Design

Library of Congress Cataloging-in-Publication Data

American Indians / consulting editor, Harvey Markowitz
    p. cm. — (Ready reference)
"A Magill Book"
Includes bibliographical references and index.
    ISBN 0-89356-757-4 (set : alk. paper) — ISBN 0-89356-758-2 (vol 1 : alk. paper)
    1. Indians of North America—Encyclopedias. 2. Indians of Mexico—Encyclopedias. I. Markowitz, Harvey.
II. Series.
E76.2.A45   1995
970.004'97—dc20   94-47633
                                                                CIP

First Printing

PRINTED IN THE UNITED STATES OF AMERICA

Publisher's Note

American Indian cultures have captured the imagination of Europeans and their American descendants ever since contact began in the late fifteenth century. Yet seldom has a collection of cultural groups been the subject of so many misconceptions as American Indians. The first Europeans to arrive in North America, believing that they had reached Asia, misnamed the people they encountered Indians. Although the inaccuracy of the name was soon realized, ethnocentrism continued to blind Europeans to the reality that the people they were meeting belonged to thousands of distinct cultures (dubbed "tribes" by the Europeans) with nearly as many languages. For the next three hundred years, American Indians were decimated by disease, massacred, driven from their homelands, and characterized as bloodthirsty warriors. At the other extreme, they were romanticized as "noble savages"—an equally unrealistic stereotype.

When the social movements of the 1960's gave birth to Indian activism and Indian studies programs, long-overdue redefinitions of Indian history and culture began to occur. Indian voices were heard as never before, both in the political arena and in the university. Scholars in Indian studies programs fought against the Eurocentric views that had long permeated such academic disciplines as anthropology and history. Tribes increasingly worked together to address such issues as Indian sovereignty and land claims. Indians used the media to educate the non-Indian public about the realities of Indian life in the twentieth century. Today, therefore, any work that attempts to survey American Indian culture and history must encompass ancient cultural traditions, historical Indian-white relations, and contemporary concerns.

In *Ready Reference: American Indians*, it was the goal of the editors of Salem Press to assemble articles on a wide range of American Indian topics—including personages, tribes, organizations, historical events, cultural traditions, and contemporary issues—and to present them in an alphabetical format for ease of access. American Indians are here considered to be the original inhabitants of the areas now included within the United States and Canada. In addition, major Mesoamerican groups such as the Aztec, Maya, and Toltec are included, as are a number of Mesoamerican archaeological sites. This three-volume set, the second installment in the Ready Reference series, contains 1,129 articles, ranging in length from 200 to 3,000 words. The encyclopedic format of this work enables readers to find information easily about subjects broad and narrow. For example, readers seeking information about food and subsistence can begin with overview articles on "Agriculture," "Subsistence," "Hunting and gathering," or "Food preparation and cooking" or can turn to such specific articles as "Acorns," "Corn," and "Squash." An article on "Feasts" expands the discussion further, and articles on specific events, such as the "Green Corn Dance," provide additional information on how food production is related to culture. Readers can also find a wide range of information on cultural groups; the types of articles that include information on the Cherokee provide an example. This publication features overview articles on the Cherokee and on the Southeast culture area; also included are shorter articles on personages such as John Ross, John Ridge, Sequoyah, contemporary principal chief Wilma Mankiller, and playwright Lynn Riggs; on events such as the Cherokee War, the Trail of Tears, and the *Cherokee Tobacco* case; on Indian Territory; and on Southeast cultural phenomena such as wattle and daub dwellings.

Each article begins with clearly marked lines of ready-reference information. Articles on people, for example, include birth and death information, alternate names, tribal affiliation, and a line that briefly states their historical or cultural significance. Articles on tribes note language groups and population (where recent figures are available); articles on events provide the date, location, and significance. Where appropriate, articles are illustrated with photographs, maps, charts, tables, and drawings; more than 200 photographs, both historical and contemporary, are included. Articles conclude with cross-references to other relevant articles in the set. Articles longer than 1,000 words conclude with a bibliography; the bibliographies of articles 2,000 words or longer include annotations.

Volume 3 contains a series of eight appendices that provide information on subjects such as educational institutions and programs; museums, archives, and libraries; and organizations. There is also a time line, glossary, mediagraphy, bibliography, and list of tribes by culture area. A comprehensive index with numerous cross-references concludes volume 3. In the front matter to each of the set's three volumes, the reader will find an alphabetical list of all entries in the set; the back matter to each volume lists the contents by category.

A few comments must be made on certain editorial decisions. Terms ranging from "American Indian" to "Native American" to "tribe" are accepted by some and disapproved of by others. We have used *American Indians* for the title of this set, as it is today the most widely accepted collective name for the first inhabitants of North America and their descendants. (It might be noted that some American Indians essentially find all such collective terms equally offensive.) We have allowed authors to use either "American Indian" or "Native American" in their articles rather than impose a term editorially, recognizing that each writer has his or her own preference. Similarly, we have used the title "Inuit" for the article on that Arctic people, but the term "Eskimo" also appears in the set, as it has a long tradition of scientific usage and encompasses a variety of Arctic peoples to whom "Inuit" does not adequately apply.

Contributors were also free to use singular or plural designations for tribal names. Spellings of tribal names, however, have been standardized throughout the set. We have attempted to use names and spellings that are both accepted by the tribes themselves and widely recognized. Parenthetical notes are occasionally provided to identify alternative names for tribes; although such alternative names ("Fox" and "Mesquakie," for example) do not always signify exactly identical groups, they are intended to help readers recognize the tribe being discussed. Finally, the abbreviations B.C.E. ("before the common era") and C.E. were used throughout the set rather than the more culturally biased B.C. and A.D. designations.

Care was taken to include articles on as many tribal groups as possible, and more than 275 North American tribes are represented by individual entries. We have provided 1990 U.S. Census figures and Canadian population figures based on the 1991 census for those tribes for whom such information was available. These figures should be used with caution, however, as they are based on "self-report"—people's individual statements of their own ethnic identification. We have included them as a point of comparison, but readers should be aware that a number of factors influence such self-identification other than a person's line of descent from members of a particular tribe.

Many authors generously contributed their time and talents in order to make this set possible, and we thank them all for their contributions in areas ranging from archaeology to contemporary Indian life. A complete list of writers appears in volume 1. We particularly wish to thank Consulting Editor Harvey Markowitz of the D'Arcy McNickle Center for the History of the American Indian, whose expertise and assistance proved invaluable.

List of Contributors

Jeff Abernathy
Illinois College

McCrea Adams
Independent Scholar

Thomas L. Altherr
Metropolitan State College of Denver

Marjorie H. Arant
Independent Scholar

T. J. Arant
Appalachian State University

Tanya M. Backinger
Jackson Community College

James A. Baer
Northern Virginia Community College

Russell J. Barber
California State University, San Bernardino

Carole A. Barrett
University of Mary

Rose A. Bast
Mount Mary College

Catherine Bereznak
Louisiania State University

S. Carol Berg
College of St. Benedict

Joy A. Bilharz
State University of New York College at Fredonia

Cynthia A. Bily
Adrian College

John A. Britton
Francis Marion University

Kendall W. Brown
Brigham Young University

Gregory R. Campbell
University of Montana

Malcolm B. Campbell
Bowling Green State University

Byron D. Cannon
University of Utah

Jack J. Cardoso
State University of New York College at Buffalo

Kelli Carmean
Eastern Kentucky University

Thomas Patrick Carroll
John A. Logan College

Ward Churchill
University of Colorado at Boulder

Cheryl Claassen
Appalachian State University

C. B. Clark
Oklahoma City University

Richmond Clow
University of Montana

Richard G. Condon
University of Arkansas

Michael Coronel
University of Northern Colorado

Patricia Coronel
Colorado State University

LouAnn Faris Culley
Kansas State University

Jennifer Davis
University of Dayton

Michael G. Davis
Northeast Missouri State University

S. Matthew Despain
University of Oklahoma

Ronald J. Duncan
Oklahoma Baptist University

Linda B. Eaton
Weber State University

Robert P. Ellis
Worcester State College

Dorothy Engan-Barker
Mankato State University

John L. Farbo
University of Idaho

James D. Farmer
Virginia Commonwealth University

Michael Findlay
California State University, Chico

Roberta Fiske-Rusciano
Rutgers University

Robert E. Fleming
Brigham Young University

William B. Folkestad
Central Washington University

Raymond Frey
Centenary College

C. George Fry
Lutheran College of Health Professions

Gregory Gagnon
Oglala Lakota College

Lucy Ganje
University of North Dakota

Lynne Getz
Appalachian State University

Jon L. Gibson
University of Southwestern Louisiana

Marc Goldstein
University of Rochester
New York University

Nancy M. Gordon
Independent Scholar

Larry Gragg
University of Missouri, Rolla

Gretchen L. Green
University of Missouri, Kansas City

William H. Green
University of Missouri, Columbia

Robert M. Hawthorne, Jr.
Independent Scholar

Eric Henderson
University of Northern Iowa

Howard M. Hensel
United States Air Force Air War College

Donna J. Hess
South Dakota State University

C. L. Higham
Winona State University

Carl W. Hoagstrom
Ohio Northern University

John Hoopes
University of Kansas

Tonya Huber
Wichita State University

William E. Huntzicker
University of Minnesota

Andrew C. Isenberg
University of Puget Sound

Robert Jacobs
Central Washington University

M. A. Jaimes
University of Colorado at Boulder

Jennifer Raye James
Independent Scholar

Helen Jaskoski
California State University, Fullerton

Joseph C. Jastrzembski
University of Texas at El Paso

Bruce E. Johansen
University of Nebraska at Omaha

Mary Johnson
Tampa College

Robert Jones
Kayenta School District

Sondra Jones
Brigham Young University

Janice H. Joy
University of North Florida

Marcella T. Joy
Independent Scholar

Charles Louis Kammer III
The College of Wooster

Richard S. Keating
United States Air Force Academy

Nathan R. Kollar
St. John Fisher College

Rosalind Ekman Ladd
Wheaton College, Massachusetts

Philip E. Lampe
Incarnate Word College

Elden Lawrence
South Dakota State University

Ronald W. Long
West Virginia Institute of Technology

Denise Low
Haskell Indian Nations University

William C. Lowe
Mount St. Clare College

Kenneth S. McAllister
University of Illinois at Chicago

Richard B. McCaslin
High Point University

Heather McKillop
Louisiana State University

Paul Madden
Hardin-Simmons University

Russell M. Magnaghi
Northern Michigan University

Kimberly Manning
California State University, Santa Barbara

Harvey Markowitz
*D'Arcy McNickle Center for the History of
the American Indian, Newberry Library*

Lynn M. Mason
Lubbock Christian University

Patricia Masserman
Independent Scholar

Thomas D. Matijasic
Prestonsburg Community College

Howard Meredith
University of Science and Arts of Oklahoma

Linda J. Meyers
Pasadena City College

David N. Mielke
Appalachian State University

Laurence Miller
Western Washington State University

David J. Minderhout
Bloomsburg University

Bruce M. Mitchell
Eastern Washington University

Robert E. Morsberger
*California State Polytechnic University,
Pomona*

Ken R. Mulliken
Brigham Young University

Michael J. Mullin
Augustana College

Molly H. Mullin
Duke University

Bert M. Mutersbaugh
Eastern Kentucky University

Eric Niderost
Chabot College

Gary A. Olson
San Bernardino Valley College

Nancy H. Omaha Boy
Rutgers University

Patrick M. O'Neil
Broome Community College

Sean O'Neill
Grand Valley State University

Max Orezzoli
Florida International University

William T. Osborne
Florida International University

Deane Osterman
Eastern Washington University

Martha I. Pallante
Youngstown State University

Zena Pearlstone
California State University, Long Beach

Francis Poole
University of Delaware

Susan Prezzano
*State University of New York
at Binghamton*

Victoria Price
Lamar University

Harald E. L. Prins
Kansas State University

Andrea Gayle Radke
Brigham Young University

Jon Reyhner
Montana State University, Billings

Jennifer Rivers
Brigham Young University

Moises Roizen
West Valley College

Fred S. Rolater
Middle Tennessee State University

John Alan Ross
Eastern Washington University

Richard Sax
Madonna University

Glenn J. Schiffman
Independent Scholar

Lee Schweninger
*University of North Carolina,
Wilmington*

Heather M. Seferovich
Brigham Young University

Burl E. Self
Southwest Missouri State University

Michael W. Simpson
Eastern Washington University

Sanford S. Singer
University of Dayton

David Curtis Skaggs
Bowling Green State University

Andrew C. Skinner
Brigham Young University

James Smallwood
Oklahoma State University

Roger Smith
Linfield College

Daniel L. Smith-Christopher
Loyola Marymount University

Robert M. Spector
Worcester State College

Pamela R. Stern
University of Arkansas

Ruffin Stirling
Independent Scholar

Leslie Stricker
Independent Scholar

Glenn L. Swygart
Tennessee Temple University

Robert D. Talbott
University of Northern Iowa

Harold D. Tallant
Georgetown College

Nicholas C. Thomas
Auburn University at Montgomery

Gale M. Thompson
Saginaw Valley State University

Leslie V. Tischauser
Prairie State College

Diane C. Van Noord
Western Michigan University

Santos C. Vega
Arizona State University

Susan Daly Vinal
University of Texas

Mary E. Virginia
Independent Scholar

Harry M. Ward
University of Richmond

R. David Weber
East Los Angeles College

Laurie Weinstein
Western Connecticut State University

Thomas F. Weso
University of Missouri, Kansas City

David E. Wilkins
University of Colorado at Boulder

List of Contributors

Raymond Wilson
Fort Hays State University

Sharon K. Wilson
Fort Hays State University

Shawn Woodyard
Independent Scholar

Susan J. Wurtzburg
University of Canterbury
New Zealand

Kari Ann Yadro
Eastern Washington University

Clifton K. Yearley
State University of New York at Buffalo

George Yonek
Louisiana State University

Dorothy Zeisler-Vralsted
University of Wisconsin—La Crosse

CONTENTS

CONTENTS

ALPHABETICAL LIST OF ENTRIES

Volume I

Volume II

Volume III

RR AMERICAN INDIANS

Abenaki: Tribe

CULTURE AREA: Northeast
LANGUAGE GROUP: Algonquian
PRIMARY LOCATION: New England, Quebec
POPULATION SIZE: 1,469 Abenaki, 2,173 Penobscot in U.S. (1990 U.S. Census); 945 Abenaki in Canada (Statistics Canada, based on 1991 census)

The Abenaki form a cross-border ethnic group that is organized in several autonomous communities. Today, there are three reservation-based Abenaki bands: Odanak (St. Francis) and Wolinak (Becancour) in southern Quebec, and Penobscot (Old Town) in Maine. The St. Francis/Sokoki band of Abenakis of Vermont is a landless group headquartered in Swanton. The total population of these groups has been estimated at fifty-five hundred. Their native tongue, spoken by few, belongs to the Eastern Algonquian language family. Calling their homeland *Wabanakik* ("Dawnland"), they draw their name from *Wabanaki* ("Dawnlanders"). Because of cultural similarities between the Abenaki and their neighbors, Wabanaki has become a collective term for western Abenaki (Odanak, Wolinak, and Swanton) and eastern Abenaki (Penobscot) as well as Passamaquoddy, Maliseet, and Micmac. Historically, it also embraced now-extinct communities at Moosehead Lake, Norridgewock (Kennebec River), Amesokanti (Sandy River), Amirkangan (Androscoggin River), Pequawket (Saco River), Pennacook (Merrimack River), Sokoki (Connecticut River), and Missisquois (Lake Champlain).

Prehistory. While tribal legends recall a culture hero, the mythic giant Gluskap (or Odzihozo, for western Abenaki), as creator of Dawnland humans, prehistoric evidence shows that Paleo-Indians migrated to this area eleven thousand years ago. It appears that Abenaki ancestors first arrived some three thousand years ago. The region features mixed spruce-fir and hardwood forests, interrupted by swamps, lakes, and rivers; it also has a long, indented coastline. Abounding with fowl, fish, and game, the region offered the migratory Abenaki a rich subsistence based on hunting (bear, deer, moose, beaver, and seals), fishing (eel, salmon, and sturgeon), collecting shellfish (lobsters, oysters, and clams), and gathering (roots, berries, and nuts). Moving about, they walked on snowshoes and pulled toboggans during winter, and they paddled birchbark canoes the rest of the year.

Periodically, Abenaki families banded together in groups of up to three hundred people, their birchbark wigwams clustered in temporary settlements. Most of the year, however, they lived in smaller units of ten to fifty people, representing one or more extended families. They elected a band chief ("sakom") to whom they turned for leadership. With the exception of pottery, introduced some twenty-five hundred years ago, Abenaki culture remained largely unchanged until the introduction of horticulture between 1200 and 1600 C.E. In the fertile valleys from Lake Champlain to the Kennebec River, Abenaki women began to raise corn, squash, and beans in fields cleared by men. Becoming semipermanent sedentary communities of up to 1,500 people, some Abenaki groups began fortifying their villages against raiders. Because hunting, fishing, and gathering remained important, families shifted residence between these villages and temporary camps in their hunting territories.

Colonial Period. In the early 1600's, Abenakis began regular trade with European newcomers, bartering beaver and other pelts for commodities such as steel knives, axes, copper kettles, woolen blankets, and alcohol. Contact brought a series of epidemics (especially smallpox) and stunning mortality rates (90 percent), reducing Abenaki numbers from about 25,000 to 2,500 in a century. By the 1620's, English colonists had begun settling "widowed" coastal lands. Meanwhile, Abenaki survivors regrouped and armed themselves with muskets acquired from French and English merchants. Paying for trade goods with furs, Abenakis and neighboring groups soon faced shortages and competed for hunting grounds. This resulted in conflicts known as Beaver Wars, pitting Abenaki warriors against Iroquois and other enemies. From the 1640's onward, French missionaries converted Abenakis to Christianity, and the baptismal ritual gave expression to their alliance with the French, which lasted throughout the colonial era. From 1675 onward, Abenakis fought repeatedly against British aggressors: King Philip's War (1675-1676), King William's War (1688-1699), Queen Anne's War (1702-1714), Governor Dummer's War (1721-1726), King George's War (1744-1748), and the so-called French and Indian War (1754-1763). During these colonial wars, they were joined by Micmac, Maliseet, and Passamaquoddy, with whom they formed the Wabanaki Confederacy. Raids by English militia and scalp bounty hunters forced the Abenaki to flee most of their traditional settlements in New England. Their famous mission village at Norridgewock, where Jesuit missionary Sebastien Rasle had been active since the 1690's, was attacked and burned to the ground in 1724.

Modern Period. When France surrendered Canada to the British, thousands of white settlers invaded Abenaki lands. In New England, only Abenakis residing in the Penobscot Valley could secure a reservation (in 1796). Having found refuge in Catholic mission villages in French Canada since the 1670's, Abenakis at Odanak and Wolinak also gained title to the small tracts where they had their settlements. In the nineteenth century, no longer able to subsist as hunters, some tried farming. Most turned to seasonal wage-labor (lumbering), guiding sport hunters, or making splint-ash basketry. Others drifted to cities such as Boston or Montreal for industrial employment.

Since the 1960's, Abenakis have embarked on a process of cultural revitalization. Fighting for native rights, they have booked numerous achievements. In 1980, the Penobscot settled an immense land claims case against the state of Maine, which gave them federal recognition and $40.3 million, mostly earmarked for land acquisition. By the mid-1990's they owned two hundred islands in their river and 55,000 acres of trust land in nearby Penobscot County. On a spiritual level, they have revived the sweat-lodge ritual and other ancient ceremonies. Similar efforts are made by their Abenaki relatives in Vermont and Quebec. —*Harald E. L. Prins*

See also Algonquian language family; Maliseet; Micmac; Passamaquoddy; Penobscot.

BIBLIOGRAPHY

Calloway, Colin G. *The Western Abenakis of Vermont, 1600-1800: War, Migration, and the Survival of an Indian People*. Norman: University of Oklahoma Press, 1990.

Day, Gordon M. "Western Abenaki." In *Northeast*, edited by Bruce G. Trigger. Vol. 15 in *Handbook of North American Indians*, edited by William Sturtevant. Washington, D.C.: Smithsonian Institution Press, 1978.

Morrison, Kenneth M. *The Embattled Northeast: The Elusive Ideal of Alliance in Abnaki-Euramerican Relations*. Berkeley: University of California Press, 1984.

Prins, Harald E. L., and Bruce J. Bourque. "Norridgewock: Village Translocation on the New England-Acadian Frontier." *Man in the Northeast* 33 (1987): 263-278.

Snow, Dean. "Eastern Abenaki." In *Northeast*, edited by Bruce G. Trigger. Vol. 15 in *Handbook of North American Indians*, edited by William Sturtevant. Washington, D.C.: Smithsonian Institution Press, 1978.

Speck, Frank G. *Penobscot Man: The Life History of a Forest Tribe in Maine*. Philadelphia: University of Pennsylvania Press, 1940.

Achumawi: Tribe

CULTURE AREA: California
LANGUAGE GROUP: Hokan
PRIMARY LOCATION: Northern California
POPULATION SIZE: 1,640 (1990 U.S. Census)

The Achumawi, also known as the Pit River Indians, live in the northeastern corner of California. They are not really one tribe, but eleven autonomous bands. "Achumawi," the name of one of these bands, serves as a kind of collective label. The other ten are the Aporige, Astarwawi, Atsuge, Atwamsini, Hammawi, Hewisedawi, Ilmawi, Itsatawi, Kosalextawi, and Madesi.

Like all California Indians, the Achumawi were well adapted to their environment. Summer houses were lashed-together poles covered by reed or tule mats; winter dwellings were semi-subterranean, with a wood frame covered by a layer of earth, tule, or bark.

The Achumawi fished, hunted, and gathered for their subsistence. Seeds, roots, and insects were collected, and game such as deer, beaver, and badger were hunted. The Achumawi dug pits to trap deer, a practice which led the first whites who came in contact with them to dub them the "Pit River people."

The Achumawi's clothing was made of deerskin and shredded juniper bark, and their basketry attained the level of fine art. Bows and arrows were used in hunting; the arrowheads were made of obsidian (a volcanic glass).

Among the Achumawi, shamans were highly respected for both religious leadership and their encyclopedic knowledge of medicine and healing. Boys would go out to the mountains to seek a *tinhowi*, or guardian spirit, when they reached adolescence. The *tinhowi* would impart supernatural powers to the young men.

Achumawi woman and her baby, in a traditional cradleboard, in the late nineteenth century. (Library of Congress)

The first whites to come to Achumawi lands were trappers in about 1828. There were about three thousand Achumawi at that time. Later, during the California gold rush, a great influx of white settlers threatened the Indians' way of life.

In spite of the problems of the past, the Achumawi are lucky enough still to be living on ancestral land. The X-L Ranch Reservation, founded in 1938, comprises 8,700 acres in six parcels. Not all Achumawi live on the reservation. The tribe maintains a health-care center and tribal office at Burney, California. In the early 1990's, there efforts by such companies as Pacific Gas and Electric to gain control of forested Achumawi reservation lands for development.

See also California; Hokan language group.

Acoma, Battle of

DATE: December, 1598-February, 1599
PLACE: Acoma Pueblo, New Mexico
TRIBE AFFECTED: Acoma (Keres)
SIGNIFICANCE: After this first major Puebloan uprising against the Spanish invaders, defeat and the Spaniards' cruel punishment of the survivors kept the Puebloans from attempting another rebellion for many decades

In May, 1598, Don Juan de Oñate, appointed by the Spanish authorities as governor and captain general of all the kingdoms and provinces of New Mexico, reached the Rio Grande valley with a large contingent of priests, soldiers, settlers, and servants as well as two nephews, Vincente and Juan de Zaldivar. Although many Puebloans fled in terror before the invaders, those who remained received Oñate and his men hospitably. In each pueblo he entered, Oñate declared that he had come to protect the Indians and save their souls, and he demanded that they swear allegiance and vassalage to their new rulers, the Spanish king and the Catholic church. At the pueblos of Ohke and Yunque, he drove the Indians from their homes and moved his own people in, leaving King Phillip's new subjects to survive as best they could in the countryside.

By October, Oñate had reached Acoma pueblo, where, after the usual ceremony of swearing allegiance to king and church, the inhabitants were asked to give generously of their food, robes, and blankets. Oñate then continued on to the Zuni and Hopi pueblos. In early December, Juan de Zaldivar and thirty soldiers, following Oñate, arrived at Acoma and demanded to be provisioned, ignoring the Indians' pleas that they had nothing left to spare. The Indians then attacked, killing Zaldivar and twelve of his men.

Oñate, vowing to avenge this serious blow to Spanish authority, called a general meeting to plan for the punishment of Acoma. He consulted the friars, who agreed that this was a "just war" under Spanish law, since the Puebloans had sworn obedience and vassalage to the Spanish crown and were therefore royal subjects who were now guilty of treason. On January 21, 1599, Vincente de Zaldivar and his forces reached Acoma, where they found the Puebloans ready to defend themselves. The Indians, fighting with arrows and stones, were no match for men armed with guns; after two days of bitter fighting, Acoma was defeated, with more than eight hundred of its people dead. The pueblo was destroyed, and some five hundred men, women, and children were captured. Those who did not immediately surrender were dragged from their hiding places and killed.

On February 12, Oñate himself decreed the punishment of the captives: All men over twenty-five had one foot cut off and served twenty years in slavery; all men between the ages of twelve and twenty-five and all women over twelve served twenty years in slavery; the old men and women were given to the Querechos (Plains Apache) as slaves; the children under twelve were given to Fray Alonso Martinez (father commissary of the Church) and to Vincente de Zaldivar; two Hopi men, at Acoma when the battle began, had their right hands cut off and were sent back to Hopi as an object lesson.

See also Indian-white relations—Spanish colonial; Missions and missionaries; Pueblo (Popé's) Revolt; Pueblo tribes, Western; Slavery.

Acorns

TRIBES AFFECTED: Tribes in California and the prehistoric Northeast
SIGNIFICANCE: Acorns provided a starchy food staple for various Indian groups

Acorns, the nuts of oak trees, average 40-50 percent carbohydrates, 3-4 percent protein, and 5-10 percent fat, making them

SEVEN OAK TREES USED BY CALIFORNIA INDIANS		
Common Name	Species	Desirability Rating
Tan oak	*Lithocarpus densiflora*	1.0
Black oak	*Quercus kelloggii*	1.5
Blue oak	*Quercus douglasii*	1.5
Valley oak	*Quercus lobata*	1.9
Coast live oak	*Quercus agrifolia*	2.0
Oregon oak	*Quercus garryana*	2.0
Engelmann oak	*Quercus engelmannii*	2.2

Source: Heizer, Robert F., ed., *California.* Vol. 8 in *Handbook of North American Indians,* edited by William C. Sturtevant. Washington, D.C.: Smithsonian Institution, 1978.

Note: Acorns were of great importance to California Indians even in areas in which not many were available. "Desirability rating" scale created by Martin A. Baumhoff (1963); the lower the number, the more preferable the acorns.

a nutritious foodstuff providing about 168 calories per ounce. This abundant and easily collected nut became the dietary mainstay for various Indian groups, particularly in the Northeast and California.

The earliest unequivocal evidence of the dietary use of acorns comes from the Lamoka culture of New York, probably around 3500 B.C.E. Archaeological sites in Massachusetts dating from a millennium later also have produced clear evidence of the eating of large quantities of acorns. By the historic period, however, Northeastern Indians were using acorns only sparingly as food.

In California, major use of acorns began later, around 1000 B.C.E., but it ultimately was more important, often forming the bulk of the diet. Six species of acorn were gathered, and families commonly obtained enough in one season to last them two years. The acorns typically were stored in baskets or wooden granaries, some as much as 5 feet in diameter and 8 feet high. To reduce infestation by vermin, the base of a granary might be painted with pitch, or fragrant laurel leaves might be included. The acorns were ground as needed, and bitter tannin was leached out by washing the acorn meal repeatedly with hot water. The acorn meal was boiled into gruel or baked into pancake-biscuits on heated rocks. This staple supported many California Indians into the late nineteenth century.

See also California; Hunting and gathering; Subsistence.

Activism

TRIBES AFFECTED: Pantribal
SIGNIFICANCE: In the mid-1960's, American Indians embarked on a new phase in their dealings with the U.S. government and its citizens, one marked by proactive insistence on rights that had been secured by treaty with the United States

During the Eisenhower Administration (1953-1961), the official U.S. government policy toward American Indians was one of "termination." By this policy, the government meant to end the special legal status of American Indians and to encourage the assimilation of native people into the U.S. citizenry. Alongside the policy of termination was the policy of "relocation," through which American Indians were to be taken off traditional land bases and relocated in urban areas for training and employment. The necessary complement to termination and relocation, in the government's view, was the abolishing of treaty rights for all the tribes. By the beginning of the Civil Rights movement, however, some American Indians were beginning to adopt some of the tactics and strategies used by Civil Rights protesters. Because many American Indians believed that most treaties had been violated over and over again, the route of active protest seemed a natural one.

Northwest Fish-ins. In 1964, the National Indian Youth Council (NIYC) organized a fish-in in Washington State. Tribes there had increasingly been prohibited from fishing in waters granted to them by treaty. Sportsmen and commercial fisheries believed that native fishers were interfering with their ability to fish for profit and fun. The native fishers, however, were most often fishing either in observation of tribal ritual or for subsistence. The fish-ins attracted widespread notice, including the appearance of celebrities such as actor Marlon Brando and Civil Rights activist Dick Gregory, and managed to bring the fishing controversies to the national headlines. Case after case was adjudicated in the following years, from the Northwest to the upper Great Lakes. Many times the decision came down on the side of the tribal treaty rights. These successes, especially between 1964 and 1966, galvanized many young American Indians. This was especially crucial because many of the elders of different tribes distrusted the course of activism. The success of NIYC leadership in the fish-in controversy legitimated more active protest.

Cornwall Bridge Blocked. Activism was not confined to the West and Midwest. In 1968, a group of Mohawks blocked the Cornwall Bridge linking Canada with New York. Their complaint was simple: Mohawks were granted free movement between Canada and the United States by treaty with Great Britain, a treaty Canada had pledged to honor. Nevertheless, Canadian police had been interfering with free transit. The Mohawks barricaded the bridge, resulting in the arrest of several of their leaders. The case was brought to trial, but the treaty issue was found to be beyond the court's jurisdiction. All charges were dropped, and the police were advised to become more conciliatory.

Birth of the American Indian Movement (AIM). In the Minneapolis-St. Paul area, in 1968, native residents had noted the extremely high rates of arrest of American Indians relative to other groups. They also heard many stories of rough and sometimes brutal police treatment of American Indians. Some Minneapolis American Indians began to follow police cruisers on weekends to document what happened. During the next ten months, police arrests of American Indians dropped to almost zero, demonstrating at least that having witnesses and advocates on the scene helped matters. This was the beginning of the American Indian Movement (AIM) organization.

The Taking of Alcatraz. None of these events was as dramatic as the November, 1969, occupation of Alcatraz Island, formerly the site of a federal penitentiary. The immediate reason for the taking of Alcatraz was that the San Francisco Indian Center had burned to the ground, leaving American Indians United, in town for a conference, without a place to stay. Fewer than twenty American Indians landed on Alcatraz and declared it Indian Territory under the Fort Laramie Treaty of 1868, a treaty that granted federal land to American Indians if it was no longer in use by the federal government. Though the island was empty two years later, the call for restoration of land by lawful treaty was once again established. Though there were successes in land restoration (for example, the return of Blue Lake to the Taos Pueblos and the return of Mount Adams to the Yakimas), the issue of land and treaty rights brought into the spotlight the U.S. government's history of treaty abridgment and effectively ended the policies of termination and relocation. There was as yet, however, no movement toward what many activists wanted—a policy of self-determination for American Indians.

Early 1970's. These were watershed years for American Indian activism. In 1970, more than 150 Pit River tribespeople occupied parts of Lassen National Park and Pacific Gas and Electric land in Northern California. Other demonstrators took over Ellis Island in New York to protest treaty violations. Lakotas briefly occupied Mount Rushmore, a sacred site to their tribe.

It is the year 1972 that claims most notice. Early that year, Chippewas had won back their rights to police fishing inside their reserve. That spring at Cass Lake, Minnesota, AIM convened to help decide how those rights would be allocated. During the convention, roads were blocked and guns were in evidence; the atmosphere was tense as AIM members battled what they saw as overly conservative traditionalists. The situation so unnerved local resort owners that they acceded to demands for absolute Chippewa control.

Shortly after the Cass Lake convention, an older Pine Ridge Sioux, Raymond Yellow Thunder, was murdered in Gordon, Nebraska, by five white men. Gordon officials did nothing about the situation, so AIM convened one thousand American Indians, who descended on the town in protest. AIM also protested the murders of American Indians in California and Arizona. After the apparent public relations successes of these protests, AIM leaders began to plan a nationwide caravan, the Trail of Broken Treaties, for the fall of 1972, before the presidential elections.

The caravan had several purposes. First, it was hoped it would create favorable public sentiment for the cause of treaty enforcement. Second, the participants hoped, by their timing, to force the U.S. government to deal with them. Third, they hoped to convert the national media to their cause.

About midway through the caravan, the group stopped in Minneapolis to release their agenda for Washington, the

"Twenty Points," to the media. Among the demands was a repeal of the 1871 ban on further treaty-making, the end of state court jurisdiction over American Indians, and a review of U.S. treaty violations of the past and redress for those violations.

Once in Washington, D.C., on November 3, the caravan had grown to numbers well exceeding expectations. There was also a high percentage of participants from reservations (about 80 percent), something most media had not predicted, since AIM was regarded primarily as an urban group. There were also a high number of eastern tribes represented, perhaps not surprising since one of the Twenty Points demanded federal services for the eastern tribes not currently receiving service.

Unfortunately, the number also exceeded what organizers had expected, with the result that there were no accommodations for many of the travelers. Eventually the Department of the Interior's auditorium was booked as a place for the activists to stay. As people began to leave the Bureau of Indian Affairs building, overzealous guards began to push people out through the doors. Believing that they might be turned over to a police riot squad on the outside, activists rushed back into the building and barricaded themselves in, breaking apart furniture in order to board windows and fasten doors.

For six days they remained inside, despite occasional police attempts to breach their security. Finally, on November 9, negotiators reached a settlement of the problem. There would be no prosecution of the Indians involved, and $66,000 was appropriated for return transportation. The Twenty Points would be considered, and a response would be made.

When the Nixon Administration replied to the Twenty Points in January, 1973, the response was disappointing to the tribes. In essence, the administration rejected any notion of treaty enforcement or treaty reform. The response noted the first Nixon Administration's accomplishments, and promised more positive action. Still, the hope represented by the drafting of the Twenty Points was dampened.

Wounded Knee II. In January, 1973, a Sioux, Wesley Bad Heart Bear, was killed under uncertain circumstances. When a white man was charged with manslaughter instead of murder, Dennis Banks and Russell Means led AIM supporters first into Buffalo Gap, South Dakota, and then into Rapid City, demanding justice. Though tension filled the air for several days, a promise of justice was finally extracted, and Banks addressed the South Dakota legislature, promising a new era in race relations between whites and American Indians.

Banks and Means repaired to the Pine Ridge Reservation to celebrate. This was unfortunate, because Tribal Chairman Richard Wilson had declared (after the Raymond Yellow Thunder celebration and the occupation of the BIA office) that Means, Banks, and the AIM were never to celebrate on Pine Ridge again.

When they arrived, tribal police began to harass them. Events escalated so much that tribal officials finally called in federal marshals to control the situation. On February 28, AIM occupied the Wounded Knee site on the reservation and an-

nounced political independence of Pine Ridge and Richard Wilson. More marshals arrived, and a number of AIM supporters from outside Pine Ridge arrived at the Wounded Knee compound, including a number of traditional holy people and a contingent from the Mohawk Nation.

The government issued several sets of ultimatums, culminating in an order during the second week that everyone leave Wounded Knee by six o'clock that day, or federal marshals would come in shooting. The National Council of Churches had representatives there, and they vowed that should such an order be implemented, they would stand between the marshals' gunfire and the activists. The ultimatum was rescinded.

On March 11, Russell Means announced to a national television audience that the Oglala Sioux Nation had been formed and declared its independence from the U.S. He described the borders of the new nation and promised to shoot anyone who crossed those borders. This action seemed finally to shift the gears of the situation toward settlement. Hank Adams, a fish-in veteran who had helped negotiate the BIA occupation, met with high-level administration officials to bring about some of the changes desired by AIM. What had begun as a local controversy between AIM and Richard Wilson ended up having national effects. The occupation lasted seventy-two days.

Legislative and Judicial Activism. American Indian issues have frequently been adjudicated, and these decisions have played a large role in how American Indians are or are not allowed to govern themselves. Because so much of American Indian activism gets its energy from the desire for self-determination, it is helpful to understand U.S. courts' actions.

The principle of tribal sovereignty was established between 1823 and 1832 in a series of cases: *Johnson v. McIntosh* (1823), *Cherokee Nation v. Georgia* (1831), and *Worcester v. Georgia* (1832). In all these cases, the operative phrasing was that tribes were "dependent, domestic nations." Though this doctrine was never challenged by subsequent courts, there was still no question of who held the power over native nations. In *United States v. Kagama* (1886), the Supreme Court ruled that the federal branch of the U.S. government, specifically the Congress, held ultimate sovereignty over tribal nations. This solidified the "plenary power" of Congress, meaning that it could legislate American Indian affairs in any way it saw fit, without regard to constitutional review (in other words, what would be unconstitutional for other Americans might well be considered appropriate for American Indians). Similarly, in *Lone Wolf v. Hitchcock* (1903), the Supreme Court ruled that Congress may abrogate at will any treaty with any tribe.

The tide in adjudication turned somewhat in the early 1900's. In *United States v. Winans* (1905), the Court recognized that tribes (specifically the Yakima) have rights reserved for them (in this case, game) even if those rights are not specifically named in a treaty. In *Winters v. United States* (1908), the Court held that water rights are included even if not named in treaties.

These decisions form the basis of law on which modern activism is based. The acknowledged beginning of the modern era of American Indian law is the landmark case *Hitchcock v. Lee* (1959). In that case, the reserved rights by treaty were held to include the right of the Navajo to try a case in their own tribal courts. The state of Arizona's position, that it alone had the right to try cases, was rebuffed.

By the 1960's, there were numerous organizations dedicated to pursuing the rights of American Indians through the courts. These included the Indian Rights Association, the Association on American Indian Affairs, the Legal Services Corporation, and the Native American Rights Fund. As described earlier, one of the persistent cases was the battle over fishing rights. This issue came before the Supreme Court three times during the 1960's. This series of cases became known as the Puyallup Series. In *United States v. Washington* (1973), the Supreme Court upheld the American Indian right to share equally in the salmon harvest in the Northwest. A subsequent case, *Washington v. Fishing Vessel Association* (1979), modified the earlier ruling somewhat by granting American Indians only a "moderate" fishing livelihood.

During the 1970's, American Indians increasingly won judicial approval for many tribal and self-determining activities. These included education, taxes, tribal governance, adoption, and revenue-generating operations of all kinds. Two particular landmark cases are *United States v. Mazurie* (1975), in which tribal courts gained the right to try a non-Indian, and *Fisher v. District Court* (1976), in which it was held that the state of Montana could not intervene in a Northern Cheyenne adoption. Finally, in 1977, the decision in *Delaware v. Weeks* ended the doctrine of plenary power, as the Court applied constitutional review to an act of Congress regarding American Indians.

Since then, three important congressional acts have been passed that seem to many to mark a new attitude toward American Indians. The 1978 American Indian Religious Freedom Act extended to American Indians the same religious freedom enjoyed by other Americans. The 1988 Indian Gaming Regulatory Act opened the door to tribal generation of revenue through the gaming industry, a boon to many tribes' coffers. The 1990 Native American Grave Protection and Repatriation Act began finally to address a problem most American Indians believed to be a symbol of American lack of respect for the First Nations. —*T. J. Arant*

See also Alcatraz Island Occupation; American Indian Movement (AIM); Banks, Dennis; Harris, LaDonna; Means, Russell; Pine Ridge shootout; Trail of Broken Treaties; Women of All Red Nations (WARN); Wounded Knee occupation.

BIBLIOGRAPHY

Deloria, Vine, Jr. *Behind the Trail of Broken Treaties: An Indian Declaration of Independence*. 2d ed. Norman: University of Oklahoma Press, 1987. Examines the Trail of Broken Treaties and the siege at Wounded Knee in the context of American Indian history.

Josephy, Alvin M., Jr. *Red Power: The American Indians' Fight for Freedom*. New York: American Heritage Press, 1971. Contains contemporary accounts of the Red Power movement.

Olson, James S., and Raymond Wilson. *Native Americans in the Twentieth Century*. Provo, Utah: Brigham Young University, 1984. A comprehensive history with a chapter specifically devoted to activism.

Ziontz, Alvin J. "Indian Litigation." In *The Aggressions of Civilization: Federal Indian Policy Since the 1880's*, edited by Sandra L. Cadwalader and Vine Deloria, Jr. Philadelphia: Temple University Press, 1984. An excellent review of judicial opinions relating to American Indians.

Adair, John L.

Adair, John L. (1828, northern Ga.—Oct. 21, 1896, Tahlequah, Okla.): Government official
TRIBAL AFFILIATION: Cherokee
SIGNIFICANCE: Adair played an important role in Cherokee affairs during the difficult years following the Trail of Tears

John Lynch Adair was born in 1828 in the original Cherokee Nation, which included northern Georgia. The Adair family, originally from Ireland, had intermarried with the Cherokee and produced numerous part-blooded Cherokee Adairs, of whom John was one.

When John was ten years old, the Cherokee were forcibly moved to the Indian Territory west of the Mississippi River. Reaching manhood there, John Adair provided needed leadership in helping the Cherokee adjust to a new environment.

In 1871, as a result of the Cherokee Treaty of 1866, Adair was appointed Cherokee boundary commissioner to work with a U.S. government commissioner in determining the boundaries between the Cherokee Nation and surrounding states. In later years, he compiled the constitution and laws of the Cherokee Nation; published in 1893, they were the major references for Cherokee law until Oklahoma became a state in 1907. Adair died in the Cherokee capital of Tahlequah in 1896.

See also Boudinot, Elias; Bushyhead, Dennis Wolf; Cherokee; Trail of Tears; Watie, Stand.

Adario

Adario (c. 1650, Ontario, Canada—Aug. 1, 1701, Montreal, Canada): Diplomat, chief
ALSO KNOWN AS: Kondiaronk, Sastaretsi, Gaspar Soiga, Le Rat
TRIBAL AFFILIATION: Petun
SIGNIFICANCE: Adario skillfully thwarted a late seventeenth century French-Iroquois alliance

Acting under a 1688 treaty, Petun leader Adario embarked on a French-sponsored military expedition against the powerful Iroquois Confederacy. Unbeknown to Adario, however, the French simultaneously were courting Iroquois alliance. While he was en route, Adario received intelligence of an Iroquois delegation led by the Onondaga Dekanisora, who was traveling to Montreal for negotiations, Adario ordered his men to ambush them. Later he claimed he was acting under French orders. As an ostensible gesture of goodwill toward Dekanisora, Adario released his Onondaga prisoners except one hostage, whom he surrendered to the French fort commander at Michilimackinac. Ignorant of machinations by the French and Adario, the commander executed the captive. Retaliating, the

Iroquois launched a massive attack on August 25, 1689, catching the French unprepared. They inflicted heavy casualties and burned Montreal.

Adario died in 1701 in Montreal while leading a treaty delegation of Huron chiefs. Unaware of Adario's duplicities, the French buried him with military honors.

See also Dekanisora; French and Indian Wars; Indian-white relations—French colonial; Iroquois Confederacy; Petun.

Adena: Prehistoric tradition
DATE: c. 1000 B.C.E.-200 C.E.
LOCATION: Southern Ohio, Indiana, Kentucky, West Virginia, western Pennsylvania
CULTURE AFFECTED: Hopewell

The Adena culture, which flourished between about 1000 B.C.E. and 200 C.E., was the first in a "spectacular series" of North American Early Woodland societies. With its classical heartland situated in a large area around Chillicothe, Ohio, the Adena culture was found in southern Ohio, eastern Indiana, northern Kentucky, West Virginia, and southwestern Pennsylvania. Its name is derived from Adena, the estate of an early Ohio governor that was situated near a mound on a hillside overlooking Ohio's first capital.

Mound Builders. The early American settlers of the trans-Appalachian West were astounded at the existence of thousands of earthen "mounds" in an area stretching from the Gulf of Mexico to the Great Lakes and from the Mississippi to the Saint Lawrence rivers. The tribes living in the region were as uninformed as to the origins of these earthworks as were the European American immigrants. Initially it was assumed that the prehistoric "mound builders" were one people. Only with the scientific exploration of these earthworks in the late nineteenth century did it become evident that there were a series of cultures represented in the construction of mounds, the earliest being the Adena. By about 500 B.C.E. they had produced the most complex and organized way of life found in the Americas north of Mexico.

Arriving in what is now the American Midwest by the start of the first millennium B.C.E., the Adenans avoided the malarial wetlands near the Great Lakes and the dense forestlands of Appalachia, preferring to settle in the open, rolling, well-drained valleys along the Ohio River and its tributaries. Here they practiced both food gathering (hunting, fishing, and harvesting fruits, berries, and herbs) and food producing (corn, squash, gourds, pumpkins, sunflowers, sumpweed, goosefoot, and, for use as a ceremonial substance, tobacco). Some mining (of gypsum) and trading (of copper, mica, and seashells) across the American heartland supplemented their economy, which was, perhaps, able to support a population density of one person per square mile.

Material Culture and Settlements. This rich and diverse economy enabled the Adenans to craft sophisticated tools and ornaments. Adenan sites have yielded such artifacts as stone and copper axes, adzes, celts, hoes, projectiles, crescents, gorgets, beads, bracelets, and carvings. Particularly remarkable are the stone tube pipes, such as one found at the Adena mound near Chillicothe, Ohio, which carries the effigy of a man wearing a set of large spool-shaped earrings and a breechcloth (decorated with the figure of a snake); he has bare feet (as if dancing), his hair is carefully braided, and his mouth is open (as if singing). Small stone blocks, deeply carved and engraved—for example with the picture of a hunting bird—have been found, perhaps having been used for printing designs on woven cloth. In addition to creating many types of woven materials, the Adenans were accomplished potters.

Adenan settlements were usually in the river valleys, near fields, gardens, and water. Both single-family units and structures capable of housing forty or more people have been found. Perhaps ten or more buildings characterize these permanent sites. The pattern of a typical Adenan house was circular in floor plan, conical in appearance. Perhaps 26 feet in diameter, the home would be sustained by six main uprights, drawing additional support from forty or fifty smaller staves around the circumference. The "roundhouse" had a hard-pounded dirt floor (with indentures for storage pits and the central hearth), with bark and thatch for a roof and walls of intertwined branches. There were also transient camps, used in hunting and trading, containing two to four dwellings.

Massive Earthworks. The Adenans are most remembered for their massive earthworks. Two major theories have been offered to explain the Adenan practice of building mounds. One, the diffusionist doctrine, suggests contact with Mexico and the dissemination of both corn cultivation and pyramid construction to the Ohio Valley at the same time. The other, the developmental theory, contends that the accumulation of surplus wealth through a successful economy enabled the Adenans to engage in gigantic public works projects. Perhaps the answer is found in a combination of both approaches. With better agricultural production, an increased population, improved social organization, and long-distance trade and communication, the Adenans had the means and the motive to engage in building monumental architecture.

Between three and five hundred Adenan mounds have been found; they vary greatly in size and purpose. Some are in ceremonial or symbolic shapes, such as the Great Serpent Mound near Peebles, Ohio. More than 1,330 feet long, 15 to 20 feet in width, and averaging a height of 4 feet, it represents an outstretched serpent (with coiled tail) with head and jaws closing on another mound, variously said to be an apple or an egg. Other Adenan mounds are circular or square, perhaps enclosing sacred sites where religious rites were conducted. Common are the tomb mounds. Some of these were burial plots for single funerals, and some were for multiple funerals. Both children and leaders (chiefs, priests, great hunters, warriors, and expedition leaders) had mound burials. Cremation and bodily burial were both practiced. From archaeological excavation it has been determined that mound construction was a community project. Initially the ground was cleared—the scrub timber being burned and the site being leveled. If entombment was planned, either graves were dug in the base or corpses were placed in a log building erected on the site. Hundreds of laborers, carrying baskets and skin aprons full of dirt, would then complete a low, rectangular ridge of dirt and begin the "inner" or "first" mound. Sticks, shells, hoes, and animal bones were used to loosen soil. Over the core mound, the outer shell was raised, often being as much as 100 feet high and covering several acres.

The fate of these brilliant prehistoric builders is disputed. Since their influence is evident in subsequent cultures in the Ohio Valley, the best guess is that they were assimilated by their successors, especially the Hopewell people, after 200 C.E.

—*C. George Fry*

See also Archaic; Effigy mounds; Hopewell; Mounds and mound builders; Prehistory—Northeast; Woodland.

BIBLIOGRAPHY

Jennings, Jesse D., ed. *Ancient Native Americans*. San Francisco: W. H. Freeman, 1978.

Kehoe, Alice B. *North American Indians: A Comprehensive Account*. Englewood Cliffs, N.J.: Prentice Hall, 1981.

Scheele, William E. *The Mound Builders*. Cleveland, Ohio: World, 1960.

Waldman, Carl. *Encyclopedia of Native American Tribes*. New York: Facts on File, 1988.

Webb, William S., and Raymond S. Baby. *The Adena People, No. 2*. Columbus: Ohio State University Press, 1957.

Webb, William S., and Charles E. Snow. *The Adena People*. Lexington: University Press of Kentucky, 1945.

Adobe

TRIBES AFFECTED: Pueblo peoples

SIGNIFICANCE: Adobe, an energy-efficient building material, made possible the typical buildings of the Puebloans of the Southwest

"Adobe" comes from the identical Spanish word, which in turn is taken from the Arabic word *attoba*, meaning "the brick." Adobe bricks are made of clay and straw mixed with water and dried in the sun. The word can be used to describe the bricks themselves or the clay or soil from which they are made, as well as the mortar sometimes made from them and the structures built with them.

Adobe is used as a building material primarily in the southwestern United States by the Pueblo peoples, which include such well-known tribes as the Hopi and Zuni. They build large community dwellings of masonry and adobe that endure, in some cases, for centuries.

Some of the oldest standing structures in the United States are made of this material. Adobe is energy-efficient, as it insulates well against both heat and cold. Buildings made of adobe can rise up to five stories in height. It is a building material well suited to the desert environments in which it is most commonly used.

See also Architecture—Southwest; Cliff dwellings; Kivas; Pueblo; Pueblo tribes, Eastern; Pueblo tribes, Western; Southwest.

Adobe Walls, Battles of

DATE: November 26, 1864, and June 27, 1874

PLACE: Texas

TRIBES AFFECTED: Cheyenne, Comanche, Kiowa

SIGNIFICANCE: The confrontations at Adobe Walls reflect a pattern of ongoing conflict between whites and Plains Indians that culminated in the decisive defeat of the latter in the Red River War

There were two engagements in present-day Hutchinson County, Texas, near Adobe Walls, which were the ruins of a trading post built in 1843 by William Bent and abandoned before 1864.

The first clash occurred when Colonel Christopher "Kit" Carson was told to attack the winter camps of the Kiowa and Comanche, who were threatening federal posts in New Mexico. Carson moved down the Canadian River into Texas with fourteen officers and 321 enlisted men of the First New Mexico Cavalry, as well as seventy-five Ute and Apache allies, two howitzers, and a wagon train. On the morning of November 26, 1864, he attacked a Kiowa encampment with his mounted troops, leaving the infantry with the wagons. The ensuing alarm brought several thousand Kiowa and Comanche warriors to confront Carson, who established a defensive position at Adobe Walls. Sporadic attacks by Kiowa and Comanche were disrupted primarily by Carson's howitzers, and at dusk he retreated to reunite his command. The next day he continued his withdrawal, having lost three killed and fifteen wounded but having inflicted perhaps a hundred casualties on his opponents. Carson was praised for extricating his force from their predicament.

The second engagement occurred nearly ten years later in 1874, after white buffalo hunters built a trading post near Adobe Walls. Angry clashes led to an attack by about seven hundred Kiowa, Comanche, and Cheyenne, led by Quanah Parker and Lone Wolf, on the post, which was occupied by about two dozen men and one woman. The warriors were told by a shaman that they could not be harmed, but heavy casualties led to the failure of their assault on June 27, 1874. After five days of siege, the hunters had lost four men, while the number of defenders had increased to about a hundred. The attackers, who had lost several dozen, withdrew. This escalating pattern of violence led to the Red River War, during which Adobe Walls was abandoned for good in August, 1874.

See also Indian-white relations—U.S., 1831-1870; Indian-white relations—U.S., 1871-1933; Lone Wolf; Parker, Quanah; Red River War.

Adoption

TRIBES AFFECTED: Pantribal

SIGNIFICANCE: Native Americans had very different ideas about family from those now accepted in America; many more people were considered family to begin with, and adoption was a widespread practice

In most American Indian cultures, a family was not only the nuclear family but also parents, parents-in-law, aunts, uncles, cousins, and other related individuals who might need the "sponsorship" of a family. An example of one to be adopted would be a great aunt whose children had died or moved to another camp or tribe. Individuals who had been adopted became part of the family.

Adoption could be temporary or permanent. For example, the Ute allowed their children to live with Spanish-speaking residents of trading partners so that the children would learn a second language and culture. These children then belonged to both families, although they continued to identify themselves as Ute. Among most nations, related children, such as a cousin's child, might be reared by the parents until a certain age and then allowed to live with relatives who might have special skills or children of similar age. While these were not considered adoptions by Indians, they are frequently cited in the non-Indian literature about Indians as adoptions. A Cheyenne girl who showed particular interest in quillwork at nine years of age might go to live with an aunt who was skilled in this work. Her parents, brothers, sisters, and cousins often continued to interact with her on a daily basis.

Adoptions, as defined by American society, also took place with orphans or captives. When a person of any age was claimed as a relative, full family status was accorded to him or her by all members of the family, and the person was treated as though he or she had been born into the family. That may be the reason that so many children who had been captured and reared by Indians preferred to stay with them, even when "rescued." The immediate love and respect they received was sometimes more endearing than the strict, relatively unaffectionate European cultures and family interactions from which they were removed. Indian families were very loving and supportive; children were cherished, and adults gave freely to all children. Among the Lakota, children without parents were taken in by relatives, but other adults continued to give them horses and beaded clothing and to treat them kindly throughout their lives.

In another form of adoption, a bereaved parent mourning the death of a beloved child might be offered another child by a friend or relative. The Winnebagos were known to have done this. Again, these children were not considered as "belonging" to the receiving family. The giving family was extending to the receiving family the right to love, educate, adore, make gifts for, share stories with, and train the child. The child did not give up his or her birth family so much as he or she added another family. The child might reside in one home or the other at different times. The benefits of both families were stronger relationships, resulting in a stronger support system.

See also Children; Education, pre-contact.

African American-American Indian relations

TRIBES AFFECTED: Pantribal; historically, primarily Southeast tribes

SIGNIFICANCE: Traditional American racial history, by focusing on Indian-white or black-white relations, has ignored the important cultural contributions of Indian-black interaction

The failure of scholars seriously to research cultural contact between Native Americans and Africans resettled in the Americas is attributable in part to disciplinary specialization, but some fault also lies with ethnocentrism. Historians and anthropologists interested in studying African Americans or American Indians usually viewed their topic in relation to white culture. The background of European colonial imperialism has also tainted scholarship by tending to portray both Africans and Indians as uncivilized peoples without histories. It has been suggested by some scholars that Africans and Indians met in pre-Columbian times as a result of transatlantic crossings by Africans; however, most contact occurred after the onset of the slave trade in the sixteenth century. It reached its apogee with the southeastern tribes' adoption of the plantation slavery system. Within this historical context, African American and Native American political alliances since the 1960's become increasingly understandable.

Historical Background. Since the 1960's, revisionist historians have shown great interest in the histories of Native Americans and African Americans. The study of the history of the contact between these two groups has been a logical development, and much new evidence has emerged. For example, significant contact between Native Americans and Africans occurred in Europe at the time of Portuguese encounters with Africans. In the sixteenth century, Native Americans were traded for West African slaves, who were needed to work on Brazilian plantations.

The Spanish were the first major users of African slaves in the New World. An initial function of Africans, because of their knowledge of Indian culture, was to aid in exploration as guides and interpreters. The first African in the New World we know by name was Estevanico, a Muslim native of Acamor. He accompanied the expedition of Pánfilo de Narváez, which was shipwrecked off the coast of Florida in 1529. Francisco Vásquez de Coronado was also accompanied by Africans as he explored central Kansas in 1541.

Indigenous forms of servitude were modified by the Spanish to serve the labor needs of their mines and plantations. Beginning with Hernando de Soto in 1538, the Spanish transported thousands of Indians from the Southeast to the West Indies. By 1540, however, Indian slavery was deemed unsuitable because of the Indians' susceptibility to disease; thereafter African labor began to be used. The mixing of Native American and African slave populations in sixteenth century Spanish America created a solidarity between the two groups, as seen in numerous revolts and insurrections.

American Colonization. Contacts among the races in the age of exploration were minor compared with those that occurred in the period of colonization. The main areas of interaction can be divided geographically into, first, New England, the middle colonies, and the Chesapeake; and second, the Southeast and Indian Territory. Except for the case of the Seminole Wars in Spanish Florida, the relations between blacks and Indians were not as amicable in English North America as they were in Spanish America. This was attributable in large part to demographics. The numbers of Indian and African slaves from New England to the Chesapeake were small in the early seventeenth century. Over time the Indian population diminished, and the black population increased. Although the two groups were initially few in number and spread over a large geographical area, there was extensive intermingling, which served to modify the physical appearance of both in Massachusetts, Connecticut, New York, New Jersey, Delaware, Maryland, and Virginia. The main form of relationship during this time was intermarriage between free blacks and reservation Indians. Reservations, in fact, were centers of racial fusion all the way from Cape Cod to the Chesapeake. Crispus Attucks, Paul Cuffe, and Frederick Douglass were famous men of mixed blood.

A mulatto named York, the first black to cross the continent, was critical to the success of the Lewis and Clark Expedition of 1804-1806. The explorers would have turned back at the Rocky Mountains had not York befriended the Shoshone, who provided needed supplies and horses. York, the son of two slaves, was known as "Big Medicine" by the Indians. He spoke several Indian languages as well as French. The Indian woman Sacagawea was his constant companion during the expedition.

Indian Slavery. The most massive contact between Indians and African Americans arose within the system of slavery developed by the so-called Five Civilized Tribes of the Southeast—the Cherokee, Chickasaw, Choctaw, Creek, and Seminole. Predominant among the Five Tribes were the Cherokee, whose 12,395-member nation held 583 slaves in 1809. By 1824 the numbers had grown to 15,560 and 1,277 respectively. Although it seems that the Cherokee were not unduly harsh masters, they refused to allow intermixture with blacks. The Chickasaw and Choctaw tribes together counted 25,000 members, with 5,000 slaves. Believing, like the Cherokee, in racial separation, these two tribes were crueler masters. The Chickasaw, who on occasion murdered the slaves of other owners, were especially cruel.

The Creek and Seminole were considered the least civilized of the Five Tribes, partly because they had the least prejudice toward blacks. This was especially true of the Seminole, who

The Creeks were said to be among the least prejudiced of the Southeast tribes, and intermarriage was common. Pictured are African Americans living in Creek territory in the late nineteenth century. (National Archives)

allowed their "slaves" to live in separate farming communities while paying a small annual tribute. The Creek, a patriarchal society, had children by slave women. The Creek reared these children as equals to their full-blooded progeny. A famous Creek chief, Tustennuggee Emartha, or Jim Boy, was of such mixed breed. The Seminole, who numbered about 3,900 in 1822, owned 800 slaves. These slaves were "maroons"—they had escaped the plantations of Georgia and the Carolinas. It was the presence of the maroons that initiated the Florida Wars.

War and Politics. Native American and African American military cooperation occurred in two campaigns closely related in time, geography, and cause. The second decade of the nineteenth century saw, in the Southeast, the outbreak of the Creek War and the First Seminole War. Both were precipitated by the anger of white slave owners who sought the return of their runaways from neighboring reservations. Andrew Jackson led the assault that crushed the Creek Red Stick Revolt in 1814, and he ended the First Seminole War in 1818 by capturing a Seminole stronghold in Florida.

African Americans figured prominently in both of these wars, since they had the most to lose in the event of a defeat. In numerous battles, Indians and blacks fought and died together. Jim Bowlegs, who was a slave of Chief Billy Bowlegs and served as his interpreter and adviser, later became a Seminole maroon leader, organizing a resettlement for his group in Mexico in 1850. The Indians and blacks continued to fight for their independence in two successive wars until the Civil War broke out.

The participation of slave-holding Indians in the Civil War was determined by their respective views on slavery. As mentioned above, the Chickasaw and Choctaw tribes were the most prejudiced against blacks, while the Creek and Seminole were the least. The former supported the Confederacy; the latter opposed it. The Cherokee held a divided position; mixed-bloods (part Indian, part white) generally supported the South, while full-bloods tended to sympathize with the North. In the confusion of war, the slaves were left largely on their own, attacking both Unionists and Confederates. After the war some blacks sought incorporation into the various tribes. This action was resisted by the Choctaw and Chickasaw. After the tribes' removal to Indian Territory, the legacy of Indian slave-holding was clearly evident. By 1907, no Seminole family was free of black intermixing, and almost no Creek families were pure-blooded. The other three tribes, however, had practically no mixture.

Since the 1960's a new alliance has occurred between Native Americans and African Americans in the arena of political activity. The Black Power and Civil Rights movements inspired Red Power organizations such as the American Indian Movement (AIM). Black theology has been the model for the development of what has been called "red theology." Such political actions have spread to international bodies such as the United Nations and the Organization of Indigenous Peoples, in which African and indigenous New World peoples sustain positive contact. —*William H. Green*

See also Cherokee; Choctaw; Creek; Osceola; Seminole; Seminole Wars; Slavery; Wildcat.

BIBLIOGRAPHY

Forbes, Jack D. *Black Africans and Native Americans: Color, Race, and Caste in the Evolution of Red-Black Peoples.* New York: Basil Blackwell, 1988. Using ethnohistorical and philological methods, the work breaks new ground in the study of American culture by stressing the Native American contributions to the tri-ethnic complexity of the nation's past.

Halliburton, R., Jr. *Red over Black: Black Slavery Among the Cherokee Indians.* Westport, Conn.: Greenwood Press, 1977. Describes how the formation of Cherokee slavery was part of an overall process of acculturation by the Cherokee Nation into American culture.

Hoover, Dwight W. *The Red and the Black.* Chicago: Rand McNally, 1976. Presents a detailed history of Indian-black interaction from the fifteenth century, with special attention to the distinct development of each culture.

Katz, William Loren. *Black Indians: A Hidden Heritage.* New York: Atheneum, 1986. This study examines how European Americans sought to discourage contacts between Indians and blacks from the age of exploration to Reconstruction.

Littlefield, Daniel F., Jr. *Africans and Creeks: From the Colonial Period to the Civil War.* Westport, Conn.: Greenwood Press, 1979. Examines the rise and development of Creek slavery from its beginnings to the aftermath of the Red Stick Rebellion.

_____. *Africans and Seminoles: From Removal to Emancipation.* Westport, Conn.: Greenwood Press, 1978. Shows the influence of African slaves on the Seminoles' activities as they fought and signed treaties with the federal government from the time of the removal policy to the Civil War.

Mulroy, Kevin. *Freedom on the Border: The Seminole Maroons in Florida, the Indian Territory, Coahuila, and Texas.* Lubbock: Texas Tech University Press, 1993. Perhaps the best study and interpretation of an example of Indian-black relations. This is a history of the long interaction between black Seminoles and their native masters as both sought to cooperate and survive the destructive federal policies.

Nash, Gary B. *Red, White, and Black: The Peoples of Early America.* Englewood Cliffs, N.J.: Prentice-Hall, 1974. The author argues that American culture arose as the product of three centuries of intense mixing and contact between three cultures: red, black, and white.

Porter, Kenneth W. "Relations Between Negroes and Indians Within the Present Limits of the United States." *Journal of Negro History* 17 (1932): 287-367. The best history of black-Indian relations available. The essay covers all geographical areas of the United States.

Perdue, Theda. *Slavery and the Evolution of Cherokee Society, 1540-1886.* Knoxville: University of Tennessee Press, 1979. This is the most detailed account of slavery in one of the Five Civilized Nations. A bibliographic essay is very comprehensive.

Agriculture

Tribes affected: Pantribal

Significance: Although the North American Indians have a long tradition of agriculture, it has not been successfully integrated with white agriculture; Indian agriculture has steadily declined

The beginnings of agriculture among the Indians of North America stretch far back into prehistory, perhaps as far back as seven thousand years. Exactly when it began—when the native peoples of North America began relying on deliberately cultivated crops for a portion of their caloric requirements—is a matter of debate. What is not in debate is where it began: Mexico is clearly the location of the earliest efforts to produce cultivated crops. From there, knowledge and seeds appear to have radiated outward, notably northward.

The progress of agriculture was very slow. It began with the domestication of one or two wild plants, the gathering of their seeds, and deliberate planting and raising of them at a prepared site in order to be able to harvest the resulting crop. Most likely the first efforts were more like gardens than agricultural fields, for the Indians were constrained by two factors that did not affect residents of the Old World: The Indians lacked metal tools and they lacked domesticated animals. All agriculture was hand labor, with tools that lacked the precise usefulness of modern, metal tools.

In time, however, the Indians were able to produce larger and larger portions of their caloric requirements from agriculture. That reduced their dependence on fruits and nuts they could gather and on game they could kill. By the time of European contact, some Indian tribes were supplying as much as 50 to 60 percent of their nutritional requirements from crops they planted, cultivated, and harvested.

The story of Indian agriculture falls naturally into three phases. The first phase, covering perhaps five thousand years, is all the time that transpired before Christopher Columbus initiated the flood of Europeans into the Western Hemisphere. The second phase (ate least in North America) is that covering the period from Columbus' discovery to the close of the American Revolution, roughly from 1500 to 1783. The third phase, in the United States, is the period after 1783, when the Indians were wards of the federal government.

Pre-contact Agriculture. The pre-contact agriculture of the North American Indians began in the highlands of Mexico. There, the earliest cultivated plants were the gourds, the cucurbits. In the earliest adaptations from wild plants, gourds were used as containers; the pulp was too bitter to eat. The seeds, however, did become a regular foodstuff, constituting the "peanuts" of Indian agriculture. As new varieties of cucurbit emerged (from careful seed selection by the Indians), squashlike vegetables were produced and eaten regularly.

During much of the millennium prior to European contact, most Indians lived in relatively permanent villages. They came to specialize in the production of food for the group. The women were responsible for the planting, cultivation, and much of the harvesting work; the men remained the hunters, going off on hunting expeditions, sometimes for weeks at a time.

The Indians settled in places where the soil could be easily worked with simple tools, often only a digging stick. The favored locations were stream bottoms, alluvial plains, and, to a lesser extent, ridge tops. These places generally had light, sandy soil that could be easily worked with tools made from forked sticks, clam shells, and stone.

If the land chosen for cultivation had shrubs and trees growing on it, the Indians generally girdled the trees and uprooted the shrubs. The latter, together with the herbaceous cover, were burned; the crops were planted around the stumps of any remaining trees. In most cases, the Indians burned over a field assigned to be cultivated each year; in this way they provided some lime and potash for the new crop.

Once the land was cleared for cultivation, a process carried out by the men of the tribe, the women took over. Planting was done with the aid of a dibble stick, thrust into the ground and worked around to provide a hole into which the seed could be dropped. Once the planted vegetables had come up, the Indian women weeded the crop at least once, sometimes twice. In the rare cases where irrigation was practiced, in the Southwest, the men were responsible for the construction and the maintenance of the irrigation ditches; otherwise agriculture was women's work.

The harvesting was also largely women's work, though the men sometimes helped with it. Depending on the crop, the harvested material needed to be prepared so that it would keep; this was usually accomplished by drying. The material was hung up in the sun until all the moisture was gone. It was then packed, often in baskets made from plant material (corn stalks, willow withes, and other flexible plant materials), and stored, frequently in pits.

By the end of the prehistoric period, the Indians were cultivating a wide variety of crops. The most important of these, squashes, beans, and corn, had all come from central Mexico. The squashes came first; beans came later, probably around 1000 C.E., but in time came to constitute an important part of the Indian diet. Their usefulness depended on the possession of pottery vessels in which they could be cooked.

Without a doubt, the most important Indian crop was maize, a cultivated version of the wild plant teosinte, a native of the central Mexican highlands. How early a cultivated maize had developed in North America is under dispute among archaeologists. There is, however, evidence that maize as a cultivated crop was widespread among Native Americans by 1000 C.E.

Prior to the development of maize, there is archaeological evidence of the cultivation of some native grasses that produced seeds rich in oil. Sumpweed (Iva annua), goosefoot (Chenopodium bushianum or berlandieri), and sunflower (Helianthus annus) were the most important of these native plants that were domesticated by the Indians. Cultivation of these native species declined after the arrival of maize, as the latter fulfilled far more easily the carbohydrate nutritional needs of the Indians.

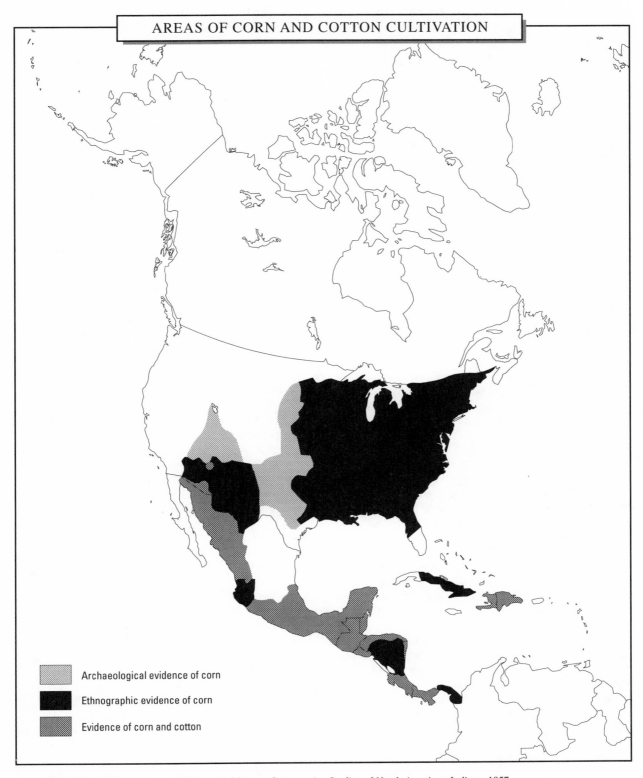

AREAS OF CORN AND COTTON CULTIVATION

Archaeological evidence of corn

Ethnographic evidence of corn

Evidence of corn and cotton

Source: After Driver, Harold E., and William C. Massey, *Comparative Studies of North American Indians*, 1957.

One important food plant that was never fully domesticated (although there is some evidence of domestication by the Chippewas) but was harvested for many centuries by the Indians of the northern tier of the United States was wild rice. The Indians of Minnesota to this day have exclusive rights to the wild rice growing in those northern swamps.

Two important crops that were not food crops were tobacco and cotton. Tobacco was grown (mostly by men, not women) for its ceremonial use. Tobacco was being grown all over what is now the United States by the resident Indians at the time of European contact. Cotton was grown only in the Southwest, generally in irrigated plots; it was developed as a crop sometime after 500 C.E. The southwestern Indians also developed the necessary skills to convert the fiber to cloth.

1500-1783. The arrival of the European colonists profoundly altered Indian agriculture in two principal ways: The Europeans, by trading manufactured items with the Indians for agricultural products, turned a portion of Indian agriculture into commercial agriculture. Additionally, the Europeans brought many new crops, some of which were eagerly adopted by the Indians.

The story of how the first Europeans to arrive as colonists survived only because they acquired food from the Indians is familiar to every American schoolchild. The Europeans brought with them manufactured products, notably axes, whose use the Indians could readily appreciate, and they were eager to acquire them. The Indians themselves had two things to offer: crops they had grown and skins from wild animals. The latter were in demand in Europe and financed much of the early development of the European colonies; the former were needed by the colonists for survival until they could develop their own fields.

One of the most important crops brought by the Europeans was wheat. The Spaniards introduced wheat to the Indians of the Southwest, and it became a major crop for the Indians of that area. The Indians of the Mississippi Valley also began growing wheat, as did the Plains Indians. The Spaniards also introduced the plow, and although some Indians (notably the Cherokee) were initially reluctant to use plows, many other tribes readily adopted plow agriculture. In some areas Indians actually traded plow services from the colonists for skins and agricultural products.

The Europeans added crops other than wheat to the traditional Indian produce. Both potatoes and tomatoes became part of the Indian diet as a result of European introduction. Watermelons and cantaloupes were also introduced by the Europeans. The Europeans introduced the idea of orchards, particularly peach orchards, and some tribes took to the idea. Peach orchards were particularly popular with the Indians of the Southwest. Apricots and apples were also grown in orchards after being introduced.

A major agricultural change introduced by the Europeans was the raising of livestock. The Indians had obtained all their meat from game prior to European contact. The Europeans brought horses, mules, cattle, sheep, and goats. Sheep and goats became particularly popular with the Indians of the Southwest, where grazing is the only possible agricultural use of much of the dry land of that area. It is widely known that the Plains Indians acquired horses from the Spaniards and that the acquisition profoundly altered their lifestyle. Some of the midwestern and eastern Indians recognized the value of oxen and began to use them for plowing.

1783-1887. The victory of the colonists in the American Revolution had a profound impact on Indian agriculture. The federal government, as soon as it was well organized, developed a definitive policy with respect to the Indians still living in the territory ceded by the British in 1783. That policy essentially involved separating the two groups—pushing the Indians into areas not inhabited by white Americans so as to open up more of the land for settlement by the colonists. With the Louisiana Purchase, this policy of separating the Indians from the white Americans became more explicit. By acquiring vast lands in the trans-Mississippi region, the federal government obtained western areas where it could establish new reservations to which the Indians could be "removed," thus effectively separating them from the European Americans.

At the same time, considerable effort was devoted to inculcating white agricultural practices. In the 1790's, Congress passed what were known as the Trade and Intercourse Acts, defining the relationship between Indians and white Americans. These acts stressed the development of white farming practices among the Indians and provided funds for tools (mostly plows and hoes) and even livestock to enable the Indians to become typical small farmers like the vast majority of white citizens of that time. The Indian agents appointed by the federal government for each tribe were instructed to promote such agricultural practices among the Indians.

1887-1934. In 1887, however, an abrupt change occurred in the Indian policy of the federal government. Although agriculture had been slowly gaining among the Indians, Congress became convinced that it could significantly lessen the costs of Indian support (needed to supplement the produce of Indian agriculture) if it created the incentive of private property. It therefore passed what was widely known, from its author, Senator Henry Dawes, as the Dawes Severalty Act, otherwise called the General Allotment Act. This act authorized the president to divide reservation land into individual allotments: Each head of household was to receive 160 acres, a single man 80 acres, and a child 40 acres. The title to the land was held in trust by the federal government for twenty-five years, at the end of which time full title to the land would be transferred to the Indian owner. If that owner should die before the twenty-five years had elapsed, the land was to be divided among all his heirs. If the reservation contained more land than was needed to allot each member of the tribe his prescribed share, then the remainder of the land was opened to white settlement. The funds derived from selling these "surplus" lands to whites were to be set aside in a trust fund for the benefit of the tribe.

Although the underlying concept of the General Allotment Act and the allotment policy was that it would hasten the time when all Indians would become at least subsistence farmers, it in fact had the opposite effect. There were a number of reasons for this failure. Most critics of the policy stress the fact that it attempted to impose, by legislation, a private-property culture on peoples whose own culture largely lacked such a concept. To Indians, the land was made available by the Great Spirit for the use of his children; that it should be used to amass individual wealth was wholly outside their sense of the appropriate.

Also crucially important was the fact that the land assigned to the Indians under the allotment system was incapable of providing subsistence for a family in the amount allotted. An allotment of 160 acres was simply too little land in an area of light rainfall, where tillage agriculture, if it could be carried on at all, depended on heavy capital investment in plows and harvesting equipment. Raising livestock was a practical option, but it required many more acres than the 160 allotted. The allotment policy discouraged the development of tribal herds run on a cooperative basis, actually the most hopeful revenue for Indian agriculture in the plains states. The result was, instead, that the Indians gave up attempts at agriculture and instead began leasing their land to whites who had the capital and the expertise to farm it.

By the 1920's, it was clear that the allotment policy was a failure. The secretary of the interior commissioned a report to be produced by a group of specialists headed by Lewis Meriam. Their report, known as the Meriam Report (1928), had three principal recommendations regarding agriculture. First, any notion of remaking the Indians into commercial farmers should be abandoned—the most that could be hoped for would be subsistence agriculture. Second, more government programs should be directed toward women to encourage subsistence gardening, poultry raising, and modern methods of food preservation. Third, the focus of Indian agriculture

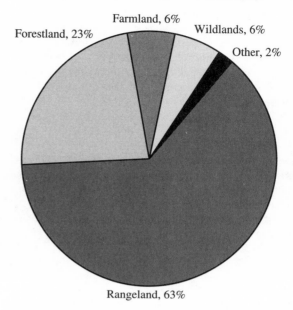

USE OF AMERICAN INDIAN LANDS, 1989

Forestland, 23%
Farmland, 6%
Wildlands, 6%
Other, 2%
Rangeland, 63%

Source: United States Department of Interior, *Bureau of Indian Affairs Natural Resource Information System Inventory and Production Report, 1989.*

Note: Includes only land under BIA jurisdiction, not privately owned lands.

should shift from tillage to livestock raising, for which the report said Indian men showed greater aptitude. The report recognized that most Indian land was only suitable for grazing anyway.

These recommendations laid the basis for a reversal of Indian agricultural policy under the New Deal of President Franklin Roosevelt. The Roosevelt Administration appointed a new commissioner of Indian affairs, John Collier, who had new ideas about how to conduct Indian policy. Collier pushed tribal initiatives, particularly cooperative agricultural efforts. These efforts had some success among Plains Indians. The Indian Reorganization Act of 1934 ended allotments for any tribes that agreed with the new policy. Any former reservation land that had been opened to white homesteading but not taken would be returned to the tribe, and some funds were provided for the purchase of additional land.

Since 1934. The steady decline in Indian land under the allotment policy was reversed, but only a modest portion of the more than 50 million acres once assigned to Indians but lost under allotment was recovered. Prior to allotment, Indians had had more than 100 million acres under their control; by the 1970's that figure had dropped to around 50 million.

The period since World War II has seen vacillating Indian policy on the part of the government. Agriculture has continued to decline among Indians, so that now no more than 10

Type of Crop	Acres	Value
Row crops	3,346,579	$49,723,580
Specialty	32,352	$33,398,568
Forage-hay-pasture	345,843	$32,756,937
Small grains	340,173	$27,598,590
Horticulture	9,880	$6,050,362
Wild rice	19,487	$1,545,950
Native hay	61,367	$648,655
Aquaculture	221,393	$143,000
Grapes	53	$90,805
Pecans	330	$20,000

PRODUCTS GROWN ON INDIAN-OWNED AND INDIAN-OPERATED LAND, 1989

Source: U.S. Department of the Interior, *Bureau of Indian Affairs Natural Resource Information System Inventory and Production Report, 1989.* Washington D.C.: U.S. Government Printing Office, 1989.

Note: Includes both Indian-owned and leased land; does not include timber or grazing lands.

percent are agriculturally active. In most recent years, the federal government, although recognizing its continuing responsibility to the Indians, has largely given up attempting to encourage agriculture among them.   —*Nancy M. Gordon*

See also Acorns; Beans; Corn; Cotton; Food preparation and cooking; General Allotment Act; Hunting and gathering; Indian Reorganization Act; Irrigation; Ranching; Reservation system of the United States; Squash; Subsistence; Wild rice.

BIBLIOGRAPHY

Carlson, Leonard A. *Indians, Bureaucrats, and Land: The Dawes Act and the Decline of Indian Farming.* Westport, Conn.: Greenwood Press, 1981. An intensive study of the effect of the allotment system on the participation of Indians in agriculture. Carlson includes an economic model of the behavioral response that might be expected to allotment-type inducements. Selected bibliography.

Ford, Richard I., ed. *Prehistoric Food Production in North America.* Ann Arbor: University of Michigan Press, 1985. A collection of papers by archaeologists involved in seeking data on prehistoric agriculture. The detail is fairly exhaustive, but the general picture is clear. Notes and bibliography.

Hurt, R. Douglas. *Indian Agriculture in America: Prehistory to the Present.* Lawrence: University Press of Kansas, 1987. A good general survey. The bulk of the book is devoted to discussing the Indian policy of the federal government as it relates to agriculture. The author is critical of the policy pursued as lacking in consideration for the special constraints imposed by Indian culture. Bibliographic note, extensive notes to text.

Russell, Howard S. *Indian New England Before the Mayflower.* Hanover, N.H.: University Press of New England, 1980. The author of the preeminent history of New England agriculture looks at the culture that preceded it. Part 4, "The Bountiful Earth," describes the agriculture of the New England Indians. Notes, extensive bibliography, and index.

Thomas, Peter A. "Contrastive Subsistence Strategies and Land Use as Factors for Understanding Indian-White Relations in New England." *Ethnohistory* 23 (1976): 1-18. A thoughtful consideration of the thorny question of whether the Indians or the European settlers were more efficient and effective users of the land. References.

Ahtna: Tribe

CULTURE AREA: Subarctic
LANGUAGE GROUP: Athapaskan
PRIMARY LOCATION: Copper River, Alaska
POPULATION SIZE: 101 (1990 U.S. Census)

The Ahtna were divided into Lower, Middle, and Upper autonomous bands, with a warlike stratified society of chiefs, nobles, commoners, and slaves organized into matrilineal clans and moieties. Their subsistence base was diversified with fishing, hunting, trapping, and gathering; their major food source was fish. They engaged in extensive trade with neighboring groups and distant Eskimo, and they utilized the potlatch to recognize status change, life crises, and for redistribution of traditional forms of wealth.

The first Ahtna-white contact was with Russian explorers in 1783, who established Copper Fort to protect fur-trading activities and who also introduced smallpox. The American fur trade began in 1876, and the 1898-1899 gold rush brought thousands of prospectors. Finally the military arrived in 1899 to explore the area and to protect the non-Indians, who had meanwhile introduced tuberculosis to the area.

The presence of the U.S. Army in Alaska during World War II intensified cultural change and the shift to a cash economy. Some employment is available through tourism, but most young people must leave to find employment in Anchorage. The number of college graduates among Ahtna youth is increasing.

See also Indian-white relations—Russian colonial; Subarctic.

Ais: Tribe

CULTURE AREA: Southeast
LANGUAGE GROUP: Muskogean
PRIMARY LOCATION: Indian River, east coast of Florida

The Ais were a Muskogean-speaking tribe who occupied the area along the Indian River on the east coast of Florida. Their principal village was located near Indian River Inlet.

They were primarily fishers and gatherers who traveled the adjacent waterways in dugout canoes. In the seventeenth and eighteenth centuries the Ais apparently dominated neighboring tribes to the north and south, while they were dominated by the Calusa to the west.

A shipwrecked Basque sailor seems to have been the first Spaniard to live with them and learn their language. In 1565, the Spanish governor, Pedro Menéndez, visited and established relations with them. A peace treaty was signed in 1570. In the 1590's the Ais sought an alliance with the Spanish, but the overtures were fruitless, as were others in later years. In 1609 an Ais chief, joined by minor coastal chiefs, visited the city of St. Augustine, where the chiefs were baptized. Evangelization by the Spanish, however, was never successful. The remaining Ais, probably numbering a few hundred, along with neighboring Indians, were removed to Cuba after Florida was ceded to Great Britain in 1763.

Information on the Ais is derived primarily from Spanish sources. The spelling of their name varies: Aix, Aiz, Alis, and Jece.

See also Muskogean language family; Southeast.

Alabama: Tribe

CULTURE AREA: Southeast
LANGUAGE GROUP: Muskogean
PRIMARY LOCATION: Alabama, Louisiana, Texas
POPULATION SIZE: 750 ("Alabama Coushatta," 1990 U.S. Census)

The Alabamas first came into contact with white explorers under Hernando de Soto in 1541, and by 1696 they were trading with Carolina traders. Later, they allied with the French. The tribe was part of the Creek Confederacy and lived on the Alabama River just below the junction of the Coosa and Tallapoosa rivers. They lived in permanent villages and were hunters, fishers, and farmers; they cultivated potatoes, corn, peas, and fruit trees.

In the mid-1700's many moved to Louisiana near the town of Opelousas, on the Opelousas River. The Alabamas who stayed took an active part in the Creek War of 1813-1814 and offered to help Andrew Jackson in the war against the Seminoles in 1828. This remnant was removed in 1836 to Indian Territory (Oklahoma).

After the Alabama migration, Louisiana was acquired by the United States in the Louisiana Purchase, and the Alabamas moved to the Spanish Territory of East Texas, near the town of Livingston. This settlement area was declared a reservation for the Alabama and Coushatti Indians in 1840. The state of Texas purchased the land in 1854 and vested the title in the Indians as a tribal unit.

The Alabamas prospered in Texas when game was plentiful but turned to farming as game decreased. The sandy soil produced poor crops, however, and poverty soon was widespread. By the late 1800's, the Alabamas were in great difficulty, surviving by finding work with logging companies. In 1928, citizens of Livingston as well as the Texas Federation of Women's Clubs succeeded in obtaining more than $100,000 from the U.S. government for the reservation, and Texas gave additional aid. When the Depression struck, the tribe suffered. Since that time, living conditions have improved. The reservation has a school and a hospital, and there are Indian-owned businesses.

The Alabamas have demonstrated remarkable patriotism. When the United States went to war in 1914, more than half the males of the tribe immediately volunteered. Many Alabamas served during World War II, and the members of the tribe bought more war bonds than the average citizen.

See also Coushatta; Creek War; Muskogean language family; Southwest.

Alaska Native Brotherhood and Alaska Native Sisterhood

DATE: Established 1912

TRIBES AFFECTED: Southeast Alaskan tribes

SIGNIFICANCE: Founded to fight social and political discrimination against Alaska Natives, the Alaska Native Brotherhood is the oldest modern Alaska Native or American Indian organization in the United States

With the stated goal of winning citizenship for Alaska Natives, twelve men and one woman formed the Alaska Native Brotherhood (ANB) in Sitka in 1912. One member was Tsimshian; the rest were Tlingit. A companion organization, the Alaska Native Sisterhood, is variously reported to have been established in 1915 or 1923. Within a decade there were chapters, called camps, throughout southeastern Alaska.

The founders of the Alaska Native Brotherhood were heavily influenced by Presbyterian missionaries, and in addition to promoting native civil rights, the organization urged the aban-

donment of traditional native languages and customs. In the 1960's, it reversed itself on this latter issue and was instrumental in the revival of many Haida and Tlingit traditions.

In the area of civil rights the ANB was active in the pursuit of voting rights and citizenship for Alaska Natives. In 1922, an ANB leader and attorney, William Paul, successfully defended his great-uncle Chief Shakes against the felony charge of voting illegally. Thus, Alaska Natives won the right to vote two years before Congress passed the Indian Citizenship Act in 1924.

The brotherhood led a series of boycotts against businesses that discriminated against natives and in 1946 lobbied successfully for the passage of the Antidiscrimination Act by the territorial legislature. It also successfully lobbied Congress to extend the 1934 Indian Reorganization Act to include Alaska. This contributed significantly to economic development in southeastern Alaska by enabling several native villages to apply for federal loans to purchase fishing boats and canneries.

The brotherhood mounted the first organized efforts to secure land rights for Alaska Natives. Its efforts were a precursor to the Alaska Native Claims Settlement Act of 1971.

See also Alaska Native Claims Settlement Act; Indian Citizenship Act; Political organization and leadership.

Alaska Native Claims Settlement Act

DATE: 1971

TRIBES AFFECTED: Ahtna, Aleut, Alutiiq, Eyak, Haida, Han, Holikachuk, Ingalik, Iñupiat, Kolchan, Koyukon, Kutchin, Tanacross, Tanaina, Tanana, Tlingit, Tsimshian, Yupik

SIGNIFICANCE: The establishment of "for profit" native corporations to replace the signing of treaties and creation of reservations set a precedent for subsequent land-claims negotiations and settlements

Although Alaska had been part of the United States since 1867, treaties had established only six small reservations in southeastern Alaska. The vast majority of Alaska's eighty thousand natives continued to claim aboriginal title (and therefore fishing, hunting, and other land rights) to the 400 million acres that make up the state of Alaska. A number of land use and aboriginal rights controversies in the 1960's led to the creation of the Alaska Federation of Natives (AFN) in October of 1966. The 1967 discovery of oil on Alaska's North Slope, and the resulting plans to build a trans-Alaska pipeline from Prudhoe Bay to Valdez, was yet another factor that initiated serious land claims negotiations between Alaska Natives and the federal government. The AFN carried out most of the formal negotiations and lobbying leading up to the signing of the Alaska Native Claims Settlement Act (ANCSA) on December 18, 1971.

ANCSA created an entirely new regime by which natives and native institutions related to themselves, the land, and the larger society. ANCSA extinguished native title to all but 44 million acres of land in exchange for $962.5 million. The previously established reservations and the existing tribal governments were dissolved. In their place, ANCSA mandated the

ALASKA NATIVES IN ALASKA NATIVE REGIONAL CORPORATIONS, 1990

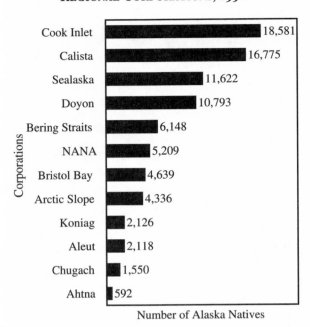

Number of Alaska Natives

Cook Inlet — 18,581
Calista — 16,775
Sealaska — 11,622
Doyon — 10,793
Bering Straits — 6,148
NANA — 5,209
Bristol Bay — 4,639
Arctic Slope — 4,336
Koniag — 2,126
Aleut — 2,118
Chugach — 1,550
Ahtna — 592

Source: U.S. Bureau of the Census, *We, the First Americans.* Washington, D.C.: U.S. Government Printing Office, 1993.

creation of twelve regional, and more than two hundred village, corporations.

The twelve regional corporations, corresponding to historical and cultural groupings of Alaska Natives, divided the land and the $962.5 million. A thirteenth corporation, established for natives living outside the state, received cash only. Of the land received, half was to be conveyed to the village corporations within each region. A portion of the cash settlement was also to be shared with the village corporations empowered to develop and operate community businesses. Since the regional corporations were expected to invest in more grandiose enterprises, they were given greater powers to develop land and to tax those operating within their zones. Both regional and village corporations were expected to make a profit for their native shareholders. Some of them, notably Sealaska in southeastern Alaska and the Arctic Slope Regional Corporation on the North Slope, have done quite well.

Initially, ANCSA provided for stock ownership only for those natives born prior to the date of enactment. It also established a twenty-year period during which corporate lands and profits could not be taxed and individual stocks could not be sold. This moratorium was set to expire in 1991, creating fears that the corporations—and most important, the lands they held—would become vulnerable to non-native corporate raiders or be sold to satisfy debts. Congress responded to some of these concerns by amending ANCSA in 1988. The amend-

ment provided for the establishment of "settlement trusts" to which corporate lands may be conveyed. The trusts, and therefore the land held by them, cannot be transferred from native control. Congress also permitted the corporations to amend their own articles of incorporation in order to issue new stock to those born after 1971 and to prevent the sale of stock to outsiders.

See also Alaska Native Brotherhood and Alaska Native Sisterhood; General Allotment Act; Land claims.

Alcatraz Island occupation

DATE: 1969-1971
PLACE: Alcatraz Island, San Francisco Bay
TRIBES AFFECTED: Various
SIGNIFICANCE: The takeover of Alcatraz Island symbolized the awakening of American Indian peoples to cultural and political concerns, even though its stated goal, the establishment of a Center for Native American Studies, was not realized

The occupation of Alcatraz Island in San Francisco Bay by an organization calling itself Indians of All Tribes was a high-profile act of self-empowerment by native American people. In 1962, the United States government closed operations of the federal penitentiary situated on the island. There were actually two subsequent occupations of the island by young American Indian people. First came a short-lived effort in 1964, then the highly publicized takeover of 1969 which lasted until June of 1971, when federal marshals and other law enforcement officials removed all American Indians left on the island.

The occupying Indians wanted the island to be transformed into a Center for Native American studies. This would involve the practice of traditional tribal spirituality; people would be trained in song, dance, and healing ceremonies. It would also be a place of training in scientific research and ecology. Also, it was to become an Indian training school whose purpose would be to teach the use of modern economics to end hunger and unemployment.

The Indians of All Tribes organization desired transfer of Alcatraz as surplus federal property, in the same manner that facilities such as Roswell Air Force Base in New Mexico, the Stead Air Force Base in Nevada, the Madera Radar Station, and Camp Parks were transferred to such profit-making organizations as Philco-Ford, Radio Corporation of American (RCA), and Litton.

Negotiations were carried out with Robert Robinson of the National Council on Indian Opportunity representing the United States. In March of 1970, the government's counterproposal included these ideas: a new name for the island, possibly from the Ohlone language; monuments commemorating noted American Indian people placed on the island park; a cultural center and museum built as an integral part of the park plan; and a number of Indians professionally trained as park rangers by the National Park Service. The federal government balked at the idea of locating an institution of higher learning on the island, noting that the first tribally controlled college was already being established at Many Farms on the Navajo Reservation and that a number of Native American studies courses were being offered at universities across the nation. This proposal was rejected by the Indians of All Tribes, and the negotiations broke down. On June 11, 1971, federal marshals arrested everyone on Alcatraz Island.

The takeover of Alcatraz Island served as a symbol in re-awakening American Indian people, as self-determination continued to replace federal policies of relocation and termination.

See also Activism; Longest Walk; Pine Ridge shootout; Trail of Broken Treaties; Wounded Knee occupation.

Alcoholism

TRIBES AFFECTED: Pantribal

SIGNIFICANCE: American Indians, whether living on or off reservations, have extremely high rates of alcoholism; many Indian problems with crime, health, and poverty are related to heavy drinking

The most severe health problem among contemporary American Indians is alcoholism. The reasons for the problem are complex, but central among them are poverty, a pervasive sense of despair (particularly among young reservation Indians), and the stresses involved in adjusting to non-Indian life. Both Indian and non-Indian sources, contemporary and historical, also point to drinking as one reaction to the profound disruption of Indian societies that began soon after Europeans landed in the Americas and which intensified through the years.

Early Contact Years. With the exception of parts of the Southwest, alcoholic beverages did not exist in North America before the Europeans came, though they were widely used by Central and South American natives. Early French and English explorers, trappers, and merchants often gave Indians liquor as a gift or exchanged it for food or furs. By the early 1600's, for example, French Canadian traders were encouraging the use of alcohol among the Huron, even though the Catholic church deplored such practices and the French government outlawed the sale or use of liquor in trade. As early as 1603, French priests in Canada reported that many natives were drinking alcohol heavily during their ceremonies and dances. Whiskey and rum quickly became prime items of trade—and killers of Indians. European traders cultivated the desire for liquor among Indians, creating a market; they realized that trading liquor was a cheap way to obtain valuable furs. John Stuart stated in 1776 that English traders obtained five times as many animal skins from the Choctaws of the Southeast through trading alcohol than through the trade of English manufactured goods of any real value. This situation, he said, was making the Choctaws "poor, wretched, . . . and discontented."

The white stereotype of the dangerous firewater-drinking Indian became established early. Regardless of what some whites believed, the truth is simply that some Indians drank and others did not. Drinking patterns varied by individual and by tribe; a number of cultures, among them the Pawnee, were

known for not drinking at all. Eighteenth century accounts suggest that, among the Iroquois, there were occasional drunken revels that would essentially engulf a whole village or town and end when the liquor was gone; life would then return to normal. Indian drinking behavior was no more dangerous or violent than that of the Europeans who lived along the frontier. A difference, however, was that Indian cultures, having no previous experience with alcohol intoxication, did not have a set of social norms or expectations governing drinking, as European cultures did. There were no religious strictures or stigma attached to being under the influence of alcohol, and being drunk may have developed religious overtones in some Indian cultures. The Lakota Sioux called alcohol "the magic water," for example, and some scholars have noted a link between drinking liquor until drunk and the traditional Indian practice of going on a vision quest seeking wisdom and strength through fasting, meditation, and prayer until a state of altered consciousness is achieved. Alcohol intoxication may also have been considered akin to being influenced or possessed by a supernatural being.

Many tribal political and religious leaders soon recognized the danger that alcohol posed to traditional culture. Many tribal leaders tried to ban alcohol from their villages, but such efforts rarely succeeded. A number of post-contact religious movements, or revitalization movements, among American Indians included abstinence from liquor as a central tenet: One was the Longhouse religion established by Handsome Lake; another was the pan-Indian movement led by Tenskwatawa.

In the Indian Trade and Intercourse Acts of 1834, the United States government prohibited the sale of alcohol to Native Americans, but enforcing the law proved impossible. Smugglers made huge profits, and bootlegging became one way of becoming very rich on the frontier. Alcohol remained illegal on Indian reservations until 1953, when Congress permitted its sale if local tribal governments voted to allow it. Easier access to alcoholic beverages led to a steady increase in cases of alcoholism among Native Americans.

Impact on the Indian Population. A report issued by the American Indian Policy Review Commission, established by Congress in 1975 to survey major reservation problems, concluded that alcohol abuse was the most severe health care problem faced by Native Americans. It found that almost one-half of Indian adults had some sort of chemical dependency, with alcohol being the chemical most often abused. Statistics at the time of the commission's report emphasized the prevalence of the problem: Seventy-one percent of all arrests on reservations involved alcohol, and the death rate from drunk driving on reservations was three times the rate for the general population. Death from cirrhosis of the liver, almost always caused by alcoholism, was more than four times greater for Indians (27.3 per 100,000) than for other Americans (6.1 per 100,000). The suicide rate among Native Americans—which drinking undoubtedly influences—was more than double the national rate. Another alcohol-related health problem, one which has been recognized relatively recently, is

ALCOHOLISM MORTALITY RATES AMONG AMERICAN INDIANS (PER 100,000 PERSONS), 1984-1988					
	Rate per Year				
Population	1984	1985	1986	1987	1988
American Indians and Alaska Natives	30.0	26.1	24.6	25.9	33.9
U.S. total	6.2	6.2	6.4	6.0	6.3
Ratio of American Indian/Alaskan Native to U.S. total	4.8	4.2	3.8	4.3	5.4

Source: Data are from U.S. Department of Health and Human Services, *Trends in Indian Health.* Washington, D.C.: U.S. Government Printing Office, 1991.

Note: Includes death from alcohol dependence syndrome, alcohol psychoses, and chronic liver disease specified as alcoholic.

fetal alcohol syndrome (FAS), a disease that stunts growth and interferes with brain development in the babies of alcoholic mothers. Native American women have been found to have babies born with fetal alcohol syndrome at a rate greater than ten times that of the rest of the U.S. population.

A 1985 study reported that one-third of all Indian deaths were related to alcohol—three times as many as the U.S. average. In 1986, recognizing the severity of the problem, Congress enacted the Indian Alcohol and Substance Abuse Prevention and Treatment Act.

Those who have studied Indian drinking generally believe that alcohol abuse among Native Americans results from the same factors that lead to high levels of alcoholism among other populations: It is a means of coping with unemployment, poverty, and alienation. The economic situation of American Indians, particularly those on isolated reservations, is grim compared with that of most Americans. In the late twentieth century, following the awakening (and oppression) of Indian activism in the 1960's and 1970's, younger Indians became increasingly aware of past injustices toward Indians and increasingly desperate regarding what seemed to be the lack of future opportunities.

Other aspects of Indian alcoholism are the social factors thought, by some, to encourage drinking actively. It has been suggested that drinking may amount to a form of social protest: By not obeying the rules of white society, a Native American displays contempt for those who destroyed his or her culture and who now do not offer opportunities in theirs. Drinking is tolerated by many adults on reservations, and there is little pressure put on alcoholics to seek help or change their ways. One study of a reservation in North Dakota found that most residents faced almost daily pressure from friends and family members to drink. Many adults supported the idea that individuals have the right to become publicly intoxicated. In addition, drunkenness was seen as a way of acknowledging

that one is no better than one's neighbor and that one knows how to have a good time; viewed in this way, drinking may be seen as representing a sense of community.

There is hope that the situation will begin to improve. Groups such as Alcoholics Anonymous have opened chapters in Indian communities. In addition, the search for an Indian answer to alcoholism has involved the reawakening of interest in Indian spiritual and cultural traditions. Because Indian alcoholism so often involves group activity, approaches involving groups and entire communities have proved more beneficial than have private counseling and treatment. As Indian cultural pride and solidarity increase, as more Indians themselves work for the Indian Health Service (which serves reservation communities), and as sufficient funding becomes available, new possibilities exist for stemming the tide of alcoholism.

—*Leslie V. Tischauser*

See also Civil rights and citizenship; Employment and unemployment; Medicine and modes of curing, post-contact; Relocation; Trade and Intercourse Acts; Urban Indians.

BIBLIOGRAPHY

Dorris, Michael. *The Broken Cord.* New York: Harper & Row, 1989.

Frederick, Calvin J. *Suicide, Homicide, and Alcoholism Among American Indians: Guidelines for Help.* Washington, D.C.: U.S. Government Printing Office, 1973.

Indian Health Service, Task Force on Indian Alcoholism. *Alcoholism: A High Priority Health Problem.* Washington, D.C.: U.S. Government Printing Office, 1977.

Leland, Joy. *Firewater Myths.* New Brunswick, N.J.: Publications Division of Rutgers Center of Alcohol Studies, 1976.

Levy, Jerrold E., and Stephen J. Kunitz. *Indian Drinking: Navajo Practices and Anglo-American Theories.* New York: John Wiley & Sons, 1974.

Shkilnyk, Anastasia M. *A Poison Stronger than Love: The Destruction of an Ojibwa Community.* New Haven, Conn.: Yale University Press, 1985.

Aleut: Tribe

CULTURE AREA: Arctic

LANGUAGE GROUP: Eskimo-Aleut

PRIMARY LOCATION: Alaska and the Aleutian Islands

POPULATION SIZE: 10,052 (1990 U.S. Census)

The Aleut, consisting of two main groups, the Atka and Unalaska Aleut, probably migrated from Siberia about 6000 B.C.E. into Alaska and moved into the Aleutian Islands around 2000 B.C.E. Their name comes from the Russian word meaning "barren rock." "Atka" is the Aleutian word for island, and "Alaska" comes from the Aleutian word for mainland. The Aleut people occupied about a dozen of the hundred or so islands (the Aleutians) that stretch from Alaska more than 1,200 miles into the Pacific. Their language resembles that of the Eskimos (Inuits). Aleuts and Eskimos moved to the New World significantly later than American Indians did. The Unalaskas live on islands close to the Alaska coast, while the Atkas live on remote islands in the Pacific.

Society and Subsistence. Aleut culture is similar to the Eskimo way of life. Both depend heavily on the sea for their existence. Seal hunting was the most important economic activity, and Aleuts became expert at this task. Most food came from the ocean, including whale meat, fish, oysters, and clams. Aleut hunters learned to navigate by following ocean currents, and they could travel on the water at night simply by feeling the direction of the wind. In times when hunting failed to bring home enough food, Aleuts ate seaweed and birds' eggs. The eggs were gathered by lowering a man on a rope over the side of a cliff to the nests, a very dangerous practice that led to many deaths and injuries.

Aleuts lived in small, isolated villages with populations of a hundred or less and no more than twelve houses. They built homes of logs, whale bones, and skins sunk at least 3 feet into the ground. A ladder from the roof provided an entranceway, and people sat inside on mats in these windowless structures. Each house contained several families, and polygamy (a man having more than one wife) and polyandry (a woman having more than one husband) were both permitted. A chief (*toyon*) headed each community, and every village had its own leader; no central authority existed among the Aleuts. The chief, who inherited his office, settled quarrels, protected village hunting grounds, and led the villagers in time of war. In return he received a portion of all foodstuffs acquired by villagers during hunts. Chiefs usually became quite wealthy but could lose their positions if they exhibited cowardice during battle.

Because of the large number of villages, there were disputes and quarrels over hunting boundaries, and Aleuts frequently fought with one another. They usually attacked their enemies at dawn, killing the warriors and taking women and children as slaves. High-ranking enemies such as a chief and his sons could also be enslaved. Aleut society had three major classes: chiefs, warriors, and slaves.

Religion. Traditional Aleut religion revolved around worship of Agudar, the creator of the universe, the provider of good fortune, and the guardian of paradise. The men worshiped in a sacred place, usually in a cave or at a certain rock, and excluded women and children. Only adult males could make offerings of sealskins and feathers and learn the sacred language of the spirits. Aleuts believed that the human spirit lived on but became invisible after death and protected loved ones still in the earthly world from harm. Death led to cremation for slaves and commoners, but important leaders and young children were mummified by removing their internal organs through a hole in the chest. Family members then laid the body in a stream until it was clean, stuffed it with grass, oiled it, wrapped it in furs, and placed it in a dry cave. They suspended the body aboveground in a cradle and left. Shamans contacted the spirits of the dead and learned about hunting prospects and what the future held. Traditional religion disappeared after initial contact with Russian fur trappers and missionaries. Most Aleuts converted, sometimes forcibly, to the Eastern Orthodox faith, and it has remained the principal religion of survivors.

Material Culture. The severe climate and shortage of natural resources placed major limitations on Aleut material culture and art. They made clothes from fur, birdskin, and whale intestines. Generally, their parkas and dresses reached to their ankles. Aleuts did not wear shoes or foot covering. They made wooden hats, and hunters wore well-designed wooded eye shades to protect their eyes from the glare while at sea. Artists produced masks and bowls from the bones and intestines of whales, sea otters, and other mammals. Pottery was nonexistent, and most food containers were skins. Aleut women made fine baskets of wild grasses, however, that became noted for their geometric designs and expert craftsmanship. Hunters built their own kayaks, an especially prized and important possession. They were light and fragile and built to individual body measurements. At sea they could travel at a relatively rapid 7 miles per hour. Hunters used spears thrown by hand from a sitting position in the kayak. Bows and arrows were used only in warfare. Aleuts killed whales with poison-pointed spears and let the bodies drift to shore, where they were butchered.

First contact with the Russians took place in the early 1700's, with devastating consequences for the native population. Between 1750 and 1780 almost 90 percent of Aleuts, who numbered about 25,000 before contact, died from smallpox, malnutrition, forced labor in Russian hunting parties, and even suicide. Aleuts proved such good hunters that Russian trappers forced them to pursue seals and otters almost constantly. The Russians forced all males to hunt seals and otters; refusal meant torture or death. Women and children left behind in isolated villages with little food during these forced hunts frequently starved to death. By the 1840's, after less than a century of Russian domination, fewer than 4,200 Aleuts remained alive. When the United States bought Alaska, which included the Aleutian Islands, in 1867, the Aleut population stood at fewer than 3,000. American control did not lead to better conditions. A tuberculosis epidemic in the 1890's and migration to the mainland reduced the number of islanders to 1,491.

Recent History. In 1911 the United States Department of the Interior prohibited the hunting of sea lions, a major resource of the Aleuts, because overhunting had led to a huge decline in their population. Two years later the Aleutian Islands became a National Wildlife Refuge, and the department banned most other hunting without a special permit. In the 1920's and 1930's a majority of Aleut males left their homes, heading for the Alaska coast to work in salmon canneries. During World War II the U.S. Navy removed all Aleuts from their island villages after the Japanese invaded Kiska and Attu in the far western Pacific and resettled them in southeastern Alaska. Only a few hundred returned to their homes when the war ended, and they found that many of their villages had been destroyed by American soldiers to prevent the Japanese from using them. Government officials gave the returnees rabbits to raise for food, but most of the animals died of disease or were eaten by rats. The experiment ended quickly. No crops could be raised in the rainy, cold (temperatures seldom get above 50 degrees), and windy climate.

Economic development was limited in the islands. The U.S. Navy built a large base on Adak Island but hired whites from the mainland for most available jobs. Work existed for only a few dozen native men, chiefly at the underground nuclear testing base on Amchitka Island. Those who remained in Alaska continued working in salmon and tuna canning factories. The death rate on the islands remained very high, especially among infants, into the 1970's, when the U.S. Public Health Service opened a facility on a remote island, the first hospital many Aleuts had ever seen. The Aleut League, formed in 1967, pressed for more economic assistance but had little success. The number of natives hovered around three thousand, far too few people to make any impression upon the federal government in Washington. Schools in the islands began bilingual education in 1972, and Aleut customs were taught, but extreme poverty remained the major problem. War on Poverty programs in the late 1960's provided some job training and literacy classes, but they created no new jobs, so out-migration continued. A majority of Aleuts now live on the mainland. Fewer than fifteen hundred live in the islands, where the only permanent jobs are found as support staff at government-owned facilities. The Department of Commerce, National Marine and Fisheries Service, controls seal hunting and pays hunters for their catches but in scrip, which can be spent only in local stores. For most Aleuts, life remains as hard and difficult as the climate in which they live.

—*Leslie V. Tischauser*

See also Arctic; Eskimo-Aleut language family; Inuit.

BIBLIOGRAPHY

Matthiessen, Peter. *Oomingmak: The Expedition to the Musk Ox Island in the Bering Sea*. New York: Hastings House, 1967.

Pallas, Peter S. *Bering's Successors, 1745-1780*. Edited by James R. Masterson and Helen Brower. Seattle: University of Washington Press, 1948.

Ray, Dorothy Jean. *Aleut and Eskimo Art: Tradition and Innovation*. Seattle: University of Washington Press, 1981.

_____. *The Eskimos of Bering Strait, 1650-1898*. Seattle: University of Washington Press, 1975.

Alford, Thomas Wildcat (July 15, 1860, near Sasakwa, Okla.—Aug. 3, 1938, Shawnee, Okla.): Educator

ALSO KNOWN AS: Gaynwawpiahsika

TRIBAL AFFILIATION: Shawnee

SIGNIFICANCE: Drawing on knowledge of white customs gained from his education with whites, Alford counseled Indians about their land rights and helped them to cope with rapid cultural changes

Born in Indian Territory, Alford was the grandson of the pan-tribal Indian leader Tecumseh. Educated in tribal customs until age twelve, he thereafter attended a mission school. In 1879, he earned a scholarship to Virginia's Hampton Institute, where he adopted Christianity. Upon returning to Indian Territory,

Alford initially was shunned by Indian traditionalists. Nevertheless, the following year, he was appointed principal of a federally funded Shawnee school, a position he occupied for five years.

In 1893, Alford chaired a federally sponsored committee designed to supersede Shawnee tribal government. Utilizing his knowledge of U.S. law, he assisted Indians in safeguarding their land rights during implementation of the allotment system. He also made trips to Washington, D.C., lobbying on behalf of his tribe. In addition, he was employed by the Bureau of Indian Affairs. Until his death, Alford continued advising his people, working to meliorate social problems exacerbated after Oklahoma achieved statehood in 1907.

See also Allotment system; Land claims; Indian-white relations—U.S., 1871-1933; Indian-white relations—U.S., 1934-1995.

Algonquian language family

CULTURE AREA: Northeast

TRIBES AFFECTED: Abenaki, Algonquin, Arapaho, Atsina, Blackfoot, Blood, Cheyenne, Cree, Fox, Illinois, Kickapoo, Lenni Lenape, Maliseet, Menominee, Micmac, Montagnais, Naskapi, Narragansett, Natick, Ojibwa, Passamaquoddy, Piegan, Potawatomi, Sauk, Saulteaux, Shawnee, Wampanoag, Wappinger

Proto-Algonquian is probably the best-known proto-language of the North American Indian languages north of Mexico, most likely because of the wide geographic spread of Algonquian tribes and the large number of researchers studying this family.

The Algonquian language family may be divided into three major groups: central, eastern, and western. The central languages are Cree, Montagnais, Naskapi, Menominee, Fox, Sauk, Kickapoo, Shawnee, Peoria, Miami, Illinois, Potawatomi, Ojibwa, Ottawa, Algonquin, Saulteaux, Delaware (Lenni Lenape), and Powhatan. The eastern group includes Natick, Narragansett, Wampanoag, Pennacook, Mohegan, Pequot, Wappinger, Montauk, Penobscot, Abenaki, Passamaquoddy, Maliseet, and Micmac. The western section consists of Blackfoot, Piegan, Blood, Cheyenne, Arapaho, Atsina, and Nawathinehena. It must be noted that scholars are not always in agreement about which ones are languages and which are dialects or subgroupings.

Culture Area. Among North American Indian groups, the tribes that speak Algonquian languages cover the largest area: They can be found from Vancouver Island and through Canada to Newfoundland, and in areas along the Atlantic Coast as far down as North Carolina. Since the time of white occupation in the United States, many changes in location and status have taken place. For example, Kickapoo, at one time contiguous with Fox and Sauk in the area of present Illinois, would later be spoken in Oklahoma and in Mexico. By the 1960's, the Arapaho were living principally in Oklahoma and Wyoming. Some five to six thousand Blackfoot were settled in Montana, Alberta, and Saskatchewan. Cheyenne had three to four thousand speakers in various states, but they were concentrated in Montana and Oklahoma. Cree also had thirty to forty thousand speakers, most of whom were in various parts of Canada; some were also in Montana. The Fox-Sauk were numerous in Iowa, Oklahoma, and Kansas. Kickapoo speakers were scattered among the central states, but some were also in Mexico, Oklahoma, and Kansas. Most of the Micmac settled in various provinces of Canada, as did the Montagnais-Naskapi. The Ojibwa (Chippewa) had a population of some forty to fifty thousand scattered across several Canadian provinces and in most of the states bordering Canada.

Status of Spoken and Written Languages. Karl V. Teeter and Wallace Chafe are but two of a number of scholars who have studied various Algonquian languages and have provided information about their status as languages still spoken by Indians of all ages. As of the mid-1970's, these were Arapaho, Blackfoot, Cheyenne, Cree, Fox-Sauk, Kickapoo, Micmac, Montagnais-Naskapi, and Ojibwa-Algonquin-Ottawa.

Nine Algonquian languages are no longer spoken: Carolina Algonquian, Connecticut-Unquachog-Shinnecock, Illinois-Peoria-Miami, Loup, Mahican, Massachusett, Mohegan-Pequot-Montauk, Nanticoke-Conoy, and Powhatan. The rest are either of questionable status—that is, as of the 1970's they were spoken only by an elderly generation—or are languages for which there is not a clear indication of status with regard to near-extinction. In the first category are Eastern and Western Abenaki, Delaware, and Menominee; in the latter are Maliseet-Passamaquoddy, Potawatomi, and Shawnee. Not surprisingly, the eastern group fares the worst, while the western languages remain the least threatened by extinction.

The most enduring Algonquian language is Ojibwa (Chippewa), which at mid-twentieth century had more than forty thousand speakers. It has a larger territorial range than any other Indian tribal language in North America. The territory extends roughly from the eastern end of Lake Ontario westward to the area around Lake Winnipeg in Manitoba and southward to the Turtle Mountains of North Dakota. The Ojibwas in Michigan have a printing of their original hymnal, which was translated by a missionary, Peter Jones, in the 1930's. Several midwest colleges and universities offer basic courses in Ojibwa.

The Cree and Ojibwa have written languages, as do the Delaware and Fox. The Cheyenne were particularly noted for the grace and fluency of their sign language.

Language Characteristics. While the Algonquian languages which survived into the 1900's obviously differ one from the other, it is nevertheless possible to make some general statements about the languages based on certain kinds of similarities. The sound systems of Algonquian languages are relatively simple, although features such as tone, accent, and voicing may cause difficulty for the non-native speaker. Proto-Algonquian has four basic vowel sounds, with a long and short version of each. Consonant clusters are subject to changes of various kinds in the modern languages. The syntax of an Algonquian word, on the other hand, is generally complex.

Nouns are differentiated according to such elements as whether a thing is animate or inanimate, singular or plural, and present or absent. The verb is central in a sentence and virtually amounts to a sentence in microcosm. The Algonquian languages are polysynthetic; that is, meaningful units are strung together so that a single word may often correspond to an entire English sentence. —*Victoria Price*

See also Algonquin; Language families; Northeast

BIBLIOGRAPHY

Bloomfield, Leonard. *Eastern Ojibwa: Grammatical Sketch, Texts, and Word List*. Ann Arbor: University of Michigan Press, 1957.

Bright, William, et al., eds. Linguistics in North America. Vol. 10 in *Current Trends in Linguistics*, edited by Thomas A. Sebeok. The Hague: Mouton, 1973.

Grinnell, George Bird. *The Cheyenne Indians: Their History and Ways of Life*. 2 vols. 1923. Reprint. Lincoln: University of Nebraska Press, 1971.

Muller, Siegfried H. *The World's Living Languages: Basic Facts of Their Structure, Kinship, Location, and Number of Speakers*. New York: Frederick Ungar, 1964.

Petter, Rodolphe. *English-Cheyenne Dictionary*. Kettle Falls, Wash.: Valdo Petter, 1915.

Voegelin, Charles F. "The Lenape and Munsee Dialects of Delaware: An Algonquian Language." *Proceedings of the Indiana Academy of Science* 49 (1940): 34-47.

Weslager, C. A. *The Delawares: A Critical Bibliography*. Bloomington: Indiana University Press, 1978.

Algonquin: Tribe

CULTURE AREA: Northeastern
LANGUAGE GROUP: Algonquian
PRIMARY LOCATION: Ontario, Canada
POPULATION SIZE: 5,780 in Canada (Statistics Canada, based on 1991 census); 1,543 in U.S. ("Algonquian," 1990 U.S. Census)

The Algonquin people, originally from eastern Canada and what would become the northeastern United States, gave their name to the language group of Algonquian speakers. Central Algonquians, including the Ottawas, Potawatomis, and Illinois, were pushed westward to the Great Lakes region by their hereditary Iroquois enemies in the mid-seventeenth century. The Algonquins proper, also enemies of the Iroquois, stayed in areas colonized by both the French and the English. Their tendency to prefer trade and military alliances with the French worked to their advantage, since French colonial rivalry with Iroquois-supporting Britain meant periodic support from a European ally in inter-Indian warfare.

Until the British finally pushed the French out of Canada in the 1760's, this pattern enabled the Algonquins to hold considerable territory in the Ontario region, communicating with other related tribes in areas that would become the United States. Prominent examples of this included the Wabanaki (most notably the Passamaquoddies and Penobscots of Maine and the Micmacs of New Brunswick) and, farther south, the

Wampanoag Federation. The latter had alliances with the famous seventeenth century tribe of Massachusetts (from the name of Massasoit, a dominant leader at the time of Pilgrim colonization).

The warring aggressiveness of the Iroquois, coupled with the already visible heavy hand of British colonialism on the Atlantic seaboard, caused the decline of the Algonquin tribal network by the end of the eighteenth century. Algonquins in Ontario, who became part of the Canadian reserve system, had a better chance of survival than those to the south in the United States.

By the nineteenth century, centuries of disruptions and dislocations had all but destroyed traditional Algonquin culture. Contemporary Algonquin population estimates vary according to what groups are considered "Algonquins." By the most inclusive definition, including the Abitibi, Kitcisagi, Nipissing, and other groups, there may be more than six thousand Algonquins in the U.S. and Canada.

See also Algonquian language family; Indian-white relations—English colonial; Micmac; Northeast; Wampanoag.

All-Pueblo Council

DATE: Established 1922
TRIBES AFFECTED: Pueblo tribes
SIGNIFICANCE: The All-Pueblo Council defended the integrity of Pueblo lands, communal life, and tribal traditions in the face of federal legislation threatening Pueblo reservation lands

The All-Pueblo Council was established in response to the proposed Bursum Bill of 1922. This legislation resulted from decades of controversy over land that had been purchased since 1848 by Hispanic and white settlers from the Pueblo Indians of New Mexico. In 1913, the United States Supreme Court ruled in the Sandoval case that the Pueblo Indians came under federal jurisdiction as wards of the government and therefore did not have the authority to sell their lands. Occasional violence broke out as Pueblos challenged the right of white settlers to be on former Pueblo lands. In 1922, Secretary of the Interior Albert B. Fall, a former New Mexico senator, asked New Mexico Senator Holm O. Bursum to introduce legislation to confirm the land titles of all non-Pueblo claimants and place Pueblo water rights under the jurisdiction of the state courts. The intention of Fall and Bursum was to settle the controversy over Pueblo lands in favor of Hispanic and white settlers and to prevent further violence.

Sympathetic whites, including the General Federation of Women's Clubs, artists from Santa Fe and Taos, and sociologist John Collier, organized a movement to stop the Bursum Bill. After Collier alerted the Pueblos to the danger of the bill, they responded by calling an All-Pueblo Council, which met on November 5, 1922, at Santo Domingo. The 121 delegates drafted "An Appeal by the Pueblo Indians of New Mexico to the People of the United States." They claimed that the Bursum Bill would destroy their communal life, land, customs, and traditions. A delegation from the All-Pueblo Council went with Collier to Washington, D.C., to testify before the Senate Committee on Public Lands. The Bursum Bill was defeated in Congress as a result of the public outcry against it. In 1923, a compromise bill, the Public Lands Act, was passed; it empowered a board to determine the status and boundaries of Pueblo lands.

See also Pueblo tribes, Eastern; Pueblo tribes, Western.

Allen, Paula Gunn (b. Oct. 24, 1939, Cubero, N.Mex.): Writer, scholar

TRIBAL AFFILIATION: Laguna Pueblo
SIGNIFICANCE: Allen's prolific works of poetry, fiction, and literary criticism have brought an influential lesbian and feminist perspective to American Indian literature

Non-Indians have often overlooked the power and significance of women in Indian communities. Paula Gunn Allen's writing has attempted to reverse this trend and has emphasized Indian women's strengths in spirituality and storytelling. Allen has also argued that Indian communities have not only included gays and lesbians but have given them respect and freedom.

Allen grew up in a multicultural household in Cubero, New Mexico. Her connection to Laguna Pueblo people comes from her mother's side of the family; her father was a businessman and politician of Lebanese descent. Since receiving her Ph.D. in American studies from the University of New Mexico in 1975, Allen, a poet, novelist, and scholar, has become one of the most influential voices in Native American literature.

Allen's best-known works include a novel, *The Woman Who Owned the Shadows* (1983); a book of essays, *The Sacred Hoop: Recovering the Feminine in American Indian Traditions* (1986); and an anthology, *Spider Woman's Granddaughters: Traditional Tales and Contemporary Writing by Native American Women* (1989). The latter won an American Book Award in 1990. Drawing on her experience as a professor of Native American literature, Allen also edited an influential volume of essays and course designs, *Studies in American Indian Literature* (1983). She has taught at San Francisco State University, the University of New Mexico, Fort Lewis College, the University of California, Berkeley, and the University of California, Los Angeles.

See also Oral literatures; Women.

Allotment system

DATE: 1887-1934
TRIBES AFFECTED: Pantribal
SIGNIFICANCE: Intended to assimilate Indians by making them small farmers, the allotment system instead led to a massive loss of Indian land

Allotment—the division of tribal lands among individual Indians—became the dominant theme in federal Indian policy in the years between 1887 and 1934. During the 1880's many whites who regarded themselves as "friends of the Indians" came to believe that Indians could be saved from extinction only by assimilation into American society. Tribal loyalties and

INDIAN LAND FOR SALE

GET A HOME

OF

YOUR OWN

✳

EASY PAYMENTS

PERFECT TITLE

✳

POSSESSION

WITHIN

THIRTY DAYS

FINE LANDS IN THE WEST

**IRRIGATED
IRRIGABLE** **GRAZING** **AGRICULTURAL
DRY FARMING**

IN 1910 THE DEPARTMENT OF THE INTERIOR SOLD UNDER SEALED BIDS ALLOTTED INDIAN LAND AS FOLLOWS:

Location.	Acres.	Average Price per Acre.	Location.	Acres.	Average Price per Acre.
Colorado	5,211.21	$7.27	Oklahoma	34,664.00	$19.14
Idaho	17,013.00	24.85	Oregon	1,020.00	15.43
Kansas	1,684.50	33.45	South Dakota	120,445.00	16.53
Montana	11,034.00	9.86	Washington	4,879.00	41.37
Nebraska	5,641.00	36.65	Wisconsin	1,069.00	17.00
North Dakota	22,610.70	9.93	Wyoming	865.00	20.64

FOR THE YEAR 1911 IT IS ESTIMATED THAT 350,000 ACRES WILL BE OFFERED FOR SALE

For information as to the character of the land write for booklet, "INDIAN LANDS FOR SALE," to the Superintendent U. S. Indian School at any one of the following places:

CALIFORNIA:
Hoopa.
COLORADO:
Ignacio.
IDAHO:
Lapwai.
KANSAS:
Horton.
Nadeau.

MINNESOTA:
Onigum.
MONTANA:
Crow Agency.
NEBRASKA:
Macy.
Santee.
Winnebago.

NORTH DAKOTA:
Fort Totten.
Fort Yates.
OKLAHOMA:
Anadarko.
Cantonment.
Colony.
Darlington.
Muskogee. GOVT. OF INDIAN AGENCY.
Pawnee.

OKLAHOMA—Con.
Sac and Fox Agency.
Shawnee.
Wyandotte.
OREGON:
Klamath Agency.
Pendleton.
Roseburg.
Siletz.

SOUTH DAKOTA:
Cheyenne Agency.
Crow Creek.
Greenwood.
Lower Brule.
Pine Ridge.
Rosebud.
Sisseton.

WASHINGTON:
Fort Simcoe.
Fort Spokane.
Tekoa.
Tulalip.

WISCONSIN:
Oneida.

WALTER L. FISHER,
Secretary of the Interior.

ROBERT G. VALENTINE,
Commissioner of Indian Affairs.

Advertisement for the government sale of "allotted Indian land"; such practices led to the drastic reduction of Indian-owned land. (Library of Congress) cultures were seen as barriers to this end. Reformers hoped that by carving up reservations and making small farmers of the Indians, they could effectively detribalize and assimilate the Indians into American culture. This policy also attracted support from those who wanted to open up tribal lands for settlement or exploitation. There were precedents for this policy. In the first half of the nineteenth century, several eastern states had broken up state-recognized reservations by dividing land among tribal members, and a number of the removal treaties of the 1830's made provision for allotments to individual Indians who wished to remain east of the Mississippi.

In 1887 Congress enacted the General Allotment Act, also known as the Dawes Severalty Act (for Senator Henry Dawes of Massachusetts, one of its proponents). The act gave the president authority to allot reservation lands in "severalty" (to individual Indians). As a general rule, heads of families would receive 160 acres, single Indians less. Title to the allotments would be held in trust by the government for twenty-five years to enable allottees to acquire the necessary skills, and the land could not be sold during the trust period. Once an Indian took up an allotment, he became an American citizen. Land not required for distribution could be sold off or opened to white settlement, with the proceeds intended to support assimilationist policies. It was suggested that the Indians, freed from tribal domination, would develop as small farmers and so be capable of taking their place in American society. The Five Civilized Tribes of Indian Territory, along with a few others, were originally exempted from the act, but in the 1890's Congress established a commission headed by Senator Dawes to negotiate allotment and thus the abolition of their tribal governments.

The actual process of allotment was complex and went on for more than forty years. Along the way Congress made several modifications: In 1900 the leasing of allotments before the end of the trust period was allowed; in 1902 heirs of allottees were permitted to sell their lands with the permission of the secretary of the interior; and in 1906 the Burke Act delayed citizenship until the end of the trust period (also permitting the secretary of the interior to cut short the trust period for Indians deemed competent to manage their own affairs).

The system did not work as intended. Many Indians came from nonagricultural tribal backgrounds and were reluctant to become farmers. Others found their allotments too small to support a family or of little agricultural value. Whites often encouraged Indians to lease or sell their lands, sometimes resorting to intimidation or outright fraud. It often proved easy to separate Indians from allotments.

The foremost result of the allotment policy was a drastic reduction in the amount of land controlled by Native Americans, from 138 million acres in 1887 to 52 million acres when the policy ceased in 1934. Of the amount lost, 60 million acres had been declared "excess land" and disposed of by the government to non-Indians. By 1934, two-thirds of Native Americans were either landless or without enough land to provide subsistence. The policy weakened tribal cultures and fostered the growth of a large bureaucracy in the Bureau of Indian Affairs.

By the late 1920's, doubts about the allotment system were growing. An investigation led by Lewis Meriam shocked many when its findings were published in 1928 as *The Problem of Indian Administration* (better known as the Meriam Report). The report detailed dismal conditions and poverty among American Indians and identified the allotment system as the major source of Indian problems. In 1934, the Indian Reorganization Act stopped the process of allotment and allowed the reorganization of tribal governments.

—William C. Lowe

See also Bureau of Indian Affairs (BIA); Burke Act; General Allotment Act; Indian Reorganization Act; Indian-white relations—U.S., 1871-1933; Meriam Report.

BIBLIOGRAPHY

Hoxie, Frederick E. *A Final Promise: The Campaign to Assimilate the Indians, 1880-1920*. Lincoln: University of Nebraska Press, 1984.

EFFECT OF ALLOTMENT ON LAND OWNERSHIP, 1890-1970				
	Indian-Owned		*Government-Owned*	
Year	*Trust Allotted*	*Tribal*	*Government-Owned*	*Total*
1890	—	104,314,000	—	104,314,000
1900	6,737,000	77,865,000	—	84,602,000
1910	31,094,000	41,052,000	—	72,146,000
1920	37,159,000	35,502,000	—	72,661,000
1930	—	32,097,000	—	32,097,000
1940	17,574,000	36,047,000	1,786,000	55,406,000
1949	16,534,000	38,608,000	863,000	56,005,000
1960	12,235,000	41,226,000	4,618,000	58,080,000
1970	10,698,000	39,642,000	5,068,000	55,408,000

Source: U.S. Department of Commerce, Bureau of the Census, *Historical Statistics of the United States, Colonial Times to 1970, Part 1.* Washington, D.C.: U.S. Government Printing Office, 1975.

Note: Figures represent acres, rounded off to thousands, under Bureau of Indian Affairs jurisdiction. Dash (—) indicates unavailable data.

Kinney, J. P. *A Continent Lost, a Civilization Won: Indian Land Tenure in America*. 1937. Reprint. Baltimore: The Johns Hopkins University Press, 1991.

McDonnell, Janet A. *The Dispossession of the American Indian, 1887-1934*. Bloomington: Indiana University Press, 1991.

Otis, Delos S. *The Dawes Act and the Allotment of Indian Lands*. Edited by Francis Paul Prucha. Norman: University of Oklahoma Press, 1973.

Washburn, Wilcomb E. *The Assault on Indian Tribalism: The General Allotment Law (Dawes Act) of 1887*. Philadelphia: J. B. Lippincott, 1975.

Alsea: Tribe

CULTURE AREA: Northwest Coast
LANGUAGE GROUP: Penutian
PRIMARY LOCATION: Oregon coast
POPULATION SIZE: 12 (1990 U.S. Census)

Alsea is the name given to the peoples of Yakonan stock occupying a small territory at (and near) the mouth of the Alsea River along the coast of western Oregon. The modern form of this name is a variant of the Alsean word *Alsi'*. Based upon linguistic classification, they are speakers of a language which is part of the Alsean family of the Penutian language phylum and appear to be most closely related to the Yaquina people.

Little is known of their early history. They remained on and around their traditional territory after they were assigned to the Siletz reservation in the mid-1800's, because their territory was part of the original reservation. When the reservation was reduced in size in 1875, they were removed to the new Siletz reservation.

Before the arrival of significant numbers of white settlers, the Alsea lived in small villages on both sides of the river and at the river mouth, engaged in a primarily riverine and woodland lifestyle based on fishing, hunting, and gathering. On the north side of the river were the villages of Kutauwa, Kyamaisu, Tachuwit, Kaukhwas, Yulehais, Kakhtshanwaish, Shiuwauk, Khlokhwaiyutslu, and Melcumtk. On the south side of the river were the villages of Yahach, Chiink, Kauhuk, Kwulisit, Kwamk, Skhakhwaiyutslu, Khlimkwaish, Kalbusht, Panit, Thielkushauk, and Thlekuhweyuk. At the mouth of the river was the village of Neahumtuk. Today the Alsea are affiliated with the larger political unit of the Confederated Tribes of Siletz Indians of Oregon. In the 1990 U.S. Census, twelve people identified themselves as Alsea.

See also Northwest Coast; Penutian language family; Siletz.

American Horse (c. 1840, Black Hills area, S.Dak.—1908, Pine Ridge, S.Dak.): Sioux spokesman

ALSO KNOWN AS: Wasechun-tashunka
TRIBAL AFFILIATION: Oglala Sioux
SIGNIFICANCE: A skilled orator and negotiator, American Horse advocated peace between whites and Sioux during the Sioux Wars of the late nineteenth century

After the 1860's, Sioux leader American Horse advocated peace with whites. (Library of Congress)

American Horse, the Younger, was probably Sitting Bear's son; American Horse, the Elder's nephew; and Red Cloud's son-in-law. As a young warrior, he fought white encroachment on Sioux hunting grounds during the Bozeman Trail War of 1866. For the remainder of his life, American Horse advocated peace with whites. In 1888-1889, after an extended and exhaustive negotiation with General George Crook, American Horse signed a treaty by which the Sioux ceded approximately half of their land in Dakota territory.

As tensions between whites and Sioux escalated, culminating in the Ghost Dance uprising of 1890, American Horse continued to advocate peace. Prior to the Wounded Knee Massacre in 1890, American Horse persuaded Big Foot's band to return to the Pine Ridge Reservation. In 1891, he led the first of several Sioux delegations to Washington, D.C., to negotiate for better Sioux-white relations. After Wounded Knee, American Horse was one of several Indian leaders who toured with Buffalo Bill Cody's Wild West show.

See also Bozeman Trail wars; Crazy Horse; Red Cloud; Sitting Bull.

American Indian

An "American Indian" is broadly defined as a member of any of the aboriginal peoples of North, Central, or South America and the West Indies. Peoples covered under this definition are also generally considered part of the Mongoloid racial subdivision. The term "American Indian" is an obvious misnomer. The word "American" refers to explorer Amerigo Vespucci, for whom the Americas were named by European explorers. The word "Indian" refers to inhabitants of the Indian subcontinent, which Christopher Columbus mistakenly thought he had reached.

As colonization of the Americas by Europeans progressed, the term continued to be used by the European immigrants, regardless of its inappropriateness. The early European explorers and colonists were not interested in exploring differences among native cultures; they simplistically perceived the hundreds of distinct indigenous cultures of North America as a singular primitive, barbaric, and uncivilized entity. "American Indian," or "Indian," became the standard term used by Europeans and European Americans simply through common usage. Many indigenous peoples, in their own languages, call themselves "the people" or "human beings," emphasizing their distinctive qualities among all living creatures, to which they believe themselves related.

In the mid-twentieth century, "Native American" became a widely used alternative collective name. By the 1990's, the popularity of this term waned, and many native people found American Indian to be relatively acceptable, even preferable. Some American Indians find all terms such as American Indian, Native American, and Amerind to be equally objectionable, as all owe a debt to European views and, at worst, to the racism of dominant American society. The most accurate—and most widely accepted—way to identify a person or tradition is simply to refer to the specific tribe or group to which the person or tradition belongs. When referring to the many indigenous cultures collectively, "American Indians" is still widely used, essentially because no consensus has been reached on a preferable term.

See also Amerind; Certificate of Degree of Indian Blood (CDIB); Indian; Native American; Tribe.

American Indian Civil Rights Act

DATE: April 11, 1968
TRIBES AFFECTED: Pantribal
SIGNIFICANCE: A move to guarantee individual Indians living under tribal governments the same civil rights and liberties guaranteed other citizens through the U.S. Constitution

A significant but controversial move toward the guarantee of individual American Indian rights came about in special Indian titles of the Civil Rights Act signed April 11, 1968. The existence of tribal governments and tribal courts had raised the issue of protection of individual rights of Indian people living in a tribal context. Tribal governments are considered inherently sovereign since they predate the Constitution and do not derive their power to exist or to govern from either federal or state government. Further, federal recognition or regulation of tribes does not make them part of the United States government or guarantee constitutional protections. Even with the Indian Citizenship Act (1924), the Bill of Rights did not extend to situations involving tribal government.

In 1968, when civil rights legislation was proposed to remedy inequal protections of some groups in the United States, Senator Sam Ervin of North Carolina proposed bringing tribal governments into the constitutional framework of the United States. Largely because of tribal protests that the full Bill of Rights would severely upset traditional governing practices, however, a blanket extension of the Bill of Rights to tribal governments was replaced by a more selective and specific list of individual rights that were to be protected.

Title II of the act, often referred to as the Indian Bill of Rights, since it is very close to constitutional provisions, stresses the rights of individuals and so limits the authority of tribal governments. It specifically authorizes a writ of habeas corpus for anyone detained by a tribe. This bill does not prohibit "establishment of religion," which would have prevented continuation of the quasi-theocracies which form the basis of government for some Indian communities, but it does guarantee "free exercise of religion." Also, persons are not guaranteed free counsel in criminal proceedings, and the right of indictment by grand jury is not guaranteed. Title III charged the secretary of the interior to draw up codes of justice to be used in courts of Indian offenses. Title IV repealed section 7 of Public Law 280, an act passed by Congress in 1953 that gave states authority to extend civil and criminal jurisdiction over reservations. This title also authorized the retrocession of jurisdiction already assumed by a state. Title V added "assault resulting in serious bodily injury" to offenses on reservations subject to federal jurisdiction. Title VI granted automatic approval of tribal contracts if the secretary of the interior did not act within ninety days.

The Indian Civil Rights Act was controversial when it was proposed and it remains so. Many Indian people view it as a violation of tribal sovereignty. Congress unilaterally imposed the bill on tribal governments and people, raising many issues of the meaning of "consent." Tribes do not seek to be protected from misuse of power, but there are questions about the legality and cultural implications of the American Indian Civil Rights Act. Tribes have questioned the legality of permitting states to have a direct role in formulating and passing this law for tribes with no mechanism for tribes to accept or reject the legislation. Tribal culture is directly affected by this law because of the stress it places on individualism. For most tribes, community needs have precedence over individual rights, yet this law stresses individualism. Many Indian leaders believe the American Indian Civil Rights Act prevents tribes from exercising their inherent sovereignty.

See also Civil rights and citizenship; Indian Citizenship Act; Public Law 280; Sovereignty.

American Indian Defense Association (AIDA)

DATE: Established 1923
TRIBES AFFECTED: Pantribal
SIGNIFICANCE: Organized by social reformer and later Bureau of Indian Affairs commissioner John Collier, the AIDA was the primary advocate for tribal revitalization

The American Indian Defense Association was organized in New York City in May, 1923, by white reformers sympathetic to Indian causes. Under the leadership of John Collier, the AIDA's founder and first executive secretary, the organization consisted primarily of wealthy, liberal Californians who joined hands in opposition to a proposed bill addressing land disputes in the Northwest that might have resulted in the loss of Pueblo lands. Led by Collier, members of the AIDA were critical of the General Allotment Act of 1887, pleading for the maintenance of Indian tribal integrity.

In 1922 Collier explicitly stated the AIDA's goals. The association was to aid in the preservation of Indian culture, including a revitalization program of Indian arts and crafts. It sought to entitle Indians to social and religious freedoms and to rejuvenate tribal governments. Provisions were also made for safeguarding Indian civil liberties. Furthermore, Indians were to be entitled to federal aid in the form of Farm Loan Bank credits, public health services, and other federal assistance programs. To break its monopoly over Indian programs, Collier suggested reform of the Bureau of Indian Affairs. Through congressional lobbying, publication of pamphlets, and advice to Indian tribes, Collier and the AIDA labored to influence federal Indian policy and to improve conditions on Indian reservations.

In its first decade, the AIDA grew to more than seventeen hundred members. Headquartered in Washington, D.C., the organization maintained branches in cities throughout the country. During the 1920's, executive secretary Collier became the nation's leading advocate of Indian rights. With the election of President Franklin D. Roosevelt in 1932, Indian reform organizations furnished candidates for appointment as commissioner in the Bureau of Indian Affairs, Collier foremost among them. Although Collier was considered controversial because of his Communist sympathies and his confrontational nature, Roosevelt nevertheless appointed him commissioner in 1933. Under Roosevelt, Collier initiated his own Indian New Deal whereby governmental Indian policy shifted away from assimilation and toward tribal revitalization. Collier's culminating triumph was passage in 1934 of the Indian Reorganization Act, the heart of the Indian New Deal. The American Indian Defense Association consistently supported Collier and the Indian New Deal, although the association was frequently critical of its application.

In 1936 the American Indian Defense Association merged with the National Association on Indian Affairs, becoming the Association on American Indian Affairs (AAIA). By the 1990's the AAIA was headquartered in New York City. There it maintained a staff of twelve employees and had forty thousand members nationwide with an annual operating budget of $1,500,000. The AAIA provided legal and technical assistance in health, education, economic development, the administration of justice and resource utilization to United States tribes. In addition, the AAIA maintained the American Indian Fund, published the newsletter *Indian Affairs*, and occasionally published books.

See also Allotment system; General Allotment Act; Indian Reorganization Act; Indian-white relations—U.S., 1871-1933; Indian-white relations—U.S., 1934-1995; Meriam Report.

American Indian Higher Education Consortium (AIHEC)

DATE: Established 1972
TRIBES AFFECTED: Pantribal
SIGNIFICANCE: The AIHEC promotes tribally controlled colleges and monitors state and federal legislation affecting Indian higher education

The American Indian Higher Education Consortium (AIHEC) was formed by six tribal college leaders in 1972 to protect the interests of tribally controlled colleges in the United States and Canada. The overall goal of the organization is to ensure survival of tribal colleges, maintain Indian control of the colleges, and secure an adequate funding base. The consortium promotes culturally meaningful training for college administrators and teachers working in the tribal colleges; it promotes and encourages the preservation and teaching of American Indian, Inuit, and Alaska Native languages, cultures, and traditions; and it encourages programs that are consistent with the inherent rights of tribal sovereignty and self-determination.

AIHEC came about at a time when Indian people were identifying common goals and establishing issue-oriented organizations that promoted sovereignty and represented both tribal and pantribal needs. Because of the complex issues connected with the implementation of the Tribally Controlled Community College Act of 1978, AIHEC has become a vital force in monitoring political and legislative issues connected with American Indian higher education at the state and federal levels. AIHEC also functions as a national forum to promote Indian higher education and recognition of the tribal college movement.

AIHEC provides considerable support to the tribal college infrastructure and sponsors annual conferences at which administrators, faculty, and students from the various colleges meet to participate in training workshops, seminars, and a variety of intercollegiate activities. AIHEC also publishes *Tribal College: Journal of the American Indian Higher Education Consortium*, which focuses on issues of Indian higher education and provides a forum to address Indian research issues. In an effort to raise money and establish endowments, AIHEC created and oversees the American Indian College Fund, intended to promote personal, corporate, and foundation gift-giving to support the tribal college movement. Through the various activities of AIHEC, the Indian tribal colleges are connected by a national organization that promotes their well-being while respecting their inherent sovereignty.

See also American Indian studies programs and archives; Civil rights and citizenship; Education, post-contact; Indian Self-Determination and Education Assistance Act.

American Indian Movement (AIM)

DATE: Established 1968
TRIBES AFFECTED: Pantribal

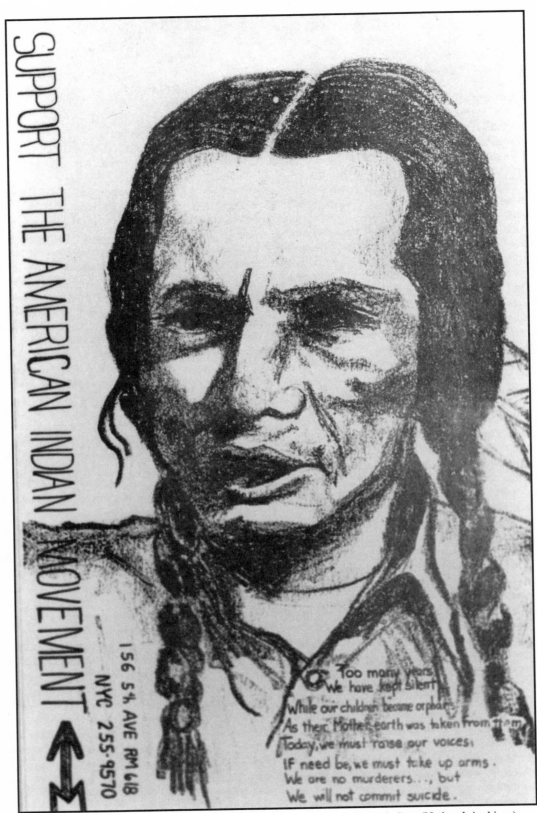

Poster urging support for the American Indian Movement in New York City. (National Archives)

SIGNIFICANCE: Creates public awareness of injustices to Indians; struggles for American Indian treaty rights; encourages self-determination among native peoples

The American Indian Movement was founded by Chippewas Dennis Banks and George Mitchell in Minneapolis, Minnesota, during July, 1968. Taking its initial ideas from the Black Panther party, AIM sought to protect urban Indians from police abuse and to create programs promoting community self-sufficiency. Inspired by the 1969 takeover of Alcatraz Island, however, the movement adopted an agenda centered on indigenous spiritual traditions, land recovery, and treaty rights.

AIM's credibility in "Indian country" was truly established in early 1972, when Russell Means led a large caravan to tiny Gordon, Nebraska, protesting the fact that two local whites who had brutally murdered an Oglala Lakota from the nearby Pine Ridge Reservation were charged only with manslaughter. As a result, the culprits became the first white men in Nebraska history to be imprisoned for killing an Indian.

In November, 1972, AIM played a key role in a spectacular seizure of the Bureau of Indian Affairs (BIA) headquarters in Washington, D.C. This was followed, in January, 1973, by a major confrontation between AIM and police in the streets of Custer, South Dakota, which left the county courthouse in flames (the issue again concerned official inaction after the murder of an Oglala). In February, 1973, while supporting Lakota treaty rights, AIM undertook a lengthy armed standoff with federal authorities at Wounded Knee. Afterward, the Federal Bureau of Investigation mounted a grim campaign of repression against "insurgents" on Pine Ridge.

Over the next three years, AIM's leadership was largely tied up in what one federal official admitted was "an effort to destroy these radicals via the judicial process." Meanwhile, more than sixty AIM members and supporters were murdered on the reservation—many of them by a federally sponsored entity calling itself "the Goon Squad"—and more than three hundred others suffered serious physical assault.

On June 26, 1975, AIM's efforts to defend itself led to a massive firefight which left an Indian and two FBI agents dead. Three AIM members—Bob Robideau, Dino Butler, and Leonard Peltier—were charged with murdering the agents. Butler and Robideau were acquitted by an all-white jury after a U.S. Civil Rights Commission representative testified that they had merely responded to a government-induced "reign of terror" on Pine Ridge. Peltier, however, was convicted and sentenced to a double-life term in a controversial process which a federal appellate court later described as "fraught with FBI misconduct."

By 1977, AIM had entered an extended period of relative dormancy. Although it has organized or participated in such events as the 1978 Longest Walk, the 1980 Black Hills Survival Gathering, the Yellow Thunder Camp occupation of 1981-1985, and the anti-Columbus demonstrations of the early 1990's, it has yet to evidence genuine revitalization.

Although it may never reconstitute itself in a form exhibiting the power it once displayed, some analysts believe that the movement had achieved its major objectives by 1975. "AIM instilled a deep sense of pride and resistance to oppression among Indians which was greatly lacking at the time," Vine Deloria, Jr., observed, "and for that we owe it a real debt." Lakota traditionalist Birgil Kills Straight concurs: "Whatever else may be said," he maintains, "AIM acted as the shock troops of Indian sovereignty at a time when we needed them most."

See also Activism; African American-American Indian relations; Alcatraz Island occupation; Banks, Dennis; Civil rights and citizenship; International Indian Treaty Council (IITC); Means, Russell; Pan-Indianism; Totem poles; Women of All Red Nations (WARN); Wounded Knee occupation.

BIBLIOGRAPHY

Churchill, Ward, and Jim Vander Wall. *Agents of Repression: The FBI's Secret Wars Against the Black Panther Party and the American Indian Movement*. Boston: South End Press, 1988.

Deloria, Vine, Jr. *Behind the Trail of Broken Treaties: An Indian Declaration of Independence*. 2d ed. Norman: University of Oklahoma Press, 1987.

Johansen, Bruce, and Roberto Maestas. *Wasi' chu: The Continuing Indian Wars*. New York: Monthly Review Press, 1979.

Matthiessen, Peter. *In the Spirit of Crazy Horse*. 2d ed. New York: Viking Press, 1991.

Weyler, Rex. *Blood of the Land: The U.S. Government and Corporate War Against the First Nations*. 2d ed. Philadelphia: New Society Publishers, 1992.

American Indian Policy Review Commission

DATE: Established 1975

TRIBES AFFECTED: Pantribal

SIGNIFICANCE: This federal commission, after two years of study, published an extensive report calling for major reforms of U.S. Indian policy

The American Indian Policy Review Commission (AIPRC) was established in 1975 as a follow-up to the Indian Self-Determination and Education Assistance Act, passed in the same year. The commission was chaired by Senator James Abourezk of South Dakota (it is sometimes referred to as the Abourezk Commission). The commission's findings were published in 1977 in its multivolume report. The report opposed assimilationist policies and recommended continuing the 1968 initiative for the establishment of permanent government units in the federal system to protect and strengthen tribal governments.

Among the factors that led to the establishment of the commission was the activism and unrest sweeping American Indian communities in the early 1970's. According to Vine Deloria, Jr., and Clifford M. Lytle (*American Indians, American Justice*, 1983; *The Nations Within: The Past and Future of American Indian Sovereignty*, 1984), the 1973 occupation of Wounded Knee in particular was a catalytic event in the decision to create a new commission to reexamine the government's Indian policy.

The AIPRC included Indian representatives in various positions; they were selected according to partisan tribal politics of the time. Indians dominated the staff; a significant number of contracted consultants were also native individuals. In addition to there being five Indian commissioners and thirty-one (out of thirty-three) Indian task force members, the commission included six members of Congress. Inevitably, complicated political dynamics plagued the commission behind the scenes.

The final report of the AIPRC generally followed the line of Indian militants who had previously been excluded from positions on commissions and task forces. The extensive document listed more than two hundred recommendations. It claimed that the relationship between American Indian tribes and the United States was political and was established via treaties, according to international law. The commission recommended that two fundamental concepts should guide all future federal policy: First, Indian tribes are sovereign political bodies having the power to enact laws and enforce them within reservation boundaries; second, the relationship between the tribes and the United States "is premised on a special trust that must govern the conduct of the stronger toward the weaker." The AIPRC report also stated that the right to choose a form of government is an inherent right of any Indian tribe.

No actual social reform directed toward improving the lot of American Indians actually took place following publication of the AIPRC report. Moreover, Congress soon afterward abolished the standing Indian Affairs Subcommittees that operated under the Department of the Interior. Eventually a Senate Select Subcommittee on Indian Affairs was authorized by Congress to sort out the many AIPRC recommendations.

The commission was not without criticism from both ends of the political spectrum. Some (including the commission's vice chair, Representative Lloyd Meems) criticized it for going too far. Others have argued that, although the commission had good intentions in its promotion of self-determination, its recommendations in reality represented a continuation of the paternalistic relationship between the U.S. government and the tribes.

See also Activism; Indian Self-Determination and Education Assistance Act; Wounded Knee occupation.

BIBLIOGRAPHY

American Indian Policy Review Commission Task Force. *Report*. Washington, D.C.: U.S. Government Printing Office, 1977.

Deloria, Vine, Jr., ed. *American Indian Policy in the Twentieth Century*. Norman: University of Oklahoma Press, 1985.

Deloria, Vine, Jr., and Clifford M. Lytle. *American Indians, American Justice*. Austin: University of Texas Press, 1983.

_____. *The Nations Within: The Past and Future of American Indian Sovereignty*. New York: Pantheon Books, 1984.

Robbins, Rebecca L. "Self-Determination and Subordination: The Past, Present, and Future of American Indian Governance." In *The State of Native America*, edited by M. A. Jaimes. Boston: South End Press, 1992.

American Indian Religious Freedom Act

DATE: August 11, 1978
TRIBES AFFECTED: Pantribal
SIGNIFICANCE: In the form of a joint resolution known as the American Indian Religious Freedom Act, Congress recognized its obligation "to protect and preserve for American Indians their inherent right of freedom to believe, express, and exercise traditional religions"

The passage of the American Indian Religious Freedom Act in 1978 formally allowed Indian tribes the freedom to practice their religions. This law also allowed tribes to regain access to sacred sites on federal lands and the right to possess certain sacred objects such as eagle feathers. This joint resolution directs all federal agencies to examine their policies and procedures and to take appropriate measures to protect Native American religious rites and practices.

Until 1934 the Bureau of Indian Affairs had regulations prohibiting the practices of Indian religion and actively pursued a policy aimed at Christianizing and "civilizing" the Indians. In order to accomplish this, the Bureau of Indian Affairs forbade the practice of most traditional religions. Violators, if caught, could be punished by fines or imprisonment. The goal of these policies, strongly supported by Christian churches, was to stamp out aboriginal religions.

The American Indian Religious Freedom Act is a key element in Indian self-determination and cultural freedom in the United States. Even with passage of this act, however, Native Americans continued to experience problems in access to sacred sites and the use of peyote. In 1994, the Native American Church's right to use peyote was an unsettled issue in both federal and state courts. Although peyote is subject to control under the Federal Comprehensive Drug Abuse Prevention and Control Act, a number of states allow its use in Native American Church ceremonies. Some courts uphold the right of Native Americans who are church members to possess and use peyote, while other courts do not grant the same recognition.

The 1978 federal statute affirms the right of Native Americans to practice their traditional religion, but it does not allow Indians to sue when federal agencies disregard Indian religious practices or when agencies pursue plans despite adverse impact on Native American religion. The extension of full religious freedom to Native Americans is an evolving concept, and the American Indian Religious Freedom Act is an important philosophical foundation.

See also Civil rights and citizenship; Native American Church; Peyote and peyote religion; Religion; Religious specialists; Sun Dance.

American Indian studies programs and archives

TRIBES AFFECTED: Pantribal
SIGNIFICANCE: American Indian studies programs, which began in the late 1960's, seek to preserve and understand American Indian history and culture

Since the late 1960's, American Indian studies (or Native American studies) programs have served as the most important scholarly approach to knowing and understanding American Indian culture, to a significant degree replacing history and anthropology. Traditional teachings of tribal and village elders remain the solid foundation of American Indian and Native American studies. These culture bearers provide the necessary understanding essential to legitimate study of the native peoples of the Americas.

Establishment of Indian Studies Programs. Dependence upon European American (notably Anglo-American) source materials has made for distortion in scholarly studies. As professor Henrietta Whiteman has stated, "Cheyenne history, and by extension Indian history, in all probability will never be incorporated into American history, because it is holistic, human, personal, and sacred. Though it is equally as valid as Anglo-American history it is destined to remain complementary to white secular American history." This specific difficulty led in large part to the creation of American Indian studies programs in existing institutions of higher learning. Despite limited funds, Native American programs began to emerge as interdisciplinary curricula. Most American Indian studies programs focus on long-term goals involved with cultural preservation, unlike Western, objective academic disciplines such as history and ethnology. American Indian studies use teaching, research, and service to cross cultural boundaries and create an atmosphere for understanding. In many instances, the American Indian studies degree programs are the only non-Western courses of study on campus.

American Indian or Native American studies programs vary considerably in method and subject matter. These also represent different degrees of institutional support, budget size, and quality of program leadership. In the late 1960's and early 1970's, various programs began to emerge at the University of California at Berkeley and the University of California, Los Angeles. Other programs developed in the California State University system on campuses at Long Beach, Fullerton, and Northridge. At that time, California had the largest Native American population in the United States. Oklahoma had the second-largest native population. Two degree programs were created in the early 1970's, one at Northeastern State University at Tahlequah, the capital of the Cherokee Nation, and one at the University of Science and Arts of Oklahoma in Chickasha. The Native American studies degree program at the University of Oklahoma was accepted by the Higher Regents in 1993. Other American Indian studies degree programs were created at the University of Minnesota, the University of Washington, Evergreen College, Washington State University, the University of Arizona, University of Illinois (Chicago), Dartmouth College, the University of North Dakota, Montana State University, the University of New Mexico, and Cornell University, among others. By the mid-1980's, eighteen programs offered a major leading to a B.A. degree. Of these, six programs also offered a M.A. degree.

Tribally Controlled Colleges. Tribally controlled colleges added new energy to American Indian studies. In 1968, the Navajo Nation created the first tribally controlled institution of

TYPES OF NATIVE AMERICAN STUDIES PROGRAMS OFFERED, 1985		
Type of Program	*Percent*	*Number*
Department status or program administered by another department	45.8	49
Major in Native American studies	16.8	18
Minor in Native American studies	37.4	40
Graduate degree in Native American studies	5.6	6
Undergraduate Indian culture specialization	28.0	30
Research unit	14.0	15
EOP or minority support program	57.9	62
Indian counselor on campus	69.2	74
Other type of program	26.2	28

Source: Guyette, Susan, and Charlotte Heth, *Issues for the Future of American Indian Studies.* Los Angeles: American Indian Studies Center at the University of California, 1985.

Note: Total number of programs is 107; many programs and departments encompass more than one type.

higher learning. Navajo Community College was a success and led to the passage of the Tribally Controlled Community College Act of 1978. This act provides for some federal support for tribally controlled colleges initiated by tribes in the western United States. Initially, this helped support thirteen tribally controlled colleges. Since the act's passage, at least nine additional colleges have been initiated. Colleges that followed the creation of Navajo Community College include Sinte Glista College, Standing Rock College, Blackfeet Community College, Dull Knife Memorial College, Salish Kootenai College, Little Bighorn College, and Stone Child College, among others. Lummi College of Aquaculture in Washington has expanded to become the Northwest Indian College. Sinte Glista College on the Rosebud Sioux Reservation has grown to become the first fully accredited tribally controlled four-year institution of higher learning.

In all these examples, the tribally based community colleges have not only aided the education of individual Indian young people but also improved the development of the tribal communities that they serve. Of primary importance is that Indian people are now controlling institutions that directly affect them. The tribally controlled colleges are far outstripping the state-supported and private colleges and universities in retention of American Indian students. The tribally controlled colleges have become important centers of research. These colleges are proving to be better suited to the needs of American Indian students and communities than their state-supported and private counterparts. The tribally controlled colleges offer hope to tribes that have, all too often, survived in a climate of despair.

Issues and Concerns. In the early 1990's, American Indian studies was in a period of questioning current methods and practices concerning spirit, philosophy, structures, roles, contexts, and intent. The quest for meaning appeared in many guises. The interest in the emotional component of community life, the expansion of traditional approaches to knowledge and wisdom, the acceptance of grammar and logic stemming from native languages, and the hope of differentiating Western-based interpretation from traditional knowledge all reflect the aim of uncovering purpose, meaning, and perspectives on truth in presentation. There is pervasive anxiety that the individual is being submerged in community. There is additional attention being given to the way people feel as well as the way they behave. There is also a movement in American Indian studies toward narrative storytelling in the literature. American Indian studies places human beings and the comprehensible

NATIVE AMERICAN STUDIES DEPARTMENTS AND PROGRAMS, 1985	
State	*Number of Programs*
Alaska	3
Arizona	7
California	19
Colorado	3
Illinois	1
Iowa	3
Kansas	2
Maine	1
Michigan	3
Minnesota	6
Montana	6
Nebraska	2
New Hampshire	1
New Mexico	7
New York	3
North Carolina	2
North Dakota	2
Oklahoma	8
Oregon	1
Pennsylvania	1
South Dakota	4
Utah	5
Washington	8
Wisconsin	8
Wyoming	1
Total	107

Source: Guyette, Susan, and Charlotte Heth, *Issues for the Future of American Indian Studies*. Los Angeles: American Indian Studies Center at the University of California, 1985.

societies in which they live into the story. These are real stories, however, not dry and forbidding pieces of analysis.

The quest for meaning only multiplies the pluralism of current research and teaching. The very process of recovering deeper motivations and attitudes, dragging the latent out of the manifest, requires such personal feats of imagination and use of language that questions about plausibility and proof are bound to arise. Senior faculty at one state-supported university in Oklahoma challenged the continuation of a B.A. degree in American Indian studies, stating, "While the program is inessential to a liberal arts education, it is not inconsistent with one." This type of Anglo-American bias makes it difficult to pursue knowledge and wisdom in an atmosphere with freedom of thought and feeling.

The obverse of the quest for meaning is an uneasiness with the material conditions of life that until recently seemed so compelling. A clear, single idea emerges from the doubts that have been expressed about the power of economic development. As American Indian studies turns to more emotional content, the demand is for a more elusive process of comprehension. Analytical and technical research is increasingly limited, as mental patterns, attitudes, and symbolic acts become more prominent.

Questions of the use of quantification arise because of the almost exclusive use of United States and Western social science data. What is at stake is a profound epistemological question, not just a disagreement over collection of data. American Indian studies many times are very personal and intuitive. The insights are justified within a specific tribal context with powerful rhetorical and imaginative methods. They appeal to an interest in behavior that is very different from Anglo-American intellectual concerns, but never claim to be definitive.

The establishment of an agenda for American Indian studies, of a set of methods or purposes indigenous to the Americas, or of a special task for its practitioners, hardly seems plausible. American Indian studies is united in its respect of tribal traditions. There is observation of certain fundamental rules for using evidence so as to be intelligible across cultural boundaries. None of these skills is difficult to learn; neither is the telling of a sustained story, which is a special mark of scholars and teachers in American Indian studies. The one form of synthesis used most often by those in American Indian studies blends the disparate methods of current research in examinations of tribally specific localities. This synthesis convincingly links physical conditions, economic and demographic developments, social arrangements, intellectual and cultural assumptions, and political behavior, with mythic patterns and images.

Archives and Tribal Records. The most important repository of American Indian knowledge remains with the tribal elders. There is no substitute for this significant information. This knowledge and wisdom can be gained only with real commitment over a significant period of time. Tribal elders have become wary of "instant experts," whether Indian or non-Indian. All scholarship must access this wisdom and knowledge to reflect tribal tradition and history.

Once removed from this vital core of information are the tribal archives and records. These are held in a variety of ways. For example, the Wichita and Affiliated Tribes maintain their tribal archives as a part of the Wichita Memory Exhibit Museum at the tribal complex on reserve land north of Anadarko. A second example is that of the Navajo Nation, which collects and preserves its records as a part of the Navajo Tribal Council Reference Library in Window Rock. A third example is that of the Cherokee Nation, which maintains a portion of its records in the Archives of the Cherokee National Historical Society in Tahlequah, while the records of the Cherokee Nation from 1839 through 1906 are held in the Indian Archives of the Oklahoma Historical Society, which functions as a trustee for the United States government. These records were placed in trust in 1906, just before Oklahoma statehood, before the National Archives of the United States was created. Each tribe maintains its records in an individual way. Contact with the tribes is the best means to understand their respective record-keeping system.

U.S. National Archives. Large numbers of records about American Indian peoples are held by the National Archives of the United States. These are housed in Washington National Records Center, Suitland, Maryland, and in eleven regional Federal Archives and Records Centers throughout the United States. Additional records holdings concerning American Indian peoples are contained at the Presidential libraries administered by the National Archives and Records Service. The papers of the presidents and many of those of other high officials, including the files of individual members of Congress, are regarded as their personal property. These personal papers are collected in large part by state-supported university manuscripts collections.

The basic organizational unit in the National Archives collections is the record group. This refers to the records of a single agency, such as the Bureau of Indian Affairs and its predecessors. The National Archives endeavors to keep records in the order in which they were maintained by the respective agency. The agency filing system was designed for administrative purposes, not for the benefit of researchers. There are important guides to assist in research efforts, however. The two most important of these are *Guide to the National Archives of the United States* (1974) and *Guide to Records in the National Archives of the United States Relating to American Indians* (1981). Another useful volume is *Indian-White Relations: A Persistent Paradox* (1976), which includes papers and proceedings of the National Archives Conference on Research in the history of Indian-White relations.

Additional materials concerning Indian-white relations are contained in the United States Supreme Court decisions, the research that was used in the Indian Land Claims Act of 1946, and in the manuscript collections of major universities throughout the western United States.

American Indian studies has long been limited in perspective because of the heavy dependence upon documents generated by Anglo-American policymakers, businessmen, and military personnel. Scholarly works accepted many of the assumptions of those who produced these sources. American Indian people were perceived either negatively as an enemy, or romantically as part of the environment. In the last decade, scholarship in American Indian studies has changed significantly from this approach. More balanced efforts are being made by American Indian scholars utilizing native languages and tribal sources. All American culture and society is being shown in a new light as of a result of the creative images and ideas of American Indian studies. —*Howard Meredith*

See also American Indian Higher Education Consortium; Civil rights and citizenship; Education, post-contact; Indian Self-Determination and Education Assistance Act; Educational Institions and Programs (appendix).

BIBLIOGRAPHY

Carnegie Foundation for the Advancement of Teaching. *Tribal Colleges: Shaping the Future of Native America.* Princeton, N.J.: Author, 1989.

Heth, Charlotte, ed. *Native American Dance: Ceremonies and Social Traditions.* Washington, D.C.: National Museum of the American Indian with Starwood Publishing, 1992.

Heth, Charlotte, and Susan Guyette. *Issues for the Future of American Indian Studies.* Los Angeles: American Indian Studies Center, University of California, Los Angeles, 1985.

Hill, Edward E., comp. *Guide to the Records in the National Archives of the United States Relating to American Indians.* Washington, D.C.: National Archives and Records Service, G.S.A., 1981.

Meredith, Howard. *Modern American Indian Tribal Government and Politics.* Tsaile, Ariz.: Navajo Community College Press, 1993.

Ruoff, LaVonne Brown. *American Indian Literatures.* New York: Modern Language Association, 1990.

Smith, Jane F., and Robert Kvasnicka, eds. *Indian-White Relations: A Persistent Paradox.* Proceedings of the National Archives Conference. Washington, D.C.: Howard University Press, 1976.

Whiteman, Henrietta. "White Buffalo Woman." In *The American Indian and the Problem of History*, edited by Calvin Martin. New York: Oxford University Press, 1987.

Wong, Hertha Dawn. *Sending My Heart Back Across the Years: Tradition and Innovation in Native American Autobiography.* New York: Oxford University Press, 1992.

Amerind

The term "Amerind" is a neologism combining the words "American" and "Indian." It came into common usage during the 1970's. A result of tribal activism meant to counter racism toward native peoples, this term was chosen as an alternative to "American Indian" and "Native American."

The people to whom this term refers include members of any of the aboriginal peoples of North America, Central America, South America, and the West Indies. Europeans and European Americans have continually sought to lump all the original inhabitants of the Americas into a convenient single group. "Amerind" represents an attempt to refer to native groups collectively with a term that could be considered (to use a post-1970's term) politically correct. Yet although the term may be descriptive and less inaccurate than others, it falls short of the redefinition needed when referring to the multitude of distinct original cultures of North America.

There are more than five hundred groups of indigenous peoples in the United States alone, each with its own name for itself, and each with a unique tribal specific cultural heritage and political legacy. Who a people are can be defined only in terms of specific environment, language, customs, traditions, taboos, and so on. Until modern Americans recognize the distinctive elements inherent in each indigenous community, any new terms such as "Amerind" will be viewed by scholars as empty generalizations. Such terms, although convenient, are more a reflection of American cultural bias than they are descriptive of the nature, quality, or diversity of the original inhabitants of the Americas.

See also American Indian; Indian; Native American; Tribe.

Anadarko: Tribe

CULTURE AREA: Southeast
LANGUAGE GROUP: Caddoan
PRIMARY LOCATION: North of Anadarko, Oklahoma; northwest of Nacogdoches, Texas

The Anadarko, or Nadako, were a tribe of the Hasinai Confederacy of the Caddo. They were first encountered by Europeans in northeastern Texas by members of Hernando de Soto's expedition in 1542. Later, in the late seventeenth century, they were living on the southern edge of what is now Rusk County, Texas.

The Anadarko and the other Hasinai formed a loose confederacy of settled farmers who lived in scattered ranchos in the bottomlands. They were primarily farmers and hunters and had elaborate religious and political systems. On a number of occasions the Spanish sought to establish missions among them, but to no avail. The French from Louisiana provided them with guns and trade goods, which allowed them to maintain their independence.

In the late eighteenth century, other Indian tribes and white Americans began to encroach on their lands. Protests to Spanish and, later, Mexican officials did little to restore their independence. Poor relations with the Republic of Texas drove the Anadarko and their Indian neighbors to central Texas. After Texas became a state, the Anadarko and other Indians were removed to Oklahoma in 1859.

After the Civil War they were finally able to obtain a reservation north of the Washita River and settled down to farming. In 1891 they ceded their lands to the government but had them restored in 1963. Today they are concentrated around their tribal center north of Anadarko, Oklahoma. The late twentieth century saw a cultural revival among Anadarko and other Hasinai.

See also Caddo; Caddoan language family; Nabedache; Texas.

Anasazi: Prehistoric tradition

DATE: c. 300 B.C.E.-1600 C.E.
LOCATION: Southwest
CULTURES AFFECTED: Navajo, Pueblo (Zuni, Hopi)

"Anasazi" is a corruption of a Navajo term meaning either "ancient ones" or "enemies of our ancient ones." The Navajo applied the term to ancient peoples responsible for extensive architectural ruins scattered throughout the modern states of New Mexico, Arizona, Utah, and Colorado. Throughout the nineteenth and early twentieth century, archaeologists believed these ruins to be a colonial or provincial extension of the Aztec or Toltec cultures of Mexico. During the 1920's, however, cultural anthropologists and archaeologists began to understand the Anasazi as an indigenous southwestern culture directly ancestral to the modern Pueblos.

Pre-contact History. Archaeologists have identified Anasazi sites throughout the southwestern United States, but the greatest concentration is in the Four Corners region of southern Utah and Colorado and northern New Mexico and Arizona. From these sites, archaeologists have reconstructed and named various stages of the evolution of Anasazi culture (some of the dates that follow are currently in dispute among archaeologists).

By 300 B.C.E., the agricultural/horticultural tradition that originated in central Mexico at least nine thousand years ago had spread to what is now the southwestern United States through cultural diffusion. Groups of Indians in the Southwest began cultivating maize, squash, and beans to augment the foodstuffs they acquired through hunting and gathering, often using primitive irrigation methods. Archaeologists call this formative period "Basketmaker I" and consider it to have begun around 300 B.C.E. (Some archaeologists consider Basketmaker I to be a part of the Archaic period.)

During the Basketmaker I period the Anasazi represented one group of agriculturalists among many in the southwestern area. Their art and architecture were virtually indistinguishable from those of other farmers scattered from present-day California to Texas: They constructed pit houses, wove textiles from wild plants, and left a few impressive paintings and carvings on rock walls.

Between 300 and 500 C.E., the Anasazi underwent a cultural revolution that made them clearly distinct from their neighbors. The Basketmaker II period among the Anasazi witnessed the introduction of large villages composed of pit houses (houses built largely underground). They began making distinctive pottery, beautiful baskets woven from native plants, and textiles woven from cotton.

During the ensuing Basketmaker III period (circa 500-750 C.E.), the Anasazi villages became larger and more numerous. Each village had a ritual room, which archaeologists call the kiva, used for religious ceremonies. The pit houses became larger and more complex, and each had an adjoining storage room for stockpiling food. Pottery making and textile weaving became more complex with the introduction of intricate designs and brilliant colors. Irrigation systems became more common and more elaborate as agriculture became the main form of subsistence, although hunting and gathering remained an important supplement to the Anasazi economy. The bow and arrow came into common use among the Anasazi during this period; they were probably imported from Mexico.

Archaeologists call the next stage of Anasazi cultural evolution the Developmental Pueblo period (circa 750-1100, called Pueblo I and Pueblo II in another common classification system). During this period, Anasazi communities greatly increased in number and size and spread as far west as Utah and northern Arizona. The pit houses gave way to multistoried houses constructed of dry masonry, adobe, or cut rocks joined to form massive structures somewhat resembling modern apartment complexes. These structures contained many kivas, some huge, some small, all increasingly elaborate, arguing for increasing religious diversity as the Anasazi absorbed neighboring tribal peoples. Famous Anasazi sites such as Chaco Canyon in New Mexico and Mesa Verde in Colorado originated during this period. Extensive trade began during the Developmental Pueblo period among the various Anasazi towns and between the Anasazi and cultures as distant as the Mississippi Valley, the Pacific coast, and Mexico. Pottery making and textile weaving became art forms as well as an integral part of the Anasazi economy.

Around 1100, Anasazi culture entered what archaeologists call the "Classic Pueblo" (Pueblo III) period, which lasted until around 1400. During this era, Anasazi architecture reached its zenith. The famous and impressive ruins at Chaco Canyon, Mesa Verde, and Kayenta assumed their modern proportions. Cut sandstone became the primary building material at many of the sites, which took on increasingly aesthetically

pleasing contours, obviously planned by the builders. Some of the towns housed populations of ten thousand or more; the total Anasazi population increased to more than a hundred thousand. Pottery and textile weaving became more refined; trade and commerce became more important to the economies of the Anasazi communities, as evidenced by a well-planned road system connecting some of the towns.

The final stage of Anasazi civilization began in the fourteenth century and lasted until about 1610. Sometimes called the Regressive Pueblo Period (Pueblo IV), the era witnessed profound changes in Anasazi culture. Many classic towns were abandoned. Neighboring communities adopted Anasazi architectural and artistic styles. More primitive hunting and gathering peoples moved into Anasazi territory, some assimilating into Anasazi culture, others apparently waging war against the Anasazi towns. New styles of pottery making and coloring replaced classic Anasazi methods, and a religious revolution (apparently imported from Mexico) occurred with the introduction of worship of supernatural beings called kachinas.

European Contact. When the Spaniards under Francisco Vásquez de Coronado penetrated the Anasazi region in the mid-sixteenth century looking for the fabled seven cities of gold, the Anasazi entered the realm of history. The Spanish described ten Anasazi provinces whose people spoke at least six different languages. Older men and clan societies governed the individual towns, with warrior societies playing an important role. Inheritance was usually matrilineal, and the Spanish noted little social/economic stratification. Each town was politically independent, but during times of war it was not unusual for several towns to ally together against nomadic peoples or against other towns, or to ally with nomadic peoples against other towns. Only once, during the great Pueblo Revolt of 1680 against the Spanish, did all or most of the Anasazi cooperate together against a common foe. By the time of the Spanish penetration, the Anasazi had abandoned most of the stone towns and moved to locations in areas which had little stone suitable for architecture. They often built their new towns from adobe brick, which led archaeologists to characterize this era as "Degenerative Pueblo," a misleading label. The art and culture of the Anasazi people during this era were in no way inferior to those of the Classic period.

Conflict and animosity marked Spanish-Anasazi relations from the first contact between the two cultures. Most anthropologists date the end of the Anasazi period to 1610, by which time Spanish dominance in the former Anasazi area had become well established. Nevertheless, in a very real sense, the Anasazi are still with us in the form of several Pueblo towns that have survived to the present. Pueblo towns such as the one at Taos, New Mexico, retain many elements of Anasazi culture, relatively untouched by modern civilization.

—Paul Madden

See also American Indian; Archaic; Canyon de Chelly; Chaco Canyon; Cíbola, Seven Cities of; Desert culture; Hohokam; Indian; Mesa Verde; Mimbres; Mogollon; Navajo;

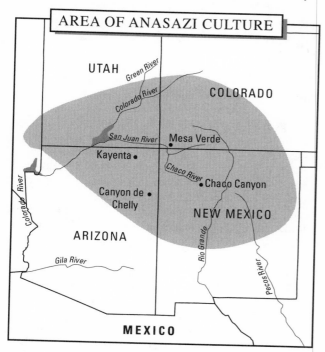

AREA OF ANASAZI CULTURE

UTAH
Green River
Colorado River
COLORADO
San Juan River
Mesa Verde
Kayenta
Chaco River
Chaco Canyon
Colorado River
Canyon de Chelly
NEW MEXICO
ARIZONA
Gila River
Rio Grande
Pecos River
MEXICO

Native American; Prehistory—Southwest; Pueblo tribes, Eastern; Pueblo tribes, Western.

BIBLIOGRAPHY

Ambler, J. Richard. *The Anasazi: Prehistoric People of the Four Corners Region.* Flagstaff: Museum of Northern Arizona, 1977.

Berry, Michael S. *Time, Space, and Transition in Anasazi Prehistory.* Salt Lake City: University of Utah Press, 1982.

Brody, J. J. *The Anasazi: Ancient Indian People of the American Southwest.* New York: Rizzoli International, 1990.

Cordell, Linda S. *Prehistory of the Southwest.* Orlando, Fla.: Academic Press, 1984.

Muench, David, and Donald G. Pike. *Anasazi: Ancient People of the Rock.* New York: Crown, 1974.

Annawan (?—c. 1676): War chief

TRIBAL AFFILIATION: Wampanoag

SIGNIFICANCE: Annawan led the war chiefs during King Philip's War

Leader of the war chiefs under King Philip (Metacomet) during King Philip's War (1675-1676) in the New England colonies, Annawan was a trusted adviser and strategist. He was acknowledged as a valiant soldier in this decisive war for the future of Indian-white relations in the Northeast.

After the death of Philip in August, 1676, Annawan became the leader of a short-lived continued Indian resistance, leading attacks on the towns of Swansea and Plymouth. Conducting guerrilla-style warfare and shifting campsites nightly, Annawan was able to evade colonial forces under Captain Benjamin Church for two weeks. Then a captive Indian led Church and a small party of soldiers to Annawan's camp, now known as Annawan's Rock. Church misled the Indians into believing that they were outnumbered, and on August 26, 1676, Annawan surrendered the tribe's medicine bundle, which included wampum belts telling the history of the tribe and of the Wampanoag Confederacy.

Church respected his defeated adversary so much that he asked for clemency for Annawan. During Church's absence, however, Plymouth residents seized Annawan and beheaded him, ending the last vestige of Wampanoag resistance.

See also King Philip's War; Metacomet; Wampanoag.

Antonio, Juan (c. 1783, Mt. San Jacinto region, Calif.—Feb. 28, 1863, San Timoteo Cañon, Calif.): Tribal chief

ALSO KNOWN AS: Cooswootna, Yampoochee (He Gets Mad Quickly)

TRIBAL AFFILIATION: Cahuilla

SIGNIFICANCE: A powerful Cahuilla chief, Antonio aided whites on several occasions in California during the turbulent 1850's

Several competing forces vied for control of California during the 1850's, including ranchers, Mexicans, miners, Mormons, outlaws, and Indians. In 1842, Juan Antonio, leader of the Cahuillas of Southern California, greeted explorer Daniel Sexton at the San Gorgino Pass, granting him permission to explore the region. Antonio likewise assisted Lieutenant Edward F. Beale of the U.S. Army in his explorations of the region, defending Beale's men against raids from Ute warriors led by Walkara. In appreciation for his aid, Beale presented Antonio with a pair of military epaulets.

Antonio continued to assist white Californians. After the outlaw John Irving and his men raided the area, stealing cattle and killing local settlers, Antonio swiftly ended the raid by killing all but one of Irving's men. White settlers, although relieved at Irving's death, nevertheless were ambivalent about Antonio's killing of whites. Consequently, Antonio was officially deposed by white Californians as chief; his Indian followers, however, ignored the white mandate and continued to view him as their leader.

As white migration increased during the Gold Rush, a Cupeño shaman named Antonio Garra organized Indian tribes to drive whites from the region. Both whites and Indians sought Antonio's assistance. Electing to help white settlers, Antonio captured Garra in 1851, thereby suppressing the uprising. In appreciation, Commissioner O. N. Wozencraft designed a treaty that would enable the Cahuilla to retain their ancestral lands. The California Senate refused to ratify the treaty, however, leading to discontent among the Cahuilla. Between 1845 and 1846, violence erupted but resistance to whites was largely ineffectual. Furthermore, by 1856 anti-Mormon sentiments had eclipsed the Indian issue, and land speculators and squatters forced Indians from their land. Already facing dispossession and inadequate provisions, California Indians were suddenly devastated by smallpox. The last of the Cahuilla leaders, Antonio died of the disease and was buried in San Timoteo Cañon. During a 1956 archaeological expedition, Antonio's body was exhumed, identified by his epaulets, and reburied with military honors.

See also Cahuilla; Garra, Antonio.

Apache: Tribe

CULTURE AREA: Southwest

LANGUAGE GROUP: Athapaskan

PRIMARY LOCATION: Arizona, New Mexico, Oklahoma

POPULATION SIZE: 50,051 (1990 U.S. Census)

The Apaches belong to the Athapaskan linguistic group, believed to be the last group to have crossed over to North America from the Asiatic continent. Most of the Athapaskan speakers spread out into northern Canada and down the Pacific coast, but ancestors of the Apaches pursued a more interior route, probably moving south along the eastern flank of the Rocky Mountains. At some point, the group that would become the Navajos split off, although retaining enough linguistic similarity to enable Navajo and Apache speakers to converse. The Apaches spread out in the Southwest, inhabiting primarily the areas now known as Arizona, New Mexico, Texas, and northern Mexico. They were driven west from the southern Plains in the eighteenth century by the Comanches.

Traditional Culture. They called themselves "Tin-ne-áh," or "the people," as many American Indian groups did in their own languages. The origin of the name "Apache" is widely disputed but is agreed to have been given to them by their enemies. The Apaches separated into two broad groups, Western and Eastern. The Eastern Apaches were the Plains groups, the Jicarilla and the Lipan, whose culture showed the influence of contact with other Plains tribes. To the west were three main divisions: the Mescaleros, the Chiricahuas, and the Western Apaches. Five major groups made up the Western Apaches. The White Mountain, which had a Western and an Eastern (often called Coyotero) band, held the largest territory. The remaining four Western groups were the San Carlos or Gileños, the Cibicues, and the Southern and Northern Tontos. These bands were further subdivided into smaller, extended family groups that supported their highly mobile existence, each designated by its own particular name, often associated with a favorite haunt. Defining early Apache bands is made difficult by the Spanish practice of naming a band for the location where they were encountered, or after a powerful chief.

Life in the deserts of the Southwest was harsh, and the Apache way of life prepared its members for survival with a rich and meaningful culture. Folktales involving Coyote and other animal spirits illustrated proper as well as improper behavior and its consequences. Spirituality was inherent in every aspect of life, and great care was taken to observe rituals and taboos. The number four was important, and the east was favored as the most holy direction.

Although bands were small and children were valued highly, a crying baby could betray the entire group to extinction by enemies. Thus, from early infancy, the Apache child was trained in self-control. The ability to remain motionless and to be quiet for long periods of time, a skill learned in the cradleboard, served the grown warrior well as he hunted or waited in ambush for an enemy.

The most important time in an Apache child's life occurred at puberty. For girls, this was marked by the onset of menses and celebrated by a puberty ceremony that lasted four days, involving blessings with sacred pollen and culminating in the girl's run to the east. During the four days, the girl assumed the identity of White Painted Woman, a supernatural figure of the Apache creation myth. An Apache boy was inducted into manhood by serving an apprenticeship to raiding warriors. The novice was required to observe certain taboos and carry special equipment on four raids, and was required to perform camp tasks such as gathering wood and cooking for the warriors.

Adult Apache men and women had clear, gender-defined tasks. Women were responsible for gathering and processing wild foods, cooking what they gathered as well as any meat brought in by the men and boys, and the manufacture of all necessary camp equipment, clothing, and personal effects—except weapons. Women also constructed the family dwelling. Although some of the Plains Apaches used the tipi, camps were usually composed of the brush-covered wickiups, easy to construct and then abandon. A man's primary task while in camp was to make weaponry, and arrow-making took up most

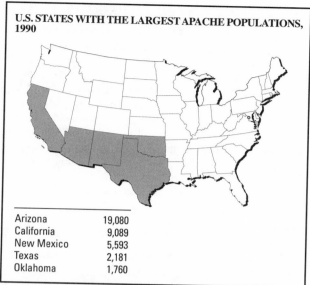

U.S. STATES WITH THE LARGEST APACHE POPULATIONS, 1990

Arizona	19,080
California	9,089
New Mexico	5,593
Texas	2,181
Oklahoma	1,760

Source: 1990 U.S. Census.

of his time. His other responsibilities were hunting and raiding or war. A married man became an economic contributor to his wife's family.

Contact and Resistance. The earliest contact of Apaches with European explorers is believed to have occurred in the sixteenth century. The Spanish were pushing north from New Spain (Mexico), and several parties encountered bands whose description matched that of Apaches. Raiding for supplies was an important part of Apache life, leading inevitably to conflict with Europeans. The earliest known violence involved Gaspar Castano de Sosa, whose party set out for adventure and were raided by a band of Apaches, who captured some stock and killed an Indian with Castano's party. Men were sent to punish the raiders; they killed and captured several of the raiding party.

As colonization progressed, Spanish soldiers were accompanied by Catholic priests eager to convert any subdued Indians. The converts were used as ready labor, often as slaves, to build missions and rancherias in the vast new country of the Southwest. In the seventeenth century, the Pueblo Revolt on the northeastern frontier sent the Spanish south, with Eastern Apaches attacking the Spaniards as they fled. The Spanish returned, however, and by 1697 once again occupied the region.

When the Mexicans won their freedom from Spain in 1824, peace agreements made with various Apache groups were abandoned. Raiding, which had never stopped, increased as the new government could not field any force to match the Apaches. Trouble on the Santa Fe Trail, which was established in 1822, led to a bounty being placed on Apache scalps. By the time the area passed into United States control after the Mexican-American War, Apaches had a reputation as fearsome enemies.

Apache and American relations were frustrating for both sides. The Apaches found that farming, which the United States government expected them to embrace as their new livelihood, did not always provide for their families—and they could not understand why the Americans opposed their continued raids into Mexico for supplies. Treaties made by the United States government were often broken for political expediency. Apache leaders were lured with promises of peace, then arrested and sometimes killed. Army officers would spend years establishing peaceful relations with key Apache leaders, only to see their efforts destroyed by a single party of drunken vigilantes bent on exterminating any Apaches they

A portrait of Chato, a Chiricahua Apache leader of the early reservation era; Chato lived until 1934. (National Archives)

could find, these generally being helpless women and children.

The course of the Apache Wars is a tangled story of capitulation, betrayal, and outbreaks of tribes believed to have been "pacified." One by one the Apache bands were subdued as the U.S. military moved relentlessly west. Treaties settled the Jicarillas and Mescaleros on reservations, but occasional outbreaks occurred. After they made peace, some of the Lipans served as army scouts, as did Apaches from other groups.

There is some evidence that hostilities were prolonged by the machinations of a secret group known only as the "Tucson Ring" or "Indian Ring"; for a time, the only lucrative business for whites in Arizona was supplying the troops who were fighting the Apaches. To the west, the Mimbres band of the Chiricahuas led by Mangas Coloradus clashed openly with the Americans over matters of justice and harassment by settlers. Cochise, another Chiricahua leader, was provoked into war by the treachery of military authorities involving a white boy who had been captured by a different group of Apaches.

The peace sought by a band of Arivaipa Apaches led by Eskiminzin was broken by an attack on their farming settlement. One hundred twenty-five sleeping men, women, and children at Camp Grant were killed by a mob of civilians from Tucson, who had taken advantage of the absence of the fort's main garrison. Among the last Chiricahua holdouts were the famous Geronimo and Naiche, last hereditary chief of the Chiricahuas. More effective fighting on foot in the rugged hills of their familiar country in both Mexico and the United States, these Apaches managed to fight and elude army troops for years, surrendering only when they could no longer escape the Apache scouts used to hunt them.

Following their military defeat, various groups of Apaches were settled on reservations in Arizona, New Mexico, Texas, and Oklahoma. The Fort Apache and San Carlos reservations in Arizona were established jointly in 1871 for Arivaipa, Chiricahua, Coyotero, Mimbreño, Mogollon, Puraleno, and Tsiltaden Apaches. This reservation was partitioned in 1897. Also in Arizona are the Fort McDowell, Tonto Apache, and Yavapai Apache reservations. The Jicarillas and Mescaleros each have reservations in New Mexico, with the Jicarilla reservation extending northward into Colorado as well. In Oklahoma, there is the Fort Sill Apache Reservation.

Modern Apaches. Far from being vanishing Americans, Apaches had grown in population to about fifty thousand by 1990. Weathering the extremes and changes of United States government policy, most Apaches have chosen to remain on their reservations. Some groups have been fortunate in the availability of natural resources; others have continued to struggle at subsistence-level poverty, assisted by government programs designed to help them with their specific needs.

The Jicarilla Apache tribe is a member of the Council of Energy Resource Tribes (CERT), founded in 1975; it obtains income from the exploitation of coal, natural gas, oil, and geothermal energy.

The San Carlos Apache Tribe is governed by a Tribal Council of elected officials serving four-year terms. Of a total reservation population of 10,000, enrolled tribal members equal 7,639; total enrolled tribal membership is 10,500. Located approximately 100 miles east of Phoenix, Arizona, the reservation has three distinct terrains: desert highlands, mountain ridges covered in grass and trees, and forested mountains abundant in wild game. The tribe has adopted an Integrated Resources Management Plan to exploit a stable economy. Timber, recreation and wildlife, agriculture, and ranching bring in revenue for the tribe and are being actively developed.

The White Mountain Apache Tribe, whose reservation is contiguous with the San Carlos, also govern by Tribal Council. They, too, benefit from the availability of exploitable natural resources, including an 800,000-acre ponderosa pine forest that supports the Fort Apache Timber Company. The tribe operates a ski resort which boasts the best ski runs in the southwestern United States and provides scenic campgrounds. Apache Enterprises operates businesses such as gas stations and restaurants throughout the reservation.

The Tonto Apaches have not been as fortunate. A small group numbering 106, with 88 members living on their reservation, they are also governed by Tribal Council. Economic development projects include a Tribal Market/Smokeshop and an eighty-unit motel, but more space is needed for housing and other development. Irrigation of a 5-acre community fruit orchard is under way, and the tribe is attempting to acquire 1,500 acres of land.

Despite relocation efforts of the twentieth century, most Apaches desire to remain on their reservations in proximity to their families. Those who have left to seek employment off the reservation often return after a short while to their more familiar lifestyle and culture. Like so many Americans, Apaches are working hard to prosper while retaining their cultural identity.

—*Patricia Masserman*

See also Apache Tribe of Oklahoma; Apache Wars; Athapaskan language family; Cochise; Council of Energy Resource Tribes (CERT); Eskiminzin; Geronimo; Indian-white relations—Spanish colonial; Indian-white relations—U.S., 1831-1870; Mangas Coloradus; Naiche; Victorio.

BIBLIOGRAPHY

Baldwin, Gordon C. *The Apache Indians: Raiders of the Southwest*. New York: Four Winds Press, 1978. Stated attempt is to be inclusive of Apache history and culture, rather than a rehash of the Apache Wars. Includes and treats the Navajo as an Apache tribe. Contains a map of "Apache Country," numerous photographs, and line drawings.

Haley, James L. *Apaches: A History and Culture Portrait*. New York: Doubleday, 1981. An excellent revisionist text that covers Apache history and culture in great detail. Intersperses narrative with brief tales gathered from Apache folklore. Draws upon a wide variety of sources, including memoirs of U.S. military participants, to detail the painful course of Apache resistance and capitulation. Contains useful notes, secondary bibliography, and comprehensive index.

Terrell, John Upton. *Apache Chronicle*. New York: World Publishing, 1972. A century-by-century account of the Apaches' contact with Europeans, beginning with the Spanish in the sixteenth century and ending with the final surrender of Geronimo in 1886. Contains notes, select bibliography, and index.

_____. *The Plains Apache*. New York: Thomas Y. Crowell Company, 1975. Finding a dearth of works focusing solely on the Plains Apaches, Terrell sets out to fill in the gap with an extensive treatment of these groups who differed in aspects of culture and experience from their western cousins. Extensive notes, select bibliography, and index.

Worcester, Donald E. *The Apaches: Eagles of the Southwest*. Norman: University of Oklahoma Press, 1979. Focuses on hostilities between the Apaches and a succession of invaders: Spanish, Mexican, and United States troops. Notes, bibliography, and index.

Apache Tribe of Oklahoma: Tribe

CULTURE AREA: Plains
LANGUAGE GROUP: Apachean (Southern Athapaskan)
PRIMARY LOCATION: Oklahoma
POPULATION SIZE: 1,400 (1993 tribal census)

The Apache Tribe of Oklahoma, or Na-i-shan Dené ("Our People"), sometimes misnamed Kiowa Apache, were a unique Apache-speaking tribe of Plains Indians distinct from the Apaches of the Southwest and politically independent of their Kiowa allies. There were a number of Apache groups on the Great Plains in the seventeenth and eighteenth centuries, but the small Na-i-shan Apache tribe was the only one to survive as Plains Indians until the reservation period. Their tribal traditions, which are supported by those of the Kiowas and other tribes, indicate northern origins for the Na-i-shan and long-term residence on the Great Plains.

History. It is difficult to identify the Na-i-shan in early documents because they were often known—both to other tribes and to Europeans—by names that also meant "Apaches" generally. They are identifiable on the northern Great Plains by 1805. At that time they were described as traders of horses to the farming tribes of the upper Missouri River. They are then recorded to have shifted their range gradually southward across the Plains until they were settled on the Kiowa, Comanche, and Apache (KCA) Reservation in present southwestern Oklahoma late in the nineteenth century. They seem to be the Apaches del Norte, whose arrival in New Mexico with a group of Kiowas was recorded early in the nineteenth century, as well as the Plains Lipans who reportedly arrived on the northern frontier of Texas at about the same time with Kiowa and Arapaho allies and were escorted farther south by Lipan emissaries.

The alliance and close association with the Kiowa tribe are said to be ancient; in the summer they joined in the Kiowa tribal Sun Dance encampment. The two tribes made an alliance with the Comanches about the year 1800 in the course of their movement southward. With the expansion of the frontier and the decimation of the buffalo, the Na-i-shan and their allies signed treaties with the United States. The last of these, the Treaty of Medicine Lodge in 1867, limited the apparently unsuspecting Kiowas, Comanches, and Na-i-shan Apaches to the reservation in present southwestern Oklahoma. That reservation was allotted in 160-acre tracts to individual members of the three tribes in 1901, over heated Indian protest. Most of the rest of the reservation was then opened to settlement by European Americans.

Traditional Culture. The nineteenth century Na-i-shan were a mounted buffalo-hunting people who lived in tipis and had Plains Indian medicine bundle, warrior, and medicine society complexes. The tribe has no traditions of a time before they lived on the northern Plains or of ever having practiced agriculture or making pottery or basketry. Their material culture was that of the Plains Indians; their economy depended upon the buffalo hunt and the trading of horses and mules taken in Mexico northward. They numbered about 350 and were unified by kinship, a common language and culture, reverence for their medicine bundles, and membership in their sodalities. Children of both sexes first joined the Rabbit Society, whose spirited dances were directed by a tribal elder. The Blackfeet Society was composed of warriors, and it acted as the tribal police. Senior warriors could belong to the *Klintidie*, whose vows required them never to retreat from the enemy. Elderly women might belong to the *Izouwe*, a secret society of grandmothers. Other societies existed as well, but little has been recorded of them. The societies generally owned certain songs, dance motifs, and regalia and met periodically, particularly when the tribe gathered for ceremonies and socializing and the summer buffalo hunt.

Recent History and Contemporary Life. The occupation of the former KCA Reservation by a flood of non-Indian homesteaders and speculators in 1901 took place when the Na-i-shan population had dwindled to its lowest point, about 150, primarily because of epidemic disease. Their twentieth century history has been one of rapid population growth, gradual adjustment to the changed circumstances of increased involvement in the affairs of American society, and determined efforts to preserve their cultural heritage.

In the 1970's a tribal government was formed to administer federal programs and otherwise benefit the tribe's members. In the 1980's the tribe's official designation was changed from the misleading term "Kiowa Apache" to Apache Tribe of Oklahoma. The people generally refer to themselves as Plains Apaches or simply as Apaches. The tribe has an administrative complex, which it also uses for educational and social activities, in Anadarko, Oklahoma, as well as a nearby bingo facility and convenience store. Tribal pow-wows take place in June and August at their dance ground west of Fort Cobb, Oklahoma. In 1993 a formal committee of elders and a tribal research committee were organized to preserve their cultural heritage and facilitate relevant research. The Na-i-shan Apaches are notable for their rich repertory of traditional music and dance. They often excel in painting, silverwork, and beadwork, as well as in other arts and crafts. —*Michael G. Davis*

See also Apache; Kiowa; Medicine Lodge, Treaties of; Plains; Sun Dance.

BIBLIOGRAPHY

Beatty, John. "Kiowa-Apache Music and Dance." In *Occasional Publications in Anthropology*. Museum of Anthropology Ethnology Series Paper 31. Greeley: University of Northern Colorado, 1974.

Bittle, William E. "A Brief History of the Kiowa Apache." *University of Oklahoma Papers in Anthropology* 12, no. 1 (1971): 1-34.

McAllister, J. Gilbert. "Kiowa-Apache Social Organization." In *Social Anthropology of North American Tribes*, edited by Fred Eggan. Enlarged ed. Chicago: University of Chicago Press, 1955.

Mooney, James. *Calendar History of the Kiowa Indians*. Bureau of American Ethnology Annual Report, 1895-1896. Vol. 2. Reprint. Washington, D.C.: Smithsonian Institution Press, 1979.

Apache Wars

DATE: 1861-1886

PLACE: Arizona

TRIBE AFFECTED: Apache

SIGNIFICANCE: A number of battles occurred between Apaches and white settlers and troops in the years between 1861 and 1886 as white settlement of the Southwest proceeded

By the year 1858, Cochise had become the main leader of the Chokonen band of the Chiricahua Apache tribes. Prior to this time his father-in-law, Mangas Coloradus, had the power to organize sizable war parties (which went into Mexico), but Cochise replaced his position of leadership. One of his chief allies, Victorio, chief of the Chihenne band, was skilled in guerrilla warfare. One of his other main allies, Geronimo, was probably the most famous of the three.

During the 1850's, European Americans were arriving in increasing numbers in the southwestern United States, traveling through Apache Pass in southeastern Arizona. Cochise first interacted with them in a congenial manner at the Apache Pass stage station, on the Butterfield Overland Mail Route. By 1860, however, after a series of incidents involving stock raids by the Apaches and retaliatory raids by the European Americans, the number of casualties had increased to the extent that Cochise became more uncomfortable with the encroachments by these new settlers. The Bascom incident of 1861 at Apache Pass caused the beginning of the Apache Wars of 1861-1886.

Lieutenant George Bascom was ordered to take appropriate actions in order to rescue a boy who reportedly had been kidnapped by some Apaches in a raid. Cochise and some of his relatives went to Bascom's camp in order to convince the lieutenant that it was not Chokonens who captured the boy, but a group of Coyoteros. Bascom, however, decided to hold them hostage until the boy was returned. Cochise escaped, but his relatives were captured and eventually executed.

Apache leaders Geronimo and Nana meeting with General George Crook and his men toward the end of the Apache Wars, probably in 1886. (Library of Congress)

Infuriated, Cochise vowed to avenge their deaths. His first battle occurred in an ambush at Stein's Peak, at the eastern end of Doubtful Canyon. Nine members of the Gidding party were killed in an attack by Cochise; about sixty warriors lost their lives. Mangas Coloradus was involved with Cochise in a number of the raids that made up the Apache Wars of this time period. For the most part, the battles consisted of raids against groups of settlers and miners.

Probably the most active period of the wars occurred in 1865, when the battles became more numerous. During December, 1865, Sonoran forces from Mexico killed thirty-nine Apaches and captured twenty-eight in a retaliatory battle. Cochise was driven from Arizona in 1866, moving into northwestern Chihuahua, and for a number of years he conducted battles in Mexico and the United States. Cochise finally signed a truce in 1872, but other Apaches continued to fight white settlers until the 1880's.

See also Apache; Cochise; Geronimo; Mangas Coloradus.

Apalachee: Tribe
CULTURE AREA: Southeast
LANGUAGE GROUP: Muskogean
PRIMARY LOCATION: Northwestern Florida

The Apalachee, a branch of the Muskogean family, lived in northwest Florida along the Apalachee Bay. Their name comes from the Choctaw word *a'palachi* ("[people] on the other side"). The Apalachee were among a group of advanced tribes who migrated from west of the Mississippi River to the Southeast around 1300.

Their first recorded contact with whites was in 1528, with an expedition led by the Spanish explorer Pánfilo de Narváez. The encounter was marked by hostility and fighting on both sides. When another Spanish explorer, Hernando de Soto, came through in 1539, he and his men were also given a hostile welcome. De Soto noted in his journal that the Apalachee were skilled agriculturalists, growing corn, beans, pumpkins, and squash. His forces walked two days through one immense stretch of corn fields. By the early 1600's, the Apalachee had been visited by missionaries, and most had converted to Roman Catholicism. While many Apalachee eagerly accepted Christianity, and at least seven chiefs were baptized, there was still tension between the Indians and the Spanish. In 1647 a rebellion occurred; several missionaries were killed, and the churches were destroyed. The missionaries persevered. In 1655, there were approximately six thousand to eight thousand Apalachee living in eight towns, each built around a central Franciscan mission.

In 1703, the Apalachee were attacked by a company of a hundred whites and about one thousand Indians of various tribes. The force was sent by the English governor of Carolina, who wanted to disrupt Spanish influence in the area. Some two hundred Apalachee were killed, and another fourteen hundred were carried off into slavery and resettled near New Windsor, North Carolina. All the major Apalachee towns, missions, groves, and fields were destroyed. A year later, another raid killed several hundred more Apalachee. Small bands drifted away, joining other tribes or establishing independent villages. When the Yamasee War broke out, those who had been made slaves joined the Lower Creeks and were eventually absorbed. By the end of the nineteenth century, the tribe was no longer a distinct entity.

See also Missions and missionaries; Muskogean language family; Southeast; Yamasee War.

Apalachicola: Tribe

Culture area: Southeast
Language group: Muskogean
Primary location: Southwestern Georgia, southeastern Alabama

The matrilineal Apalachicola raised the "three sisters"—beans, corn, and squash—but were also river-oriented. They had individual and large communal hunts for deer, which supplemented their food bases and provided needed by-products. There were probably four large, permanent, and politically independent villages that maintained exchange of resources and alliances. According to oral history, when the Muskogee encroached upon Apalachicola territory a peace treaty resulted, which the Apalachicola negotiated and which led to the Creek Confederacy.

The Apalachicola were first contacted by the Spanish in the late sixteenth century, then by the French, and eventually by the British. After conflict with encroaching European Americans in 1706, the Apalachicola were resettled on the Savannah River. After the Yamasee War of 1716, they returned to their aboriginal area. During the years 1836-1840 they were forced onto the northern part of the Creek Reservation in Oklahoma, where they were gradually absorbed into other ethnic groups.

See also Creek; Southeast; Yamasee War.

Apes, William (Jan. 31, 1798, Colrain, Mass.—?): Writer

Also known as: William Apess
Tribal affiliation: Pequot

Significance: Apes, a nineteenth century political protest writer, produced the first published autobiography by an American Indian

Little is known of William Apes outside his own account in his autobiography, *A Son of the Forest* (1829), which recounts his youth and early adulthood. He spent his first four years with intemperate grandparents, reporting that they often beat him and his siblings. While growing up, he recalled, his indenture was sold several times to different families in Connecticut. He had only six years of formal education, took part in the War of 1812, had bouts with drinking, and was reformed by his introduction to Christianity. In 1829, he was ordained as a Methodist minister.

In May, 1833, he traveled to the Massachusetts community of Mashpee, where he immediately took part in a revolt against the Massachusetts Commonwealth. In the context of organizing and leading this revolt, he published an account of Indians' grievances against whites in *Indian Nullification of the Unconstitutional Laws of Massachusetts, Relative to the Mashpee Tribe* (1835). Like the earlier "An Indian's Looking-Glass for the White Man" (1833), this book turns on his political astuteness and sense of fairness. At the Odeon in Boston in 1836, Apes preached *Eulogy on King Philip*, a political and historical account of the Indian wars of the previous century; it was published the same year. Apes returned to autobiography in *The Experiences of Five Christian Indians* (1837), in which he accuses whites of racism based primarily on skin color. After about 1838, Apes disappeared from the public eye, and nothing is known of his later life.

See also Indian-white relations—Spanish colonial; Pequot.

Bibliography

Apess, William. *On Our Own Ground: The Complete Writings of William Apess.* Edited by Barry O'Connell. Amherst: University of Massachusetts Press, 1992.

Appliqué and ribbonwork

Tribes affected: Northwest Coast, Eastern Woodlands, Southeast tribes
Significance: The personalized designs for these traditional garment decorations both express individual style and maintain group identity

Clothing is a silent communication of personal or cultural values and beliefs. Observers may not understand the meanings being expressed, but they are usually aware that a certain style is not accidental. Decorations such as appliqué and ribbonwork may lend similarity (if not uniformity) to the clothing of a people. Styles of clothing and decoration may be maintained over time as part of a people's culture; some garments themselves are literally passed down through many generations. Since such garments are usually handmade, they are a visible history of a family, clan, or a people and are thought to carry the essence of the original wearer.

Appliqué. Appliqués are cutout decorations of contrasting color or fabric stitched to a garment. They are often embellished with stitching, beads, or shells. The Kwakiutl people of the Northwest Coast are famous for their appliquéd button blankets. Worn as ceremonial shawls, the red blankets carry large blue or black appliquéd crests of Raven, Wolf, or Eagle Clans. Outlines of gleaming mother-of-pearl and abalone buttons (as many as three thousand) emphasize the crests and trim the edges of these magnificent blankets. In addition to expressing wealth, the wearing of these blankets imparts the qualities of clan animals.

The Kwakiutl people are well known for the ceremonial potlatch, an extravagant giveaway once banned by the Canadian government. On the eve of the potlatch, women wear button blankets as they dance in the smoke-filled great house. While the women sing mourning songs, the iridescent buttons sparkle in the firelight, helping to drive away sadness so the celebration can proceed. The next day, the men in their crested button blankets perform the Chiefs' Dance to begin the potlatch.

After contact with Europeans provided new fabrics, Eastern Woodlands women put aside their deerskin outfits and decorated their cotton shawls and skirts with wide borders of silk appliqué. These formal outfits are worn in ceremony and at social gatherings. In the mid-twentieth century, younger Woodlands women adapted this style to create the cape dancer's outfit now often seen at pow-wows. The young dancers whirl in their one-of-a-kind satin shawls decorated with bright, bold appliqués and yards of fringe. For ceremonies and pow-wows, Woodlands men wear aprons and leggings of black velvet decorated in stylized nature designs. These are typically rendered in colorful combinations of appliqué, embroidery, and beads.

Ribbonwork. Seminole and Miccosukee women of Florida have raised the use of decorative ribbons to an art form. One of the most recognizable styles in North America, some of these attractive designs have been used for many decades. The practice may have begun after contact with Spanish officials who wore striped brocade on dress uniforms. In the trading days of the late 1800's, the hand-cranked sewing machine was readily adopted by Southeast women to adorn calico skirts and shirts. The early patterns of wide bands of single contrasting colors soon evolved into elaborate multicolored patchwork strips. The strips are combined with bands of ribbon in a manner similar to that used in quilting and sewn together.

Both men and women wear garments of this distinctive type. The early tradition was knee-length shirts for elderly men and longer shirts for younger men. Women and girls wore full-length ribbon skirts topped with a lightweight cape edged in ribbons. Later a popular waist-length jacket was rendered in a Seminole ribbon style for men.

Traditional Seminole patterns are still used and are often altered as the tailor expresses her own ideas. Complex designs have names, such as *checkers* or *rattlesnake*, suggested by something they resemble. Designs are treasured but are not claimed as personal property. They are shared with friends and handed down within families. Copying of designs by those who admire them is considered an honor to the originator.

The use of ribbons in ceremonial dress was carried to Oklahoma by the Creek, formerly of the Southeast. In the Ribbon Dance, women wear rainbow-colored headdresses of cascading ribbons as they parade through the public square. The annual ceremony reaffirms and honors the role of women within the community. —*Gale M. Thompson*

See also Beads and beadwork; Creek; Dress and adornment; Headdresses; Kwakiutl; Pow-wows and contemporary celebrations; Quillwork; Seminole; Shells and shellwork.

BIBLIOGRAPHY

Billard, Jules B., et al. *The World of the American Indian*. Washington, D.C.: National Geographic Society, 1974. More than 440 color illustrations, maps of culture areas, poems and chants, and tribal location supplement. Back-pocket map, index, and acknowledgments.

Garbarino, Merwyn. *The Seminole*. New York: Chelsea House, 1989. Culture, history, and effect of European contact on the Seminole people; Seminole resistance under leader Osceola; color and black-and-white photographs; and designs of Seminole ribbonwork clothing.

Maxwell, James A., et al. *America's Fascinating Indian Heritage*. Pleasantville: Reader's Digest, 1978. Comprehensive account of culture areas, prehistory (including Mesoamerican), cultural, political, and social issues of early twentieth century. Includes more than seven hundred color illustrations as well as descriptions of ceremonies. List of museums, historic villages, and archaeological sites.

Owen, Roger G., et al. *The North American Indians: A Sourcebook*. Macmillan: New York, 1967. Collection of original (edited) articles dating from 1888 to 1963 and arranged by culture areas; history, evolution, and demography; and social perspectives of the mid-twentieth century. Includes references, additional reading list, and a directory of 250 educational films.

Underhill, Ruth M. *Red Man's America: A History of Indians in the United States*. Sixth impression. Chicago: University of Chicago Press, 1960. Surveys origins, history, social customs, material culture, religion, and mythology. Written from the perspective of the first peoples of North America.

Arapaho: Tribe

CULTURE AREA: Plains
LANGUAGE GROUP: Algonquian
PRIMARY LOCATION: West-central Wyoming, Western Oklahoma
POPULATION SIZE: 6,350 (1990 U.S. Census)

The Arapaho were Plains Indians with a classical buffalo (bison) economy. They are closely related to the Atsina and were close associates of the Cheyenne. The Utes, Shoshones, and Pawnees were their constant enemies. Their relationship with the Sioux, Kiowa, and Comanche varied. The Arapaho were probably pushed west and south by the Sioux in their early days on the Plains, and in turn they pushed the Comanche and Kiowa south. At other times, they were allied with each tribe against other Indians and white Americans.

Early History and Traditional Lifestyle. Exactly when the Arapaho moved into the Plains is not clear, but at the end of the eighteenth century, when they first came to the attention of white Americans, they were established in eastern Colorado, southeastern Wyoming, and extreme western Nebraska and Kansas. They may have lived as farmers in western Minnesota until the sixteenth century and then moved west and south into the Plains, probably because of pressure from eastern tribes moving west under pressure from European immigrants. On the Plains, they established a nomadic lifestyle, almost entirely dependent on buffalo. Eventually, northern and southern subdivisions developed.

The Arapaho's early Plains lifeways are not well known either, but they probably followed buffalo herds, using travois pulled by dogs to move their belongings. They lived in lodges (tipis) made of buffalo hides stretched over a set of poles. Their hunting tactics included driving buffalo into enclosures and killing them with arrows and spears; they also drove groups of buffalo over cliffs.

Sometime before the middle of the eighteenth century, by raiding or trading, the Arapaho obtained horses from southwestern tribes. This acquisition changed their lives dramatically. The travois was adjusted to fit horses, so moves could be made rapidly. More important, the horses became their vehicle for hunting and fighting. The Arapaho were not the best-known horse Indians of the Plains; nevertheless, they were highly skilled at hunting and fighting from horseback.

Men hunted buffalo by separating the target individual from the herd and killing it with arrows and spears. Alternatively, if a large group of horsemen was available, the buffalo herd was surrounded and arrows were fired into the herd. Those wounded too seriously to keep up with the escaping herd were killed. Guns became available to the Arapaho shortly after they obtained horses, and buffalo hunting became even more efficient. The men butchered the buffalo at the site of the kill.

In camp, the women cooked some of the meat for immediate use and smoked or dried the rest. Women also scraped and treated the hides for use as tipi covers, clothing, or pouches for carrying various materials. They gathered and preserved berries, roots, and other plant foods. Tools, such as knives, scrapers, and arrowheads, were initially made of flint or buffalo bones. After trade was initiated with whites, metal was often used.

An 1870 photograph of an Arapaho camp near Fort Dodge, Kansas; note the buffalo meat drying on poles. (National Archives)

An artist's rendition, based on photographs, of an Arapaho Ghost Dance ceremony. (National Archives)

The Arapaho lived in groups of twenty to eighty families. Several such groups came together in spring and summer to hunt buffalo and for ceremonial events. The groups separated for winter, each moving to a stream in a protected valley in the foothills of the Rocky Mountains. The men, often on snowshoes, hunted deer, elk, and small game. The women cooked and made and decorated clothes and other articles.

Ceremonial and Religious Life. The Arapaho were deeply religious, holding ceremonies for each stage of life (the birth of a child, the child's first steps, selected stages of male maturity) and for every important event (the buffalo hunt, an individual's pledge of service to—or plea for help from—the Creator). Music and dance were important parts of all these ceremonies. The Flat Pipe, the most sacred symbol of the Arapaho Nation, is kept by an elder of the Northern Arapaho in a sacred bundle and is still used in a number of the nation's most sacred ceremonies. The Sacred Wheel is maintained and used in the same way by the Southern Arapaho.

Arapaho men were almost all members of age-graded societies or lodges. These were of particular importance in the organization of the tribe and in assigning duties to the various tribal members. The first two were youth societies. Membership in the six adult male lodges was achieved with age and demonstration of responsible behavior, especially generosity. Regular demonstration of generosity was essential for becoming an Arapaho leader. There were specific rituals associated with each lodge, and members of each had certain responsibilities in war and peace. The highest lodge comprised the seven Water Sprinkling Old Men and was attained by a few spiritual leaders. Each was responsible for a medicine bundle which contained items of spiritual importance to the tribe.

Arapaho women belonged to the buffalo lodge. There were also Seven Old Women, who, though they did not form a lodge, were the female counterparts to the Water Sprinkling Old Men. Their medicine bags contained the materials needed to teach the skills of making and decorating tipis, clothes, bags, and other tribal materials. The symbolic decorations were of great importance in tribal culture.

A vision quest was a personal religious undertaking. To gain insight into his particular role in life, a man would fast and pray alone in the plains until he received a vision. Often a small animal would be involved in the vision, and the man made his medicine bag from that animal's skin.

The best-known Arapaho ceremony was the Offerings Lodge, also called the Sun Dance. It was an elaborate, week-long ceremony initiated when an Arapaho, called the lodge builder, vowed to pay for the ceremony. This was done to petition the Creator for success in battle, recovery from sickness, or satsifaction of some other need or desire. Self-torture was the most infamous part of the Offerings Lodge. A man pushed skewers through his chest muscles, tied the skewers to the center pole, and hung suspended until the skewers tore through his flesh. According to one explanation, the man was asking the Creator to forgive and favor the tribe.

The Offerings Lodge was important in social as well as spiritual life, especially in maintaining the unity of the tribe. All Arapaho bands gathered for the ceremony. The other lodges were important in maintaining order and organization in Arapaho life. Tribal history, skills, and customs were passed from generation to generation by way of the age-graded societies and the Buffalo Lodge. Some authorities believe that the organization of the age-graded societies spared the Arapaho the conflicts between generations that other Plains tribes suffered during the transition from buffalo hunting to reservation life.

Transition and Contemporary Life. The Arapaho fought ably against other American Indian tribes and, as allies of the Sioux, Cheyenne, and Comanche, against white encroachment. Some raided settlements and wagon trains, stole livestock, and participated in battles with white Americans. They were less aggressive than some other tribes, however, and put more effort into trading than fighting. Friday, a Northern Arapaho, and Left Hand, a Southern Arapaho, spoke English and had many white friends. They counseled for peace throughout the white invasion. Northern Arapaho men were important scouts for the United States Army, and relationships between Arapahos and whites were often friendly.

The Arapaho's most important encounter with the U.S. Army was at Sand Creek, Colorado, on November 29, 1864. A group of Cheyenne and Arapaho, camped under the flag and protection of the U.S. government, were attacked by troops led by Colonel John Chivington. The chiefs in the camp, Left Hand and Black Kettle, a Cheyenne, were known advocates of peace, and the Indians present were primarily women and children. Chivington probably knew this before the attack. Most of the Indians killed were women and children, and soldiers mutilated the dead Indians. Left Hand died as a result of his wounds.

In response, many Arapaho joined the Cheyenne and Sioux in the Plains Indian wars, which finally ended in 1890, at Wounded Knee, South Dakota. Most Arapaho, however, followed chiefs Little Raven, of the southern group, and Medicine Man and Black Coal from the north and pursued peace. In 1869, the Southern Arapaho and Cheyenne were assigned to a reservation in Oklahoma; in 1878, the Northern Arapaho were placed on the Shoshone (Wind River) Reservation in western Wyoming. These areas were a minute fraction of the land that had been promised in the 1851 treaty of Horse Creek.

In response to settlers' demands for land from the new reservations and because of a determination to assimilate the Indians into white society, the General Allotment Act (Dawes Severalty Act) was passed in 1887. It gave a parcel of reservation land to each individual American Indian. Not coincidentally, there was reservation land left after all Indians had received allotments, and the law allowed whites to buy or lease the leftover land. Both Northern and Southern Arapaho were cheated by unfair loan, lease, and sale agreements, but the burden fell most heavily on the southern group.

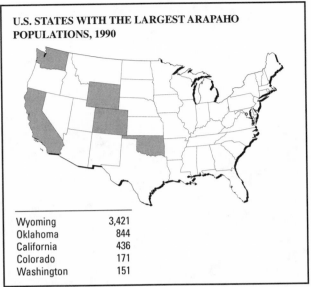

U.S. STATES WITH THE LARGEST ARAPAHO POPULATIONS, 1990

Wyoming	3,421
Oklahoma	844
California	436
Colorado	171
Washington	151

Source: 1990 U.S. Census.42

The Northern Arapaho succeeded in retaining control of most reservation land through a long period of abject poverty. In the 1940's, a tribal business council of six elected representatives, working with the tribal elders and a similar Shoshone council, convinced the federal government to allow payments to individual families from reservation income. The income is derived from oil and gas production, land rental, and tribally owned businesses. In 1961, the Arapaho and Cheyenne won millions of dollars in compensation for broken treaties. As a result of these and other astute political maneuvers, Northern Arapaho economic conditions improved considerably. Many old problems continued, however, especially undereducation, unemployment, and attendant poverty.

The Southern Arapaho also received individual allotments, but for reasons unique to their situation, they were unable to maintain an intact reservation. Reservation land left after allotment was sold to white ranchers and farmers; in addition, many individual Arapaho sold their allotments. Because of extensive fraud, sale prices were often well below market value. As part of the continuing attempt to assimilate American Indians into white society, the reservation was abolished in 1890. The Southern Arapaho subsequently scattered around western Oklahoma, and tribal unity, so important to the maintenance of Arapaho culture, was lost. An elected Cheyenne-Arapaho Business Committee now manages tribal resources. Many Arapaho live in the towns of Geary and Canton, Oklahoma, and the tribal offices are in Concho. Many tribal members are undereducated, unemployed, and living in poverty.

The two branches of the tribe maintain contact with each other. The Offerings Lodge is celebrated in Wyoming each year, and some southern members make the trip north to join in the celebration. The Arapaho language is on the verge of extinction, but members of both branches are striving to maintain their heritage while living in the modern world.

—Carl W. Hoagstrom

See also Atsina; Cheyenne; Left Hand the First; Left Hand the Second; Little Raven; Plains; Sand Creek Massacre; Sun Dance.

BIBLIOGRAPHY

Bass, Althea. *The Arapaho Way*. New York: Clarkson N. Potter, 1966. A description of Arapaho life based on the memory of a Southern Arapaho, Carl Sweezy. Illustrated with his paintings.

Coel, Margaret. *Chief Left Hand: Southern Arapaho*. Norman: University of Oklahoma Press, 1981. An outline of Southern Arapaho life and history, centered on the first Chief Left Hand and on the Sand Creek Massacre and its aftermath. Index, bibliography, maps, illustrations.

Fowler, Loretta. *The Arapaho*. New York: Chelsea House, 1989. A summary of everything Arapaho. Short index, bibliography, glossary, maps, and many illustrations.

_____. *Arapaho Politics, 1851-1978*. Lincoln: University of Nebraska Press, 1982. An excellent account of the Arapaho political system before and during reservation life. Index, bibliography, maps, illustrations.

Shakespeare, Tom. *The Sky People*. New York: Vantage Press, 1971. A description of Arapaho life written by a Northern Arapaho.

Trenholm, Virginia Cole. *The Arapahoes: Our People*. Norman: University of Oklahoma Press, 1986. History of the Arapaho, including both northern and southern groups. Index, bibliography, and illustrations.

Zdenek, Salzmann. *The Arapaho Indians: A Research Guide and Bibliography*. New York: Greenwood Press, 1988. An invaluable source for nearly everything written on the Arapaho before 1988. Including U.S. government documents and archive and museum holdings.

Arapoosh (c. 1790, northern Wyo.—Aug., 1834): War chief

ALSO KNOWN AS: Rotten Belly, Sour Belly

TRIBAL AFFILIATION: Crow

SIGNIFICANCE: Revered for his extraordinary spiritual powers, Arapoosh was believed to be virtually invincible in battle

Known to whites as Rotten Belly or Sour Belly, Arapoosh apparently earned his name through his disposition: He was surly, ill-tempered, and impatient. He was also known to be extraordinarily brave. The foremost warrior among the River Crow who lived along the Big Horn, Powder, and Wind rivers in present-day northern Wyoming and southern Montana, Arapoosh led his people against their traditional Indian enemies, the Blackfeet, Sioux, and Northern Cheyennes.

After receiving a guardian spirit vision from the "Man in the Moon," Arapoosh adopted that symbol, painting it on his medicine shield. Before battle, Arapoosh would roll his shield along a line of tipis, using its position as it fell as an omen for the coming battle. If it landed with his insignia facing down,

the project was doomed and consequently abandoned; face up, however, augured well for the engagement and the battle was waged.

Believing his tribe's future was threatened by the proposed reservation, and voicing his suspicions of the ultimate intentions of whites, Arapoosh in 1825 refused to sign a treaty of friendship negotiated between the Crow and the United States. Instead he continued to protect the lush Crow territory from other tribes as well as from whites.

At Pierre's Hole, Idaho, Arapoosh met the trader and Hudson's Bay Company representative William Sublette, who was much impressed with his bearing and reputation.

During a war between the Crow and the Blackfeet in 1833, Arapoosh prophesied his own death. Resting his shield on a pile of buffalo chips, he claimed that he would die in the coming battle if his shield rose into the air of its own volition. Purportedly it did just that, rising to a height level with his head. Arapoosh died in the battle.

See also Crow.

Archaic: Prehistoric tradition

DATE: Beginning 8000 B.C.E.

LOCATION: North, Central, and South America

CULTURES AFFECTED: All

The term "Archaic" was designated by archaeologists Gordon Willey and Philip Phillips as nomenclature for the period between the end of the Paleo-Indian big-game hunting and gathering period and the beginnings of settled, agriculture-based village life. It has roughly the same meaning in the New World as the term "Mesolithic" does in the Old World. The Archaic tradition covers several millennia and is broadly construed. It includes societies that were highly nomadic, such as those of the Desert culture, as well as more sedentary groups, such as riverine and coastal shell-fishing peoples of the southeastern United States. Archaic cultures ranged from small, mobile bands that utilized sites such as Bat Cave to relatively large groups such as those who constructed Poverty Point.

A number of characteristics were shared by societies of the Archaic tradition. First and foremost of these was a reliance on wild plant and animal resources. Archaic peoples subsisted primarily by hunting (sometimes with domesticated dogs) and gathering. Strategies ranged from bison hunting on the central Plains and shellfishing on the Florida coast to intensive gathering of marsh elder in eastern Illinois.

The technology of the Archaic tradition included artifacts made of chipped and ground stone, bone, wood, shell, gourds, and a variety of fibers. Among these were ground-stone manos and metates, for grinding seeds and nuts, and polished axes. Over time, ground-stone techniques extended to the manufacture of elaborate stone bowls, axes, and adzes as well as objects such as birdstones and banner stones. Archaic peoples were adept at the use of leather, sinews, and plant fibers. Basketry was used for containers, sandals, and even shelters. Leatherwork, as well as twining and weaving, was used to make bags, hats, clothing, and sandals. Pottery was invented by Archaic peoples. In the lower Mississippi Valley, fired clay was used to make boiling "stones," while fiber-tempered vessels were manufactured in the Southeast. Simple metallurgy was also practiced in the Great Lakes region, where Archaic peoples made ornaments of hammered native copper.

Archaic peoples initiated the processes that resulted in the domestication of plant and animal species. In Mexico these included maize, beans, squash, chiles, avocados, amaranth, and goosefoot, as well as turkeys. In South America they included gourds, cotton, potatoes, chiles, the guinea pig, llama, and muscovy duck, while in eastern North America they included squash, marsh elder, amaranth, goosefoot, and sunflowers. Other Archaic period innovations were the emergence of early social ranking, as evidenced by marked differences in the quality of burial goods found in cemeteries, and long-distance trade in rare minerals or craft items. It is likely that many of the religious traditions that became focal points of community activity in later times had their origins in Archaic times.

The Archaic tradition ends with the emergence of communities that relied more heavily on agricultural products than on wild resources. It is fair to say that it continued into the historic period among groups such as fishing societies of the Northwest Coast and can still be found today in remote regions of South America.

See also Bat Cave; Clovis; Desert culture; Folsom; Paleo-Indian; Poverty Point.

Architecture—Arctic

Tribes affected: Aleut, Inuit, Yupik

Significance: Although the domed snow house is the most widely recognized Arctic habitation, a number of other types of structures have been used by groups in the Arctic culture area

Throughout the Arctic, housing styles were largely a function of four factors: local weather conditions, availability of raw materials, requirements for mobility, and household size and organization. While the domed snow house (in common parlance, the igloo) is the form of shelter most commonly associated with the Arctic, it actually had a very limited distribution. Many Arctic groups, such as the Yupik of southwestern Alaska, the Aleut, and the West Greenlanders, never built snow houses. Rather, there was a wide range of architectural styles, including aboveground plank houses, semi-subterranean sod and rock houses, semi-subterranean log houses, and walrus-skin houses elevated on stilts.

Snow Houses. Without a doubt, the dome-shaped snow house was the most remarkable architectural achievement of Arctic populations. At the time of European contact, the snow house was the primary winter shelter in most areas of the Central and Eastern Canadian Arctic. In these areas, a typical strategy involved building large snow house communities on the ocean ice from which hunters would depart daily to engage in breathing-hole seal hunting. It was essential that the right kind of snow be used: hard-packed, granular snow that was uniformly compressed by blowing winds. The snow house was built by arranging the snow blocks, cut with a large snow knife, in a circular pattern spiraling upward. The spiral ensured that each snow block placed in line had another block to lean against. This made the construction process easier and maximized the structural integrity of the shelter.

Any snow house that was to be occupied for more than one or two nights would have a porch attached to provide storage space and protection from the wind. The entrance generally sloped downward so as to create a cold trap. At least half of the interior included a raised sleeping and sitting platform, which provided protection from the cold air on the floor below. Caribou skins or musk ox skins would be placed on the sleeping platform for additional insulation. Often, a small hole would be punched through the roof to provide some air circulation and hence a guarantee against asphyxiation. A piece of ice might also be placed into the wall to provide natural lighting.

Semi-Subterranean Houses. Far more common than the snow house was the semi-subterranean house, found from East Greenland to South Alaska and the Aleutian Islands. Excavated several feet into the ground, these shelters generally consisted of a wood, stone, or whalebone framework covered with insulating sod. Because of the great effort involved in building and maintaining such shelters, they tended to be used by groups with year-round or seasonally occupied villages. In North Alaska, houses were rectangular and constructed of a whalebone and driftwood frame covered by sod. A wood planked floor marked the main living area, which included a raised sleeping platform. Entrance to the house was through a passageway which sloped from ground level downward to a depth of about 4 to 5 feet. On either side of this passageway were side rooms used for storage, cooking, and food preparation. The long tunnel ended under the main living area, which was entered through a trapdoor in the floor. This main living area was usually kept warm by a soapstone lamp, although body heat alone was sometimes adequate to keep it warm. A membrane-covered skylight provided light to the interior.

In the Bering Sea region, easier access to wood resulted in this material being a more significant component in house construction. These houses tended to be slightly larger and were often made with a frame of whole logs covered with sod. The main living areas often had sleeping platforms on all three sides as opposed to the single sleeping platform of the North Alaskan house. A central fireplace fueled by wood and placed under a square smoke hole in the roof was the primary source of heat. Such dwellings occasionally had two entrances: a ground-level entrance for summer use and an underground passageway for winter use. Farther south, among Chugach and Koniag Eskimos, wood was even more evident in house construction. Although these houses were semi-subterranean, they lacked the sloping entranceways characteristic of more northern groups. Even in winter, entry was generally through a ground-level doorway.

The Aleut constructed large semi-subterranean houses which have been documented to range between 70 and 200 feet in length. These houses had log supports and roof frames made of either wood or whalebone. Woven grasses were placed on the roofs, which were then covered with sod. Since the Aleut lived in a far milder climate than most Eskimo groups, an underground passageway was not necessary. Rather, entrance into the house was down one or more notched log ladders positioned under the structure's smoke holes. Since these longhouses generally accommodated a large number of related families, often an entire village of thirty to forty people, each family was assigned a living area along the outside walls. Grasses were woven into partitions to separate the living areas.

Semi-subterranean longhouses were also used in Labrador, West Greenland, and East Greenland, but these generally had underground passageways to function as cold traps. In East Greenland, these longhouses invariably housed an entire village. Given the scarcity of wood, house walls were constructed of stone and sod, while roofs were made of sod placed over driftwood rafters.

In North Greenland, the Polar Eskimo had extremely limited access to wood, so they constructed their semi-subterranean winter houses of cantilevered stone covered by sod and snow. These shelters tended to be small and triangular-shaped, rarely housing more than one nuclear family, and were often dug into a hillside. A similar style of structure, called a *qarmaq*, was used by certain Central Arctic groups. Usually occupied only during transitional seasons, the qarmaq was made of a circular wall of stone, sod, or snowblocks covered over with a skin roof.

Aboveground Wood Houses. Aboveground wood houses had a limited distribution, since they required ready access to timber. They were the dominant form of summer residence among Yupik groups in southwestern and southern Alaska. In the Yukon-Kuskokwim region, for example, these houses were built with horizontally placed logs for the side walls and with vertically placed planks for the front and back walls. The gabled roof was covered with wood planks and bark. Since the houses were occupied only during the warm months of the year, they were built aboveground with ground-level entrances. These houses were typically found at spring and summer fishing camps.

Tents, Stilt Houses, and Men's Houses. Skin tents were ubiquitous throughout the Arctic region. Typically made of caribou or seal skin, they were the primary form of summer residence throughout much of the region, especially among those groups that were highly nomadic in summer. Even the Alaskan Yupik, with their wooden summer houses, used tents while traveling or hunting over long distances.

Perhaps the most unusual houses in the Arctic were the summer stilt houses of King Island, located in the Bering Strait. These small houses were usually erected next to the semi-subterranean winter houses and were boxlike structures with walrus hide walls. Their elevation on wooden stilts was necessary given the steep coastline of the island and the lack of level ground for building.

Ceremonial men's houses constituted an important part of village life throughout most of Alaska. Although large ceremo-nial snow houses were sometimes built by Central Arctic groups for midwinter games and dances, permanent ceremonial houses were not found anywhere in the Central or Eastern Arctic. Throughout Alaska, ceremonial houses were built in a style similar to regular residences, although somewhat larger. They were regarded as men's houses, but women were allowed to visit and participate in certain ceremonies. In North Alaska, each ceremonial house (*karigi*) was associated with one or more whaling crews. Among the Yupik of southwestern Alaska, the men of the village slept and ate in the ceremonial house (*qasgi*). These houses were also used for sweatbaths and for important religious ceremonies such as the Bladder Feast. Some of these houses are reported to have been large enough to seat up to five hundred people.

—*Richard G. Condon and Pamela R. Stern*

See also Aleut; Arctic; Igloo; Prehistory—Arctic.

BIBLIOGRAPHY

Crowell, Aron. "Dwellings, Settlements, and Domestic Life." In *Crossroads of Continents: Cultures of Siberia and Alaska*, edited by William Fitzhugh and Aron Crowell. Washington, D.C.: Smithsonian Institution Press, 1988.

Damas, David, ed. *Arctic*. Vol. 5 in *Handbook of North American Indians*. Washington, D.C.: Smithsonian Institution Press, 1984.

Nabokov, Peter, and Robert Easton. *Native American Architecture*. New York: Oxford University Press, 1989.

Nelson, Edward. *The Eskimo About Bering Strait*. Eighteenth Annual Report of the Bureau of American Ethnology for the Years 1896-1897. Reprint. Washington, D.C.: Smithsonian Institution Press, 1983.

Oswalt, Wendell H. *Alaskan Eskimos*. San Francisco: Chandler, 1967.

Architecture—California

TRIBES AFFECTED: Achumawi, Atsugewi, Chemehuevi, Chumash, Costano, Cupeño, Gabrielino, Hupa, Juaneño, Kamia, Karok, Kateo, Luiseño, Maidu, Mattole, Miwok, Patwin, Pomo, Quechan, Salinan, Serrano, Shasta, Tolowa, Tubatulabal, Wailaki, Wintun, Wiyot, Yahi, Yana, Yokuts, Yuki, Yurok

SIGNIFICANCE: Indian architecture in California was of a wide variety because of climatic variations throughout the state

The Indians of California lived in climates ranging from foggy, damp coastlands in the north to dry desert regions in the south. Using materials available in their natural environment, they constructed homes of earth, wood, brush, sand, or bark. Buildings were used for summer and winter houses, dance chambers, food storage, and sweatbaths.

In the north, large rectangular plank houses were made of cedar, sometimes having several pitched roofs and excavated floors. Sweathouses for male clan members were made of wood and had wood or earth floors. Earth-covered semi-subterranean houses were common. These had circular side door openings which had to be crawled through.

A Mono wickiup-style brush structure; both the dwelling and the baskets in front are representative of central California styles. (Library of Congress)

The most common form of Indian architecture in the California region, and most characteristic of the central region, was the earthlodge. This pit house was a small structure with an excavated earth floor, an earth roof, and a roof smoke hole, which was also used for entry. Ladders ran up the sides of such dwellings in order to gain access to the entry hole. Small slat openings in the lower sides of the earthlodges could be used to crawl through.

Dwellings made of willow poles, tule, brush, or bark had round or cone-shaped roofs and were used by the California region Indian. These structures were covered with bark slabs in winter for greater protection from the cold and could house many families. Ceremonial halls and men's sweathouses were smaller circular or rectangular buildings of the same type.

In the southern regions, dome-shaped brush structures such as the wickiup as well as four-post sand-roofed houses were built. After the arrival of the Spanish, adobe bricks were used and made into mud-thatched one-room homes much like those found in neighboring Mexico.

The roundhouse, largely the result of European contact, was a large, round assembly or dance hall made of wood with metal nails and split shingles.

See also Adobe; California; Earthlodge; Grass house; Pit house; Plank house; Sweatlodges and sweatbaths; Tule; Wickiup.

Architecture—Great Basin

Tribes affected: Bannock, Gosiute, Kawaiisu, Mono, Numaga, Paiute, Shoshone, Ute, Walapai, Washoe

Significance: In the sparsely populated Great Basin region, Indians lived in grass huts, wickiups, tipis, or low, flat-roofed houses

The Great Basin area north of the Colorado River, basically comprising present-day Utah and Nevada, mostly consists of hot, dry desert and continental steppe. The Indians inhabiting this wide area never settled long in one place but constantly moved about in search of fresh food sources. For all but those Indians living along the Colorado River, mobility was a significant factor in the design of their dwellings.

The Paiute made a fiber structure known as the wickiup with small forked branches twisted into the shape of a small cone or dome and then covered with grass and brush with an open door space. This structure was used for sleeping, cooking, and storage, as well as for protection from the sun. The wickiup was either left in place when they moved or carried with them to a new location. In the hot summer, Great Basin Indians also made grass huts with a center ridgepole, slanted roof, open ends, and open side walls made of vertical poles; they looked much like an open-sided tent. In the winter, frame homes near the foothills were covered with mud thatch for greater protection and warmth.

Those who lived near other geographical regions often borrowed the architectural styles of the neighboring Indian tribes. Structures included the tipi of the Plains, the earthlodge of California, the adobe of the Southwest, and the pit house of the Plateau.

Along the Colorado River, Indians developed low, flat sand-roofed homes built on poles with excavated floors. The roofs were used for food storage and socializing as well as for protection. These houses also included open ramadas for additional living space.

See also Architecture—California; Architecture—Plateau; Earthlodge; Great Basin; Pit house; Wickiup.

Architecture—Northeast

TRIBES AFFECTED: Abenaki, Algonquin, Cahokia, Cayuga, Erie, Fox, Huron, Illinois, Iroquois, Kickapoo, Lenni Lenape, Lumbee, Mahican, Maliseet, Massachusett, Mattaponi, Menominee, Metis, Miami, Micmac, Mohawk, Mohegan, Moneton, Montagnais, Montauk, Mountain, Nanticoke, Narragansett, Nauset, Neutral, Niantic, Nipissing, Nipmuc, Nottaway, Ojibwa, Oneida, Onondaga, Ottawa, Passamaquoddy, Pennacook, Penobscot, Pequot, Susquehannock, Tobacco, Wampanoag, Wappinger, Winnebago

SIGNIFICANCE: The woodlands of the Northeast provided basic building materials, such as saplings, brush, and bark, for a variety of buildings, including the wigwam and the longhouse

The buildings of the Northeast region Indians were constructed in woodlands, on mountains, along the Atlantic coast, and along inland lakeshores. Architectural styles were versatile, adapting to the particular climate and the social, religious, and economic needs of the particular tribe. Primarily used for protection, architecture also expressed the Indians' way of life.

In the eastern portion of this region, the Iroquois and Huron built long communal buildings which were used year-round by clan groups. The longhouse, which varied in length and accommodated more than a hundred people, could be enlarged to make room for newly married couples. The pole-framed structure had a barrel or vaulted roof. Smoke holes placed about 25 feet apart represented the space given to an individual family. The smoke holes were also sources of light. Sleeping bunks ran along the sides of the building. Doors and storage areas were at each end.

A typical dwelling structure of Northeast region Indians was the wigwam. Its simple construction of a frame and covering could be easily moved. The basic structure of the wigwam was made of sapling frames bent into arches and tied together with fibercord and then covered with rolls of bark or reed mats. A central fire was used for cooking and heating, and smoke escaped through a parting of the mats. There were many different styles of the basic domed wigwam.

The Algonquin used a variety of bark-covered and mat-covered wigwams and barrel or gabled roofs as well as conical tipis using straight poles covered with bark. Along the North Atlantic coast, tipis were made by leaning straight poles vertically together; at the top, these poles met at the center point of a circular shape on the ground, on the circumference of which were positioned the poles' ends. Sapling stringers were lashed to the frame for stability. They were sometimes insulated by laying grass over the frame and covering this with sheets of birchbark. The smoke hole was at the top of the tipi where the poles met, the floor was covered with fir boughs, and an opening in the side provided a doorway.

The Great Lakes region had several basic house types. These were the domed wigwam, used mainly in winter, the conical wigwam, an extension of the domed type by use of a ridge pole, and the summer square bark house, with vertical walls and a gabled roof. Ceremonial lodges and many-sided dance lodges were the largest structures built by the Great Lakes Indians. They were made with poles of cedar, considered to be sacred. A small religious structure called the shaking tent was a single-person hut. Used by the shaman, it was made of a sapling frame covered with bark or canvas, and it shook while the shaman was moving and speaking inside as he performed a rite.

Where the Northeast region came closer to the Plains region, the Indians also used the tipi type of dwelling, often covered with canvas or animal hides.

See also Birchbark; Longhouse; Northeast; Tipi; Wigwam.

BIBLIOGRAPHY

Bushnell, David I., Jr. *Native Villages and Village Sites East of the Mississippi.* Washington, D.C.: Government Printing Office, 1919.

Kubiak, William. *Great Lakes Indians: A Pictorial Guide.* Grand Rapids, Mich.: Baker Book House, 1970.

Morgan, Lewis H. *Houses and House-Life of the American Aborigines.* Chicago: University of Chicago Press, 1965.

Nabokov, Peter, and Robert Easton. *Native American Architecture.* New York: Oxford University Press, 1989.

Russell, Howard S. *Indian New England Before the Mayflower.* Hanover, N.H.: University Press of New England, 1980.

Architecture—Northwest Coast

TRIBES AFFECTED: Chinook, Cowlitz, Haida, Haisla, Kwakiutl, Nisqually, Nootka, Quileute, Salish, Samish, Siuslaw, Snohomish, Tillamook, Tlingit, Tsinshian, Umpqua, other Northwest Coast tribes

SIGNIFICANCE: The abundance of the environment and the ready availability of wood enabled groups in the Northwest Coast area to construct large, permanent plank buildings Primary living quarters for Northwest Coast Indians accommodated large extended families up to fifty or more persons. Family houses served also as meeting halls for clan events as well as theaters for annual performances. Houses faced the shoreline, with a lineage leader's house in the middle and less important family homes on the perimeter. Houses varied in size depending upon the wealth and status of the owner, with the chief having the largest house. Cedar, the prevalent building wood, was hewn into planks to create rectangular, gabled longhouses that regionally varied but could average 60 by 100 feet in area. The commissioning of a house was restricted to the wealthy, and the building of houses was designated to trained specialists, usually of no relation to the owner. Every workman, from skilled craftsman to manual laborer, was paid for each assigned task. Architectural relief carvings or paintings required additional artists and ceremonial feasting at its completion. A potlatch celebration, often including the erec-

tion of a totem pole, was expected by the community in order to consecrate the house and the status of the owner. At this time, principal houses were given names that referred to totemic crests of the lineage or to a distinct quality of the house.

Northern House Style. Among the Tsimshian, Haida, Tlingit, and Haisla (the northern Kwakiutl), large houses for wealthy extended families measured up to 50 feet by 60 feet and had gabled roofs and vertical plank walls. The first elements constructed on the site were the corner poles. These were raised into foundation holes by pulling and wedging them into position. Tall ridgepoles supported heavy posts at the front and back, which in turn supported the roof planks with a central opening for a smoke hole. The horizontal beams were elevated into the notched holes of the vertical uprights, followed by the elevation of cross beams. Once the structural framework was constructed, the tapered vertical wall planks were put into place. The entrance was an oval or circular doorway cut into the base of the center ridgepole facing the shoreline. The interior contained a planked, platform floor with bench steps (sometimes movable) leading down to a central fire pit located di-

An engraving of a Chinook lodge in the Oregon Territory based on a sketch from the 1830's. (Library of Congress)

rectly below the roof smoke hole, which, often fitted with a movable shutter, allowed directed interior ventilation. The upper platform provided assigned sleeping space for each family, with the lineage head and his family occupying the rear. The center ridgepole, interior vertical support poles, interior planked screen, and the house front typically exhibited elaborate carved and painted totem crests that validated the ancestral legacy of the house owner. By the nineteenth century, European architectural influences were evident in the introduction of framed doorways and windows in traditional houses, the use of nails instead of notched joints, commercially sawed lumber, and stoves (replacing the central fire pit).

Southern House Style. Two types of house construction differentiate the southern style that dominated throughout the Coast Salish region: the shed roof and the Wakashan. Unlike the northern house style, the walls of horizontal planks created a shell around the house frame. The pitch of the shed roof houses was created by the shoreline vertical poles being taller than the rear support poles. The center-sloping gabled roof of the Wakashan house was created by the center ridge beam being of a larger diameter than the two eave beams. Shed-roof houses averaged about 38 by 80 feet, though they were sometimes much longer when expanded by building end on end. The Wakashan house measured from 36 to 40 feet wide by 40 to 150 feet long.

Secondary Structures. The most common secondary architectural structures included summer houses, sweatlodges, smokehouses, mortuary houses, and decks. Roughly built structures, often without flooring, served to house families during the summer fishing and gathering activities. When summer activities occurred annually in the same place, the framework for these houses was frequently permanent, while the planks and materials for the side and roof were brought by the owners each season. Additionally, a summer house could serve as a drying area for the fish in the absence of a separate drying structure. A smokehouse was a plank framework with horizontal poles functioning as drying racks for smoking fish. Rough, enclosed plank structures on stilt poles served as warehouses for fish storage. Sweatlodges were typically walled with tightly fitted planks or logs supporting a roof of boards and earth. With sand floors, fire pit, and an entrance toward the water, this structure made a controllable interior space for steambaths. Small house replicas (8 feet by 6 feet) or small shed-roof shelters built of logs or planks, with platforms to hold the deceased, functioned as grave houses. Open-deck structures or raised platforms on stilts constructed on the beach provided designated gathering areas in fair weather.

—Michael Coronel and Patricia Coronel

See also Longhouse; Northwest Coast; Plank house; Sweatlodges and sweatbaths; Totem poles.

BIBLIOGRAPHY

Drucker, Philip. *Indians of the Northwest Coast.* Garden City, N.Y.: Natural History Press, 1963.

Emmons, George Thornton. *The Tlingit Indians.* Edited by Fredrica de Laguna. Seattle: University of Washington Press, 1991.

Highwater, Jamake. *Arts of the Indian Americas: Leaves from the Sacred Tree.* New York: Harper & Row, 1983.

Olsen, Ronald L. *Adze, Canoe, and House Types of the Northwest Coast.* Seattle: University of Washington Press, 1991.

Stewart, Hillary. *Cedar: Tree of Life to the Northwest Coast Indians.* Vancouver, B.C.: Douglas & McIntyre, 1984.

Architecture—Plains

TRIBES AFFECTED: Plains tribes

SIGNIFICANCE: Plains tribes used a variety of temporary and permanent dwellings, including earthlodges and grass houses; the best-known Plains dwelling is the tipi

Plains Indian architecture is marked by contrasts between mobile and permanent constructions. Evidence suggests that both types of dwelling have a long history in the Plains region. Prehistoric tribes constructed brush-covered lodges supported by stationary cones of branchless trees. They also left "tipi rings," circles of rocks probably used to hold down the sides of small hide-covered dwellings.

Medicine wheels, circular constructions of boulders with both terrestrial and celestial alignments, were another early architectural achievement. The best-known of these is in the Bighorn Mountains of northern Wyoming. Petroforms, rock designs resembling animal and human figures, suggest a southeastern Indian cultural influence in the Canadian and Dakotan plains.

Along the Missouri River, the typical house type was the earthlodge. From the Dakotas to the northeast, the earthlodges of the prehistoric seminomadic agricultural communities were primarily rectangular and consisted of wooden uprights joined by cross beams and rafters covered with sticks, grass, and sod. Along the upper Missouri, villagers used the terrain to augment defenses consisting of dry moats or log palisades.

Palisades protected the Mandans' earthlodge dwellings, which surrounded plazas dominated by a wooden shrine honoring the mythic hero Lone Man. Mandan post-and-beam construction was overlaid by wooden rafters supporting willow branches, grass, and sod. The rectangular format of the Mandans' sacred Okeepa lodge was a reminder of its prehistoric architectural origins.

The Caddo, Kichai, and Wichita of the southern Plains constructed permanent grass houses of thatch bundles fixed to a wood pole frame. Other permanent Plains structures were the ceremonial Sun Dance lodge (of the Kiowa, Arapaho, Shoshone, and Cheyenne), menstrual huts, funerary platforms, religious structures, and sweathouses, such as the Sioux inipi, made of bent willow saplings covered with buffalo hides.

The tipi, a cone of poles covered by sewn and tanned buffalo hides and staked to the ground, was widely used for temporary shelter and later became a year-round mobile dwelling. Tipis developed from the "tipi ring" shelter and the Northeastern Woodlands three-pole conical tent. With the arrival of horses to serve as transportation, tipis became larger and more elaborate.

A Pawnee earthlodge, photographed in Nebraska around 1870. (National Archives)

See also Earthlodge; Grass house; Medicine wheels; Plains; Tipi.

Architecture—Plateau

TRIBES AFFECTED: Bannock, Gosiute, Kawaiisu, Paiute, Panamint, Shoshone, Ute, Washoe

SIGNIFICANCE: Plateau architecture was characterized by circular pit houses

The principal structures within the Plateau culture area were sleeping dwellings, the ubiquitous sweatlodge, isolated menstrual huts, excavated food storage pits, food-drying scaffolds and racks, and temporary lean-to shelters. Though architecture type varied through time and spatial distribution, there were essentially two types of winter dwelling: the circular semi-subterranean pit house and the inverted-V rectangular tule mat lodge. The older pit house was an excavated, flat, circular pit measuring 9 to 15 feet in diameter, with gradually sloping earthen walls of 3 feet. The aboveground shape was achieved by erecting three or four top-forked poles which, when secured, accommodated smaller lodge poles to support cedar planks, which were covered with sewn willow mats. The exterior was made of layered sewn tule mats, with the apex of the structure being open to serve as a smoke hole and entrance up or down a notched log or hafted, runged ladder. Various grasses, old tule mats, and bear skins covered the dwelling floor.

The second type of winter village dwelling was the tule mat-covered, inverted-V type pole-constructed lodge, usually with no ridge pole. Often the floor was excavated to a depth of one foot. These rectangular structures averaged 30 feet in length and approximately 10 feet in width; they could accommodate three to six extended families. Entrance was usually from both ends, where firewood was kept; food was stored in hemp and pliable root bags suspended from the ceiling. This structure was often used for large gatherings and ceremonial rituals.

A major influence on southern Plateau architecture was the introduction of the horse, permitting greater involvement with Plains culture through trade and bison hunting, as evidenced by the adoption of the tipi. In the mid-1800's, bark, tule, and cattail mats began to give way to canvas as a preferred covering material for sweatlodges, tipi dwellings, and longhouses.

See also Pit house; Plateau.

Architecture—Southeast

TRIBES AFFECTED: Southeast tribes

SIGNIFICANCE: Wattle and daub structures, chakofas, and chickees were among the dwelling types of the Southeast, but the best-known Southeast constructions were large earthen mounds, some of which can still be seen

Southeastern tribal architecture is distinguished by a tradition of monumental mound building. Southeastern mound construction may have originated with Mexican Indians who moved to this locale to participate in the trade that occurred from the Great Lakes region to Florida. The concentric ridges of shaped soil that define a large central plaza at Poverty Point,

Louisiana, are associated with this cultural influence. They date from about 1200 B.C.E.

The Adena culture of the Ohio River valley (1000 B.C.E.-200 C.E.) raised cone-shaped burial mounds. They also built dwellings that were 20 feet to 70 feet in diameter and had clay-covered latticework walls, a type of construction called wattle and daub. The dwellings were covered with thatched roofs. Adena effigy mounds, known as geoforms, depicting bears, panthers, reptiles, and birds, survive, from Wisconsin to Louisiana. The Great Serpent Mound (800 B.C.E.-400 C.E.) in southern Ohio is 1,247 feet in length and portrays the serpent clutching an egg in its mouth. The Hopewell culture's funerary mounds, monumental circles, squares, and pentagonal geoforms, found in the Ohio Valley, succeeded the Adena constructions.

Under the Mississippi tradition (700-1000 C.E.), communities periodically enlarged their flat-topped trapezoidal mounds. The Cahokia site (800 C.E.) near St. Louis, Missouri, was the political, religious, and econom1ic center of the Mississippi tradition. Cahokia's central pyramid is the largest manmade structure north of Mexico, measuring more than 1,000 feet in length, 700 feet in width, and 100 feet in height, the result of fourteen different building campaigns over three centuries.

When European explorers first arrived in the Southeast, they encountered Indian townsites with shaped mounds dominating the community and its plaza. These mounds supported chieftains' houses and public buildings or contained burials. The Natchez Indians of Mississippi continued the temple mound building tradition into the early eighteenth century.

Creek and Yuchi Indians built large villages with ceremonial plazas and ball courts. The Creek chakofa was a communal structure with a thatched conical roof. The Cherokees also built communal structures on low earthen mounds to house sacred fires.

By the nineteenth century, many southeastern tribes had adopted European-style buildings. One notable exception was in Florida's southern marshes, where the Seminoles built wide-eaved, open-sided dwellings with elevated platforms of cypress poles and palmetto thatch known as chickees.

See also Adena; Chickee; Hopewell; Mississippian; Mounds and mound builders; Moundville; Southeast; Wattle and daub.

Architecture—Southwest

TRIBES AFFECTED: Anasazi, Eastern Pueblo, Hohokam, Hopi, Mogollon, Zuni, other Southwest traditions and tribes

SIGNIFICANCE: Architecture in the Southwest evolved from the crude pit house to the magnificent stone pueblos of the prehistoric Anasazi, and then to pueblos built in the historic period in the Rio Grande Valley and at Zuni and Hopi

All three prehistoric cultures in the Southwest were pit house builders. The Mogollon constructed circular pit houses grouped in small villages of fifteen to twenty families. The Hohokam built square or rectangular pit houses randomly

scattered over a large area (the settlement at Snaketown covers almost a square mile).

Basketmaker and Developmental Pueblo. Basketmaker Anasazi (circa 1-700 C.E.) in the Four Corners area built crude circular subterranean structures with flat roofs, entered by ladder through the smoke hole. Later in this period, three major Anasazi centers developed: Mesa Verde, Chaco Canyon, and Kayenta. In these villages, circular pit houses were as much as 25 feet in diameter and often were divided into ceremonial space and living space.

During the Development Pueblo period (700-1100), the Anasazi evolved building techniques which resulted in structures that were considerably more complex and sophisticated. The pit house continued as a kiva, but dwellings were now aboveground, consisting of slightly curved rows of contiguous flat-roofed rooms, each housing an entire family. The earliest utilization of stone was in "jacal," a method similar to wattle and daub, with the addition of stone slabs placed against the bottoms of walls and held in place with adobe. A true masonry technique evolved from jacal, wherein large, irregular rocks were laid end to end and packed solidly with adobe.

Stone Masonry. Toward the end of this period, the Anasazi shaped sandstone rocks into building blocks, using stone tools not much harder than the sandstone itself. At first, only the load-bearing surfaces were shaped, but eventually both visible surfaces were smoothed as well, producing a wall that was both aesthetically pleasing and strong. This new masonry technique resulted in an increase in both the size and complexity of the pueblos; some were as large as thirty or more contiguous rooms and were two stories high. Stone masonry also affected the kiva, whose walls and floor were now lined with carefully shaped and fitted stone blocks, with a stone bench and stone pilasters to support the flat roof.

During the Classic Pueblo period (1100-1300), the Anasazi refined their masonry further, developing walls built with a three-ply construction: an inner and outer facing of shaped sandstone blocks with an interior filling of loose stones and adobe. Varying the shapes of the blocks created linear patterns, adding visual interest to the walls. Pueblos of this period often rose to as many as five stories, with heavy beams set into the walls to support the floors above ground level. Flat roofs were constructed with beams laid across with poles and brush and covered with several inches of clay and mud. Chaco Canyon, Mesa Verde, and Kayenta continued to be major centers of Anasazi culture; their influence had spread from the upper Rio Grande Valley to Texas and Nevada and to central and southern Arizona.

Pueblo Bonito in Chaco Canyon was the largest pueblo in the Southwest, housing more than one thousand people and covering almost four acres, with eight hundred rooms rising in tiers from a single frontal story to five stories at the back. The Anasazi at Mesa Verde built large stone pueblos on the mesa tops but abandoned them a hundred years later in favor of the cliff dwellings—stone buildings erected in irregularly shaped caves in the cliff faces. They apparently made the move for reasons of defense, because the caves were much less desirable places to live, being without sunlight much of the day, difficult to reach, and limited in size. Even so, some of the cliff dwellings contained as many as two hundred rooms, twenty-three kivas, and both square and round towers. Having been built in haste in a less desirable location, the stonework was not as skillful as that of the earlier pueblos. Keet Seel and Betatakin were the largest pueblos at Kayenta, a center that was never as populous as Chaco Canyon or Mesa Verde, probably because crops grew less abundantly there. Pueblos both in the open and in the cliffs were built with masonry that was inferior to the other sites.

Anasazi Influence. As Anasazi culture spread during the Pueblo period, it transformed the architectural styles of both the Mogollon and the Hohokam. The Mogollon abandoned their pit houses in favor of aboveground masonry structures, such as those at Gila Cliffs in southern New Mexico. There they built forty rooms in five deep caves 150 feet above the canyon floor. The Hohokam were also influenced by Anasazi pueblo architecture, as evidenced by the ruins of Casa Grande in the Arizona desert. Built of caliche, a subsoil with high lime content, Casa Grande has deeply trenched walls 4.5 feet thick at the bottom, tapering to 2 feet at their height. The main two-storied structure was set on a base of earth 5 feet high. A single room atop the building had holes in one wall that lined up precisely with sunset at the equinoxes, suggesting that it may have served as an observatory. Pueblo Grande, on the outskirts of Phoenix, was built of adobe and stone masonry on an earthen platform, providing an unobstructed view of the surrounding countryside. The platform was retained by a massive adobe and rock wall, with a second wall built around the pueblo itself.

About 1300, the Anasazi began to leave their major centers to migrate elsewhere. There are several theories which attempt to explain this, among them drought, invasion, or plague. In any case, Pueblo culture was reestablished in large communities in the Rio Grande Valley from Isleta Pueblo to Taos, in the Zuni Mountains, along the Little Colorado River, and in the area of the Hopi Mesas. Although construction varied according to time and place, pueblos generally followed the traditions established at Chaco Canyon, Mesa Verde, and Kayenta: large communal structures with hundreds of rooms, often multistoried, built around a central plaza. Some continued the techniques of stone masonry, while others were built with solid adobe or mixed adobe and stone construction. Kivas either were above ground and incorporated into the room blocks or were square or circular subterranean structures located in the plazas.

The Puebloans of the Southwest and many of their pueblos survived the Spanish, the Mexican, and finally the United States' occupation of their lands. The traditions that evolved in the fourteenth and fifteenth centuries formed the basis for the Pueblo cultures that exist in these areas today.

—LouAnn Faris Culley

See also Anasazi; Chaco Canyon; Cliff dwellings; Kivas; Hohokam; Pit house; Pueblo.

BIBLIOGRAPHY

Ambler, J. Richard. *The Anasazi: Prehistoric People of the Four Corners Region*. Rev. ed. Flagstaff: Museum of Northern Arizona, 1989.

Taos Pueblo in New Mexico. (Library of Congress)

Amsden, Charles A. *Prehistoric Southwesterners from Basketmaker to Pueblo*. Los Angeles: Southwest Museum, 1949.

Brody, J. J. *The Anasazi: Ancient Indian People of the American Southwest*. New York: Rizzoli International, 1990.

Frazier, Kendrick. *People of Chaco: A Canyon and Its Culture*. New York: W. W. Norton, 1986.

Jones, Dewitt, and Linda S. Cordell. *Anasazi World*. Portland, Oreg.: Graphic Arts Center, 1985.

Lister, Robert H., and Florence C. Lister. *Chaco Canyon: Archaeology and Archaeologists*. Albuquerque: University of New Mexico Press, 1981.

Nabokov, Peter, and Robert Easton. *Native American Architecture*. New York: Oxford University Press, 1989.

Stuart, David. *The Magic of Bandelier*. Santa Fe, N.Mex.: Ancient City Press, 1989.

Architecture—Subarctic

TRIBES AFFECTED: Algonquin, Beaver, Beothuk, Carrier, Chilcotin, Chipewyan, Cree, Dogrib, Han, Hare, Ingalik, Kaska, Koyukon, Kutchin, Naskapi, Slave, Tanaina, Tutchone, Yellowknife

SIGNIFICANCE: The architecture of the sparsely populated, expansive Subarctic region was primarily wigwams, lean-tos, log houses, and tipis

Geographically, the Subarctic region, comprising much of present-day Canada, is a land of mountains, tundra, evergreen forests, lakes, and streams, with cold winters and heavy snow. Raw materials used for dwellings were saplings, bark, brush, planks or logs, and animal skins.

In the Northwest, basically three types of shelters were used. Double lean-tos made of wooden frames were covered with bark, animal skins, or brush. As a result of contact with Northwest Coast Indians, Subarctic Indians made wooden plank houses. Portable tents for summer and winter were used in the northwest Subarctic with snow piled against the sides for winter insulation.

In the eastern Subarctic region, the cone-shaped wigwam was covered with birchbark rolls. Framed with wooden arched poles, the wigwams were covered with rolls of bark which had been sewn together. The floors were layered with pine boughs, and the larger wigwams had central hearths or family fires. Double walls filled with brush in the wigwams provided cooling in the warm months. Brush-covered conical lodges and tents were also used as summer dwellings, and earth-covered conical structures and log cabins with moss-covered roofs were used in winter.

In the Subarctic, some Indians migrated to warmer climates during the winter. Tipis were used throughout the region by those who moved often because they were quickly built and portable; they were made of wooden poles and animal skins.

A basic need of Subarctic community was safe food storage. A simple log building constructed on poles off the ground provided a place for food to be stored out of the reach of animals.

See also Birchbark; Earthlodge; Plank house; Subarctic.

Arctic: Culture area

LANGUAGE GROUPS: Eskimo-Aleut (Aleut, Inuit-Iñupiaq, Yupik)

TRIBES AFFECTED: Aleut, Inuit, Yupik

The Arctic culture area encompasses a vast region of treeless, windswept tundra stretching across the northern coast of North America. It includes most of the Alaskan coastline from Prince William Sound in the southeast to the Arctic coast in the north, continues across the Canadian Arctic archipelago and mainland coast down into Labrador, and includes all of Greenland. While some parts of this culture area are more appropriately labeled Subarctic in terms of climate and vegetation (most specifically the Aleutian Islands, South Alaska, Southern Labrador, and South Greenland), the linguistic, cultural, and physical similarities among the native inhabitants are such that this region can be considered a highly integrated cultural unit.

Terminology. The term "Aleut" is of uncertain origin and appears to have been used first by the Russians to describe the inhabitants of the Near Islands. It was later extended to all Aleuts and even to the Pacific Eskimos (Koniag and Chugach). The result has led to some confusion, since today the Koniag Eskimos refer to themselves as "Alutiiq" (an "Eskimoization" of Aleut in the current orthography) even though they are culturally and linguistically distinct from the Aleut. The term "Eskimo" is most often cited as originating from the Subarctic Montagnais (speakers of an Algonquian language) and has been purported to mean "eaters of raw meat." Two major cultural-linguistic groups of Eskimos are recognized: the Yupik of southwestern and southern Alaska and the Inuit of North Alaska, Arctic Canada, and Greenland. It should be noted that the term "Eskimo" has engendered some controversy (with many Canadian Arctic natives, for example, preferring "Inuit"), but it is used here because it incorporates a large number of groups that cannot easily be united under any other term and because it has a long scientific tradition of usage.

Environment. The Arctic culture area includes a wide range of environments both above and below the Arctic Circle and the tree line. In the northern regions of Alaska, Canada, and Greenland, treeless Arctic tundra and a severe climate dominate. The combination of permafrost, extreme cold, and prolonged periods of midwinter darkness result in low levels of biological productivity, making adaptation to this region a great challenge to both humans and animals. The climate is less severe farther south. The coastlines of the Aleutian Islands, southern Alaska, southern Labrador, and western Greenland have a milder climate and less pronounced seasonal variation in temperature and photoperiod. These areas usually have access to open water all year round, with the result that their climates are heavily maritime-influenced. In southern Alaska, for example, Koniag and Chugach Eskimos are reported to have gone much of the year in bare feet. In the High Arctic and interior regions of Canada and Alaska, a cold continental climate prevails.

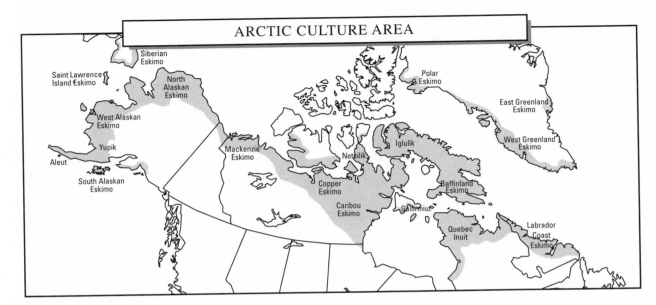

ARCTIC CULTURE AREA

Language. On the basis of sound and grammar, Eskimo and Aleut are recognized as being related. Although regarded as a unified language family, they are mutually unintelligible. Linguists generally agree that Eskimo and Aleut diverged at least four thousand years ago.

Within Aleut there is a high degree of uniformity. Today it is a single language with only two dialects: a western dialect and an eastern dialect. Much greater variation exists within Eskimo, which is divided into two main languages: Yupik and Inuit-Iñupiaq. The distance between the two is very similar to the distance between German and English. Lexicostatistical studies suggest a divergence dating to between eight hundred and eighteen hundred years ago. The dividing line between these two languages is located around the Norton Sound region of western Alaska. Yupik displays much more variability than Inuit-Iñupiaq and is composed of five fairly distinct languages. The Inuit-Iñupiaq branch of Eskimo is characterized by a higher degree of uniformity, representing more a series of interconnecting dialects. The mutual intelligibility of these dialects is the result of the spread of Thule culture across Arctic Canada and Greenland.

Population. The Arctic culture area was not uniformly populated. At contact, the region was inhabited by about twelve thousand to fifteen thousand Aleut on the Aleutian Islands, twenty to twenty-five thousand Yupik in southern and southwestern Alaska (including St. Lawrence Island), twelve thousand Iñupiat in northwestern and northern Alaska, nine to twelve thousand Canadian Inuit, and nine to twelve thousand Greenlandic Inuit divided among 140 to 200 fairly distinct societies (or tribal groupings). The most densely populated regions were those with a relative abundance of food resources, more often than not with access to a combination of marine and riverine products. Prior to contact, the greatest populations could be found on the Aleutian Islands, southern and southwestern Alaska, and the southwest coast of Green-

land. The areas with the lowest population densities included the Central Canadian Arctic (associated with the Copper and Netsilik groups), the Barren Lands west of Hudson Bay (Caribou Eskimos), and North Greenland (Polar Eskimos). These groups lived in extremely marginal areas and were therefore forced to a high degree of nomadism. Starvation was probably relatively common, and the practice of infanticide has been well documented in these areas. Many of those Aleut and Eskimo in more abundant environments were able to live much of the year in relatively permanent houses (either above-ground wood-plank houses or semi-subterranean sod houses) within sedentary villages.

Economy and Subsistence. The stereotype of highly nomadic, snowhouse-building, dogsledding Eskimos actually applies to only a small number of Inuit groups in the Central Canadian Arctic. Many Eskimo groups, most notably in southern and southwestern Alaska, never built a snowhouse, never traveled with dogs, and never even saw a polar bear. Despite a common cultural template, hundreds of years of adaptation to markedly different environments and contacts with different neighboring groups gave rise to distinct cultural forms, expressed in material culture, housing styles, and subsistence strategies.

While the primary economic focus in this culture area was (and continues to be) a maritime one oriented toward hunting of whales, seals, walruses, narwhales, and so on, a number of groups subsisted primarily from riverine or terrestrial resources. Yupik groups in the middle Yukon-Kuskokwim River region and Iñupiat groups on the Noatak and Kobuk rivers were heavily dependent upon fish resources at the expense of marine mammals. In the Barren Lands west of Hudson Bay, the Caribou Eskimo maintained a heavy reliance upon seasonally migrating caribou herds. The typing of Eskimo groups as either maritime, riverine, or terrestrially focused can, however, be misleading, since many groups maintained a seasonal round in which all of these items were exploited. Longer exploitation cycles were also maintained, since certain resources that were abundant for one generation could easily disappear a generation or two later. Since marine and terrestrial ecosystems in the Arctic are extremely fragile, population crashes of certain important animal species could and did occur.

The Aleut appear to have had the most developed maritime adaptation, a fact reinforced by their mastery of kayak (*baidarka*) construction and their reputation for long-distance ocean travel. Their skill in adapting to a high-risk/high-yield maritime ecosystem ensured high population densities and a relatively high quality of life compared with those of most Eskimo groups. Other Arctic groups with a maritime adaptation included West Greenlandic and North Alaskan whaling communities which were oriented toward spring and fall hunting of large bowhead whales from open, skin-covered umiaks.

The seasonality of Eskimo subsistence is most vividly seen with Central Canadian Arctic groups such as the Netsilik and Copper Eskimo. Since these groups lived in an extremely marginal environment, they were forced to a high degree of nomadism. Winters were generally spent in large snowhouse communities on the ocean ice, where hunters engaged in breathing-hole sealing. Summers, however, were usually spent inland dispersed in small family groups in search of fish, fowl, and caribou. Although these groups do not display the maritime skills of the Aleut or North Alaskans, they nevertheless had a clear maritime focus at certain seasons.

Material Culture and Trade. The material culture of all these groups was technologically sophisticated and highly functional. The toggle-headed harpoon, kayak, tailored clothing, semilunar woman's knife (*ulu*), and soapstone lamp are typical of much of the area. Throughout the region, there was heavy reliance upon animal products such as bone, horn, antler, and skin for the manufacture of clothing, hunting tools, and household goods. In the High Arctic, wood was an extremely valuable commodity and could be obtained only through trading networks or long trips to the tree line. For this reason, among groups such as the Polar Eskimo, Copper Eskimo, and Baffin Island Eskimo, wood was heavily curated.

Inuit woman chewing seal skin to prepare it for sewing. (George Comer, American Museum of Natural History)

Prior to European contact, meteoric iron found in the Cape York region of North Greenland was cold hammered into hunting implements, while the Copper Inuit were known for surface mining deposits of copper, which was used for knives, scrapers, and harpoon points.

Despite the isolated nature of the Arctic culture area, intergroup trade was quite extensive. Elaborate trade networks and regional fairs facilitated the distribution of raw materials and manufactured goods. Iron from iron-working centers in Siberia was traded across the Bering Strait into Alaska, while high-quality soapstone lamps from Coronation Gulf in the Central Canadian Arctic were traded into Alaska, where such materials were scarce. Even before the arrival of Russian, European, and American traders, the Seshalik fair in Northwest Alaska attracted two thousand or more individuals each summer in what has been described as the largest regular trade gathering anywhere in the Arctic culture area. Formalized trading partnerships were typical throughout the region. In the absence of trading fairs, individuals would initiate their own trading expeditions for desired resources.

Political Organization and Leadership. Forms of political organization and leadership varied greatly throughout the region. Egalitarianism defined the social relations of most Central and Eastern Arctic groups. An *isumataq* ("one who thinks") would often assume an informal leadership position over a number of related families. The degree of authority that the isumataq held varied from region to region, being relatively low among the Copper Inuit and high among the Iglulik and Baffin Island Eskimos. As one travels into Alaska, more formalized leadership structures appear. In North Alaska, the successful whaling captain (*umialik*) was an influential leader over both his family and the community as a whole. Some researchers have even suggested that the North Alaskan Eskimo, far from being an egalitarian society, were actually a highly ranked society. In South Alaska and the Aleutian Islands, leadership forms were even more formalized and appear to have been heavily influenced by the ranked societies of the Northwest Coast. In all regions, leaders were expected to be generous to the point of sharing their resources with all community members. Such sharing is most dramatically seen in North Alaska with the distribution of whale meat and muktuk from the successful whaling captain to the entire community.

Post-contact. The first contacts between Eskimos and Europeans probably occurred soon after the establishment of the Norse colonies in South Greenland in 985. From the sixteenth century onward, numerous expeditions ventured into the Canadian Archipelago seeking the Northwest Passage. These expeditions resulted in contacts between Europeans and Canadian Inuit, but most of these meetings had minimal long-term impact upon the Inuit.

A more significant influence was the establishment of a mission in West Greenland by the Danish missionary Hans Egede in 1721. Although he had hoped to minister to the (by then long-extinct) Norse colonies, he ended up converting the Greenlandic Inuit to Christianity and initiated the Greenlan-

ders into a period of intimate cultural, economic, and political involvement with Denmark that continues to the present day.

In Alaska, the arrival of Russian fur traders soon after Vitus Bering's discovery of Alaska in 1741 had a devastating impact upon the Aleut, who were once quite numerous throughout the island chain. It is generally agreed that 80 to 90 percent of the Aleut population was wiped out from a combination of disease, warfare, and forced labor. Similar processes resulted in deaths among the Pacific Yupik, who were in the direct path of the Russian traders' advance. A smallpox epidemic in the 1830's wiped out a large portion of the Aleut and Yupik populations over a wide area of southern and southwestern Alaska, including many areas well outside the Russian sphere of influence.

Farther north, Inuit people were heavily impacted by the intensification of whaling in the late nineteenth century. Scottish and American whalers were active in Baffin Bay and Davis Strait from the 1830's on, while American whalers had established themselves in North Alaska by the 1880's and 1890's. These contacts had a significant impact on the Eskimos. Not only did infectious diseases take a heavy toll in many areas, but also the whalers introduced the Inuit to highly desirable material goods. Population losses were profound in some areas, such as Southampton Island, the Mackenzie Delta, and North Alaska. Many Inuit were hired by whalers either as meat and fish providers or as laborers. With the collapse of whaling at the turn of the century, most whalers left the Arctic permanently, while others turned to trading activities. This marked the period when many Eskimo groups made the transition to trapping, as furs became a highly desirable commodity on the international fashion market. The 1940's and 1950's continued to be a difficult time for many Inuit and Yupik, who were plagued by poverty, high infant mortality, and high rates of tuberculosis. In Canada, increased government involvement in the late 1950's and early 1960's brought wage employment, social assistance, schools, medical facilities, and government-subsidized housing, all of which were designed to encourage the Inuit to move from their isolated hunting camps into centralized communities. Since the 1960's, the populations and infrastructure of these communities have grown at a rapid rate.

—*Richard G. Condon and Pamela R. Stern*

See also Aleut; Architecture—Arctic; Arts and crafts—Arctic; Dorset; Igloo; Inuit; Prehistory—Arctic; Whales and whaling.

BIBLIOGRAPHY

Balikci, Asen. *The Netsilik Eskimos.* Garden City, N.Y.: Natural History Press, 1970. This ethnographic classic provides a detailed analysis of the material culture, social organization, and religious beliefs of a stereotypically classic Inuit group adapted to one of the harshest environments of the Arctic region.

Burch, Ernest S., and Werner Forman. *The Eskimos.* Norman: University of Oklahoma Press, 1988. Written for a nonprofessional audience, this work is a highly readable and informative introduction to the Eskimo culture area. The text is accompanied by 120 striking photographs by Werner Forman.

Damas, David, ed. *Arctic*. Vol. 3 in *Handbook of North American Indians*. Washington, D.C.: Smithsonian Institution Press, 1984. This work is undoubtedly the definitive resource on the Arctic culture area and contains detailed articles on prehistory, language, and contemporary issues as well as ethnographic chapters on each of the Eskimo groups. An extensive bibliography, which covers all relevant material published up to the early 1980's, is extremely useful.

Fitzhugh, William W., and Aron Crowell, eds. *Crossroads of Continents: Cultures of Siberia and Alaska*. Washington, D.C.: Smithsonian Institution Press, 1988. Designed to accompany the Smithsonian exhibition "Crossroads of Continents," this edited volume includes chapters written by international experts on the cultures of Alaska and Siberia and on the ancient contacts which have been maintained by the natives of the two continents. It is a highly informative work that contains a large number of useful maps, figures, and photographs.

Laughlin, William S. *Aleuts: Survivors of the Bering Land Bridge*. New York: Holt, Rinehart, & Winston, 1980. This work, written by one of the world's leading authorities on Aleut culture, describes the archaeology, linguistics, physical anthropology, and culture of the Aleuts.

Arikara: Tribe

CULTURE AREA: Plains
LANGUAGE GROUP: Caddoan
PRIMARY LOCATION: North Dakota, South Dakota
POPULATION SIZE: 1,583 (1990 U.S. Census)

The Arikara, or Ricaree, lived along the lower Missouri River basin in what is presently North and South Dakota. This is prairie country, which was conducive to the Arikara hunting and agriculture practices. The tribe had originally been Pawnee but had at some point moved north up the Missouri to form their own tribe, maintaining much of the Pawnee language yet being influenced by the neighboring Sioux and various other tribes.

Hunting, farming, and fishing were all practiced by the Arikara. During the winter, the tribe spent its time on the hunt, ranging as far as forty miles in search of buffalo. During this time, the people lived in lodges constructed of animal hides. Yet these Indians were not renowned as great hunters, nor did they keep many horses in their own possession. Rather, they served as middlemen in the distribution of horses from the nomadic tribes south and west of the Missouri to other nomadic tribes north and east of the river.

When they were not engaged in hunting, the Arikara's housing was more permanent. Huts were constructed by driving four posts into the ground and laying timbers lengthwise between them. Smaller twigs were then filled in and overlaid with rushes, willows, and grass. The entire structure was plastered thickly with mud, with a hole left in the top for smoke and one in the side for a door. The finished home was round in shape. Each hut was excavated inside to a depth of 2 to 4 feet, making the interior tall enough for people to stand up and walk around in. Beds were located around the extremity of the interior circle. A covered passage about 10 feet in length was then constructed outward from the side opening, sloping gently from the exterior to the interior, with a wooden door helping to shut out the elements. Trenches were dug around the outside of the huts to guide rainfall away. Huts were placed randomly within the village, 15 to 20 feet apart, with no paths of any regularity among the dwellings. Cellars were dug within the houses for the storage of corn and other produce.

Corn was grown on family farms of about one acre each. Farming plots were separated by brush and rudely built pole fences. Women did the majority of the farming chores, using hoes and pickaxes made from shoulder blades of cows and deer, and rakes made from reeds. The corn, a variety of Indian corn with a small hard grain and stalks only 2.5 to 3 feet tall, was planted in April or May and then picked around the first part of August. The Arikara women picked the corn when it was still green, boiled it slightly, dried it, shelled it, and then stored it. Other popular crops were squashes, either boiled or eaten green, and pumpkins. Crops were subject both to occasional floods by the Missouri River and to drought. The Arikara held various rites and ceremonies related to the production of crops.

They also capitalized on their agricultural successes by trading crops with the American Fur Company for knives, hoes, combs, beads, paints, ammunition, and tobacco. In addition, they traded with the Sioux for buffalo robes, skins, and meats—and then, in turn, traded these items with whites for guns and horses.

The Arikara were known to be good swimmers and fishermen. The men would place willow pens in eddies of the river, and then throw the caught fish to shore. In the spring, the men would sometimes float out on melting ice cakes and gather rotting buffalo which had died in the winter, stack them on the shore, and then feast on the carcasses with fellow tribe members. Women were known to float out on ice floes in much the same manner to collect driftwood.

The Arikara were adept at making fired, unglazed pots; pans, porringers, and mortars for pounding corn; ornaments of melted beads; and skin canoes of buffalo hide and willows for hunting along the banks of the Missouri River. They made good use of the resources available to them and were generally considered to be a peaceful people.   *—Ruffin Stirling*

See also Hidatsa; Mandan; Pawnee; Plains; Sioux.

Arpeika (c. 1760, Ga.—1860, Fla.): Medicine man

ALSO KNOWN AS: Aripeka, Apayaka Hadjo (Crazy Rattlesnake), Sam Jones
TRIBAL AFFILIATION: Seminole
SIGNIFICANCE: Arpeika was the only Seminole leader successfully to resist removal to the West

Arpeika probably was born in Georgia and moved into Florida in the late eighteenth century as part of the migration of Creeks that created the Seminole Nation. A *hillis haya*, or medicine man, he became a revered figure among the Seminoles and was an ardent opponent of attempts by the U.S. government to remove the tribe to Indian Territory (modern Oklahoma). During the Second Seminole War (1835-1842) he became a military leader despite his advanced age, leading his warriors in a number of battles while unsuccessfully warning Osceola and other Seminole leaders not to trust the American flags of truce.

While most Seminoles were being removed to the West after the war, Arpeika led his band into the Everglades and eluded U.S. forces. In the Third Seminole War (1855-1858) he again fought to avoid removal, fighting beside Billy Bowlegs. The only major Seminole leader to survive the Seminole Wars and remain in Florida, Arpeika died of natural causes near Lake Okeechobee in 1860. He was thought to be one hundred years old.

See also Bowlegs, Billy; Micanopy; Osceola; Seminole Wars.

Art and artists, contemporary

TRIBES AFFECTED: Pantribal

SIGNIFICANCE: Drawing both on antiquity and on the present, Indian artists depict their history, legends, insights, and sorrows

Contemporary American Indian art was spawned by the mid-1960's Civil Rights movement and the 1962 founding of the Institute of American Indian Arts in Santa Fe, New Mexico. By the late 1960's, the innovative work of Fritz Scholder (Luiseño) and his student T. C. Cannon (Kiowa/Caddo) had alerted other American Indian artists to new ways of depicting the world. Today's Indian artists balance the traditional and the contemporary, seeing these times as aspects of merging and intersecting cycles.

Individuality. In the new atmosphere created by the Civil Rights movement and its aftermath, artists feel free to pursue their own views and concerns rather than having their lives and traditions expressed, often stereotypically, by others. They are doing this in many different ways. There is no singular position from which to examine American Indian art and artists, no distinctive style, materials, or outlook. Today's American Indians belong to or are descended from hundreds of unique peoples, each with their own culture, language, and history. It can never be assumed that all have a similar history or see themselves unilaterally in relation to European Americans or other American Indians.

Many speak through their art to their individuality, which may be woven from a number of different cultures. In *Kaaswoot* (1982), a self-portrait, Edna Jackson reflects both her Tlingit and European ancestry. Some artists draw on traditions other than their own. Sylvia Lark (Seneca) has been attracted to the arts of Asia. Lark's fellow Seneca, Peter Jemison, on the other hand, continues the Northeast tradition of artful containers by placing his self-portrait on a paper bag (*Aotearoa/Ganondagan*, 1986). Those who redefine the old ways, like Jemison, generally attract more critical attention than those who follow the old ways. Thus, Florence Riggs (Navajo), who weaves the life around her—a circus, a trading post—is distinguished from those who reproduce traditional patterns. Political and social statements are often conveyed through these modern interpretations. Many artists, however, do continue the traditional arts and ideas of their culture and gender; women, for example, continue to weave or sculpt with clay, sometimes drawing on ancient forms and styles. Subscribing to another position are those who define themselves as American rather than American Indian, and who may believe that cultural identity has no place in the definition of their art.

Shared Concerns. While American Indian art can never be funneled into a single definition, many of these artists do share a sense of community resulting in part from a common history. American Indians are sensitized to the past and present manipulation of their land, peoples, religion, culture, and social position at the hands of the politically and economically dominant. As the only group in America who live on and visit their ancestral lands, American Indians are particularly responsive in their work to the loss of their lands and the destruction of the environment. Edgar Heap of Birds (Cheyenne/Arapaho) in *Native Hosts* (1988) put up aluminum signs in New York parks with messages such as NEW YORK TODAY YOUR HOST IS SHINNECOCK to indicate to today's residents whose land they occupy. Part of the text is written backward to force the viewers to face the past. Jean La Marr (Paiute/Pit River) in *They're Going to Dump It Where?* (1984) shows, reflected in the eyeglasses of a Paiute woman, the Diablo Canyon nuclear facility being struck by lightning—a statement against the destruction of sacred sites for the fostering of European American technology. At the same time, some American Indian artists continue, in both traditional and contemporary styles, to acknowledge the land as sacred, intertwined with culture and religion.

Since the earliest days of European conquest, there has been a tendency by European Americans to objectify all American Indians, assuming similarities across social class, education, personal taste, degree of assimilation, and dozens of other factors. The cultures of the Iroquois, Sioux, Hopi, and others have been compressed, standardized, and packaged. Addressing this objectification in *The Good Doctor's Bedside* (1983), Lance Belanger (Maliseet) documents the stitchwork of a physician who closed the operation scar of a native woman with beads. Jimmie Durham (Cherokee), in his installation *On Loan from the Museum of the American Indian* (1986), speaks to the dominant view that anything Indian is worth collecting and displaying; the piece includes "Pocahontas Underwear," which is decorated with feathers, beads, and pottery shards labeled "Scientifacts" and "Real Indian Blood." James Luna (Diegueño/Luiseño) in 1986 took the ultimate step in illustrating this objectification when he put himself on display, with the appropriate labels, as an American Indian artifact (*The Artifact Piece*). Some artists with wry humor turn the tables. T. C. Cannon's *The Collector (or Osage with Van Gogh)* shows an elder in traditional dress sitting in his comfortable Western living room with his European American possession, a Van Gogh painting.

Jaune Quick-to-See Smith (Cree/Flathead/Shoshone) powerfully addresses past maltreatments of her people in *Paper*

Dolls for a Post-Columbian World with Ensembles Contributed by U.S. Government (1991), in which sets of dolls' clothes are labeled "Special Outfit for Trading Land with the U.S. Government for Whiskey with Gunpowder in It" and "Matching Smallpox Suits for All Indian Families After U.S. Government Sent Wagon Loads of Smallpox Infected Blankets to Keep Our Families Warm." Other artists address the present conditions of American Indians. Richard Ray Whitman (Yuchi/Pawnee) presents the plight of the urban homeless in a set of photographs entitled *Street Chiefs Series*, 1988. Ron Nogonosh (Ojibwa), on his *Shield for a Modern Warrior or Concession to Beads and Feathers in Indian Art* (1984-1985), makes reference to Plains art and Dada sculpture; but most poignantly, the crushed beer cans in the center speak to the past and ongoing tragedy of alcoholism among native peoples.

Most American Indian artists today, whether they live in a city, on an Indian reservation, or both, speak from two worlds. In works that call on antiquity and the present, they depict their history and their legends, their insights and their sorrows.

—*Zena Pearlstone*

See also Appliqué and ribbonwork; Arts and crafts; Paints and painting; Pottery; Symbolism in art.

BIBLIOGRAPHY

Brody, J. J. *Indian Painters and White Patrons*. Albuquerque: University of New Mexico Press, 1971.

Contemporary Native American Art. Stillwater: Gardiner Art Gallery, Oklahoma State University, 1983.

Hammond, Harmony, and Jaune Quick-to-See Smith, curators. *Women of Sweetgrass, Cedar, and Sage*. New York: Gallery of the American Indian Community House, 1985.

Lippard, Lucy R. *Mixed Blessings: New Art in a Multicultural America*. New York: Pantheon Books, 1990.

Rushing, W. Jackson. "Recent Native American Art." *Art Journal* 51, no. 3 (Fall, 1992): 6-15.

Art and artists, traditional. *See entries under Arts and crafts.*

Articles of Agreement

DATE: Established 1730

TRIBES AFFECTED: Cherokee

SIGNIFICANCE: Although not a major treaty between Indians and the English, the Articles of Agreement were unique in that they were engineered by one man and the Cherokees went to England to sign it

During the late 1720's it became evident that stronger ties were needed between the English colonists and the Cherokee Nation. The increasing conflict between France and England over interests in North America necessitated that each country have the loyalty of Indian tribes.

Colonel George Chicken, English commissioner of Indian Affairs, obtained Cherokee loyalty. In 1728 when he left the Cherokee, several French emissaries began working within the tribe. The French influence among the Cherokees became so great by 1730 that an alarmed English government dispatched

Sir Alexander Cumming for the purpose of bringing the tribe into sure alliance. Upon Cumming's arrival in the province, a council of the entire Cherokee Nation was called to meet at Keowee, and allegiance was sealed with the English. The Cherokees' Nequasse crown, a construction of opossum fur and feathers, and some scalps and feathers were laid at Cumming's feet along with a request that they be delivered to the king of England. Six Cherokee chiefs were selected to accompany Cumming to England. A seventh chief, plus Indian trader Eleazer "Old Rabbit" Wiggins and an interpreter, joined them at the Port of Charleston on May 13, 1730. They set sail, landing in Dover in June. The seven Indians remained in England for three months, visiting all the important places and inciting curiosity among the English. They were presented to King George II on September 7 and gave him the crown and artifacts; each signed the Articles of Agreement, a treaty of friendship and commerce.

The treaty consisted of a preamble of friendship and devotion along with the following six provisions.

(1) The English and Cherokee shall live in peace and trade with each other. The Indians and English may live wherever they please, but the English are forbidden to live near the Cherokee towns. (For that pledge the Cherokees were given two pieces of white cloth, dyed red.)

(2) The Cherokee pledge to fight against any enemy of the English, white or red. (For that pledge the Cherokees were given twenty guns.)

(3) The Cherokee pledge not to interfere with other Indians trading with the English. (For that pledge the Cherokees were given four hundred pounds of gunpowder.)

(4) The Cherokee will not be permitted to trade with any other white nation nor allow any other nation to build forts or cabins, or even plant corn near them. (For that pledge the Cherokees were given five hundred pounds of shot and five hundred pounds of bullets.)

(5) The Cherokee will return any runaway "Negro slaves" to the English. For each returned slave, a reward of a gun and coat will be paid. (For that pledge the Cherokees were given ten thousand gun flints and six hatchets.)

(6) The English government, through English law, is responsible for the trial and punishment of an Englishman should he kill a Cherokee and a Cherokee if he should kill an Englishman. (For that pledge, the Cherokees were given twelve dozen spring knives, four brass kettles, and ten dozen belts.)

The 1730 Articles of Agreement had little influence on the entire Cherokee tribe. It was signed by only seven of their chiefs, and to be binding on the entire tribe it would have had to have been signed by all chiefs. The seven chiefs returned to their people and told of the greatness and splendor of England, contrasting it to the primitiveness and struggles of the Cherokee people. As a result of this visit and treaty, the English acquired only five years of allegiance from the Cherokee people.

See also Cherokee; Indian-white relations—English colonial.

Arts and crafts—Arctic

TRIBES AFFECTED: Aleut, Inuit, Yupik

SIGNIFICANCE: Art of the Arctic, including prints, basketry, tapestries, and sculpture of stone, bone, and ivory, is exhibited and sold throughout the world; it grew in commercial importance in the years after World War II

Visitors to nearly any Canadian city cannot help but notice the ubiquitous small black and gray stone carvings of polar bears, walruses, seals, and fur-clad hunters. These hastily made souvenirs of the Canadian Arctic may be the best-known objects of Eskimo tourist art, but they are hardly representative of the great variety and fine quality of representational art from the Arctic region. Sculptures of stone, bone, and ivory, tapestries of wool and fur, wood and skin masks, baskets, dolls, and prints are widely exhibited in art museums and galleries.

Historical Roots. The manufacture of arts and crafts, first for trade and later for cash sale, can be traced to early contacts between Arctic peoples and European explorers, whalers, and traders. Visitors to the region sought souvenirs of their adventures, and native residents quickly discovered that they could obtain desirable trade goods by providing those souvenirs, often in the form of miniatures of native material culture. In Alaska, this trade accelerated and grew in importance at the beginning of the twentieth century. The export of arts and crafts from the North remained modest until after World War II, when a time of economic hardship existed for Arctic natives because of the dramatic drop in fox pelt prices. In 1948, a young Canadian artist named James Houston traveled to Port Harrison in northern Quebec, where he became entranced by the miniature carvings made by local Inuits. He returned to Montreal, where he organized an exhibition sponsored by the Canadian Handicrafts Guild. Public reaction to the fine carvings was so exuberant that Houston returned to the Arctic the following year to encourage Inuits to produce more of these pieces, which were shipped south for sale. At the same time, the federal government of Canada, concerned about the dire financial situation of most Inuit communities, hired Houston to act as a roving arts and crafts officer. As the volume of arts and crafts exports increased each year, Inuit artists began experimenting with larger carvings made from soapstone and serpentine. Houston was later instrumental in starting the printmaking industry in the Baffin Island community of Cape Dorset.

Throughout the late 1950's and early 1960's, the Canadian government was instrumental in the establishment of arts and crafts cooperatives in most Canadian Inuit communities. An umbrella organization known as Canadian Arctic Producers was established to assist in the purchase of raw materials and the distribution of finished products. Although the organization of arts and crafts production varies somewhat from one northern community to another, in Canada the cooperatives continue to play a vital role in the training of artists and the marketing of their work.

Throughout the Arctic culture area, much of the early tourist or souvenir art consisted of models or miniatures of items of traditional material culture. For generations, natives had manufactured and decorated highly sophisticated utilitarian objects. Thus, the skills necessary to produce artwork were widely distributed. Scholars generally agree that throughout the Arctic, fine craftsmanship in the manufacture of everyday items was highly valued. The hunting cultures of the region believed that animals preferred to be killed by individuals who took the time to produce beautifully designed and decorated weapons. Yupik legend, for example, relates that seals would give themselves up to men whose wives sewed with skill but would avoid men whose wives were slovenly in their sewing habits.

As natives accepted more southern manufactured goods and produced fewer utilitarian objects, artwork for local consumption became less common. Commercial art, however, grew in importance as people sought the cash with which to purchase the imported goods. Consequently, the forms that arts and crafts took were heavily influenced by the demands of the marketplace. It is ironic that natives were often encouraged to produce images depicting a traditional way of life that, increasingly, they no longer followed. There have been a number of well-known instances in which native-produced art was believed to have been overly influenced by Western styles or motifs and was therefore rejected by the market as not native enough.

Contemporary Forms. There is considerable variation in both motifs and materials among the three native groups of the region. On both the eastern and western extremes of the Arctic culture area the art forms draw heavily on spiritual motifs. This is seen most clearly in the *tupilak* sculptures from East Greenland. These small, often grotesque, figurines are generally carved from sperm whale teeth. Although the tupilaks are physical representations of Inuit helping spirits, they have always been produced, not as amulets, but for sale. To the contrary, the spirit masks produced by Alaska's Yupik Eskimos were (and to some extent, still are) an integral part of the dance and ceremonies that accompanied the annual subsistence cycle. Often made of driftwood, the masks are representations of plants, animals, and helping spirits.

Printmaking is most developed in several Canadian Inuit communities, including Holman, Baker Lake, Povungnituk, and Cape Dorset. Prints are produced in series of fifty per image, and stone block printing, stenciling, and lithography are the most common printmaking methods. Although there are clearly developed community styles, many of these tend to be artifacts of local printmaking techniques. The primary differences in artistic style are those of gender—men tend to produce scenes of hunting and other "male" activities, while women more often depict relationships, families, and spirits.

Sculptures of fossil whalebone and soapstone are produced from St. Lawrence Island in the west to Baffin Island in the east. Most carvers are male and, as with printmaking, many of the images are of animals and hunting. Some notable recent pieces have depicted social concerns such as alcohol abuse. Graceful birds delicately shaped from musk ox horn are also a recent innovation.

Dolls, jewelry, and baskets are also produced in the region. Twined Aleut baskets are among the most delicately woven in the world. Generally woven from wild rye beach grasses, the almost clothlike baskets require great skill, time, and patience. Few Aleut women continue this painstaking activity.

Among the Iñupiat of North Alaska, there are also a few makers of coiled baleen baskets. The first baleen baskets were produced in Barrow around 1914 at the request of the trader Charles Brower. The stiff baleen is extremely difficult to work, and a finely made basket commands a high price. In the Iñupiat community of Anaktuvuk Pass, located in the Brooks Range of North Alaska, residents make a unique caribou-skin mask that is pressed into the shape of a human face and decorated with sealskin and fur for the eyebrows, hair, and beard. *—Pamela R. Stern and Richard G. Condon*

See also Aleut; Architecture—Arctic; Arctic; Inuit.

BIBLIOGRAPHY

Black, Lydia T. *Glory Remembered: Wooden Headgear of Alaska Sea Hunters*. Juneau: Friends of the Alaska State Museums, 1991.

Canadian Museum of Civilization. *In the Shadow of the Sun: Perspectives on Contemporary Native Art*. Mercury Series Paper 124. Hull, Quebec: Canadian Ethnology Service, 1993.

Driscoll, Bernadette. *I Like My Hood to Be Full*. Winnipeg, Canada: Winnipeg Art Gallery, 1980.

Goetz, Helga, ed. *The Inuit Print/L'Estampe Inuit*. Ottawa: National Museum of Man, 1977.

Graburn, Nelson H. H. "Inuit Art." In *Arctic Life: Challenge to Survive*, edited by Martina M. Jacobs and James B. Richardson III. Pittsburgh: Carnegie Institution Press, 1983.

Hudson's Bay Company. *Beaver* 298 (1967). Special issue on Canadian Inuit arts.

Iglauer, Edith. *Inuit Journey*. Seattle: University of Washington Press, 1979.

Ray, Dorothy Jean. *Aleut and Eskimo Art: Tradition and Innovation in South Alaska*. Seattle: University of Washington Press, 1981.

_____. *Eskimo Art: Tradition and Innovation in North Alaska*. Seattle: University of Washington Press, 1977.

Arts and crafts—California

TRIBES AFFECTED: Chumash, Cupeño, Fernandeño, Gabrielino, Hupa, Kato, Luiseño, Maidu, Miwok, Modoc, Patwin, Pomo, Salinan, Tolowa, Wintun, Yana, Yokuts, Yurok

SIGNIFICANCE: Californian tribes are known for fine rbasketry work and rock art

California tribes hunted, gathered, and fished, and they were divided into many relatively small groups. Although they neither produced monumental art nor possessed a complex art tradition as did the tribes of the Southwest or the Plains, they were nevertheless masters in basketry. Artistic traditions were divided into three geographical zones within the state of California. The southernmost groups had poorly made pottery, carved stone bowls and figures (including stone effigies), rock art, and basketry. The central groups, especially the Pomo, were master basketmakers. The northern groups were influenced by Northwest Coast arts and crafts and made plank houses, dugout canoes, slat armor, and basketry hats.

Basketry. The preeminent craft of Native Americans in California has been basketry. They used both coiling and twining techniques, with coiling being done by the southern groups and twining by the northern ones. Basketry was used to make most containers and to provide many other functional necessities, including mats, baby boards, and boats. Basketry was also used to make decorative objects such as headdresses, and was a part of religious rituals and the life passage rituals of birth, puberty, marriage, and death.

Basketry has always been a woman's art among the California groups, and it provided the women with their primary means of aesthetic expression. Basket designs, considered to be the property of women, were usually geometric and abstract, including circles, crosses, steps, and parallel line designs. Stylized figures of plants and people were also made. Natural vegetable colors were used to achieve the designs. The aesthetic accomplishment in the finer baskets from this region goes far beyond the functional needs for which the basketry was made.

The finest examples of basketry are the "jewel" or "gift" baskets made by Pomo women. These special baskets incorporated feather mosaics into the design along with clam and abalone shells. Red, white, black, blue, and green feathers were used. In some cases the feathers and shells were used sparingly to heighten the basketry design, but in others they became a second layer which totally covered the basket and formed designs of their own. Shells hung along the rim or sides of the basket as ornamentation.

These "jewel" baskets were not only made by women, but were also made as gifts for other women. They were seen as a special ceremonial gift for a woman at important life passage points in her life, such as birth, puberty, and marriage. These baskets had emotional importance for Indian women, probably forming part of self-identity. They were usually cremated along with the woman at death.

Baskets also play a crucial role in mythology. One story says that the earth did not originally have the light of the sun. The original culture hero and creator discovered a village where there was light which was kept in baskets in a sacred sweatlodge. Able to steal one of the magic sun baskets, he hung it in the sky so that all would have light.

Functional baskets were important to the economy of the California groups. Since most groups did not have pottery, baskets were used for cooking and domestic purposes which included storing, grinding, toasting, and boiling food. Water containers were also made from baskets. Although some groups sealed their baskets with pitch or tar, the Pomo, Patwin, and other groups from central California made coiled baskets so tightly bound that they were naturally waterproof.

Rock Art. Rock art consisted of painting highly personalized dream images onto rocky cliffs or overhangs. The Chumash seem to have been the only group to practice it. This art may have reproduced hallucinogenic images seen by men after the ceremonial taking of datura. Rock art consists of compositions of geometric forms, including circles, zigzags, diamonds, chevrons, and crosses, juxtaposed with figures of animals, plants, and people. The colors normally used were strong, saturated hues of red, yellow/orange, black, white, and blue, and the paints were made from minerals and bonded with vegetable and animal oils. The practice of this art seems to have died out in the late 1800's without the meanings being explained in historical records. *—Ronald J. Duncan*

See also Baskets and basketry; California; Pomo.

Arts and crafts—Great Basin

TRIBES AFFECTED: Bannock, Gosiute, Kawaiisu, Mono, Numaga, Paiute, Paviotso, Shoshone, Ute, Walapai, Washoe

SIGNIFICANCE: The arts and crafts of the Great Basin are primarily baskets and other objects created through basketry techniques, reflecting a material culture adapted to a desert environment

The arts and crafts of the tribes of the Great Basin represent the highest degree of dependence on basketry techniques of any of the Native American culture areas. Many different kinds of baskets were made, including carrying baskets, serving baskets, and water jars; basketry techniques were also used for making other items, from clothing to boats and houses. Although most baskets were coil made, some were made by the twining technique.

Decorative Baskets. Some of the earliest baskets collected from the Paiutes in the nineteenth century were decorated, and since that time there has been an evolution in designs. The earliest baskets known from this region used the stacked rod coiling technique, which refers to the plaiting of two or more coils. The early decorated baskets were made with a technique different from the one normally used, which suggests that the early decorative patterns were borrowed from neighboring basket-maker groups; the baskets themselves may even have been made by other groups.

By the 1890's, the Paiutes were making decorated baskets for the Navajo, especially wedding baskets, and this relationship continued throughout the twentieth century. In addition to that design, the Paiute basket makers borrowed others from Navajo textiles. The designs on Paiute baskets during the twentieth century seem to have been largely borrowed.

The wedding basket is an interesting case of one cultural group doing important ceremonial craftwork for another group. The wedding basket is a tray or open bowl shape of twelve to fourteen inches in diameter; it was used by the Navajo to serve cornmeal mush to the honorees and guests at important ceremonies. It is characterized by a circular band of deep red that is bordered by black triangles along both the inside and outside edges. A break in the encircling band is left to provide an opening from the center of the basket outwards, and it is sometimes called the door. During ceremonial use of the basket, the "door" is pointed eastward. Star or snowflake patterns may be created by the black triangles in the center of the basket if the encircling red band is small and the triangles are large. Wedding baskets are made with coils of three bunched rods of sumac. The sewing splints are narrow, and the rims are finished in a herringbone design with diagonal plaiting.

Decorative trade baskets have also been made by various groups during the twentieth century, including the Washoe and the San Juan Paiutes. There was a period of outstanding Washoe decorative baskets during the early part of the century. Since traditional Washoe baskets were undecorated, the styles of California tribes were imitated initially; however, the Washoe baskets were distinctive because of their large size, fine stitching, and red and black decoration. Some Washoe baskets were characterized by bold designs, a style that continued throughout the remainder of the century. The San Juan Paiutes experienced a period of florescence during the latter part of the twentieth century based on the borrowing of design patterns, including the use of Navajo *yei* figures, the Navajo Spider Woman cross, and Havasupai angular designs, among others.

Utilitarian Basketry. The largest utilitarian baskets were the conical burden baskets carried on the back with supplies of nuts, roots, or other foods. They were often about 18 inches high and 16 inches across at the opening, and they were made by coiling or twining. Burden baskets could be made with a tight weave for the carrying of seeds and small nuts or made with an open weave for carrying heavier roots. Although utilitarian baskets were rarely decorated, some burden baskets were made with dyed splints.

Basket bowls and shallow circular trays were used for preparing seeds and nuts for eating; food was sometimes cooked or parched with hot stones in the lined baskets. The trays were also used for winnowing out chaff from eatable food. There were also seed beaters in various shapes, ranging from "snowshoe" to handfan designs. These were used to knock seeds off grasses into a conical carrying basket. Pot-shaped storage baskets with tight weave and small necks were used to protect food; water jars were sealed inside with pitch. Scoops, brushes, toys, and other small objects were also made from basketry techniques.

Cradleboards, Canoes, and Houses. The people of the Great Basin could live in basket-made structures from the cradle to death. A cradleboard for a small infant was made completely by basketry techniques, with a curved hood to protect the head and a soft back. The cradleboard for a larger infant was made with a wooden frame onto which a basketry back and hood were woven.

Houses were also made with basketry techniques and were essentially upside-down baskets. A willow frame was made by setting up twelve or more vertical willows that were approximately 10 feet long. They were tied together by other willows running horizontally—just above the ground, midway up, and near the top. The top of the frame was tied inward to form a closed-in shape. Cattail leaf mats were woven around other willows, and the mats were tied into place to form the walls. Long grass could also be used to form the walls.

Examples of Chemehuevi (a Southern Paiute offshoot) basketry in the 1890's. (Museum of New Mexico)

Small canoes were also made with bulrushes (or tule), similar to reed boats made in Peru. Armload bundles of bulrush were tied together with twisted cattail leaf ropes in such a way that a narrow prow was formed, leaving a broader stern where a person could sit and direct the craft. Bulrush duck decoys were also made.   —*Ronald J. Duncan*

See also Baskets and basketry; Great Basin; Tule.

BIBLIOGRAPHY

Arkush, Brooke S. "The Great Basin Culture Area." In *Native North Americans: An Ethnohistorical Approach*, edited by Daniel L. Boxberger. Dubuque, Iowa: Kendall/Hunt, 1990.

Cohodas, Marvin. "Washoe Innovators and Their Patrons." In *The Arts of the North American Indian: Native Traditions in Evolution*, edited by Edwin L. Wade. New York: Hudson Hills Press, 1986.

Feder, Norman. *American Indian Art*. New York: Harry N. Abrams, 1965.

Wheat, Margaret M. *Survival Arts of the Primitive Paiutes*. Reno: University of Nevada Press, 1967.

Whiteford, Andrew Hunter. *Southwestern Indian Baskets: Their History and Their Makers*. Santa Fe, N. Mex.: School of American Research Press, 1988.

Arts and crafts—Northeast

TRIBES AFFECTED: Algonquin, Cayuga, Fox (Mesquaki), Huron, Iroquois, Kickapoo, Lenni Lenape, Lumbee, Menominee, Miami, Micmac, Mohawk, Narragansett, Oneida, Onondaga, Ottawa, Potawatomi, Sauk, Seneca, Shawnee, Susquehannock, Tuscarora, Winnebago

SIGNIFICANCE: The baskets, quillwork, beadwork, and masks of the Northeast tribes are among the finest in North America

The Northeast covers New England, New York, and the eastern Great Lakes region down to the Ohio River valley. The art of Native Americans from the northeastern area of the United States used themes associated with nature, mythology, and the supernatural. It might represent otherworldly themes, such as a quillwork ornament representing a thunderbird which protected the wearer from the panther spirit of the other world. It might also represent everyday themes, such as beadwork showing the multicolored hues of flowers and vines that were a natural part of the flora. Included in this rich array of arts were birchbark boxes, quillwork, beadwork, and wood carvings. Pottery was lost in this region soon after contact was made with European groups who introduced the Indians to metal containers.

Masks. Iroquois-made wooden and cornhusk masks are the most striking art form in this region. Men carve and paint wooden masks, while women braid cornhusk ones. These masks are still worn by contemporary members of the Society of Faces in dances that are intended to cure people and drive disease from their homes. Characteristics include strong, staring eyes, heavy wrinkles, and horse-mane hair. Although some have sober, dark colors and small mouths, others are brightly painted and have big ear-to-ear mouths. The features may be distorted.

Wooden masks, made and worn only by men, represent many different spirits, including those of trees, plants, waterfalls, unusual rocks, and other special features of the landscape. They are carved from living trees, and the traditional belief was that they embodied a living spirit. Tobacco was tied into the hair for use by the spirit, and the mask was fed regularly. Cornhusk masks may be made and worn by men or women, and they represent the spirits of vegetation which work to heal people.

Various features of the mask identify the spirit portrayed by it. For example, a broken nose and wide crooked mouth represent a spirit called the "Great Defender" or the "Rim Dweller," who was transformed from a malevolent spirit into one which helped people. Wood carving was also used to make clubs and carved figures for knife handles and other uses. Carvings commonly represented hands, the human body, bears, and horses.

Bark boxes and baskets. Bark was a favorite material for making boxes, baskets, and even canoes. Birchbark was used in the Great Lakes area, and elm bark was used by the Iroquois and other groups in the East. These barks are soft and pliable when peeled, which permits them to be shaped into square and round designs for containers. Bark can be bent, rolled, and stitched, and it provides a good surface for drawing or incising. Quillwork was frequently used to decorate the surface. Both covered boxes and open baskets made use of this material. Splint basketry was also made in this area.

Beadwork. Both quillwork and small stone beads were originally used to create designs and decorative bands on clothing. After the introduction of European glass trade beads, this art medium went through a spectacular development. The original work was limited to the muted colors of autumn earth tones, but the glass beads permitted the introduction of the saturated hues of spring flowers and berries. Ribbons were introduced along with beads; combined, they gave many more opportunities for the ornamentation of clothing.

Beads have been used to represent both the geometric designs found in earlier ceramic patterns and the floral motifs with which the eastern groups are identified. The latter may have developed out of an earlier tradition of naturalistic representations. There were also European models for the floral motifs which may have been the ecclesiastical attire of priests, but other floral patterns incorporated later may have referred to local medicinal plants. The idea that there were European sources for the floral patterns is reinforced by the fact that they were commonly used on shoulder-strap bags, adapted from European military pouches, and on European-style deerskin coats. Indigenous belts and trumplines decorated with quillwork later evolved into beaded and beribboned votive belts by which people expressed their devotion.   —*Ronald J. Duncan*

See also Baskets and basketry; Beads and beadwork; Masks; Northeast; Quillwork.

Arts and crafts—Northwest Coast

TRIBES AFFECTED: Bella Bella, Bella Coola, Haida, Haisla, Kitamat, Kwakiutl, Makah, Nitinat, Nootka, Tlingit, Tsimshian

The totem poles flanking this bridal party are representative of Northwest Coast art. (Edward S. Curtis, American Museum of Natural History)

SIGNIFICANCE: The people of the Northwest Coast have one of the most recognizable art styles of the world and produced the most important monumental art of the indigenous North American groups

The people of the Northwest Coast are identified by their art, especially painted house facades, masks, and the monumentality of the totem poles. They are the outstanding wood carvers of North America, and their art treats the themes of cosmology and origins, social status and prestige, and shamanistic power. Both sculpture and painting are characterized by strong colors and shapes.

Totem Poles. Totem poles stand in front of houses as a statement of the sacred history of the family. The vertical series of figures making up the pole traces the family to the time the lineage was founded in the mythic past. The origin story usually tells about the original ancestor encountering a spirit who gave him and his descendants a special power, as well as the image of the spirit as a heraldic crest for the family. Each family may possess more than one crest; crests are inherited by the children in each generation. Multiple crests may be represented on a pole, and common ones include the bear, mountain lion, eagle, frog, and wolf. The totem pole seems only to have developed during the nineteenth century, but similar poles were carved earlier as the crest poles of houses.

The totem poles were carved and erected as memorials to men of chiefly status who had died, and they were mnemonic devices to record the heritage of the family. The pole became a public proclamation of ancestry and the rights to positions of prestige along with their benefits, obligations, and supernatural characteristics. The carver of a totem pole was expected to be a relative of the man honored. If the man chosen to be the carver did not have the required skill, he could conceptualize the piece and name a skilled carver to execute it. The authorship of a pole was assigned to the one who conceptualized it. The poles were as much as 60 feet tall, and they were carved lying on the ground.

House Facades and Crest Poles. The house itself was the cosmos in a microcosm, with the hearth being the navel of the world; the house posts were the supports of the earth and sky, and the smoke hole was the connection between the earth and the heavenly world, forming a vertical cosmic axis. The facades of chiefly houses could be painted with the images of mythical animals who were the head of the lineage. In the nineteenth century and earlier, the crest poles of houses were carved, and sometimes a large entrance hole was cut into it, which served as the door for the house. The opening was frequently portrayed as the mouth or the vagina of the animal lineage head of the family, and going in and out of the house represented death and rebirth from the lineage totem. In some instances the door hole represented the hole of creation through which the original ancestor passed to enter this world. Another version interpreted it as the hole through which the original shaman passed back and forth to the other world to learn the sacred knowledge, ceremonies, and masks that characterized ritual.

Masks and Hats. Masks have been the most common art form among the peoples of the Northwest Coast. Like the motifs of the totem poles, masks belong to families and were originally given to the founding ancestor because of a victory over an adversary. Masks and the accompanying costumes create a figure who was an actor in a myth; songs and dances are also inherited with the mask to dramatize the myth. Masks represent the shamanic power of transformation from the earthly present to the mythic past or to the supernatural world. In the ephemeral other world of the masks, the heroic exploits of the original people are acted out, and the myths reconfirm the fundamental principles of the cosmos. Masks may represent supernatural animal spirits, shamans, or important people. In addition to being carved, many are painted with strong primary colors. Some have movable parts.

The shaman's quest for spiritual powers is also a common theme of mask-myth performances. The shamanic regalia included special masks, costumes, drums, and rattles. The rattles are especially striking because of their elaborate and complex carving. The basic figure shown in the rattle was frequently a water bird, and the shaman is shown on its back with other animals. The tongue of a goat or a frog may become a bridge through which the shaman transforms the power of that animal into his own.

Carved wooden hats and war helmets were traditionally important, and some are essentially variations on the idea of the masks. War helmets have not been made since the nineteenth century, but they represented ancestors or other effigy beings who could give strength to the warrior. Conical clan hats were also important, and they represent the animal of the family crest. Like masks, these hats sometimes had movable parts. These family crest hats are among the most dramatic pieces of Northwest Coast art, possessing abalone-shell inlays, stylized bodies, and polychrome painting.

Domestic Crafts. Weaving, basketry, and the carving of wooden household utensils were also common crafts. During historical periods woven tunics frequently included the family crest motifs, similar to the totem poles, masks, and hats. Spindle whorls for spinning the thread were elaborately carved in wood. Women were accomplished basket makers, and their twined work with grasses and other fibers were as fine as woven cloth.   —*Ronald J. Duncan*

See also Architecture—Northwest Coast; Masks; Northwest Coast; Tlingit; Totem Poles; Tsimshian.

BIBLIOGRAPHY

Carlson, Roy L., ed. *Indian Art Traditions of the Northwest Coast.* Burnaby, B.C.: Archaeology Press, Simon Fraser University, 1982.

Furst, Peter T., and Jill L. Furst. *North American Indian Art.* New York: Rizzoli International, 1982.

Holm, Bill. *Crooked Beak of Heaven: Masks and Other Ceremonial Art in the Pacific Northwest.* Seattle: University of Washington Press, 1972.

_____. "The Dancing Headdress Frontlet: Aesthetic Context on the Northwest Coast." In *The Arts of the North American Indian: Native Traditions in Evolution*, edited by Edwin L. Wade. New York: Hudson Hills Press, 1986.

King, J. C. H. *Portrait Masks from the Northwest Coast of North America.* London: Thames & Hudson, 1979.

Suttles, Wayne, ed. *Northwest Coast.* Vol. 7 in *Handbook of North American Indians.* Washington, D.C.: Smithsonian Institution Press, 1990.

Arts and crafts—Plains

TRIBES AFFECTED: Arapaho, Arikara, Assiniboine, Atsina, Blackfoot, Caddo, Cheyenne, Comanche, Cree, Crow, Hidatsa, Iowa, Kiowa, Mandan, Missouri, Omaha, Osage, Pawnee, Ponca, Sioux, Tonkawa, Wichita

SIGNIFICANCE: The beadwork and headdresses of the Plains are a dramatic statement of personal aesthetics, and they are the primary association with Native American art for many people

The arts and crafts of the Plains tribes were small in scale and highly transportable because of the largely nomadic Plains existence. The arts had supernatural relationships with the spirit world; for example, beautifying the skin of a slain animal was thought to please its spirit and avert retaliation. Ghost Dance shirts and dresses also demonstrate the close relationship between art and the spiritual world.

Clothing and Bags. Clothing, moccasins, and bags were made of skins, and most were decorated with geometric designs by women using quills, beads, or paint. Plains art is most known for the beadwork on clothing and other personal items and the earlier work with porcupine quills. By the early nineteenth century, colored beads of Venetian glass had been introduced by the Europeans as trade items, and by midcentury they had been replaced by even smaller "seed beads," which led to a new style of beadwork that covered entire surfaces.

The elongated shape of the quill was used to decorate medallions, boxes, and cradleboards, among other items, and resulted in geometric designs or highly stylized figures. Beadwork portrayed such things as floral patterns, the tipi, crosses, the United States flag, and lightning. Dresses, shirts, and parfleches were frequently painted. The parfleche was a thick-skinned, folding bag which was capable of withstanding arrows and lances.

Narrative Art. Narrative paintings were done by men on skins, especially on robes and tipis. These narrated calendrical histories (called winter counts), important tribal gatherings, personal visions, mythological events, and important battles, raids, and hunts. The calendar drawings have mnemonic value for remembering the major events that occurred in a tribe or band over a number of years. The winter camps were the fixed points between which yearly events were remembered. Battle scenes, as well as raids and hunts, narrate the personal bravery and skill of a specific warrior, and these were usually painted by the same warrior on his personal buffalo robe or on his tipi cover. He would usually portray the most important moment of his triumph. Tribal gatherings were also portrayed in narrative detail, describing features of the landscape, placing of tipis, clothing, and tribal paraphernalia. The describing of personal visions and mythological events was done with less narrative detail; it was left to the imagination of the viewer to complete the story. Vision paintings were frequently done on shields or tipis.

As the independent lifestyle of the Plains people came to an end and the people were settled around forts, the art of skin painting was lost. This happened in part because the personal exploits narrated by the men in battle and hunting no longer happened and in part because the skins were no longer available. In its place, ledgerbook painting was developed among the Southern Plains tribes; among the Northern Plains tribes, men adapted to painting on cloth. Ledgerbook art typically narrates the experience of Native Americans with the European American world. Instead of the horses, tipis, and buffalo of the skin paintings, the ledger paintings portray forts, trains, wagons, and even towns. The most famous collection of ledger art comes from the seventy-two warriors from five Southern Plains tribes who were sent to Fort Marion in Florida after their surrender in 1875.

Pipes as Miniature Sculpture. The pipe was the single most important art object made by the Plains groups, and it explored the relationship between humans and the sacred in the earth and sky, including the concept of the universe. Each man carved his own private ceremonial pipe, and sometimes one would be made as a special gift for another person. The holiest pipes were common property and were considered to be especially powerful. The bowls were usually carved from reddish pipestone, which was considered to be blood colored and therefore to represent life. They were usually plain bowls but could include complex carvings of animals or humans. The stems were also elaborately carved and could be two feet long or more; sometimes they were of greater importance than the bowl itself. Stems were carved in a number of imaginative designs, including spiral stems, mazeway puzzle stems, and stems with figurative carvings of animals and guardian spirits. Since the power of the pipe was activated when the stem and bowl were united, they were usually separated when stored. Pipe bags show some of the most important Plains beadwork and quillwork, which indicates the significance of pipes.

Gender and Art. Women beautified clothes and other items of domestic use with geometric designs in their media of bead and quillwork, with occasional painting. Craft and skill were definitive of women's work, and they used the geometric signs that communicated the important concepts of nature and the supernatural. Many incorporated the United States flag into their beadwork during the late 1800's, perhaps as a statement of peace. The women's art uses collective designs, and it does not emphasize the individuality of the piece. In contrast, men's narrative art is individualistic and boasts of personal exploits. Craft seems to be less important in the narrative art, which is done with lines that are rigid and awkward. Men's pipe carvings are carefully crafted, however, and rival the quality of the women's beadwork. —*Ronald J. Duncan*

See also Beads and beadwork; Dress and adornment; Plains; Quillwork.

BIBLIOGRAPHY

Coe, Ralph T. *Sacred Circles: Two Thousand Years of North American Indian Art*. Kansas City, Mo.: Nelson Gallery Foundation, 1977.

Catlin, George. *Indian Art in Pipestone: George Catlin's Portfolio in the British Museum*. Edited by John C. Ewers. Washington, D.C.: Smithsonian Institution Press, 1979.

Furst, Peter T., and Jill L. Furst. *North American Indian Art*. New York: Rizzoli International, 1982.

Penny, David W. *Art of the American Indian Frontier*. Seattle: University of Washington Press, 1992.

Wade, Edwin L., ed. *The Arts of the North American Indian: Native Traditions in Evolution*. New York: Hudson Hills Press, 1986.

Arts and crafts—Plateau

TRIBES AFFECTED: Cayuse, Chilcotin, Klikitat, Lillooet, Nez Perce, Shuswap, Umatilla, Walla Walla, Wasco, Wishram, Yakima

SIGNIFICANCE: The arts and crafts of the Plateau effectively preserved traditional design styles and techniques longer than most other Native American culture areas

The people of the Plateau have produced bags, basketry, beadwork, and wood carving of excellent quality. Their work reflects the influences from neighboring culture areas and demonstrates the diffusion and acculturation of arts and crafts traditions across culture lines among Native Americans. Contact with European groups occurred later here than in most other areas, and this fact permitted a greater preservation of traditional arts and crafts.

Woven Bags. The Plateau bag is the most distinctive art and craft medium of this culture area. These bags are known for their geometric designs and skillful color patterns. The women makers of these bags are known for their weaving skill, and many of them achieved personal visions of aesthetic excellence in geometric and color composition. Along with Navajo blankets and rugs, these bags represent the finest designs in North American weaving. Plateau people have also made blankets but never with the same sophistication with which they weave bags.

The first European Americans to arrive in the area were Meriwether Lewis and William Clark in 1805, and they mentioned the woven bags made by the Nez Perce. The twined or woven bags are made with the beige background of hemp but then decorated with bear grass and cattails dyed with vegetable colors. After corn was introduced into the area in the early nineteenth century, corn husks were used for the bags; later, yarn was also incorporated. After that they were sometimes referred to as cornhusk bags. They were made in varying sizes, ranging from 8 by 8 inches to 18 by 22 inches. Some large versions of the bag are as much as 36 inches long, and they were usually carried vertically. They were originally used for carrying food that had been collected. After horses arrived in the region, they were used as saddlebags. In the twentieth century they became decorative handbags carried by women.

The designs were traditionally geometric, but figurative motifs were introduced in the late nineteenth century. The bag was continuously woven in the round, with the front side being more elaborate than the back. Triangles and diamond shapes were especially popular, and they were sometimes combined to form star, butterfly, cross, chevron, or arrow designs. Smaller designs were incorporated within or around the larger main design, which added complexity and visual interest. Long straight lines were frequently serrated, also creating more visual interest. Bag designs also emphasize the play between positive and negative spaces so that the viewer must shift his or her vision between the two.

The introduction of figurative designs including plants, animals, and humans reflected European American influences, especially the floral designs of the Victorian period. Since weaving lends itself more to the representation of geometric shapes than to reproducing organic ones, geometric forms continued to be important into the twentieth century. The ability to make organic, figurative shapes was the sign of a skillful weaver.

Baskets and Basketry. Both coiling and twining were used to make basketry items. Twining was used to make soft fiber objects such as hats and bags, as discussed above. Coiling was used to make more rigid basket containers, ranging from small bowls to large storage baskets. A technique of decoration known as "imbrication" is distinctive to the Plateau area. Imbrication is a process of creating a second decorative layer on top of the coil-made basket by stitching it into the surface of the basket. Since the decorative layer has no important structural problems to solve, it can be designed purely for aesthetic purposes. The imbricated layer has a continuous surface not interrupted by the dominant coil lines of the coil-made basket. Mats were also made by some groups and were traditionally used to cover the walls of tipis.

Beads and Beading. Beading was done on clothes, bags, baskets, and horse trappings, among other things, and represents an influence from the Plains tribes to the east. Similar to the Northern Plains people, both men and women of the Plateau used buckskin clothing decorated with beadwork. Originally beads were added to fringes, but later overall beading was used for shirts, cuffs, headbands, belts, and other accesso-ries. Beading was used for horse trappings, including bridles, mane covers, shin straps, stirrup covers, and saddle bags. Beading was also used to cover coiled baskets. The bead designs were geometric during the nineteenth century, but figurative motifs became increasingly important in the twentieth century. The Plateau bead workers used triangles, diamonds, squares, and crosses to create geometric designs, and the figurative patterns incorporate floral motifs, eagles, and the U.S. flag, among many other patterns.

Carving. Figures, grave marker totems, scoops, and small bowls were carved of wood and horn, reflecting influences from the neighboring Northwest Coast peoples. Human figures carved of wood represented ancestral spirits or beings, and shaman's wands included anthropomorphic forms. Small wooden bowls included figures carved in relief on the surfaces as well as decorative patterns of parallel or serrated lines. Occasionally figures were carved in three dimensions on the sides of bowls. The handles of scoops and spoons were carved with animal and human figures. The handles of wood-carving tools were themselves elaborately carved.—*Ronald J. Duncan*

See also Baskets and basketry; Beads and beadwork; Plateau; Weaving.

BIBLIOGRAPHY

Coe, Ralph T. *Sacred Circles: Two Thousand Years of North American Indian Art.* Kansas City, Mo.: Nelson Gallery Foundation, 1977.

Feder, Norman. *American Indian Art.* New York: Harry N. Abrams, 1965.

Kehoe, Alice B. *North American Indians: A Comprehensive Account.* 2d ed. Englewood Cliffs, N.J.: Prentice Hall, 1992.

Linn, Natalie. *The Plateau Bag: A Tradition in Native American Weaving.* Kansas City, Kans.: Johnson County Community College, Gallery of Art, 1994.

Penney, David W. *Art of the American Indian Frontier.* Seattle: University of Washington Press, 1992.

Arts and crafts—Southeast

TRIBES AFFECTED: Alabama, Anadarko, Apalachee, Catawba, Cherokee, Chickasaw, Chitimacha, Choctaw, Creek, Guale, Mobile, Natchez, Powhatan, Seminole, Tuskegee, Yamasee, Yazoo, Yuchi

SIGNIFICANCE: The Indians of the Southeast are especially known for baskets, beaded sashes and bags, carving, patchwork, and ribbon work

The artists of the Southeast tribes are the heirs to one of the richest artistic traditions in North America, but much of it has disappeared over the last few centuries because of acculturation and the dislocation of tribes. Elaborate earthen mounds, excellent stone-carved sculptures, copper sheets cut like mythical animals, baskets, and painted ceramics were made in the period before contact with Europeans. This early art incorporated motifs that suggested contact with the complex civilizations of Mexico. During the historic period, these tribes have been known for their work in belts and bags, baskets, carving, and sewing.

Belts and Bags. Creek, Cherokee, and Choctaw women, taking advantage of the creative possibilities of small seed beads, made sashes and shoulder bags that were well known for their elaborate flowing designs. These women were exceptional colorists and exploited the many colors made available with glass beads. They fashioned complex sashes with beads worked into the designs, and they made shoulder bags with beaded decoration. These were some of the finest bags produced in North America, and they competed with those of the Great Lakes area for aesthetic and technical excellence.

The double-ended scroll is a characteristic design from the Southeast tribes, and the beaded designs on belts and bags frequently use it. It is a linear design 8 to 10 inches long and 3 to 4 inches wide, consisting of a spiral or circle at each end with a line uniting them diagonally. The cross in a circle design surrounded by emanating sun rays was also used in beadwork, and both this design and the scroll pattern were used in other media, such as ceramics. Another common design pattern is the diamond, used especially by the Choctaws but also by Creeks and Seminoles. Creek sashes line up ordered rows of diamonds embroidered in seed beads, similar to the rows of diamonds that Choctaws sew onto the hems of dresses and onto the decorative bands of shirts. All of these designs were also used by prehistoric groups in the region.

Shoulder bags were made from wool or velvet, backed with a cotton lining and embroidered with seed beads in designs of flowing lines that suggest floral patterns but are in reality abstract. The patterns were bold and asymmetrical and the designs seem more individually expressive than the patterned formality of designs of the Northeast. In some designs the lines seem to meander, following their own will and resulting in amorphous "figures" that give a sense of elegant playfulness distinctive to these pieces.

Baskets. Southeastern basketry is especially known for the use of the split and plaited cane technique, which produces a flexible basket of considerable strength. The altering of colors between the warp and the weft gives ample opportunity for the creation of patterns and decoration. Covered baskets were made as containers for storage and protection, and open baskets were made for gathering and carrying food products. A gathering basket made by various tribes in the region has a square base which changes into a round shape for the top half of the basket. It is known for fitting well to the back, making it easier to carry loads. Common design motifs include the diamond, chevron or zigzag lines, crosses, and angular spirals.

Sewing. Patchwork dresses and shirts and elaborate ribbonwork decoration are also associated with the work of women in tribes of the Southeast. The Seminoles are most known for this type of patchwork, which was borrowed from European patchwork quilting. The patching together of hundreds of small pieces of colored cloth has been appropriated to form an aesthetic which is particular to this area and is now considered traditional. In the latter part of the twentieth century, ribbons have also been used in a similar way to create the patterns. Neighboring groups such as the Choctaws have adopted a similar practice of sewing diamond patch designs on dresses and shirts to give them tribal identity.

Carving. Men's craft consisted of carving, and they made stylized figures in wood and pipestone. Effigy pipes, representing bears and other animals from the region, were carved until the nineteenth century, following long Eastern Woodlands traditions. Other pipes were carved in geometric designs.

—*Ronald J. Duncan*

See also Baskets and basketry; Beads and beadwork; Dress and adornment; Southeast.

Arts and crafts—Southwest

Tribes affected: Apache, Navajo, Pueblo (including Hopi, Zuni)

Significance: The arts and crafts of the Southwest are a thriving and coherent representation of Native American art that has continuity with its prehistoric cultural roots

Southwest Native American art can be traced back to prehistoric groups that lived in the area. The prehistoric groups developed pottery, basketry, weaving, and jewelry making, and the contemporary Pueblo groups have continued the designs and techniques inherited in those media. The Navajos and Apaches have a different history, having entered the area only six hundred to eight hundred years ago. Although they originally practiced basketry, they acquired weaving from the Pueblo people and, later, silversmithing from the Spanish.

Eastern Pueblos. The Eastern Pueblos live on or near the Rio Grande River near Santa Fe, and they were most affected by the Spanish. They have had commercial success with arts and crafts in the twentieth century. The Eastern Pueblos have the richest pottery tradition, but they also make jewelry, baskets, and weaving.

Pueblo pottery is made with the prehistoric techniques of coil building, slip painting, and open-air firing. The pots are elaborately painted, usually iron oxide red, white, or black colors. Pueblo designs may use geometric forms or stylized figures of animals, birds, or plants. Border lines are usually drawn as a frame to define the area to be decorated. The designs frequently play back and forth between positive and negative fields, resulting in complex symmetries, and they are usually subdivided into smaller and smaller units. Women are the traditional makers of pottery, but men may paint it and fire it. The most common types of pots are water jars, dough bowls, and storage pots. Although each type was originally made for functional purposes, in the twentieth century they were made primarily for artistic purposes. The pottery tradition from this area is divided into a number of styles, including blackware, redware, and polychrome ware.

Blackware pottery was traditionally made in the Pueblos north and west of Santa Fe, especially Santa Clara, San Juan, and San Ildefonso, where the tradition was made famous by María and Julián Martínez. Santa Clara Pueblo is famous for both blackware and redware pottery, and it is well known for the deep carving of designs in the surface of pots. Rain serpents and the bear paw are popular designs. Polychrome pottery is most associated with the pueblos located to the south and west of Santa Fe, most notably Zia and Acoma. The colors are typically red and/or black on a white background. Border lines frame the painted areas of the pots, and within those borders designs may include floral patterns, animal figures (especially deer), birds, and geometric forms. Cochiti is the only pueblo to make figurative pieces, and in the last half of the twentieth century it was particularly known for the storyteller figure.

Navajo women spinning, carding, and weaving in the 1940's. (Museum of New Mexico)

The most traditional jewelry of the Southwest is made by people of the Eastern Pueblos, particularly Santo Domingo, and it characteristically includes strings of turquoise for necklaces and other pieces made of mosaics of turquoise. Although weaving and basketry were traditionally important, they have largely disappeared among these pueblos.

Western Pueblos. The Zuni and the Hopi were more isolated than the Eastern Pueblos and continued many of their traditions until the twentieth century. These Pueblos make polychrome ware, and Zuni pottery is distinguished by the motif of the deer with a red heart-line going from the mouth into the torso and the rosette design. Hopi pottery is made primarily on the First Mesa by Hopi-Tewa descendants, and it is noted for the flat, broad shape of its pots. Surface designs are geometric and in the twentieth century have largely followed the designs of the Sikytki revival pottery.

The Western Pueblos are most known for jewelry making. The Zunis do lapidary work and silversmithing, while the Hopis focus primarily on silver work. The Zunis are famous for carving fetishes in stone which are sometimes made into necklaces of turquoise, coral, and other stones. These fetishes depict bears, mountain lions, foxes, frogs, and owls among other animals. They also set turquoise and other fine stones in silver, sometimes in complex patterns called clusterwork, and they do stone inlay jewelry.

The Hopi make jewelry with overlay designs in silver, sometimes including stones. They are most known, however, for making kachina dolls, which are carved, painted, and dressed. The kachinas incorporate rain and cloud symbols and represent the hope for well-being and plenty, and they are used to teach children about the supernatural. The Hopi also do basketry and weaving.

Navajos and Apaches. Although the Eastern and Western Pueblos do weaving, the Navajos have most excelled in this media. The designs are primarily geometric and include stepped frets, crosses, and butterflies. There are complex patterns of repetition and contrasts of positive-negative fields. A number of regional styles exist throughout the Navajo area. Occasionally, the weaving incorporated designs from sand paintings, which have special ritual and healing significance. The Navajo are also famous for turquoise and silver jewelry, especially the squash blossom necklace. The wide range of Apache baskets includes trays, carrying baskets, and pitch-sealed water bottles. The designs include geometric and highly stylized figures.

—Ronald J. Duncan

See also Baskets and basketry; Navajo; Pottery; Pueblo tribes, Eastern; Pueblo tribes, Western; Weaving.

BIBLIOGRAPHY

Eaton, Linda B. *Native American Art of the Southwest.* Lincolnwood, Ill.: Publications International, 1993.

Furst, Peter T., and Jill L. Furst. *North American Indian Art.* New York: Rizzoli International, 1982.

Wade, Edwin L., ed. *The Arts of the North American Indian: Native Traditions in Evolution.* New York: Hudson Hills Press, 1986.

Whiteford, Andrew Hunter. *Southwestern Indian Baskets: Their History and Their Makers.* Santa Fe, N. Mex: School of American Research Press, 1988.

Wyckoff, Lydia L. *Designs and Factions: Politics, Religion, and Ceramics on the Hopi Third Mesa.* Albuquerque: University of New Mexico Press, 1990.

Arts and crafts—Subarctic

TRIBES AFFECTED: Beaver, Beothuk, Carrier, Cree, Dogrib, Han, Hare, Ingalik, Neskapi, Ojibwa, Ottawa, Sekani, Slave, Tahltan, Tanaina, Tsetsaut, Tutchone, Yellowknife

SIGNIFICANCE: Subarctic artisans were especially known for their quillwork and birchbark baskets

The arts and crafts of the Subarctic Indians included quillwork, beadwork, bags, birchbark baskets and boxes, and wood carving, but because of the sparse population and the demands of a hunting and gathering life, this work did not exist in quantity. Most of the arts and crafts from this area are known to be from the Algonquian-speaking tribes (Cree and Ojibwa) who occupied the eastern area and were influenced by the arts of the Northeast and Plains culture areas. Athapaskan-speaking tribes (Beaver, Han, Ingalik, Tahltan, Tanaina, Tutchone, and Sekani) occupied the western Subarctic and were influenced by the material culture of the neighboring Northwest Coast groups as well as the Aleuts and the Eskimos (Inuits).

Quillwork and Embroidery. Porcupine quillwork was particularly well developed among the eastern groups, and it was in wide use at the time of the earliest contact with the Europeans. Women used these techniques to decorate the surfaces of birchbark boxes, moccasins, decorate bands (such as wampum belts), and clothing. Designs were made by plaiting the quills in patterns that may have developed out of basketry techniques, and they were sewn to the surfaces.

Designs were primarily geometric and included diamonds, chevrons, parallel lines, crosses, crossbars, cross-hatching, step design, and the double-ended swirl. The sides and lids of boxes were frequently covered with overall decoration. For example, the side of a box could be covered with various parallel bands of quills and the top with concentric circles. The artists varied the density of the plaiting of the quills to make tightly packed patterns or open-weave patterns, which produced different textures.

Quillwork clothing decoration was also geometric. The Cree copied European-style officers' coats in buckskin, which reached the knees and were decorated with quills and paint. Elaborate designs were placed along the bottom edge and the front borders of the coat. Three or four bands of design were frequently used, and it sometimes took on the compositional look of Plains hide paintings, although there were no figures. The designs on coats tended to be bold and clearly visible from some distance, but the designs on moccasins were smaller, intricate, and tightly finished. The decorative bands and epaulets for coats were similarly more intimate in scale.

Eventually, embroidery and beads replaced quillwork on clothing. Moose-hair embroidery was common in earlier periods, and in the twentieth century women were still doing silk embroidery. The quillwork and embroidery from this area is known for its beauty of line and fine stitching.

Beads and Bags. The Ojibwa (or Chippewa) and the Ottawa developed a rich tradition of decorating shoulder bags, also called bandoleer bags. Early buckskin versions were commonly decorated in geometric patterns with quills, but stylized representations of mythological beings were also used. Later versions were beaded and made of cloth, and they incorporated floral patterns. Especially complex versions of these items were called "friendship bags," and they were worn by men as a demonstration of prestige. In the nineteenth century, floral designs were increasingly used, and floral and geometric designs were sometimes incorporated into the same bag. During this period, geometric designs were adapted to represent floral-like patterns. Fringe was frequently added to bags, and in some cases fringe flaps became narrow bands of pure geometric design.

Birchbark. Birchbark was used to make most containers for normal domestic use. Made by peeling birchbark, folding it into the form desired, and sewing it with spruce root, these containers were used as gathering and storage baskets. Since birchbark was both pliable and strong, it was even used to make canoes and houses. It was because of this material's adaptability that these tribes did not make pottery or many baskets. Birchbark designs could be made by scraping the outside layer of the bark, which was white, to reveal the brown layer beneath. Animal and plant figures from the area were normally shown on birchbark, and in keeping with the quillwork tradition, these figures were highly stylized.

Woodwork. Some Subarctic groups did wood carvings of small objects, such as knife handles and spoons, similar to those of the Northeast culture area. Human and animal figures were carved, and both were highly stylized. Simple sgraffito drawings were also done occasionally on wooden surfaces, showing stylized images from the natural worlds, geometric signs, and pictographs.   —*Ronald J. Duncan*

See also Baskets and basketry; Beads and beadwork; Quillwork; Subarctic.

Asah, Spencer (c. 1908, Carnegie, Okla.—May 5, 1954, Norman, Okla.): Painter

ALSO KNOWN AS: Lallo (Little Boy)

TRIBAL AFFILIATION: Kiowa

SIGNIFICANCE: Asah was one of a group of Kiowa artists who initiated the flat style of easel painting, or traditional American Indian painting

Spencer Asah was the son of a medicine man. He completed six years of schooling at Indian schools in the Anadarko area, including St. Patrick's Mission School. He, along with other Kiowa youths, joined Susan C. Peters' Fine Art Club. She was the Indian Service field matron stationed in Anadarko who, with the assistance of Willie Lane, gave the students formal instruction in the arts, including drawing, painting, and beadwork. Peters took Asah to the University of Oklahoma to explore the possibility of his receiving further art instruction. Asah, Jack Hokeah, Stephen Mopope, and Monroe Tsatoke began private lessons in painting in the fall of 1926 with Edith Mahier of the art department, using her office as a studio. They publicly performed dances to raise money for expenses. The four boys were joined by James Auchiah in the fall of 1927. This group is often known as the Kiowa Five; it is also referred to as the Kiowa Six when Lois Smoky, who came to the university in January of 1927, is included.

The Kiowa flat style that the Kiowa Six created was illustrative watercolor, with little or no background or foreground and with color filling in outlines, depicting masculine activities. Asah depicted recognizable people. The group's work was shown nationwide and at the 1928 First International Art Exhibition in Prague. Asah was hired to paint murals for various Oklahoma buildings during the Depression. Later he farmed. Asah fathered four children.

See also Art and artists, contemporary; Auchiah, James; Hokeah, Jack; Mopope, Stephen; Tsatoke, Monroe.

Assiniboine: Tribe

CULTURE AREA: Plains

LANGUAGE GROUP: Siouan

PRIMARY LOCATION: Alberta and Saskatchewan (Canada), Montana (U.S.)

POPULATION SIZE: 5,274 in U.S. (1990 U.S. Census); more than 3,000 in Canada

The Assiniboine (including groups sometimes called the Stoneys) lived in northeastern Montana, northwestern North Dakota, and adjacent Canada. They spoke a language of the Siouan language group, but their associations with the Sioux were generally antagonistic, as were their relations with the Blackfoot. They had a close and long-standing alliance with the Cree and became friendly with the Atsina after decades of fighting them. The Assiniboine were not important participants in the Plains Indian wars and were assigned to several reservations in Montana, Alberta, and Saskatchewan.

Early History and Traditional Lifestyle. The Assiniboine separated from the Sioux in the mid-seventeenth century while still living in the eastern woodlands. They moved into southern Ontario, where they became associated with the Cree. They trapped furs for Europeans and acted as intermediaries between western Indians and European traders until the establishment of trading posts on western rivers gave the traders direct access to those Indians.

With the westernmost members of the Cree, they moved into the northern Plains and took up buffalo hunting, at first on foot using dogs to bear their belongings on their treks across the Plains. Around the middle of the eighteenth century they obtained horses, and although they probably never had as many as other Plains Indians, the buffalo hunt and tribal movements in pursuit of the buffalo became easier and more efficient.

They followed the buffalo herds across the prairies and plains and obtained most of their food and material goods

An engraving of Assiniboines in traditional clothing. (Library of Congress)

from them. They lived in tipis of buffalo hides sewn together and stretched across a group of poles. Readily put up and taken down, the tipi was ideal housing for a mobile society. Men hunted, butchered their prey, defended the tribe in war and made weapons and shields. Women cooked; gathered seeds, fruits, and vegetative parts of plants; preserved foods for future use; made clothing and tipi covers; struck camp; and put up camp with each move. They gathered in large groups to hunt buffalo, and broke up into smaller groups for the winter.

The Assiniboine fought almost constantly with the Blackfoot, Crow, Sioux, and Atsina over buffalo ranges and horses. These wars, and diseases (especially smallpox and measles) introduced by Europeans, precipitated a decline in the Assiniboine population and in the tribe's ability to hold its territory. Around 1870, the Atsina-Blackfoot alliance disintegrated and the Assiniboine and Atsina became allies. This association may have been what enabled the two small tribes to resist constant Blackfoot and Sioux aggression.

Assiniboine ceremonial and spiritual life was typical of plains Indians. They held the Sun Dance, an elaborate spiritual ceremony lasting for days. Generally held when the tribe was gathered for the buffalo hunt, the Sun Dance was intended to assure a successful hunt; it was also used to invoke supernatural assistance in other undertakings, or to express gratitude for past assistance. Individuals went on vision quests, which involved days of fasting and praying in a secluded place, to obtain their personal "medicine" or source of power. The message, or inspiration, they received on the quest gave subsequent direction to their lives.

Men were organized into warrior societies, each with a particular responsibility in the life of the tribe. Men became eligible for membership as they accomplished feats of bravery, and practiced generosity. Chiefs were also chosen on the basis of these characteristics. While masks were not generally a part of Plains Indian ritual, members of the Assiniboine Fool Society (who mocked and acted contrary to societal standards to emphasize their importance) wore masks.

Transition and Contemporary Life. The Assiniboine contributed little resistance to the European American conquest of the Plains, in part because of the early interaction between Assiniboines and whites in the fur trade, as well as the reduced Assiniboine population because of disease and Indian warfare. They were placed on several reservations, representing a small fraction of the land over which they once hunted, in Montana, Alberta, and Saskatchewan.

Assiniboines face the poverty, unemployment, lack of education, and threats to their culture that other Indian groups face. Yet they have clung to their culture throughout government attempts at assimilation. One aspect of that culture in which they take particular pride, a willingness to assist one another in times of trouble or need, will be a great help in efforts to improve the tribe's condition and conserve Assiniboine culture.
—*Carl W. Hoagstrom*

See also Atsina; Cree; Indian-white relations—Canadian; Plains; Siouan language family.

Astronomy

Tribes affected: Pantribal

Significance: The ancient people of the Americas observed the heavens carefully, and many built structures for observing or measuring the movement of the sun and stars

Early Native American knowledge of the heavens ranged from the complex Mayan calendars to more simple markings of the solstices. Throughout North America, references to the sun, moon, stars, and planets occur in creation accounts and other cultural practices.

In Central America, the Mayan calendar influenced civilizations from 100 B.C.E. to the time of the Spanish Conquest (1519-1697). Guatemalan "daykeepers" still use the original astronomical system for divination. The four extant books, or codices, in the hieroglyphic Mayan language are almanacs. The Dresden Codex records the revolution of Venus. Mayans observed the solar year as well as lunar cycles and the movements of stars. The Mayan creation account, the *Popol Vuh*, includes references to the Pleiades, the Big Dipper, and Ursa Minor (Draco). The twin heroes of the Mayan creation story are associated with the sun and moon as well as with Venus.

In the northern plains of Canada and the United States, medicine wheels attest an ancient knowledge of astronomy. The prehistoric wheels are spoked circles outlined by stones, up to 60 yards in diameter. About fifty medicine wheels are known to exist, most of which are on the eastern slopes of the Rocky Mountains. The oldest medicine wheel, in Majorville, Alberta, dates to 4,500 years before the present, and it has a central cairn made of 50 tons of stones. Many medicine wheels mark sunrise points of equinoxes and solstices, while a few mark summer stars. The Bighorn Medicine Wheel in Wyoming has cairns that correspond to paths of Aldebaran, Rigel, and Sirius. These three stars rise a month apart during the summer.

In the Midwest, prehistoric mounds in the Mississippi and Ohio river valleys also reflect astronomical understanding. Hopewellian and Mississippian mounds are often in the shapes of animals or stepped temples, but the Marching Bear mounds in McGregor, Iowa, correspond to the stars in the Big Dipper. At Cahokia, Missouri, where 120 earthen mounds formed a large village, a circle of cedar posts marked sunrise solstices and the equinox. Archaeologists have nicknamed the reconstructed site Woodhenge, after Stonehenge.

Stars had sacred meanings to the Skidi Pawnee, who lived in the river valleys and plains of Nebraska. This band arranged their villages in the pattern of the North Star, evening star, and morning star. They arranged the posts of their earthen lodges in the same pattern, so each home repeated the cosmic arrangement. A painted hide at the Field Museum in Chicago records the Milky Way and many Pawnee constellations.

Ancient Anasazi sites in the Southwest still show the yearly cycle of the sun. A stone house at Hovenweep, Utah, has ports through which sunlight enters during the solstices and equinox. Stars were important to the nomadic Navajos. Their creation account describes how Black God made stars from crystals. He placed constellations in the sky, including First Big

One (Scorpio), Revolving Male (Ursa Major), Revolving Female (part of Ursa Minor), Slender First One (in Orion), Rabbit Tracks (near Canis Major), and the Pleiades. Star charts on cave roofs had ceremonial importance. —*Denise Low*

See also Cahokia; Mathematics; Maya; Medicine wheels; Mounds and mound builders.

Atakapa: Tribe

CULTURE AREA: Southeast
LANGUAGE GROUP: Atakapan
PRIMARY LOCATION: Southwestern Louisiana, southeastern Texas

The Atakapa lived in small groups scattered across southwest Louisiana and southeast Texas. Most of the Texas Atakapa were called Akokisa or Deadose by the Spanish.

According to Atakapa oral tradition, their ancestors were stranded in Texas after a great flood, and they later spread eastward. At the time of European contact, Atakapa subsistence depended on collecting wild plants and hunting (bison and deer) across the grasslands and swamps of southeast Texas and southwestern Louisiana. Unlike their neighbors to the east, such as the Chitimacha, the Atakapa did not depend on agriculture and had a less sedentary lifestyle. In common with other southeastern cultures, the Atakapa traded with neighboring peoples. Despite their contacts with the hierarchical societies of the Mississippi River, Atakapan sociopolitical organization was not stratified to the same degree. The seeming simplicity of their lifeways (hunting and gathering rather than farming and inhabiting permanent villages) meant that the European settlers recorded little information concerning them, and since their culture had vanished by the twentieth century, no other data were forthcoming.

The word *Atakapa* is Choctaw, meaning "people eater," and their cannibalistic reputation is upheld in the account of Simars de Belle-Isle, who was captured and enslaved by the Akokisa (the Atakapa on the Louisiana-Texas border) from 1719 to 1721.

The Louisiana Atakapa inhabited terrain deemed inappropriate for early European settlement, so they were initially spared the depredations suffered by other southeastern Native Americans. The Akokisa and Deadose of Texas were not so lucky. They were missionized in 1748-1749, from the San Ildefonso Mission in Texas. The combined influence of additional missions (begun during the middle to late eighteenth century) and an epidemic (1777-1778) resulted in the Akokisa and the Deadose no longer being mentioned in colonial records by the 1800's.

The Louisiana Atakapa were affected by European incursions dating from the mid-eighteenth century onward. The locations of several Louisiana Atakapa villages are recorded for the period 1760 to 1836, but afterward there are only scattered reports of Atakapa. In 1885, for example, two Atakapa speakers were living in the vicinity of Lake Charles, Louisiana. By the early twentieth century, the Atakapa had been absorbed into the European population or joined other Native American groups.

Atakapa lifeways and history are described in John R. Swanton's *The Indians of the Southeastern United States* (1946).

See also Atakapa language family; Southeast.

Atakapa language family

CULTURE AREA: Southeast
TRIBES AFFECTED: Atakapa, Akokisa

The Atakapan language group includes the Atakapa and the Akokisa (Orcoqisac in Spanish texts), closely related to the Opeloosa and the Bidai. The language areas in the early modern period (circa 1500 through 1840) existed along the western coast of the Gulf of Mexico, reaching from Vermillion Bayou to West Galveston Bay. The tribes occupied land along the Mermentou River, the Calcasieu River, the Sabine River, the Trinity River, and the Houston Bayou along the coast and as much as 100 miles inland. In the twentieth century, Atakapa has been a designate in the present parishes of St. Mary, Iberia, St. Martin, Lafayette, and Vermillion of Louisiana.

The principal villages of the Atakapa were situated on the Vermillion Bayou, the Mermentou River, the Calcasieu River, and the lower Sabine River. The Opeloosa village was situated at the location of the present town of Opelousa in Louisiana. The villages of the Akokisa existed on Galveston Bay, near the courses of the Trinity River and the Houston Bayou, as well as near Dollar Point and Shoal Point in present Texas City (across from Galveston) in Texas. The research of H. E. Bolton on Spanish missionary documents linked the Bidai language with that of the Akokisa.

The knowledge of these tribal languages rests almost entirely on the work of A. S. Gatschet of the Bureau of American Ethnology in the late nineteenth century. Besides the material collected by Gatschet, there exist the Akokisa word lists of the French sea captain Jean Berenger and the Atakapa word lists collected by Martin Duralde, the Spanish commandant at the Atakapa Post in 1802. The Akokisa of the late eighteenth century differed slightly from the Atakapa in the area of Lake Charles where the materials were collected in the early nineteenth century.

Atakapa makes frequent use of stems indicating certain general concepts (such as to sit, to go, to come, and to stand), accompanied by a single suffix. Verbalization of nouns is important to Atakapa. In fact, verbalization of all kinds of elements is accomplished with exceptional freedom. In the verb complexes, suffixes are more numerous than prefixes. The principal verb stem is placed near the beginning of the phrase. Plural forms and emphasis are constructed by simple duplication of the verb stem, as in *its* ("to wake"), *wicakitsitso* ("I wake someone repeatedly"); *kuts* ("red"), *kutskuts* ("red things"); and *ak* ("green"), *akak* ("very green or green things"). There are a few verb forms with distinct stems, singular and plural, such as *itol*, *iwil* ("to arrange, to put in order"); *kau*, *pix* ("to die"). The Atakapa numeral system is decimal.

Atakapa and Akokisa use both independent personal pronouns and pronominal affixes. Distinct independent pronouns are used in the first-person singular and the first-person plural, though the independent forms for the second and third persons of both numbers are closely related to the objective forms. The concept of self, as in myself, yourself, is represented by a separate word after the appropriate independent pronoun. Atakapa also employs reflexive affixes. The word "thing" is employed frequently in close connection with the verb so as to assume the appearance of an affix.

See also Atakapa.

Athapaskan language family

CULTURE AREAS: Southwest, Subarctic
TRIBES AFFECTED: Ahtna, Apache, Beaver, Han, Hare, Ingalik, Kaska, Koyukon, Kutchin, Nabesna, Navajo, Slave, Taina, Tanaina, Tuchone

The Athapaskan language family is spoken by a small number of people spread out over a very large area. The origins of this language group are obscure, since none of the tribes speaking Athapaskan languages had developed writing before the arrival of European settlers. There is some evidence, however, of a relationship to native languages spoken in Siberia.

The largest group of Athapaskans still speaking their original languages in modern times inhabit the interior of the Subarctic and Arctic areas. They speak about a dozen dialects, with great enough differences to make the languages mutually unintelligible in some cases, though neighboring tribes can communicate with no great difficulty. Along the Atlantic, Pacific, and Arctic coasts, however, the natives are mostly Eskimos and Aleuts, whose languages are not apparently related to the Athapaskan group in any way.

For reasons that have not been made clear, Athapaskan languages are also spoken by Apaches, Navajos, and related tribes in the Southwest of the United States. There is a large amount of territory between the Subarctic Athapaskan group and that of the Southwest where apparently unrelated languages are spoken. Along the west coast of southern Canada and the Northwest United States, for example, Northwest Coastal languages are spoken.

Athapaskan languages, though still spoken by some of the older members of the Arctic and Subarctic tribes and still used for traditional ceremonies, are rapidly losing ground to English. The major reason that these languages survived into the twentieth century is that the territory on which these people live was largely inaccessible before then, and Americans from outside Alaska showed little interest in the area until gold was discovered at the end of the nineteenth century. Late in the twentieth century, oil was discovered, and roads were built through the tundra. As a result, the old culture and languages are quickly being submerged.

See also Apache; Language families; Southwest; Subarctic.

Atlatl

TRIBES AFFECTED: Pantribal
SIGNIFICANCE: The atlatl was an ancient and widespread hunting and warfare weapon throughout the Americas

The term "atlatl," applied to many versions of the implement, is derived from Nahuatl, the language spoken by the Aztecs of sixteenth century central Mexico. Synonymous terms include spear thrower and dart thrower. Originating from Old World prototypes and brought to the New World by the earliest paleolithic inhabitants, it was gradually replaced by the bow and arrow as the preferred hunting weapon throughout the Americas by 1100 C.E., except in central Mexico, where the Aztecs still used it along with other weapons in the sixteenth century.

The atlatl was a straight or slightly curved wooden stick averaging 24 inches in length. One end was notched and wrapped with hide for a handle, and the opposite end bore a hook or barb. Different versions included loops for finger holes. While the user gripped the handle, the feathered end of a long dart or spear was mounted against the barb, and the dart was hurled overhand in slingshot fashion, significantly increasing its range and power. Small stones were sometimes attached to the atlatl as weights and balances to increase efficiency. In South America, Moche atlatls were elaborately decorated in painted and carved designs.

Atlatl imagery held great symbolic importance, particularly for warrior cults and hunting societies. Atlatls appear frequently in pre-Columbian paintings and in ceramics and relief sculpture from the United States, central and western Mexico, the Maya area, and Peru. In the American Southwest, atlatl depictions are common in rock art, and actual atlatls were frequently included in Anasazi burials. In the Eastern Woodlands, the atlatl weights, called banner stones, were frequently carved in the form of animals from brightly colored stone. Maya and central Mexican artists frequently depicted ruling elites proudly displaying atlatls as signs of military and social status.

See also Banner stones; Hunting and gathering; Lances and spears; Projectile points; Weapons.

Atotarho (fl. 1500's, present-day New York State): Sachem

ALSO KNOWN AS: Tadodaho (Snaky-Headed, or His House Blocks the Path)
TRIBAL AFFILIATION: Onondaga
SIGNIFICANCE: Atotarho was one of three central figures who established the Iroquois Confederacy

Atotarho is a historical figure for whom there is no historical record. Oral tradition stories hold that Atotarho was a brutal, evil sorcerer. These stories relate that Atotarho had snakes growing out of his head, that he was a cannibal, and that he was soothed by magical birds sent by Deganawida (the Peacemaker) and Hiawatha, the other two principal architects of the Iroquois Confederacy. It is probably true that he was a cannibal.

Atotarho was bitterly opposed to the formation of the confederacy. He insisted that certain conditions be met before the Onondagas would join. The Onondagas were to have fourteen chiefs on the council, the other nations only ten. It was also a condition that Atotarho be the ranking chief on the council—only he would have the right to summon the other nations. In addition, he demanded that no act of the council would be valid unless ratified by Onondagas.

A sketch depicting the snakes that oral tradition said grew from Atotarho's head. (Library of Congress)

The Onondagas were given the role of central fire-keepers of the confederacy, and to this day they retain not only that role but also the role of keepers of the wampum belt, which records and preserves the laws of the confederacy.

See also Deganawida; Hiawatha; Iroquois Confederacy.

BIBLIOGRAPHY

Wilson, Edmund. *Apologies to the Iroquois.* New York: Farrar, Straus, Cudahy, 1960.

Atsina: Tribe

CULTURE AREA: Plains
LANGUAGE GROUP: Algonquian
PRIMARY LOCATION: Montana
POPULATION SIZE: 2,848 (1990 U.S. Census)

The ethnological origins of the Atsina, or White Clay People, are mysterious. The Atsina, also known as the Gros Ventre, once belonged to an Algonquian parent tribe that included the Arapaho. Until the seventeenth century, the Arapaho-Atsina hunted, gathered, and perhaps planted near the Red River of Minnesota. In the late seventeenth or early eighteenth century, the Atsina broke off from the Arapaho and moved northward and westward to the Eagle Hills in Saskatchewan. There the Atsina probably subsisted by gathering and pedestrian buffalo hunting, although they evidently also planted tobacco. In the middle of the eighteenth century, the Atsina acquired horses

and became equestrian buffalo hunters. In the late eighteenth century, the Cree and Assiniboine pushed the Atsina from Saskatchewan southwest to the Upper Missouri River.

Like other Plains tribes, the Atsina alternately battled and allied with their neighbors. Atsina bands were often allied with the closely related Arapaho and the Algonquian-speaking tribes of the Blackfeet Confederacy. In 1861, however, the Atsina sought an alliance with their erstwhile enemies, the Crow. At some point in the mid-nineteenth century, the Atsina allied with their former enemies, the Assiniboine, to resist the encroachments of the Sioux into their hunting territory.

Atsina religion and social organization revolved around two medicine bundles containing the Flat Pipe and the Feathered Pipe. Stewardship of the bundles, which combined both religious and political authority, rotated among certain adult men every few years.

In the second half of the nineteenth century, the territory under the control of the Atsina steadily eroded. An executive order by President Ulysses Grant in 1873 established a large reservation for the Blackfoot, Assiniboine, and Atsina in northern Montana. In January, 1887, representatives of the federal government met with the Atsina and Assiniboine at the Fort Belknap Agency to negotiate the cession of most of the Indians' reserve. President Grover Cleveland signed the Fort Belknap agreement into law on May 1, 1888, reducing the

The Atsina Crazy Dance as photographed circa 1908 by Edward S. Curtis. (Library of Congress)

Atsina and Assiniboine to a shared reservation of approximately 600,000 acres. Despite the diminution of their territory, the Atsina and Assiniboine of the Fort Belknap Reservation won an important United States Supreme Court decision in the early twentieth century that became a landmark in American Indian law. On January 6, 1908, the Supreme Court ruled in *Winters v. United States* that the Indians of Fort Belknap Reservation, rather than nearby white settlers, had first rights to the contested water of the Milk River.

In 1934, Fort Belknap became the first reservation in the Plains to establish a government under the auspices of the Indian Reorganization Act. For the Atsina, reorganization had the unanticipated consequence of merging their reservation government with that of the Assiniboine. Economic conditions at Fort Belknap languished until the mid-1960's, when many Atsina were able to take advantage of federal War on Poverty programs. By 1980, Fort Belknap had the highest percentage of college graduates of any reservation of the northern Plains.

See also Algonquian language family; Arapaho; Assiniboine; Buffalo; Plains.

Atsugewi: Tribe

CULTURE AREA: California
LANGUAGE GROUP: Palaihnihan
PRIMARY LOCATION: Burney Valley and Mount Lassen, California

Prior to European contact, the Atsugewi were a socioeconomically stratified society, divided into two territorial groups: the Atsuge ("Pine Tree People"), most of whose population was confined to five main villages, and the Apwaruge ("Juniper Tree People"), who occupied more extensive territory. People lived in either bark or earth lodges, with the village being the principal autonomous political unit. Traditional forms of wealth could be acquired and accumulated by anyone willing to be industrious. Fish and acorns, the staple foods, were acquired and stored by elaborate technologies, particularly the leaching of tannic acid from acorns and horse chestnuts.

First contact with European Americans was in 1827 with Peter Skene Ogden. By the 1830's, the Hudson's Bay Company was trapping in the area and had established a trail from Klamath to Hat Creek, which provided access to prospectors entering the area in 1851. Conflict erupted with settlers, some of whom were killed at Fall River, which led to a punitive war by white volunteers. Some Atsugewi were removed to the Round Valley Reservation, and many participated shortly after in the Ghost Dance revival of 1890.

See also Acorns; California.

Auchiah, James (1906, Medicine Park, Okla. Territory—Dec. 28, 1974, Carnegie, Okla.): Artist

TRIBAL AFFILIATION Kiowa
SIGNIFICANCE: Auchiah was one of the Kiowa artists who created the Oklahoma style of Native American painting in the early to mid-twentieth century

Auchiah was a Kiowa and a grandson of Chief Satanta. He was an authority on Kiowa history and culture and also a leader of the Native American Church. He took noncredit art classes with the Kiowa Five group at the University of Oklahoma in 1927.

In 1930, Auchiah won an award at the Southwest States Indian Art Show in Santa Fe, New Mexico, which led to commissions to paint murals in a number of public buildings, including the Fort Sill Indian School, Muskogee Federal Building, Northeastern State University (Oklahoma), and St. Patrick's Mission School. The most important of his murals was a commission in Washington, D.C., for the Department of the Interior, in which the Bureau of Indian Affairs is located. This mural, which is 8 feet high and 50 feet long, represents the theme of the Harvest Dance.

Auchiah's work is included in public and private collections, including the National Museum of the American Indian (Smithsonian), University of Oklahoma Museum of Art, and the Castillo de San Marcos National Monument (Florida). He served in the U.S. Coast Guard during World War II and later worked for the U.S. Army Artillery and Missile Center Museum, Fort Sill, Oklahoma.

See also Art and artists, contemporary; Asah, Spencer; Hokeah, Jack; Mopope, Stephen; Tsatoke, Monroe.

Awa Tsireh (Feb. 1, 1898, San Ildefonso Pueblo, N.Mex.— Mar. 12, 1955, San Ildefonso Pueblo, N.Mex.): Artist, painter
ALSO KNOWN AS: Alfonso Roybal
TRIBAL AFFILIATION: San Ildefonso Pueblo
SIGNIFICANCE: Alfonso Roybal, who signed his paintings Awa Tsireh, gained widespread recognition as a painter during the 1920's and 1930's; his paintings are included in many major museum collections

As a child in San Ildefonso Pueblo, Awa Tsireh sometimes painted pottery made by his mother, Alfonsita Martínez. Even before attending San Ildefonso Day School, where he was given drawing materials, Tsireh made sketches of animals and ceremonial dances. After completing day school, he began painting watercolors with his uncle, Crescencio Martínez, who, in 1917, was commissioned by anthropologist Edgar Hewett to paint a series of depictions of ceremonies held at San Ildefonso.

Awa Tsireh's meticulously precise but sometimes whimsical paintings attracted the attention of Edgar Hewett and other influential art patrons in nearby Santa Fe. Hewett hired him to paint at the Museum of New Mexico; in 1920, Tsireh's work was included in exhibitions of Indian art at the Society of Independent Artists in New York and at the Arts Club of Chicago. In 1925, his paintings were exhibited in a one-man show at the Newberry Library in Chicago. In 1931, he won first prize at the opening of the Exposition of Indian Tribal Arts in New York, a show that went on to tour major cities in the United States and Europe.

Tsireh traveled frequently but made San Ildefonso his home for life. Around the time of his death, he was still painting and continued to be among the most popular of Pueblo painters.

See also Arts and crafts—Southwest; Martínez, Crescencio; Paints and painting.

Awatovi: Archaeological site
DATE: 1150-1700
LOCATION: Northeastern Arizona
CULTURES AFFECTED: Anasazi, Hopi

The ruins of Awatovi pueblo are spread over approximately 23 acres near the southwestern tip of Antelope Mesa, one of the easterly fingers of the great Black Mesa, in the Jeddito drainage of northeastern Arizona. Situated at an altitude of about 5,600 feet above sea level, it was the easternmost of the Hopi villages. Awatovi was initially founded during the Pueblo III period, at around 1150 C.E. It was continuously occupied until its violent and tragic destruction in 1700. Archaeological excavations were undertaken at the site beginning in 1935 under the direction of J. O. Brew of the Peabody Museum at Harvard University. These resulted in the excavation of several hundred rooms of the pueblo and a complete excavation of the mission complex at the site.

Awatovi was within the territory of the Western Anasazi and represented one of several villages along the southeasterly edge of Antelope Mesa. Pottery studies have revealed a wide variety of styles, and detailed analyses include a study of the distinctive "corrugated ware" by archaeologist James Gifford. Kivas at Awatovi have also yielded examples of late prehistoric mural paintings.

The pueblo's first European visitor is believed to have been Don Pedro de Tovar, who led the initial Spanish expedition into Hopi territory in 1540 under the service of Francisco Vásquez de Coronado. It was visited again in 1583 by Antonio de Espejo and eventually became the site of a Franciscan mission, called San Bernardo de Aguatubi. The mission period lasted from 1629 to the Pueblo Revolt of 1680, when the mission was destroyed.

The destruction of Awatovi in 1700 was precipitated by the activities of two Franciscan friars who reportedly converted and baptized several hundred Indians. This angered neighboring Hopi chiefs, who entered Awatovi when the friars left to seek military protection for the pueblo. Hopi warriors from other villages raided and burned the pueblo, killing many people and carrying off women and children. Archaeological investigations at the site confirmed the destruction of Awatovi, with evidence that individuals of both sexes and all ages had been violently mutilated and slaughtered. They also revealed evidence for the construction of a military barrack and stable complex, suggesting that the friars had intended to use Awatovi as a base for the reconversion of the Hopi.

See also Anasazi; Pueblo tribes, Western.

Aztalan: Archaeological site
DATE: 1100-1300
LOCATION: Jefferson County, Wisconsin
CULTURES AFFECTED: Mississippian, Oneota

Aztalan was a colony of Cahokia that flourished between 1100 and 1300 C.E. At its height the population reached around five hundred people, living within an area of 21 acres. The site was stockaded and encompassed houses, at least three platform mounds, and crop fields. Additional burial mounds were located beyond the palisades. Immigrants from the Mississippian tradition probably ascended the Mississippi, Rock, and Crawfish rivers to establish Aztalan on the banks of the Crawfish in Jefferson County, Wisconsin.

The site was initially described by Nathaniel Hyer in 1837. Hyer named it Aztalan because the pyramidal mounds resembled Aztec temple mounds. Excavations were done in 1919, 1920, and 1932 by S. A. Barrett and in 1949-1952 by the Wisconsin Archaeological Survey. Aztalan State Park opened in 1952 and features restored mounds and a partially restored stockade. Aztalan Museum is adjacent to the restoration.

Aztalan's inhabitants displayed the characteristic features of Middle Mississippian culture: agriculture, pottery, an extensive lithic complex, pyramidal mound building, burial mounds, fortification, trade, and a core Mississippian population. Apparently the colonists quickly fused with or adapted to the extant Woodland cultures surrounding Aztalan. Artifacts indicate that pottery styles were combined and lithic complexes were shared between formerly distinct cultures.

Warfare and trade were probable concomitants of Aztalan's existence. Evidence of cannibalism, violent deaths, the stockade, artifacts including copper, and burned houses and fortifications are indicative of this relationship, common to other Mississippian sites as well. A crematorium located on the northwest pyramid is consistent with Mississippian practice and contained eleven burials. There was considerable variety in the house styles, which may indicate sharing between two cultures but which is not an uncommon feature of Mississippian sites. The degree of trade is also difficult to assess. It is clear that the inhabitants of Aztalan were manufacturing more stone items than needed and that they were receiving other items from their Woodland neighbors.

Aztalan poses a number of problems. The site was considerably disturbed before excavations occurred. The coexistence of distinct cultural artifacts is difficult to interpret. It is not clear how long the site was occupied by the Mississippian colonists; it is also not possible to determine the sequence of occupation by previous or successor cultural traditions. Additional uninterpreted sites which seem to indicate coexistence of cultures or intermingling of cultures are scattered throughout southern and central Wisconsin.

Aztalan was vacated around 1300. Whether this abandonment was a result of war, natural disaster, or a constricting of Mississippian colonies cannot be determined. Aztalan stands, however, as evidence that the Middle Mississippians extended their influence and people widely.

See also Mississippian; Oneota; Prehistory—Northeast.

Aztec: Tribe

CULTURE AREA: Mesoamerica
LANGUAGE GROUP: Uto-Aztecan
PRIMARY LOCATION: Central Mexico

The Aztecs, or *Mexica* (Me-shee-ka) as they called themselves, became the most important tribe in Central Mexico and created a powerful empire that would last until the arrival of the Spanish in the early sixteenth century. The Aztec state disappeared, but the people and their culture left an important legacy; modern Mexicans refer to the founding of Tenochtitlán by the Aztecs in 1325—not the arrival of the Spanish—as the beginning of their nation. Moreover, more than a million people still speak Nahuatl, the Aztec language (a part of the Uto-Aztecan family).

Early History. Aztec origins are unclear. The people entered the Valley of Mexico in the thirteenth century from what is now northern Mexico, or perhaps Southwestern United States, from a land they called Aztalán, or Aztlán. They would later create an elaborate legend to describe how their principal god, Huitzilopochtli (the left-handed hummingbird), led them to a site where an eagle stood on a cactus with a serpent in its beak. This scene, pictured on the present-day flag of Mexico, marked the location of Tenochtitlán, capital city of the Aztecs and, today, Mexico City.

Archaeologists tell a simpler story, suggesting that the Aztecs were a relatively unimportant Chichimec tribe from the north that entered the Valley of Mexico looking for more fertile land. Many important cities already existed around the great lake in the valley, and the Aztecs became tributaries of a more powerful tribe, serving them as mercenaries. The city of Tenochtitlán was originally a muddy mound in the middle of the lake, where the tribe could find protection after antagonizing important Indian leaders. They flourished in their new home, and their city expanded.

Society. The Aztecs were divided into clans, or *Capulli*, each related by blood and engaging in a specific economic activity. The capulli were led by a council of elders, called the *Tlatocan*, who made the important decisions for the community. Though still under the domination of other tribes, the Aztecs chose Acamapichtli (who ruled from 1375 to 1395) as their leader. A new warrior class was created from these ruling families, known as the *Pipiltin*. When Acamapichtli died, his son became chief, beginning the Clan of the Eagle, a royal lineage that would last 125 years, until the defeat of the Aztecs by the Spanish.

Aztec nobles were priests, warriors, and judges. They were trained in a school called the *Calmécac*, where they learned discipline and special skills. Beneath the nobles in Aztec society were the merchants. Because they traded with distant lands, they were able to serve as spies for the expanding empire. Called *Pochteca*, these merchants amassed wealth but were denied the dress or status of nobility. Members of lesser groups could be put to death for wearing dress reserved for the nobility. Sandals, jewels, and feathered headdresses were the prerogative of the upper class.

Craftsmen formed a separate group in Aztec society. They worked with jade, gold, and feathers to make ceremonial costumes and jewelry. Commoners, the largest group, worked the fields, performed construction duties, and served the nobility. Their day began at dawn; rising from sleeping mats in small huts and wearing simple loincloths, they went out to work without any breakfast. At ten in the morning the first meal was taken, consisting of a simple bowl of porridge. The main meal was eaten at midday, during the hottest hours of the day. This meal consisted of maize cakes, beans, pimento, and tamales. Meat from turkeys or small game, routine fare for the upper classes, was rare among the commoners. Everyone would squat on a mat and eat quickly, drinking only water. This meal would often be the last of the day.

Nobles, by contrast, lived in larger homes and ate better meals. Their midday meal included meat and fruit as well as more common dishes made from corn. Nobles drank cocoa, at that time a bitter drink taken without sugar. Occasionally there were feasts that lasted most of the night at which pulque, a fermented alcoholic beverage, was consumed. The drug peyote was used, but only for religious ceremonies.

Religious Beliefs. The Aztecs believed that life was a struggle, and their religion was based on the need to appease the gods. They thought that the sun's journey across the sky would continue only if the gods were offered human sacrifice. The belief in human sacrifice was not unique to the Aztecs, but it became bound up with their expanding empire and came to dominate their society to a greater extent than in other tribes. In fact, much of Aztec culture, including their gods, was derived from earlier peoples of the Valley of Mexico. One aspect of this common culture was a calendar that combined the lunar and the solar years in fifty-two-year cycles. On the eve of the last year of the cycle, all the fires in the land were extinguished, symbolizing the people's fear that the world was about to end. Crowds gathered silently on the hillsides as priests climbed to the top of a mountain to await the hoped-for dawn. When the sun rose, and time did not end, a human sacrifice was conducted and a new fire kindled. The flame was used to relight fires throughout the land, and the people rejoiced. The Aztecs believed that only human sacrifice could save their society from destruction. They also believed that there had been four previous cycles of time, and that they were living in the fifth and final period.

Rise to Power. In the early 1400's the Aztecs, along with the people from the cities of Texcoco and Tlacopán, rebelled against the overlordship of Azapotzalco, the most powerful city in the Valley of Mexico. Once successful, the three cities formed a Triple Alliance to dominate the area around the great lake. The alliance was short-lived, however, and the Aztecs subdued the other tribes to emerge by 1440 as the greatest power in Central Mexico. At this time a shift occurred among the Aztecs that necessitated further expansion. In response to a number of natural disasters, Aztec priests claimed that additional sacrifices were needed to please the gods. Thus, the Aztecs began to combine wars of conquest with capture of warriors to be used as human sacrifices. Some estimates indicate that tens of thousands of sacrifices were conducted in

major ceremonies such as those marking the dedication of temples. Even after the Aztecs had conquered most of the tribes in Central Mexico they conducted ceremonial "Flower Wars," whose purpose was to take prisoners for sacrifice. For more than half a century the Aztecs ruled this expanding empire, facing much discontent among their subject peoples who were seldom integrated into Aztec society.

Conquest and Legacy. When Hernán Cortés arrived in 1519 he heard about the wealthy city of Tenochtitlán and the great lord Montezuma. Cortés, with a small group of Spanish soldiers and a growing number of Indian allies hoping to be freed from Aztec rule, entered Tenochtitlán, which he described as one of the largest and most beautiful cities he had ever seen. Undaunted by the power of the Aztecs, and fully aware that Montezuma thought him to be the god Quetzalcóatl returning from the East, Cortés took the Aztec leader prisoner and attempted to control his empire. An Aztec assault forced him out of Tenochtitlán, but Cortés returned with more Indian allies and destroyed the city in 1521. The last of the Aztec leaders, Cuauhtémoc, was taken prisoner by the Spanish.

Cortés chose the site of Tenochtitlán for his new capital, Mexico City. Although many Aztecs died in the assault or later perished from disease, their language and many of their customs remained to influence the development of Mexican society.
—*James A. Baer*

See also Ball game and courts; Chichimec; Codices; Mathematics; Pochteca; Tenochtitlán; Teotihuacán; Toltec; Tula.

BIBLIOGRAPHY

Caso, Alfonso. *The Aztecs: People of the Sun.* Translated by Lowell Dunham. Norman: University of Oklahoma Press, 1958. The focus is on Aztec religious beliefs. Recounts creation stories. Good color illustrations and plates. Lists gods of fire and gods of death.

Leon-Portilla, Miguel, ed. *The Broken Spears: The Aztec Account of the Conquest of Mexico.* Translated by Lysander Kemp. Expanded ed. Boston: Beacon Press, 1992. Offers an unusual account of the conquest by providing the background and events from an Aztec perspective.

Marrin, Albert. *Aztecs and Spaniards: Cortés and the Conquest of Mexico.* New York: Atheneum, 1986. A general history of the Spanish conquest that focuses on relations between Aztecs and Spaniards, especially Cortés and Montezuma.

Soustelle, Jacques. *Daily Life of the Aztecs on the Eve of the Spanish Conquest.* Translated by Patrick O'Brian. Stanford, Calif.: Stanford University Press, 1961. Presents much information on the society and beliefs of the Aztecs at their peak of power. Gives details about dress, food, housing, and commerce.

Townsend, Richard F. *The Aztecs.* London: Thames and Hudson, 1992. A general history of the Aztecs, with information on religious beliefs, families, and society. Good illustrations.

Bacon's Rebellion

DATE: July, 1675-September 1676
PLACE: Virginia, Maryland
TRIBES AFFECTED: Nanticoke, Pamunkey, Powhatan Confederacy, Susquehannock
SIGNIFICANCE: Bacon led attacks, conducted largely against peaceful tribes, that revealed English settlers' willingness to raid and destroy American Indian groups indiscriminately

Despite their dwindling numbers, some tribes in Virginia and Maryland in the 1670's were willing to contest further white expansion onto their land and to avenge wrongs committed against them by whites. When the Nanticoke tried to collect a debt from a Virginia planter, they set in motion a series of conflicts that escalated into Bacon's Rebellion.

In July, 1675, some Nanticokes, who lived just across the Potomac River in Maryland, crossed the river and attempted to steal Thomas Mathew's hogs to satisfy a debt. Some of Mathew's neighbors intercepted the Nanticokes and killed at least one of them. In retaliation, the Nanticokes killed Mathew's overseer, Robert Hen. Virginia militiamen responded by crossing into Maryland and killing at least twenty-four Nanticokes and Susquehannocks, the latter considered a friendly tribe by Virginia authorities.

In August, Virginia's governor, Sir William Berkeley, ordered two militia officers to investigate the episode. Instead, the two men joined with militia units from Maryland to form a one-thousand-man army, which marched on a Susquehannock fort. When five chiefs came out of the fort under a flag of truce to discuss the escalating conflict, the militiamen killed them and laid siege to the fort. After several weeks, the Susquehannock, near starvation, escaped at night, killing ten sleeping militiamen. In January, 1676, several Susquehannock raiding parties killed or captured thirty-six frontier settlers. They explained to the governor that the attacks were in revenge for the murder of their chiefs. In response to the attacks, Berkeley implemented a cautious defense, the construction of forts along the frontier, manned by a roving five-hundred-man army.

Angry frontiersmen, wanting a more aggressive approach, took matters into their own hands. Convincing a recent arrival in Virginia, Nathaniel Bacon, to take command, an army of planters and indentured servants set out on a war of revenge. The force led by Bacon slaughtered a peaceful tribe of Ocaneechi who had destroyed a Susquehannock encampment as a goodwill gesture toward the English. When Governor Berkeley declared him a rebel, Bacon marched on the capital at Jamestown and obtained a commission to lead his army by threatening the assembly.

In September, Bacon led his army against the peaceful Pamunkey tribe, killing eight and capturing forty-five when they tried to escape into the Great Dragon Swamp between the Rappahannock and Potomac rivers. When Governor Berkeley rescinded Bacon's commission, the rash commander marched on Jamestown, which he captured and burned. Bacon died at the height of his power on October 26, 1676, from dysentery.

Although Bacon and his men killed relatively few natives, the conflict demonstrated that the English settlers in the Chesapeake area were willing to attempt to exterminate any tribe, friendly or hostile. Beyond the devastating effects of European diseases, the native peoples in Virginia had suffered significant losses, particularly during the Powhatan Wars (1622-1646), in their confrontations with the English. Their population dropped steadily. At the conclusion of Bacon's Rebellion, there were fewer than three thousand natives in Virginia. Whether pushed to the margins of white settlement or employed as servants or day laborers, there were too few natives left in Virginia in 1677 to pose a threat to continued white expansion.

See also Nanticoke; Ocaneechi; Powhatan Confederacy; Powhatan Wars.

Bad Heart Bull, Amos (c. 1869, present-day Wyo.—1913): Tribal historian

ALSO KNOWN AS: Tatanka Cante Sica (Bad Heart Buffalo), Eagle Lance
TRIBAL AFFILIATION: Ite Sica band of Oglala Lakota (Sioux)
SIGNIFICANCE: Amos Bad Heart Bull kept an extensive pictographic history of the Oglala Lakota that spanned the last half of the nineteenth century and the beginning of the twentieth

Amos Bad Heart Bull was born into a noted Oglala family. His father, also called Bad Heart Bull, was a band historian who kept a historic record in pictographic form. His uncles, He Dog and Short Bull, and cousin Crazy Horse were noted warriors active in opposing United States encroachments on Lakota lands. Born about 1869 in the final years of the traditional Lakota lifestyle, Amos Bad Heart Bull was too young to take part in the Sioux Wars (1864-1876) but was present at many of the battles, particularly Little Bighorn. His father and older male relatives were prominent warriors in these battles.

From 1890 to 1891, Amos Bad Heart Bull served with his uncle Short Bull as a scout for the United States Army at Fort Robinson, Nebraska. During this time he purchased a ledger book from a clothing store owner in Crawford, Nebraska, and began to record the recent history of the Oglala Lakota in the traditional Plains art genre of pictography. Because his father was dead, Bad Heart Bull's primary informants for this work were his uncles Short Bull and He Dog. Bad Heart Bull's drawings convey an extensive narrative history of Oglala social and political history, religious ritual and ceremony, methods of warfare, and battles. This extensive record of over four hundred drawings is unique in its scope and in its intent to be a complete historic record. Artistically, Bad Heart Bull provided greater action, realism, and attention to detail than previous artists of this genre.

Amos Bad Heart Bull died in 1913, and his manuscript passed to his sister Dollie Pretty Cloud. In 1926, a graduate student at the University of Nebraska, Helen Blish, studied and photographed the manuscript in *A Pictographic History of the Oglala Sioux*. This photographic record is all that remains.

The original ledger was buried with Dollie Pretty Cloud in 1947 at her request.

See also Bozeman Trail wars; Indian-white relations—U.S., 1871-1933; Little Bighorn, Battle of the; Sioux; Sioux uprisings.

Ball game and courts

DATE: 500 B.C.E.-1200 C.E.
LOCATION: Mesoamerica
CULTURES AFFECTED: Aztec, Maya, Olmec, Toltec

The "ball game," or *tlachtli*, and the elaborate courts in which it was played constitute one of the most distinctive cultural phenomena of Mesoamerican cultures. The game had social, political, mythological, and religious significance. Originating with the Olmecs ("rubber people") of Veracruz, the ball game was played in every major center as far north as modern Arizona and south to Honduras. The Mayan center of Chichén Itzá had seven courts, including the largest in Mexico—480 by 120 feet.

The H-shaped ball court was enclosed by high vertical or sloping walls on which spectators sat to watch players attempting to knock a solid rubber ball into the vertical stone ring in the center, a rare event which immediately determined the winner. The heavy ball could not be touched with the hands or feet—only knees, elbows, and hips—so players wore protective gloves, knee pads, helmets, and a thick leather belt around their hips. *Tlachtli* was probably a fierce game; injuries, and even death, seem to have been fairly common. In spite of its violence, the game was played with great enthusiasm.

In their recreational games, players from the ruling class made huge bets of their valuable clothing, prized feathers, gold, and even slaves. With such passion for gambling, one could begin the game a rich man and end it a pauper. Also, winners and spectators could claim garments and adornments of their opponents, so feather capes and gold jewelry were often confiscated. Ritual games had even more serious results: death to the losers or, in some cases, the winners. In a culture preoccupied with death, this ultimate sacrifice was the highest tribute one could pay.

Mythological and religious meanings of the ball game were revealed during ritual play; the court represented earth, and the ball was the sun or moon. At the Mayan center of Copan, priests divined the future from results of ritual games. Among the Aztecs, chief deities were sky gods who constantly fought a battle between polarities of light and darkness, day and night. The sky was their sacred *tlachtli*, and a star was the ball.

Games were used symbolically to explain natural events. Drought and famine were supposedly the result of a legendary ball game between Huemac, last ruler of the Toltecs, and Tlaloc, the rain god. When Huemac won, Tlaloc offered corn as the prize, but Huemac refused it, demanding jade and feathers. Tlaloc gave them, telling Huemac that leaves of corn *were* precious green feathers and that green corn was more valuable than jade. Huemac got his jade and feathers, but the people starved because the corn would not grow.

Victory was sometimes fleeting, according to the story of Mexican emperor Axayacatl, who played against the lord of Xochimilco, betting his marketplace against this lord's elaborate garden. Axayacatl lost. The next day he sent his soldiers to the palace to honor the winning lord with presents. One gift was a garland of flowers which contained a rope. The soldiers placed it around Xochimilco's neck and strangled him.

See also Aztec; Chichén Itzá; Copan; Maya; Tenochtitlán; Teotihuacán.

Banks, Dennis (b. Apr. 12, 1937, Leech Lake, Minn.): Activist

TRIBAL AFFILIATION: Chippewa (Ojibwa)
SIGNIFICANCE: One of the founders and leaders of the American Indian Movement (AIM), Dennis Banks has drawn attention to the plight of contemporary Indians

Dennis Banks, born on the Leech Lake reservation in northern Minnesota, was one of the founders of the American Indian Movement (AIM) in 1968. During the summer of 1972, Banks and about fifty other native activists met in Denver to plan a Trail of Broken Treaties caravan. Their hope was to marshal thousands of protesters across the nation to march on Washington, D.C., dramatizing the issue of American Indian self-determination. Banks was also a principal leader of AIM in 1973 during the occupation of the hamlet Wounded Knee on the Pine Ridge Sioux Reservation.

Banks eluded capture during a Federal Bureau of Investigation (FBI) dragnet following the deaths of two agents at Pine Ridge in 1975. He went underground before receiving amnesty from Edmund G. Brown, Jr., governor of California. Banks earned an associate of arts degree at the University of California's Davis campus and, during the late 1970's, helped to found and direct Deganawidah-Quetzecoatl University, a native-controlled college.

After Brown's term as governor ended, Banks was sheltered in 1984 by the Onondagas on their reservation near Nedrow, New York. In 1984, he surrendered to face charges stemming from the 1970's in South Dakota. He served eighteen months in prison, after which he worked as a drug and alcohol counselor on the Pine Ridge Reservation. Banks remained active in Native American politics in the 1990's, although he was not as often in the national spotlight. He also had acting roles in several films, including *War Party, The Last of the Mohicans*, and *Thunderheart*.

See also Activism; American Indian Movement (AIM).

Banner stones

TRIBES AFFECTED: Prehistoric tribes of the Eastern Woodlands
SIGNIFICANCE: Banner stones were part of the technology for casting spears, though their beauty led early archaeologists to imagine them as emblems of chiefly office

Early archaeologists in eastern North America discovered a class of ground and polished stone artifacts that were unknown among historic American Indians. These "banner stones" varied widely in shape but shared several characteristics. They usually were made of visually appealing stone such as the banded slate of Hamilton County, Ohio, which was carefully ground and polished to a high luster. Averaging about 3 inches wide and 3 inches long, banner stones were always symmetrical and had a single hole passing through their length, about three-fourths of an inch in diameter. Sometimes found elsewhere, they often were found in graves.

Believing that their beauty had some meaning other than the technological, archaeologists invented the term "banner stone" to reflect their belief that they had been mounted on short handles and held as emblems of office by chiefs. That interpretation was abandoned in the twentieth century when unusual conditions preserved the wooden parts associated with banner stones. It then became obvious that they were spear-thrower ("atlatl") weights, designed to assist an individual in casting a spear with great power. Their primary period of use was between 1000 B.C.E. and 700 C.E.

See also Atlatl; Lances and spears.

Bannock: Tribe

CULTURE AREA: Great Basin
LANGUAGE GROUP: Uto-Aztecan
PRIMARY LOCATION: Fort Hall Reservation, southeastern Idaho
POPULATION SIZE: 218 (1990 U.S. Census)

The name "Bannock" derives from the tribe's Indian name, Banakwut. Originally a branch of the Northern Paiute tribe in southeast Oregon, they acquired horses in the eighteenth century and moved to Idaho.

The Bannock were closely allied with the Shoshone. They were primarily horsemen and ranged widely throughout Idaho, Montana, and Wyoming. Family units were organized into at least five larger bands. Each band was headed by a chief, who inherited his position through the male line subject to approval by band members. The Bannock traveled with the Shoshone to hunt buffalo, trade, or do battle against their common enemies, the Blackfoot—and sometimes the Crow and Nez Perce.

In the winter—and while traveling—the Bannock lived in buffalo-skin tipis, which they adorned with pictures of their personal exploits. In the summer they lived in dome-shaped grass-and-willow houses. The Bannock fished for salmon in the spring, gathered seed and roots in the summer, and communally hunted buffalo in the fall.

Their major ceremonies were four seasonal dances. The dead were buried with their heads pointed west, since souls were thought to journey west along the Milky Way to the land of the dead. Both men and women served as shamans responsible for healing illness, conducting ceremonies, and controlling the weather.

The California gold rush and opening of the Oregon Trail in the mid-nineteenth century brought hordes of whites through Bannock lands, with devastating results. Wagon trains destroyed their pastures and smallpox reduced their population

from about 2,000 to 500. The Bannock and Shoshone fought in vain to protect their way of life. Finally, in 1868, they signed the Fort Bridger Treaty, agreeing to relocate to the Fort Hall Reservation. Adverse conditions there and bitterness over their losses led them to revolt in 1878 (the Bannock War). The revolt was suppressed by 1880, and the Bannock returned to their 500,000-acre Fort Hall Reservation, where most live today with the Shoshone.

See also Bannock War; Datsolalee.

Bannock War

DATE: 1878
PLACE: Idaho, Oregon
TRIBES AFFECTED: Bannock, Paiute, Sheepeater, Umatilla
SIGNIFICANCE: The Bannock War ended a series of resistance efforts by the northern mountain tribes of the Idaho/Oregon/Wyoming area and resulted in permanent relocation to reservations

The Bannocks, a northern mountain branch of the Paiute language group, originally occupied the mountain areas of southern Idaho and northwestern Wyoming. In the 1850's they had accepted treaties that limited their area to southern Idaho. During the 1850's, raids by Bannock, Shoshone, Paiute, and others occurred often along the trails to Oregon and California. By the 1860 Pyramid Lake and 1863 Bear Paw campaigns and the victories of George Crook in the Snake War of 1866-1868, European Americans were in control of the area and the Bannock had peacefully begun drawing meager rations that amounted to two and a half cents per person per day. They supplemented this with their traditional hunting and gathering.

The 1877 escape attempt by their northern neighbors, the Nez Perce, caused considerable upset among the Bannock, but they did not join the resistance that year. The immediate cause of the Bannock War of 1878 was the issue of digging camas roots on the Camas Prairie, located about 90 miles southeast of Fort Boise. The right to dig camas roots had been guaranteed by earlier treaties, but hogs owned by white settlers were now eating many of the roots. In May, a Bannock wounded two whites, an event that led to the creation of a two-hundred-man war party under Buffalo Horn. This unit was defeated by Idaho volunteers, and Buffalo Horn was killed in June. The warriors moved to southeastern Oregon and joined Paiute from the Malheur Agency under the leadership of Chief Egan and medicine man Oyte. The regular army units from Fort Boise were mobilized under General Oliver O. Howard. A chase through southern Idaho and eastern Oregon ended with the defeat of the Indians at Birch Creek, Oregon, on July 8, 1878. Some of the Indians escaped to the Umatilla Agency near Pendleton, Oregon, where Chief Egan was killed by the Umatillas, and the rebels were betrayed and captured. Another smaller group of Bannock had escaped and were captured east of Yellowstone Park in September, 1878.

A subsidiary war developed with the smaller Sheepeater group in the extremely rugged Salmon River Mountains of central Idaho. The fifty warriors eluded the cavalry under

Captain Reuben Bernard and defeated another unit under Lieutenant Henry Catley, but persistent tracking forced their surrender in October of 1878.

The Paiute reservation at Malheur in southeastern Oregon was terminated and the Paiute prisoners were placed on the Yakima reservation in central Washington. The Bannock were held at various military posts for a time and then returned to their reservation on the Snake River in southern Idaho, where the Sheepeaters soon joined them. Except for some outbreaks by the Ute to the south, this ended the northern mountain Indian wars.

See also Bannock; Nez Perce; Oregon Trail; Paiute, Northern; Paiute, Southern; Umatilla.

Barboncito (c. 1820, Canyon de Chelly, present-day Ariz.—Mar. 16, 1871, Canyon de Chelly, present-day Ariz.): War chief, religious singer

ALSO KNOWN AS: Barbon, Bislahani (The Orator), Hastín Daagii (Man with Whiskers), Hozhooji Naata (Blessing Speaker)

TRIBAL AFFILIATION: Navajo

SIGNIFICANCE: Barboncito was a major war chief during the 1863-1866 Navajo War, and he signed the 1868 treaty establishing the Navajo Reservation

At the age of twenty-six, Barboncito agreed to terms of friendship with whites when he signed a treaty with the American representative to the New Mexico territory during the Mexican War. Barboncito came to the attention of American army officers when, in April of 1860, he joined forces with Manuelito on the attack of Fort Defiance. After the skirmish, Barboncito and his brother Delgadito tried to work for peace. During the campaign for "resettlement" to Bosque Redondo, in eastern New Mexico, however, the brothers defiantly rejoined Manuelito.

In 1864, Barboncito was captured and forced to resettle at the Bosque. Unbearable living conditions forced him and five hundred followers to escape. In November of 1866 he surrendered for the second time. In 1868, while signing the treaty establishing the Navajo Reservation, Barboncito eloquently articulated the desires of his people when he said, "We do not want to go to the right or left, but straight back to our country."

See also Delgadito; Manuelito; Navajo War.

Basketmaker: Prehistoric tradition

DATE: 1-750

LOCATION: Arizona, New Mexico, Utah, Colorado

CULTURES AFFECTED: Anasazi, Pueblo

The term "Basketmaker" is used to refer to pre-Pueblo ancestors of the Anasazi culture in the Four Corners region of the American Southwest. The name is based on archaeological sites in the region that lacked pottery but had evidence of the production of basketry, nets, and sandals. It was introduced as part of a nomenclature for prehistoric peoples at the first Pecos Conference (1927), organized by archaeologist Alfred V. Kidder. Basketmaker I (Early Basketmaker), a designation that has since been dropped, was proposed for a preagricultural stage that is now recognized as the Archaic period. Basketmaker II (Basketmaker) refers to a pre-pottery agricultural stage during which time the atlatl, or spear thrower, was introduced. Basketmaker III (Post-Basketmaker) refers to the earliest pottery-making village farmers, who lived in characteristic pit house dwellings. The Basketmaker stages were followed by the Pueblo I through IV periods, corresponding to the appearance and growth of agricultural villages with contiguous, aboveground rooms.

Among the differences between Basketmaker and Pueblo peoples was their physical appearance. Basketmaker peoples had longer skulls, while skulls of the Pueblo period were flattened. This was originally thought to indicate genetic differences between the earlier and later populations. Actually, however, these differences are attributable instead to the adoption of hard cradle boards and their resultant modification of cranial shape. A continuity in population from the Basketmaker through the Pueblo periods is now widely accepted, and together these are referred to as part of the Anasazi tradition.

Basketmaker II: 1-450 C.E. The Basketmaker II period is transitional between the nomadic hunting and gathering patterns of the late Archaic period and later sedentary lifeways. Villages were small and widely spaced, with circular pit houses that were deeper in the west than in the east. Natural caves and rock shelters were favored locations for campsites and burials. Food was often stored in caves, using large, jar-shaped pits excavated into the floors and bins made of stone slabs and mud.

The most characteristic trait of Basketmaker II occupations is the absence of pottery at all but a few sites. The principal containers were coiled baskets, nets, and fiber bags. The former included a wide variety of useful containers, including large trays for winnowing grain, conical baskets for collecting seeds, and a range of serving bowls. As noted above, the atlatl, or throwing stick, was utilized during Basketmaker II times. This device improved the leverage of spears tipped with projectile points, increasing the speed, distance, and accuracy with which a spear could be thrown. Flaked projectile points of this period are typically side- or corner-notched, and they were attached to spears with hardwood foreshafts. Ground stone tools represent a continuity of Archaic technology and included a variety of milling stones, with large, basin-shaped grinding slabs and manos (handstones) made from large cobbles. At some sites, trough-shaped metates approach shapes typical of later periods.

The Basketmaker II people were the first people in the Anasazi tradition to utilize agriculture, but wild plant foods and hunting resources remained a significant part of the diet. Among the plant foods collected by Basketmaker II peoples were grass seeds, chenopodium, amaranth, and piñon nuts. There is some evidence for the cultivation of maize and squash, although beans are reportedly absent at this time. The transition to agriculture may have occurred as a response to pressures on wild resources that resulted from growing populations, periods of environmental deterioration, or a combination of the two. Experimentation with cultivated species, farming, and food storage would have provided an adaptive advantage in the face of diminished resources. As these strategies became more efficient, especially with changes in environmental conditions, agricultural populations grew in size and complexity.

Basketmaker III: 450-750. By 450, there was a noticeable preference for settlement near well-watered soils, probably because of an increased reliance on agriculture. Sites are found in both alluvial valleys and upland regions such as mesa tops. With greater utilization of cultivated foods as opposed to wild resources, there was less concern for access to a diversity of natural regions. Sedentism led to an increase in the size and density of settlements. Although some sites consist only of isolated pit houses and hamlet clusters, some villages had more than fifty structures for estimated populations of more than two hundred people. There is evidence for communal construction activities, such as an encircling stockade found at the Gilliland site in southwestern Colorado, and the building of ceremonial structures.

The typical dwellings of Basketmaker III people were pit houses with either circular or rectangular plans and antechambers or large ventilator shafts. These were often augmented with auxiliary storage units, built of jacal (poles and mud) on stone slabs. At Mesa Verde (Colorado), pit houses contained banquettes, clay-lined central hearths, wing walls, and four-post roof supports. In general, the plans of Basketmaker III villages do not indicate any type of organized arrangement. Exceptionally large pit houses, however, have been interpreted as the precursors to great kivas, used for councils and sacred rituals.

The subsistence patterns of this period differ from those of the preceding one in their emphasis on the cultivation of maize, squash, and beans. There is evidence for the keeping and possible domestication of turkeys, which would have replaced meat from hunting activities as the latter became less frequent. Bows and arrows, indicated by the use of basal-notched projectile points, replaced atlatls as the favored hunting weapon. The technology for food processing was modified by the introduction of two-handed manos and an increase in the use of trough-shaped over slab metates. The crafts of twined woven bags, nets, sandals, and coiled basketry continued, but Basketmaker III peoples also made and used pottery containers. The most common vessels were jars and bowls of a plain gray ware, although vessels decorated with simple black designs on a white base also appear during this period. In southeastern Utah, orange pottery with red designs appears toward the end of this period. The adoption of pottery use and changes in ground stone tools have been interpreted as signalling an intensification in household labor that accompanied village sedentism and an increased reliance on agricultural products. —*John Hoopes*

See also Agriculture; Anasazi; Pit house; Pottery; Prehistory—Southwest; Pueblo tribes; Southwest.

BIBLIOGRAPHY

Glashow, Michael. "Changes in the Adaptations of Southwestern Basketmakers: A Systems Perspective." In *Contemporary Archaeology*, edited by Mark P. Leone. Carbondale: Southern Illinois University Press, 1972.

Guernsey, Samuel J., and Alfred V. Kidder. "Basket-maker Caves of Northeastern Arizona." In *Papers of the Peabody Museum in American Archaeology and Ethnology*. Vol. 8, No. 2. Cambridge, Mass.: The Museum, 1921.

Martin, Paul S. "The Hay Hollow Site, 200 B.C.-A.D. 200." *Field Museum of Natural History Bulletin* 38, no. 5 (1967): 6-10.

Morris, Earl H., and Robert F. Burgh. *Basket Maker II Sites near Durango, Colorado*. Carnegie Institution of Washington Publication 604. Washington, D.C.: Carnegie Institution of Washington, 1954.

Rohn, Arthur H. "A Stockaded Basketmaker III Village at Yellow Jacket, Colorado." *The Kiva* 40, no. 3 (1963): 113-119.

Baskets and basketry

TRIBES AFFECTED: Pantribal

SIGNIFICANCE: Baskets and basketry formed one of the most important utilitarian crafts throughout native North America, and in some areas they were also an important art form

Basketmaking is one of the most characteristic crafts of Native American groups, and it is a craft that is considered a woman's activity by most groups. Early Native American people made baskets for thousands of years before ceramics were developed. Basketry techniques were used primarily to make containers, but they were also used for making other objects, ranging from hair brushes to clothes and canoe-like boats. Some early pottery seems to have been shaped around baskets and then fired. Among the historic tribes, the basketry of the West is more widely known than that of the eastern tribes. What is known of basketry today comes primarily from the last two hundred years, and many of the eastern traditions had been lost or significantly acculturated by the late 1700's.

Techniques. Twining and plaiting are related early techniques, while coiling is a later development. Twining is a process similar to weaving in which warp and weft strands are interwoven in various patterns, while plaiting is a simple process of passing a warp and weft alternately over and under each other. In contrast, coiling involves wrapping fibers into coils and stitching them together. To do coiling, a basketmaker gathers a group of fibers, probably grass stems, and wraps them with another long grass stem or yucca fiber. She then wraps the coil in on itself to form a spiral which is stitched together; another bunch of fibers is added and wrapped to lengthen the coil, and so on until the basket is formed. Since the fibers that form the coils are wrapped, a wider range of materials can be adapted to coiling than is the case with twining, and this may be the reason for its popularity. Groups of coils can be stacked one on top of the other, and sometimes two are bunched side by side as they are stitched; this variation in technique is frequently associated with style differences.

Examples of Hupa basketry; the Hupas are a Northern California tribe. (Ben Klaffke)

Eastern Woodlands. Twining and plaiting were frequently used basket techniques in the East, and the basketry of this area was especially affected by the easy availability of wooden materials. Birchbark was popular for making basket-boxes among groups that lived across the northern sections of the United States in which the tree grew, and these baskets were frequently decorated with porcupine quills. The Micmac, Montaignais, Cree, and others worked with birchbark. Split-cane techniques were used by the Cherokee, Choctaw, and Chitimacha of the Southeast to make plaited baskets of wood splints, and this technique was borrowed by other tribes. The Cherokee were well known for baskets made of fine, even splints of cream, red, and black colors that were plaited to form interesting visual patterns. Along with more standard shapes, the Cherokee made an unusual shape in which a square base was transformed into a round, bowl-like upper half that was easy to carry as a burden basket.

Southwest. The best basketmakers of the Southwest have been the nomadic peoples living in arid, agriculturally marginal regions—the Apache, Paiute, Hualapai, Havasupai, Pima, and Tohono O'odham (Papago). The Navajo had stopped making baskets by the end of the nineteenth century and now buy baskets made in their own designs from the Paiute. Although the Pueblo peoples are basically pottery makers and produce little basketry, the Hopi are known for basketry. In the last half of the twentieth century the most successful basketmakers in this region have been the Tohono O'odham, San Juan Paiute, Havasupai, and Hopi.

Twining, plaiting, and coiling are all common basketmaking techniques in the Southwest, but the latter is used most frequently. The basket forms include the tray and open bowl shapes, deep bowl shapes, closed neck water bottles, conical burden baskets, and vase-shaped baskets. Designs are usually geometric or represent stylized figures. Recurring design motifs include petal designs, butterflies, star or cross, whirlwind, zig-zags, squash blossom, birds, and animal figures.

The most complex designs have been those of the Pima, and they use a complex layering of positive and negative images created by black and beige patterns. Although the Navajo have not been active in basketmaking since the nineteenth century, they are famous for the wedding basket design, which is a band of deep red lined with black triangles around the inside surface of a tray. The band is incomplete, so that a small opening or "door" is left. Traditional Apache baskets include elegant petal and zig-zag designs on open trays, but the most distinctive form is a large pot-shaped basket which may be 30 inches high and almost as broad in diameter.

Great Basin and Plateau. Basketry in this region was largely utilitarian, and it was used for a wide variety of purposes. Large burden baskets were made to be carried on the back for seeds, roots, and other gathered foodstuffs. Carrying bags were made by twining from grasses and other fibers. Winnowing trays and toasting trays were used in the preparation of food. Clothing, housing, and boats were also made using basketry techniques.

Pacific Coast. Some of the finest basketry in North America was produced in California by the Pomo, Tulare, Washo, and Karok. Baskets were made by both coiling and twining; the latter sometimes resulted in baskets of fine woven quality. They made trays, deep bowls, covered baskets, and vase forms and adorned special baskets with elaborate feather designs. The people of the Northwest Coast also made good baskets, but they were not equal to the complexity of their carved art.

—*Ronald J. Duncan*

See also Arts and crafts—California; Arts and crafts—Great Basin; Arts and crafts—Northeast; Arts and crafts—Plateau; Arts and crafts—Southeast; Arts and crafts—Southwest; Datsolalee.

BIBLIOGRAPHY

Boxberger, Daniel L., ed. *Native North Americans: An Ethnohistorical Approach.* Dubuque, Iowa: Kendall/Hunt, 1990.

Coe, Ralph T. *Sacred Circles: Two Thousand Years of North American Indian Art.* Kansas City, Mo.: Nelson Gallery Foundation, 1977.

Feder, Norman. *American Indian Art.* New York: Harry N. Abrams, 1965.

Furst, Peter T., and Jill L. Furst. *North American Indian Art.* New York: Rizzoli International, 1982.

Whiteford, Andrew Hunter. *Southwestern Indian Baskets: Their History and Their Makers.* Santa Fe, N.Mex.: School of American Research Press, 1988.

Bat Cave: Archaeological site

DATE: 4000-200 B.C.E.

LOCATION: New Mexico

CULTURES AFFECTED: Cochise culture, Desert culture

The site of Bat Cave, on the plains of San Agustin in southwestern New Mexico, has provided some of the most complete evidence for manifestations of the Cochise culture, a regional variant of the more widespread Desert culture of the Archaic period in western North America. Although the Cochise were primarily a hunting and gathering culture, carbonized floral samples from dry deposits in the cave have yielded remains of squash, beans, and maize. These provide valuable information about the origins of agriculture in the Southwest. Although the age of the earliest remains of maize at the site is the matter of some debate, these remains represent some of the earliest examples of this cultigen north of Mexico. Experimentation with maize cultivation by Cochise culture peoples is interpreted as representing early stages in the growth of agricultural practices that became the foundation of settled village life in the southwestern United States.

Archaeological remains at Bat Cave, excavated by archaeologist Herbert Dick, span a period of almost four thousand years. These include a series of projectile points together with abundant scrapers, blades, and other chipped stone tools. Ground and pecked implements include milling stones and manos for processing seeds and other plant foods. The dry environment of the cave created an ideal situation for the preservation of organic remains. Bone, horn, and shell were used to make punches, needles, scrapers, ornaments, and gaming pieces. Well-preserved basketry, both coiled and twilled, and three dozen fiber sandals were recovered. Other organic artifacts included squash and leather containers, eagle feathers wrapped in grass, arrow shafts, and fire-making tools.

Perhaps the most important evidence from Bat Cave was the large amount of remains from subsistence activities. Noncultivated plant remains included piñon nuts, juniper berries, yucca quids, walnuts, acorns, prickly pears, and various grasses and seeds. Abundant animal remains consisted of bison, mountain sheep, deer, antelope, elk, wolf, badger, porcupine, jackrabbit, cottontail, gophers, and rats.

The earliest maize at Bat Cave was reportedly found in the context of the Chiricahua phase (3000 to 1500 B.C.E.). Radiocarbon dates associated with the remains of maize are internally inconsistent; the site's excavator interpreted them as dating the appearance of this cultigen to around 3500 b.c.e. A more recent appraisal, however, concludes that the remains of cultigens at Bat Cave cannot be demonstrated to date any earlier than 500 B.C.E., appearing during the San Pedro phase (1500 to 200 B.C.E.). This does not alter the significance of Bat Cave maize as the earliest yet documented for the Southwest region, but it has a profound effect on how one interprets the introduction of this cultigen from its hearth of domestication in central Mexico and its relative importance during the late Archaic period.

The area in which Bat Cave is located was later the homeland of the Mogollon cultural tradition, which corresponds to the establishment of pottery-producing sedentary villages reliant on the rainfall cultivation of maize, squash, and other crops.

See also Archaic; Corn; Desert culture; Mogollon; Prehistory—southwest.

Bayogoula: Tribe

CULTURE AREA: Southeast
LANGUAGE GROUP: Muskogean
PRIMARY LOCATION: Alabama

The Bayogoula were largely dependent upon garden products, mainly maize, beans, squash, and different roots, berries, and nuts gathered by women. Men hunted, particularly for deer, and utilized various fishing technologies. The Bayogoula are known to have engaged in almost continual conflict with various neighboring tribes. In fact, oral history states that the Bayogoula nearly exterminated the Mugulasha people; later, the remaining Mugulasha deceived and massacred many of the Bayogoula.

The Bayogoula were probably first encountered by the explorer Pierre le Moyne Iberville in 1699. It is documented that the Houma inflicted considerable loss of life with a surprise attack upon the Bayogoula in 1700. The remaining Bayogoula were eventually removed to an area near New Orleans, but later they settled to the north between the Houma and Acolapissa tribes. There is debate as to the date, but probably by the early 1730's, the Bayogoula were decimated by a smallpox epidemic. The Bayogoula eventually merged with the Houma.

See also Muskogean language family; Southeast.

Beads and beadwork

TRIBES AFFECTED: Pantribal
SIGNIFICANCE: Beadwork is one of the most distinctive decorative techniques used among Native Americans for clothing and other objects of personal and ritual use

Beadwork was a popular decorative technique before the arrival of the Europeans, and beads were traditionally made of shell, stone, bone, teeth, hoofs, and seeds. These were used to make necklaces, pendants, fringes, belts, and ornaments on clothing. Quillwork, a related decorative technique, was used in a similar way. Today beads and beadwork normally refer to the glass beads of European origin.

Historical Background. Although glass beads were traded with Native Americans during the eighteenth century, little is known about beadwork from that time. The production of traditional beads was difficult and slow, since each one had to be shaped by hand and then hand drilled. The imported glass beads were preferred because of their color and reflectiveness. About 1800 a large-sized bead made in Venice became available, and beaded artifacts using this type of bead represent the oldest examples of beadwork in collections today. This bead was referred to as the "pony bead" because it was brought by traders on pony pack teams. These beads were one-eighth inch in diameter, and they came in white, sky blue, dark blue, light red, dark red, and beige. They were used to make bands of decoration for clothing, bags, cradles, and moccasins.

About 1840 the smaller "seed bead" that is used today became available; it, too, was made of Venetian glass. It was half the size of the earlier beads and permitted making more delicate designs. Since these beads were partly made by hand, they could be slightly irregular in size and shape. In the 1840's and 1850's they were used to make bands of decoration similar to those made with pony beads.

By 1860 beads were more commonly available, and their smaller size permitted the introduction of a new all-over pattern of beadwork. Indians beaded clothing, bags, horse trappings, and ceremonial objects, among other things. During this period Czechoslovakian (Bohemian) glass beads were introduced; they are darker and more bluish. By 1870 translucent beads had become available, and by the mid-1880's silver- and gold-colored beads were traded. French and British manufacturers also entered the trade, and a wide variety of colors and sizes were available. In the twentieth century the production of beadwork became much more commercialized. Japanese beads entered the market, as did inexpensive Japanese and Chinese reproductions of Native American designs.

Culture Areas. Beadwork has been done in most culture areas. The French fur traders introduced trade beads to the tribes of the Northeast Woodlands in the seventeenth century. The beadwork that was to become distinctive of this area displayed the foliate patterns of the Algonquian (Potawatomi, Sauk and Fox, Kickapoo) and Chippewa groups of the western Great Lakes region. The beadwork of the southeastern tribes (especially Creek and Seminole) is related to the floral patterns of the Northeast but is less ordered and symmetrical than that

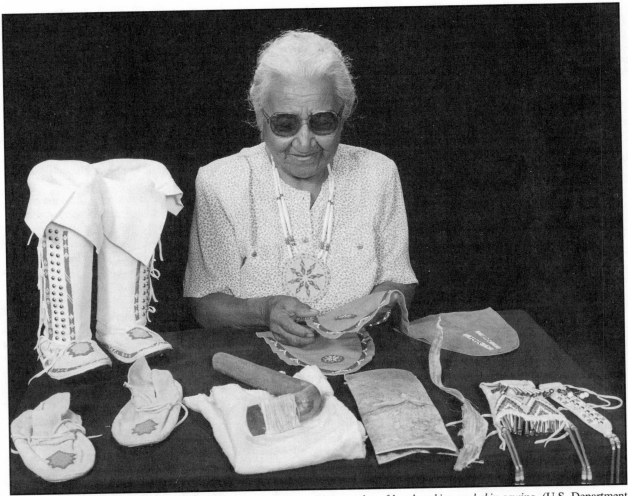

Alice Littleman, a Kiowa woman, demonstrating the northern Plains styles of beadworking and skin sewing. (U.S. Department of the Interior Indian Arts and Crafts Board)

of the north. Plains beadwork has the most complex, detailed patterns, some made with thousands of beads. There is a division between the northern Plains style, which tends to be conservative, and the bolder, more individualized Southern Plains style. Beadwork in the Southwest, Great Basin, and Plateau is usually done by tribes that have had contact with the Plains groups and have borrowed designs from them. In these latter three areas, beading tends to be limited to small-scale work.

Designs. Both geometric and floral designs are given names by the people who use them, and within each culture there is a repertoire of recognized design elements and full design patterns. The fact that the designs were given names has led many students of design to assume they also had symbolic significance. It seems, however, that a given design motif may have been used with a decorative intent by some beadworkers and with symbolic intent by others. Some foliate designs of the western Great Lakes region seem to have represented local flora, perhaps some used for medicinal purposes. Others may

have been copied from print designs on manufactured cloth or the designs of vestments of priests. The geometric motifs of the Plains have names that refer to the natural world, such as eye, buffalo, wolves, eagle, turtle, butterfly, centipede, person, and buffalo track.

Techniques. Beads may be embroidered onto a cloth or skin backing, woven to form a beaded band independent of the backing, or attached to fringes. Two basic embroidery stitches are used, the spot stitch and the lazy stitch. The spot, or overlay, stitch means that a beaded thread is attached to the backing by a second thread sewn in an over-and-under stitching pattern. In finely sewn work the overlapping stitch which holds the beaded thread to the backing may come every second, third, or fourth bead. This is especially used with floral designs and curving lines among the Chippewa, Algonquian, and some northern Plains groups.

In contrast, the lazy stitch is used more for overall designs that include straight lines and geometric patterns, and it is used more by the Western Sioux, Cheyenne, Arapaho, Crow, and

Kiowa. In this stitching pattern, the thread that carries the beads is itself stitched into the backing, with five or six beads added to the thread between each stitch.

Bead weaving is used to make headbands, armbands, legbands, or belts that do not have backing material. Band weaving is easier and faster than the stitching techniques, but it requires a weaving frame. The warp, or base threads, are wrapped onto the frame, and the weft with beads is woven into it. This technique lends itself best to straight-line geometric shapes; floral designs must be stylized to adapt to it.

—*Ronald J. Duncan*

See also Arts and crafts—Northeast; Arts and crafts—Plains; Dress and adornment; Quillwork.

BIBLIOGRAPHY

Coe, Ralph T. *Sacred Circles: Two Thousand Years of North American Indian Art.* Kansas City, Mo.: Nelson Gallery Foundation, 1977.

Furst, Peter T., and Jill L. Furst. *North American Indian Art.* New York: Rizzoli International, 1982.

Lyford, Carrie. *Quill and Beadwork of the Western Sioux.* Edited by Willard W. Beatty. Boulder, Colo.: Johnson, 1979.

Penney, David W. *Art of the American Indian Frontier.* Seattle: University of Washington Press, 1992.

Whiteford, Andrew Hunter. "The Origins of Great Lakes Beaded Bandolier Bags." *American Indian Art Magazine* 2, no. 3 (1986): 32-43.

Beans

TRIBES AFFECTED: Most agricultural tribes
SIGNIFICANCE: Beans were a significant source of nutrition for agricultural tribes in Mesoamerica, Peru, and North America

While fava beans and a few other bean species were domesticated in the Old World, most beans are American. Four major species were domesticated and used by Indians in pre-Columbian times. Common beans (*Phaseolus vulgaris*) are highly variable, including pinto, kidney, navy, black, and many other varieties. This bean was domesticated by 5000 B.C.E. in Mexico and was the most commonly used bean in most parts of the Americas; it was the only bean in most of North America. Tepary beans (*Phaseolus acutifolius*), a small species not used in modern commerce, were domesticated by 3000 B.C.E. in Mexico and used in the American Southwest and western Mexico. Lima beans (*Phaseolus lunatus*) were domesticated separately in Peru (3300 B.C.E.) and Central America (200 C.E.) and were used there and in Mexico. Runner beans (*Phaseolus coccineus*) were domesticated in Mexico by 200 B.C.E. and spread to Peru, Central America, and the American Southwest.

Beans were important for the nutrition of Indian agriculturalists, providing protein and lysine, a critical amino acid lacking in maize, the primary starchy staple. While diffusing to North America separately, beans, squash, and corn were grown together virtually everywhere that crops were cultivated.

Shucked and dried, beans could be stored for a full year and reconstituted by boiling, either with or without presoaking. Most tribes ate beans boiled and mashed, added to soups, or mixed with corn and other ingredients as succotash.

See also Acorns; Agriculture; Corn; Food preparation and cooking; Subsistence.

Bear Hunter (c. 1830, present-day Utah—Jan. 27, 1863, near present-day Preston, Idaho): War chief

ALSO KNOWN AS: Wairasuap, Bear Spirit
TRIBAL AFFILIATION: Shoshone
SIGNIFICANCE: War chief Bear Hunter was killed during the Bear River Campaign, which secured the Great Basin for white expansion

Located along the Bear River in southeastern Idaho, Bear Hunter's village was near the Great Salt Lake, which had become the focal point for Mormon expansion. The village was crossed by the Central Overland Mail Route and the Pony Express, each bearing stagecoaches carrying mail to California. Although some Shoshone leaders, including Washakie of the Wind River Shoshone and Tendoy of the Lemhi Shoshone, were friendly toward whites, Bear Hunter led his people in active resistance to white encroachment into the Great Basin.

Largely unimpeded by sparsely stationed federal troops during the early years of the Civil War, on several occasions Shoshone war parties attacked mail carriers and emigrants. In order to protect the telegraph lines and mail coaches, their only communication with the east, the Third California Infantry under Patrick E. Connor and a portion of the Second California Cavalry, a volunteer force of more than one hundred troops, traveled to Utah to reinforce federal troops at several forts.

In January, 1863, Connor led more than three hundred men 140 miles through deep snow from Fort Douglas north to Bear Hunter's village. Although Bear Hunter's people had fortified their village with barricades of rock, they were unable to defend themselves against Connor's superior manpower and arms. After four hours of relentless shelling, 224 Indians including Bear Hunter were killed and more than 150 women and children were taken captive. Following the Bear River Campaign, Indians were forced to cede most of their lands in the Great Basin.

See also Bear River Campaign; Tendoy; Washakie.

Bear River Campaign

DATE: 1863
PLACE: Idaho
TRIBE AFFECTED: Shoshone
SIGNIFICANCE: As did the Sand Creek Massacre, the Bear River Campaign exemplified the antagonistic nature of military leadership when state militias replaced federal troops in the West during the Civil War

With the Civil War, some twenty-five hundred federal troops under General Albert Sydney Johnston left Utah to fight in the East. Utah Territory, like the West in general at the time, was placed militarily under a volunteer state militia. The regarrisoning of Utah fell to the volatile California businessman and former Mexican-American War veteran, Colonel Patrick Edward Connor. Connor organized his California volunteers, numbering about a thousand, and marched them to Salt Lake City in 1862 to assume the task of policing the Overland Mail Route across Utah. Connor held even more contempt for American Indians than he did for the Mormons, and both experienced his fiery temper and decisive, vicious action. At one time Connor had a number of Indians hanged or shot, leaving their bodies exposed as an example.

At the time, the Shoshone and Bannock held a somewhat amicable relationship with the Mormon settlers, but occasionally they committed depredations on the Oregon and California trails as well as on the mail and telegraph routes—enough to cause Connor to muster his energies against them. Connor dispersed his forces throughout the region in an attempt to control the Indians, yet reports of belligerent activity continued. Incensed, Connor determined to deliver a decisive blow to the Shoshone and Bannock.

In the dead of winter, he marched a detachment of three hundred men, mostly cavalry, northward from Salt Lake City to attack the village of Shoshone leader Bear Hunter on the Bear River near Preston, Idaho. At daybreak on January 27, 1863, the Shoshone were in wait as Connor pressed his attack. About two-thirds of Connor's men forded the ice-choked Bear River and commenced a frontal assault on the village, but they met heavy resistance. Connor sent detachments to flank the village, thus trapping the Indians in the large ravine where they were wintering. As troops sealed off any escape routes, others swept over the rims of the ravine, pouring a murderous volley into the encampment. The Shoshone fought back desperately, having no alternative. Most were slain defending their positions. Others, who attempted to escape, were shot trying to swim the icy river. By mid-morning the fight was over.

Connor's troops counted 224 bodies, including that of Bear Hunter, though the death toll was higher. The troopers destroyed the village (seventy lodges), seized 175 ponies, and captured more than 150 women and children, who were then left in the razed village with a small store of food. Connor's losses were only 14 dead, 53 wounded, and 75 with frostbite. Connor's attack upon the village gained him the War Department's praise as well as quick promotion to brigadier general. Today the Bear River Campaign is perceived in much the same light as the Sand Creek Massacre, as an act of pointless, excessive bloodshed.

See also Bannock; Bear Hunter; Shoshone.

Bear's Heart, James (1851—Jan. 25, 1882, Darlington, Indian Territory): Warrior, artist

ALSO KNOWN AS: Nock-ko-ist

TRIBAL AFFILIATION: Cheyenne

SIGNIFICANCE: A prolific artist, James Bear's Heart combined Indian symbolism with formal Western techniques

Young James Bear's Heart was a noted warrior, having fought against the Utes, Texans, Mexicans, and U.S. Rangers. During the Red River War of 1875, he was accused of complicity in the murder of white settlers in Indian Territory and sent to the Fort Marion military prison in St. Augustine, Florida. He was confined for three years as a prisoner of war. While imprisoned, he participated in an educational and vocational program designed by U.S. Army Lieutenant Richard Henry Pratt. For their artistic pursuits, American Horse and fellow warriors Cohoe, Howling Wolf, and Zotom became known as the Florida Boys. Bear's Heart discovered a substantial market for his artwork.

After release from prison in 1878, Bear's Heart attended Virginia's Hampton Institute, where he converted to Christianity and adopted the name James. In 1881, Bear's Heart returned to Indian Territory, where he practiced carpentry, another skill learned under Pratt's tutelage while imprisoned. Bear's Heart died of tuberculosis in 1882.

See also Art and artists, contemporary; William Cohoe; Howling Wolf; Zotom.

Beaver: Tribe

CULTURE AREA: Subarctic

LANGUAGE GROUP: Athapaskan

PRIMARY LOCATION: Northeastern Alberta and northeastern British Columbia, Canada

POPULATION SIZE: 1,405 (Statistics Canada, based on 1991 census)

The Beaver lived as three composite bands along the Peace River; their fundamental socioeconomic unit was the bilaterally extended family group, which was dependent upon bison, woodland caribou, moose, beaver, and hares. Their worldview, associated behaviors, and socioeconomic activities emerged from this dependence upon game. Social control, kinship, and traditions were maintained through stories, vision quests, food and behavioral taboos, dreaming, consensus of opinion, and threats of sorcery.

The Beaver, after being forced from their aboriginal area by the Cree in the mid-eighteenth century, displaced the Sekani on the eastern slopes of the Rocky Mountains. In the nineteenth century, the Beaver became increasingly involved in fur trading, and were influenced by Catholic missionaries in 1845.

In 1900, treaties which established reserves were signed. By 1930, European American farmers had settled on most of the Beaver territory, and in 1942 construction of the Alaskan Highway further disrupted their lives. Most Beaver by the 1960's earned a living by guiding hunters and clearing brush for roads, pipelines, and powerlines. Although the number of Athapaskan-speaking Beaver has declined, some traditions remain viable.

See also Subarctic.

Beaver Wars

DATE: 1642-1685

PLACE: Northeastern woodlands, from the Hudson River west to the Great Lakes and from the Ohio River north to Ontario

TRIBES AFFECTED: Cayuga, Erie, Huron, Miami, Mohawk, Neutrals, Oneida, Onondaga, Ottawa, Petun, Seneca, Susquehannock

SIGNIFICANCE: The Beaver Wars involved the Five Nations (Iroquois) and their Algonquian neighbors; the Iroquois' objectives combined economic and demographic motives

Dates vary for when the Beaver Wars actually began. Some scholars say 1638, but a generally accepted date is 1642. In that year a Seneca war party that included warriors from other Iroquois nations attacked the Huron village of Arendaronon. At the same time, Mohawk and Oneida warriors began a systematic blockade of the St. Lawrence River, attempting to confiscate all furs being brought to Montreal and Quebec. By 1648 the Five Nations were concentrating their attacks on the Huron Confederacy. Scattering the Hurons, the Iroquois turned their attention to the Petuns (1650), the Neutrals (1651), and the Eries (1657).

Justification for the Wars. The Five Nations justified their attacks on the grounds of the traditional mourning war. By 1662, the Iroquois had pushed their attacks into Virginia and into New England. In this initial phase, Five Nations warriors sought three things: prisoners for either adoption or revenge, beaver pelts, and hunting rights to the vacated lands of their enemies. Initially successful in their pursuits, after 1685 the Five Nations found themselves on the defensive. Iroquois desires to replace lost members with captured prisoners for adoption seemed to override economic considerations.

Political Consequences. As for the Iroquois enemies, many Algonquian-speaking groups from the Great Lakes into the Ohio Valley migrated westward. These Algonquian refugees formed new, often heterogeneous, communities. These new refugee communities sought ties with strangers, often in the form of Algonquian kinship terms. One such relationship was with the French. It was this relationship that allowed the western Indians to turn the tide against the Five Nations at the end of the Beaver Wars.

Five Nations politics were transformed as the Beaver Wars continued. One such transformation concerned the creation of the "Covenant Chain" between 1675 and 1677. The chain referred to a diplomatic initiative between anti-French Iroquois headmen and the governor of New York, Edmund Andros. Andros and the Iroquois created the chain during the struggles of the Beaver Wars, Metacom's (King Philip's) War, and Bacon's Rebellion, and it simplified the complexities of Indian affairs for the English. It gave the Five Nations a preeminence among Indian peoples in dealings with the English. By 1680 the Mohawks had used this preeminence to become the dominant Indian power in eastern New York and colonial New England. For both groups it served an economic purpose: Iroquois traders had safe access to Albany. The original chain was an "iron" chain. The original chain was transformed into one of "silver" by the end of the Beaver Wars. Whatever the chain's material, the Five Nations covenant with New York allowed them to serve as the dominant Indian polity in future Anglo-Indian relations for nearly a century. It also

allowed New York to dominate the colonial side of Indian relations until the Seven Years' War.

The Beaver Wars altered traditional Iroquoian politics. By 1685 a new political structure was operating among the Five Nations. This new structure was the Iroquois Confederacy. The confederacy differed from the original "Iroquois League." For one thing, the confederacy's leadership was fluid. The confederacy dealt with external matters, while the league continued to operate as a "peace council" for internal matters. Three things account for the confederacy's development. First were the Europeans' decisions to "treat the Five Nations as . . . a single political entity." Second, debates between competing Iroquoian factions at the local level forced headmen to seek alliances outside their immediate community. Third, the loss of so many elders as a result of the wars and disease allowed younger leaders to shape a new political structure. The Iroquois Confederacy allowed historically independent communities to coordinate their strategy in dealing with foreign polities. This new confederation convinced English officials that the Five Nations Iroquois dominated the Indian polities in the interior of North America.

The Intertwining of War and Trade. The Beaver Wars illustrate how traditional native antagonisms became intertwined with the new European trade. The Iroquois attacked their traditional enemies and continued to perceive their actions within a traditional framework. Iroquois clans adopted prisoners to replace lost relatives, Iroquois hunters trapped on lands vacated by their enemies. Nevertheless, as hunters moved westward and northward, they inevitably came into contact with other hunters. Often the result was another conflict and the loss of warriors. This produced the need for more prisoners, which again led to conflict. The quest for furs, therefore, led to renewed conflicts to secure prisoners. In this manner the quest for prisoners and the fur trade become intertwined.

As the wars continued, various factions emerged among the Five Nations, often labeled Francophile, Anglophile, or neutralist. These factions tried to direct or redirect communities toward either the French or English, or away from both. These factions attempted to create opportunities for the Five Nations that would secure their objectives, rather than those of the Europeans. Nevertheless, the Beaver Wars produced a need for European goods and technology. The Five Nations were materially dependent on European goods when the Beaver Wars finally ended. Firearms had replaced bows and arrows. European missionaries competed for converts, and their efforts often split whole communities. For some converts, Christianity became a means for maintaining a separate identity despite new circumstances.

—*Michael J. Mullin*

See also Bacon's Rebellion; Huron; Iroquois Confederacy; King Philip's War.

BIBLIOGRAPHY

Hunt, George T. *The Wars of the Iroquois: A Study in Intertribal Trade Relations.* Madison: University of Wisconsin Press, 1940.

Richter, Daniel K. *The Ordeal of the Longhouse: The Peoples of the Iroquois League in the Era of European Colonization*. Chapel Hill: University of North Carolina Press, 1992.

Schlesier, Karl H. "Epidemics and Indian Middlemen: Rethinking the Wars of the Iroquois, 1609-1653." *Ethnohistory* 23, no. 2 (Spring, 1976): 129-145.

Trigger, Bruce G. *The Children of the Aataentsic: A History of the Huron People to 1660*. 2 vols. Montreal: McGill-Queen's University Press, 1976.

White, Richard. *The Middle Ground: Indians, Empires, and Republics in the Great Lakes Region, 1650-1815*. New York: Cambridge University Press, 1991.

Bella Bella: Tribe

CULTURE AREA: Northwest Coast
LANGUAGE GROUP: Wakashan (Heiltzuk dialect of Kwakiutl language)
PRIMARY LOCATION: British Columbia, Canada
POPULATION SIZE: 1,580 ("Heiltsuk," Statistics Canada, based on 1991 census)

The Bella Bella originally lived on Milbank Sound in British Columbia. They were divided into three subtribes, the Kokatik, Oeltik, and Oealitk, and three matrilineal clans, the Haihaiktenok (Killer Whale), Koetenok (Raven), and Wikoktenok (Eagle).

The Bella Bella were a Kwakiutl tribe, and their cultural and social lives were similar to those of other Kwakiutl tribes. Central to their social life were secret societies, potlatches, and a highly developed mythology featuring a folk hero named Raven and a creator god. The Bella Bella lived in villages. Their houses were made of cedar planks and decorated with totem poles and the crests of their clan. They subsisted primarily on salmon and other wild animals and plants; their primary means of transportation was the dugout canoe, which they used for fishing, warfare, travel, and trade.

During their early history the Bella Bella were a warlike tribe. They were flanked on either side by the Tsimshian and Bella Coola, and they had to contend with Haida war parties. It is believed that this constant threat of war was responsible for the founding of the secret societies, the most important of which originated in war customs.

Europeans eventually moved into the area, attracted by Milbank Sound, which provided one of the few good openings into the inner passage to Alaska. The effects of this contact with Europeans were similar to the dismal effects visited on other tribes in the area: decline in population from war casualties, disease, and confinement to reservations. Additionally, the Bella Bella were largely Christianized by Protestant missionaries, such that most of their ancient culture, customs, and mythology have been largely forgotten.

Today the Bella Bella live primarily on a 1,622-acre reserve. The remaining Bella Bella live on numerous small reserves, totalling 1,759 acres, in British Columbia.

See also Bella Coola; Kwakiutl; Northwest Coast; Tsimshian.

Bella Coola: Tribe

CULTURE AREA: Northwest Coast
LANGUAGE GROUP: Coast Salish
PRIMARY LOCATION: Bella Coola Valley, British Columbia
POPULATION SIZE: 980 (Statistics Canada, based on 1991 census)

The Bella Coola occupied approximately sixty permanent villages built of split/hewn rectangular cedar houses along the major rivers and streams in the narrow Bella Coola Valley; they intermarried and traded with the Carrier, Chilcotin, and Bella Bella. A wide variety of fish was their major source of food, supplemented by various animals—particularly the mountain goat, which provided food, horn, and wool that was woven into blankets and capes. Both sexes wore fur robes and capes of woven cedar or rabbitskin.

Kinship was based on lineal ascent, and social organization centered on the extended household. Marriage was usually monogamous, though polygynous households existed. Though Bella Coola society was divided into nobility, commoners, and slaves, social mobility was possible. Potlatches acknowledged change of status; they also served to redistribute goods and wealth and commemorate rites of passage. Each stage of life—birth, puberty, marriage, and death—called for a specific ritual. Status was gained through family affiliation, hunting skills, shamanism, oratory, and wealth—the latter counted in pleated red woodpecker scalp capes, obsidian blades, copper, dentalium, and slaves.

Captain George Vancouver first met and traded with the Bella Coola in 1793 while surveying. Alexander Mackenzie came overland, establishing the Hudson's Bay Company post in 1869. The Bella Coola invited a Methodist minister, the Reverend William Pierce, a mixed-blood Tsimshian, to establish a mission in Bella Coola. The people experienced drastic change with depopulation and disease, and by the 1900's their traditional hunting, gathering, and fishing way of life had changed to one dominated by commercial fishing and logging.

Musical recordings, legends, and records of older art forms have become important in the revitalization of past woodworking and weaving skills, singing, Indian rights, and a renaissance of traditional medicine and beliefs during the 1970's. In 1980 the Bella Coola Band Council, in establishing their sovereignty, referred to their people as the Nuxalk Nation.

See also Bella Bella; Carrier; Chilcotin.

Beothuk: Tribe

CULTURE AREA: Northeast/Subarctic
LANGUAGE GROUP: Algonquian
PRIMARY LOCATION: Newfoundland, Canada

The Beothuk lived in small villages in Newfoundland prior to the arrival of Europeans in the late 1500's. Each village consisted of three or four wigwams, cone-shaped houses made of sticks and birch bark, with a hole in the top to let out smoke. The Beothuk slept in trenches dug in the floor around a fireplace for cooking. They fished for salmon and hunted seal, birds, and caribou; they also gathered eggs, roots, and berries.

The meat and fish were frozen or smoked for winter consumption. Little is known of where the Beothuk originated or of their history before contact with whites.

Their customs are known only through reports made by early missionaries. They had twenty-four-hour wedding ceremonies with much dancing and feasting. The men conducted purification ceremonies in dome-shaped sweatlodges. Inside the skin-covered huts were hot rocks and water to make steam. Individuals would enter for a while, then run out to jump in the snow, believing that this would cleanse their bodies of evil. Tribal members dressed in caribou-skin robes, with leggings, mittens, and fur hats for winter. They sewed together birch and spruce bark for dishes, buckets, and cooking pots. The Beothuk buried their dead with their weapons and tools and small, carved wooden figures probably representing a god or goddess, but little is known about Beothuk religion. They placed the deceased in a wooden box and carried the body to a cave, setting it aboveground on a small scaffold.

English explorers made first European contact with the Beothuk and called them "red men" because they covered their bodies and hair with a reddish powder to repel insects. By the early 1700's, French fur-trappers from Labrador began trading with the Beothuk. Conflict with the Micmac who were also trapping furs for the Europeans, erupted into warfare and many deaths. By 1800, the Beothuk—who probably never numbered more than five hundred—were almost wiped out because of war, disease, and starvation. A few survivors migrated to Labrador, where they were absorbed into the Montagnais.

See also Beothuk language; Micmac; Montagnais; Northeast; Subarctic.

Beothuk language

CULTURE AREA: Northeast/Subarctic
TRIBE AFFECTED: Beothuk

The Beothuk language was spoken by the Beothuk people of Newfoundland. It apparently was an isolate (having no demonstrable ties to other known languages), although a relationship to the Algonquian family has been suggested by some, notably linguist John Hewson. Others argue that the language has no readily apparent links to Algonquian and that, if it is related, the relationship is quite ancient.

The language became extinct before linguists began the careful study of American Indian languages. The last speaker of Beothuk, whose name was Shananditti (also spelled Shanawdithi), died in the mid-nineteenth century, perhaps in 1829. From Shananditti, James P. Hawley compiled a vocabulary list which is the primary source of information on Beothuk. About four hundred items from the Beothuk language were collected from Shananditti and three other sources (mostly captive Beothuks), but no standard orthography can be compiled because of the relatively poor quality of the lists. In general, study of the Beothuks and their language has been hampered by the group's very early contact with Europeans and the disruption and depopulation that resulted.

See also Beothuk; Northeast; Subarctic.

Beringia

DATE: Late Pleistocene epoch, 25,000-12,000 B.C.E.
LOCATION: Arctic Circle, North Atlantic, region between Siberia and Alaska
CULTURES AFFECTED: All

Beringia is the name given to a land bridge that once existed in the region now known as the Bering Strait. It was periodically exposed toward the end of Pleistocene epoch, when water deposited through precipitation on the polar ice caps resulted in a lowering of global sea levels as much as 400 feet below what they are now. With the rise in global temperatures that occurred around 12,000 years ago, Beringia was submerged as sea levels rose.

Only about 60 miles separate Asia and North America in the Bering Strait today. At the time Beringia existed, the land between them was continuous. The land bridge at its maximum extent would have measured more than 600 miles wide from north to south, representing an expanse of territory indistinguishable from the areas of Siberia and Alaska it connected.

Warmed by the Japanese Current, Beringia had a tundra-like climate. It was occupied by migratory herds of Pleistocene animals, including woolly mammoth, bison, and reindeer. These animals provided food and clothing for nomadic peoples of northeast Asia, who were drawn to the hunting grounds of Beringia. Over time, these peoples moved east and south into the North American continent, where they became the ancestors of American Indian populations.

The Asian ancestry of American Indians is supported by dental patterns, blood group markers, and other physical and genetic characteristics which indicate that American Indians are more similar to Asians than to any other human populations. The wide diversity of indigenous physical types and languages found throughout the Americas resulted from the wide dispersion of the descendants of the original migrants. Cultural similarities between widely separated native populations of the Americas may be attributed to their ancient common origins.

Conflicting evidence has led to wide disagreement about the timing and number of migrations across Beringia, which may have occurred as early as 28,000 years ago or as late as 11,000 years ago. The vast majority of radiocarbon dates from secure archaeological contexts in the Americas favor migration dates in the latter half of this range.

See also Archaic; Migrations; Paleo-Indian.

Big Bear (1825, near Fort Carlton in present-day Saskatchewan, Canada—1888, near Fort Pitt, present-day Pittsburgh): Chief

ALSO KNOWN AS: Mistahimaskwa
TRIBAL AFFILIATION: Cree
SIGNIFICANCE: Big Bear was a war chief during the Second Riel Rebellion of 1885

At a council of two thousand Indians in 1876, Big Bear denounced the newly formed Canadian government for dishonesty and urged armed resistance. He joined Louis Riel, Jr., leader of the Metis uprisings against white encroachment. The Metis were people of mixed French, Scottish, and Indian ancestry whose land and trade rights had been guaranteed after the First Riel Rebellion. Unremitting white encroachment, particularly during the construction of the Canadian Pacific Railway, precipitated a second rebellion.

Big Bear's warriors raided a settlement at Frog Lake on April 2, 1885. Although Big Bear attempted to prohibit violence, there were several white mortalities, provoking retaliation by Canadian Mounties. On May 28, Big Bear's group was attacked near Fort Pitt, escaped, and was relentlessly pursued northward, where they were attacked at Lake Loon. On June 18, Big Bear released several white prisoners, who bore his request for mercy to the commander at Fort Pitt. He surrendered on July 2 and was sentenced to three years' imprisonment. He died while imprisoned.

See also Poundmaker; Riel, Louis, Jr.; Riel Rebellions; Treaties and agreements in Canada.

Big Bow (c. 1830—c. 1900): Chief
ALSO KNOWN AS: Zipkoheta
TRIBAL AFFILIATION: Kiowa
SIGNIFICANCE: During the Central Plains Indian wars, Big Bow was the most militant Kiowa chief and the last to surrender to reservation settlement

Big Bow's parentage and heritage are unknown. He gained an early reputation as one of the most hostile and violent Indian war chiefs after killing and scalping countless whites. With Big Tree, Satanta, Satank, and Lone Wolf, he fought settlers in Texas, Kansas, and Oklahoma.

Big Bow refused to honor the Treaty of Medicine Lodge (1867), which assigned Indians to two reservations in southern Kansas and which was endorsed by leaders of the Arapaho, Kiowa, Comanche, and Kiowa-Apache (Apache of Oklahoma). Instead, he continued attacking settlers and battling U.S. troops. After an aggressive U.S. Army campaign to subdue the Kiowa in 1870-1871, Big Bow was the last major war chief to capitulate. In 1874, he joined the Comanches in the Red River War. Later in 1874, at the urging of the peace leader, Kicking Bull, he moved his people to the reservation. Subsequently he was granted amnesty and served as an army Indian scout.

See also Big Tree; Lone Wolf; Red River War; Satanta.

Big Foot (c. 1825—Dec. 29, 1890, S.Dak.): Tribal chief
ALSO KNOWN AS: Si Tanka, Spotted Elk
TRIBAL AFFILIATION: Minneconjou Sioux
SIGNIFICANCE: Big Foot was the leader of the band of nearly two hundred men, women, and children who were killed by the U.S. Seventh Cavalry at Wounded Knee Creek, South Dakota, on December 29, 1890

Big Foot is primarily remembered as a central figure in the 1890 massacre at Wounded Knee Creek. Born around 1825, he became a tribal leader upon the death of his father in 1874. Shortly after the Sioux wars of 1876, he began farming and was one of the first Sioux to raise corn. In the year 1889, however, conditions for the Sioux became nearly intolerable, with failed crops and threats from the U.S. government to take over much of the remaining Sioux land. Into this situation came the hope offered by the Ghost Dance of the prophet Wovoka. The Ghost Dance was among the things that struck fear into white settlers in the area.

A resolution by the citizens of Chadron, Nebraska, in November, 1890, requested that the secretary of war order all Sioux in the area be disarmed and deprived of their horses (Chadron is on the border with South Dakota). The Sioux people of the Pine Ridge, Rosebud, and Standing Rock reservations frequently visited the town. The suggestion of the Chadron citizens' committee initiated a chain of events that included the murder of Sitting Bull by reservation police, the flight of his people to Big Foot's camp, and the tragic massacre of Sioux under the leadership of Big Foot by the U.S. Seventh Cavalry at Wounded Knee Creek, South Dakota, on December 29, 1890.

Many have tried to decipher what happened that day. Most accounts agree that Big Foot was dying of pneumonia. One thing is certain: In the confusion of the military chain guard that surrounded the Sioux council that day, military gunfire took the lives of nearly two hundred Sioux men, women, and children. Twenty-five soldiers died as well—many of whom fell in the crossfire, killed by comrades. The inscribed monument erected at Wounded Knee Cemetery by survivor Joseph Horn Cloud bears the names of 185 Indian people killed that day. Other estimates, however, have placed the number at three hundred or higher.

See also Ghost Dance; Wounded Knee Massacre.

Big Tree (c. 1847, Tex.—Nov. 13, 1929, Fort Sill, present-day Okla.): War chief
ALSO KNOWN AS: Adoltay, Adouette
TRIBAL AFFILIATION: Kiowa
SIGNIFICANCE: Big Tree ambushed General William Tecumseh Sherman's wagon train as it was en route to Fort Sill, Texas, during the Kiowa raids

As a young Kiowa war chief, Big Tree raided soldiers and settlers in present-day Texas. After ambushing William Tecumseh Sherman's wagon train on May 18, 1871, chiefs Big Tree, Satanta, and Satank were arrested for murdering seven white men. Satank was killed while attempting escape; Big Tree and Satanta were tried and sentenced to die. Leaders of the Kiowa militants, as well as of the peace faction, protested their sentence. During negotiations in Washington, D.C., Lone Wolf negotiated the men's prison release subject to their agreeing to remain in Texas. After violating their parole during a hunting trip to Kansas, Big Tree was imprisoned at Fort Sill, Texas; Satanta committed suicide. Following his release in 1875, Big Tree married Omboke, a Kiowa woman, and settled peacefully on the Kiowa reservation, where he farmed and ran a supply train between Kansas and Texas. After converting to Christianity, he became a Baptist deacon and Sunday school teacher.

See also Fort Atkinson, Treaty of; Kicking Bird; Kiowa; Satanta.

Big Warrior (?—Mar. 8, 1825, Washington, D.C.): Tribal chief

ALSO KNOWN AS: Tustennugee Thlucco
TRIBAL AFFILIATION: Creek
SIGNIFICANCE: Big Warrior's decision to fight on the American side in the Creek War of 1813-1814 contributed to the defeat of the Red Sticks

Of Shawnee ancestry, by 1802 Big Warrior had become principal chief of the important Upper Creek town of Tukhabahchee. In 1811, as a religious revival and resentment at white encroachments swept through Indian country, Big Warrior hosted the Shawnee pan-Indian leader Tecumseh at Tukhabahchee. Many thought that he would join the anti-American Red Stick faction. In 1812, however, his warriors carried out the order of the Creek National Council to punish Creeks who had attacked white settlers. This helped to bring on a Creek civil war, in which Big Warrior became a target of the Red Sticks. Tukhabahchee was besieged, but Big Warrior was able to escape and fight on the American side of the Creek War.

Big Warrior signed the Treaty of Fort Jackson in 1814. He was angered, however, at the American demand for a large land cession that penalized friendly Creeks as severely as Red Sticks. Opposing further land cessions, he died in Washington in 1825 while arguing against ratification of the Treaty of Indian Springs.

See also Creek; Creek War; McIntosh, William; Tecumseh; Weatherford, William.

Biloxi: Tribe

CULTURE AREA: Southeast
LANGUAGE GROUP: Siouan
PRIMARY LOCATION: Louisiana, Mississippi

French explorers first encountered a Biloxi village on the Pascagoula River about 1700. The Biloxi at that time were one of only two groups in the area that spoke a language from the Siouan linguistic family; the other was the Ofo. Both probably migrated from the Ohio River valley. The name Biloxi was a corruption of their own word for "first people"; others wrote it as "Moctobi."

The French observed that the Biloxi village contained thirty to forty cabins and was surrounded by a palisade that was 8 feet in height. Security was enhanced by the presence of three square watchtowers. During the French occupation, there were no more than five hundred Biloxi at any time, and they usually lived between the Pearl River on the west and the Pascagoula on the east, though there was an abortive attempt by the French to settle them closer to New Orleans.

The culture exhibited by the Biloxi fascinated the French. They were organized by clans with animal names, and kinship was traced through the mother. Chiefs were assumed to have religious as well as secular power, and after death their bodies were dried before a fire and stored in a temple with the remains of their predecessors. The Biloxi were adept at making pottery and weaving baskets, and their adornment included feather headdresses, tattoos, nose rings and earrings of bone, and necklaces of bone and bird beaks. One of their more enduring rituals proved to be stickball, which was abolished in the twentieth century because of the gambling associated with it.

After the French lost the area east of the Mississippi River in 1763, the Biloxi moved to Louisiana, together with other Indians from the Gulf Coast. Many Biloxi joined the Tunica and Choctaw Indians there, while some moved to Texas and the Indian Territory and blended with other groups. In 1975, the state of Louisiana officially recognized the Biloxi-Tunica tribe. At that time, there were about two dozen people who claimed Biloxi ancestry.

See also Choctaw; Southeast; Tattoos and Tattooing; Tunica.

Birchbark

TRIBES AFFECTED: Tribes throughout the Northeast and Great Lakes areas
SIGNIFICANCE: Birchbark served a wide variety of purposes for the northeastern and boreal Indians, from roofing material to the covering of canoes

The image of figures gliding silently along a river in a birchbark canoe, as depicted in thousands of stories and films, is one of the most common images people throughout the world have of American Indians. Indeed, in the Northeast and Great Lakes regions, birchbark canoes were widely used both for personal travel and for transporting goods. The canoes were made by first fashioning a framework of cedar, comprising the keel and the ribs; over this framework, sheets of birchbark, stripped from the trees in seven-foot-long sheets, were stretched tight and bound together with cordage made from the inner bark of the basswood tree. Pitch from evergreens was used to caulk the seams to make the canoe water-tight.

Birchbark canoes were highly maneuverable, though it took some skill to navigate them. Because they were so light in weight, a single person could carry one over a portage. They were so ideal for use in northern waters that they were adopted by the French fur traders for use throughout Canada.

Birchbark was also used to cover the tipis of the Algonquian tribes. Four basic framing poles were connected together, and additional "leaner" poles were positioned around them. The whole was covered with sheets of birchbark. Among the tribes that constructed longhouses, birchbark was used, along with elm bark, for the roofing material.

Birchbark was used by northeastern Indians to make a wide variety of containers. Before pottery, cooking pots were made of birchbark. The contents were heated by dropping hot stones into the mixture. Birchbark containers were used by many tribes as tubs to hold dried food to be set aside for use during the winter; sometimes these tubs were buried in underground pits to protect the contents from freezing. The Indians of Maine used small birchbark pouches to carry tobacco; drinking cups were also made of birchbark.

The Iroquois were in the habit of steeping birchbark in boiling water to make a popular drink with medicinal qualities. Birchbark could be fashioned into a kind of whistle that served as a moose caller. It was also used to make floats for fishnets. The Indians of the northern Great Lakes region used birchbark to make fans. These were used to winnow the wild rice they harvested from the swamps. Feathers were attached to the sheets of bark to stir the air. A personal fan could be made by attaching a stick, as a handle, to a piece of birchbark.

In order to ensure a steady supply of birchbark, the Indians would have needed to clear areas and burn the brush, for the birch is a shade-intolerant tree and will only grow in the open sunlight. It is, however, able to tolerate soils that have modest nutritional capabilities. The fact that the Indians could make such great use of birchbark says much about their environmental management. The range of the paper birch extends from the Atlantic Ocean to the Great Bear Lake in western Canada.

See also Boats and watercraft; Fish and fishing; Northeast; Wigwam; Wild rice.

Black Drink

TRIBES AFFECTED: Southeast tribes
SIGNIFICANCE: Black Drink was the main ceremonial beverage of Southeastern Indian tribes

Black Drink was a ritual beverage consumed by many Southeast tribes before and during important occasions such as certain council meetings. It was called "Black Drink" by the Europeans because of its color, but Indians called it "White Drink," referring to its purity and medicinal properties. Consuming the drink purified men of any pollution, made them hospitable, and served as "symbolic social cement."

Black Drink was made of holly leaves and twigs gathered along the Atlantic and Gulf coasts. Inland tribes traded for the holly plants and transplanted them. Some tribes, for example the Seminole, combined the holly with other medicinal herbs. To prepare Black Drink, the holly plant was dried and roasted in earthen pots to a parched brown. The roasted leaves and twigs were then boiled in water until the liquid was dark brown. It then was strained and generally consumed hot and fresh.

Black Drink was a stimulant, with one cup containing as much caffeine as eighteen to twenty-four cups of coffee. It was also a diuretic and brought on profuse sweating. If an important man in the tribe died, friends would consume Black Drink for eight successive mornings. A practice of the Timucuans was to consume large quantities and after about fifteen minutes cross their hands on their chests and vomit six to eight feet. The Chickasaw would place a little Black Drink into their ceremonial fire to provide social purification for all present.

See also Chickasaw; Southeast; Timucua.

Black Elk (c. 1866, S.Dak.—Aug. 17, 1950, near Manderson, S.Dak.): Holy man

ALSO KNOWN AS: Hehaka Sapa
TRIBAL AFFILIATION: Lakota (Sioux)

SIGNIFICANCE: Black Elk, one of the greatest of Lakota holy men, witnessed and described many of the most important events of nineteenth century Lakota history

At the time of Black Elk's birth, the Lakota and other Indian peoples were already suffering from the encroachment into their territory by European Americans. In spite of the constant threat of conflict between the U.S. Army and the Indians, Black Elk lived in traditional Lakota fashion until he became a young adult. His was the last generation to live in that way.

When he was about five years old, Black Elk had a vision in which two men came down from the clouds, "headfirst like arrows slanting down." There was thunder that sounded like drumming, and the two men sang a song, telling Black Elk, "A sacred voice is calling you." Black Elk did not know what to make of his vision, and he was afraid to tell anyone what had happened. From that point on, however, he could hear and see things that no one else could perceive. He sometimes heard voices; he had the feeling that the voices wanted him to do something, but he did not know what.

When he was nine years old, Black Elk had a great vision that was to shape his life for many years. The vision was long and complex; it is described in detail in *Black Elk Speaks* (1961), by John Neihardt. In the vision, Black Elk was summoned by the six grandfathers: the powers of the four directions, of the sky, and of the earth. Black Elk was made to understand that he was being given abilities that would enable him to help the Lakota people in times of trouble. He still did not know what to do, however, and it was not until he was seventeen that he began to put what he had learned in his vision into practice.

Black Elk became a warrior by 1876, and he fought in the famous Battle of the Little Bighorn, which is called the Battle of the Greasy Grass by the Lakota, during which General George Armstrong Custer and all his troops were killed. Custer had moved, on June 25, 1876, to attack the camps of Crazy Horse (Black Elk's second cousin) and his followers, but the Indians far outnumbered Custer's troops, and they responded quickly and effectively to Custer's attack. Black Elk's account of the battle, as given by John Neihardt in *Black Elk Speaks*, is one of the most important descriptions of that famous event.

On September 5, 1877, Crazy Horse was arrested and taken to Fort Robinson, where he was murdered when he refused to enter a jail cell. With his death, serious resistance to the U.S. Army ended. It was clear that the traditional Lakota way of life was coming to an end, but Black Elk's family stayed away from the Indian agencies that had been set up by the U.S. government and lived as they always had.

It was during this period that Black Elk told another holy man of his great vision and learned that the vision had to be performed as a dance by the Lakota people. A horse dance based on his vision was performed when Black Elk was about seventeen. Other visions and dances followed, and Black Elk began to work as a healer, using the understanding that had come to him in his visions.

In 1886, Black Elk joined the performing troupe organized by Buffalo Bill Cody. He traveled to England, France, and Germany, where he hoped to learn more about the ways of white people in order to help the Lakotas. Once, he performed for Queen Victoria of England, who impressed him as a good woman.

When he returned to South Dakota in 1889, Black Elk continued to work as a healer. He was frustrated, however, because he believed that he had not lived up to the requirements that his vision had made of him. He was convinced that he had been given the opportunity to save his people but that he had not been strong enough to do so.

On December 29, 1890, a band of 250 to 350 Indians led by the Minneconjou chief Big Foot was massacred by troops commanded by Colonel James W. Forsyth. Black Elk witnessed and fought in this one-sided engagement, which marked the end of the traditional way of life for the Lakota and the other tribes in the area, who from that point on lived as they were told to by the U.S. government.

In 1904, when Black Elk was attempting to heal a sick boy, he was interrupted by a Catholic priest, Father Lindebner, who had baptized the boy. Lindebner caught the healer by the neck and said, "Satan, get out!" The priest gave the boy Communion and prayed with him, after which he took Black Elk to the Holy Rosary Mission, where he gave him clothing and religious instruction. Black Elk stayed there for two weeks, and on December 6, 1904, he willingly accepted the Catholic faith.

For the next forty-five years, Black Elk was a devout Catholic. He did his best to convert other Lakotas and to encourage them to live virtuous lives, although he respected those who adhered to traditional Lakota belief. He was most disturbed by those people who had no belief of any kind. Until the end of his life, Black Elk served as a catechist, assisting the priests and teaching Catholicism.

Black Elk died on August 17, 1950, apparently of old age. He had told Joseph Epes Brown, "You will know when I am dying, because there will be a great display of some sort in the sky." Indeed, after his wake, a spectacular phenomenon was observed in the night sky. The Jesuit brother William Siehr, who attended the wake, described it as follows: "There were different formations in the sky that night which, to me, looked like spires, like tremendous points going up—then flashes. And it seemed like they were almost like fireworks in between. It was something like when a flare goes off in the sky—some sparkle here and there, but spread over such a vast area. And it was not just momentary. We all seemed to wonder at the immensity of it."
—*Shawn Woodyard*

See also Little Bighorn, Battle of the; Religious specialists; Sioux.

BIBLIOGRAPHY

Brown, Joseph Epes, ed. *The Sacred Pipe: Black Elk's Account of the Seven Rites of the Oglala Sioux*. Baltimore: Penguin Books, 1971.

DeMallie, Raymond. *The Sixth Grandfather: Black Elk's Teachings Given to John G. Neihardt*. Lincoln: University of Nebraska Press, 1984.

Neihardt, John G. *Black Elk Speaks: Being the Life Story of a Holy Man of the Oglala Sioux*. Lincoln: University of Nebraska Press, 1961.

Powers, William K. *Oglala Religion*. Lincoln: University of Nebraska Press, 1975.

Steltenkamp, Michael F. *Black Elk: Holy Man of the Oglala*. Norman: University of Oklahoma Press, 1993.

Black Hawk (c. 1767, near present-day Rock Island, Ill.— Oct. 3, 1838, near Iowaville, Iowa): War chief

ALSO KNOWN AS: Makataimeshekiakiak

TRIBAL AFFILIATION: Sauk

SIGNIFICANCE: Black Hawk led a band of Sauk and Fox against the Americans in an attempt to regain their traditional village sites along the Rock River in Illinois; the destruction of his band marked the end of armed Indian resistance in the Old Northwest

Black Hawk was born near the mouth of the Rock River in Illinois. He took his name early in life, after realizing that his guardian spirit would be the sparrow hawk. Little is known about Black Hawk's early life. He earned his right to be considered a warrior at the age of fifteen; after demonstrating his valor, he joined his father in a war against the Osages. It was during this war that Black Hawk killed and scalped the first of his opponents. By the time he reached his mid-thirties, Black Hawk was recognized as one of the most able war chiefs of the Sauk nation.

Black Hawk's hostility toward European Americans began in 1804, when a party of five Sauk and Fox leaders journeyed to St. Louis to negotiate the release of a Sauk brave accused of murder. Governor William Henry Harrison of the Indiana Territory took advantage of the situation. After encouraging the Indian leaders to drink heavily, Harrison managed to get their signatures on a treaty under which the two tribes ceded all their land east of the Mississippi River. Most of the money promised to the delegation was used to pay for the whiskey they drank. The Sauk and Fox were permitted to use the ceded land until American settlers moved into the region.

When the Sauk and Fox delegation returned to their homeland, they told their people little about the treaty. Upon learning of the terms the following year, more than 150 natives went to St. Louis to protest that the chiefs sent to the city the previous year had no power to sell land.

Inspired by the anti-American message of Tecumseh, Black Hawk led an attack on Fort Madison in 1811. When the War of 1812 began, Black Hawk assembled more than two hundred Sauk and Fox warriors and led them to Green Bay in order to fight alongside the British.

During the War of 1812, Black Hawk and his warriors fought with distinction in Tecumseh's Indian army. The Sauk warriors participated in the battles of the Raisin River, Fort Meigs, and Fort Stephenson. During Black Hawk's absence, many Sauk moved west of the Mississippi in order to seek the protection of the United States. Those who remained at Saukenuk, east of the river, chose Keokuk as their new war

An 1836 drawing of Sauk leader Black Hawk. (Library of Congress)

chief. When Black Hawk and his warriors returned to their homes in 1814, they were surprised by the election of Keokuk.

In spite of Keokuk's new position, it was Black Hawk who rallied the Indians of the region in their efforts to turn back two American invasion forces. Black Hawk was stunned to learn of the Treaty of Ghent. For a time, the Sauk warrior continued his personal war against the Americans. Both Black Hawk and Keokuk traveled to St. Louis with a delegation of civil chiefs in May 1816. The civil chiefs signed a document reaffirming the Treaty of 1804.

By the 1820's, the United States government was placing an increased amount of pressure on the Sauk to abandon their Rock River villages and move west. Keokuk urged cooperation with the Americans, but Black Hawk protested the increasing encroachment by pioneer settlers.

When the Sauk returned from their winter hunt in the spring of 1829, they discovered that white families had established themselves in Saukenuk. Most of the Sauk decided to move to new homes along the Iowa River. Black Hawk refused to abandon his village, and his followers took up residence in lodgehouses not occupied by white families. Black Hawk's band returned again in the spring of 1830.

When the British returned to Saukenuk in the spring of 1831, Illinois governor John Reynolds called out the militia. After a futile meeting between General Edmund Gaines and Black Hawk, the militia army destroyed Saukenuk. Black Hawk's people escaped across the Mississippi. Black Hawk was forced to sign a promise never to return.

Inspired by White Cloud, a Winnebago prophet, Black Hawk attempted to forge an alliance of tribes against the Americans. When he recrossed the Mississippi with six hundred Sauk and Fox warriors in April, 1832, his allies failed to come to his aid. Black Hawk's reappearance in Illinois sparked alarm among the settlers, and a militia army, supplemented by several regiments of the U.S. Army, quickly assembled.

Black Hawk's band was forced to fight their way up the Rock River into southern Wisconsin. Facing near-starvation in the marshes of Wisconsin, Black Hawk attempted to lead what remained of his band west across the Mississippi. The Sauk attempted to cross the river on August 1, 1832, near the mouth of the Bad Axe River. The Indians were forced to battle the armed steamboat *Warrior* during most of the day.

On August 2, General Henry Atkinson's force of more than sixteen hundred men attacked the Sauk. An estimated two hundred Indians were killed, including women and children. Many who managed to get across the Mississippi were attacked by Sioux warriors. Black Hawk managed to escape to a Winnebago village, but he soon surrendered to the Americans at Prairie du Chien. Placed in chains, he was transported by the *Warrior* to Fort Armstrong.

After several months of confinement, Black Hawk was taken to meet President Andrew Jackson. The president confined him in prison at Fortress Monroe for a year, then sent him on a tour of the East Coast.

The old warrior lived out his remaining years on the Sauk reservation in Iowa. He made a second trip to Washington in 1837 and was invited to speak at a banquet in Madison, Wisconsin, a year later. Unfortunately, real power within his nation had passed to his rival, Keokuk.   —*Thomas D. Matijasic*

See also Black Hawk War; Fox; Indian-white relations—U.S., 1831-1870; Keokuk; Sauk; White Cloud.

BIBLIOGRAPHY

Black Hawk. *Black Hawk: An Autobiography*. Edited by Donald Dean Jackson. Urbana: University of Illinois Press, 1964.

Drake, Benjamin. *The Great Indian Chief of the West: Or, Life and Adventures of Black Hawk*. Cincinnati: H. M. Rulison, 1856.

Josephy, Alvin M., Jr. *The Patriot Chiefs: A Chronicle of American Indian Resistance*. New York: Viking Press, 1961.

Tebbel, John W. *The Compact History of the Indian Wars*. New York: Hawthorn Books, 1966.

Waters, Frank. *Brave Are My People: Indian Heroes Not Forgotten*. Santa Fe, N.Mex.: Clear Light Publishers, 1993.

Black Hawk War

DATE: 1832
PLACE: Illinois, Wisconsin
TRIBES AFFECTED: Fox, Sauk, Winnebago
SIGNIFICANCE: Defeated by U.S. troops, the Sauks, Fox, and Winnebagos lost most of their land in futile resistance to white settlement

Into the early nineteenth century, the Sauks, Fox, and Winnebagos were relatively free of white pressure, most warfare being against such enemies as the Sioux or Osage. Their traditional world remained strong until the post-revolutionary decades. Yet soon American settlers, migrating west in steady streams, threatened to destroy the old ways.

Historical Background. Fleeing powerful eastern rivals, the Sauks (Black Hawk's people) and their main allies, the Fox (Mesquakies), had migrated into parts of Michigan, Wisconsin, Illinois, and Iowa by the late 1600's. They became farmers and trappers, trading regularly with the French, whose hunger for furs and competition with the British would embroil the tribes in warfare.

By the time of Black Hawk's birth in 1776, the Sauks were settled near present-day Rock Island, Illinois, and in eastern Iowa. His childhood and youth were years of seasonal moves dictated by farming, fishing, and trapping. Frequent warfare gave warriors a high status within the tribe, and Black Hawk joined a war party at fifteen, seeking family and tribal respect. By his thirties, he was a premier war leader and a committed traditionalist who, at a terrible cost to his people, would resist change.

Before 1800, neither the Sauks nor the Mesquakies had signed a peace treaty with the United States, resenting bitterly the seeming American favoritism toward the hated Osages. In 1804, however, the United States, Sauk, and Mesquakie leaders signed a treaty wherein the chiefs ceded fifty million acres of

An engraving of the Battle of Bad Axe, the fight that ended the Black Hawk War on August 2, 1832. (Library of Congress)

land. Disregarding any Indian rights, white settlers poured into the territory. They burned Indian homes and cornfields while the Indians received neither adequate compensation nor protection from the federal government. Black Hawk protested, claiming that the chiefs had not understood the full implications of the 1804 treaty and that his people were being cheated.

Tribal cohesion was splintering among the Sauks and the Mesquakies. Traditionalists—with Black Hawk as their main spokesman—wanted to retain the old ways and therefore sought to resist the Americans. Nontraditionalists—led by a young Sauk warrior named Keokuk—called for accommodation with the Americans. Keokuk had visited Washington and feared the strength of the government, but Black Hawk and his followers, relatively isolated, refused to compromise.

The rivalry between Black Hawk and Keokuk broke the Sauks into factions; gradually Keokuk's influence grew stronger. In a council held at Prairie du Chien in 1825, Keokuk was a major spokesman for the Sauks and the Mesquakies. Black Hawk refused to attend and brushed aside the council's decisions for peace. He was further enraged when, in 1827, the government began plans to remove all Indians from Illinois as of 1829.

The 1832 War. White squatters moved into Saukenuk, Black Hawk's home and the major Sauk village. In July, 1829, the United States General Land Office announced that the land around Saukenuk would go on sale in October. Black Hawk and his people—some three hundred warriors and their families—vowed to reoccupy their land. General Edmund P.

Gaines, commander of the army's Western Department in St. Louis, led troops to the area.

Gaines and Black Hawk confronted each other, the latter insisting that the treaty of 1804 was invalid and that he would not leave Saukenuk. Gaines, in turn, warned that he was there to enforce the treaty, either peacefully or by force. Keokuk persuaded some Indian families to join his peace faction, but Black Hawk resisted removal, counting on aid from nearby Winnebagos and Potawatomis.

On June 25, 1831, soldiers attacked Saukenuk at dawn. Black Hawk and his followers had left during the night, crossing to the west side of the Mississippi. His village in ruins, Black Hawk signed a peace treaty with Gaines on June 30. Gaines then ordered white settlers at Rock River to provide the Indians with corn. Only token amounts were sent, however, and Black Hawk's band faced starvation.

Convinced by his chief lieutenant, Napope, that the British would assist him and that the Potawatomis and Chippewas were also ready to enlist, Black Hawk chose to go to war. By early 1832 he commanded some six hundred warriors and prepared to retake Saukenuk. Hoping to defuse the situation, General Henry Atkinson called on friendly Sauk and Mesquakie chiefs to negotiate and warned that if Black Hawk crossed to the east side of the Mississippi his troops would attack. Neither the Potawatomis nor the Winnebagos gave Black Hawk the help he expected.

General Atkinson had mustered more than seventeen hundred Illinois militia into federal service in early May, 1832, combining them with his regular army troops, numbering three hundred. By late May he led these forces toward Rock River. The militia was in advance, and, fearing treachery, they killed several of Black Hawk's scouts carrying a flag of truce. The Sauks fought back, defeating the militia in what is called the Battle of Stillman's Run. The Sauks kept on the move, eluding Atkinson and his men.

During the summer, Black Hawk's band raided frontier settlements for food and livestock. Atkinson sent Colonel Henry Dodge to lead a militia against the band. Weakened by malnutrition, Black Hawk and his band were overtaken by the militia in late July, 1832. As the band began crossing the Wisconsin River, the militia attacked. Although most of the band escaped, many lives were lost. The remainder pressed on toward the Mississippi, reaching it on August 1.

The Battles of August 1 and 2. While the Sauks were crossing the river, the steamboat *Warrior* appeared with troops aboard. They opened fire, and a fierce battle ensued. The *Warrior* broke off the fight when it ran low on fuel. The main battle between the Sauks and the army began on the morning of August 2. Atkinson's and Dodge's men, supported by the *Warrior*, trapped the Sauks and began a systematic slaughter. The Battle of Bad Axe, resulting in some 150 to 300 Sauk deaths, ended the Black Hawk War. Black Hawk and perhaps fifty others escaped, heading for LaCrosse, Wisconsin, site of a Winnebago village. There they decided to surrender, traveling to Prairie du Chien, headquarters of the Indian agency.

Black Hawk, two of his sons, and eight other ringleaders were imprisoned, but all were released within a year.

A treaty, signed on September 21, 1832, formally ended the war. The Sauks, Mesquakies, and Winnebagos lost approximately six million acres of land—most of eastern Iowa—receiving in return a promise of an annuity of $20,000 for thirty years. Broken in spirit and poverty-stricken, the Sauks and their allies never again attempted armed resistance against the United States.

—*S. Carol Berg*

See also Black Hawk; Fox; Indian-white relations—U.S., 1831-1870; Keokuk; Sauk; White Cloud.

BIBLIOGRAPHY

Gurko, Miriam. *Indian America: The Black Hawk War*. New York: Thomas Y. Crowell, 1970.

Jackson, Donald, ed. *Black Hawk*. Urbana: University of Illinois Press, 1964.

Josephy, Alvin M., Jr. *The Patriot Chiefs: A Chronicle of American Indian Resistance*. New York: Viking Press, 1961. Reprint. New York: Penguin Books, 1976.

Nichols, Roger L. *Black Hawk and the Warrior's Path*. Arlington Heights, Ill.: Harlan Davidson, 1992.

Utley, Robert M., and Wilcomb E. Washburn. *The Indian Wars*. Rev. ed. New York: American Heritage, 1985.

Waters, Frank. *Brave Are My People: Indian Heroes Not Forgotten*. Santa Fe, N.Mex.: Clear Light Publishers, 1992.

Black Hills

TRIBES AFFECTED: Lakota and Teton Sioux

SIGNIFICANCE: The Black Hills have had both economic and spiritual significance to the Sioux; the U.S. Congress took the Black Hills with no compensation in 1877, violating an earlier treaty

The Black Hills are located in southwestern South Dakota along the Wyoming and Nebraska borders. Formed in the Pleistocene era, they form a remote ridge of limestone and granite 110 miles long, 40 miles wide, and 4,000 feet high. They provided a panoramic view of the vast prairie of buffalo grass below. The hills themselves were heavily wooded with dark pine and contained abundant animal and plant life as well as numerous springs and small lakes.

The Black Hills were reached in the late 1700's by the Sioux chief Standing Bull and his followers as the Sioux migrated westward. The Sioux called these hills *Paha Sapa* (Black Hills) because they were so heavily wooded with dark pine that from a distance they looked black. The Sioux had expelled the Kiowa from the area by 1814 and extended this border further west in the next few years.

The Black Hills acquired a special significance to the western Sioux and were perhaps the most loved area in the Sioux domain. They provided water and abundant food, lodgepoles for tipis, and medicinal plants for healing. The steep canyons provided protection from the severe winter weather. Spiritually, the Black Hills were holy. They were the site of vision quests and the home of *Wakan Tanka*, the Great Spirit. According to legend, two-legged animals raced four-legged animals to see who would dominate the earth. The thunder-being proclaimed that the Black Hills were the heart of the earth and that the Sioux would come back some day and live there. The hills were seen as a reclining female figure whose breasts provided life-giving forces and to whom the Teton went as a young child would go to its mother.

White encroachment into Sioux territory led to war in the mid-nineteenth century. The Treaty of Fort Laramie in 1868 ended this war and created the permanent Great Sioux reservation, of which the Black Hills formed a part. The pressures of white settlement and the discovery of gold in the Black Hills, however, led the government to try to purchase or lease them. The Sioux refused. In 1877 Congress ratified the Manypenny Agreement, which took the Black Hills without compensation. This violation of the 1868 treaty was upheld in the 1903 Supreme Court decision *Lone Wolf v. Hitchcock*. In 1911 the Sioux began what was to become a protracted legal process to regain the Black Hills. In 1980 the Supreme Court affirmed a 1979 Court of Claims ruling that the Sioux were entitled to $106 million in compensation for the taking of the Black Hills. Various attempts to have the Black Hills returned to the Sioux, such as Senator Bill Bradley's land return legislation in 1985, have not succeeded.

See also Fort Laramie Treaty of 1868; Little Bighorn, Battle of the; *Lone Wolf v. Hitchcock*; Sioux.

Black Kettle (1803?—Nov. 27, 1868, Washita River): Chief

ALSO KNOWN AS: Moketavato

TRIBAL AFFILIATION: Southern Cheyenne

SIGNIFICANCE: Cheyenne leader Black Kettle, who struggled to maintain peace with white settlers and soldiers, was one of the few survivors of the Sand Creek Massacre

Black Kettle was one of the most noted of the traditional chiefs of the Cheyenne Nation, who were known as "peace chiefs." The Cheyenne were originally part of the larger complex of Algonquian-speaking peoples of the Canada/Minnesota region surrounding the Great Lakes. They were encountered in this region as late as 1667 by French explorers but were soon driven southward by British distribution of guns to more northern peoples.

Cheyenne oral tradition holds that the first such peace chief was appointed by Sweet Medicine, who left a code of conduct for the peace chiefs. A peace chief was to abandon all violence, even in the face of imminent danger to himself or his family. Yet he was also to stand firm, even if nonaggressively, against opponents of his people, even when the soldier societies among the Cheyenne had retreated. He was to persist in peacemaking efforts despite total opposition by the soldier societies of the younger Cheyenne warriors—seeking peace with native and settler alike in all circumstances. Finally, he was to show generosity in dealing with his own people, particularly toward the poor.

From U.S. military sources, Black Kettle appears to have been recognized as the main leader of the Cheyenne people of the western Plains by 1860. Therefore, he was the main authority in the crisis years of 1860 until his death in 1868. Reports of his age at death vary from fifty-six to sixty-one. Little is known about his early life except that he was an able warrior in the traditional Cheyenne manner.

Black Kettle was distinguished in his dealings with white settlers by his courage in the face of superior firepower and his willingness to negotiate release of captives, often by purchasing them at his own expense (even the chief was subject to Cheyenne economic law) in order to present them to white authorities.

In the midst of serious hostilities and severe food shortages, Black Kettle traveled to Fort Lyon, where he was refused food rations by Major Scott Anthony and Colonel John Chivington. He was instructed to take his people to Sand Creek village, where he had assurances that they would be allowed to hunt and would not be endangered by American military operations. On November 28, 1864, American soldiers attacked the Sand Creek village. Severely injured, Black Kettle was among the few survivors. During the attack, Black Kettle tried to hoist an American flag presented to him by American authorities, believing that these were soldiers who did not know about the agreement at Fort Lyon. He was to discover, however, that it was Anthony and Chivington themselves who led the unprovoked massacre of the Cheyenne people at Sand Creek. There followed a period of serious warfare, and for the next eight years, Black Kettle was frequently involved in attempting to mediate disputes between the Cheyenne and the American military. The constant movements imposed upon the Cheyenne made it increasingly difficult for Black Kettle to control the younger soldiers, as was also often the case with the lack of central control of the American military raiding parties. On November 27, 1868, George Armstrong Custer led a surprise attack at dawn on the encampment at Washita River, where Black Kettle's band was located. Black Kettle and his wife were killed.

See also Cheyenne; Sand Creek Massacre.

BIBLIOGRAPHY

Stan Hoig. *The Peace Chiefs of the Cheyennes*. Norman: University of Oklahoma Press, 1980.

_____. *The Sand Creek Massacre*. Norman: University of Oklahoma Press, 1961.

Blackfoot and Blackfeet Confederacy: Tribe and confederacy

CULTURE AREA: Northern Plains

LANGUAGE GROUP: Algonquian

PRIMARY LOCATION: Montana (U.S.), Alberta (Canada)

POPULATION SIZE: 32,234 in U.S. (1990 U.S. Census); 11,670 in Canada (Statistics Canada, based on 1991 census)

The Blackfeet Confederacy consisted of four Algonquian tribes: the Siksika (Blackfeet Proper), Kainah (Blood), Northern Piegan, and Southern Piegan. Siksika is a Cree word meaning "people with black feet," which probably referred to moccasins dyed black or that turned black after contact with prairie fire ashes. "Piegan" means "poorly dressed robes" and referred to tribal members who lived in the foothills of the Rocky Mountains. The Blackfeet originally came from somewhere in the east and had a common language and similar religious beliefs; they frequently intermarried. Geography separated the tribes, particularly in the mountains where each branch of the Confederacy lived in a separate valley or along a different river. The Blackfeet came together to fight invaders, to hunt for food, and to celebrate weddings and successful hunts. The tribes moved about frequently in search of their primary source of food and clothing, the American bison (buffalo).

Customs and Culture. The four major tribes separated into smaller groups, the Northern and Southern Piegans having twenty-three bands, the Blood seven, and the Blackfoot or Siksika six. Each band had a headman, chosen because of bravery in battle. The headman took care of the poor and disabled and sponsored social and religious ceremonies. The headmen met together as a tribal council to decide on questions such as war and trade relations with neighboring tribes. Within each band, warriors were divided by age into military societies, dance groups, and religious clubs.

In traditional Blackfoot religion, the Sun Dance played a prominent role as it did in many Plains tribes. A woman—the "vow woman"—sponsored the event, usually after a great disaster such as a tornado or the loss of many lives in battle. In honor of the survivors she prepared a sacred dish of buffalo tongue and pledged to live a life of purity. A Sun Dance ceremony consisted of three days of preparation and four days of dancing. Male members of the tribe constructed a medicine lodge (okan) of a hundred newly cut willows and dedicated it to the sun, the source of all power and knowledge. They covered the okan with offerings of food and drink. Inside they said prayers and conducted secret purification rites. The "vow woman" fasted while the lodge was built and presented herself to the assembled worshippers on the fourth day, wearing a sacred headdress, and led the people in prayers. If the prayer was not uttered precisely right or if too few presents, such as horses, blankets, and clothes, were given away by the woman and her family, more terrible disasters could strike the tribe. The Blackfoot Sun Dance did not include incidents of self-torture, such as among the Mandan. It remained the most important event in the yearly cycle of life, however, until ended by missionaries in the 1890's.

When a Blackfoot died, the body was placed in a tree and a horse was killed to accompany the deceased into the land of the dead. If the death took place in a tipi, the tipi was burned. Surviving relatives and friends mutilated themselves to show their grief—slashing their arms or legs, cutting their hair, or cutting off their fingers.

The Blackfeet lived in tipis made of skins. Women built the tipis; men painted them with sacred signs, including star constellations and animals. The men spent much of the summer hunting buffalo. In the fall and spring they gathered turnips, onions, cherries, plums, and berries. Women made clothing, cooked, sought out wood and water, and made pemmican, a favorite food made of dried meat pounded together with blueberries. Besides buffalo meat, the tribe also consumed deer, elk, and antelope. The buffalo, however, provided far more than food. Tribal members found more than sixty uses for various parts of the animal. The buffalo provided clothing and shelter (from the hides), tools (from the bones), and utensils, bags, and storage containers. Before horses were introduced, warriors hunted buffalo by chasing them on foot and stampeding them over cliffs. The Blackfeet learned how to use horses in the early 1700's from other tribes. Hunting strategies changed quickly; warriors now drove the buffalo into a box canyon where they shot them from horseback with bows and arrows. Their hunting territory now spread from central Montana to northern Saskatchewan.

Historical Period. The first contact with whites came in 1806 when Meriwether Lewis reported meeting people called Piegans. Not until the 1830's, however, did the tribe become involved in trade with white Americans. At this time John Jacob Astor's American Fur Company, headquartered in St. Louis, opened a series of trading posts in the northern Great Plains. The company sought buffalo robes and paid for them with guns, blankets, and ammunition. The Blackfeet gained control of a vast area of buffalo range through successful wars with the Flathead, Nez Perce, Crow, Cree, and other Plains tribes. Wealth and weapons acquired in the robe trade enabled the Blackfeet to keep their traditional customs, at least as long as the buffalo herds existed. The coming of the railroads and the increasing number of white farmers moving into the area greatly threatened those herds.

In 1855, the Blackfoot headman (chief) Lame Bull signed a treaty with United States government agents allowing con-

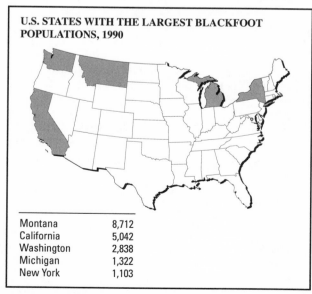

U.S. STATES WITH THE LARGEST BLACKFOOT POPULATIONS, 1990

Montana	8,712
California	5,042
Washington	2,838
Michigan	1,322
New York	1,103

Source: 1990 U.S. Census.

struction of a railroad through tribal lands. American citizens would be able to travel through the territory unharmed. According to the terms of the treaty, the confederacy would receive $20,000 in useful goods and services immediately and $15,000 each year in the future "to promote civilization and Christianization." The United States promised the Blackfeet schools, agricultural training, and perpetual peace. The army established an office at Fort Benton in northern Montana Territory to distribute the goods and services. Beginning in 1856 about seven thousand Blackfeet a year received aid, though many crossed the border from Canada to get their annuities. The Indians, having never recognized such a border, ignored army agent complaints about giving aid to "Canadian" citizens.

In the years after the American Civil War (1861-1865), more and more whites moved into the region and demanded added protection from "savage Indians." Especially troublesome for the Blackfeet were the increasing numbers of cattle ranchers who fenced their lands with barbed wire to keep buffalo out. In 1870, war broke out in Montana after a massacre of 173 Blackfoot men, women, and children by a white volunteer militia. In addition to the dead, 140 women and children were driven from their village into the subzero weather, where they suffered horribly. In 1874, President Ulysses S. Grant issued an executive order moving the reservation boundary much farther north than had been agreed upon by the Blackfeet. No payment was offered to the Indians. A smallpox epidemic in the new reservation reduced the tribe's population to three thousand, about one-fifth of what it had been a hundred years earlier. At this point, Chief White Calf ordered a halt to any more resistance; "further war would only result in our extermination," he explained.

The Blackfeet living in Canada managed much better than their American brothers. In 1877, the Canadian government signed a treaty creating a reserve on which Blackfeet could live, hunt, raise cattle, and receive government rations. Only at this point did the American-Canadian border achieve any significance in tribal history, as people north of the line improved the quality of their lives while those living south of it suffered a continuing population decline. By 1880, only twenty-two hundred Blackfeet lived on the United States reservation surrounded by a white population of over twelve thousand. The buffalo had practically disappeared, in all of North America only a few hundred having survived the hunters. With the annihilation of their main source of subsistence, the Blackfeet became impoverished; more than six hundred suffered horrible deaths in the "starvation winter" of 1883-1884. Rations provided by the army allowed 1.5 pounds of meat, half-a-pound of flour, and smaller amounts of beans, bacon, salt, and coffee for each individual. Another bitter winter hit the reservation in 1886-1887, but the rations still were not increased and hundreds more died.

The Roman Catholic church provided much of the education on the reservation in the early days. An elementary school had opened in 1859, but after thirteen years a new agent, the Methodist minister John Young, closed the school and opened one of his own. Catholics were forced to attend school off the reservation. Jesuit missionaries built a school a few miles away, but refused to allow parents the right to visit students during the school term. Isolating children from parents, it was hoped, would break down old loyalties and habits and encourage young Indians to adopt white ways. The reservation school taught English, Christianity, and "modern" ways. Whichever institution the students attended, any connection with their past customs and traditions was effectively torn away from them.

Reservation Life. In 1895, Blackfoot leaders leased thousands of acres of land back to the federal government, with Indians retaining the right to hunt, fish, and cut timber on the property. The leased land supposedly contained large deposits of gold, but prospectors actually found little of value in the territory. Much of this land became Glacier National Park a few years later.

After 1900, economic conditions on the reservation became even worse, largely because of a failed attempt by the Indian Office in Washington, D.C., to "civilize" the Blackfeet by teaching them how to farm. The leasing of land for grazing cattle had at least provided a meager income to the tribe, but now some experts in the Indian office believed that collecting grazing fees just made the Indians "lazy." Farming, it was decided, was a manlier, healthier, more appropriate way to make a living. Accordingly, the local agent contracted to have a huge irrigation system built. The reservation, however, had little water of its own. It was also windy and subject to extremes of temperature, and crops could not be grown. The irrigation project proved to be a costly waste of time and effort.

The agent in charge of the reservation then encouraged cattle ranching. In 1904, the Blackfeet paid to have their land fenced to keep out non-Indian cattle, but a drought that year, a tough winter the next, and an epidemic disease the next killed thousands of reservation cattle. The Blackfeet stayed poor. Other problems resulted from a rapid turnover in agents; from 1905 to 1921 ten different men filled the post. Some of the agents quit after being charged with corruption, while others were simply weak or incompetent. Weather continued to have a devastating impact on reservation life. The 1920's saw a long dry spell bringing fires and tremendous heat as well as grasshoppers, cutworms, and other plagues to the area. Grain and cattle prices fell, and many surrounding communities became ghost towns. The Blackfeet, of course, could not leave. Poverty, sickness, and hunger spread. Two out of three Blackfeet were living entirely on government rations.

A new agent in the late 1920's improved conditions somewhat by encouraging small gardens for each household and the raising of chickens and pigs. He also promoted adult education and literacy programs. Then the Great Depression hit, its impact on the reservations mirroring that on American society at large. The Indian Reorganization Act of 1934 promoted self-government and a return to cultural traditions. It also brought some money into the community for small construction projects. These helped many Blackfeet survive the worst ravages of the Depression years, but hunger and poverty persisted for many on the reservation.

The Great Northern Railroad provided some help by hiring Blackfeet to give performances at its lodge in Glacier National Park. The park had opened in 1910 and lay outside the territory the Blackfeet had actually lived in, but tourists enjoyed the Indian dances all the same. The Blackfeet still performed the Sun Dance but by the 1930's had moved the date of celebration to July 4. Missionaries who formerly had denounced the dance as heathen could hardly object when the dancers insisted that their only motive was to celebrate the birthday of their new homeland. Allowing Indians to practice their traditional religions, as provided for by the 1934 act, came too late to save many Blackfeet customs. Poverty, death, and disease had already taken their toll; meanwhile, white schools had ruined any opportunity for the Blackfeet to maintain their traditional language. Few young Blackfeet could speak the old tongue anymore, and with its passing went most of the traditions of Blackfoot life.

Conditions on the reservation improved somewhat after World War II, and only a few tribal members participated in the disastrous resettlement plan of the 1950's when the Bureau of Indian Affairs tried to force Indians from their reservations and place them in cities. In the 1960's, many Blackfeet got jobs through the War on Poverty as Head Start teachers, firefighters, and government welfare agents. Others obtained employment in the sugar-beet and hay fields of northern Montana. A few became teachers, doctors, lawyers, and engineers. Still, the per capita income on the reservation was well below the poverty level, and many Blackfeet in the late twentieth century found themselves trapped in joblessness and hopelessness. —*Leslie V. Tischauser*

See also Algonquian language family; Plains; Reservation system of the United States; Reserve system of Canada; Sun Dance.

BIBLIOGRAPHY

Brandon, William. *The Indian in American Culture*. New York: Harper & Row, 1974. A massive volume covering the entire period of Indian-white relations, with a few pages devoted to the Blackfeet. Useful for placing the confederacy into the overall picture of Indian life in North America. Good index and bibliography.

McFee, Malcolm. *Modern Blackfeet*. New York: Holt, Rinehart and Winston, 1972. A scholarly, well-researched, and very readable volume on the problems of assimilation faced by the Blackfeet Confederacy. A look at life on the reservation, and a history of Bureau of Indian Affairs policies toward the Blackfeet. A detailed bibliography and useful index.

Washburn, Wilcomb E. *The Indian in America*. New York: Harper & Row, 1975. Essential reading for anyone interested in any tribe in North America. The best single-volume history of American Indians from their origins to the 1970's. Contains a comprehensive bibliography and detailed index.

Wissler, Clark. "Material Culture of the Blackfoot Indians." In *Anthropological Papers of the American Museum of Natural History, No. 5*. New York: American Museum of Natural History, 1910. Still-useful compilation of field notes and observations by an early student of American Indian ways of life. Good sections on the Sun Dance and Blackfoot customs and economics.

Blacksnake (c. 1760, Cattaraugus, N.Y.—Dec. 26, 1859, Cold Spring, N.Y.): War chief

ALSO KNOWN AS: Thaonawyuthe, Chain Breaker
TRIBAL AFFILIATION: Seneca
SIGNIFICANCE: Blacksnake was present at, and later recalled in memoirs, many significant events involving the Iroquois between 1775 and 1850

A principal chief of the Seneca, Chain Breaker, or Governor Blacksnake, was an honored warrior and leader in combat, but he was not one of the fifty sachems of the confederacy. The exact date of his birth is not known, but he is thought to have lived almost a hundred years. He was present on the English side at the battle of Oriskany, New York, in 1777, and his memoirs discuss the Wyoming and Cherry Valley, Pennsylvania, "massacres" of 1778 and the Sullivan-Clinton campaign against the Iroquois in 1779. He fought on the American side in the War of 1812. Blacksnake's autobiographical account of his war experiences, dictated at age ninety-six and told to a Seneca native with limited English, contains unique insights into Indian character and thought during the American Revolution. His opinions of Joseph Brant, Old Smoke, Cornplanter, Handsome Lake, Red Jacket, and well-known British loyalists are especially perspicacious. Blacksnake was present when the prophet Handsome Lake fell into the trance that provided the visions for the Longhouse religion, and his perspective tempers the force of those revelations. Among the Americans Blacksnake met were George Washington and possibly Thomas Jefferson. Some of Blacksnake's war accounts are quite lurid and graphic; in other cases he sets the record straight, especially regarding the "massacre" at Cherry Valley.

Because Cornplanter, Handsome Lake, and Red Jacket were related to him through his mother (an important relationship in a matrilineal society), Blacksnake was allowed to be present at nearly every council meeting, treaty negotiation, and battle undertaken by the Seneca during his active years. Blacksnake was in a central position to relate the historical events of the time from the Indian perspective. His story is one of violence and war, of military alliances, and finally of building peace. Fortunately, Blacksnake was often in the right place at the right time, and he was a careful observer.

See also Cornplanter; Handsome Lake; Iroquois Confederacy; Red Jacket; Seneca.

BIBLIOGRAPHY

Ables, Thomas, ed. *Chainbreaker: The Revolutionary War Memoirs of Governor Blacksnake as told to Benjamin Williams*. Lincoln: University of Nebraska Press, 1989.

Caswell, Harriet. *Our Life Among the Iroquois*. Chicago: Congregational Sunday School and Publishing Society, 1892.

Graymont, Barbara. *The Iroquois in the American Revolution*. Syracuse: Syracuse University Press, 1972.

Hodges, F. W., ed. *Handbook of American Indians North of Mexico*. New York: Pageant Books, 1959.

Stone, William L. *The Life of Joseph Brant—Thayendanega*. 2 vols. 1838. Reprint. St. Clair Shores, Mich.: Scholarly Press, 1970.

Bladder Festival

TRIBES AFFECTED: Yupik (Eskimo)

SIGNIFICANCE: As the major religious event of the traditional Yupik, the Bladder Festival not only expressed the cosmology of the Yupik but also reiterated the social and economic relationships between people and between humans and animals

The Bladder Festival, which occurred at the winter solstice, was perhaps the most elaborate and most important of the traditional Yupik religious festivals. Called *Nakaciuq*, meaning "something done with bladders" in the Yupik language, the annual festival consisted of gift giving, feasting, and ritual performances of songs and dances. The festival lasted five or six days, depending upon the community. It culminated with the return to the sea of the bladders of all the seals and walruses harvested in the previous year. In this respect, the Bladder Festival symbolized the close of one subsistence cycle and the start of the next. It was last celebrated in the early part of the twentieth century.

Like other Arctic peoples, the Yupik believed that future hunting success depended upon a hunter's respectful attitude toward the caught game. The Yupik believed that each animal possessed a soul, or *Inua*, that resided in its bladder. These Inuas were finite in number and in order for future seals and other sea mammals to be caught, the Inuas of previously harvested animals must be returned to the sea. Furthermore, the Yupik believed that the game animals whose souls were well treated by humans would willingly give themselves up again to those humans. Good treatment was evidenced by the observance of hunting rituals, the careful and aesthetic use of the animal's pelt, and the public honoring of the animal at celebrations such as the Bladder Festival.

In the months and weeks leading up to the Bladder Festival, new songs were composed, new bowls, ladles, and buckets were carved, and new clothes were sewn. The semi-subterranean men's house, or *qasqi*, which was the primary site of the festival, was cleaned and purified. Although most of the festival occurred in and around the men's house, everyone in the village—men, women, and children—participated. Each of the bladders was inflated, decorated, and displayed in the *qasqi*. Ritual meals were served to the inflated bladders, and they, along with the human hosts, were entertained with songs and dances. At the conclusion of the festivities, each hunter removed the bladders of the animals he had killed through the smoke hole in the roof of the *qasqi* and carried them to the ice. Once on the ice, he speared the bladders to deflate them and dropped them into a hole in the ocean ice. This was done in order to release the Inua and return it to the sea.

The themes of renewal and regeneration were pervasive throughout the festival. Most important was the recognition that human livelihoods were dependent upon maintaining respectful relationships with the natural and supernatural worlds. The Bladder Festival also provided an opportunity for hunters within a community to compare their abilities as providers. Since each man displayed all the bladders of the sea mammals he had harvested that year, each person's hunting success became common knowledge. Thus, the Bladder Festival provided opportunities for the reaffirmation of, or the reordering of, status among hunters.

See also Arctic; Inuit.

Blankets

TRIBES AFFECTED: Pantribal

SIGNIFICANCE: American Indian trade blankets were manufactured by non-Indians and used as a commodity in trade dealings between the U.S. government and Native Americans

The earliest known use of European and English commercially made blankets in North America was in the fur trade with American Indians in the late seventeenth century. The use of the trade blanket as payment for treaties between the U.S. government and Native Americans began in 1776. Small manufacturers of blankets were established in the United States by the early 1800's. About the same time, trade stations were being established across the country for the nonprofit exchange of goods between the government and the Indians. By the 1820's, however, private businesses had replaced the government-controlled trade, and the trade blanket became a profit-making commodity. The market for trade blankets continued to expand with the opening of the West by the railroads, bringing more competition among manufacturers and a greater variety of colors and designs.

At the beginning of the twentieth century, there were five major U.S. manufacturers (one of which was Pendleton) that produced only trade blankets. By the end of the twentieth century, Pendleton was the only company still in business producing "trade" blankets.

The finely woven, double-faced blankets were used by Indians as clothing that provided both warmth and a means of expression. They replaced the use of robes made of animal hides by the Plains Indians and the hand-woven blankets of the Navajo; they were also used as highly valued gifts. Blankets conveyed different moods, depending on the style in which they were worn. They were thrown over the shoulder, belted at the waist, wrapped around the waist, or worn as a hooded robe. Blankets were also used as infant and child carriers, covers for the bed, and saddle blankets. The blankets also were a measure of wealth or status and could be used as statements of tribal unity or individual identity.

There were six general categories for design in trade blankets. These include the striped, banded, and nine-element de-

Navajo blankets and rugs, woven on looms such as this, had become valuable trade and sale items by the late nineteenth century.

signs used in chief's blankets, as well as center point, overall, and framed designs. Bright earth tones plus white, blue, and black were the predominant colors and were often woven into intricate design patterns. Design elements include motifs such as the cross, swastika, arrow, zig-zag, and banding that formed geometric patterns symbolizing mountains, paths, clouds, stars, birds, and the four cardinal directions. Some designs were believed to express stories and myths and were made for Indians by using Indian symbols and colors.

Trade blankets continue to be highly valued by Indians and non-Indians, both as collectibles and as usable blankets. They became known as "Indian blankets" long ago because American Indians made them a distinct part of their lives and cultures.

See also Chilkat blankets; Dress and adornment; Gifts and gift giving; Trade; Weaving.

Bloody Knife (c. 1840, N.Dak.—June 25, 1876, Little Bighorn, Mont.): Army scout

TRIBAL AFFILIATION: Arikara, Hunkpapa Sioux

SIGNIFICANCE: A skilled army scout, Bloody Knife served with George Armstrong Custer and fought at the Battle of the Little Bighorn

Bloody Knife was born about 1840 to a Hunkpapa Sioux father and an Arikara mother. Taunted by his peers for his mixed heritage, he returned at age twelve with his mother to her people in Missouri. He carried a hatred for the Hunkpapa, especially Gall and Sitting Bull. By 1860, he was working as a mail carrier between forts and settlements along the Missouri River, where he developed skills in avoiding Sioux patrols. He

enlisted as an army scout and received the commendation of several generals. In 1865, while at Fort Berthold, North Dakota, he led an army patrol to Gall's encampment. Gall was shot as he emerged from his dwelling and pronounced dead. To be certain, Bloody Knife put his shotgun to Gall's head and fired. An army officer kicked the gun and it discharged harmlessly in the snow. Gall recovered.

By 1876, Bloody Knife had become one of Custer's best scouts. He rode with Custer from Fort Abraham Lincoln as Custer set out in search of Gall and Sitting Bull. Bloody Knife expressed concern about the possible size of the Sioux party they were pursuing and recommended against attack. On June 25, he was deployed with Major Marcus A. Reno's detachment as Custer split his command. Bloody Knife rode with the advance attack, which Custer had hoped would disperse the Sioux in panicked flight. The Sioux, however, counterattacked. Early in the fighting, Bloody Knife's skull was shattered by a shot from Gall's warriors, causing Reno's detachment to disperse in their own chaotic retreat. Bloody Knife was then beheaded and his head paraded among the victorious Sioux.

Following his death, it took his wife, She Owl, four years to collect the less than one hundred dollars the army owed Bloody Knife in back wages.

See also Arikara; Gall; Little Bighorn, Battle of the; Sitting Bull.

Blue Eagle, Acee (Aug. 17, 1907, Wichita Reservation, Okla.—June 18, 1959, Muskogee, Okla.): Painter, lecturer

ALSO KNOWN AS: Chebona Bula (Laughing Boy), Alex C. McIntosh

TRIBAL AFFILIATION: Pawnee, Creek

SIGNIFICANCE: The flamboyant Acee is probably the best-known Oklahoma Indian painter; he also taught and lectured widely

Acee Blue Eagle was reared by a guardian in Henryetta, Oklahoma. His education included coursework at Bacone College, University of Oklahoma, and Oxford University (1935). His art career began in the 1920's. Acee studied with Oscar Jacobson at the University of Oklahoma and continued to paint in the Kiowa flat style. He created numerous murals, including those for a commission from the Works Progress Administration (1934), in addition to many canvases.

In 1935, Acee toured the United States and Europe, lecturing and exhibiting on the life, dances, and stories of American Indians, often in costume. He spent three years in the Air Force during World War II. From 1947 until 1949, he free-lanced in New York and Chicago and then was artist-in-residence at Oklahoma Technical College from 1951 to 1952. From 1950 to 1954, he hosted a television program. He toured the West Coast, lecturing about improving television programs for children. Blue Eagle wrote and illustrated *Ecogee, the Little Blue Deer* (1972), a children's book, drew a cartoon carried in Oklahoma newspapers, and edited *Oklahoma Indian Painting-Poetry* (1959). Referred to as flamboyant and as the foremost living Indian painter, he was named "Outstanding Indian in the United States" in 1958.

See also Art and artists, contemporary; Auchiah, James; Hokeah, Jack; Mopope, Stephen.

Boats and watercraft

TRIBES AFFECTED: Widespread but not pantribal

SIGNIFICANCE: Many native peoples used watercraft for hunting and transportation

Native American watercraft generally fall into three basic types: dugout canoes, birchbark canoes, and kayaks. The word "canoe" is a general term that refers to many different types of light, narrow boats with pointed ends that are propelled by paddling. Christopher Columbus first recorded the word *canóoa*, which was used by natives in the West Indies to describe their dugout boats.

Canoes. Because of their heavy weight and the difficulty of overland transport, dugout canoes were primarily used by more stationary tribes or by those who fished or navigated on the oceans and thus needed a very strong craft. The Tlingit, for example, who lived in the area of present-day southeastern Alaska along the Pacific coast, constructed canoes for fishing and coastal voyages out of large red cedar trees, which they felled by building a fire at each tree's base. They then hollowed out the log with a stone axe and sometimes added planks along the sides or fastened two canoes together, side by side, with spars made from sturdy branches for more stability in rough waters. Smaller canoes for two or three persons were fashioned from cottonwood logs and used for river travel and fishing. The larger oceangoing canoes could carry as many as sixty people and measured up to 45 feet in length. A dugout canoe on display in New York City's Museum of Natural History from Queen Charlotte's Island, off the coast of British Columbia, Canada, measures 63 feet long, 8 feet, 3 inches wide, and 5 feet deep; it was cut from a single log. Along the eastern coast of the United States, dugout canoes made from pine, oak, chestnut, or tulip wood were common. It took one man ten or twelve days to make a dugout canoe by lighting a small fire in the center of the log and then chopping out the charred wood with an axe. Dugout canoes were heavy but sturdy, and predominated in areas where birchbark was scarce.

The birchbark canoe was first used by the Algonquin Indians in what is now the northeastern United States and Canada, where birch trees were plentiful. They were extremely buoyant and sturdy, yet light enough to be carried over land, which

A Kutenai duck hunter in a canoe; the photograph is from circa 1910. (Library of Congress)

made them particularly useful for exploration and trade and for hunting and trapping in smaller rivers. The early French missionaries, fur traders, and explorers in North America all used birchbark canoes, and the adoption of the bark canoe by European explorers is in large part responsible for the rapid exploration and development of the continent.

Indian birchbark canoes varied in length from 15 to almost 100 feet for canoes built to carry warriors. The Ojibwa (Chippewa), once one of the largest tribes north of Mexico, were master canoe makers. They would first outline the craft's shape by driving wood stakes into the ground; then thick, pliable sheets of birchbark were placed inside and fastened to wooden gunwales (the upper edge of the canoe). The frame was fortified with cedar ribs, and the bark was sewn with strings made from spruce roots. Finally, the seams were made watertight with sap from spruce trees. Other tribes substituted bark from elm, hickory, spruce, basswood, or chestnut when birch was unavailable, but barks other than birch absorbed water quickly. Often such canoes were built for limited use and then simply abandoned as they became waterlogged and heavy.

Kayaks and Umiaks. One of the most significant achievements of the Eskimos (Inuits) was the invention of the kayak, which is perhaps the most seaworthy watercraft ever built. Most were about the size of a small canoe and were made from a frame of driftwood, saplings, or whalebone, over which sealskin was tightly stretched and made waterproof by rubbing it with animal fat. Kayaks were commonly built for one occupant but could be designed for two or three. They were first used as hunting boats for walrus and seals by the Eskimos of Greenland and later also used by Alaskan Eskimos. Some scholars suggest that the design of the birchbark canoes used by tribes in the more southerly areas of North America was adapted from the kayak.

The kayak is completely covered except for a hole in which the paddler sits, which the Eskimos made watertight by lacing their clothing over the rim of the hole. Since they were completely waterproof and highly maneuverable, kayaks could be launched in rough surf and navigated through ice-infested ocean waters that would quickly swamp an open boat. Since the paddler sat low in the center, kayaks were also useful in rivers with swift waters and rapids. Propelled by a double-bladed paddle, a capsized kayak could be righted by a skillful person without taking in any water by rolling full circle.

When pursuing seal or walrus, the hunter would lean forward, concealed behind a small sail-like blind attached to the bow. As he drew close, he would hurl a wooden spear attached to the boat by a line coiled in a tray on the deck.

The Eskimos also used a larger, open boat covered with animal skins called a "umiak," which is Eskimo for "woman's boat," as it was most often piloted by the women in the group. The umiak was used for carrying families and supplies and was propelled by both paddles and oars—the only known instance of the use of oars by Native Americans before the coming of the Europeans. Some of the Eskimo boats may also

have been powered by sails; among the other native peoples of the American continents, only the Mayas of the Yucatán Peninsula and the natives of the coast of Peru were known to have used sails before the Europeans arrived. Most Eskimos today have replaced their kayaks with wood or aluminum boats, and their sails and paddles with outboard gasoline motors.

The modern descendants of Native American canoes and kayaks are made from wood, aluminum, canvas, or fiberglass, and are used for sport, recreation, or competition.

—Raymond Frey

See also Birchbark; Transportation modes.

BIBLIOGRAPHY

Adney, Edwin Tappan, and Howard I. Chapelle. *The Bark Canoes and Skin Boats of North America*. Washington, D.C.: U.S. Government Printing Office, 1964.

McPhee, John. *The Survival of the Bark Canoe*. New York: Farrar, Straus, Giroux, 1975.

National Geographic Society. *National Geographic on Indians of the Americas*. Washington, D.C.: Author, 1955.

Oswalt, Wendell H. *This Land Was Theirs: A Study of North American Indians*. New York: John Wiley & Sons, 1966.

Weyer, Edward Moffat. *The Eskimos: Their Environment and Folkways*. New Haven, Conn.: Yale University Press, 1932.

Bonnin, Gertrude Simmons (Feb. 22, 1875, Pine Ridge Reservation, S.Dak.—Jan. 25, 1938, Washington, D.C.): Writer, activist

ALSO KNOWN AS: Zitkala Sa (Red Bird)

TRIBAL AFFILIATION: Sioux

SIGNIFICANCE: In the early twentieth century, Gertrude Bonnin became a successful author and an influential advocate of Indian policy reform

Gertrude Bonnin belonged to a generation of Indian leaders who survived an educational process whose aim was to assimilate Indian youth into European American life. Bonnin put her education to use by urging tolerance for Indian cultural differences and by trying to reform prevailing policy regarding Indians.

The daughter of a Sioux woman, Ellen Simmons, and a European American settler, Bonnin left Sioux country at the age of eight to attend a Quaker missionary school for Indians in Indiana and went on to attend Earlham College. As a young woman, Bonnin taught at the Carlisle Indian School, studied violin at the Boston Conservatory of Music, and began a career as a writer. She published autobiographical essays and stories based on tribal legends in *The Atlantic Monthly* and *Harper's*. Bonnin's publications include two books, *Old Indian Legends* (1901) and *American Indian Stories* (1921).

After returning to live among the Sioux in the early twentieth century, Bonnin married a Sioux employee of the Indian service, Raymond Talesfase Bonnin, and joined the Society of American Indians. In 1916, she moved to Washington, D.C., where she spent the rest of her life as an activist, writer, and lecturer. In the 1920's and 1930's, Bonnin worked with numer-

An 1899 portrait of Gertrude Bonnin in traditional Sioux clothing. (National Archives)

ous groups involved in reforming Indian policy and, in 1926, she organized the National Council of American Indians.

See also Education, post-contact; National Congress of American Indians (NCAI).

Booger Dance

TRIBE AFFECTED: Cherokee

SIGNIFICANCE: The Booger Dance is a major symbolic feature of Cherokee night dances

The term "booger," equivalent to "bogey" (ghost), is used by English-speaking Cherokee for any ghost or frightful animal. The Booger Dance originated among Eastern Mountain Cherokee as a way to portray European invaders as awkward, ridiculous, lewd, and menacing. The dance dramatizes hostility and disdain for white culture by mocking elements that cause cultural decay and defeat.

The dance is preceded by a ritual of divination. Should divination devices conclude that an illness was caused by "boogers" (bogeymen), the Booger Dance is then determined to be the means of relief. The dance is conducted to "scare away" the spirit causing the sickness. It is a masked dance, in which masks made from gourds are often garishly painted with hideous designs. The dance is not an independent rite but is a major symbolic feature of Cherokee night dances. Early forms of the Booger Dance were limited to winter performances, as killing frost and bitter cold were associated with ghosts. The dance then evolved during the nineteenth century to deal with the appearance of whites. Performed by four to ten men and sometimes two to four women, it incorporates profane, lewd, even obscene dramatic elements.

See also Dances and dancing; Medicine and modes of curing, pre-contact.

Boudinot, Elias (c. 1803, near Rome, Ga.—June 22, 1839, Park Hill, Indian Territory): Editor, writer

ALSO KNOWN AS: Galegina

TRIBAL AFFILIATION: Eastern Cherokee

SIGNIFICANCE: Boudinot was editor of, and a frequent contributor to, the Cherokee newspaper, the *Cherokee Phoenix*; he collaborated in translating parts of the New Testament into Cherokee and was a signer of the Treaty of New Echota

Elias Boudinot was born Galegina or Kilakeena Watie in northwestern Georgia in 1803, to a full-blooded Cherokee father and a half-blood mother. He became a Christian and attended the Moravian mission school at Spring Place. Upon graduation in 1818, he and his cousin John Ridge, with Leonard Hicks, enrolled at the Foreign Mission School at Cornwall, Connecticut. At this time, Galegina adopted the name Elias Boudinot from one of the benefactors of the school.

After graduation, Boudinot attended the Andover Theological Seminary. When he became engaged to Harriet Gold of Cornwall, townspeople hostile to racial intermarriage burned them in effigy, but Harriet married Elias on March 28, 1826. They had six children, one of whom (Elias Cornelius Boudinot) became a noted Indian lawyer. En route back to Georgia, Boudinot delivered a notable address at the First Presbyterian Church of Philadelphia in which he spoke of the progress and prosperity of the Cherokees and their desire to live in friendship with their white neighbors. Part of that progress was Sequoyah's devising an eighty-six-character syllabary, which soon enabled many Cherokees to read and write their own language. Consequently, the Cherokees started a newspaper, the *Cherokee Phoenix*, printed partly in English and partly in Cherokee, which Boudinot edited from February 21, 1828, until its suppression by the Georgia Guard in October, 1835. Boudinot frequently wrote for the paper and, in 1833, published in Cherokee a book, *Poor Sarah: Or, The Indian Woman*. With the Reverend Samuel Worcester, a close friend and neighbor, Boudinot worked on translating the New Testament into Cherokee.

When gold was discovered in Cherokee lands in the late 1820's, Georgia began an intense effort, supported by President Andrew Jackson, to force the Indians to give up their lands and move west. The principal chief of the Eastern Cherokees, John Ross, stubbornly resisted removal, even after his own plantation was confiscated and sold at lottery. Eventually, Boudinot, John Ridge, and Boudinot's uncle, Major Ridge, concluded that it might be better to go west and make a new start, free from persecution. Despite a "blood law" decreeing death for anyone selling Cherokee lands without the full consent of the nation, Boudinot and the Ridges signed the Treaty of New Echota in December, 1835, selling the Cherokee land in Georgia for five million dollars, comparable land in Indian Territory, and transportation there. John Ross and most Cherokees were not at New Echota and did not endorse the treaty, so the Ridge party was subject to the death penalty. In 1836, Harriet Boudinot died as a complication of childbirth. Boudinot married Delight Sargent and shortly thereafter journeyed with the Ridges to what is now eastern Oklahoma. When Ross and his followers continued to resist removal, President Martin Van Buren in 1838 sent troops to collect the remaining seventeen thousand or so Cherokees in concentration camps until they could be marched under armed guard to Indian Territory west of the Mississippi. The Trail of Tears in the autumn and winter of 1838-1839 became a death march in which about a third of the Cherokees died. In retaliation, militants of the Ross faction, without Ross's knowledge, carried out the blood law by murdering Boudinot, Major Ridge, and John Ridge on June 22, 1839.

See also Journalism; Removal; Ridge, John Rollins; Ross, John.

Boudinot, Elias Cornelius (Aug. 1, 1835, near Rome, Ga.—Sept. 27, 1890): Businessman, lawyer

TRIBAL AFFILIATION: Cherokee

SIGNIFICANCE: Boudinot, a lawyer and tobacco factory owner, was involved in a Supreme Court case with far-reaching implications

The son of Elias Boudinot, one of the signers of the Treaty of New Echota, Elias Cornelius Boudinot was one of the first relocated Cherokees to realize the possibility of great profits in Indian Territory. As a young man, Boudinot worked briefly as an engineer, but he soon changed careers. Settling in Arkansas, he studied law and was admitted to the bar in 1856. He also worked as a journalist, writing editorials for newspapers in Arkansas. During the Civil War, he served in the Confederate Army.

The Treaty of 1866 between the U.S. government and the Cherokees allowed manufacturing and merchandising to proceed on Cherokee land without excise tax being levied by the U.S. government. In the late 1860's, Boudinot and his uncle, Stand Watie, created the Watie and Boudinot Tobacco Company. They found that the cost of manufacturing chewing tobacco was forty-three cents per pound. Competing firms' product, after federal excise taxes were added, sold at seventy-five cents per pound. Boudinot quickly realized that he could sell his product at a significantly lower price. He used his profits to stake out extensive land claims of his own.

On December 20, 1869, however, U.S. marshals seized the Watie and Boudinot Tobacco Company after competitors claimed that the company had an unfair advantage. The case came before the U.S. Supreme Court, which ruled in 1871 that an act of Congress can supersede any treaty previously entered into and that the Watie and Boudinot Tobacco Company could be held *post facto* for unpaid excise taxes. This court decision ended one of the few economic advantages held by the Cherokees.

In the years after the case, Boudinot was a controversial figure, disliked by many Cherokees, as he advocated dividing Indian lands into individual allotments. He continued to farm and practice law in Indian Territory into the 1880's.

See also Boudinot, Elias; *Cherokee Tobacco* case; Watie, Stand.

Elias Cornelius Boudinot, cofounder of the Watie and Boudinot Tobacco Company. (Library of Congress)

Bowl (1756, N.C.—July 16, 1839, near present-day Overton, Tex.): Military leader

Also known as: Diwali, Colonel Bowles

Tribal affiliation: Cherokee

Significance: Leader of a large band of Cherokee militants, Bowl fought Americans throughout his life

The son of a Cherokee woman and a Scots-Irish trader named Bowles, Bowl was born in North Carolina and grew up in Chickamauga, Tennessee.

While most Cherokee sided with the Americans or remained neutral during the American Revolution, Bowl aided the British. In 1794, at the Massacre of Muscle Shoals, he attacked a white settlement along the Tennessee River in present-day Alabama. Thereafter, rather than surrendering to the Cherokee Council, which demanded his arrest, Bowl conducted his people across the Mississippi River to Spanish Territory. In 1824, after his new home in the Louisiana territory became a U.S. possession, Bowl again led his people westward, settling on the Angelina River in Texas, where Mexican authorities encouraged Indian settlement as a buffer to American expansion. Bowl's band was granted land near Overton, Texas, and in 1827, Bowl was commissioned a lieutenant colonel in the Mexican army. With Texan independence in 1835, white settlers demanded removal of Indians to reservations. Bowl retreated to Indian Territory, where he was killed in a battle against Texas troops in 1839.

See also Dragging Canoe; Indian-white relations—U.S., 1775-1830.

Bowlegs, Billy (c. 1810, northern Fla.—1864, Kans.): Resistance leader

Also known as: Holatamico, Halpatter-Micco

Tribal affiliation: Seminole

Significance: Billy Bowlegs was the principal leader of the Seminoles in Florida during the Third Seminole War, 1855-1858

Bowlegs was a Miccosukee, or Hitchiti-speaking Seminole, who was related to other prominent leaders of the tribe. His Indian name, Holatamico, is a Creek corn dance title for a leader with influence over several villages.

Bowlegs first emerged as a leader in 1832, when he signed the Treaty of Payne's Landing. He led other Seminole warriors during the Second Seminole War and remained in the field after Osceola was captured. In 1839, he directed a force of two hundred in an attack on a federal trading post, killing most of the garrison. He surrendered in 1842 and was given a grant of land in Florida. By this time he was recognized as the most prominent leader of the Seminoles who remained in Florida, and as such he went to Washington to speak with federal officials in 1842.

Government officials in 1850 began pressuring Bowlegs to take his people to the Indian Territory. They offered him $215,000 and sponsored him on a tour of several cities, including a stop in Washington, where he met President Millard Fillmore. Bowlegs would not move, so the government in 1853 declared that all Indians in Florida were outlaws.

Seminole leader Billy Bowlegs in an 1858 Harper's Weekly *portrait.* (Library of Congress)

The Third Seminole War erupted in 1855 when a party of federal surveyors and soldiers penetrated the region inhabited by Bowlegs and his people. Bowlegs led an attack on the intruders, and three years of guerrilla warfare ensued. The federals greatly outnumbered Bowlegs' tiny force, but they never inflicted a decisive defeat.

In 1858, Bowlegs accepted a large financial settlement from the government and moved his followers—thirty-three warriors, eighty women and children—to the Indian Territory, where he remained a prominent leader. When the Civil War began, he spurned the Confederates and led his group to Kansas, where he became a captain in a Union regiment mustered from among the Indians. He died of smallpox in 1864 while still serving in the army.

See also Seminole; Seminole Wars.

Bows, arrows, and quivers

Tribes affected: Pantribal

Significance: The bow and arrow was the most important missile weapon used by North American Indians

Archery was universal in native North America, and the bow and arrow was by far the most important missile weapon complex in use. The bow and arrow was of tremendous importance in hunting, which was vital to procuring the food supply in all parts of the continent. Archery was also essential in warfare, where it existed, and was rich in symbolism. The making of bows and arrows involved highly valued knowledge and skills. The materials from which archery tackle was made were often important in trade, as were the finished products. The design and scale of bows, arrows, and quivers varied regionally, as did the materials utilized. Both bows and arrows were made in proportion to the archer's body; the formulae used varied with the size of tackle desired.

Bows were of several types. Most common was a selfbow (a bow made of a single piece of wood with no laminating materials) of springy wood tapering toward both ends and sometimes narrowed at the grip. This bow type seems to be virtually the only one definitely recorded for the eastern United States, southeastern Canada, and most of Mexico. In the north and west, wooden bows and generally shorter bows of horn, antler, or bone were reinforced with sinew. In the Arctic, the sinew was commonly attached in the form of many strands of a slender

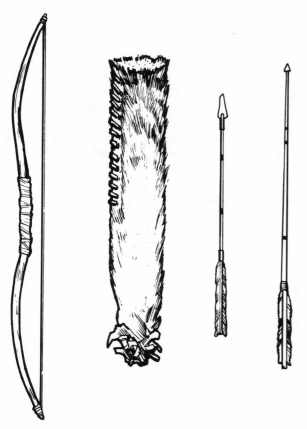

Southern Paiute (Great Basin) hardwood bow, animal skin quiver, and arrows; the left arrow is wooden with an iron point, the right is a cane arrow tipped with stone.

cable laced to the back of the bow so that its tension could be adjusted to suit the archer. Elsewhere the sinew was applied directly to the back of the bow with glue and sometimes with lashings as well. An alternative bow type utilized sinew lashings to reinforce the bow but lacked the sinew backing. In general, bows were longer in the east. Bowstrings were made of sinew, plant fiber cordage, hide, or gut. Bracers were often simple hide straps, but other types were known as well.

Arrows were predominantly of wood, but reed- or cane-shafted arrows with wooden foreshafts into which points might be set were common in the western and southern United States and southward. Arrow points were of many types and were made of bone, antler, hardwood, and other materials as well as stone. Points and fletching were attached with lashings of sinew and sometimes with pitch or glue.

Quivers were generally narrow bags of animal skin that could be conveniently slung over the shoulder for ease in carrying. In the north and west, a common quiver type was a fur bag that sheltered both the bow and its arrows from the weather. In the central United States and neighboring regions a separate case for the bow was sometimes attached to the quiver. Other quivers were simply arrow cases. Accessories, such as sinew and arrow points or a fire drill, were often carried in the quiver or in bags attached to it.

Boys commonly practiced archery from early childhood and began hunting small game while still very young. The bow and arrow was the constant companion of men of all ages. Native archery is said to have been deadly at a distance of fifty yards. The form employed in shooting varied both between and within tribes.

See also Atlatl; Hunting and gathering; Lances and spears; Projectile points; Warfare and conflict; Weapons.

Bozeman Trail wars

DATE: Summer, 1866-fall, 1868
PLACE: Montana, Wyoming
TRIBES AFFECTED: Arapaho, Cheyenne, Sioux
SIGNIFICANCE: One of the first instances of Plains tribes uniting to thwart white expansion, proving their ability to pose a significant barrier to that expansion

During the summer of 1866, U.S. government peacekeepers gathered at Fort Laramie along with numerous Sioux leaders, including Young Man Afraid of His Horses and Red Cloud. Their goal was to gain Indian consent to opening the Bozeman Trail to white travelers and allowing the establishment of military posts along it. They purposely obscured their intentions until the arrival of Colonel Henry B. Carrington's command exposed the deceit (Carrington had presumed that negotiations would be finished before he arrived). Red Cloud wrathfully broke off negotiations and vowed violence against any whites who traveled the route. Regardless, Carrington established Fort Reno on the trail's southern end on the Powder River, Fort C. F. Smith on its northern end on the Bighorn River, and Fort Phil Kearny between the two. This was the area of the Bozeman Trail wars (the eastern slope of the

Bighorn Mountains), the conflict's epicenter being Fort Phil Kearny.

Indian forces led by Red Cloud soon struck and took control of the region. The forts became islands in a sea of hostility. By the fall of 1866, the Indians had devised plans against Fort Phil Kearny using a decoy tactic requiring uncustomary discipline and coordination on the Indians' part. On the morning of December 21, the Indians, with roughly 1,750 warriors, lured Captain William J. Fetterman and his command of eighty-one from Fort Phil Kearny with a decoy party led by a young Crazy Horse, surrounded the command, and wiped them out to the last man.

The army, determined to command the region, established Fort Fetterman at the lower end of the trail. Nevertheless, the Sioux and Cheyenne controlled the region through persistent attacks, and they literally closed the road. By the summer of 1867, the Indians' hatred for the forts had swelled, and in July, following their annual Sun Dance, plans were laid to destroy Forts Phil Kearny and C. F. Smith altogether. It was decided that some five hundred to eight hundred Cheyenne would attack Fort C. F. Smith while another thousand Sioux under Red Cloud would strike Fort Phil Kearny. The battles that ensued were the Hayfield Fight, near Fort C. F. Smith, and the Wagon Box Fight, near Fort Phil Kearny. The battles bore remarkable similarities. Both military detachments that were attacked numbered approximately thirty and were severely outnumbered. Both groups also had the new breech-loading Springfield rifles (not muzzle loaders, as had Fetterman's troops) and were able to repel numerous charges from the Indians while inflicting severe casualties. Even so, Red Cloud and other leaders remained unmoved in their demands for abandonment of the forts as conditions to any treaty agreements. The army finally decided to abandon the forts, realizing their cost inefficiency as well as the fact that the railroads would soon make the road obsolete. As the troops abandoned the forts, the Indians put them to torch. The ensuing treaty agreements ultimately became the (second) Treaty of Fort Laramie (1868). Red Cloud himself submitted to the agreements and to reservation life, thus ending the Bozeman Trail wars.

See also Crazy Horse; Fort Laramie Treaty of 1868; Indian-white relations—U.S., 1831-1870; Red Cloud; Wagon Box Battle; Young Man Afraid of His Horses.

Brant, Joseph (c. 1742, Ohio Valley—Nov. 24, 1807, Grand River, Ontario, Canada): Unofficial chief

ALSO KNOWN AS: Thayendanegea (Two Sticks of Wood Bound Together for Strength)

TRIBAL AFFILIATION: Mohawk

SIGNIFICANCE: An unofficial leader of the Mohawk tribe and of the Six Nations Iroquois Confederacy, Brant led most of the Iroquois in siding with the British during the American Revolution

Born into the matrilineal and matrilocal Mohawk tribe, and into a leading political family, Joseph Brant's status as a chief or "sachem" of the Mohawk tribe was unorthodox. Because of his position within his family, he had no chance of inheriting a formal position as sachem. Instead, Brant was the most famous of the "pine tree chiefs," men whose political power rested on recognition by European American and European Canadian political or military leaders rather than from within their own nation or tribe.

Brant was born in 1742, while his family was on a seasonal hunting trip in the Ohio Valley. His older sister was Molly Brant (Degonwadonti), who inherited the political office of matron from her family line. While growing up at Canajoharie, the Mohawk village on the Mohawk River in present-day upstate New York, both Joseph and Molly Brant were exposed to two worlds and two cultures. They lived in the Mohawk village but may have attended an Anglican mission school and church nearby. A close family friend was Sir William Johnson, Superintendent of Indian Affairs for the British colonial administration from the 1750's to the 1770's. Molly Brant married Johnson according to Mohawk rite, probably in 1758, and young Joseph, now Johnson's brother-in-law, became William Johnson's protégé.

With his mentor leading the way, thirteen-year-old Joseph Brant experienced the terrors of battle at Lake George, New York, in 1755. Johnson led a group of Mohawk warriors, including Brant, in a victory over the French in this important engagement of the French and Indian War (1754-1763), in which the British defeated the French. In 1757, Brant was commissioned as a captain in His Majesty's Royal American Regiment. In this capacity, he and other Mohawks accompanied Johnson on a campaign to capture Forts Oswego, Miami, Duquesne, Detroit, and Niagara from the French. Brant proved a courageous warrior during this campaign.

At the close of the war, Sir William sponsored Brant's continued formal education at Moor's Charity School (later to become Dartmouth College). The school curriculum emphasized English, Latin, Greek, and mathematics, as well as practical training courses. Christianity was also emphasized; Brant attended Bible study and catechism classes and was baptized, probably in 1763. In that year he returned to his homeland to rally support among the Mohawks and the other Iroquois tribes (Oneidas, Onondagas, Cayugas, Tuscaroras, and Senecas) for a steadfast alliance with the British. This support was needed against the confederacy of tribes rallying around Pontiac for war against the British. Although Joseph Brant was gaining in reputation as an accomplished warrior and unofficial leader of the Mohawks, his popularity within the Iroquois Confederacy at large was limited because many of them sided with Pontiac. Many non-Mohawk Iroquois leaders such as Cornplanter, a Seneca, were growing wary of Brant.

Brant first married an Oneida woman with whom he had two children, Isaac and Christine. Isaac inherited his mother's fiery temper, and when she died of tuberculosis, he blamed his father. Brant then married his deceased wife's half-sister, but she also died of tuberculosis within a year. In 1775, a year after the death of his mentor, William Johnson, Joseph married Catharine Croghan, daughter of a Mohawk woman and an

Mohawk leader Joseph Brant urged the Iroquois to side with the British in the American Revolution. (Library of Congress)

Irish man. She was to bear him seven children in the 1780's and 1790's. Before he could start a family, however, the American Revolution took up much of Brant's time and proved to be extremely disruptive not only to the Brant family but also to the Mohawk and Iroquois nations in general.

As the patriots and loyalists formed sides around 1775, few of the former wooed Iroquois leaders to their side. Most were disdainful of Indians, seeing them as a nuisance to be gotten rid of to make way for European American farms. Consequently, and also perhaps because leaders such as Brant were hand-in-glove with the British Indian Department, most sided with the British. Guy Johnson, Sir William's nephew and successor in his post as head of the Indian Department, made Brant his secretary. The Indian Department operated during the American revolutionary war mostly as a military force for fighting non-Indians. Brant was also recognized as a leader of the Mohawk warriors, and in that capacity British officials invited him to Montreal in 1774 to persuade him into solid support of the British cause against the Americans. Sir Guy Carleton, governor of the colony of Quebec, and Major-General Frederick Haldimand, commander-in-chief of the military forces, displayed the power of the British army for Brant and others. Haldimand even promised that the Iroquois would not lose their lands at the end of the war. Brant and others wanted assurances directly from the British crown, so they journeyed to England in 1775 and held meetings with King George III.

These combined efforts convinced the Mohawks to promise Iroquois support for the British in the impending war. Brant returned to the Mohawk Valley convinced of British victory.

Brant's sister Molly also lobbied among all the Iroquois nations for a strong contingent of warriors to join the British forces. Eventually most, except one large faction of the Oneidas, agreed. During the war, Joseph Brant was extensively involved in military operations in the Mohawk Valley, most notably at Oriskany, Cherry Valley, and German Flats. Patriot legend had it that Brant participated in a British raid on Wyoming, a hamlet south of the Mohawk River, committing horrible atrocities against American settlers there; it was later proved that he had not been there. In fact, he was known for his humanity in the face of war, more than once sparing innocent women and children from the brutality of his fellow non-Indian officers (such as Walter Butler, Jr.).

When the Clinton-Sullivan expedition invaded Iroquois territory and wreaked havoc on Seneca towns and food supplies in the far west of Iroquoia, Red Jacket, a Seneca chief long opposed to Brant for his too-close ties to the British, blamed Brant's policies for the revenge of the Clinton-Sullivan patriots. Red Jacket even attempted to engineer a separate peace with the Americans. Brant heard of the plan and headed it off, only to discover that during the treaty negotiations between the Americans and the British in 1783 the Iroquois Confederacy had been forgotten.

Brant spent much of his time after the American Revolution trying to rectify this injustice. Most of the Iroquois people took refuge at British Fort Niagara at the end of the war, and holding onto Haldimand's promise, Brant convinced him to grant a huge tract of land west of the fort, in a newly formed British colony (upper Canada, now Ontario), to the Six Iroquois Nations. In 1784, the Iroquois were granted a large tract of land along the Grand River: about six miles wide from the river's source to its mouth on Lake Erie. The town which grew up near this reserve became known as Brant's Ford—Brantford. Brant, in order to make the reserve a success, sold parcels of it to non-Indians in order to raise money for needed supplies. Many Mohawks and other Iroquois who settled there criticized him for this, as they did for his grandiose style (he dressed and furnished his estate in the manner of an English gentleman) and for his posturing with British colonial and American officials. Brant had personally received from the British government a tract of land at Burlington Bay, east of Grand River, for an estate of his own, and therefore was distanced geographically as well as in outlook from his people. While many of them wanted to maintain as much of their traditional culture as possible, Brant arranged for English-language schools, Christian missionaries, and other elements of European culture at Grand River.

Brant remained a controversial figure until his death in 1807. He was seen by many Iroquois as a self-promoter who sold out his people to the British. Nevertheless, he was an extremely influential figure in a turbulent period of North American history.
—*Gretchen L. Green*

See also Brant, Molly; Cornplanter; Fort Stanwix, Treaty of; French and Indian Wars; Iroquois Confederacy; Mohawk; Pontiac's Conspiracy; Red Jacket.

BIBLIOGRAPHY

Graymont, Barbara. *The Iroquois in the American Revolution.* Syracuse, N.Y.: Syracuse University Press, 1972.

Green, Gretchen. "Molly Brant, Catharine Brant, and Their Daughters: A Study in Colonial Acculturation." *Ontario History* 81, no. 3 (1989): 235-250.

Hamilton, Milton W. *Sir William Johnson: Colonial American, 1715-1763.* Port Washington, N.Y.: Kennikat Press, 1976.

Kelsay, Isabel Thompson. *Joseph Brant, 1743-1807: Man of Two Worlds.* Syracuse, N.Y.: Syracuse University Press, 1984.

O'Donnell, James H. "Joseph Brant." In *American Indian Leaders: Studies in Diversity*, edited by R. David Edmunds. Lincoln: University of Nebraska Press, 1980.

Stone, William L. *The Life of Joseph Brant—Thayendanegea.* 2 vols. 1838. Reprint. St. Clair Shores, Mich.: Scholarly Press, 1970.

Brant, Molly (c. 1753, Canajoharie, N.Y.—Apr. 16, 1796, Kingston, Ontario, Canada): Tribal matron

ALSO KNOWN AS: Mary Brant, Degonwadonti (Many Opposed to One), Gonwatsijayenni

TRIBAL AFFILIATION: Mohawk

SIGNIFICANCE: Brant was a leading Mohawk political figure during the time of the American Revolution. She was instrumental in convincing the Mohawks and the Iroquois Confederacy to side with the British

Little is known of Molly Brant's early childhood, except that she lived with her family at the Mohawk village of Canajoharie and frequently traveled to the Ohio Valley for winter hunting trips. Brant's childhood was one of mixed Mohawk and English/Dutch influences; she may have attended an Anglican mission school at Canajoharie and therefore learned how to read and write English, since her letters written in later years displayed excellent penmanship. Her family was prominent within Mohawk society; consequently, she was destined to become a matron (a female political role in traditional Iroquois culture). Her younger brother, Joseph Brant, was to become a prominent politician and war leader.

Brant's stepfather was a close personal friend of Sir William Johnson, Superintendent of Indian Affairs for the British colonial administration in North America from the 1740's to the 1770's. Brant married Johnson according to Mohawk marriage customs, probably in 1758, and although he was against female involvement in politics, Brant stubbornly refused to let her marriage prevent her from exercising her political power. In addition to bearing eight children with Johnson, Brant took advantage of the opportunities available at her new residence, Johnson Hall, which was also the headquarters of the British Indian Department. She used these opportunities, some of them in the form of access to information, some in the form of material goods, to increase her own political influence among

the Iroquois people. After her husband's death in 1774, she was said to be the heir of his influence among the Iroquois. Patriot revolutionary war politicians and military strategists feared this influence, since Brant was loyal to the British.

When hostilities broke out between the British and the Americans, Brant refused to leave her homeland. She aided the British cause by informing British rangers of an impending American attack on a New York village, as well as by working to convince the Mohawk tribe and the Iroquois Confederacy that their interests could best be served by siding with the British against the Americans. Most were reluctant to agree with her, although gradually they were forced by circumstances to make a decision. Most decided to ally with the British; both Molly Brant and her brother Joseph played large roles in this outcome.

Brant received a military pension from the British government following the American Revolution, and lived, courtesy of the British, in a substantial European-style house in Kingston, Ontario. She attended the Anglican church, which she had helped to establish, until her death in 1796. Despite Brant's apparent assimilation, she dressed Mohawk-style throughout her life, and often insisted on speaking only Mohawk, even though she could speak English. Her legacy among the Mohawk people is controversial, however. She is viewed by some as having sold out her people by convincing them to fight on the British side in the American Revolution, after which they were forgotten at the treaty negotiations in 1783. She did protest this omission, and the treatment of Iroquois people by the British, on numerous occasions after 1783, but her influence among her people had declined by that time. Brant may not have been popular among her kinspeople after the Revolutionary War, since she chose not to live on one of the two Mohawk reserves set up in Upper Canada (Ontario) by the British government in the 1780's.

See also Brant, Joseph; Iroquois Confederacy; Mohawk.

Bronson, Ruth Muskrat (Whitewater, Okla., 1897—June 24, 1982, Tucson, Ariz.): Educator

TRIBAL AFFILIATION: Cherokee

SIGNIFICANCE: Bronson educated Native American youth in their culture and heritage

Beginning her career as a playground supervisor, Ruth Bronson went on to obtain an A.B. degree from Mount Holyoke College in Massachusetts. She taught at the Haskell Institute in Kansas in 1935. She also worked with the Bureau of Indian Affairs, starting in 1931 as director of the bureau's scholarship program, a position she held until 1943, after which she was executive secretary of the National Congress of American Indians. From 1957 until she retired in 1962, she was health education specialist for the San Carlos Apache Reservation in Arizona. After retirement, she continued her work as an educator, serving the Tohono O'odham and Yaqui in Arizona as a representative of the Save the Children Foundation. She died in a nursing home in Tucson.

See also Education, post-contact.

Bruce, Louis R. (Dec. 30, 1906, Onondaga Reservation near Syracuse, N.Y.—May 20, 1989, Arlington, Va.): Native American leader, BIA commissioner

ALSO KNOWN AS: Agwelius (Swift)

TRIBAL AFFILIATION: Mohawk, Oglala Sioux

SIGNIFICANCE: Bruce served as commissioner of the Bureau of Indian Affairs (BIA) during a time of considerable Native American activism

Louis R. Bruce was reared on the Saint Regis Mohawk reservation in upper New York state; his father was a Methodist minister there. Bruce's mother was an Oglala Sioux, and he considered himself a Sioux; his paternal grandfather was a Mohawk chief. Bruce was graduated from Syracuse University in 1930; in 1935 he was appointed the New York state director of Indian projects for the National Youth Administration, a position he held for seven years.

Bruce was named commissioner of the Bureau of Indian Affairs by President Richard Nixon in 1969. He set out to "Indianize" the bureau by appointing Native Americans to influential positions. His policies encountered considerable opposition from interests that had benefited from keeping Indians in subordinate positions. Bruce's tenure coincided with Indian activist movements in the late 1960's and early 1970's; in 1972, for example, the BIA building in Washington was occupied by native militants. Bruce and most of his top assistants were subsequently fired by Nixon, less than a week before the 1972 presidential election.

See also Bureau of Indian Affairs (BIA); Trail of Broken Treaties.

Buffalo

TRIBES AFFECTED: Plains tribes

SIGNIFICANCE: Until the nineteenth century, Plains tribes subsisted largely on the buffalo (or bison); by the 1870's, the combination of the fur trade and white hide hunters had nearly exterminated the herds, forcing Plains tribes to submit to the reservation system

From the end of the last Ice Age until the late nineteenth century, the American buffalo, also called the bison, was the dominant species in the Great Plains. While some estimates of the historic bison population have ranged as high as one hundred million, increasingly accurate assessments of the carrying capacity of the grasslands have suggested that the historic bison population in the Great Plains was not more than thirty million. Native Americans hunted bison on foot for thousands of years by surrounding a herd until the animals were within

The hunting of buffalo, which could provide food, clothing, and shelter, was central to the plains culture of the late eighteenth and early nineteenth centuries. (American Museum of Natural History)

Buffalo Depletion from 1850 to 1895

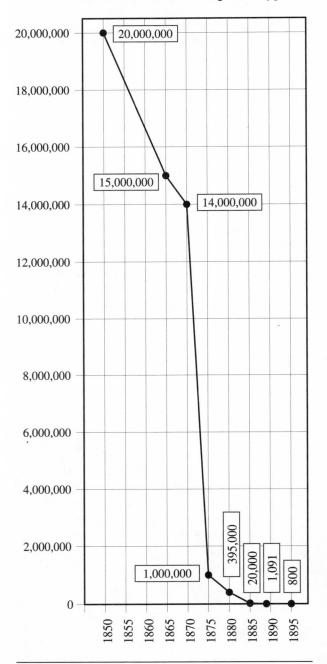

Source: Data are from Thornton, Russell, *American Indian Holocaust and Survival: A Population History Since 1492* (Norman: University of Oklahoma Press, 1987); Thornton, Russell, *We Shall Live Again: The 1870 and 1890 Ghost Dance Movements as Demographic Revitalization* (New York: Cambridge University Press, 1986).

Note: In the twentieth century the buffalo population began to rebound from its 1895 low of about 800; in 1983 it was estimated at 50,000.

range of bows or by setting a fire to stampede a herd over a bluff.

Following the diffusion of horses into the Great Plains in the first half of the eighteenth century, a number of tribes—among them the Arapaho, Assiniboine, Atsina, Blackfeet Confederacy, Cheyenne, Comanche, Kiowa, Apache of Oklahoma (Kiowa-Apache), and Sioux—became almost exclusively nomadic, equestrian buffalo hunters. Others—among them the Arikara, Hidatsa, Mandan, and Pawnee—maintained their gardens in the river valleys of the Plains while adapting from pedestrian to equestrian buffalo hunting. The nomadic tribes adapted their social organization to the habits of the bison. They assembled as a tribe only during the summer, when the bison were congregated for the rutting season. During the rest of the year they were divided into bands, reflecting the actions of the herds, which divided to search for winter forage.

In response to the fur trade, Indian hunting of the buffalo accelerated during the nineteenth century. By the 1840's, the Plains Indians were providing between 150,000 and 200,000 buffalo robes each year to European American fur traders along the Missouri River. By the 1850's, Indian commercial hunting had markedly reduced the number of bison in the eastern Great Plains.

White hide hunters delivered the final blow to the herds in the 1870's and early 1880's. As many as two thousand buffalo hunters armed with large-caliber Sharps or Winchester rifles blanketed the southern Great Plains in the early 1870's. The hide hunters were extraordinarily destructive: In the early years of the slaughter, every hide shipped to market probably represented five dead bison. In the late 1870's, having largely extirpated the bison from the southern Great Plains, the hide hunters moved to the north, where they destroyed the remaining herds by 1883. By 1889, there were fewer than three hundred of the animals remaining in remote areas of the Texas panhandle, Colorado, Montana, and Wyoming. Once the herds were destroyed, the Plains Indians were reduced to extreme poverty and had little alternative to the reservation system.

See also Buffalo Dance; Horses; Plains.

Buffalo Dance

Tribe affected: Mandan

Significance: The Buffalo Dance and ceremony were meant to ensure an adequate supply of buffalo for the hunt

The Mandan, a hunting people of the northern Great Plains, performed the Buffalo Dance before the yearly hunt to ensure success. A special society, the Bull Dancers, wore buffalo head masks with eye and nose holes. The dancers carried buffalo hide shields and long lances. They had buffalo tails tied around their knees and danced until they fell to the ground from exhaustion. Then they were dragged away by other members of the tribe and symbolically skinned and butchered. According to Mandan tradition, the dance originated when a white buffalo took a shaman to the home of the "buffalo people" in the sky. Here he was taught the dance, and he brought it back to his people. As part of the dance ceremony, Mandan women prepare two large kettles of corn meal mush—which buffaloes like very much—and set them out at the edge of the village. Women in the White Buffalo Calf Society then lure buffalo to the camp by putting on buffalo robes and dancing wildly. As the dance ends, the performers say a prayer to the gods thanking them for all they have provided and asking for their help in living as the gods wish. The dancers then eat the mush.

Buffalo dancing had stopped by 1900—the buffalo were gone, so there was no longer a reason to perform the dance. White reservation officials had already banned buffalo dancing because of its "pagan" nature. Only in the 1930's, with buffalo herds restored to a few areas of the Great Plains, was the dance performed again, though mostly for the benefit of tourists.

See also Buffalo; Mandan; Plains.

Buffalo Hump (c. 1800, Indian Territory, present-day Okla.—after 1865): War chief

ALSO KNOWN AS: Bull Hump, Pochanaw-quoip
TRIBAL AFFILIATION: Comanche
SIGNIFICANCE: A leader in the early Comanche Wars, Buffalo Hump was most active from the 1830's through the 1850's

With the exception of his exploits as a leader during the early Comanche Wars, little is known of Buffalo Hump's life. After proving himself in battle against Mexicans, Texans, Cheyennes, and Arapahos, Buffalo Hump became principal chief of the Peneteka band of Comanches in 1849.

In the 1830's, he led more than one thousand men on raids for horses and slaves in Chihuahua, Mexico. During the same period, he also raided other Indians, particularly the Southern Cheyenne under Yellow Wolf. In 1840, Buffalo Hump participated in establishing peace between the Cheyennes, Kiowas, and Comanches.

After an incident in 1838 known as the Council House Affair, in which Texas Rangers attempted to force Comanche release of several white hostages by seizing chiefs who had gathered under truce at San Antonio, Buffalo Hump led his forces to the Gulf of Mexico. After raiding several villages and coming under attack by Rangers, Buffalo Hump returned north.

Texas Rangers led a coordinated campaign against the Comanches in the 1850's. Although his band was badly defeated at Rush Springs, Oklahoma, Buffalo Hump escaped. With representatives from other Southern Plains tribes, including the Comanches, Kiowas, Cheyennes, and Arapahos, Buffalo Hump, in October, 1856, signed the Little Arkansas Treaty, by which a reservation was established in Kansas and Indian Territory. The resulting peace was short-lived, however, as the promised reservation was never established. Buffalo Hump's son, also named Buffalo Hump, fought with war chief Quanah Parker.

See also Comanche; Parker, Quanah; Yellow Wolf.

Bull Bear (c. 1840, Kans.—after 1875, Cheyenne Reservation, Indian Territory): Military leader

TRIBAL AFFILIATION: Cheyenne
SIGNIFICANCE: One of the principal leaders of the elite Cheyenne Dog Soldiers, Bull Bear participated in numerous battles during the Cheyenne Wars for the Great Plains

With Tall Bull and White Horse, Bull Bear led the society of warriors known as the Dog Soldiers. Functioning partially as an internal Cheyenne police force, the Dog Soldiers were also known for their battles against the U.S. Army during the wars for domination of the Plains. After his brother, peace chief Lean Bear, was murdered in 1864, Bull Bear became increasingly militant and thereafter was arguably the most powerful Dog Soldier.

Although he negotiated with Colorado governor John Evans at Camp Weld in 1864, Bull Bear nevertheless continued raiding whites. He participated in the Hancock Campaign of 1867, which sought to eliminate all non-reservation Indian presence in Kansas, and (although he signed the Medicine Lodge Treaty in 1867) he fought against the Sheridan Campaign, including the Battle at Summit Springs, Colorado, on July 11, 1868, during which Tall Bull was killed. In 1869, he led his people to Indian Territory, but returned in 1871. During the Red River War of 1874-1875, he aided the Comanches and Kiowas, thereafter retiring to the Cheyenne Reservation.

See also Cheyenne; Lean Bear; Medicine Lodge, Treaties of; Roman Nose; Tall Bull.

Bundles, sacred

TRIBES AFFECTED: Pantribal
SIGNIFICANCE: Sacred bundles contain objects that represent the power or medicine of their owner; assembled under the guidance of spirit beings, they are used in ceremonies to assure the well-being of an individual, clan, or tribe

Sacred bundles were believed to have supernatural power to cure the sick, win the affections of another, get revenge on an enemy, gain possessions, or even assure long life for an individual or a whole tribe. Wrapped in the hide of a deer or the whole skin of an otter, some tribal bundles were large enough to hold hundreds of items, while personal bundles were often small enough to carry in one hand. (Although the use of sacred bundles is treated as historical here to emphasize their great importance in many traditional American Indian cultures, it is important to note that many practices involving sacred bundles still occur today.)

Sacred bundles required special care. They were considered to be "alive" with supernatural power. Some personal bundles were displayed in the owner's lodge or hung outside the tipi, but the great tribal bundles were secluded from everyday view. Because of their magical quality they were surrounded with taboos. Bundles represented an important link with the past and supernatural beings and could be opened only under prescribed circumstances to benefit the person or the tribe.

Traditionally, a personal bundle was acquired through a vision quest. One went out alone for several days and fasted and prayed until the guardian spirit was encountered. A relationship was established and directions were given for the spiritual path of the seeker. Upon return from the quest, objects were gathered for the medicine bundle as symbols of the experience. An item representing the guardian spirit was usually worn to assure ongoing contact. The primary item in a medicine bundle symbolized the guardian spirit. Tobacco, feathers, fur, stones, or anything of special meaning could become part of the bundle. Often a song was given by the spirits as part of the seeker's medicine.

Something of the vision experience, such as a song, a painting on a shield, a dance, or the telling of a particular incident, was shared with the tribe. In this way others received some of the power that was available as long as requirements were met for keeping the bundle.

In some tribes a bundle could be inherited through the father's lineage, captured during a battle, purchased, or received in exchange for horses. A powerful bundle could be duplicated for one or two others with permission of the spirits. The owner could remake a bundle that was lost or taken in a fight. Unless the bundle, with its power, was willingly given to someone, it belonged to the owner until death.

Personal Bundles. Objects in a sacred bundle filled a definite purpose, either spiritual or practical. A large medicine-pipe bundle belonging to a member of the Blackfoot tribe, for example, contained a decorated pipe stem along with a tobacco cutting board and pipe stokers. Animal spirits were represented by an elk hide, bearskin, mountain-goat headdress, eagle-wing feather, head of a crane, skin of a loon (used as a tobacco pouch), fetus of a deer, and skins of prairie dog, squirrel, mink, muskrat, and owl. Other ceremonial tools were a rattle, a rawhide bag of roots for making smudge (sacred incense), a bag of pine needles, and tongs for placing coals on the smudge. Personal items included necklaces, a wooden bowl for food, a horse whip, a thong lariat, and a painted buffalo robe. A sacred song was also given by the spirits and was sung any time the bundle was displayed. In Blackfoot tradition, the pipe bundle could be opened on four occasions: when the first thunder was heard in the spring; when the bundle was being transferred to a new leader; when tobacco in the bundle was renewed; and when the pipe was used in keeping a vow.

Tribal Bundles. The great tribal bundles, such as the Blackfoot Sacred Pipe bundle or the Pawnee Evening Star bundle, were sometimes displayed at ceremonies, but they were opened only on special occasions. In some Plains tribes bundles were used to "keep the world together." The people believed that the tribe's well-being depended on the proper care and protection of those bundles because the items within them symbolized life itself. The Kiowas had a small stone image resembling a man that was shown to the people only once a year at the Sun Dance.

The Fox of the Great Lakes had forty sacred bundle groups in eleven major categories. For the Pawnee of the Plains, the stars were important in sacred traditions, and the Evening Star bundle was assembled under the direction of that highly revered star guardian. A Cheyenne bundle contained the four Medicine Arrows, and an Arapaho bundle held a special flat pipe, an ear of corn, and a stone turtle.

The summer Green Corn Dance was a time of cleansing and renewal for the Seminole of Florida and Oklahoma. Meeting at sacred places in woods and near creeks, they danced and recited oral history to honor their mystical origin. Just before dawn on the fourth day, the sacred bundle was blessed and opened. Nearly seven hundred items wrapped in buckskin or white cloth contained sacred knowledge and medicine for the health of the tribe. The Seminole believed that this renewal of the sacred bundle assured that the people would not die and the tribe would not disappear.

The power within sacred bundles was regarded with wonder, respect, and sometimes fear. The sacred practitioners who worked with this secret and often dangerous knowledge learned by experimenting with natural forces after much ritual preparation. An untrained person would resist contact with this potent knowledge because, as one individual put it, "the power might come back at me if I exposed myself to it when I was not prepared, or not ready to know about it"; another said, "I wouldn't want to go near those medicine bundles if I didn't know how to act."

—*Gale M. Thompson*

See also Calumets and pipe bags; Ethnophilosophy and worldview; Medicine bundles; Religion; Sacred, the.

BIBLIOGRAPHY

Beck, Peggy V., Anna Lee Walters, and Nia Francisco. *The Sacred: Ways of Knowledge, Sources of Life*. Redesigned ed. Tsaile, Ariz.: Navajo Community College Press, 1992.

Brown, Joseph Epes. *The Spiritual Legacy of the American Indian*. New York: Crossroad, 1982.

Garbarino, Merwyn S. *Native American Heritage*. Boston: Little, Brown, 1976.

Radin, Paul. *The Story of the American Indian*. Deluxe illustrated ed. Garden City, N.Y.: Garden City Publishing, 1937.

Underhill, Ruth Murray. *Red Man's America: A History of Indians in the United States*. Chicago: University of Chicago Press, 1953.

Bureau of Indian Affairs (BIA)

DATE: Established March 11, 1824

TRIBES AFFECTED: Pantribal

SIGNIFICANCE: The BIA is the central U.S. federal agency for the management of Indian affairs

Attempting to centralize Indian administration, previously controlled by a bewildering array of government and military officials, Secretary of War John C. Calhoun in 1824 created the Bureau of Indian Affairs. Although authority over Indians initially resided in the Secretary of War, the fledgling bureau controlled all annuities and expenditures, managed funds for the civilization of Indians, mediated disputes between Indians under the trade and intercourse laws, and handled all correspondence. In 1832 the president was empowered to appoint a commissioner of Indian affairs.

In 1849 the BIA was transferred to the newly created Department of the Interior. Thereafter authority descended from the president of the United States to the secretary of the interior to the commissioner of Indian affairs. The coordination of field superintendents, agents, missionaries, traders, and local Indians was entrusted to a field superintendent who corresponded directly with the commissioner. The BIA grew rapidly, from its original three members to six thousand employees in 1911. By the late twentieth century it had thirteen thousand employees and controlled a budget of nearly $900 million.

Designed to implement federal policy, the BIA has historically reflected prevailing government attitudes toward Indians. Initially it oversaw funding under the 1819 civilization plan designed to aid assimilation through education. Similarly, under the General Allotment Act, passed in 1887, the BIA was charged with the mammoth task of preparing a list of members of tribes as well as classifying and appraising Indian lands.

After World War I, responding to government economizing mandates, the BIA decentralized its operations. Regional offices were superimposed over the existing administrative structure, and further reorganization in 1946 provided for separate geographical divisions with regional headquarters.

Surveys and studies during the 1920's, including the scathing Meriam Report, revealed the appalling conditions of Indian life under the allotment plan, thereby giving impetus to fresh reforms. Between 1933 and 1945 during Commissioner John Collier's tenure, the BIA for the first time turned from its assimilationist policy. Because of Collier's influence, the Indian Reorganization Act (IRA) of 1934 provided for a revitalization of tribal government and social customs. The IRA also granted Indians priority hiring within the BIA. Indeed, by 1982, Indians accounted for 78 percent of BIA personnel.

Since the 1960's the BIA's influence over Indian affairs has eroded, thereby favoring a shift of responsibility to Indians themselves. In 1975, for example, the Indian Self-Determination and Education Assistance Act encouraged Indians to assume control over pertinent government programs. In the 1990's dispersion of BIA activities to states, to other agencies, and to Indians continued, yet the bureau remained a vast organization supporting twelve regional offices and eighty-two agencies headed by a commissioner. The BIA still oversaw several features of Indian life, including education, law enforcement, and the mobilization of public and private funds for economic development and natural resource management.

See also Bruce, Louis R.; General Allotment Act; Indian Reorganization Act; Indian-white relations—U.S., 1871-1933; Indian-white relations—U.S., 1934-1995; Termination policy; Trail of Broken Treaties.

Burke Act

Date: May 8, 1906
Tribes affected: Pantribal
Significance: Passed to improve the process of allotting tribal lands to individual American Indians, the Burke Act contributed to the large-scale loss of Indian land between 1887 and 1934

In 1887 Congress passed the General Allotment Act (or Dawes Act). This act sought to make small farmers out of American Indians by dividing tribal lands into individual allotments. Indians taking allotments received United States citizenship; the government held the title for the lands in trust for twenty-five years, during which time they could not be sold. At the end of the period, the Indian would receive a fee patent giving him full ownership of the land.

The administration of the General Allotment Act prompted considerable criticism. Many of those sympathetic to the Indians were concerned at the distinction between citizenship, which was taken up at the outset, and ownership, which came at the end of the trust period. The discrepancy became a source of worry in 1905 when the Supreme Court ruled that citizenship exempted an Indian from direct federal supervision, thus invalidating federal restrictions on liquor on allotments. Other people simply thought that the trust period postponed too long the time when an Indian might sell his allotment.

In 1906 Congress passed the Burke Act, named for South Dakota Congressman Charles Henry Burke. The act provided that the trust period could be extended indefinitely on presidential authority, though it also permitted the secretary of the interior to cut the period short if requested, provided an individual Indian could prove that he was competent to manage his own affairs. In either case, there would be no citizenship until the end of the trust period, during which the Indian would remain subject to federal control.

The Burke Act had a major effect on the awarding of allotments, though not the one that some of its supporters had hoped. Though certificates of competency (and fee patents) were awarded cautiously at first, there were clear signs that many allotments quickly passed out of Indian possession once they could be sold or mortgaged. During the act's first decade of operation, roughly ten thousand fee patents were issued, the vast majority of allotments passing out of Indian ownership. When the ardent assimilationist Fred K. Lane became secretary of the interior in 1917, the process speeded up. Competency certificates and fee patents were often given without the requisite individual investigation, sometimes to Indians who had not asked for them. In four years twenty thousand fee patents were issued, again with much of the land quickly alienated.

During the 1920's, when the Burke himself was commissioner of Indian affairs, the process slowed, but the overall trend of allotment lands passing into the hands of non-Indians continued. By 1934, when the Indian Reorganization Act finally stopped the allotment process, Indians had lost 86 million of the 138 million acres they had controlled in 1887. In the meantime the citizenship available under the Burke Act had been made redundant by Congress's grant of citizenship to all Indians in 1924.

See also Allotment system; General Allotment Act; Indian Reorganization Act; Indian-white relations—U.S., 1871-1933; Meriam Report.

Bushyhead, Dennis Wolf (Mar. 18, 1826, near Cleveland, Tenn.—Feb. 4, 1898, Talequah, Okla.): Tribal chief

ALSO KNOWN AS: Unáduti

TRIBAL AFFILIATION: Cherokee

SIGNIFICANCE: Bushyhead was one of the leading political figures of the Cherokee Nation during the last half of the nineteenth century

Dennis Wolf Bushyhead, a mixed-blood Cherokee, was born near the present-day town of Cleveland, Tennessee, in 1826. When he was twelve years old, he and his family were rounded up and sent west on the infamous Trail of Tears with thousands of other Cherokees. Bushyhead reached manhood in the Indian Territory of present-day eastern Oklahoma.

Bushyhead assumed a leadership role in helping the Cherokees solve the numerous problems related to their forced move to a strange land. During the 1870's, Dennis helped found the National Independent Party, partly to challenge an attempt by full-bloods to take control of all Cherokee affairs.

In 1879, Bushyhead began serving two elected four-year terms as principal chief. His major goal was to preserve Cherokee sovereignty, which was becoming increasingly difficult to do. The General Allotment Act, passed by Congress in 1887, led to denationalizing the tribes in the Indian Territory and eventually to the establishment of the state of Oklahoma in 1907.

See also Adair, John L.; General Allotment Act; Ridge, John Rollins; Trail of Tears.

Cacique

TRIBES AFFECTED: Tribes of Spanish America

SIGNIFICANCE: Originally a term applied to Caribbean tribal chiefs, "cacique" was adopted by the Eastern Pueblo peoples, to whom it designates a religious-secular office

In the Caribbean, the Spanish encountered Arawak Indians who applied the term "cacique" to their chiefs. The Spanish subsequently used the term wherever they went to designate leaders with varying degrees of authority. Among North American Indians, the term has been adopted only by the Eastern Pueblo tribes along the Rio Grande of New Mexico. There, it refers to the male religious-secular leader of a community. The Puebloan cacique is probably an outgrowth of a native office, namely the peace leader of the community, whose title and duties were modified by the Spanish. The modern cacique serves as a representative of the pueblo as a whole and is said to have the duty of "looking after the people." This entails presiding at various religious ceremonies, allocating certain rights to agricultural fields, representing the pueblo in dealings with outsiders, and appointing and training one's successor. The degree of power wielded by a cacique varies with that cacique's personality.

See also Political organization and leadership; Pueblo tribes, Eastern.

Caddo: Tribal group

CULTURE AREA: Plains

LANGUAGE GROUP: Caddoan

PRIMARY LOCATION: Oklahoma

POPULATION SIZE: 2,549 (1990 U.S. Census); 2,500 according to Caddo tribal roll

The Caddo Nation historically included the Hasinai, Kadohadacho, and Natchitoche alliances of peoples. It existed for centuries before the modern era in what is now the northwest portion of Louisiana, east Texas, southwest Arkansas, and southeastern Oklahoma. In this region of river valleys and upland forests, the Caddo hunted and cultivated the rich fauna and flora in a sustainable manner. They hunted deer, peccary, and bear as well as small game animals. Long expeditions were sent out on the Southern Plains to hunt buffalo and antelope in the spring and the fall. In early spring, migrations south to the Gulf Coast were made to feast on turtles, sea bird eggs, and early spring fruit. Vegetables, fruit, and berries were cultivated in riverine areas in great variety, including amaranth, blackberries, and potatoes.

With the introduction of bows and arrows, hunting became more efficient. Agricultural innovations made it possible to sustain larger populations. Especially important was the introduction of corn and pumpkin. The Caddo planted and harvested two varieties of corn, one smaller and early maturing, the other larger and more abundant. Intensive agricultural methods provided a reasonable harvest yet did not deplete the soil, especially when the corn was grown with beans. Corn and pumpkin were preserved through drying and roasting methods. Food surpluses strengthened the place of the Caddo Na-

tion in relation to other peoples. Food was preserved and stored for future use or traded for items that further enriched the Caddo people. Agriculture continued as a principal means of supporting life for the Caddo well into the twentieth century. Agricultural patterns were based on observation. Each person was taught never to be false with the earth, for lack of respect only leads to destruction.

Classic Villages and Ceremonial Complexes. The classic Caddo villages and ceremonial centers dominated the river courses of the ancient landscape in the Arkansas, Red, Sabine, Neches, and Angelina valleys. Towns were surrounded by the fields given over to intensive forms of agricultural production of maize or corn, beans, pumpkins, squash, and other foodstuffs. Inside the circle of houses of extended families was the central plaza, the public meeting buildings, monuments, and community storage houses. Walkways connected the village's living areas with its community service areas, the fields, and the water courses.

Architectural and artistic evidence of the classical forms of Caddoan culture have been collected from villages and centers throughout the region of their existence. In the eastern and southern portions of the region, styles closely resemble those of the region of the Mississippi River populations, but in the core Caddo areas their own styles dominate, expressing genius in engraving and design. Elements of design unlike those originating elsewhere appear in important sites such as *Keewut'* (the Davis site near Alto, Texas, in the Neches River valley) and *Dit-teh* (the Spiro mound complex in the Arkansas River Valley in present-day Oklahoma).

The Davis site is on a high alluvial terrace above an old stream bed about a mile from the present course of the Neches River. The remains of this ceremonial complex extend over approximately 60 acres. The most prominent architectural fea-

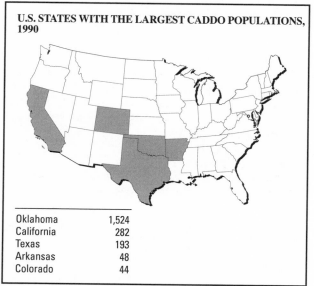

U.S. STATES WITH THE LARGEST CADDO POPULATIONS, 1990

Oklahoma	1,524
California	282
Texas	193
Arkansas	48
Colorado	44

Source: 1990 U.S. Census.

tures are three large mounds constructed of rammed earth, clay, and ash. Two of the mound structures are considered to be temple platforms. The third is defined as a burial mound. The outlines of houses and other material remains are concentrated around and between the mound structures. These include the remains of pottery and stone implements as well as marine shell, copper, high-quality flint, and galena, which were imported into the area.

The Spiro mound complex is dominated by two large monumental structures and a series of seven smaller mounds. The burial mound at the extreme eastern edge of the site is the largest in the ceremonial complex. It measures approximately 91 meters in length, 37 meters in width, and 10 meters in height at its highest point. Architectural features found within the burial mound structure are the primary mound, a clay basin area, a central chamber, and an earthen ramp extending northeast from the main structure. In the central chamber archaeologists found thousands of pearls, elaborate shell engravings, copper images, and carved cedar as well as shaped flint, stone celts, and axes. It is one of the most treasured collections of pre-Columbian art in North America.

Another way to look at the story of the Caddo Nation is through the facts and philosophies that are found within the framework of Caddo dance patterns and songs, notably the traditional Turkey Dance and Drum Dance. Some stories that form parts of the dances and songs relate specific events in the lives of the people, locating them in space and time. Others are historical only in that they communicate a sense of the meaning of history rather than present a record of events. Still others record natural events that have affected the lives of the people. The sequence of songs and dances is destroyed if the stories that speak to the meaning of the people's existence are ignored and only events themselves are expressed.

The Turkey Dance: Historical Insight. The Turkey Dance is always done in the afternoon. It relates the stream of events in relationship to the land through time that defines the Caddo peoples within the centering device of song and dance. The women dance the principal sequences expressing the active logic of the Caddo people.

For the dance, the drum is placed in the center of the dance ground. Male singers sit around the drum. They begin by calling the dancers through several songs. The first of these songs translates as "Come, you turkeys." As the women dancers begin to arrive in the dance plaza, they start to dance in a circle, dancing on the balls of their feet in a clockwise direction, in harmony with the earth.

The singers continue, describing the movement of the dancers. The next songs repeat the message of the first, but in the dialects of the various tribes within the Caddo Nation, including the Haish or Eyeish, Neche, Hainai, Yona, Ceni, and Keechi (Kichai). The Keechi are now affiliated with the Wichita Nation but are still remembered as part of the Caddo Nation. Only the Hasinai, Hainai, and Haish dialects are still spoken with any frequency today, although each of the dialects is used in the song sequence.

By the end of the first sequence of songs, the dance ground is filled with the color and movement of the women in their traditional dresses. The Turkey Dancers wear clothing of every color—purples, reds, yellows, greens, and blues. The dresses are usually of one piece, with unmarried women having their clothing buttoned in the back and married ones having theirs buttoned in the front. Over the dresses are long aprons that are tied at the waist. The most distinctive feature of their clothing is the *dush-tooh*, a butterfly-shaped board tied to a silver crown worn in the hair. This is decorated with ribbon pendants and streamers with attached shell or small round mirrors.

The next cycle of songs is the longest. The women in single file follow the lead dancer, imitating the turkey's gait. They dart each foot forward in turn, then quickly draw it back before planting it on the ground. The feet then alternate in rapid succession. During this phase, the songs relate events and insights from the Caddo collective past. These are records of significant occurrences and understandings in the history of the people. These range from single military engagements to major natural phenomena. Songs carry the story of events that occurred both before and after the forced removal into Indian Territory that climaxed in 1859.

An example of the pre-removal record is that of an eyewitness account of the creation of Caddo Lake. The lake exists on the present Louisiana-Texas border northwest of Shreveport. Two brothers watched as the Caddo people danced through the night in the traditional sequence of dances that includes the Drum Dance, the Bear Dance, the Corn Dance, the Duck Dance, the Alligator Dance, the Women's Dance, the Stirrup Dance, the Quapaw Dance, the Vine Dance (sometimes known as the Cherokee Dance), the Bell Dance, and the Morning Dance. Several village populations were present at the dance. As it proceeded, the water near the dance ground began to rise. The brothers watched as the people continued to dance while the water rose around them. The older of the two brothers called out: "Let's go to higher ground—we might all drown." The people went on dancing despite his efforts. It was then that the brothers noticed movement to the east of the dance ground. They perceived something like a great serpent writhing across the stream bed. This undulating form was holding back the water. The dancers continued to dance, even as they disappeared beneath the surface of the water.

Finally, the younger brother went for help, but he did not return until after dawn. The lake was formed where the people had danced through the night. As the people surveyed the scene they found no serpent, but a natural ridge of land retaining the water, as it does to this day. Some say the people still dance beneath the surface of the water. Others say that the older brother was frozen in fright as he continued to watch the scene. His form is said to be found in stone on the high ground above the lake.

At times during the dance sequence, the women can go to the center of the dance plaza to give the singers some tobacco and tell a story involving an event or insight that further carried the Caddo sense of heritage. These stories are sometimes incorporated into the collected public history of the Caddo Nation in the form of a new song. (At other times, the woman may give tobacco to the singer and simply say, "I have no story.") In this way new materials are added to the history as the Caddo moved from their place of origin in southeastern North America up the valleys of the Red River, the Sabine River, and the Neches and Angelina rivers, out onto the southern Great Plains. The dance cycle continues until the end of the historical song sequences.

After an extended pause, the third sequence of songs begins. During this phase of the Turkey Dance, the singers relate a basic philosophical outlook. The dancers move to and from the center of the dance ground examining the singers at the center. As they continue, the dancers examine the center from a variety of perspectives around the dance plaza. The underlying thought is that the Caddo should examine every concern from a variety of perspectives, up close and far away, until they can bring about a decision that is appropriate for the community.

A final segment of the dance begins with a song that tells the women to select a male partner. They dance in a counterclockwise fashion around the dance ground. Sometimes the women must choose the man and catch him for the dance. If he still refuses, he must offer her an article of clothing, which he must redeem at the end of the dance.

At the foundation of the Turkey Dance is the feeling that the Caddo people can find the center for the community in this analog. Throughout the centuries, all Caddo people have repeated these patterns in dance and song so that they know who they are. Without the Turkey Dance and the other dance sequences, the individuals are lost. The historiography of the dance and its songs provides a civilized frame of reference for lifeway concerns—for public and private decision making.

The Drum Dance: Governance and Development. The initial dance of the night-time dance sequence is the Drum Dance. It tells of the origins of the Caddo people as they emerged from the world of darkness into the world of light. It patterns the nature and structure of governance among the Caddo as well as the spiritual and economic underpinnings of traditional society. The patterns of the dance represent the self-organizing thought patterns that are critical to thought and feeling. The dance refers directly to the emergence of the sun in the universe, the place of emergence of the Caddo people, the ecology of sustainable development, and the village system of life. It also refers to cultural heroes such as Medicine Screech Owl, who introduced the bow and arrow and provided a code of behavior for the Caddo. It also refers to the importance of dreams and visions to appropriate behavior as well as to the symbolic loss and reintroduction of the drum in Caddo lifeways.

Tribal and International Relationships. The Caddo Nation maintained generally harmonious relations with the tribes in the region of the Mississippi Valley and the Southern Plains. They have had close associations with the Wichita Nation for centuries. They also worked with other tribes as they appeared on the Southern Plains, such as the Comanche, Kiowa, and Apache. The Caddo had more strained relations with the Chickasaw and the Osage as they were forced to hunt farther and farther west in the modern era.

Of the European nations, the Caddo Nation was recognized by both the Spanish and the French as the dominant force in the region between the Mississippi River and the Rio Grande. The Spanish named the province of Texas using a corruption of a Hasinai word for "friends," *ta'-sha*. While the Spanish attempted to introduce European feudal practices among the Caddo people, the French traded on a commercial scale which brought about more favorable relations. U.S. relations with the Caddo Nation primarily involved forceful removal from Louisiana to Texas and then to Indian Territory or Oklahoma, where the Caddo tribe is one of several federally recognized tribes in the area of Anadarko, Oklahoma.

In 1938, a measure of home rule was afforded the Caddo under the Oklahoma Indian Welfare Act of 1936 when it was accepted by the Caddo voters. A Caddo constitution was drawn up and accepted in 1938 along with an economic charter that provided for economic development. The Caddo constitution has been revised several times since the New Deal era to provide more effective governance. The constitution remains true to the federated style of government that has been Caddo tradition for centuries. The tribal council is chosen according to the district in which the member lives. The parliamentary style of governance is headed by the tribal chairperson, who is a member and chief officer of the council. The tribe supports a number of social and economic programs for the benefit of the Caddo people. It also enables cultural retention through the preservation of the Caddo languages, customs, music, dances, crafts, and values. In this way the Caddo maintain a bicultural perception of the world around them.

—*Howard Meredith*

See also Oklahoma Indian Welfare Act; Southeast; Spiro.

BIBLIOGRAPHY

Dorsey, George A., comp. *Traditions of the Caddo*. Washington, D.C.: Carnegie Institution of Washington, 1905. This material was collected by George Dorsey from Caddo informants in Indian Territory in the early twentieth century.

Gregory, H. F., ed. *The Southern Caddo: An Anthology*. New York: Garland, 1986. This is an excellent source of a variety of materials on ethnohistory, sociological tracts, linguistics, physical anthropology, archaeology, material culture, and arts.

John, Elizabeth A. *Storms Brewed in Other Men's Worlds: The Confrontation of the Indians, Spanish, and French in the Southwest, 1540-1795*. College Station: Texas A&M University Press, 1975. A narrative history of Indian-white relations that heavily involved the Caddo Nation.

Meredith, Howard. *Southern Plains Alliances*. Lawrence: University Press of Kansas, 1994. This is an interdisciplinary study of the intertribal relationships of the Southern Plains tribes in which the Caddo Nation has participated from the early centuries of the modern era to the early 1990's.

Moss, William. *The Wisdom of Oat*. Austin, Tex.: Triangle Books, 1993. William Moss, a Caddo, is a direct descendant of Oat, a Caddo signer of the United States-Caddo Treaty of 1835. This is a reflection of the leadership tradition passed down through that family.

Newkumet, Vynola Beaver, and Howard L. Meredith. *Hasinai: A Traditional History of the Caddo Confederacy*. College Station: Texas A&M University Press, 1988. This is the first academically published interpretation of the Caddo Nation and people by a Caddo author.

Perttula, Timothy K. *The Caddo Nation: Archaeological and Ethnohistoric Perspectives*. Austin: University of Texas Press, 1992. A sensitive overview of Caddoan cultural materialism that corresponds to tribal tradition. It contains useful maps and statistical information.

Story, Dee Ann, ed. *Archeological Investigations at the George C. Davis Site*. Austin: University of Texas Press, 1981. This is a very readable study of a specific classical Caddoan site; it offers an excellent overview of Caddoan studies.

Swanton, John R., comp. *Source Material on the History and Ethnology of the Caddo Indians*. Washington, D.C.: Government Printing Office, 1942. Edited material collected from Caddo informants and foreign observers about the Caddo, which was deposited at the Smithsonian Institution, Bureau of American Ethnology.

Whitebead, Irving, and Howard Meredith. "*Nuh-Ka-Oashun*: Hasinai Turkey Dance Tradition." In *Songs of Indian Territory: Native American Music Traditions of Oklahoma*, edited by Willie Smyth. Oklahoma City: Center of the American Indian, 1989. This is a study of the historical tradition of the Caddo by one of the most important lead singers of the Caddo tribe.

Caddoan language family

CULTURE AREA: Plains

TRIBES AFFECTED: Arikara, Pawnee, Wichita

The original geographical area in which Caddoan languages were spoken spanned what eventually became Arkansas, Kansas, Oklahoma, and parts of East Texas. By the twentieth century, the Caddoan group had become quite limited, both in the number of languages still traceable and the number of remaining speakers of each. Today, three key Caddoan languages survive: Caddo proper, Pawnee, and Wichita. Some experts extend the list to include Arikara (or Ree), a nearly distinct tongue originally related dialectically to Pawnee. Use of the term Caddoan as a general classification came after the research into Indian language groups undertaken by John Powell in the 1890's. Before then, the term Pawnee was applied to both Caddo and Wichita, as well as to Pawnee itself. Historically, the ancestors of today's Caddoan speakers referred to themselves as Hasinai, a name apparently applicable to tribes in the East Texas area, or Kadohadacho, a more general grouping covering the area from East Texas eastward and northeastward.

Linguists assume that when European explorers first recorded their observation of Caddoan speakers—possibly as early as Hernando de Soto's expedition of 1541, and certainly by Sieur de La Salle's expedition of 1687—several other languages existed that have now disappeared.

Several features link the four surviving languages linguistically. Although all share certain phonetic or grammatical family traits, it is important to note that they are distinct enough to be mutually unintelligible.

The main sound system, or phonology, of the Caddoan languages is based on only three vowels (*i, u,* and *a*) and about twenty consonants. Among the latter are voiced and unvoiced consonants, glottalized stops, two sibilants, and four affricates (sounds produced by stopping all breath flow, then releasing at the moment of articulation, as in the "tch" combination in the English word "clutch").

A common grammatical pattern in Caddoan languages is absorption into the verb of elements that—without being semantically linked to the verb—lend their meaning to the action which the verb denotes. A typical case would be the prefixes *awis-, anikis-,* and *ini-* (approximate phonetic renderings), which indicate that certain verbal conditions (for example, "to be something," as in the expression "to be angry") occur "while sitting," "while standing," or "while lying." Other prefixes that can affect the way a conjugated verb is understood include *tak-* and *tuk-,* which imply possibility or probability (as in "I *might* see," contrasted with "I *probably will* see"). A different prefix would be attached to obtain the same nuance, but in negative form (as in "I am *not likely* to see").

The earliest attempts to collect samples of Caddoan vocabulary came only after the United States' acquisition of the Louisiana Territory in 1801. John Sibley provided President Thomas Jefferson (himself a collector of a wide variety of cultural and linguistic "memorabilia") with a small body of words and their definitions. The tongue he transcribed as a branch of Caddo was, he said, called Natchitoches. Later evidence suggested that Sibley's word list was not actually Caddoan, but Adai, with some Caddoan borrowings.

A second early vocabulary list, this time indisputably Pawnee with some samplings of the Arikara dialect, was collected by a German traveler to what was considered the western United States in the 1830's. Alexander Philipp Maximilian, Prinz von Weid, depended on a non-Indian who spoke Pawnee to provide him with terms that were mainly practical in nature. A near-contemporary American traveler in 1836, Albert Gallatin, was aware that the Arikara (located quite far north, in what became North and South Dakota) spoke a language that was close to Pawnee, but he remained convinced that none of their vocabulary had been collected for comparison. This is precisely what von Weid was doing. Publication of his work three years later made it linguistically possible to prove that Arikara had, in fact, branched off from the main Pawnee groups and migrated north.

Incomplete collections of Caddoan terms, without any accompanying efforts at linguistic analysis, were provided by a number of military and ethnographic observers by mid-century. Two individuals in particular, Randolph B. Marcy (author of the 1853 *Exploration of the Red River of Louisiana*) and Amiel Weeks Whipple (author of the 1856 *Reports of Explorations . . . for a Railroad from the Mississippi River to the Pacific Ocean*), worked to collect Wichita vocabulary. Whipple's work took on added significance after a few generations' time, since he worked among speakers of Waco, a Wichita dialect that subsequently became extinct.

Unfortunately, the only substantial studies involving systematic phonemic analysis (for accurate pronunciation of words that never appeared in writing) would not be realized until the second half of the twentieth century, when the number of Caddoan speakers had dwindled seriously.

—*Byron Cannon*

See also Arikara; Caddo; Pawnee; Wichita.

Cahokia: Archaeological site

DATE: c. 900-1250
LOCATION: East bank of Mississippi River, Illinois
CULTURES AFFECTED: Cahokia, Illinois

Cahokia is a large urban site on the east bank of the Mississippi River valley in what is now Illinois, across the river from St. Louis, Missouri. It is the site of one of several Native American cultural and commercial centers that existed in an area bounded by the Gulf of Mexico and the present states of Oklahoma, Wisconsin, and Georgia.

Large public structures dominate the central part of the site, with smaller ones located at or near the community periphery. Large storage facilities were concentrated in two areas in the northwestern portion of the site. Near the southern edge of the urban complex is the area interpreted as a locus for butchering and meat-processing.

The Cahokia site is the largest pre-Columbian site in North America north of Central Mexico, encompassing some 3,700 square miles. It contains more than one hundred carefully constructed mounds of rammed earth and clay of various shapes and sizes. The largest of the mounds, which dominates the site, is known as Monks Mound. This monumental structure covers fifteen acres of ground and rises more than one hundred feet above the valley floor. Among structures in North America, it is second in size only to Cholula and the Pyramid of the Sun at Teotihuacán.

At the time of modern European contact, Cahokia was settled by the Cahokia tribe, which made up a part of the Illini or Illinois Nation. Other tribes in the Illinois Nation included the Kaskakia and Peoria. The Illinois Nation, along with the Wea and Piankashaw tribes, were removed in the nineteenth century to lands west of the Mississippi. These various tribal peoples are known presently as the Consolidated Peoria Tribe of northeastern Oklahoma.

The population of Cahokia at its height is estimated to have been in the tens of thousands. Numerous plazas, ceremonial areas, and ritual spaces have been excavated. These are protected as a part of the Cahokia Mounds State Park and Museum, supported by the state of Illinois and private donations. A full program of events is run on a scheduled basis, including the summer solstice celebration, storytelling and stargazing, Summer Games Field Day, Native Harvest Festival, Native American Crafts Days, and archaeological field schools.

See also Illinois; Mounds and mound builders.

Cahuilla: Tribe

CULTURE AREA: California
LANGUAGE GROUP: Uto-Aztecan
PRIMARY LOCATION: Southern California
POPULATION SIZE: 1,418 (1990 U.S. Census)

Cahuilla Indians lived at the southern tip of California. Men used the bow and arrow to hunt deer, rabbits, and mountain sheep; women roasted and dried surplus meat for winter use and gathered acorns, piñon nuts, seeds, beans, fruit, and berries. Many of the goods so gathered were ground into flour and stored in pots and baskets.

Cahuilla villages were situated near water, which became scarce in summer. The homes were constructed of brush gathered together and formed into dome-shaped structures; there were also some larger dwellings, rectangular in shape, that could be as long as twenty feet. Men wore deerskin loincloths; women wore skirts made from mesquite bark or deerskin. Rabbitskin blankets provided winter warmth.

Cleanliness was very important to Cahuilla. They regularly bathed and sweated in village sweathouses. It was a great

A Cahuilla woman, photographed in 1905, carrying nuts or berries in a traditional basket. (Library of Congress)

disgrace for any foreign particles to be discovered on household utensils and baskets. They believed in supernatural spirits and a universal power which explained unusual or miraculous events. Elderly tribe members were greatly respected; they taught values and skills to the young and were regarded as repositories of knowledge.

In 1774, Spanish explorer Juan Bautista de Anza made the first documented contact with Cahuilla Indians. Because Cahuilla and other local tribes were hostile to Europeans, white settlers avoided the area for many years. Cahuilla Indians finally did become involved with Europeans through the Spanish missions. They adopted certain aspects of Spanish culture, including trade, Catholicism, animal husbandry, and wage labor.

In 1863, a smallpox epidemic struck the Cahuilla, cutting their population in half. Its reduced size left the tribe defenseless against the increasing number of Americans who began to settle in their region. After 1891, the U.S. government began overseeing Cahuillan life and activities. Schools and Protestant missions were opened, and several traditional practices—particularly Cahuilla religious activities—were discouraged.

During the 1960's, federal resources provided significant improvements in health, education, and general welfare. In the second half of the twentieth century, the Cahuillas raised cattle and worked in civil service, construction, social work, and blue collar jobs. Despite such modernization, a number of traditional foods were still favored and Cahuilla songs and dances were performed on holidays.

See also Baskets and basketry; California; Missions and missionaries; Pottery; Uto-Aztecan language family.

California: Culture area

LANGUAGE GROUPS: Athapaskan, Chimariko, Chumashan, Esselen, Karok, Maiduan, Palaihnihan, Pomoan, Salinan, Shastan, Uto-Aztecan, Wintun, Wiyot, Yanan, Yokutsan, Yukian, Yuman, Yurok

TRIBES: Achumawi, Atsugewi, Cahuilla, Chemehuevi, Chumash, Costano, Cupeño, Diegueño, Esselen, Fernandeño, Gabrielino, Hupa, Juaneño, Kamia, Karok, Kato, Luiseño, Maidu, Mattole, Miwok, Patwin, Pomo, Quechan, Salinan, Serrano, Shasta, Tolowa, Tubatulabal, Wailaki, Wappo, Wintun, Wiyot, Yahi, Yana, Yokuts, Yuki, Yurok

The California culture area corresponds closely to the modern boundaries of that state. Approximately 300,000 people lived there when the Spaniards arrived in 1769, making it the most densely populated area within the present boundaries of the forty-eight contiguous United States.

Material Culture. The technology of the native people of California may have been among the least sophisticated in North America. The wheel, pottery, and metallurgy were rare or unknown. Furthermore, the people had not yet achieved any form of systematic agriculture, but relied on hunting (of almost all animal life in the area), fishing (in ocean, lake, and river), and gathering (primarily of acorns, but also of pine cones and other plants) for their basic sustenance.

Nevertheless, many artifacts of pre-contact years have survived into the modern era and provide insight into the lives of California's original people. Archaeologists have uncovered a large number of arrow points made of chipped stone; a wide variety of hooks and other fishing implements; mortars and pestles (although in many cases the grinding was done on a fixed mortar of bedrock with a grinding stone); bowls and eating implements made of such materials as wood, bark, steatite, and shells; combs or brushes of soap plant root; wedges of deer horn; and awls of bone.

Probably the most common surviving artifacts are the many baskets now on display in museums and other collections. Curiously, native Californians seem not to have utilized the simplest and easiest method of basketmaking: a basic in-and-out weave. Instead, more complex coiling or twining techniques prevailed. The materials were as diverse as the native vegetation of the region, with tule reeds, grass stems, and various barks serving as the ingredients for the baskets. Lacking pottery and metallurgy, native Californians utilized baskets for almost every conceivable purpose. In the richness and elaborateness of their basket decorations, Californians exceeded all other native people of North America.

Art and Architecture. Aside from the decorations on baskets, most California material culture is of a practical, rather than purely decorative and artistic, nature. One of the few art forms was rock painting and carving. Petroglyphs, or peckings in rock outcroppings, have been recorded at more than one thousand sites throughout the state, and many others were destroyed by urbanization before archaeologists could record and study them. The distribution of such rock art is somewhat uneven, with heavy concentrations in some areas (north coast, southwest coast, and central Sierra) but total absence in others. Pictographs, or painted rocks, are also scattered unevenly, with the heaviest concentrations in the extreme northeast, the southwest coast, the southern Sierra, and most spectacularly in the caves of the Chumash tribe on the central coast. Although some naturalistic or animalistic representations appear in both the pecked and painted art, most of the work appears in abstract styles, possibly with religious significance.

Artistic expression also manifested itself in body painting, beads, and clothing. Because the mild climate permitted men to go naked and women to wear a simple apron, clothing was limited. In colder weather, animal skins and furs provided the raw material for woven blankets or robes and provided some opportunity for creative artistry, usually with decorative uses of feathers.

The housing of California also provided little opportunity for creative expression because of its modest form. The structures varied, from quadrangular in some instances to circular and domed in others. Building materials were usually limited to available vegetation, with bundles of tule thatching serving as the most common fabric. Most houses were only about ten feet square, intended only for sleeping quarters for a single family. When houses became uncomfortable because of dirt or

CALIFORNIA CULTURE AREA

Tolowa

Karok Shasta

Yurok

Hupa Achumawi

Wiyot Wintun Atsugewi

Mattole

Sinkyone Yana

Wailaki Yahi

Yuki

Maidu

Pomo Patwin

Wappo

Coast
Miwok

Miwok

Costanoan

Monache

Yokuts

Esselen

Tubatulab

Salinan

Chemehuevi

Chumash

Fernandeño Serrano

Gabrielino

Luiseño

Juaneño Cahuilla

Cupeño

Diegueño Kamia Quechan

pests, they were simply burned and rebuilt. Few other structures were part of native villages.

Social and Political Organization. The typical form of social organization was the tribelet or village, usually of one hundred to five hundred residents. Although people were not nomadic, neither were they completely immobile. Entire villages were occasionally burned and rebuilt at another location; trading ventures required long trips within and outside of California; men often embarked on extensive expeditions in search of fish and game; even excursions to gather acorns and other plants occasionally required coverage of extensive areas.

Although men thus enjoyed mobility and movement over long distances, women were more typically confined to their home villages. Their lives revolved around the laborious and tedious processes of grinding acorns, leaching out the poisonous tannic acid, baking bread, and otherwise preparing food. Women also took on the chores of rearing children (usually in a communal fashion), weaving baskets, and obtaining wood and water.

Relations among the sexes were usually governed by marriage practices and rules that did not differ markedly from those of other Native Americans. People married soon after puberty, with families choosing the partners and the groom paying a bride price. Customary incest taboos prevailed, and marriages with partners of equivalent social class were encouraged. Monogamy was the norm, but exceptions did exist, especially for people of higher social rank. Divorce was readily available to either partner, although the necessity of refunding the bride price somewhat limited the freedom of women in such matters.

Several variables, especially wealth and inherited rank, determined social status. Wealth was measured by possession of a variety of tangible objects, including shells that acted as a form of money for the facilitation of trade. Although birth was normally the determinant of status, some social mobility was possible for people who worked hard and accumulated wealth or demonstrated special skills.

At the top of the social hierarchy in nearly every village were two officials: the chief and the shaman. The position of the chief, always a male, was normally inherited and usually correlated with wealth. Since warfare played a negligible or even nonexistent role for native Californians, the responsibility of the chief involved mostly the administration of the economic functions of the tribelet. He supervised food-gathering and hunting activities, directed trade with other peoples, and generally assumed responsibility for the economic survival of his people. His position carried with it several wives, the largest and most luxurious house, and possession of the largest store of wealth goods.

Religion. The other post of highest status was that of shaman. Although the position was essentially a religious one, its functions mostly involved healing, both physical and psychological. The shaman's knowledge of the healing properties of various herbs and other plants, along with sacred objects and chants, was essential to the performance of his duties.

As people close to nature, native Californians felt a part of it, and utilized animals for most of their myths. Typically, they believed that animals preceded men in occupation of the earth and were responsible for creation of both the earth and its human occupants. Natural phenomena all had explanations in mythology, although the accounts of the causes of earthquakes, thunder, phases of the moon, and similar events varied from tribe to tribe.

Religious ceremonies played a smaller part in the lives of the native people of California than for many other Native Americans, but they did exist. Puberty rites, funerals, marriages, and births were among the events that served as occasions for some type of ceremony. Because the allocation of functions between the sexes left men with more free time than women, they were able to engage in more frequent religious activity. Especially popular in much of the area was the use of the *temescal*, or sweathouse. A fire provided the heat and smoke (not steam) that caused the men to sweat and cleanse themselves, after which they took a dip in a nearby source of water. The function of the temescal is not entirely clear; it probably served both a social and ritualistic role.

History. White contact began in 1769 when Spanish missionaries, led by Father Junípero Serra, arrived to begin a process of Hispanicizing the Indians. By 1823, the Spanish had established a chain of twenty-one missions, generally near the coast from San Diego to just north of San Francisco. The tribes within the Spanish area included the Chumash, Costanoan, Cupeño, Diegueño, Esselen, Fernandeño, Gabrielino, Juaneño, Luiseño, and Salinan. In 1821, Mexico became independent and sought to reduce the power of the Spanish missionaries, eventually by secularizing the missions around 1834. By that time, the population within the mission range had declined from about seventy-two thousand to approximately eighteen thousand. The causes of the decline are uncertain, but most likely disease, poor diet, psychological stress, and declining female fertility all played a part. Faced with disappearing converts, missionaries went on raids into the Central Valley to recruit Yokuts, whether by persuasion or force.

By the time of the U.S. invasion in 1846, the total native population of California had shrunk to less than 150,000, but that included people outside the coastal strip who were still living largely as they had for centuries. The discovery of gold shortly after the American conquest brought thousands of whites into the area, especially the Sierra foothills of the Miwok and Yokuts. Americans regarded the natives as "diggers," an inferior people suitable as targets for mass destruction. By 1900, the Indian population had reached its nadir at 15,500.

In the 1870's, the U.S. government began its policy of establishing reservations and, in at least a few instances, forcing people away from other land. Despite the harsh conditions on the reservations, the native population gradually rebounded in the twentieth century, reaching nearly twenty-two thousand on the first "Great Roll," conducted between 1928 and 1933, more than thirty-six thousand on the second roll, taken from

1950 to 1955, and more than ninety-one thousand in the census of 1970. The last figure reflects the influx into California of Native Americans from other culture areas, a process that continued throughout the 1970's and 1980's. The census of 1990 recorded the presence of approximately 236,000 American Indians within California; that figure is still less than the population in pre-contact times. —*R. David Weber*

See also Acorns; Architecture—California; Arts and crafts—California; Baskets and basketry; Indian-white relations—Spanish colonial; Petroglyphs.

BIBLIOGRAPHY

Cook, Sherburne F. *The Conflict Between the California Indian and White Civilization.* Berkeley: University of California Press, 1976. A collection of six articles, originally published in *Ibero-Americana* from 1940 to 1943 by the preeminent demographer of California's native peoples.

Harrington, John P. *Karuk Indian Myths.* Washington, D.C.: Bureau of American Ethnology, 1932. One of the few published works by one of the three great anthropologists of California natives. Harrington, working for the Smithsonian Institution, recorded vast amounts of linguistic and other data in California and other parts of the Southwest, but he infuriated his superiors by his general failure to write up his findings.

Heizer, Robert F., ed. *California.* Vol. 8 in *Handbook of North American Indians.* Washington, D.C.: Smithsonian Institution, 1978. The eighth volume in the comprehensive series by the Smithsonian, this encyclopedic work includes articles on each of the tribes as well as on such topics as environmental background, historical demography, trade and trails, and intergroup conflict. Complete with maps, photographs, tables, and bibliography.

Kroeber, Alfred Louis. *Handbook of the Indians of California.* Reprint. Berkeley: California Book Company, 1953. Originally published in 1925 as Bulletin 78 of the Bureau of American Ethnology, this remains a standard reference work. It includes fifty-three chapters on tribes as well as other general sections. The author, another of the three great figures in California anthropology, taught for many years at the University of California.

Merriam, C. Hart. *Studies of California Indians.* Berkeley: University of California Press, 1955. Written by the third of the three giants in the field, this is a series of his papers published posthumously. Privately funded by a wealthy woman, Mary Harriman, Merriam often feuded with Kroeber.

Calumets and pipe bags

TRIBES AFFECTED: Pantribal
SIGNIFICANCE: The calumet (sacred pipe) was the most widely used ceremonial object among North American Indians, and it has been a central symbol of modern Pan-Indian movements

Calumet, from the French for reed pipe, refers to pipes with long wooden stems and detachable clay or stone bowls. Widely used for both personal and ceremonial purposes, calu-

met refers to only the sacred pipes. Archaeological evidence shows extensive use throughout North America that may date back four thousand years. Most tribal groups have myths similar to a myth of the Lakota Sioux in which a sacred being, such as White Buffalo Woman, brings the pipe at the time of the creation of the people, or during a time of hardship. The pipe serves as an ongoing means of communication with the spirit beings.

Ceremonial pipes were understood to have a special power and were kept in bags (bundles) tended by specially trained women and men. The bowl and stem were joined only for ritual use, symbolizing the merger of earth and sky, male and female. In most ceremonies, the lit pipe was offered to the six directions (north, south, east, west, up, and down) and then passed in the direction of the sun to all those gathered. Some pipes were so powerful that only certain sacred persons could smoke them. The bowls were often carved in the images of animals or persons, although *L* shapes and inverted-*T* shapes were also common. Red pipestone was prized material for bowls, and many of the carvers were men with disabilities who could not participate in war. The long wooden stems were usually decorated with feathers or ornaments. The decorations revealed when the pipe was to be used: for healing, before the hunt, before war, to bind together confederacies, or to make peace (the peace pipe). Smoking the pipe was understood to link those present and the spirit beings in a cosmic harmony. After a period of decline, pipe carving has been revived, and sweatlodges and pipe ceremonies have become central symbols in pan-Indian movements such as the American Indian Movement (AIM).

See also Bundles, sacred; Kinnikinnick; Pipestone Quarries; Religion.

Calusa: Tribe

CULTURE AREA: Southeast
LANGUAGE GROUP: Muskogean (probable)
PRIMARY LOCATION: Florida

The Calusa were a nomadic people who inhabited the south Florida peninsula from the Tampa Bay area to Lake Okeechobee, including the Florida Keys. They may have been related to the Muskogee family in North America. Stories of their cannibalism, human sacrifice, and piracy suggest a connection to the South American or Caribbean Indians.

Historians believe the Calusa numbered about three thousand at the time of their first contact with whites (around 1513), when the Spanish explorer Juan Ponce de León attempted to enter Calusa land. The Calusa lived up to their name, which means "fierce people," and forced Ponce de León to retreat after a prolonged battle. Spanish missionaries made several forays into the area but abandoned the attempt to convert the Calusa around 1569.

The Calusas' success in repelling the European invaders also depended upon their reliance on hunting and fishing instead of agriculture. The tribe roamed freely throughout south Florida, harvesting the bounty of the sea and native plants that grew year-round, rather than building more permanent villages and planting crops; sites of Calusa settlements along the Florida coast are marked by huge shell mounds. This nomadic life made them less vulnerable to the Spanish, who often subjugated the Indians by burning their storehouses, leaving the tribes without food for the winter.

Like most Southeastern Woodlands tribes, the Calusa probably followed a matrilineal clan structure: Familial relationships depended on the mother's connections. Calusa women prepared and preserved food, though they did not have to plant and cultivate like women of other tribes. The men, through their intimate knowledge of the sea, became excellent swimmers and divers, made strong, seaworthy canoes, and plundered sunken Spanish ships for gold and silver to make jewelry (as well as making captives of stranded crew members).

In spite of their independence, the Calusa population seems to have dwindled rapidly, probably from diseases introduced by the European invaders; by the time the Seminoles entered the area in the late 1700's, few members of the tribe remained. These few were probably assimilated into the Seminoles; some may have moved to Cuba.

See also Seminole; Southeast.

Campbell, Ben Nighthorse (b. Apr. 13, 1933, Auburn, Calif.): Jeweler, politician

TRIBAL AFFILIATION: Northern Cheyenne
SIGNIFICANCE: Campbell, elected to the U.S. Senate in 1992, was successful in the jewelry business before winning elective office in Colorado

Ben Campbell was the son of Portuguese immigrant Mary Vierra and Albert Valdez Campbell, of Scottish-Mexican descent; his paternal grandmother is said to have been Yellow

In 1987, Congressman Campbell observes the removal of a painting that he felt was offensive from the House interior committee room. (AP/Wide World Photos)

Woman, a Southern Cheyenne. He was entered on the Northern Cheyenne tribal roll in 1980.

After stints as an Air Force military policeman during the Korean War, a San Jose State University student, and a member of the 1964 U.S. Olympic Judo Team, Campbell taught martial arts near Sacramento. Thereafter, he married, worked as a shop teacher, moonlighted in law enforcement, and began making jewelry with American Indian motifs. In 1970, he first announced his identity as a "closet Indian" and took the name "Nighthorse." In 1977, with his jewelry business extremely successful, Campbell and his wife moved to a ranch near Durango, Colorado. They raised quarter horses and opened a gallery to display and sell his work. Campbell had become a millionaire by 1980.

Campbell was elected to the Colorado state legislature in 1983 and served until 1986. He was also an adviser to the Colorado Commission on International Trade and the Arts and Humanities. He was elected to the U.S. House of Representatives in 1987. During his time in the House he was a member of the House Committee on Agriculture and the Committee on Interior and Insular Affairs. He was elected to the U.S. Senate in 1992; Campbell was the first Native American since Charles Curtis to be elected a U.S. senator.

See also Curtis, Charles.

BIBLIOGRAPHY
Viola, Herman J. *Ben Nighthorse Campbell: An American Warrior.* New York: Orion Books, 1993.

Canonchet (c. 1630—Apr., 1676, Stonington, Conn.): Chief

ALSO KNOWN AS: Nanuntenoo
TRIBAL AFFILIATION: Narragansett
SIGNIFICANCE: Canonchet is best known for his interactions with the British colonists during King Philip's War

Initially the settlers convinced Canonchet, sachem of the Narragansett, to remain loyal to the British cause. He signed a treaty in July, 1675, promising to turn over to the British their enemies and agreeing to fight against those Indians the colonists deemed enemies. Canonchet evidently agreed, however, to shelter women and children of the Wampanoag tribe, thereby breaking the agreement. The following December (1675), in retaliation, the British attacked and killed about one thousand Narragansett. Canonchet survived and, in March, 1676, led an ambush of about forty of Captain Michael Pierce's troops.

While organizing an effort to replace the corn the British had destroyed, Canonchet was spotted in April by Captain George Denison, who chased and captured him. Upon learning that he was to be executed, Canonchet is reputed to have replied that he "liked it well, that he should die before his heart was soft, or had spoken anything unworthy of himself." The sachem was turned over to the Pequots and Mohegans, who shot and beheaded him. Canonchet's execution in 1676 coincides with the dispersal of the Narragansett and essentially signals the end of what was formerly the strongest tribe in New England.

See also Indian-white relations—English colonial; King Philip's War; Metacomet; Narragansett.

BIBLIOGRAPHY

Drake, Samuel G. *The Book of the Indians*. 1832. Reprint. New York: AMS, 1976.

Hubbard, William. *The History of the Indian Wars in New England*. Roxbury, 1865. Reprint. New York: Kraus, 1969.

Canonicus (c. 1565—June 4, 1647): Chief

TRIBAL AFFILIATION: Narragansett
SIGNIFICANCE: Canonicus kept the Narragansetts at peace with the British colonists for the twenty-seven years between their arrival in 1620 and his death; he befriended Roger Williams, giving him the land on which stands present-day Providence, Rhode Island

Canonicus shared the leadership of the Narragansetts with his nephew Miantonomo at the time of English arrival. While Miantonomo dealt with the colonists and the other tribes, Canonicus ruled at home. Colonist Edward Winslow gives an account of how Canonicus had a bundle of arrows wrapped in snake skin delivered to the Plymouth pilgrims, a gesture the pilgrims interpreted as hostile. No hostilities came of the act, however, nor did hostilities result from Canonicus' 1632 threat of three settlers near Plymouth. Besides maintaining a friendship and alliance with the pilgrims, Canonicus befriended Roger Williams and his fellow outcasts in 1636, giving them the land that is now Providence, Rhode Island.

Despite the Narragansetts' having been betrayed by the colonists in the death of Miantonomo, Canonicus remained faithful to a peace compact, though his tribe did avenge the death of Miantonomo by Uncas in June, 1644. Also in 1644, Canonicus made a treaty accepting the sovereignty of England and its king.

Noting his death, New England historian John Winthrop wrote: "Canonicus, the great sachem of Narrangansett [*sic*], died, a very old man." Roger Williams recalled Canonicus as a great and benevolent friend to him and the British.

See also Indian-white relations—English colonial; Miantonomo; Narragansett.

BIBLIOGRAPHY

Drake, Samuel G. *The Book of the Indians*. 1832. Reprint. New York: AMS, 1976.

Hodge, Frederick W., ed. *Handbook of American Indians*. 2 vols. 1907-1910. Reprint. Totowa, N.J.: Rowman and Littlefield, 1975.

Winslow, Edward. *Good News from New England*. London: John Dawson, 1624.

Canyon de Chelly: Archaeological site

DATE: Since 350
LOCATION: Near Chinle, Arizona
CULTURES AFFECTED: Mescalero Apache, Navajo

Canyon de Chelly, located near Chinle, Arizona, and now designated a U.S. national monument, was first inhabited by the Navajo as early as 350 C.E. Traditionally, the Navajo were at war with the people to the south, first with bands of the Western Apache, later with the Spanish. The Navajo learned to withdraw into the mountains for defense, and they turned Canyon de Chelly into a defensive stronghold. Though the Spanish and later Americans raided the cliff dwellings, Canyon de Chelly remained a feasible defensive stronghold until the era of the American Civil War.

The first treaty between the U.S. government and the Navajo was signed in 1846, but each Navajo chief was willing to commit only for his own band or village. All Navajo chiefs never reached a consensus, so the 1846 treaty never was fully implemented. In 1863, Colonel Christopher "Kit" Carson, leading U.S. Army troops, raided the cliff dwellings at Canyon de Chelly. Carson, perhaps anticipating General William Tecumseh Sherman's march of the following year, first destroyed the Navajo sheep and orchards and captured as many horses as possible. The Navajo finally surrendered, in early 1864, as a preferable alternative to possible starvation in the blockaded canyon. All eight thousand members of the Navajo tribe were forced to walk 800 miles to the northeast to Fort Sumner, New Mexico. After this "Long Walk," the Navajo remained imprisoned at Fort Sumner—with their traditional enemies, the Mescalero Apache, sharing their incarceration—for five years.

In 1868, a new and binding treaty was signed between the U.S. government and the Navajo Nation. The treaty allowed the Navajo to return to their ancestral lands in Arizona and stipulated that no one else was to enter Canyon de Chelly without the express permission of the Navajo Nation. The Navajo, in return, were to pledge eternal peace, a promise which they kept even during the so-called Indian Wars that occurred in the two decades after the 1868 treaty was signed.

See also Cliff dwellings; Long Walk; Mesa Verde; Navajo; Prehistory—Southwest.

Cape Fear: Tribe

CULTURE AREA: Southeast
LANGUAGE GROUP: Siouan
PRIMARY LOCATION: Cape Fear River, North Carolina

The proper name of this tribe is unknown; they were designated "Cape Fear" by European Americans. The matrilineal Cape Fear group gained their subsistence primarily from different types of maize, squash, beans, and other plants tended by women, who also gathered numerous types of nuts, seeds, and roots. Hunting, trapping, and fishing supplemented their diet.

English settlers from New England may have been the first to contact the Cape Fear people in 1661, but they were driven away after the settlers kidnapped several Indian children, under the pretense of civilizing them. A small colony of settlers from Barbados arrived in 1663 but soon left. Numerous settlements were attempted by European Americans. In 1695 the Cape Fear asked Governor Archdale for protection, which was granted after the Cape Fear Indians rescued fifty-two passengers from a wrecked New England ship. After the 1716 Yamasee War they were moved inland from Charleston, South

Carolina. Records indicate that by 1808 only twenty Cape Fear people remained.

See also Yamasee War.

Captain Jack (c. 1840, Lost River, Northern Calif.—Oct. 3, 1873, Fort Klamath, Oreg.): Tribal chief

ALSO KNOWN AS: Kintpuash (Having Indigestion)

TRIBAL AFFILIATION: Modoc

SIGNIFICANCE: Chief and leader of the Modoc War of 1872-1873, Captain Jack engaged in a lifelong struggle to preserve Modoc independence

Born near the California-Oregon border, Kintpuash (nicknamed Captain Jack by whites) became a Modoc chief when his father was killed by whites. Believing in peace, he encouraged trade with the white settlers. In 1864, however, Schonchin Jim surrendered Modoc lands and moved the Modoc to the Klamath reservation in Oregon. The Modoc were denied food and supplies, and disputes developed with the more favorably treated Klamath Indians. In 1865, denied permission for a separate Modoc reservation, Kintpuash led his people back to California. In November, 1872, troops ordered to return the Modoc to Oregon were engaged in a skirmish. Captain Jack led the main group to a natural rock sanctuary in the lava beds near Tule Lake. Hooker Jim led a separate group which took revenge by killing white settlers. Seeking refuge, Hooker Jim joined Captain Jack.

Modoc leader Captain Jack, or Kintpuash, led the tribe in the Modoc War. (National Archives)

During January, 1873, soldiers tried unsuccessfully to dislodge the Modocs. General Edward Canby was then ordered to end the uprising. He convened peace talks which included Kintpuash's cousin, Winema. While the talks proceeded, Canby surrounded the Modoc with a thousand soldiers. On February 28, Kintpuash requested a separate Modoc reservation and amnesty for Hooker Jim's band. Both requests were refused. Believing that Canby was stalling for time, Hooker Jim convinced the majority of warriors that they needed to kill Canby. Facing tribal pressure, Captain Jack agreed. At a meeting on April 11, Kintpuash and his warriors drew hidden pistols, killing Canby and several others.

In an act of betrayal, Hooker Jim later agreed to lead soldiers to Captain Jack in exchange for amnesty. On June 1, surrounded, Kintpuash surrendered. The resisting Modocs were tried without legal defense. Kintpuash and three of his warriors were sentenced to death and hanged on October 3. His body was stolen from its grave and displayed by an eastern carnival.

See also Hooker Jim; Modoc; Modoc War; Scarface Charlie; Winema.

Captivity and captivity narratives

TRIBES AFFECTED: Pantribal

SIGNIFICANCE: Captivity narratives provide cultural data concerning Native Americans and early contacts with Europeans, although these narratives were often biased and many of them perpetuated stereotypes of Indians

Captivity narratives are accounts written by Europeans who were captured by Native Americans. They provide informative vignettes of Native American life, since in many cases captives were adopted into families and learned the languages and aboriginal cultures. In this way, cultural outsiders became insiders who were later able to write about their experiences. There is a risk, however, in relying too directly on these captivity accounts for objective information on Native Americans. Many of the captives were taken during hostile interactions between the Europeans and the indigenous peoples, and thus they did not always relish their enforced observation of another culture. In addition, captivity narratives were often published for the purpose of providing moral guidance to the masses (and were generally sensationalized for entertainment value), and this agenda seriously affects some of the data reported. A prime example is an early captivity narrative published by a minister's wife under the title *The Soveraignty and Goodness of God, Together with the Faithfulness of His Promises Displayed: Being a Narrative of the Captivity and Restauration of Mrs. Mary Rowlandson; Commended by Her, to All That Desire to Know the Lord's Doing to, and Dealings with Her* (1682). It may be found in Charles Lincoln's *Narratives of the Indian Wars (1675-1699)* (1913). This genre of literature served to warn erring Christians of the dangers in straying from a religious life; Indians served as the stereotype of extreme waywardness.

The commercial success of the earlier captivity accounts resulted in further publications, and by the nineteenth century hundreds of pamphlets and anthologies were available. Many of these were written by women or featured a female heroine; if the typical plot is to be believed, generally the purity of the protagonist allowed her to overcome the dangerous ordeal and to return unscathed to her former lifestyle. Those with a male hero often had the man being seduced by the freedom of the wilderness and its native inhabitants to become one with his aboriginal hosts. Occasionally, these men "reformed" and attempted, with difficulty, to return to their former societies, as in Edwin James's *John Tanner's Narrative of His Captivity Among the Ottawa and Ojibwa Indians* (1830). A history of captivity narratives appears in Robert F. Berkhoffer, Jr.'s "White Conceptions of Indians" in volume 4 of the *Handbook of North American Indians*, entitled *History of Indian-White Relations* (1988), published by the Smithsonian Institution.

See also Adoption; Scalps and scalping; Warfare and conflict.

Carib: Tribe

CULTURE AREA: Mesoamerica
LANGUAGE GROUP: Cariban
PRIMARY LOCATION: Lesser Antilles

The Caribs, the third Indian group to migrate from the north coast of South America through the Lesser Antilles, began their move northward in the fifth century; by the end of the fourteenth century they had expelled or incorporated the Arawaks in the Lesser Antilles.

The Caribs, who were farmers and fishermen, located their villages high on the windward slopes of mountains near running water. Land was communally owned, but canoes and ornaments were personal property. Tobacco was used as money. The Caribs erected small, wood-framed, oval or rectangular houses with thatched roofs around a plaza with a communal fireplace. The plaza served as the center of ceremonies and social life. Furnishings were few: small wooden tables, metates (grinding stones), griddles, stools, hammocks, gourds, and pottery. Their diet consisted of fish, lizards, crabs, agouti, corn, sweet potatoes, yams, beans, and peppers. Turtles and manatees were forbidden foods because of the fear that eating them would make a person slow. Men and women shared the tasks of making canoes, beer, baskets, and textiles. Both sexes shaped their skulls, wore amulets and charms, and decorated their bodies with flowers, coral or stone, gold dust, and red, white, and black paint. Persons of rank wore crescents of gold or copper.

The Caribs were closely related culturally to the Arawaks but were less organized socially. Their villages were small, usually populated by an extended family. The leader, often head of the family, supervised the activities of the village and settled village disputes. He also served as military chief and led raiding parties.

War was the main activity of the Caribs, who were fierce fighters. Their weapons included bows, poisoned arrows, javelins, and clubs embedded with sharpened flint. The Caribs were excellent sailors and could construct a war canoe capable of carrying more than a hundred warriors from the trunk of a single tree. They also lashed canoes together to form rafts for longer voyages. The Caribs raided Arawak settlements, reaching Puerto Rico by the 1490's. Captured Arawak men were killed and sometimes cooked and eaten. Captured women and children were taken away as slaves; the women were settled in breeding colonies which the Carib warriors visited periodically.

Carib religion had no elaborate rituals. Each individual Carib had a personal deity that could take many forms and to which the Carib sometimes offered cassava (a plant with a nutritious edible root). Good and evil spirits fought constantly, both within the body and everywhere in nature. Shamans attempted to ward off the evil spirits and to please the good ones.

The Spaniards did not settle the Lesser Antilles, but the Caribs' skill as fighters and their reputation as cannibals did not prevent other European nations from displacing them later. The Caribs were limited to the islands of St. Vincent and Dominica. On St. Vincent they mixed with shipwrecked slaves and became known as the "Black Caribs," who in 1795 were transferred by the English to Roatan Island off Honduras. They spread onto the mainland and northward into Guatemala. Today a small Carib population lives on a reservation on Dominica.

Carlisle Indian School

DATES: 1879-1918
TRIBES AFFECTED: Pantribal
SIGNIFICANCE: The Carlisle Indian School sought to assimilate Indian children into white society; it served as a model for many other Indian boarding schools

In 1879, a U.S. military officer, Captain Richard Henry Pratt, opened a school for Indians in a military barracks in Carlisle, Pennsylvania. Pratt belonged to a generation of policy-makers working for what many believed to be a more humane, progressive approach to Indian policy. Unlike many of his predecessors, Pratt believed that Indian people were capable of being transformed into the European American model of the law-abiding, Christian, wage-earning citizen. According to Pratt, this was the only way for Indian people to survive—by leaving behind everything that distinguished Indian people as "Indian," including language and spirituality.

Pratt first experimented with Indian education by training Plains Indian prisoners being held at Fort Marion in Florida. After persuading the federal government to allow eighteen male prisoners to attend Hampton Normal Institute, an all-black school in Virginia, Pratt recruited both male and female students from Indian communities across the country for enrollment in the Carlisle Indian Industrial School. At Carlisle, students were required to speak only English and to adopt middle-class European American ways of living. Students did not, however, follow a middle-class curriculum: In addition to very basic academic skills, girls were trained in domestic skills such as ironing and cooking, while boys learned industrial

A group of Sioux boys being "civilized" at the Carlisle Indian School. (Library of Congress)

skills. Such a curriculum did little to prepare students for life in Indian communities.

Students, however, proved much more able to maintain strong Indian identities than Captain Pratt had expected. Pratt was disappointed that so many students left Carlisle to return to their tribal homelands. The Carlisle experience also fostered new forms of Indian identity. Bringing together students from many different Indian communities, Carlisle tended to encourage students to form new bonds with members of other tribes and to work together, not just as members of specific tribes and local communities, but as American Indians with certain interests in common. Although Carlisle required a traumatic isolation from family and community, some students did, nevertheless, emerge from the experience with new skills and a determination to improve political and social conditions for other native people.

See also Education, post-contact.

Carrier: Tribe

CULTURE AREA: Subarctic
LANGUAGE GROUP: Northern Athapaskan
PRIMARY LOCATION: British Columbia, Canada
POPULATION SIZE: 6,910 (Statistics Canada, based on 1991 census)

The Carrier, members of the Northern Athapaskan language group, got their name because widows of the tribe carried the bones of their deceased husbands in a small bag on their backs during a one-year mourning period. The original location of the Carrier remains unknown, though they moved into the area of north-central British Columbia between the Rocky Mountains and the Coastal range several hundred years before first contact with whites. The Carrier lived in small subtribal groups in isolated villages. Ideas of individual ownership did not exist, and land belonged to the people using it. The Carrier fished for salmon; hunted caribou, mountain goats, and sheep; gathered berries and turnips; and—in the hard times of winter—survived by eating the bark of hemlock trees.

Carrier religion centered on a belief in a vast spirit world. Spirits could be talked to during dreams. A young man found a guardian spirit of his own after a two-week-long period of fasting, praying, and dreaming in the wilderness. This spirit was said to remain with a person for his entire life, offering protection and guidance. Potlatches were held every year by clan chiefs and wealthy tribe members, who gave away huge amounts of food and property to demonstrate their power and generosity. Individuals gained status by giving away goods rather than accumulating them as in European value systems.

Europeans first contacted the Carrier in 1793 along the Fraser River. The Carrier wanted guns and horses and gave furs to the whites in exchange. Until the 1850's, the Hudson's Bay Company provided the only contact with white civilization. Still, the trappers brought measles and smallpox with them which severely reduced the Indian population. A gold rush in 1858 brought thousands of prospectors, and then farmers and ranchers. The Carrier population continued to decline.

The Canadian government established a reservation in 1876. Sawmills opened, and the lumber industry provided most of the employment for the Indians—though the greatest cash income for the tribe came from old-age assistance programs and welfare.

See also Athapaskan language family; Subarctic.

Catahecassa (c. 1740, Fla.—c. 1831, Wapakoneta, Ohio): War chief

ALSO KNOWN AS: Black Hoof
TRIBAL AFFILIATION: Shawnee
SIGNIFICANCE: A principal chief and spirited orator, Catahecassa fought against white settlers during several Indian rebellions

Although forced to move north due to white expansion, Catahecassa was originally from Florida. During the French and Indian war, Catahecassa aided the French, thereby helping ensure General Edward Braddock's defeat at Fort Duquesne in 1755. Following the ultimate French defeat, Catahecassa supported Pontiac in his pantribal rebellion against the British in 1763. He also aided Shawnee chief Cornstalk and Tarhe of the Wyandots during Lord Dunmore's War, 1773-1774, in which Indians unsuccessfully fought to retain their land rights in Kentucky.

During the American Revolution, Catahecassa assisted the British against the Americans. With the Shawnee Blue Jacket, he again fought Americans during Little Turtle's War, 1790-1794. After General "Mad" Anthony Wayne marshaled two thousand highly disciplined troops, Indians suffered a devastating loss at the Battle of Fallen Timbers, August 20, 1794. On August 3, 1795, the allied leaders signed the Treaty of Fort Greenville, by which their territory, including more than half of Ohio, was ceded for lands farther west.

Thereafter, Catahecassa sought to maintain peace. To that end, like the Wyandot Tarhe, he refused to join Tecumseh in his rebellion during 1809-1811.

See also Fallen Timbers, Battle of; Little Turtle; Lord Dunmore's War; Pontiac; Tarhe; Tecumseh.

Catawba: Tribe

CULTURE AREA: Southeast
LANGUAGE GROUP: Siouan
PRIMARY LOCATION: South Carolina
POPULATION SIZE: 1,078 (1990 U.S. Census)

The Catawba (or Katapu) tribe is the largest of the eastern Siouan tribes, the only one to have survived into the twentieth century under its original name. Like most Southern Woodlands tribes, the Catawba grew corn, beans, and squash, and were known for their skill in pottery-making and basket-weaving. The Catawba inhabited the area that would become the North/South Carolina border. The Catawba were sometimes known as Isswa, "the river people." The Catawba River and Catawba grape are both named for this group. First contact with whites probably occurred in the 1560's, when Spanish explorers occupied the region. The Catawba were generally friendly to the English, becoming their allies during skirmishes with the Tuscarora tribe in the early 1700's and later joining them against the French and northern Indians.

The Catawba, whose name means "strong" or "separated people," had a history of enmity with other tribes. A long-standing state of war existed between them and several other tribes, among them the Cherokee, the Iroquois, and the Shawnee. Battles were often prompted by white settlers' encroachment into Indian territory, forcing one tribe to move into another's domain. The Catawba took several smaller tribes (the Congeree, Sugaree, Wateree, Sewee, Santee, and others) under their protection and probably later assimilated the remnants of these groups. Between 1738 and 1776, the Catawba were ravaged by smallpox; the tribe never recovered their previous numbers or importance. In 1840, they were tricked into signing over their land in South Carolina in exchange for land in North Carolina. The North Carolinians refused to honor the treaty, however, and the Catawba were forced to retreat, homeless. They were eventually granted a reservation in York County, South Carolina, where some members of the tribe still remain. Others moved west, to Oklahoma, Arkansas, and Utah; many joined the Choctaw. In 1970, only seventy Catawba Indians lived on the South Carolina reservation (some records indicate that only mixed-blood descendants of the tribe existed); by the mid-1980's, they numbered more than a thousand and were engaged in a legal battle to regain some 140,000 acres of their homeland.

See also Choctaw; Southeast.

Cayuga: Tribe

CULTURE AREA: Northeast
LANGUAGE GROUP: Iroquoian
PRIMARY LOCATION: New York State, Ontario
POPULATION SIZE: 1,048 in U.S. (1990 U.S. Census); estimated 1,000 in Canada

One of the original five tribes of the Iroquois Confederacy, the Cayugas occupied a homeland between the Senecas to their west and the Onondagas to their east in what is now west-central New York State. The Cayuga language is very closely related to those of the other Iroquois tribes and to other Iroquoian languages. The name Cayuga is thought to mean "where the boats were taken out," "where the locusts were taken out," or "mucky land." The Iroquois Confederacy Council name for the Cayugas refers to them as "those of the great pipe." Like their fellow Iroquois, the Cayugas were divided into matrilineal clans, with a spokesman for each clan in the political system appointed by the matron of each clan. The Cayugas were matrilocal—a marrying couple would live with the wife's family. Consequently, married men were guests in their wives' extended family households.

Men in Cayuga society traditionally spent much of their time away from the village hunting, fishing, trading, and engaging in warfare. Women were the primary breadwinners, raising the staple crops of corn, beans, and squash as well as tobacco and other agricultural products. Cayuga villages were composed of twenty to fifty longhouses, extended-family dwellings made of poles and bark coverings. Each longhouse housed between fifteen and thirty people. The Cayuga population was estimated at 1,500 in 1660, after the first epidemics of European diseases had taken their toll. For most of the eighteenth century, the Cayugas occupied only one village, and their population fell partly because of disease but also from extensive warfare. The Iroquois Confederacy was engaged in a series of wars with both other tribes and European powers, most notably the French. They initiated the "Beaver Wars" of the mid-1600's and were periodically involved in military expeditions until the American Revolution. In the war of American independence, the Cayugas and most other Iroquois sided with the British, and they lost most of their homelands in what is now New York State. Most Cayugas moved to the Grand River in what is now Ontario, Canada, and settled on a large reserve set aside for the Six Nations of the Iroquois Confederacy. Many still reside there. A few remained in New York, and some moved to Sandusky, Ohio, in the early nineteenth century with some Senecas, eventually moving to Oklahoma. A few remain in Oklahoma. Some traveled with a group of New York Oneidas to Wisconsin in the 1830's, their descendants remaining there. The Cayugas still living in New York and Ontario retain much of their traditional culture: Their language is still spoken, and traditional ceremonies such as the Green Corn Ceremony and the Midwinter Festival are still held. Cayugas all live with other Iroquois people and must strive to maintain their distinctiveness in the face of larger numbers of Onondagas and Senecas.

Cayuga contact with the French, Dutch, and English in the colonial era was not as great as it was for the Onondagas and Mohawks. The Cayugas often were overshadowed by the larger Onondaga and Seneca tribes. Nevertheless, the Cayugas did deal with the French and succeeding English and American missionaries, who at times attempted to change their culture as well as their religious beliefs. Handsome Lake, a Seneca prophet who revitalized traditional Iroquois spiritual beliefs and blended them with Quaker Christian ideas in the early nineteenth century, had an impact on many Cayuga people; some today adhere to this Longhouse religion. Others are nominally Christian, a legacy of the various missionary attempts to proselytize the Iroquois.

See also Beaver Wars; Indian-white relations—Dutch colonial; Indian-white relations—English colonial; Indian-white relations—French colonial; Iroquois Confederacy; Longhouse; Longhouse religion; Mohawk; Oneida; Onondaga; Seneca; Tuscarora.

Cayuse: Tribe

CULTURE AREA: Plateau
LANGUAGE GROUP: Penutian, Sahaptian
PRIMARY LOCATION: Oregon and Washington
POPULATION SIZE: 126 (1990 U.S. Census)

The Cayuse tribe is generally considered a Plateau tribe, but some scholars consider the Cayuse a Great Basin group. The Cayuse were called "Cailloux," meaning "People of the

A Cayuse mother and child, photographed by Edward S. Curtis in 1910. (Library of Congress)

Stones," by early French-Canadian fur traders. They were closely related to the Walla Wallas of southeastern Washington and to the Nez Perce, with whom they intermarried and whose more flexible language they eventually adopted. They lived primarily near the headwaters of the Walla Walla, Umatilla, and Grande Ronde rivers. The Cayuse acquired the horse relatively early and became known as expert riders (the term "cayuse" was eventually adopted by whites to refer to Indian ponies generally).

Little is known of the pre-contact history of the Cayuse. Some of the earliest information about the tribe was recorded in the journals of the Lewis and Clark expedition and in historical documents describing the activities of missionary Marcus Whitman in the Walla Walla, Washington, region.

By 1844, the number of European Americans arriving in Cayuse territory had escalated to the point that a dramatic increase in confrontations was occurring between the two groups. In the mid-nineteenth century, the Cayuse became regarded by whites as one of the more fierce and warlike tribes. Two sources of tension were the activities of missionaries and, later, the fact that whites repeatedly sought to move the Cayuse from their land. Among the missionaries in the area were Whitman, Samuel Parker, and Catholic priests François Norbert Blanchet and Modeste Demers. In 1841, the two priests baptized several Cayuse chiefs and the baby of Chief Tauitau. In 1847, a group of Cayuse killed missionary Whitman along with thirteen others, beginning what is known as the Cayuse War (1847-1850). The Cayuse were angry and worried that he and other missionaries, in attempting to win converts, were beginning to destroy traditional Cayuse beliefs and lifeways. In return, a vigilante army launched a devastating attack on the Cayuse.

In 1856, about a year after the Walla Walla Treaty, a general war broke out among the Plateau tribes, who essentially wanted their lands back. The Cayuse were unable to keep their lands in the Walla Walla valley, however, and they had to move to the Umatilla reservation. In 1886, because whites wanted land that was part of the Umatilla reservation, the reservation was reduced to about one-fourth of its original size.

The contemporary Cayuse population is small. Through the years, tribal members have intermarried with other groups, and their descendants tend to be scattered among the Colville, Nez Perce, Coeur d'Alene, and Umatilla reservations.

See also Cayuse War; Plateau; Walla Walla Council.

Cayuse War

DATE: 1847-1850
PLACE: Southeastern Washington State
TRIBES AFFECTED: Cayuse, Tenino
SIGNIFICANCE: The Cayuse War began when the Cayuse attacked a mission because they were angry about the disruption and disease that had come with the whites; the war gained the Cayuse a reputation as a fierce and warlike tribe

The Waiilatpu Mission was established near Fort Walla Walla in southeastern Washington by a medical doctor, Marcus Whitman. The mission was located on Pasha Creek (called Mill Creek by most European Americans). The land on which the mission was built was actually part of the ancient Cayuse lands, a situation which would later lead to friction between the missionaries and the Cayuse. The Cayuse land was in the center of an area through which many Europeans passed on their way to a number of destinations in the Pacific Northwest, another cause of friction between the two groups.

Whitman's preachings in the mission were designed to persuade the Cayuse to forsake their traditional ways and adopt his version of "Christian values." Gradually, the Cayuse became convinced that Whitman was an evil man. To make matters worse, many Cayuse tribal members contracted measles, and some of them blamed Whitman. He returned to his mission during the fall of 1847 after ministering to the sick at Umatilla. His mission complex was attacked by the Cayuse, and the Whitmans and twelve others were killed.

A retaliatory effort was mounted against the small group of Cayuse and the dissidents, but it was repulsed. On January 28, 1848, a group of Cayuse warriors and some recruited Teninos defeated a volunteer party under the command of Major Henry Lee; although the Cayuse tried to persuade other area tribes to join them in the battle, only a few did.

The Cayuse later suffered a defeat during the Sand Hollow battle of 1848, in which Cayuse chief Gray Eagle was killed. A number of other skirmishes ensued during the remainder of 1848 and in 1849. The refusal of other tribes to join the Cayuse would ultimately lead to their downfall.

In a message to the territorial legislature in 1850, Joseph Lane, the new governor of Oregon Territory, declared that the entire Cayuse tribe would be considered responsible for the deaths of the European Americans in the Whitman mission attack until the guilty parties were turned over to the government for trial. An increasing number of Cayuse and other bands attempted to capture the members of the Cayuse tribe who had attacked the missionaries. Finally, five of the attackers were captured after being pursued by members of their own tribe. They were turned over to the Oregon territorial government for trial. It has been speculated that the accused Cayuse had little understanding of the American legal system which would judge their case. They were provided defense council by the Oregon territorial government. On May 24, 1850, the jury pronounced them guilty as charged, and they were hanged on Monday, June 3, 1850.

See also Cayuse; Walla Walla Council.

Certificate of Degree of Indian Blood (CDIB)

TRIBES AFFECTED: Pantribal
SIGNIFICANCE: Of all the ethnic and racial groups in the United States, only American Indians are issued cards by the government stating their ethnic identity

A Certificate of Degree of Indian Blood is a card issued by the U.S. Bureau of Indian Affairs. The card indicates that the bearer is entitled to be called "Indian." It states the cardholder's tribal affiliation and blood quantum—the percentage of Indian blood the person possesses. One purpose of the CDIB is to establish who is eligible for the various governmental services available to Indians. State legislatures have also enacted laws that specify (with varying degrees of precision) who is considered an Indian in that state.

See also American Indian; Tribe.

Chaco Canyon: Archaeological site

DATE: 900-1200
LOCATION: New Mexico
CULTURES AFFECTED: Anasazi, Pueblo

Chaco Canyon is the site of some of the finest ruins in the United States and is an example of the zenith of pre-Columbian Pueblo civilization. Located in northern New Mexico, the canyon is roughly 10 miles long and a mile wide, surrounded by sandstone cliffs and traversed by the seasonal Chaco River. Within the area are located six large pueblos—Pueblo Bonito, Chetro Ketl, Una Vida, Peñasco Blanco, Hungo Pavi, and Kin Bineola—and many smaller towns connected by a network of roads.

The Anasazi (Navajo for "ancient ones") inhabited the site back to 900 C.E. They farmed the lowlands, began constructing the great masonry towns, and within a century had created an economic and political center at Chaco Plateau. It has been estimated that between two thousand and five thousand people were living in some four hundred settlements in and around Chaco. Although archaeological work went back to the Hyde Expedition (1896-1899), the question of the "Chaco Phenomenon" persisted: How could so many people live in such an inhospitable land? Beginning in 1972 the National Park Service, in conjunction with the University of New Mexico, sought to explain the Chaco Phenomenon.

One theory is that the site was an administrative and ritual center that oversaw the agricultural life of the region. Food was gathered, stored, and distributed as needed. Remains exist of an extensive, well-planned 400-mile road system which connected Chaco with seventy-five other communities constructed in the eleventh and twelfth centuries, creating an integrated society. From the evidence, these people conducted extensive trade as far south as Mexico. Final answers as to how the Chaco Phenomenon fit into the larger world outside the San Juan Basin remain to be found.

Between 1130 and 1180 a prolonged drought, and possibly an overtaxed environment in the San Juan Basin, brought about the decline of the Chaco Phenomenon. Social disintegration set in, and the Anasazi moved to better lands in the Rio Grande Valley, where their descendants remain. Chaco Culture National Historical Park was made part of the National Park Service by presidential proclamation in 1907.

See also Anasazi; Prehistory—Southwest.

Chantways

TRIBE AFFECTED: Navajo
SIGNIFICANCE: "Chantways" is the term used to refer to the Navajo ceremonial healing system based on creation myths, using a combination of singing, sand painting, prayer, and sacred objects

The Navajo ceremonial system is composed of rites, chants, and rituals for restoring balance and harmony to life. Based on Navajo creation myths that explain their understanding of the reciprocity of the natural and supernatural worlds, religious rituals requiring from two to nine days and nights are conducted that are both curative and preventative.

Belief. The Navajo believe that the universe is interrelated. All of creation is maintained by a delicate balance of natural and supernatural elements that results in a state of harmony and well being. The natural and supernatural operate in a system of mutual interchange in order to achieve this ideal state of health.

In this system, it is believed that people become ill as a result of disharmony in the world caused by such things as bad dreams, evil spirits and sorcery, excesses in activities, and the hoarding of property. Navajos adhere to a rule of moderation in living to avoid sickness, injury, and other misfortune. For those who are suffering, the sacred ceremony centering on the sand painting is the means to physical, emotional, and psychological restoration.

Sand Paintings. Sand paintings are freehand drawings which serve three main purposes: to attract "the supernaturals"; to identify the patient with them; and to serve as a medium of exchange, absorbing evil or imparting good. Completed sand paintings obligate the Holy People to come and infuse the sand painting with their power. Because of the sacred and powerful nature of this exchange, complete and accurate sand paintings are always used only in a ritual context.

Sand paintings are a type of ritual altar on the floor of the hogan, and they are the center of activity and power in the Chantways ceremonials. The symbols and images used in sand painting are irresistible for the supernaturals; they are compelled to come to their likenesses in the painting. A painting can take from thirty minutes to ten or more hours to complete, often with several apprentice assistants working on it. The average painting takes about four hours. When the painting is completed it is inspected, sanctified, and used immediately.

Practice. Chantways, so called because of the singing and shaking of rattles during the ceremonials, are organized into ceremonial categories or complexes based on the interrelatedness of procedure and myth. Of twenty-four known complexes, about half are well known, with seven of these performed often. These seven are called Shootingway, Mountainway, Nightway, Flintway, Hand-tremblingway, Navajo Windway, and Chiricahua Windway. They are used to treat such ailments as respiratory disease, arthritis, head ailments, emergencies, nervousness, and heart and lung trouble, respectively. They are regulated by one of three rituals, called Holyway, to attract good, Evilway to drive away evil, or Lifeway, for injuries. Holyway uses the greatest variety of sand paintings and is performed at such events as marriage, childbirth, and the consecration of a new home. Rites included in these rituals are

Blessingway rites to ensure peace, harmony, and good and Enemyway rites, used to exorcise evil spirits or ghosts from outside the Navajo tribe. Every ceremonial ends with a Blessingway rite.

Holy People are supernaturals composed of two groups. One is represented by mythological figures such as Sun, Changing Woman, and their twin children, Monster Slayer and Born-for-Water. The other group is called the "Yei"; the Yei are led by Talking God and Calling God (who participate in the Nightway chant wearing masks).

Participants include the singer and his assistants, the patient, family members, a diagnostician, and the supernaturals. Trained singers possess the knowledge of the ritual and have undergone a long apprenticeship. Many singers learn only a few ceremonials, each of which involves songs, prayers, plant medicine, sand paintings, sacred objects, and the correct ritual procedure. The singing must be complete and correct to attract the Holy People. If the Holy People are pleased, they are obligated to come and infuse the sand paintings with their power and restore health and harmony to the patient.

Services are performed when needed. Men are usually the singers. Women are allowed to participate, but extreme care is taken to protect them from contacting and absorbing any evil spirits. Pregnant women are not allowed to participate.

The ceremony is held in the family or relative's home, or hogan, which has been ritually consecrated. A diagnostician determines what has caused the patient's illness or trouble and which Chantway is needed to effect the cure. The sand painting is made, and prayer sticks are placed where the supernaturals will see them and be compelled to come. The patient is prepared for the ritual by being cleansed physically and spiritually; the individual then sits almost naked facing east on a specific part of the painting determined by the singer to relate most directly to the patient's trouble. The patient is touched by the singer and his medicine bundle and is sprinkled with sand from appropriate parts of the sand painting. After the patient leaves, the painting is erased in the order in which it was made, and the sand from the sand painting is deposited at a distance from the hogan. Blessingway paintings, however, may be left on the floor of the hogan to become part of the home's floor, continuing to impart their good.

The Chantway system is unique to the Navajo and reflects a holistic approach to health and healing. In spite of the availability of modern medicine to today's Navajo, they continue to preserve this method of bringing harmony to their world.

—*Diane C. Van Noord*

See also Navajo; Religion; Religious specialists; Sacred narratives; Sand painting.

BIBLIOGRAPHY

Circle, Black Mustache. *Waterway*. Recorded by Berard Haile. Flagstaff: Museum of Northern Arizona Press, 1979.

Parezo, Nancy J. *Navajo Sandpainting*. Tucson: University of Arizona Press, 1983.

Reichard, Gladys A. *Navaho Religion: A Study of Symbolism*. 2 vols. Princeton, N.J.: Princeton University Press, 1950.

Sandner, Donald. *Navaho Symbols of Healing*. Rochester, Vt.: Healing Arts Press, 1991.

Wyman, Leland C. *Southwest Indian Drypainting*. Santa Fe, N.Mex.: School of American Research Press, 1983.

Charlot (c. 1831, northern Idaho—1900, Jocko Reservation): Tribal chief

ALSO KNOWN AS: Clem-hak-kah (Bear Claw)
TRIBAL AFFILIATION: Flathead/Salish (possibly Kalispel)
SIGNIFICANCE: Charlot fought against removal by white settlers

Charlot (sometimes called Martin Charlot) was among the Flathead/Salish people in the Bitterroot Mountains of Montana who created fertile farms only to have them seized by immigrants. In the early 1890's, he was among those who were told to move to less fertile land on the Pend d'Oreille reservation. The dissident band of Flathead/Salish led by Charlot managed to delay relocation for several years. Charlot even traveled to Washington, D.C., in 1884 with Indian Agent Peter Ronan to discuss the issue. He still refused to cooperate in removal to a reservation. As whites usurped their homeland, many of Charlot's followers moved in the 1880's, but he and a few followers held out until 1900, when they were finally removed by force.

See also Flathead.

Charlot and his followers resisted removal to a reservation until 1900. (Library of Congress)

Chasta Costa: Tribe

CULTURE AREA: Northwest Coast
LANGUAGE GROUP: Athapaskan
PRIMARY LOCATION: Rogue River and Chasta Costa Creek drainages, Oregon

Living in a mountainous area throughout their history, the socially stratified Chasta Costa were dependent upon trading with the Upper Coquille, the Galice to their southeast, and the coastal Tututni. These patrilineal groups were headed by polygamous chiefs whose position was maintained through consensus of opinion, oratorical skills, and leadership. The groups had complex ceremonies and engaged in warfare, primarily for status and for acquiring slaves. Subsistence was diversified through fishing, hunting land and sea mammals, and gathering of roots, tubers, berries, nuts, and acorns. Annual controlled burning improved resource areas; deer-hunting areas were burned over every five years. Permanent winter dwellings were of split cedar planks; the size of the structure was determined by one's status.

In April of 1792, Robert Gray began trade with people of this area, but little ethnographic information was recorded. These tribes were devastated by gold seekers, who introduced disease. The Rogue River War (1855-1856) was also destructive, as Chasta Costa were moved from their traditional territories. By 1871 the Ghost Dance was introduced, followed by the Warm House Dance in 1873.

Chehalis: Tribe

CULTURE AREA: Northwest Coast
LANGUAGE GROUP: Coast Salish
PRIMARY LOCATION: Harrison River below mouth of Chehalis to Harrison Lake, Washington
POPULATION SIZE: 484 (1990 U.S. Census)

The marine-oriented Lower Chehalis lived, during the winter, in permanent gable-roofed dwellings of split cedar, each housing eight to twelve families. The inland Upper Chehalis were located on major streams and used similar structures. Marriage was outside the kin group and the village was the main socioeconomic and political group. Fish was the principal food, as reflected in fishing technology, ceremony, and various behavioral prohibitions and divisions of labor. Smelt, herring, lamprey, and shellfish were taken. Women collected roots, berries, and fruit.

Several other expeditions had made contact with the Chehalis before Meriwether Lewis and William Clark visited them in 1805. By 1811, Astoria was established, and fur traders began to exploit the area. The establishment of Fort Vancouver in 1825 by the Hudson's Bay Company encouraged further white settlement and use of the Cowlitz Trail, which traversed Lower Chehalis territory. The Chehalis Reservation was established in 1864, and in 1866 a smaller reservation was also established. Until Prohibition, most employment was in picking hops. By the late twentieth century, the Chehalis were earning their income in urban employment, logging, and fishing.

See also Salishan language family.

Chemakum: Tribe

CULTURE AREA: Northwest Coast
LANGUAGE GROUP: Chemakum
PRIMARY LOCATION: Hadlock Bay and Port Townsend, south to Port Gamble, Washington

Little is known of the lifeways of the Chemakum before contact with European Americans. They were a marine-oriented society and lived in a stockaded village on Chimacum Creek. The area was sometimes subject to drought, placing an emphasis upon fish and sea mammals for food and various byproducts. The Chemakum had linguistic and cultural connections with the Quileute.

European American disease and intertribal warfare reduced the Chemakum population. They were reported to be an aggressive people, having conflict with the Clallam, Duwamish, Makah, Snohomish, and Twana. By 1850, it was apparent that their decline was partially attributable to assimilation by other ethnic groups. In 1855, part of the Point No Point Treaty placed them on the Skokomish Reservation. By 1860, there were only seventy-three surviving Chemakum; that same year they dispersed north and relocated in eighteen lodges at Point Hudson, where they intermarried with the Clallam and Twana-Skokomish. Some Chemakuan people took up residence on the Skokomish Reservation.

See also Clallam; Quileute.

Cheraw: Tribe

CULTURE AREA: Southeast
LANGUAGE GROUP: Siouan
PRIMARY LOCATION: Head of Saluda River, South Carolina

The matrilineal, horticultural Cheraw were socioeconomically stratified and had centralized authority. They lived in palisaded permanent riverside villages, with fields of maize, squash, beans, and other cultivated food plants. Men hunted and trapped large and small animals throughout the year to supplement stored foods. Principles of usufruct applied to acorn forests, deer-hunting areas, and berrying patches.

Hernando de Soto first mentioned the Cheraw in 1540, calling them Xuala. European American disease came in the late sixteenth century, reducing the Cheraw population. By 1700 they moved from their aboriginal territory to Dan River, and in 1710, after continual conflict with the Iroquois, they moved southeast and joined the Keyauwee. This close association of the tribes alarmed colonists of North Carolina, who declared war on the Cheraw. The Iroquois also maintained their attacks on the Cheraw, who between 1726 and 1739 became affiliated with the Catawba for protection. By 1768 only a few Cheraw were remaining.

See also Catawba.

Cherokee: Tribe

CULTURE AREA: Southeast
LANGUAGE GROUP: Iroquoian
PRIMARY LOCATION: North Carolina, Oklahoma
POPULATION SIZE: 308,132 (1990 U.S. Census)

The largest and most powerful of the Eastern Woodland tribes in what is now the southeastern part of the United States was the Cherokee. Their population in the sixteenth century is estimated to have been about twenty-five thousand. Between their first major contact with Europeans in 1540 and their forced removal to the west in 1838-1839, the Cherokee adopted many aspects of European civilization. The Cherokee, Creek, Choctaw, Chickasaw, and Seminole, all southeastern tribes, became known as the Five Civilized Tribes.

Background and Tradition. The Cherokee language belongs to the Iroquoian language group, found primarily in the Northeast. Apparently a major war, perhaps against the Delaware (Lenni Lenape) along the East Coast, separated the Cherokee from the other Iroquoian tribes and led to their migration to the southern Appalachian highlands. Traditions of both the Delaware and the Cherokee support this theory.

The early Cherokee called themselves Ani-Yun-Wiya, which means "principal people." Neighboring tribes of the Muskogean language group called them Chilikee, or "people of a different speech." The chroniclers of Hernando de Soto in 1540 called the area Chalique. "Cherokee" is an Anglicized form of these last two names.

The Cherokee lived in approximately eighty towns, scattered over a large area of the southern Appalachians. There were three basic groups of towns, each speaking a distinct dialect. The lower towns were along the Tugaloo River in northeastern Georgia and the Keowee river in northwest South Carolina. The middle-valley towns were in western North Carolina, along the Nottely River, the upper Hiwassee River, and the Valley River. Across the mountains in eastern Tennessee was the third group, the upper or Overhill towns, which were located around the Little Tennessee River, the Tellico River, the lower Hiwassee River, and the headwaters of the Tennessee River. Although the Cumberland Plateau formed the western boundary of all Cherokee towns, their hunting grounds spread far beyond the plateau into middle Tennessee. The dialect of the middle-valley towns has been preserved by the Qualla Cherokee in North Carolina; the Cherokee Nation of Oklahoma has retained the Overhill dialect. The lower town dialect has disappeared.

Although the Cherokee had a loosely organized tribal government, most affairs were conducted at the town level. Both levels had a dual organization, one for peace and one for war. At the town level, the peace chief was an elder who also served as the chief priest. The war chief was a younger and highly successful warrior; he wielded great power in town affairs. Each town had a council, which met in a seven-sided town house, composed of seven clans: Deer, Wolf, Long Hair, Red Paint, Blue, Bird, and Wild Potatoes.

The customs of the Cherokee were similar to those of the other Eastern Woodland tribes. They lived in mud and thatch houses that were easy to build yet designed to be permanent. Marriage and family traditions were matriarchal and matrilineal. Women often rose to influential positions in town and tribal affairs, acquiring such titles as Ghighau (beloved or greatly honored woman). These women had an active role in town councils and could decide the fate of prisoners.

The major occupations of Cherokee men were hunting and warfare. Some historians classify them as the warlords of the southern Appalachians. Although most wars occurred on the town level, there were basic tribal rivalries, especially with the Creek, who lived south of the Cherokee, which led to major tribal wars. Honorary titles, such as Mankiller, Bloody Fellow, and The Raven were given to outstanding warriors.

Cherokee religion was polytheistic, but major emphasis was placed on Yowa, the creator god. Seven religious festivals, with elaborate ceremonies and artistic dancing, were held each year. One of the most beautiful of all Native American dances is the Cherokee Eagle Dance. Many elements of Cherokee religion, including Yowa, made it comparatively easy for many Cherokees later to convert to Christianity. In spite of this conversion, much religious tradition has been retained by modern-day Cherokees.

On the eve of their first contacts with Europeans, the Cherokee seemed to be at peace with their environment, contented with their lifestyles, and prosperous in their economic development. Beginning in 1540, these conditions began to change—first slowly, then very rapidly.

European Contact, 1540-1775. Although there are legends of white-skinned people visiting the southern Appalachians as far back as the twelfth century, the first documented contact was with the Spanish explorer and conqueror Hernando de Soto. De Soto landed at Tampa Bay in 1539, fought his way up the East Coast with an army of six hundred men, and entered Cherokee country in May, 1540. Along the way, several hundred other Native Americans had been enslaved as burden-bearers for de Soto's army. The goal of de Soto's expedition was gold, such as had already been discovered by other Spaniards in Central and South America. As he drew near to the Cherokee and heard accounts of their power, de Soto thought he had found what he was seeking.

The Cherokee were initially awestruck by the sight of de Soto's armor-clad warriors, thinking that they had been sent by the gods to punish them for their sins. Later, realizing the true nature of the Spaniards, the Cherokee goal was to get their uninvited guests through and out of their territory as quickly as possible. This they accomplished by being hospitable but pressing de Soto to move on, which he did when he found no gold. De Soto moved west into Chickasaw territory, where, in 1542, he was buried in the Mississippi River. Twenty-five years after de Soto, another Spaniard, Juan Pardo, visited the Cherokee, also looking for gold (and also finding none). Following the exit of Pardo in 1567, the Cherokee enjoyed more than a century with no significant European contact.

That serenity ended in 1673, when Abraham Wood, a trader in the English colony of Virginia, sent two men to establish a commercial relationship with the Overhill Cherokee in eastern Tennessee. With the taste of the Spanish still lingering in their tribal memory, the Cherokee killed one of the men and made a

Yayahsti, a Cherokee boy, performing a traditional dance at a 1977 pow-wow in Maryland. (AP/Wide World Photos)

temporary prisoner of the other. In spite of this rough beginning, commercial ties were soon established that endured until the American Revolution.

In 1730, six Cherokee warriors were taken on a visit to Great Britain, where they signed the Articles of Friendship and Commerce. This treaty, after being approved by the chiefs at home, meant that the Cherokee would trade only with—and fight only for—the British. For the next fifty years, the Cherokee tried to keep their word, even when the British were negligent of theirs. This period included the French and Indian War (1754-1763), in which the Cherokee fought with the British against the French and their Indian allies. In the midst of that conflict, however, mistreatment by the British led to the brief Cherokee War (1759-1761) against the British. Following the end of the French and Indian War in 1763, peaceful cooperation between the Cherokee and the British was restored.

One of the warriors who visited Great Britain in 1730 was Attakullakulla, later called the Little Carpenter by the British because of his ability to build mutually beneficial relationships between his own people and the European settlers. Until his death in 1778, at about ninety-two years of age, Little Carpenter performed this task well.

The Cherokee were perplexed by the outbreak of the American Revolution in 1775, not understanding why British settlers were fighting Great Britain. When they did understand, true to the Articles of Friendship and Commerce, they gave support to the British. The desire of Little Carpenter and most other leaders was that the Cherokee would not become militarily involved. The British also, believing that the revolution would soon collapse, believed that it would be in the best interests of the Cherokee to remain neutral. One group of Cherokee warriors, however, had no desire for neutrality.

The Chickamauga, 1775-1794. On March 19, 1775, exactly one month before the first shots of the revolution were fired, the Treaty of Sycamore Shoals was signed in present-day Elizabethton, Tennessee. This treaty was between the Cherokee and their white neighbors, and it involved the sale of about twenty million acres of Cherokee hunting grounds to white leaders. The land, about half of the area originally claimed by the Cherokee, included much of Kentucky and middle Tennessee. Little Carpenter led the majority of the Cherokee in approving the sale. Dragging Canoe, the outspoken son of Little Carpenter, led the minority who opposed it. When he realized that his views were not going to prevail, Dragging Canoe left Sycamore Shoals, with a bitter warning of the violence to be expected when whites tried to settle the land being purchased.

In June, 1776, a delegation of northern tribes, led by a Shawnee chief named Cornstalk, visited the Cherokee capital of Chota, on the Little Tennessee River. Taking advantage of the American Revolution, Cornstalk was forming a coalition to drive the white settlers back across the Appalachian Mountains. Little Carpenter and other peaceful chiefs listened to Cornstalk's appeal, then watched in sad silence while Drag-

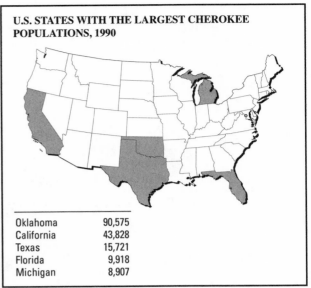

U.S. STATES WITH THE LARGEST CHEROKEE POPULATIONS, 1990

Oklahoma	90,575
California	43,828
Texas	15,721
Florida	9,918
Michigan	8,907

Source: 1990 U.S. Census.

ging Canoe accepted the war belt offered by the Shawnee chief.

Within a month of the meeting at Chota, Dragging Canoe was leading raids against the white settlements in east Tennessee. The settlements, however, were usually warned by friendly Cherokees such as Nancy Ward, a Ghighau (beloved woman). After being wounded in a raid that became an ambush, Dragging Canoe and his followers withdrew from Cherokee territory. Their new home was along Chickamauga Creek, a tributary of the Tennessee River. They occupied several abandoned Creek sites and began to call themselves the Chickamaugas, a name that means "river of death."

The raids against the settlements in east Tennessee continued until the original Chickamauga towns were destroyed by a retaliatory raid in April, 1779. After moving west to their Five Lower Towns, the Chickamauga launched new raids, this time against Fort Nashborough and the Cumberland River settlements on land bought at Sycamore Shoals. The raids, which continued for about ten years and covered a distance of about one hundred miles each way, could not prevent the settlement of that part of middle Tennessee.

In September, 1794, two years after the death of Dragging Canoe, the Five Lower Towns were destroyed by a surprise attack from Fort Nashborough. The surviving Chickamaugas were gradually assimilated back into the mainline Cherokee.

Cherokee Civilization, 1775-1830. The Long Island Treaty, signed in July, 1777, kept the majority of the Cherokee out of the American Revolution. By the terms of the Treaty of Hopewell, in 1785, the Cherokee recognized the supreme authority of the new government of the United States, which in turn promised to protect the rights of the Cherokee to the twenty million acres of land that they still possessed. In spite of this promise, by 1817 Cherokee lands had been reduced to about seven million acres in southwest North Carolina, southeast Tennessee, a large portion of north Georgia, and the northwest corner of Alabama. The reduction in the size of Cherokee land led to major changes in their lifestyle. The basic means of support shifted from hunting to agriculture. Many Cherokee continued to supplement their income by trading with their white neighbors, who constantly moved closer and closer to the Cherokee towns.

Soon after the American Revolution, the Cherokee began adopting European standards of civilization. Their hope was that by so doing they would be able to remain in their homelands. The first step in civilization was the acceptance of Christianity. The evangelization of the Cherokee was begun by the Moravians in 1802. The most effective attempt was by the Brainerd Mission, beginning in 1817 in present-day Chattanooga; this was also the major source of education for young Cherokee men and women. Later Cherokee leaders such as Elias Boudinot and John Ridge began their formal education at Brainerd.

During the War of 1812, the Cherokee were given the chance to prove their loyalty to the United States. One of their traditional tribal enemies, the Creek, were fighting in Alabama. The Cherokee joined the volunteers of Andrew Jackson to defeat the Creek at Horseshoe Bend in 1814, a battle in which Yonaguska, a future Cherokee chief, saved the life of Jackson, a future American president.

Cherokee educational development took a major step forward in 1826, when Sequoyah, a part-blood Cherokee, invented a syllabary for the Cherokee language. With this creation, the first for any Native American tribe, the Cherokee soon began publishing their own newspaper: the *Cherokee Phoenix*, edited by Elias Boudinot.

The next significant step was the Cherokee adoption, on July 4, 1827, of a democratic constitution. This document was patterned after the U.S. Constitution. It established a national capital at New Echota, in north Georgia, and led to the election of John Ross as the first principal chief. Although only an eighth-blood Cherokee, Ross was pure Cherokee at heart, and he became the tribe's major protector and spokesman during the trying years that followed.

The Trail of Tears, 1830-1839. Beginning with the Georgia Compact in 1802, signed by President Thomas Jefferson, the United States government promised to aid in the eventual removal of the Cherokee from Georgia. The Jackson-McMinn Treaty in 1817 was the first step in that process; it provided for the voluntary relocation of Cherokee to the western territory, present-day Oklahoma. Between two and four thousand Cherokee accepted this offer; about sixteen thousand remained on their ancestral land.

The urgent demand to remove all Cherokee began in 1828, when gold was discovered on their land near Dahlonega, Georgia. In 1830, Congress passed the Indian Removal Act, authorizing President Andrew Jackson to pursue Cherokee removal vigorously. A representative of the president met with a pro-removal minority of Cherokee leaders at New Echota on December 29, 1835. The resulting treaty was ratified by the U.S. Senate; it gave the entire tribe until May, 1838, to move voluntarily to the west. The majority, led by John Ross, refused to move.

The forced removal began when the deadline expired. After a heartless roundup of unoffending Cherokee families, the deadly journey began. Under the guard of federal soldiers, the Cherokee were taken, first by water, then by land, to their new homes in the west. When the "trail where they cried" ended, in March, 1839, there were four thousand unmarked graves along the way. About one thousand Cherokee escaped the removal by fleeing into the mountains. They later became the nucleus of the Eastern Band of the Cherokee, on the Qualla Boundary in North Carolina.

A New Life. The tragedy of the Trail of Tears did not end with the arrival in the west. Those who had been forced to travel the trail harbored deep bitterness toward those who had signed the New Echota Treaty. The brutal assassinations of the leaders of the Treaty Party on June 22, 1839, did not end the bitterness. The murderers of Major Ridge, John Ridge, and Elias Boudinot were never identified or punished.

There was also friction between the Old Settlers, who had been in the west since 1817, and the more numerous arrivals of 1839. On July 12, 1839, the Act of Union, under the leadership of John Ross, helped create a unified direction for the uncertain future. On September 6, the first united council was held at Tahlequah, their new capital. Ross was elected as the first principal chief, and David Vann, an Old Settler, was chosen as assistant chief. The constitution for the tribal government was similar to the one adopted in 1827. A new treaty signed in 1846 helped to heal the rift with the Treaty Party.

A new Cherokee schism developed in connection with the U.S. Civil War. Both the Union and the Confederacy courted Cherokee support. John Ross, still the principal chief, led those who backed the Union. Stand Watie, the brother of Elias Boudinot, became a Confederate general.

Traditional tribal government for the western Cherokee Nation ended in 1907, when Oklahoma became a state. From that date until 1971, the principal chief was appointed by the president of the United States. In 1971, the Cherokee regained the right to elect their chief and a tribal council.

The last capital of the Cherokee before the Trail of Tears had been at Red Clay in east Tennessee. In 1984, an emotional meeting was held at the same location. It was the first full tribal council since 1838, with delegates from both Oklahoma and North Carolina attending. An eternal flame was lit to symbolize the new united spirit of all the Cherokee. In December, 1985, another history-making event occurred in Oklahoma, when Wilma Mankiller became the first female chief of any North American tribe. She was re-elected to four-year terms in 1987 and 1991.

A 1989 U.S. Census Bureau publication listed the population of the western Cherokee Nation at 87,059. According to the 1990 U.S. Census, the Qualla Boundary in North Carolina had a population of 5,388. The 1990 census figure for the total

Wilma Mankiller, principal chief of the Cherokee Nation, conferring with Choctaw leader Phillip Martin in 1989. (AP/Wide World Photos)

Cherokee population was much higher (308,132), because it included anyone who identified himself or herself as Cherokee.

—*Glenn L. Swygart*

See also Boudinot, Elias; *Cherokee Tobacco* case; Cherokee War; Mankiller, Wilma Pearl; Ridge, John Rollins; Ridge, Major; Ross, John; Sequoyah; Trail of Tears; Ward, Nancy; Watie, Stand; Yonaguska.

BIBLIOGRAPHY

Corkran, David H. *The Cherokee Frontier: Conflict and Survival, 1740-62.* Norman: University of Oklahoma Press, 1962. Corkran's research emphasizes the effect of European contacts on the Cherokee. Special attention on their alliance with England and involvement in the French and Indian War.

Finger, John R. *The Eastern Band of the Cherokee, 1819-1900.* Knoxville: University of Tennessee Press, 1984. Covers the Cherokee in North Carolina, emphasizing problems after the Trail of Tears. Gives the reader a good picture of traditional Cherokee life.

McLoughlin, William G. *The Cherokee Ghost Dance.* Macon, Ga.: Mercer University Press, 1984. An interesting collection of essays covering Cherokee relations with other tribes, involvement in slavery, and contact with missionaries (1789-1861). Good tables.

Malone, Henry. *Cherokees of the Old South.* Athens: University of Georgia Press, 1956. Presents a clear picture of the origin and pre-removal history of the Cherokee. Stresses tribal customs and civilization.

Wilkins, Thurman. *Cherokee Tragedy.* New York: Macmillan, 1970. Based on the Ridge family. A very emotional account of the Cherokee during the years preceding removal. Good photographs.

Woodward, Grace Steele. *The Cherokees.* Norman: University of Oklahoma Press, 1963. An excellent picture of Cherokee development up to Oklahoma statehood. Emphasizes internal problems. A help in understanding present-day Cherokee. Good bibliography.

Cherokee Tobacco case

DATE: Argued April 11, 1871; decided May 1, 1871

TRIBES AFFECTED: Cherokee directly; pantribal by implication

SIGNIFICANCE: This case, also known as *Boudinot v. United States*, established the "last-in-time" precedent—the concept that later statutes overrode earlier treaties—and the rule that tribes are "included" in congressional acts unless they are specifically "excluded"

In the *Cherokee Tobacco* suit, two Cherokee nationals, Elias Cornelius Boudinot and Stand Watie, challenged the imposition of an 1868 federal tax law on their tobacco factory, which had been established in the Cherokee Nation under provisions of the Cherokee/U.S. Treaty of 1866. (Although the year 1870 is often given for this case, it was actually argued in 1871; it was received by the Court in 1870.)

Article ten of the 1866 treaty stated that Cherokee citizens had the right to sell any product or merchandise without having to pay "any tax thereon which is now or may be levied by the U.S." Two years later, Congress enacted a general revenue law which imposed taxes on liquor and tobacco products "produced anywhere within the exterior boundaries of the U.S." Justice Noah Swayne, speaking for a deeply fractured court (three justices concurred with Swayne, two dissented, and three did not participate), said that the case boiled down to which of the two laws—treaty or general domestic—was superior. (Swayne created this scenario even though there was no evidence that Congress in enacting the 1868 revenue law intended to abrogate Article ten of the treaty.)

"Undoubtedly," said Swayne, "one or the other must yield. The repugnancy is clear and they cannot stand together." Swayne then developed what has been termed the "last-in-time" rule. In effect, whichever is latest in time, be it treaty or statute, stands.

This was a catastrophic precedent for tribes, since the treaty termination law, which had been attached as a rider to the March 3, 1871, Indian Appropriation Act, had closed the door on Indian treaties, although preexisting ratified treaties were still to be honored by the U.S. This law effectively froze tribes in political limbo: They were no longer recognized as nations capable of treating with the federal government, yet they remained separate sovereignties outside the pale of the federal Constitution.

Tribes, as a result of this decision, were virtually bereft of legal or political protection. The federal government could hereafter explicitly or implicitly abrogate treaty provisions and tribes had little recourse, save returning to the corridors of the very Congress that had enacted the abrogating legislation. The Supreme Court generally deferred to the political branches on Indian matters, going so far as to say that "the act of Congress must prevail as if the treaty were not an element to be considered."

This opinion ignored the historical and political reality that the Cherokee Nation was a separate and autonomous political entity not subject to general domestic laws unless they had given their express consent; it denied the fact that Congress itself had not explicitly stated in the 1868 law that the revenue act applied to Indian Territory. Moreover, it disavowed the general principle that specific laws, such as treaties, which create special rights are not to be held "repealed by implication by any subsequent law couched in general terms."

Notwithstanding earlier U.S. guarantees of the sanctity of treaty rights, *Cherokee Tobacco* announced that those hard-fought-for rights, often secured at the cost of great amounts of tribal land and the loss of other rights, could be destroyed by mere implication.

See also Boudinot, Elias Cornelius; *Lone Wolf v. Hitchcock*; Watie, Stand.

Cherokee War

DATE: 1759-1761

PLACE: Eastern Tennessee, western Virginia, North Carolina, South Carolina, Georgia

TRIBES AFFECTED: Cherokee, Creek

SIGNIFICANCE: This war placed pressure on the Cherokees to cede eastern lands

Encroachment of white settlements, abuses by traders, French intrigue during the French and Indian War, and frontier violence led to deterioration of relations between the Cherokees and the southern colonies in the mid-eighteenth century. The South Carolina government had built two forts in the Cherokees' territory—Fort Prince George (present mid-South Carolina) in 1753 and Fort Loudoun (present eastern Tennessee) in 1757. Although the Cherokee War involved mainly South Carolina, it started in Virginia. Virginia had recruited four hundred Cherokee warriors to accompany the British-American expedition against the French in western Pennsylvania in 1758. Unpaid for their services (they had been promised pay), the major part of the Cherokee contingent defected from the army and drifted home through western Virginia. Indian thefts sparked violence with frontier farmers. Some thirty Cherokees died in Virginia during 1758. Cherokee leaders sought revenge, resulting in Indian raids on the back settlements on the Yadkin and Catawba rivers. Indian attacks spread along the frontier as far south as Georgia; in Georgia, however, the Creeks, declaring neutrality, served to constrain Indian hostilities. Cherokees cut off Forts Loudoun and Prince George from communications.

From October to December in 1759, Governor William Henry Lyttleton of South Carolina marched into the Indian country and relieved the siege of Fort Prince George. He secured twenty-four Indian hostages, to be detained at Fort Prince George, until the Indians surrendered those accused of murdering whites.

Indian hostilities, led by Osteneco, resumed in early 1760. The new South Carolina governor, William Bull, dispatched a fifteen-hundred-man force of royal troops and South Carolina militia into Indian country under Lieutenant Colonel Archibald Montgomery. Montgomery destroyed some towns and crops and, proceeding through the Little Tennessee River valley, defeated the Cherokee on June 27, 1760, though at the cost of heavy casualties on the British side. The battle occurred at the Cherokee village of Etchoe (present Franklin, Tennessee). The invaders then returned to Charleston. On August 9, Cherokees led by Oconostota captured Fort Loudoun and killed most of the captives in retaliation for the British having murdered the Indian hostages at Fort Prince George.

In early 1761, General Jeffrey Amherst, commander-in-chief of British forces in America, sent Lieutenant Colonel James Grant and twelve hundred royal troops to South Carolina. Joined by Carolina militia and some Indian auxiliaries (including Catawbas and Chickasaws), with a force now numbering three thousand, Grant attacked Indian settlements along the Tennessee and Tuckaseegee valleys in June, 1761, driving five thousand Indians into the mountains and destroying fifteen Indian villages and 1,400 acres of Indian crops. Indians under Attakullakulla (Little Carpenter) sued for peace. The treaty, signed on December 18, gave the British the right to build forts anywhere in Cherokee country, restored trade, and redefined the Cherokee-South Carolina boundary line westward.

During the war a Virginia force headed by William Byrd and then Adam Stephen was sent to join the Grant expedition. The Virginia contingent, aided by some North Carolina troops, went no further than the Great (or Long) Island (Kingsport, Tennessee) on the Holston River. There, on November 17-19, 1761, Stephen concluded peace with Osteneco, Oconostota, and other tribal leaders representing the Overhill Cherokees (the northernmost branch of the tribe). Frontier encroachments upon Indian land continued, however, and a Cherokee war again erupted in 1776-1777, from western Georgia to western North Carolina, culminating in the Cherokees surrendering all their lands east of the Blue Ridge.

See also Cherokee; Oconostota.

Cheyenne: Tribe

CULTURE AREA: Plains
LANGUAGE GROUP: Algonquian
PRIMARY LOCATION: Montana, Oklahoma
POPULATION SIZE: 11,456 (1990 U.S. Census)

The Cheyenne originally lived in woodland country in what is now southeastern Minnesota. The name "Cheyenne" comes from the Dakota Sioux, who called the Cheyenne *Shahiyena* or *Shahiela*, which means "people who talk differently," "people of alien speech," or, literally, "red speakers." They probably lived in permanent, small villages of two to three hundred and hunted, harvested, and gardened.

Early History. By the late 1600's the Cheyenne began to be displaced from their homeland by hostile neighboring tribes of Woodland Sioux, Cree, and Assiniboine. The Cheyenne sought escape by migrating westward to the prairie country in the southwestern corner of present-day Minnesota; however, they were forced by hostile Sioux to migrate northwest to the prairies of the Sheyenne River in the Dakotas. From 1725 to

1775 they established a number of fortified earthlodge villages along the river. They established cordial relations with, and learned horticultural techniques from, a number of tribes in the area, including the Oto, Iowa, Mandan, and Hidatsa. They also acquired horses and used them for hunting and war. Once again, however, they were forced to abandon their prosperous life, this time because of the depredations of the Chippewa and the European diseases of smallpox and measles.

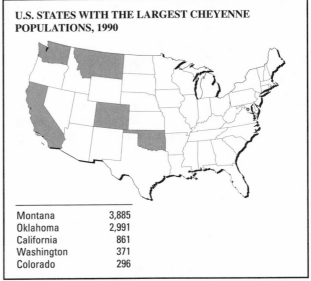

U.S. STATES WITH THE LARGEST CHEYENNE POPULATIONS, 1990

Montana	3,885
Oklahoma	2,991
California	861
Washington	371
Colorado	296

Source: 1990 U.S. Census.

Plains Phase. The Cheyenne left the prairie in the late 1700's and moved west across the Missouri River. A number of villages may have been established for a time on the Missouri River, but the Cheyenne had become a predominantly nomadic tribe. Upon crossing the Missouri into the Great Plains they encountered the Sutaio, who had been living on the plains for some time. The Sutaio also spoke an Algonquian dialect, and the two tribes became closely allied. By 1820 the two tribes had united, and the Sutaio became one of several distinctive bands within the Cheyenne.

The Black Hills, located in the northwest corner of South Dakota, became a spiritual and geographical center of the Cheyenne. The Cheyenne roamed over a vast area approximating a semicircle to the west, south, and east of the Black Hills. The half century from 1800 to 1850 represents the apex of Cheyenne culture. It was a period of stabilization, solidification, and prosperity. In 1840 the Cheyenne reached an accord with their traditional enemies the Kiowa and Comanche in order to fortify their southern flank against the Pawnee, Cherokee, and other tribes. They made peace with the Sioux to oppose their mutual enemies to the north, the Crow and Shoshone. By 1830 the Cheyenne had obtained sufficient numbers of horses to abandon village life completely and become nomadic hunters and traders. Sufficient firearms had been obtained that they were able to become a formidable warrior nation.

Culture in the Early Nineteenth Century. The Cheyenne lived in tipis made from animal skins by the women. The women were also responsible for dressing skins for clothing and for gathering various edible plants. The men hunted game, fought battles, and performed most of the tribal ceremonies. The Cheyenne fought in order to acquire access to new territory to hunt, to maintain their traditional territory, to obtain horses, and to revenge previous defeats and deaths. Military virtue and bravery were glorified. In a sense, warfare was a game or competitive activity in which the Cheyenne counted the number of "coups" a warrior accumulated. A coup could include killing or scalping an enemy but could also involve "show-off" accomplishments such as touching the enemy or being the first to find him.

The Cheyenne consisted of ten bands, including the Sutaio. The bands lived separately in the winter but came together in the summer for the communal buffalo hunt and to perform sacred ceremonies (the Great Ceremonies) of unity and renewal, such as the Sacred Arrow Renewal and the Sun Dance, which they learned from the Sutaio. A large circular camp was constructed, and each band had a particular position it occupied within the circle. The circle symbolized the family tipis and reinforced the belief that the tribe was one large family.

Bands were composed of closely related kindreds which customarily camped with one another. Kindreds were composed of individual conjugal and composite families. Each of the ten bands had a name, such as Eaters, Burnt Aorta, or Hair Rope Men. These were nicknames, often referring to a particular, unique characteristic of that band and emphasizing that each band had a distinctive identity and its own customs.

Each band was presided over by a chief, the man considered to be most outstanding in that band. A few members from each band were chosen as members of the Council of Forty-Four. This council had the responsibility of maintaining peace, harmony, and order among the Cheyenne bands and so was the supreme authority in the tribe. The Council of Forty-Four was composed of chiefs committed to peace. It was separate from the Society of War Chiefs, who were chosen from the seven military societies to which males belonged. All peace chiefs were warriors. Upon joining the council they could keep their membership in the war society but had to resign any position held. The Cheyenne recognized the virtues of separating civil and military powers. Each band contributed about four members to the council.

A council member served a ten-year term but could be reelected. A member had to be a man of highest virtue: even-tempered, good-natured, energetic, wise, kind, concerned for others' well being, courageous, generous, altruistic, and above reproach in public life. The council chose one of its members to be the head chief-priest of the entire tribe, the Sweet Medicine Chief. Four other chiefs chosen by the council served as the head's associates and were known, along with the Sweet Medicine Chief, as the five sacred chiefs. The tribal chief could not be deposed or impeached during his term, even if he committed a grievous crime such as murder.

The Council of Forty-Four symbolized the melding of spiritual, democratic, and moral values that characterized the Cheyenne. When the council was in session, the chief sat at the west side of the lodge, the center or zenith of the universe (*heum*). The five sacred chiefs were considered cosmic spiritual beings, and a number of other council members represented various spirits of the supernatural and mystical world. The council consisted of the wisest men and men in touch with the positive life forces from which emanated the good things which the Cheyenne desired. The high virtue of the council members symbolized the values the Cheyenne placed on dignity, chastity, courage, rationality, harmony with their environment, and a democratic tribal government.

1830's to 1870's. In the late 1830's, the Bent's Fort trading post was established in southern Colorado. Many Cheyenne moved south near the fort to establish a primary position of access to trade. This taxed the solidarity of the tribe because of the great distance separating those remaining in the north (who eventually became known as the Northern Cheyenne) from those who moved south (who eventually became known as the Southern Cheyenne). It became increasingly difficult for the whole tribe to assemble for the Great Ceremonies of early summer. Also, the tribal council met less frequently and thus lost much power in regulating tribal affairs. One of the last unified gatherings for the Great Ceremonies occurred in 1842. The Northern and Southern Cheyenne then separated from each other and went their own ways.

In the 1840's the westward movement of white settlers and gold seekers drastically upset traditional Cheyenne culture. Hunting areas were distributed, and a cholera epidemic in 1849 exterminated nearly half the tribe. The Santa Fe Trail ran through the heartland of Cheyenne territory. In 1851 the Cheyenne and eight other tribes signed the first Fort Laramie Treaty with the United States. The treaty formalized the separation of Northern and Southern Cheyenne, merged the Southern Cheyenne and Arapaho for treaty purposes, and assigned 122,500 square miles of territory (not a reservation) to them. It also permitted the United States to establish roads and forts on their territory (which had already been done).

The steady influx of settlers continued to disrupt tribal life, however, bringing the Southern Cheyenne and Arapaho to near starvation in 1853. The Indians retaliated, and wars broke out between 1856 and 1878. Notable events included the massacre at Sand Creek in 1864 and the death of Black Kettle in 1868 at the hands of Colonel George Armstrong Custer. The United States assigned the Southern Cheyenne and Arapaho to reservations in 1869, but they resisted until finally subdued in 1875. Some warriors were considered prisoners of war and sent to Florida.

The Northern Cheyenne joined with the Sioux in resisting the encroachment of gold seekers and settlers. Attempts by the army to confine them to reservations culminated in the Battle of the Little Bighorn in 1876. They were captured and confined to reservations by 1884.

Since the 1870's. Confinement to reservations effectively ended traditional Cheyenne culture. The Northern Cheyenne fared much better than did their southern brethren. They eventually settled in 1884 on the Tongue River in Montana in an area they chose and which was isolated from whites. Most of their land remained unallotted. Unallotted lands were not made available to whites. The Northern Cheyenne own more than 275,000 acres of tribal land held in common and have been buying back parcels of the more than 150,000 acres of allotted land. Mineral resources, farming, and stock raising are the main sources of income.

The Southern Cheyenne and the Arapaho were confined to a reservation in the Indian Territory in 1875. Their traditional nomadic hunting society was stripped from them as the federal government tried to assimilate them into American society by molding them into educated Christian farmers. Religious ceremonies were banned. The Council of Chiefs had disappeared by 1892. The military societies were disbanded. Additionally, the government consistently failed to provide adequate support services so that hunger, disease, and hopelessness became daily miseries. The 1887 Dawes Act (General Allotment Act) ultimately resulted in the loss of 3,500,000 acres of unallotted reservation land that was bought by the government.

The Indian Reorganization Act of 1934 and the Indian Claims Act of 1947 redressed these injustices somewhat and encouraged increased self-government and the assumption of control over a number of services. This process was given further impetus by the 1975 Indian Self-Determination and Education Assistance Act. Economic development is a high priority, but success has been spotty and many Indians still live in poverty. Nevertheless, through all this the Cheyenne have retained their essential identity, character, and courage.

—Laurence Miller

See also Algonquian language family; Black Kettle; Buffalo; Fort Laramie Treaty of 1851; Fort Laramie Treaty of 1868; Horses; Little Bighorn, Battle of the; Plains; Sand Creek Massacre.

BIBLIOGRAPHY

Berthrong, Donald J. *The Cheyenne and Arapaho Ordeal*. Norman: University of Oklahoma Press, 1976. Describes in detail the life of these tribes on the reservation from 1875 to 1907 as they were subjected to government attempts to assimilate them into the population.

Boxberger, Daniel L., ed. *Native North Americans: An Ethnohistorical Approach*. Dubuque, Iowa: Kendall/Hunt, 1990. Contains an excellent chapter on Plains Indian history, culture, and contemporary life.

Hoebel, E. Adamson. *The Cheyennes: Indians of the Great Plains*. New York: Holt, Rinehart and Winston, 1978. This second edition of a classic work adds chapters on contemporary life and issues through the mid-1970's, in addition to chapters on history and culture. Thorough, informative, and readable.

Josephy, Alvin M., Jr., ed. *The American Heritage Book of Indians*. New York: Simon & Schuster, 1961. Contains general information on the Cheyenne and other Plains Indians. Contains numerous excellent illustrations.

Swanton, John R. *The Indian Tribes of North America*. Washington, D.C.: Government Printing Office, 1953. This standard reference contains brief but very informative accounts of the Cheyenne. Concentrates on a brief history, derivation of the name, location, and subdivisions and villages.

Waldman, Carl. *Atlas of the North American Indian*. New York: Facts on File, 1985. Contains general information on Cheyenne life and their wars. Distinguished by excellent illustrations and maps.

Chiaha: Tribe

CULTURE AREA: Southeast
LANGUAGE GROUP: Muskogean
PRIMARY LOCATION: Chattahoochee River, Georgia/Alabama border

The Chiaha (or Chehaw) were a horticultural people who lived in raised dwellings located in several large permanent villages within sight of their extensive fields of maize, beans, squash, and other plants (including tobacco). For men, hunting and trapping was a favorite pastime, and it encouraged relationships which were critical in trading and in political alliances. Chiaha society was somewhat stratified, but with central authority that was influenced by consensus of opinion. Men gained status through warfare, hunting, oration, and generosity. Women who were industrious and skillful were accorded status.

Hernando de Soto's narratives of 1540 provide the first description of these people, suggesting that the Chiaha were already members of the Creek Confederacy. The Spanish later established a fort in Chiaha territory in 1567, which the Chiaha later destroyed. Because of ongoing conflict, numerous demographic changes affected the Chiaha, who eventually moved to Oklahoma and settled in the northeastern corner of the Creek Reservation. After the Civil War, many remaining Chiaha moved to Florida and settled among the Western Seminole.

Chichén Itzá: Archaeological site

DATE: Eighth to thirteenth centuries
LOCATION: Northern Yucatán
CULTURES AFFECTED: Chontal (Putun) Maya or Itzá

Human settlement probably began earlier at Chichén Itzá, but the city started its rise to prominence with the arrival of Chontal Maya in the late eighth or early ninth century. Sometimes calling themselves the "Putun" and referred to by later Mayas as the Itzá, the Chontal were traders who helped link the Maya lowlands with Teotihuacán and Central Mexico. When Teotihuacán collapsed in the 700's, however, the Chontal began to expand their commercial networks into the Yucatán and eventually some settled at the *cenote*, or great well, where Chichén Itzá is located. The earliest clearly legible date found in the city's architecture and sculpture is 867, with another inscription perhaps dating to 842.

The site became known among later inhabitants of the region as Chichén Itzá, or "Well of the Itzá." Archaeologists have partially excavated only the central remains, but at its peak the city covered 25 square kilometers (9.6 square miles). It was a commercial entrepôt and textile center, judging from the cotton whorls found there.

Two distinct styles of architecture are present at Chichén Itzá, Puuc and Toltec, a situation which has led to considerable controversy over the history of the site. The traditional view held that the Itzá were Toltecs from Central Mexico who conquered Maya Chichén Itzá. These newcomers then built in their style a group of structures north toward the cenote: El Castillo, the four-sided temple which rises in pyramid form to dominate the site; the largest ball court in Mesoamerica; the skull rack, or *tzompantli*, where the heads of sacrificial victims were displayed; and the Temple of the Warriors, whose bas-reliefs depict scenes of war and sacrifice. A path of 300 meters (328 yards) leads north to the Sacred Cenote. To the south are the Puuc remains, including the high priest's grave, the *caracol* (observatory), *las monjas* (the nunnery), *la casa colorada* (the pink house), and several other temples. The artwork contains many hieroglyphics, something much rarer in the Toltec section. Nevertheless, study of inscriptions and ceramics indicates that the two styles were probably contemporaneous rather than sequential. Furthermore, the artwork is more sophisticated than that found at Tula, the Toltec center. These facts cast doubt on the traditional chronology assigned to Chichén Itzá and raise questions about the presence of any direct Toltec influence.

Chichén Itzá was the only known center of a "conquest state and hegemonic empire" among the Maya, according to archaeologist Linda Schele. During Classic times, the Mayas lived in independent city-states with no political centralization over broad territories. A divine king ruled the city-state. Chichén Itzá broke with this pattern, with power shared between the king and nobles in "joint rule" or *mul tepal*. Evidently the lords of different lineages lived and ruled together at Chichén Itzá.

In the early thirteenth century Chichén Itzá was abandoned. Later Mayas knew of the site, however, visited by John L. Stephens and Frederick Catherwood in 1842 during their famous exploratory travels in the Yucatán.

See also Maya; Toltec; Uxmal.

Chichimec: Tribe

CULTURE AREA: Mesoamerica
LANGUAGE GROUP: Nahuatl (Otomian)
PRIMARY LOCATION: Northern Mexico
The name Chichimec is used to describe several different tribes of northern Mexico, most of whom spoke the Nahuatl language. They were nomadic and were considered barbarians by the more developed tribes of the Valley of Mexico. Chichimec, in fact, means "people of dog lineage."

The city of Teotihuacán acted as a buffer between the Valley of Mexico and the Chichimecs. When it fell in 650 C.E., the way was opened to invasions by Chichimecs. An early group was the Tolteca-Chichimeca, or Toltecs. Beginning in the tenth century, they entered the Valley of Mexico under the leadership of Mixcóatl (Cloud Serpent), who has been called a "Mexican Genghis Khan." He established his capital at Culhuacán.

After Mixcóatl was assassinated by his brother, his pregnant wife fled into exile and bore a son, Ce Acatl Topilzin, who as a young man defeated his uncle and ascended the throne. He became a follower of the Feathered Serpent god Quetzalcóatl, assuming the name Topilzin-Quetzalcóatl. A dispute between the followers of two gods split the people. Topilzin-Quetzalcóatl was tricked by opposing priests into committing the sins of drunkenness and incest. He voluntarily went into exile, promising to return from the east in the year Ce Acatl to resume his rightful place on the throne. In 1519, the year Ce Acatl, the Spaniards appeared from the east, raising the question of whether Hernán Cortés was Topilzin-Quetzalcóatl returned.

From the late eleventh century to 1156, droughts and famine weakened the Toltecs. Wars discouraged them until they abandoned their capital Tula, and the great Toltec diaspora began. The fall of Tula again opened the Valley of Mexico to invasions by primitive Chichimecs. By the first part of the thirteenth century, several Chichimec tribes had conquered the desirable areas; however, by the early fifteenth century, all the Chichimec cities had declined.

The most famous and successful of the Chichimec tribes was the Mexica, or Aztecs. The Aztecs were the last of the important nomadic Chichimecs to enter the Valley of Mexico. In 1111, the Aztecs migrated from Nayaret southward. From their capital, Tenochtitlán, on an island in Lake Texcoco, they conquered their neighbors, creating an empire that extended from the Pacific to the Gulf Coast and from the Valley of Mexico to the coast of Guatemala.

After their conquest of the Aztecs, the Spanish controlled the sedentary Indians, leaving the north-central plateau in the hands of the Chichimecs. After the silver strike at Zacatecas in 1545, Spain began to expand northward into the Gran Chichimeca. Between 1550 and 1590, the War of the Chichimeca occurred, the longest and most costly in money and lives of the frontier conflicts. Their military efforts were unsuccessful, so Spanish officials changed their policy in the decade of the 1590's to pacification by gifts of food and clothing and by conversion, using the mission system and sedentary Indians from the south. By 1600 the Chichimecs were incorporated into pacified Mexico.

See also Aztec; Quetzalcóatl; Tenochtitlán; Toltec.

Chickasaw: Tribe

CULTURE AREA: Southeast
LANGUAGE GROUP: Muskogean
PRIMARY LOCATION: Oklahoma
POPULATION SIZE: 20,631 (1990 U.S. Census)
At the beginning of the historic period, the Chickasaws inhabited an area encompassing modern western Tennessee and

Kentucky, northern Mississippi, and northwestern Alabama. They are closely related linguistically to the Choctaws, and the two tribes may once have been one. The Chickasaw way of life was similar to that of other southeastern tribes. They lived in towns and pursued an economy based on farming, especially corn, and hunting. Chickasaw social structure was based on a clan system. One's clan was derived from one's mother, and marriage between clan members was forbidden. While most affairs were handled locally, the High Minko, or principal chief of the tribe, was chosen by a council of clan elders. Though a relatively small tribe (around forty-five hundred at the time of European contact), the Chickasaws had a reputation among neighboring tribes as fierce warriors.

The Chickasaws were visited by Hernando de Soto's expedition in 1540, and they nearly annihilated the Spaniards the following year. In the seventeenth century, the Chickasaws became involved in a series of wars against the French and their Indian allies. Having established contact with English merchants, the Chickasaws became British allies in the eighteenth century and remained loyal to them through the American Revolution. By the late eighteenth century, a mixed-blood, acculturated minority was becoming increasingly influential in tribal affairs.

In 1786, the Chickasaws signed the Treaty of Hopewell with the new United States, acknowledging themselves to be under American protection and selling a small area at Muscle Shoals (modern Alabama) to the United States. The Chickasaws fought on the American side in the Creek War of 1813-1814; however, they soon came under pressure to part with more and more of their land. In 1818, General Andrew Jackson persuaded the tribe to sell all of its lands in Tennessee and Kentucky. After Jackson became president, the Chickasaws were pressured to sell the remainder of their lands east of the Mississippi. In 1832, the Chickasaws agreed to sell out and move to the Indian Territory (modern Oklahoma), where they would settle on land bought from the Choctaws. It took five years to work out mutually acceptable arrangements, but in the 1837 Treaty of Doaksville the Choctaws agreed to sell to the Chickasaws a large tract of land to the west of their Oklahoma settlements for $530,000 and to accept the Chickasaws as tribal citizens. A tribal census taken at the time of removal in 1838 counted approximately five thousand Chickasaws.

Though the Chickasaws had an easier "Trail of Tears" than other southern tribes did, they faced problems once in Indian Territory. They resisted absorption by the Choctaws and faced threats from the Plains tribes who were used to roaming the area. Only after army posts were established did full-scale resettlement take place. Friction with the Choctaws continued until, in 1855, the two tribes reached a relatively friendly divorce, and a separate Chickasaw Nation was constituted in what is today south-central Oklahoma.

The Chickasaws had brought about a thousand slaves with them on their trek west, and when the Civil War broke out in 1861, they allied with the Confederacy. The Chickasaw Nation was relatively unscathed by the fighting, but at the end of the war the tribe had to make peace with the United States. The tribe lost its claim to a large tract of southwestern Oklahoma, and accepted the end of slavery. Pressured to incorporate its former slaves (freedmen) into the tribe, the Chickasaw—alone among slaveholding tribes—avoided doing so.

In the later nineteenth century the tribe once again found itself in the path of expansionist policy. During the 1890's Congress moved to extend the policy of allotment (the division of tribal lands among individual Indians, with "surplus" land being sold off) to Indian Territory. Tribal powers were reduced, and the Dawes Commission was established to negotiate allotment terms. In 1906 a tribal roll was drawn up, counting 6,319 citizens of the Chickasaw Nation (1,538 of them full-bloods); the roll of Chickasaw freedmen numbered 4,670. On March 4, 1906, the tribal government came to an end. Each Chickasaw received 320 acres of land (each freedman got 40 acres). By 1934, 70 percent of the land had passed from Chickasaw ownership. Tribal government was eventually reorganized in the 1960's. —*William C. Lowe*

See also Allotment system; Choctaw; Creek War; Green Corn Dance; Muskogean language family; Natchez; Trail of Tears.

Bibliography

Foreman, Grant. *The Five Civilized Tribes*. Norman: University of Oklahoma Press, 1934.

_____. *Indian Removal: The Emigration of the Five Civilized Tribes of Indians*. Norman: University of Oklahoma Press, 1932.

Gibson, Arrell M. *The Chickasaws*. Norman: University of Oklahoma Press, 1971.

Hudson, Charles. *The Southeastern Indians*. Knoxville: University of Tennessee Press, 1976.

Perdue, Theda, ed. *Nations Remembered: An Oral History of the Cherokees, Chickasaws, Choctaws, Creeks, and Seminoles, 1865-1907*. 1980. Reprint. Norman: University of Oklahoma Press, 1993.

Chickee

Tribes affected: Calusa, Seminole, Timucua, Choctaw, Chickasaw, Chitimacha

Significance: The chickee, a dwelling on poles or stilts, is well suited to a wet climate

The chickee is a type of dwelling that was used in the wetter areas of the Southeast culture area. It consists of a platform built on top of four or more posts. The posts are made of trimmed saplings sunk into the earth. These are reinforced by cross members. Beams are cut and laid on top of the posts, and planks are lashed to the beams with braided cords to create a platform that serves as the floor.

A framework of saplings is lashed together, and poles are laid on top of them to support the roof. The roof is then thatched with fronds of palm or grasses. They are arranged in layers that shed water. The walls are open, as the southeastern climate is usually warm and moist. Woven mats are sometimes used in place of walls; mats are also used to cover the floor.

Chickee

The chickee was well suited to subtropical environments where seasonal flooding of rivers or marshy lands is common. Often a dugout canoe or other water conveyance was tied to the stilts upon which the dwelling sat to serve as transportation when waters are high.

During floods, the residents often obtained food by using the chickee as a fishing platform. Families could thus be self-sustaining for long periods of time during the wet seasons. Chickees were often built in groups of several, but they could also be isolated. Similar types of dwellings were built by indigenous peoples throughout the Americas who live in wet environments.

See also Architecture—Southeast; Seminole.

Chilcotin: Tribe

CULTURE AREA: Subarctic
LANGUAGE GROUP: Northern Athapaskan
PRIMARY LOCATION: British Columbia, Canada
POPULATION SIZE: 1,705 (Statistics Canada, based on 1991 census)

The Chilcotin, named for a river flowing through their homeland, originally came from an area north of their present reservation in British Columbia. They fished for salmon, hunted caribou, elk, and deer, and gathered roots and berries. The Chilcotin had no group leaders. No one could force another tribal member to do anything. They lived in small isolated camps made up of brothers and sisters and their husbands, wives, and children. These camps grew larger in the winter when a number of family groups lived together in a cluster, but when spring came they moved to their separate hunting areas again. Parents usually arranged marriages. Sharing was a cultural the ideal; if people had things to spare, they gave them away.

The Chilcotin believed that ghosts and monsters filled the universe but had no direct influence in human affairs. No single, all-powerful supreme being was thought to exist. Individuals could acquire a "guardian spirit" while teenagers—but only after fasting, meditating, and bathing during a vision quest lasting several weeks. This spirit protected an individual from harm and helped bring success in fishing, hunting, and gambling. Chilcotin art consisted of human heads carved in tree stumps, basketry, dancing, and drums for music.

White trappers first contacted Chilcotin along the Fraser River in the late 1700's. Until the 1850's, however, they had little contact with Europeans. Then, in 1857, a gold rush brought prospectors and railroad surveyors onto Chilcotin land. Within two years, a smallpox epidemic reduced the tribe's numbers from 1,500 to 550. The Chilcotin fought a brief war against white settlers in 1864, but after five Indians were hanged the war came to an end. In the 1870's, Roman Catholic missionaries established schools, and the Chilcotin moved onto a reservation in the 1880's. Ranching replaced hunting as the most important economic activity, and many of the natives became cowboys. In the 1960's, several resorts opened in the area and many Chilcotin found jobs as maids, cooks, and fishing guides.

See also Athapaskan language family; Subarctic.

Children

TRIBES AFFECTED: Pantribal
SIGNIFICANCE: American Indian children, reared with love and gentle guidance to respect nature, their elders, and tribal customs, were an integral part of the community.

Children born into traditional American Indian societies represented part of the never-ending chain of life, and their births were greeted with community pride. The sometimes dangerous nature of Indian life increased the importance of children and made high birthrates common. Considered a gift from sacred forces, children entered the physical world under the guidance and protection of a spiritual guide, and a child's name reflected the qualities of that guide (an adult name would frequently be taken at puberty or when a major accomplishment was noted).

Early Years. For most Indian children, the first year of life was spent strapped to a cradleboard. These rigid carriers could be fastened to the mother's back, stuck upright in the ground, or attached to horse packs. Once out of the cradleboard, children were allowed to discover their world freely. Although welcomed and cherished, babies represented a potential danger to the tribe: Crying children might reveal the tribe's position to enemies. Therefore, it became a common practice among some tribes (as among the Cheyenne and Sioux) to pinch babies' nostrils to quiet them. Infants were often nursed up to the age of four, helping to create a strong bond between mother and child.

Children flourished in a world surrounded by love and gentle care. Strong extended-family ties brought loving guidance and stability into the child's life. Toilet training was not

A 1910 photograph of a Flathead girl in traditional clothing. (Library of Congress)

stressed; children frequently remained naked until four or five years of age, and in some cases, such as the Algonquian peoples, children were occasionally naked until age ten.

Under the direction of their mothers, Indian children were taught the beauties of nature and a deep respect for their elders. Many hours were spent with their elders, especially grandparents, learning tribal history and myths. Children were the key to the future, and elders sought to instill in them the tribe's ancient traditions. Since survival was directly related to what was available and useful from their surroundings, children were directed from an early age to take only what they absolutely needed from Mother Earth.

Preparing for Puberty. Around the age of five, children began to learn the practical knowledge needed for adult life. Tribal society could not tolerate unproductive members, so even small children contributed by picking berries, hunting small game, and assisting their families in chores. Young girls erected miniature tipis and learned through imitating their mothers' daily routine, such as preparing food, caring for smaller children, and tanning hides. Tending small gardens also helped eastern Indian girls learn to grow crops. After the introduction of the horse into Indian cultures, young boys learned to ride early in life. In addition, competitive sports taught the boys vital warrior qualities such as self-sufficiency, strength, endurance, and accuracy in the hunt. Adults encouraged this education, which would prepare children for their future tribal roles.

Art was also an important element of this stage of childhood. Mothers passed down their talents in beadworking, painting, and weaving. Both sexes grew up around religious and social forms of music. Boys began to learn the drum music associated with tribal ceremonies, while girls learned chants and lullabies. Children were also taught the ceremonial dances of their tribe.

Discipline. Discipline among the Indian people was based on respect. Children were born by the good graces of the spirit world, and physical punishment was rare. Many tribes feared that this form of discipline would cause children's souls to depart from their body and thus harm their personality and health. Instead, discipline typically consisted of verbal reprimands designed to teach a lesson. Even with a societal preference for avoiding corporal punishment, however, some children faced harsh treatment, including beatings, scarring from hot stones, or public lashings for severe offenses.

The responsibility of disciplining children was often undertaken by other family members or tribal elders, who interceded on the parents' behalf. Storytelling and legends were frequently used to shape the character of young minds and to teach the difference between good and evil. For example, the

Apache told of Mountain Spirits that dictated proper behavior, while the Hopi related tales of the Soyoko (a "boogeyman" type of figure) to persuade children to follow a moral code. Some parents used disguised tribesmen to educate children about expected behavior. Often representing supernatural spirits, these dressed-up tribesmen warned, frightened, or, in rare cases, even whipped disobedient children.

Modern Indian Children. Reservation life threatened the existence of American Indian culture. Forced into an unfamiliar, constricted way of life and facing the loss of their freedom, tribe members had to find new means to pass their culture on to the next generation. Tribal elders encouraged children to carry on the ancient rituals (sometimes with revisions) and to maintain the tribal bloodline.

The art of hunting became increasingly difficult to teach, as game was scarce on the reservations; children spent less time in nature and more time in school. The skills and values emphasized during the pre-reservation period, such as self-sufficiency, had to be taught through planned events instead of everyday activities. Many tribes found it hard to maintain their ancient traditions while living in an increasingly modern world. As a result, many tribes lost touch with their heritage. Revivals in the late twentieth century, however, have created new awareness of tribal traditions and customs.

—*Jennifer Davis*

See also Education, pre-contact; Games and contests; Gender relations and roles; Hand games; Names and naming; Puberty and initiation rites; Toys.

BIBLIOGRAPHY

Coles, Robert. *Eskimos, Chicanos, Indians: Children of Crisis.* Vol. 4. Boston: Little, Brown, 1977.

Driver, Harold E. *Indians of North America.* 1961. Rev. ed. Chicago: University of Chicago Press, 1969.

Erdoes, Richard. *The Sun Dance People.* New York: Alfred A. Knopf, 1972.

Gill, Sam D. *Dictionary of Native American Mythology.* Santa Barbara, Calif.: ABC-Clio, 1992.

Lowie, Robert H. *Indians of the Plains.* New York: McGraw-Hill, 1954.

White, Jon Manchip. *Everyday Life of the North American Indian.* New York: Holmes & Meier, 1979.

LANGUAGE SPOKEN IN AMERICAN INDIAN OR ALASKA NATIVE HOMES BY CHILDREN AGES FIVE TO SEVENTEEN, 1980

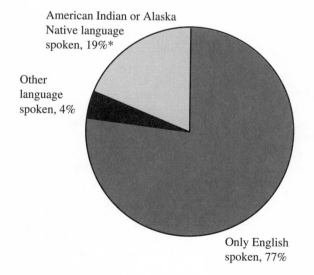

American Indian or Alaska Native language spoken, 19%*

Other language spoken, 4%

Only English spoken, 77%

Source: Data are from U.S. Bureau of the Census, *1980 Census of Population, Volume 2, Subject Reports, Characteristics of American Indians, by Tribes and Selected Areas: 1980.* Washington, D.C.: U.S. Government Printing Office, 1989.

Note: Total number of American Indian/Alaska Native children ages five to seventeen in 1980 was 413,614.

*Nearly 85% also speak English well.

Chilkat blankets

TRIBES AFFECTED: Tribes of the Northwest
SIGNIFICANCE: Chilkat blankets represent some of the finest and most visually impressive handwoven Indian artifacts

The Chilkat Tlingit were a Northwest Indian tribe. The accumulation and display of wealth was an important aspect of their tribal life. Chilkat chieftains commissioned the finest weavers their clan could afford to prepare ceremonial robes. The robes were worn and displayed to symbolize the wealth and status of the owner. The robes were illustrated with depictions of animals and objects that represented the chief's crests. Some of the most popular designs included ravens, whales, drums, bears, and wolves.

A traditional Chilkat blanket with multicolored designs and long fringe. (Boltin/Rota, American Museum of Natural History)

Weavers applied twining techniques used in basketry to craft technically intricate blankets. Goat wool, and later commercial yarn, was dyed white, green, black, yellow, and blue with native dyestuff. Weavers decorated the robes with long fringe sewn onto the bottom and sides. The fringe, crafted of cedar bark and mountain goat wool, was a very important aspect of the robe. When chieftains danced, they lifted and swung their robes so that the fringe swung freely and created an impressive effect.

By the 1980's, only one Chilkat robe weaver, Jennie Thlunaut, continued to produce blankets. In the last quarter of the twentieth century, however, interest among collectors renewed, and the number of weavers increased.

See also Arts and crafts—Northwest Coast; Blankets; Northwest Coast; Weaving; Tlingit.

Chinook: Tribe

CULTURE AREA: Northwest Coast
LANGUAGE GROUP: Chinookan (perhaps Penutian)
PRIMARY LOCATION: Oregon/Washington coast
POPULATION SIZE: 798 (1990 U.S. Census)

The Chinook, a southern tribe of Northwest Coast Indians, controlled the Columbia River waterway from The Dalles (the location of a major waterfall) to the Pacific Ocean and lived on the coast in the area of the present states of Washington and Oregon. The Chinook charged a toll to other tribes who used the river for commerce and became principal traders in the area, partly because the falls at The Dalles made portaging necessary. The Chinooks' trade included slaves, canoes, and dentalia shells.

The first documented contact that the Chinook had with European Americans was with explorer John Meares at Willapa Bay in 1788. The Chinook later met the overland Astor fur expedition as well as, in 1805, explorers Meriwether Lewis and William Clark. References in Chinook oral tradition imply earlier contact with Russian and perhaps even with Spanish ships.

The Chinook shared many characteristics with other tribes of the Northwest Coast—living in plank houses, building seaworthy canoes, telling Coyote stories, and participating in potlatch distributions of property. The Chinook, however, did not generally enjoy the wealth or possess the artistic skills of coastal tribes to the north. While the Chinook produced twine basketry and sewed rush mats, they did not create the totemic art of the northern coastal tribes.

Salmon provided sustenance—spiritual and physical—to the Chinook. An important ceremony in the Chinook religion is the first salmon rite, which heralds the annual salmon run. The Chinook supplemented their diet with clams, crabs, oysters, seals, and small game hunting on land.

The Chinook language is unique in a number of respects and has been only tentatively affiliated with the widespread Penutian stock. "Chinook jargon," spoken from California to Alaska, bases its lexicon on the Chinook language but has characteristics of French, English, and Indian (especially Nootka) languages.

See also Athapaskan language family; Chemakum; Flathead; Plank house; Salish; Salmon.

Chipewyan: Tribe
CULTURE AREA: Subarctic
LANGUAGE GROUP: Athapaskan
PRIMARY LOCATION: Saskatchewan, Manitoba
POPULATION SIZE: 9,350 (Statistics Canada, based on 1991 census)

The early Chipewyans occupied the edge of the northern subarctic forests and the tundra beyond, where the winters were long and severe and the summers moderate. By the late 1700's, some Chipewyans had moved into the forests. These people were nomadic hunters and fishermen. The most important animal was the caribou; it was the focus of their religious belief and oral literature, and it structured their life cycle and population distribution.

The Chipewyan tribe had no central organization but lived in regional bands, the size of which depended on the concentration of the caribou. Bands were larger during the caribou migrations and smaller when the caribou were dispersed. Hudson's Bay Company officials recognized two divisions: the Northern Indians (Chipewyans) and the Yellowknife. Chipewyan means "pointed skins," a term referring to the form of their dried beaver skins.

Early contact with Europeans came as a result of fur trading and brought both good and hardship. Furs were traded for basic necessities, but in 1781 smallpox, caught from the Europeans, destroyed a large number of the Chipewyans.

The Chipewyans had few ceremonies to mark life's events. If the band was traveling, a woman would give birth and continue traveling within a few hours. No ceremonies marked puberty or marriage. The husband hunted with the woman's family until the birth of the first child. Polygamy was permitted, and wives, especially the young and childless, were sometimes prizes in wrestling matches. The old and feeble had little value and could be abandoned if they could not keep up when traveling.

By the mid-1800's, the Chipewyans were divided into five regional bands, and their territories existed primarily within the forests. They were divided between living on the forest edge because of hunting on the tundra and living deep within the forest close to trading posts and missions. In the 1960's there was an attempt to move some of the bands into towns. This was only partly successful; many families returned to their traditional areas and have remained hunters and fishermen. Some of the bands engage in commercial fishing.

See also Athapaskan language family; Subarctic; Yellowknife.

Chippewa. See Ojibwa

Chisholm, Jesse (c. 1805, southeastern Tenn.—Mar. 4, 1868, near Norman, Okla.): Trader, interpreter
TRIBAL AFFILIATION: Cherokee
SIGNIFICANCE: Chisholm's work as a trader and his ability as an interpreter carried his influence far beyond the reach of his own Cherokee tribe

Jesse Chisholm, a half-blood Cherokee born in Tennessee, traveled to the western Indian Territory before the Trail of Tears of 1838-1839. After marrying a Creek woman, he traded with the Plains Indian tribes of the West. In the course of that work, he learned fourteen different languages, which enabled him to become an interpreter.

Chisholm's language abilities made him a vital part of Creek efforts to establish peace among the tribes of the Plains. In 1853, he was sent to the Comanche to help make arrangements for the Grand Council, which was held at the Salt Plains in June, 1853. Here Creek leaders met with delegations from many of the Plains tribes. Chisholm was the interpreter for all of the tribes.

Chisholm had a trading post near Wichita, Kansas. In 1865, he drove a wagon from Texas to his trading post. Texas cattlemen followed the ruts left by Chisholm's wagon to get their cattle to Wichita, and the route became the famous Chisholm Trail. Jesse Chisholm died in 1868.

Chitimacha: Tribe
CULTURE AREA: Southeast
LANGUAGE GROUP: Chitimacha
PRIMARY LOCATION: Chitimacha Reservation, Charenton, Louisiana
POPULATION SIZE: 618 (1990 U.S. Census)

Today, the Chitimacha are found on their reservation at Charenton, Louisiana. According to Chitimacha oral tradition, their homeland was in the Natchez, Mississippi, region. By the time of European contact (in the early 1700's), they occupied an extensive territory on the western side of the Mississippi River in southern Louisiana. Bayou Lafourche, a principal drainage flowing south from the Mississippi River, was known as the River of the Chitimacha.

The traditional lifeways and material culture are described in John R. Swanton's *The Indians of the Southeastern United States* (1946). Chitimacha subsistence involved agriculture, fishing, hunting, and gathering. They lived in palmetto hut villages, some with dance houses for religious celebrations.

There is limited information concerning their complex social, political, and religious organization, although there are suggestions that in these matters they may have resembled the Natchez (a well-documented group at Natchez, Mississippi).

During the early years of colonialism, the European settlers were often short of food, and they relied upon the Indians initially to provide sustenance and later to exchange deerskins. As a result of this lucrative trade, Native Americans relocated to settlements more convenient to the foreigners, and farming groups, such as the Chitimacha, planted more extensive fields.

Despite initially peaceful interactions, the relationship between the Chitimacha and the Europeans became increasingly antagonistic. By 1706, a dispute between the Chitimacha and the Taensa had resulted in several French deaths. Chitimacha warriors attempted to retaliate against the Taensa (or Bayogoula) but were unable to locate them; instead, by chance, they encountered the French Jesuit Jean François Buisson de Saint-Cosme and his companions. As a result of this unfortunate meeting, Saint-Cosme and most of his party were killed. After this event, Jean Baptiste le Moyne, Sieur de Bienville, created a coalition of Mississippi tribes to revenge the French deaths. In 1707, they raided a Chitimacha village. From this time until 1718, the Chitimacha battled with the French.

In 1727, Father du Poisson made a trip up the Mississippi River and contacted the Chitimacha. His account mentions a chief named Framboise, who had been a French slave. The case of Framboise's enslavement was not an isolated incident, since many Chitimacha had been captured during the war with the French. In 1769, Governor Alejandro O'Reilly proclaimed that Indian slavery was forbidden, but as late as 1808, there were still Native American slaves.

Through the late eighteenth and nineteenth centuries, European settlement encroached further upon Chitimacha territory. In response, some Chitimachas retreated to more remote locations; others moved to New Orleans.

In 1925, the Chitimacha received federal recognition, and they later complied with the Indian Reorganization Act of 1934. Chitimacha property near Charenton consists of 262 acres and approximately three hundred people, although another few hundred may reside outside the reservation. The reservation possesses a school and a branch of the Jean Lafitte National Park. The Chitimacha are probably best known for their basket-making skills.

See also Baskets and basketry; Chitimacha language; Indian Reorganization Act.

Chitimacha language

CULTURE AREA: Southeast
TRIBE AFFECTED: Chitimacha

Chitimacha is an extinct language that was spoken in southern Louisiana. Although there are a few hundred members of the Chitimacha tribe, with its reservation at Charenton, Louisiana, the language is no longer spoken. The Chitimacha people lived along Bayou Teche at the time of their first encounter with the

French in the 1600's; the tribe was then composed of about twenty-six hundred people, scattered along bayous in several villages. Eventually French replaced their native language, and in the 1930's, when Morris Swadesh studied the language, there were only two speakers left.

Chitimacha is a language isolate; that is, it has no known relatives. Several attempts have been made to associate it with other languages. For example, John Swanton tried to relate Chitimacha to Tunica and Atakapa as part of the Tunican group, which Edward Sapir placed in his Hokan-Siouan superstock; Mary Haas included Chitimacha in her Gulf proposal and later in her even broader Algonquian-Gulf grouping. None of these relationships, however, has been accepted.

A problematic aspect of Chitimacha is that very little documentation has been published. The language has been studied by a number of noted linguists, including Albert Gatschet as well as Swanton and Swadesh. Swadesh conducted the most extensive study, but most of his research remains unpublished.

Chitimacha had a five-vowel system with a vowel length distinction (similar to Latin). It utilized glottalized consonants—one speaker with whom Swadesh worked used glottalized nasals and glides which the other speaker had lost. Nouns are generally uninflected, except that nouns referring to humans are sometimes marked for plural. Word order is flexible, but the basic order seems to be subject-verb-object, with postpositions (as opposed to prepositions) which express relations such as location, direction, means, and purpose. The verbs are inflected with suffixes for person (first person versus non-first person) and number (singular versus plural) of subject and for tense-aspect. Swadesh, in 1933, also described a set of Chitimacha verbs which are marked as having a derogatory or abusive connotation when applied to humans. Chitimacha shares a number of traits with other, genetically unrelated languages of the southeastern linguistic area, features usually assumed to have been diffused among the languages.

See also Chitimacha; Prehistory—Southeast; Southeast.

Choctaw: Tribe

CULTURE AREA: Southeast
LANGUAGE GROUP: Muskogean
PRIMARY LOCATION: Oklahoma, Mississippi, Louisiana, Alabama
POPULATION SIZE: 82,299 (1990 U.S. Census)

The Choctaw, a linguistic subgroup of the Muskogean people, first occupied portions of present-day Mississippi, Arkansas, and Alabama. By 1820 the Choctaw were considered part of the so-called Five Civilized Tribes because of their rapid adaptation to European culture. By 1830 the Choctaw were forced to cede all lands east of the Mississippi; their removal to Indian Territory (Oklahoma) took place between 1831 and 1833. Today tribal lands and businesses of the Choctaw are textbook examples of progressive farming, ranching, and industrial development. The Choctaw have grown from a few thousand to more than 82,000 persons, making them the fifth largest tribe in the United States.

Prehistory and Traditional Life. The prehistory of the Choctaws centered on farming communities in the modern state of Mississippi. Their culture was an integral part of a large ethnolinguistic area stretching from the Atlantic Coast to the Mississippi Valley. A portion of this region was also occupied by other tribes of the Muskogean branch of the Gulf language stock, the Seminole, Chickasaw, and Chitimacha. Sixteenth century Spanish arrivals found the Choctaw in the last stages of mound building. They were preeminent agriculturalists and hunters, having an abundance of food, including sunflowers, corn, beans, and melons, as well as tobacco. Favored dietary items included bear ribs, turkey, venison, root jelly, hominy, corn cakes, and soup. In 1729 the Choctaw aided the French in a war against the Natchez Indians. Later they signed a treaty with the British, although they continued to support the French until defeat by Britain in 1763. During the American Revolution, Choctaw warriors served under the command of four American generals. (Choctaws continued to provide meritorious military service in World Wars I and II, Korea, Vietnam, Grenada, Panama, and the Persian Gulf.) The Naniaba (fish eaters) were a riverine Choctaw tribe; in the early 1700's they were located in close proximity to the Mobile and Tohome tribes in southern Alabama. Their earlier home was on a bluff (Nanna Hubba) near the confluence of the Alabama and Tombigbee rivers.

Removal. The Naniaba had provided fierce opposition to Hernando de Soto's advance in 1540, but by 1761 both the Naniaba and Mobile were lost to history as tribes. The Indian Removal Act of 1930, urged on Congress by President Andrew Jackson, provided for forcing southeastern natives to give up their ancestral homelands. The Treaty of Dancing Rabbit Creek, signed later that same year, officially legalized the deportation of the Choctaws. A small amount of land was reserved for Choctaw chiefs and other individuals; this land

A Choctaw woman, at a fair at the Pearl River Reservation, weaves baskets in the traditional way. (Elaine S. Querry)

formed the basis of the present-day Mississippi Band of Choctaws. Although the Choctaw had never fought against the United States, they were forced to cede their lands in a series of treaties starting in 1801 and culminating in 1830. The forced deportation of the Choctaw, under army escort, to Indian Territory was cruel and involved bitter hardship and death from exposure and starvation. The road they and other tribes followed to Indian Territory has forever since been known as the Trail of Tears.

Contemporary Life. Today the Choctaw are divided into three areas: southeastern Oklahoma, with tribal headquarters located at Durant; Mississippi, with the band administrative center at Philadelphia; and the Apache, Jena, and Clifton bands of Louisiana and the Mowa band of Alabama. The Choctaw also reflect the geographic mobility of Americans in general. Most Choctaws live outside tribal enumerated census areas.

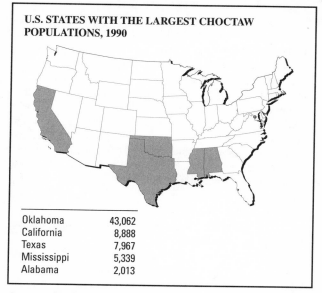

U.S. STATES WITH THE LARGEST CHOCTAW POPULATIONS, 1990

Oklahoma	43,062
California	8,888
Texas	7,967
Mississippi	5,339
Alabama	2,013

Source: 1990 U.S. Census.

MAJOR TREATIES AND LEGISLATION AFFECTING THE CHOCTAWS, 1786-1934	
1786	Hopewell Village (Smoky Mountains) Treaty provides protection against white settlers.
1801	Fort Adams (Mississippi) Treaty. Choctaws relinquish to United States land identified in 1765 treaty with Great Britain.
1802	Fort Confederation (Mississippi) Treaty confirms the 1765 cession made to Great Britain.
1803	Hoe Buckintoopa (Mississippi) Treaty. Cession of land to pay debts.
1805	Mount Dexter, or Pooshapukanuk (Choctaw County) Treaty. Choctaws cede all land in southern Mississippi.
1816	Choctaw Trading House (Choctaw Nation) Treaty. Cedes all land near boundary with Chickasaws.
1820	Doak's Stand (Choctaw Nation) Treaty. Cedes land in central Mississippi.
1825	Washington, D.C., Treaty. Cedes all land in Arkansas, totalling nearly two million acres.
1830	Indian Removal Act orders tribes to leave their lands in the Southeast and move to new lands in Indian Territory (present-day Oklahoma).
1830	Treaty of Dancing Rabbit Creek (Mississippi). Choctaws cede all Southeast land and agree to move to Indian Territory as soon as possible.
1837	Doaksville (Indian Territory) Treaty. Establishes Chickasaw Tribal Council within Choctaw Nation.
1866	Washington, D.C., Treaty. Choctaw Nation agrees to receive 10,000 Indian refugees (including Kickapoo, Iowa, and Shawnee) and to provide a railroad right of way.
1907	Oklahoma statehood and the end of the Choctaw Nation.
1934	Indian Reorganization Act slows acculturation of American Indians into mainstream American culture. Choctaw government strengthened and Mississippi Choctaw government established.

Figures from the 1990 census include 82,299 persons total: Oklahoma, 28,411; Mississippi, 3,932; Louisiana, 1,048; and Mowa Band of Alabama, fewer than 100 persons (total 33,400). Choctaws living outside enumerated areas totaled 48,899.

The Choctaw, rich in cultural heritage and spirit, are today successful developers and managers of an array of cultural and business activities in Oklahoma, Mississippi, and Louisiana. Choctaw leaders have particularly focused their development efforts on a valuable commodity, the intellect and drive of the Choctaw people.   —*Burl Self*

See also Dancing Rabbit Creek, Treaty of; Mounds and mound builders; Muskogean language family; Removal; Southeast.

BIBLIOGRAPHY

Debo, Angie. *The Rise and Fall of the Choctaw Republic*. Norman: University of Oklahoma Press, 1934.

De Rosier, Arthur H., Jr. *The Removal of the Choctaw Indians*. Knoxville: University Press of Tennessee, 1970.

Kappler, Charles. *Indian Affairs, Laws, and Treaties*. 4 vols. Washington, D.C.: Government Printing Office, 1929.

Morrison, James D. *The Social History of the Choctaw Nation, 1865-1907*. Durant, Okla.: Creative Informatics, 1987.

Nelson, Will T., ed. *English Choctaw Dictionary*. 5th ed. Reprint of *A Dictionary of the Choctaw Language*, by Cyrus Byington. Oklahoma City: Council of Choctaws, 1975.

Chumash: Tribe
CULTURE AREA: California
LANGUAGE GROUP: Chumashan
PRIMARY LOCATION: Ventura, Santa Barbara, and San Luis Obispo counties, California
POPULATION SIZE: 2,981 (1990 U.S. Census)

The Chumash were one of the largest (fifteen thousand is a likely estimate) and most sophisticated California Indian tribes at the time of European contact. Of the many unique features of their culture, two stand out as distinctive: their extensive rock art and their construction of boats. The Chumash area abounds in pictographs, mostly of abstract forms. By the time of the arrival of Europeans, no Indians were still living who could recall the origins or meaning of the paintings, and vandals have destroyed many of the sites. Many of the Chumash lived on islands in the Santa Barbara Channel, and trade and communication between those islands and the mainland was extensive. The Chumash became very proficient in making canoes of pine planks stitched together with deer sinews and sealed with thick asphaltum. Canoes varied in length from 8 to 25 feet, were usually painted red with shell decorations, and held two to twenty people.

While some scholars have attempted to identify and preserve native terms for regional subdivisions, others have simply borrowed the names of the five Spanish missions in the region: Tsoyinneahkoo or Obispeño for the San Luis Obispo mission (founded 1772); Aḧmoo or Purisimeño for Purísima Concepción (1787); Kaḧshakompéah or Ynezeño for Santa Ynéz (1804); Kaśswah or Barbareño for Santa Barbara (1786); and Chumahs or Ventureño for San Buenaventura (1782). Inland territorial districts have been named Hooíkookoo or Emigdiano and Kaḧshenahsmoo or Cuyama.

The Spanish expedition of 1769 reported the Chumash as friendly and peaceful, so missionaries were eager to enter the area. By the 1820's nearly all the Chumash, including those of the Channel Islands and the inland mountainous areas, had become part of the mission system. As happened elsewhere, however, the Chumash preserved many features of their own culture. Although they generally proved to be, as anticipated, a very peaceful people who quietly accepted Hispanization, the most serious uprising in the entire history of the California missions occurred in 1824 when a violent Chumash revolt at several missions resulted in the death of a number of Indians and whites. Historians are uncertain about the cause of that rebellion, but one explanation is that the Chumash were fighting to preserve some of their traditional social and marital patterns.

Despite their efforts to maintain their traditional lifestyle, the Chumash population experienced the familiar pattern of decline during and after the mission period. By 1832 they numbered only 2,471, by 1865 only 659, and by 1920 a mere 74. The federal roll of 1928 identified 31 Chumash, of whom only 8 were of unmixed ancestry. In May, 1941, Juan Justo, identified as the last surviving full-blood Chumash, died in Santa Bar-

bara. The federal government had established the Santa Ynéz Reservation near the mission of that name on December 17, 1901. As of March 15, 1993, that reservation provided a home for 195 people of Chumash ancestry, with another 28 registered members living in adjacent areas. The 1990 U.S. Census reported a much larger population, with nearly three thousand people identifying themselves as Chumash.

See also California; Missions and missionaries; Prehistory—California.

Cíbola, Seven Cities of
DATE: Sixteenth century
LOCATION: Southwest
TRIBES AFFECTED: Pueblo, Zuni

With their conquest of Mexico and Peru, sixteenth century Spaniards expected to find other rich cultures in the New World, including the Seven Cities of Cíbola. They believed that when the Moors had invaded the Iberian Peninsula in the eighth century, seven Portuguese bishops fled toward the west and established the Seven Cities of Antilia. Early explorers of the Caribbean, including Christopher Columbus, searched for the bishops' cities. They also named some of the islands after them—the Antilles.

In 1529 a Mexican Indian told the Spanish that his father had traded in the north with seven rich cities. Perhaps, they thought, these might be the land of Antilia. Further confirmation arrived in 1536. Eight years after being shipwrecked on the Gulf of Mexico, Alvar Núñez Cabeza de Vaca, a black

Spanish gold seekers, with Esteban, in search of the Seven Cities of Cíbola. (Associated Publishers)

slave named Esteban, and two companions made contact with Spaniards in northwestern Mexico. From their wanderings through what is now the southwestern United States, they brought reports of rich civilizations.

Viceroy Antonio de Mendoza sent Esteban and Friar Marcos of Nice to investigate the story and appointed Francisco Vásquez de Coronado to organize an exploratory expedition. In March of 1539 Marcos, Esteban, and accompanying Indians began their trek northward. They made their way through eastern Arizona, with the slave traveling ahead. Esteban sent reports to Marcos that the Seven Cities lay ahead, although he referred to them as Cíbola rather than Antilia. Then an Indian messenger arrived to report that the people of Cíbola had killed Esteban and many of those with him. Friar Marcos proceeded until the first city came within view. He then returned to meet Coronado's expedition.

Encouraged by the friar's report, Coronado and his men pushed ahead. They met fierce resistance outside the first city, entering it on July 7, 1540. To their dismay, it was neither large nor wealthy. The other cities proved equally disappointing. They had discovered instead what scholars have generally (although not unanimously) identified as the land of the Zunis. Received hospitably for four months after the initial hostilities, Coronado's forces eventually moved eastward into the pueblos of north-central New Mexico. Afterward, the Spaniards abandoned the land of Cíbola until 1581-1582, when a missionary and trading expedition arrived. Its chronicler, Hernán Gallegos, referred to the people for the first time as the "Suni."

In 1540 there were six Zuni cities clustered south of modern Gallup, New Mexico. The three largest were Halona, Matsakya, and Kyakina (where Esteban died, according to Zuni tradition). Others were Kwakina, Kechipbowa, and Hawikuh, where Coronado fought his battle. The total population of the villages probably amounted to about three thousand people, living in houses of three or four stories. The Zuni probably descended from intermixing of Anasazis and Mogollon migrants from the south. Their dietary staples were corn, beans, squash, and turkeys. They traded salt (collected from a nearby lake) and turquoise, obtaining buffalo hides from the Pueblos and other items from the Mexicans. The Spanish explorers may have derived Cíbola from *cíbolo*, their term for the American bison.

See also Anasazi; Indian-white relations—Spanish colonial; Southwest; Zuni language.

Civil rights and citizenship

TRIBES AFFECTED: Pantribal

SIGNIFICANCE: Indian activism, federal legislation, and tribal activities have all been important in the struggle of American Indians for equality under U.S. law and for true equality in education, employment, and health

The concept of civil rights may be construed in two ways: narrowly, as referring to guaranteed equal rights under the law (as guaranteed, for example, by laws against discrimination), and more broadly, as referring to whether a group has in fact achieved equality. Civil rights includes access to such things as education, employment opportunities, and adequate health care. American Indians, despite considerable federal legislation addressing such issues as discrimination, education, and health care, still experience poor health, poor education, and high unemployment, mortality rates, poverty rates, and rates of child abuse. These ongoing problems raise a twofold question: How can Native Americans solve these problems in the midst of a non-Indian industrial United States without surrendering their own cultural and religious traditions?

Three generalized historical phases of federal Indian policy can be identified. First, before 1890, American Indians were either exterminated or forced onto reservations. Second, between 1890 and 1934, attempts were made to Christianize Indians and assimilate them into white culture. To this end, "termination" of federal relations with tribes became the policy during the 1940's and 1950's. Finally, when this did not work, policy changed to direct assistance to the reservations to help them achieve self-determination. In accordance with a multicultural society, tribal governments have been reestablished and strengthened, and Native American cultures have been revived. Today, American Indian policy is complex, involving the Bureau of Indian Affairs (BIA) and a number of other federal agencies, hundreds of "federally recognized" tribes, more than half the states, various interest groups, and the court system.

Most of the people who identify themselves as American Indians do not live on reservations but are spread throughout the country. Whereas the average American has two citizenships, federal and state, the reservation Indian has three: federal, state, and tribal. By 1961, termination had gone far enough to alarm many Indians, who believed that too much discretionary power in the states over reservation Indians would replace the federal government and that the answer to the problems of American Indians lay not in termination of federal services but in better legislation.

Activism. American Indian activists, beginning in the late 1960's, began to call attention to the injustices still faced by Indians and to demand legislation to correct the situation. A group called Indians of All Tribes took over abandoned Alcatraz Island on November 9, 1969, and remained there for nineteen months. Following a demonstration at Mount Rushmore in 1971, Indian interest groups organized the Trail of Broken Treaties march on Washington to bring further attention to the American Indian situation. Its specific purposes were stated in Denver, Colorado, on October 2, 1971: fulfillment of treaty obligations; genuine fulfillment of trust responsibility for Indian lands, Indian resources, and the rights of individual Indians; removal of Indian matters from the BIA and placement directly under the president of the United States; no termination of federal services without a referendum; increase of congressional appropriations to the same level of others in American society; and passage of special laws guaranteeing education at the highest level for any Indian who wants it.

Supporting the march, which took place in August, 1972, were more than fifteen groups, but the American Indian Movement (AIM), founded by Dennis Banks and George Mitchell in 1968, was the dominant participant. The march ended with the November 2, 1972, seven-day occupation of the BIA building in Washington. About six months later, on February 27, 1973, about two hundred armed Indians of AIM seized the small town of Wounded Knee on the Pine Ridge Reservation in South Dakota. The occupation ended by peaceful negotiation seventy-one days after it began.

The Longest Walk started on February 11, 1978, when about 180 people set out from San Francisco, California, to walk across the continent to Washington, D.C., to commemorate all the forced walks the Indian people had made in the past, such as the Trail of Tears in the 1830's. The organizers of the Longest Walk included such leaders of AIM as Vernon Bellecourt and Dennis Banks but no tribal leaders. About five to ten thousand people were estimated to have reached Washington by July 15, 1978.

Indian Reorganization Act and Federal Acknowledgment Program. In mid-1994 there were 543 tribes that were "federally recognized" and received the services of the BIA. The Indian Reorganization Act (1934) delineated steps by which any "Indian tribe . . . residing on the same reservation" might formally organize for recognition. In 1978, the Federal Acknowledgment Program was established, delineating seven mandatory criteria for federal recognition. In the mid-1980's, about 125 American Indian groups were trying to meet these seven criteria. One should emphasize that termination did not mean that a tribe no longer existed; it meant that the federal government had terminated its relationship with the tribe. If the tribe wished to end termination, it had to meet the criteria listed.

Legislation. During the 1960's, federal programs designed to aid chronically depressed areas, such as the Area Redevelopment Act (1961) and the Economic Opportunity Act (1964), were made applicable to American Indians. Indians gradually took a larger role in planning and administering these programs, as, for example, when in 1970, BIA commissioner Louis R. Bruce signed contracts with the Zuni, Salt River Pima, and Maricopa permitting them to administer all programs previously operated by the BIA. Experimentation was also launched in New Mexico and Arizona in which all-Indian school boards were given full authority over curriculum, expenditure of school funds, and hiring and firing of teachers.

Indians, along with Latinos, African Americans, and other minorities, took advantage of the Voting Rights Act of 1965. Since passage of the Fifteenth Amendment to the federal constitution in 1870, a variety of methods, such as literacy tests and gerrymandering, had been employed to prevent Native Americans from voting. A Navajo tribal chairman estimated that in the decade of the 1960's, half the otherwise eligible Navajo voters were barred the franchise by the literacy requirement in Arizona. The Voting Rights Act outlawed literacy tests. Later, the 1975 renewal of the Voting Rights Act outlawed gerrymandering and required bilingual ballots and voting information. Racial discrimination, however, continued to inspire new ways of maintaining white political control over areas of heavy Indian population.

The American Indian Civil Rights Act of 1968 unilaterally extended many of the provisions of the Bill of Rights to members of Indian tribes in order to protect them from arbitrary actions of their own tribal councils. Although the government meant well, critics argued that the federal government lacked understanding of or sympathy with tribal traditions, which were not the traditions of white society: Unilateral imposition without tribal voting was the exact opposite of the self-determination policy.

In July, 1970, President Richard M. Nixon presented a message to Congress requesting repudiation of the termination policy; legislative authority to empower any tribe to accept responsibility for the operation of federally funded programs in the Department of the Interior and the Department of Health, Education, and Welfare; authority to channel federal education funds to Indians in public schools through tribal governments rather than through local public-school districts; and authority for Indians to enter into long-term leases of their lands. These policies strengthened the right of the recognized Indian tribes to determine their own futures within the context of United States citizenship as well as the right of tribes to exist as tribes.

The process of bringing the tribes into the American system has been labeled co-option by critics. Co-option may be defined as a situation in which a powerful government or system voluntarily brings a less powerful but threatening organization into its operation as a means of lessening the threat. In this case the threat was not only the rise of Indian protest groups but also the desires of other radical groups that wished to include Native Americans as another exploited minority.

Nixon left the presidency on August 9, 1974, but his message produced the Indian Self-Determination and Education Assistance Act of 1975, which provided statutory authority to permit tribes to assume responsibilities formerly reserved to officials of the BIA and other departments of the government. Although theoretically sound, the Self-Determination Act did not operate as well as it might have. Conflict developed between tribes seeking full implementation of self-determination and the reluctance of the BIA to surrender its dominance in Native American affairs. The BIA retained its position through increased bureaucratization, requirements that the BIA approve tribal contracts with non-Indian parties, lack of tribal power over their own resources, the vagaries of congressional appropriations, and so on. This proved to be especially true of the criminal justice operation on reservations, where the Division of Law Enforcement Services of the BIA devised its own Reservation Law Enforcement Improvement Plan. Between Nixon's message to Congress and the Self-Determination Act, an Office of Indian Rights was established within the civil rights division of the Justice Department to develop expertise

TWENTIETH CENTURY LEGISLATION AFFECTING AMERICAN INDIAN CIVIL RIGHTS

Date	Legislation	Results
1934	Indian Reorganization Act	Provides for formal, legal organization of tribes.
1961	Area Redevelopment Act	Provides aid to depressed areas.
1964	Economic Opportunity Act	Provides aid to depressed areas.
1965	Voting Rights Act	Specifically outlaws voting practices that discriminate against minorities.
1968	American Indian Civil Rights Act	Extends Bill of Rights provisions to tribal members.
1972	Indian Education Act	Provides financial grants to schools with significant numbers of Indian students.
1975	Indian Self-Determination and Education Assistance Act	Allows tribes to assume responsibilities previously held by federal government agencies.
1975	Voting Rights Act (renewal)	Outlaws gerrymandering and requires bilingual ballots where needed.
1978	Tribally Controlled Community College Assistance Act	Provides incentives for the establishment of community colleges to teach native languages and traditions.
1978	American Indian Religious Freedom Act	Protects and encourages the expression of traditional Native American religious beliefs.
1986	Indian Civil Rights Act	Amends 1968 act to allow tribal courts to impose fines and jail time for criminal offenses.
1988	Indian Education Act	Provides financial assistance to local educational agencies serving Indian children.
1988	Tribally Controlled School Grants Act	Assures maximum Indian participation in provision of educational services.
1988	Indian Gaming Regulatory Act	Allows gambling on Indian land to promote tribal economic self-sufficiency.
1990	Indian Child Protection and Family Violence Prevention Act	Authorizes procedures to ensure child protection and provide programs to prevent and treat family violence.
1991	Criminal Jurisdiction Act	Establishes that tribes can exercise criminal jurisdiction over members.
1992	Indian Resources Act	Provides assistance to foster tribal control in developing and administering natural resources.

in the area of Indian civil liberties, but the office was not funded until 1981.

The Indian Education Act of 1972 was really a failure. Although intended to make financial grants more available to school districts with large numbers of Indian students, the act failed to define the beneficiaries sufficiently, so that school districts which did not suspect themselves of having any significant numbers of Indian students soon found themselves besieged by students claiming Indian blood. The Education Act of 1988 proved more successful.

Congress passed the Tribally Controlled Community College Act in 1978, which encouraged tribes to establish community colleges where native languages, culture, and history could be taught. The American Indian Religious Freedom

Act, also of 1978, aimed at encouraging Indians to worship in accordance with their ancestral forms and beliefs. The federal government committed itself to "protect and preserve for Native Americans their inherent right of freedom to believe, express, and exercise the traditional religions" and directed federal agencies to make certain that Native Americans were not deprived of access to their sacred sites on federal land. As there was no enforcement section to the act, however, it remained more a statement of policy than anything else.

In the meantime, a variety of United States Supreme Court cases returned to John Marshall's view in *Worcester v. Georgia* (1832) that recognized tribes were sovereign entities that should be within themselves largely free from restrictions by both federal and state governments. *Santa Clara Pueblo v. Martinez*, 436 U.S. 49 (1978), upheld the right of a tribe to be governed by its own traditional laws and to determine its membership, even if such procedures conflicted with the civil rights of individual tribal members or other Americans under the federal Constitution. Other significant cases include *Oliphant v. Suquamish Tribes* (1978); *Merrion v. Jicarilla Apache Tribe* (1982); *Arizona v. California* (1983); *Nevada v. U.S.* (1983); *Montana v. Blackfeet Tribe of Indians* (1985).

The Indian Alcohol and Substance Abuse Prevention and Treatment Act (1986) was passed to develop a comprehensive coordinated attack on the illegal narcotics traffic in Indian country and the deleterious impact of alcohol and substance abuse on Indian tribes and their members. It was to provide guidance in the way of schools, tribal offices, the BIA, and the Indian Health Service (IHS), and to establish Indian Youth Programs, emergency shelters, and rehabilitation services.

On April 28, 1988, Congress passed two important acts. First was the Tribally Controlled School Grants Act, to respond to the obligation of the Indian people for self-determination by assuring maximum Indian participation in the direction of education services so as to render such services more responsive to the needs and desires of Indian communities. Second was the Indian Education Act, intended to provide financial assistance to local educational agencies to develop and carry out elementary and secondary school programs specially designed to meet the special educational and cultural academic needs of Indians. An Office of Indian Education was established in the Department of Education to encourage fellowships for Native Americans and adult education.

The Indian Gaming Regulatory Act of October 17, 1988, declared federal policy as promoting tribal economic development, tribal self-sufficiency, strong tribal government, and, if not specifically prohibited by federal law, the allowance of gambling on Indian land under the supervision of a National Indian Gaming Commission. This led to a lucrative source of funding for Indian projects. In 1989, only a few reservations offered a form of gambling, but by the end of 1992 about 140 tribes maintained gaming operations. Annual wagering on reservations, according to an article in *The Christian Science Monitor* (David Holmstrom, March 18, 1993), was estimated to be as high as five billion dollars.

Senate hearings in 1988-1989 on continuing Indian problems in the areas of health, education, religion, culture, employment, and tribal sovereignty led to considerable legislation. The Indian Child Protection and Family Violence Prevention Act (1990) sought to require reports of abused Indian children, establish reliable data on the topic for statistical purposes, authorize procedures to ensure effective child protection, establish an Indian Child Abuse Prevention and Treatment Grant Program for technical assistance, and provide for treatment and prevention of incidents of family violence. In 1992, the Indian Employment, Training, and Related Services Act demonstrated how Indian tribal governments can integrate the employment, training, and related services they

provide in order to improve the effectiveness of those services and reduce joblessness in Indian communities.

On finding that the increasing numbers of Indian students who qualified for postsecondary education far outpaced the resources available, and that tribes showed an increasing interest in administering programs to serve these individuals, Congress passed the Indian Higher Education Programs Act (1992), providing financial assistance to individual Indians either wishing to attend or attending institutions of higher education. The Indian Resources Act (1992) enabled the secretary of energy, in consultation with the secretary of the interior, to cooperate with and provide assistance to Indian tribes for the purpose of assisting Indian tribes in the development, administration, and enforcement of tribal programs to promote energy self-sufficiency on reservations. An Indian Resource Commission was established; it included the secretary of the interior and the secretary of energy or their designates. Problems, nevertheless, continued to plague the Indian community.

Social Conditions. Senator John McCain of Arizona reported in 1992 that from 40 to 45 percent of reservation Indians and 22 percent of off-reservation Indians in the United States live below the poverty line. The BIA reported that as of 1985 there was a 39 percent unemployment rate among Indians, three times the rate for the United States as a whole. Twenty-five percent of Indian reservation households were receiving food stamps. Of the working-age population on Indian reservations, only about 40 percent were employed more than forty weeks out of the year, and the majority of those who worked earned less than $7,000 per year. The rate of alcoholism on reservations was 438 percent greater than the national average, tuberculosis 400 percent higher, diabetes 155 percent higher. There were 131 percent more accidents on reservations, 57 percent more homicides, 27 percent more suicides, and 32 percent more cases of pneumonia and influenza.

Health. A number of governmental agencies provide health services for American Indians; the most important is the Indian Health Service (IHS), within the Public Health Service. It operates a program of comprehensive health services for eligible American Indians and Alaska Natives. It provides hospital and medical care, rehabilitative services, and disease control activities and assists in the development of water supply and waste disposal. It provides for the training of health personnel and promotes tribal self-determination in health care. The 1976 Indian Health Care Improvement Act "authorized resources to carry out the objectives of Indian Self-Determination" and established national goals for programs providing health care to Native Americans. Under this act, some tribes have chosen to operate their own health systems directly; some run their own hospitals, and various tribes and Indian organizations operate about 250 health clinics.

Yet statistically, the Indian population dies young. Most deaths of Indians under the age of forty-five have been attributed to six causes: unintentional injuries, cirrhosis, homicide, suicide, pneumonia, and complications of diabetes. According

AMERICAN INDIAN AND NON-HISPANIC WHITE DEATH RATES PER 100,000 POPULATION FROM SIX MAJOR CHRONIC DISEASES, 1987

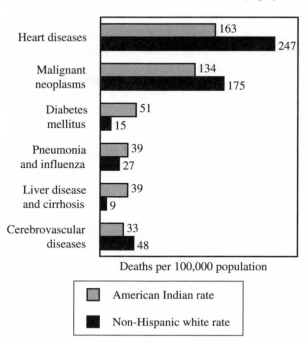

Deaths per 100,000 population

■ American Indian rate

■ Non-Hispanic white rate

Source: U.S. Department of Health and Human Services, Public Health Service. *Health Status of Minorities and Low-Income Groups.* 3d ed. Washington, D.C.: U.S. Government Printing Office, 1991.

Note: Rates are age-adjusted to the 1986 U.S. population.

to the Indian Health Service in 1992, Indian people have the highest mortality rates in the United States.

Education, Employment, and Housing. The 1991 Digest of Education Statistics reported that during the 1988-1989 school year, for every ten thousand bachelor's degrees awarded, only forty went to American Indian students; in that year, only forty-seven Indians in ten thousand were undergraduate students. More than 44 percent of Indian adults age twenty-five and older had not been graduated from high school.

The BIA in 1992 estimated that an average of 48 percent of the available workers on or near reservation areas had no jobs, while the conditions of Indians in many urban areas was little better. In 1992, Congress passed the Indian Employment, Training, and Related Services Demonstration Act to demonstrate how Indian tribal governments can integrate to improve the effectiveness of employment and training services and to reduce joblessness in Indian communities.

Representative Doug Bereuter of Nebraska, taking his information from the U.S. Census Bureau, stated in 1992 that almost 24 percent of all Indians living in Indian communities or on reservations lacked adequate shelter. While the national average of homelessness was estimated at 6.4 percent, Indians had nearly four times the amount of homelessness of the general population. In addition, many houses on Indian reservations lacked running water or indoor plumbing of any kind.

Finances and Claims. *Time* magazine reported in 1992 that although Indian governments controlled about 40 percent of the Bureau of Indian Affairs' $1.9 billion budget, self-government had merely given many Indians the responsibility to administer their own poverty, since they still had the shortest life spans, highest infant-mortality rate, highest high school dropout rate, and most extensive health problems of any United States ethnic group. The article saw the situation changing with the spin of roulette wheels, however: As of 1992, about 140 Indian tribes operated 150 gambling casinos, and revenue grew from $287 million in 1987 to more than $3.2 billion by 1993, making some tribes rich.

Indian claims after World War II were assisted by the establishment, after decades of Indian dissatisfaction, of an Indian Claims Commission. Although intended to operate for five years, the commission was inundated with so many claims against the government that its life was extended four times, to 1978; thereafter, major cases were referred to the U.S. Court of Claims. By that time approximately 40 percent of the claims filed had been adjudicated. —*Robert M. Spector*

See also Activism; American Indian Civil Rights Act; American Indian Religious Freedom Act; Indian Act of 1876 (Canada); Indian Act of 1951 (Canada); Indian Act of 1989 (Canada); Indian Citizenship Act; Indian Education Acts; Indian police and judges; Indian Self-Determination and Education Assistance Act; Sovereignty; Termination policy; Voting rights—Canada; Voting rights—United States.

BIBLIOGRAPHY

Bolt, Christine. *American Indian Policy and American Reform.* London: Allen & Unwin, 1987. Deals in part 1 with the history of Native Americans along the road to self-determination in the 1960's. Part 2 is devoted to case studies of specific topics, such as Indian education in the twentieth century, Indian women, urban Indians since World War II, and Indian protest groups. There are a few charts and maps.

Deloria, Vine, Jr., ed. *American Indian Policy in the Twentieth Century.* Norman: University of Oklahoma Press, 1985. An anthology of eleven essays on various topics of Native American life, such as Indian voting, the evolution of federal Indian policy making, the crisis in tribal government, and an overview of American Indian policy. Particularly valuable is the essay on federal Indian policies in the setting of international protection of human rights.

Deloria, Vine, Jr., and Clifford M. Lytle. *American Indians, American Justice.* Austin: University of Texas Press, 1983. Particularly valuable for the white justice system and relationship with the Native American both as an individual and as a member of a tribe.

A Matter of Fact 17 (1992). This semiannual periodical has been published since 1984. Valuable because it brings in brief form up-to-date comments of public figures such as congressmen and senators on various aspects of American life, including the social conditions of Native Americans.

Nabokov, Peter, ed. *Native American Testimony: A Chronicle of Indian-White Relations from Prophecy to the Present, 1492-1992*. New York: Viking Penguin, 1991. An anthology of Indian-white relations as seen by Native Americans from 1492 to 1992. Chapter 19, "Facing the Indian Future," is especially valuable for the period of the 1960's on.

Nichols, Roger L. *The American Indian Past and Present.* 4th ed. New York: McGraw-Hill, 1992. An anthology of essays dealing with the history of Native Americans, such as urban Native Americans, 1920-1950; building toward self-determination; Jim Crow, Indian style; and Nichols' own article dealing with Indians in the post-termination era. The book does not sufficiently discuss the policy of termination, however, leaving a gap that should be filled. No maps, tables, or charts.

Taylor, Theodore W. *American Indian Policy*. Mt. Airy, Md.: Lomond, 1983. Excellent for a quick insight into the legislation of the federal government regarding its Indian policy, as well as policies of the states, since the 1960's. The footnoting is particularly good. Very good on Indian health. Many charts and tables.

Thornton, Russell. *American Indian: Holocaust and Survival*. Norman: University of Oklahoma Press, 1987. This book deals with a population history of Native Americans since 1492 and is filled with statistics in a demographic overview of Native American history. It describes the holocaust that white society brought to the American Indian. Valuable reading.

Clallam: Tribe
CULTURE AREA: Northwest Coast
LANGUAGE GROUP: Salishan
PRIMARY LOCATION: North side of Strait Juan de Fuca
POPULATION SIZE: 3,800 (1990 U.S. Census)

Prior to European American contact, the Clallam—including the Klallam, Skallam, and Tlallum—inhabited approximately a dozen permanent villages while intermarrying with other Central Coast tribes and thus encouraging trade and ritual exchange of wealth. They hunted inland to the Olympic Mountains and used dugout canoes to hunt seals, porpoise, sea lions, and sturgeon. They gathered numerous plant foods and by-products. Various complex ceremonies recognized status change and redistribution of food and goods.

By the 1820's, the Hudson's Bay Company had explored the area and established Fort Langley on the Fraser River in 1827. The Central Coast Salish territory was divided in 1846 by the Treaty of Washington. In 1855 the Clallam signed the Point No Point Treaty, consenting to cede their lands and live on the Skokomish Reservation. Most Clallam earned wages by hop and berry picking, working in canneries, and selling fish.

Economic depression in the 1920's and 1930's coincided with the spread of the Indian Shaker Church. Issues of gaming and gill-netting confront these groups today, as well as land claim settlements against the federal government.

See also Hudson's Bay Company; Salishan language family.

Clans
TRIBES AFFECTED: Widespread but not pantribal
SIGNIFICANCE: In societies with these unilineal descent groups, clan membership provides an individual with social identity and regulates marriage choices; clans sometimes own property, perform ceremonies, and control political offices

Clans are unilineal descent groups into which a person is born. In a matrilineal society, one is a member of one's mother's clan; in a patrilineal society, one is a member of one's father's clan. In nearly all societies with clans, the clans function to regulate marriage. Clans may also hold property and perform specific rituals. Clans often have distinctive symbols.

Definitions. Colloquially, "clan" often connotes a clique of kin who avoid contact with outsiders. Among members of American Indian tribes with clans, however, and for anthropologists working with such tribes, the term "clan" has a different connotation: two or more lineages closely related through a common traditional bond, usually belief in a common ancestor. Thus, a clan is a unilineal descent group: a group of people who trace relationship to one another through either the mother's line (matrilineal) or the father's line (patrilineal) but not both. A clan, in which the precise genealogical links among members are unknown, is distinguished from a lineage, in which each individual can trace descent from a known common ancestor.

Some anthropologists, following the work of George Murdock in the 1940's, define a clan as a "compromise kin group" that combines principles of descent and residence. The core of the group is a unilineal descent group, but the clan also includes the in-marrying spouses of descent group members. Today, however, most anthropologists have abandoned Murdock's definition of clan. Moreover, most Indians from groups with unilineal descent groups use the term to refer to the descent group rather than to the residential group. For example, when a Navajo says that her "clan" is "Edgewater," she means that she is related, by matrilineal descent, to all "Edgewater" people regardless of where they reside.

Distribution. There can be lineages without clans; this is the case in most of aboriginal California and among the Bering Sea Eskimo. There cannot, however, be clans without lineages. Groups with bilateral descent systems (in which descent is traced equally through both parents) have no lineages and, hence, no clans. Bilateral descent commonly occurs in Great Basin, Plateau, Plains, Arctic, and Eastern Subarctic cultures.

Hunting and gathering societies usually lack clans. Among the primary exceptions to this generalization are some Northwest Coast cultures and adjacent Athapaskan peoples of the Subarctic, which had matrilineal clans. Each Tlingit clan had a symbol ("crest" or "totem") and unique mythic traditions.

Many agricultural peoples of the East (such as Iroquoians and the Creek) and some in the Southwest (Western Pueblos, Navajo, and Western Apache) had matrilineal clans, as did the Mandan and Hidatsa of the Missouri River. The Crow, close linguistic relatives of the Hidatsa, retained matrilineal clans when they shifted from agricultural pursuits to bison hunting on the Great Plains.

Patrilineal clans were found mainly in two areas of North America: among Prairie farming tribes (such as the Omaha and Mesquakie, or Fox) and the adjacent Subarctic Ojibwa, and in the Southwest among Yumans and Pimans.

Clans and Marriage. The most common clan function involves marriage rules, especially clan exogamy (the requirement that one marry a person of a different clan). Because members of the same clan consider themselves to be closely related, marriage to a member of the same clan would be considered incestuous. Various additional restrictions based on clan relationships may also exist. Many matrilineal societies (Hopi, for example) prohibit marriage into the father's clan, while many patrilineal systems (as with the Omaha) prohibit marriage into the mother's clan. Such rules tend to increase the number of families which are allied by marriage, thereby increasing the network of kinship relations throughout the society.

The Navajo clan system illustrates the operation of marriage rules. There are more than fifty matrilineal clans. Sets of clans are linked into one of eight or nine groups ("phratries"). A Navajo is "born into" his mother's clan and is "born for" his father's clan. Notions of kinship are extended to members of these two clans and, more generally, to linked clans (phratry mates). A Navajo cannot marry someone in either of these two clans or phratries. Beyond marriage rules and the idioms of kinship and hospitality, Navajo clans have few functions.

Clans as Corporate Groups. In many tribes, however, clans have functions in addition to marriage regulation. The Hopi also have more than fifty matrilineal clans grouped into nine phratries. Hopi clan-related marriage rules and hospitality are similar to those of the Navajo, but Hopi clans are also corporate groups which hold land, own houses and sacred property, perform rituals, and maintain clan symbols. The eldest competent female of a clan's highest ranking lineage is the "clan mother." She lives in the clan house and, with her brother or maternal uncle, manages clan property. These two are stewards of clan property and agents of the clan considered as a corporation.

Each Hopi clan has its own migration legend. The sequence of the arrival of the clans in Hopi country is a rough measure of the prestige of the clans. For example, Bear clan, acknowledged as the first to arrive, should provide the village chief and the leader of the important Soyal ceremony.

The Siouan-speaking Winnebago and Omaha have twelve and ten patrilineal exogamous clans, respectively. Each Winnebago clan is associated with an animal that serves as a clan symbol or clan totem. According to ethnologist Paul Radin, individual Winnebagos conceive of the relationship to the clan animal as one "of descent from an animal transformed at the origin of the present human race into human beings." The Omaha conform less well to clan totem symbolism. Some Omaha clans are named after animals; others take their names from human attributes or natural phenomena such as lightning. Winnebago and Omaha clans, like those of the Hopi, have ceremonial property and political functions. For example, Winnebago village chiefs are Thunderbird clan, while Bear clan has disciplinary functions. *—Eric Henderson*

See also Adoption; Incest taboo; Kinship and social organization; Marriage and divorce; Names and naming; Societies, non-kin-based.

BIBLIOGRAPHY

Barnes, Robert H. *Two Crows Denies It: A History of Controversy in Omaha Sociology*. Lincoln: University of Nebraska Press, 1984.

Driver, Harold E. *Indians of North America*. 2d rev. ed. Chicago: University of Chicago Press, 1969.

Drucker, Philip. *Indians of the Northwest Coast*. 1955. Reprint. Garden City, N.Y.: Natural History Press, 1963.

Eggan, Fred. *Social Organization of the Western Pueblos*. Chicago: University of Chicago Press, 1950.

Murdock, George Peter. *Social Structure*. 1949. Reprint. New York: Macmillan, 1967.

Radin, Paul. *The Winnebago Tribe*. 1923. Reprint. Lincoln: University of Nebraska Press, 1970. A reprint of part of the 37th Annual Report of the Bureau of American Ethnology, Smithsonian Institution, 1923.

Schusky, Ernest L. *Manual for Kinship Analysis*. 2d ed. New York: Holt, Rinehart and Winston, 1972.

Clatskanie: Tribe

CULTURE AREA: Northwest Coast
LANGUAGE GROUP: Athapaskan
PRIMARY LOCATION: Chehalis River and mouth of Shockumchuck River, Washington

The Clatskanie (or Tlatskanai) were a riverine and maritime people, living in permanent frame, rectangular post and lintel dwellings. They depended largely on fish for subsistence, but also hunted. The women exploited the large root fields of their territory. Unfortunately, little ethnographic data was collected before their culture's demise. It is estimated that their population of approximately two thousand in 1780 had declined to 336 by 1904; by 1910, only three Clatskanie were living; this decline was primarily the result of disease introduced by European Americans and of conflict with other ethnic groups of the region. It is believed that the Clatskanie may have enforced a toll on people using the Columbia River for trading of goods.

Cliff dwellings

DATE: c. 500-1400
LOCATION: Colorado plateau in Arizona, Colorado, New Mexico, Utah
CULTURES AFFECTED: Anasazi, Western Pueblo tribes (Hopi, Navajo, Zuni)

Cliff dwellings identified with the Southwest's Anasazi culture were constructed between 500 C.E. and the climax of what archaeologists define as the Pueblo III period, between 1100 and 1300. While remains of these dwellings, some remarkably intact, have been found over a wide area of the Colorado plateau, the most notable sites are found in the Four Corners area, where the boundaries of Arizona, Colorado, New Mexico, and Utah meet. The largest and best-preserved (or restored) of these ruins include Betatakin, Cliff Palace, Fire Temple, Oak Tree House, Spruce Tree House, and Square Tower House. During the twentieth century the ruins of nearly all cliff dwellings have been incorporated either into National Historical Parks, as at Capitol Reef (Utah), Chaco Culture Historical Park (New Mexico), and Mesa Verde (Colorado), or into National Monuments, as at Bandelier (Colorado), Canyon de Chelly (Arizona), Gila Cliff Dwellings (New Mexico), Hovenweep (Colorado and Utah), Montezuma Castle (Arizona), Navajo (Arizona), Tonto (Arizona), and Walnut Canyon (Arizona).

A culture based on settled agriculture combined with supplemental hunting and gathering, and distinguished by its versatile and beautifully crafted basketwork, the Anasazi originally lived in pueblos of circular pit houses constructed in communal clusters. From as early as 500 C.E., some of these dwellings were built in the numerous cliff overhangs and caves common to the Colorado plateau, particularly in the Four Corners area. Early Anasazi housing was represented by pit houses lined with stone slabs and with wooden roofs and entrances through the roof or passageways. In time, the construction of these structures was carried above ground, retaining the sunken portions as kivas—sacred rooms for men. Built of stone, mud, and wood, some of them three stories high, cliff dwellings, with their terraced apartments, housed scores of people—more than two hundred in Mesa Verde's Cliff Palace—and included courtyards, storage rooms, and kivas. In these regards they continued the essentials of older pueblo architectural traditions. There is only informed speculation about why the cliff dwellings were abandoned during the 1300's.

The "opening" of the Southwest by white Americans, facilitated in the nineteenth century by the Gadsden Purchase, the discovery of gold in California, and the Mormon settlement of Utah, drew attention to previous occupants of the region, beginning with Lieutenant James Simpson's descriptions of the cliff dwellings and other ruins in Canyon de Chelly and Chaco Canyon, written while he was fighting the Navajos in 1849. Subsequent archaeological interest was stimulated by the explorations of John Wesley Powell and early archaeological work by Cosmos and Victor Mindeleff in the early 1890's. These studies were expanded by Richard Wetherill, Adolph Bandelier, Gustav Nordensjold, and (most important for preservation of the cliff dwellings) Jesse Walter Fewkes.

See also Anasazi; Architecture—Southwest; Canyon de Chelly; Chaco Canyon; Kivas; Mesa Verde; Pueblo; Pueblo tribes, Western.

Cloud, Henry Roe (Dec. 28, 1884, Thurston County, Nebr.—Feb. 9, 1950, Siletz, Oreg.): Educator, Bureau of Indian Affairs official
ALSO KNOWN AS: Wonah'ilayhunka
TRIBAL AFFILIATION: Winnebago
SIGNIFICANCE: Henry Roe Cloud was instrumental in expanding Indian educational opportunities

Henry Cloud's parents were Nah'ilayhunkay and Hard to See. He later added "Roe" to his English name in honor of his adoptive parents, missionaries Dr. and Mrs. Walter C. Roe. He was educated at the Indian school in Genoa, Nebraska, the Santee Mission School in Nebraska, and Dwight Moody's Academy at Mt. Hermon, Massachusetts. He was the first Indian to graduate from Yale, in 1910. He went on to receive a Bachelor of Divinity degree from Auburn Theological Seminary in 1913, and was ordained a Presbyterian minister the same year. He received an M.A. from Yale in 1914 and a Doctor of Divinity degree from the College of Emporia. In 1915, he married Elizabeth A. Bender (a Chippewa), a graduate of the Hampton Normal Training School. They had four daughters and a son who died in infancy.

In 1915, Henry Roe Cloud founded the Roe Indian Institute in Wichita, Kansas. He remained the Institute's superintendent until 1931, when he became a special representative of the Bureau of Indian Affairs. Roe Institute, which became the American Indian Institute in 1920, was unique for the time in that it promoted an academic rather than a vocational curriculum, with the aim of developing Indian leaders.

From 1933 to 1936, Henry Roe Cloud was superintendent of Haskell Institute in Lawrence, Kansas. Appointed Haskell's superintendent under the administration of John Collier to help change the direction of Indian education, he was unhappy with Haskell's vocational emphasis and wanted Indian education to help develop Indian leaders. His pioneering work in that direction helped lead to Haskell eventually becoming a junior college in 1970 and Haskell Indian Nations University in 1993. Henry Roe Cloud was appointed assistant supervisor of Indian education at-large for the Bureau of Indian Affairs in 1936. In 1947, he became superintendent of the Umatilla Indian Agency, where he served until his death.

Throughout his life, Henry Roe Cloud was active in Indian affairs. In his twenties he was a leader in the Society of American Indians, which preceded the National Council of American Indians. He served as chairman of the Winnebago delegation to the President in 1912, was a member of the Commission of Federal Survey of Indian Schools in 1914, was a member of the Standing Committee of One Hundred on Indian Affairs in 1920, and was a co-author of the Meriam Report of 1928. While he called for Indian leadership, he also promoted cultural assimilation both as a Presbyterian minister and as a Bureau of Indian Affairs employee.

See also Education, post-contact.

Clovis: Prehistoric tradition

DATE: 10,000-9200 B.C.E.

LOCATION: Most of continental North America

CULTURES AFFECTED: Paleo-Indian

Archaeological evidence of Paleo-Indian peoples was unearthed near Clovis, New Mexico, in 1931, and subsequent discoveries of related artifacts at kill sites across the continental United States justified the designation of a Clovis cultural tradition. In the west the best-known Clovis sites are Blackwater Draw, New Mexico; Naco, Lehner, Murray Springs, and Escapule, Arizona; Union Pacific, Montana; Dent, Nebraska; and Domebo, Oklahoma. Of the many sites excavated in the east, rich Clovis finds have been unearthed at Plenge, Port Mobil, Dutchess Quarry, and West Athens, New York, as well as at Reagan, Vermont; Williamson and Flint Run, Virginia; Bull Brook, Massachusetts; Shawnee-Minisink, Delaware; Shoop, Pennsylvania; and Hardaway, Tennessee. Related discoveries have been found at a score of other locations.

The Clovis tradition apparently was short-lived, lasting from circa 10,500 B.C.E. to 9200 B.C.E., giving way to the somewhat different Folsom and then Plano traditions. Clovis peoples have been characterized chiefly as roving mammoth hunters, although they also stalked camelids, horse, bison, tapirs, caribou, giant armadillo, four-horned antelope, sloths, and dire wolves. Some kill sites continued in use for thousands of years, providing ample evidence of their distinctive Clovis fluted projectile points, prismatic and edge-chipped, flat-flaked knives, smooth or bone cylinders, burins, cleavers, picks, and uniface chipped scrapers. Quarries where the chert and jasper preferred for such toolmaking were obtained have likewise been found. The Clovis culture was well-acquainted with fire, and there are findings at the Thunderbird site at Flint Run, Virginia, as well as at locations in Massachusetts and Nova Scotia, which suggest that the Clovis tradition may have included construction of the earliest known houses in the Americas. Developed south of, though often close to, continental glaciation, the Clovis culture yielded to other adaptations as its chief prey, mammoths, disappeared.

See also Folsom; Paleo-Indian; Plano; Projectile points.

Clowns

TRIBES AFFECTED: Pantribal, but especially Apache, Navajo, Pueblo, Seminole, Sioux

SIGNIFICANCE: Through their behavior, clowns reinforce a sense of order and the need for personal responsibility; they can also serve as powerful healers

Clowns are an important part of Indian mythology and ritual. While there is great variation in costuming, ranging from the famous mud-head clowns of the Hopi and Zuni to the black-and-white-striped clowns of the Koshare and Apache, clowns perform similar functions in all tribal groups. Most creation stories include the creation of a clown figure. As in the Keresan story of the clown being created from the epidermal waste of the creator, Iatiku, the clown figure usually has unusual beginnings. While sometimes associated in mythology with the sun, clowns are more often associated with water and water rituals, as are the Sioux heyoka, who receive their power from the Thunderbeings. In most tribes, one must be selected to be a clown and receive years of training in one of the clown societies.

Clowns engage in various forms of outrageous behavior. Often, like the Contrary Society of the Cheyenne, clowns will do everything backward—walk backward, ride a horse backward, and wear winter clothing in the summertime. Also common is scatological behavior such as eating dirt or excrement, drinking urine, cavorting naked, and simulating sexual acts in public. They may also, like the Apache Crazy Dancers, follow behind ceremonial dancers, healers, and tribal leaders, mimicking their behavior.

While part of the clown's intent is to entertain and generate laughter, they do have a more serious purpose. Through humor, they are trying to teach important lessons to the tribe. Most important, they reinforce the need for personal responsibility, tribal rules, and tribal order. By doing things backward and by violating rules, they show that chaos develops when rules are not maintained. Additionally, through their humor, they show the danger of human vices such as greed, gluttony, and sexual promiscuity. Finally, clowns serve to keep the powerful in check through their mimicking. They remind the healers and tribal leaders that, despite their special gifts, they are only human. By making them look foolish, clowns demystify their power.

Although clowns are humorous figures, they are viewed as very powerful. Their participation in ceremonies helps to assure fertility, a good harvest, and good health. Because of their association with water, they are especially important in bringing rain and performing cleansing rituals. Like the koshare, who are part of the Acoma Medicine Society, they are often powerful healers as well. The Navajo clown, Watersprinkler, is an important figure in the Night Chant ceremony, one of the tribe's most important healing rituals.

While the clowns are usually men, there have been women clowns in the Pacific Northwest. Like many other aspects of Indian culture, recent decades have seen a recovery and revival of the clown tradition and activities. Clown figures often figure prominently in cartoons in contemporary tribal newspapers.

See also Humor; Masks; Societies, non-kin-based; Tricksters.

Coast Yuki: Tribe

CULTURE AREA: California

LANGUAGE GROUP: Yuki

PRIMARY LOCATION: Drainage of the Eel River, northwestern California

The coast Yuki, or Ukhotnom, were shell-mound dwellers. They comprised eleven groups who occupied approximately fifty miles of the Mendocino Coast. They lived in conical redwood bark-covered dwellings; in summer they utilized brush huts for privacy and windbreaks. Men hunted and fished, while women collected and gathered essential plant foods. Each group had its own elected headman and territory. Groups visited, traded, and had usury rights to resources of other villages. Though a marine-oriented people, they had no boats. Their diet consisted primarily of acorns, grass seeds, salmon, and mussels. Deer and elk were important for food and by-products.

In the early 1850's, the Coast Yuki were intruded upon by white lumbermen and ranchers, whose activities destroyed many natural resources. Many Indians were interned on the Mendocino Reservation in 1856, though some continued to work on white ranches. The Coast Yuki joined the Pomo Earth Lodge cult, a derivative of the Ghost Dance, and revitalized some traditional ways, but by the 1970's they were no longer considered a distinct group.

See also California; Yuki.

Cochise (c. 1812, Chiricahua Mountains of present-day southern Ariz.—June 8, 1874, Chiricahua Apache Reservation, Ariz. Territory): Tribal chief

ALSO KNOWN AS: Goci (His Nose)

TRIBAL AFFILIATION: Chiricahua Apache

SIGNIFICANCE: As principal chief of the eastern Chiricahua Apaches from 1860 to 1872, Cochise orchestrated and led raids against U.S. and Mexican settlements

Cochise was born in the Spanish colony of Sonora (in present-day Arizona) during the revolution of 1810-1821, which eventually established the modern nation of Mexico. Although details of his ancestry remain uncertain, Cochise was probably the son of Pisago Cabezon, the leader of one of four bands of the Chiricahua Apaches who ranged over the area that is now southern Arizona and New Mexico and the northern Mexican states of Sonora and Chihuahua. As he grew to manhood, the long peace that had marked Mexican-Chiricahuan relations since around 1790 was coming to an end. By 1830, a bloody cycle of raiding, plundering, and murder had begun between the Apaches and Mexicans that determined the course of Cochise's life.

Virtually nothing is known about Cochise's life before 1835. He almost certainly received the special training his people reserved for the sons of chiefs, who were expected to become leaders when they matured. Such a child learned more discipline than other children, including controlling one's temper, patience with other children, and respect for the property of others. Religious ritual accompanied every phase of the instruction of all Apache children.

Cochise entered the pages of history for the first time in 1835, when Mexican documents mention him as a leader of the Chokonen band of Chiricahua Apaches raiding in Sonora. His name appears again on the lists of those Apaches drawing rations from the Mexican government at Janos in modern Chihuahua in 1842 and 1843. By that time, the Apaches were in an almost perpetual state of war with the Mexican population of the area. Beginning about 1830, raiding (what Cochise called in his later years "making a living"), livestock stealing,

and plundering became an integral part of the economies of many Apache tribes.

The man who was most likely Cochise's father died by treachery during the Mexican-Apache wars in 1845 or 1846. Cochise never forgave the Mexicans and continued to raid south of the U.S. border until almost the end of his life.

After the Mexican-American War in 1846-1848, the United States acquired the territory known as the Mexican Cession (modern New Mexico, Arizona, Colorado, Utah, Nevada, and California). The Apache bands quickly learned that they could raid in northern Mexico, flee across the border into Arizona or New Mexico, and have relative immunity from Mexican pursuit. The Apaches also found unscrupulous U.S. citizens eager to buy their Mexican plunder.

The Chiricahuas continued to live in the United States and raid primarily in Mexico for the next eight years, with Cochise probably a subchief in large frequent raiding parties led by his father-in-law, Mangas Coloradus. In 1857, the U.S. Army launched its first large-scale campaign against the Apaches in reaction to raids in New Mexico. Cochise joined other Chiricahuas in making a temporary peace with the Mexicans and fled across the border. This began a pattern that continued throughout the next decade: The Apaches would make peace on one side of the border for a while and then raid on the other.

By 1859, Cochise had become the principal chief of the Chokonen band. He negotiated a peace with the U.S. troops that lasted until 1861, although members of his band occasionally raided north of the border. Early in 1861, with the American Civil War only days in the future, an event occurred that launched the so-called Cochise wars between the U.S. government and the Chiricahuas: the Bascom Affair.

Although accounts of the affair vary, American troops led by Lieutenant George Nicholas Bascom apparently captured Cochise by treachery during a peace parlay on February 6, 1861, near Apache Pass in southern Arizona. Bascom ordered the execution of three of Cochise's relatives in retaliation for the torture deaths of three U.S. citizens. Cochise escaped and spent the next decade pursuing vengeance against the Americans. For the next four years, the American governments (both U.S. and Confederate) focused most of their attention on fighting each other. As a result of American distraction, the Apaches raided with relative impunity throughout New Mexico and Arizona.

Cochise led or planned many of the Apache raids during this period. He became not only the principal chief of the Chokonen, but of the entire Chiricahua tribe. Apache warriors from other Apache tribes such as the Mescaleros and White Mountain groups often joined his raiding parties because of his reputation as a leader. He became the most famous (or infamous) Indian leader of the 1860's, often mentioned prominently in the American press by newspapers as far away as San Francisco and Missouri. He also continued to plan and lead raids into Mexico. The Mexicans, their attention diverted by the French Emperor Napoleon III's attempt to establish himself as emperor of Mexico, became easy prey for Apache raids.

After the Civil War ended and the French were expelled from Mexico, both governments began devoting more men and resources to stopping the Apache depredations in the Southwest. American and Mexican officials began cooperating more closely to eliminate the Apache scourge. As a result of this cooperation, Cochise found it more difficult to make peace with one country and raid in the other. Despite large expenditures by both governments on troops and costly expeditions, Cochise managed to evade the American and Mexican armies for several years. Cochise was growing old, however, and his health was deteriorating. He also supposedly confided to his subchiefs that the Apache way of life was coming to an end. Finally, largely through the efforts of Thomas J. Jeffords, General Oliver Otis Howard negotiated a lasting treaty with Cochise on October 10, 1872, at Cochise's camp in the Dragoon Mountains in southern Arizona.

The terms of the treaty allowed Cochise and his people to live at peace in his beloved Chiricahua Mountains, drawing rations from the U.S. government. In return, he agreed to use all of his influence to halt Apache raids in both the United States and Mexico. For the remainder of his life, the raids virtually ceased in Arizona and New Mexico, but continued sporadically in northern Mexico. On June 8, 1874, Cochise died in bed of a stomach ailment, an ironic end for a man who spent virtually his entire adult life at war.   —*Paul Madden*

See also Apache; Apache Wars; Geronimo; Guadalupe Hidalgo, Treaty of; Mangas Coloradus; Victorio.

BIBLIOGRAPHY

Cremony, John C. *Life Among the Apaches*. Tucson: Arizona Silhouettes, 1954.

Lockwood, Frank C. *The Apache Indians*. New York: Macmillan, 1938.

Sweeney, Edwin R. *Cochise: Chiricahua Apache Chief*. Norman: University of Oklahoma Press, 1991.

Thrapp, Dan L. *Conquest of Apacheria*. Norman: University of Oklahoma Press, 1967.

Tyler, Barbara Ann. "Cochise, Apache War Leader, 1858-1861." *Journal of Arizona History* 6 (Spring, 1965): 1-10.

Cocopa: Tribe

CULTURE AREA: Southwest
LANGUAGE GROUP: Yuman
PRIMARY LOCATION: Sonora, Mexico
POPULATION SIZE: 640 in United States (1990 U.S. Census); most live in Mexico

The Cocopas, sedentary dwellers of the Southwest, inhabited the region along the lower stretch of the Colorado River in what is presently Sonora, Mexico, bordered on the south by the Gulf of California. Along with the nearby Mojaves, Halchidhomas, Maricopas, and Yumas, the Cocopas were Yuman-speaking and were ancient inhabitants of this hot and dry region. Another neighboring tribe was the Chemehuevis of the Uto-Aztecan language family.

Because of their efficient use of the land and water resources available to them, the Cocopas were able to remain in one place, and didn't have to roam for hunting or gathering purposes. They utilized the annual flooding of the Colorado River, rather than irrigation, for the watering of their crops which included corn, beans, pumpkins, gourds, and tobacco. Both men and women took part in tending the fields. Limited hunting of small game, including rabbits, supplemented the agricultural production for the tribe, as did the gathering of mesquite beans and other wild foods by the women. The Colorado River provided fish, which were caught by the men with seines, basketry scoops with long handles, weirs made from interlaced branches, and dip nets.

Because of the intense heat of the area, the men wore only narrow breechcloths, while the women wore front and back aprons. Sandals were worn while traveling. Men and women painted their faces and wore tattoos. Hair was worn with bangs covering the forehead. The men twisted their hair in back into many thin strands, while the women wore their hair long.

The housing of the Cocopas also conformed to the hot, dry weather. Houses were little more than flat-roofed structures for shade, with open sides. In winter, rectangular structures with sloping sides and ends, all covered with earth, were utilized. Rabbitskin blankets provided warmth in winter.

The Cocopas lived with little formal government. They held a strong sense of tribal unity, with the family being the basic unit within the tribe. Chiefs held an advisory role, maintaining intratribal peace and conducting religious ceremonies. Shamans were held in high regard and accompanied chiefs on war parties. War raids were well organized, with the warriors using bows and arrows, clubs, heavy sticks, round hide shields, and feathered staves.

Today most Cocopa people live in Sonora, Mexico; the 1990 U.S. census also reported 640 living in the southwestern United States.

See also Mojave; Quechan; Yuman language family.

Codices

TRIBES AFFECTED: Aztec, Maya, Mixtec
SIGNIFICANCE: Codices were the books of the pre-Hispanic Aztec, Maya, and Mixtec cultures; they describe events of historical, ritual, or calendrical significance

The pre-Hispanic cultures of the Aztecs, Mayas, and Mixtecs of Mexico produced written literature called codices (the singular form is "codex"). Aztec and Mixtec codices were made of either deerskin or agave paper; the Maya made theirs from paper made from tree bark covered with a thin layer of lime. Only three pre-Hispanic Mayan codices still survive, while there are no surviving pre-Hispanic Aztec codices; most codices were destroyed by the Spanish in the sixteenth century. Following the Spanish conquest, however, a number of codices were produced by Hispanicized Aztecs which describe the pre-Hispanic culture; several of these texts also survive.

Codices were folded accordion-fashion and were read from right to left. Surviving codices range in length from 4 to 24 feet. Individual pages range from 4 to 8 inches in width and from 8 to 10 inches in height. Pre-Hispanic cultures in Mexico did not use a phonetic alphabet (in which each written symbol represents a sound). Rather, they used a logographic writing system in which each symbol represented a word or concept, or occasionally a syllable. Logographic writing systems are often called pictographic or hieroglyphic. Literacy was not widespread, and codices were probably read only by a specialized class of scribes, who produced them, and the upper classes, who commissioned them. Someone reading a codex would begin with the logographs pictured in the upper right corner of a page and would then move down one column of figures and up the next. Following the Spanish conquest, some Aztec codex authors began to write their native language, Nahuatl, in a phonetic alphabet borrowed from the Spanish; this new writing was largely confined to place names and personal names.

The content of codices varied greatly. Many described the histories or genealogies of rulers or important nobility. As an example, the most famous surviving Mixtec codex tells the history of a chieftain named Eight-Deer from his birth in 1011 C.E. to his death by sacrifice at age fifty-two, following his capture in battle. The codex describes his rise to power, the expansion of his realm through conquest and strategic marriages, and the birth of his children. Some codices describe rituals and mythology, while others outline calendrical or astronomical events. Some codices apparently served as primers, or teaching devices, for the children of nobility or scribes; these primers described rituals, stories, and etiquette with which the children were to be familiar. Codices were not comprehensive texts. Rather, they provided the main outline of their content; readers had to provide many details of a narrative from their own memories. Aztec, Mayan, and Mixtec codices were destroyed by the Spanish priesthood in order to undermine the pre-Hispanic religions and to encourage the conversion of the Indians to Christianity.

See also Aztec; Indian-white relations—Spanish colonial; Maya; Mixtec.

Coeur d'Alene: Tribe

CULTURE AREA: Plateau
LANGUAGE GROUP: Salishan
PRIMARY LOCATION: Northwestern Idaho
POPULATION SIZE: 1,048 (1990 U.S. Census)

The Coeur d'Alene, an Interior Salishan-speaking people, called themselves "Schitsu' Umsh." They occupied an area east of the Spokane River, around Coeur d'Alene Lake and all its tributaries, including the headwaters of the Spokane River, with eastern boundaries to the Bitterroot Mountains. Aboriginally they were composed of three distinct geographical bands with a population of approximately 3,500 until the smallpox epidemics of 1831, 1847, and 1850 reduced the population by half. After acquiring horses in the late 1700's, they, like the Flathead and Nez Perce, adopted a war ethos. At the time of European American contact, they had adopted many Plains traits, including the hide tipi, scalp-taking, reed armor, and Plains-style clothing and ornaments. Their culture was further influenced when they ventured annually onto the western Plains for hunting bison and trading out roots, salmon pemmican, bows, and hemp.

They possessed bilateral descent, sexual equality, a strict division of labor, polygyny, rule by consensus of opinion, and elaborate ceremonialism that emphasized the Bluejay Ceremony, First-Fruit Ceremony, and Midwinter Ceremony. Other aspects of their culture included shamanism, the vision quest for skill-related tutelary spirits, an animistic belief system with a complex pantheon, the sweathouse complex, a trickster, and social control by public opinion and threats of sorcery.

First mention of the Coeur d'Alene was by Meriwether Lewis and William Clark in 1805, and their first contact with European Americans was with David Thompson, who surveyed the area in 1811. The first permanent white settler was Father Nicholas Point, who in 1842 established a Catholic mission on the banks of the St. Joseph River. It was built by the Coeur d'Alene from 1843 to 1853 under the supervision of Father Anthony Ravalli and was later moved to the present Cataldo site; it is the oldest standing building in Idaho. The area was periodically exploited by encroaching settlers and miners, a situation which in 1877 caused the Sacred Heart Mission to be moved to its present location at De Smet, Idaho. An executive order of November 8, 1873, established the Coeur d'Alene Reservation, and the existing boundaries were ratified by Congress in 1894; it covers an area of 345,000 acres. In 1903 the Historic Sisters' Building was constructed by the Sisters of Providence and functioned as a boarding school for Indian girls until 1973.

The Coeur d'Alene, a sovereign nation created by executive order, are consolidated on the Coeur d'Alene Reservation on the southern portion of Coeur d'Alene Lake, Idaho. Tribal headquarters, containing the tribal archives, museum, and library, is southwest of Plummer, and the elected tribal council administers finance, planning, natural resources, a tribal farm, education, and social and health services. The Benewah Center features an Indian specialty store, post office, medical center, and supermarket. The two major employers are the Coeur d'Alene Tribe and Pacific Crown Timber Products, with additional monies gained from the successful management of agriculture, minerals, and water recreation facilities on adjacent Coeur d'Alene Lake.

See also Plateau; Salishan language family.

BIBLIOGRAPHY

Chalfant, Stuart A. "Ethnological Field Investigation and Analysis of Historical Material Relative to Coeur d'Alene Aborginal Distribution." In *Interior Salish and Eastern Washington Indians*, edited by D. A. Horr. Vol. 4. New York: Garland, 1974.

Peltier, Jerome. *Manners and Customs of the Coeur d'Alene Indians*. Spokane: Peltier Publications, 1975.

Ross, John Alan. "An Ethnographic and Ethnohistorical Survey of the Proposed Washington Centennial Trail Corridor." In *Archaeology of the Middle Spokane River Valley: Investigations Along the Spokane Centennial Trail*, edited by

John A. Draper and William Andrefsky. Pullman: Center for Northwest Anthropology, Dept. of Anthropology, Washington State University, 1991.

Walker, Deward E., Jr. *American Indians of Idaho*. Anthropological Monographs of the University of Idaho, 2. Moscow: University of Idaho Press, 1971.

Colorow (c. 1810, northern Mexico, in present-day northern Colo.—Dec. 11, 1888, Uintah Reservation, Utah): Chief

ALSO KNOWN AS: Colorado (Red)

TRIBAL AFFILIATION: Ute

SIGNIFICANCE: Colorow was an influential chief among northern Colorado Ute bands and a leader in an attack on U.S. troops in 1879; he clashed with game wardens while leading his band to hunt off the reservation in 1887

Colorow rose to prominence among the isolated northwestern Colorado Ute bands as a chief of the Yampa band, which ranged the Yampa River. After 1868, his band was consolidated with other northern Ute bands as part of the White River Ute agency (White River Utes) near present-day Meeker, Colorado.

Colorow signed as subchief to a treaty in 1863 and as a Yampa Ute chief in 1868. He was one of the prominent Ute leaders who were passed over as spokesman for all Utes when the U.S. government sought a head chief with whom to negotiate and settled on the more conciliatory leader Ouray.

Colorow was known for his large size and often belligerent and threatening manner. In 1879, he joined Captain Jack and Antelope in ambushing U.S. troops under the command of T. T. Thornburgh as they entered the Ute reservation at the request of White River agent Nathan C. Meeker. The Ute bands were fearful that the soldiers were coming to transport them forcibly to Indian Territory in Oklahoma. When, after negotiations with Colorow and Captain Jack, the troops crossed the reservation boundaries anyway, the Utes attacked and besieged them for six days. Meanwhile, other Utes attacked the agency and massacred white workers and took their women captive.

As punishment for the massacre, the U.S. government removed the White River Utes from Colorado and resettled them on the Uintah Reservation in Utah; however, Colorow switched his allegiance to the central Colorado Uncompaghre Ute band to avoid removal. Nevertheless, by 1881, this band had been maneuvered out of Colorado too. On the day the Utes were to begin their exodus into Utah, Colorow led his warriors in a charge against U.S. troops, but they were quickly and ignominiously repulsed by a show of power.

While on the Uintah Reservation, Colorow led his band back into northern Colorado for annual fall hunts, as was provided in their 1873 agreement and never rescinded. In 1886, however, Colorado passed legislation binding all Indians to local laws when off reservations; this was interpreted as including game laws, so Colorado game wardens and a posse were waiting for Colorow's band in 1887. Shots were exchanged and a squaw camp burned with its accumulated hides. The Utes fled back toward Utah, chased by state troops and a local posse. The band was engaged in battle just before the Utah border where at least fifteen Indians were killed and a substantial amount of Indian livestock was confiscated. Troops from Fort Duchesne, Utah, eventually arrived and escorted the band home. According to tradition, it was at this battle that Colorow received the wound from which he would die a year later.

See also Captain Jack; Ouray; Ute.

Columbia: Tribe

CULTURE AREA: Plateau

LANGUAGE GROUP: Salishan

PRIMARY LOCATION: Northeastern Washington

POPULATION SIZE: 441 (1990 U.S. Census)

The so-called Columbia Indians were composed of seven bands who lived on the Columbia River and collectively called themselves Sinseloxw'i't ("big river people"). They numbered about twelve hundred at the time of contact with European Americans, and are generally considered to have included the Sinkiuse, Chelan, Methow, Sinakakaius, and Wenatchi. These hunters and gatherers had a definite annual subsistence round, regulated through marriage, trade, and availability of resources. Social control was achieved through threats of sorcery, gossip, consensus of opinion, behavioral and dietary taboos, high division of labor, and a complex mythical charter. Villages were autonomous, with chiefs, and descent was bilateral. The aboriginal population was drastically reduced by seven major epidemics; the first, in 1782-1783, was estimated to have reduced their population by one-half.

The first European Americans to spend time with the Columbia peoples were Alexander Ross of the Pacific Fur Company in 1810 and David Thompson in 1811. White incursion increased throughout the first half of the nineteenth century until it resulted in a series of wars involving Columbia peoples from 1855 to 1858. Eventually the militaristic, nontreaty Columbias were settled on the Colville Indian Reservation in 1884 under the leadership of Chief Moses after the July, 1884, "Moses Agreement." There are no full-blooded Columbias today, and those people with Columbian ancestry live mostly on the Colville Reservation.

See also Colville; Methow; Moses; Wenatchi.

Colville: Tribe

CULTURE AREA: Plateau

LANGUAGE GROUP: Salishan

PRIMARY LOCATION: Washington State

POPULATION SIZE: 7,140 (1990 U.S. Census)

The Colville, one of the largest branches of the Salishan family, lived between Kettle Falls and the Spokane River in eastern Washington. They spoke the same language as another Salishan tribe, the Okanagan. "Colville" is the name of the fort of the Hudson's Bay Company near which they lived, in villages of varying size. Because they relied on hunting and fishing—salmon was a chief staple of their diet—as well as on gathering roots and berries, they were forced to move throughout the year to find food in different seasons. This prevented the villages from growing and developing as political or social centers. The Colville do not seem to have relied on agriculture. They were skilled with horses and used them in their travels seeking food. Generally, Salishan tribes enjoyed relatively peaceful lives. They were involved in no protracted struggles with their neighbors; there seems to have been enough food to go around, so no major disputes arose over hunting territory. The American explorers Meriwether Lewis and William Clark encountered the Colville in 1806. In 1872 the Colville Reservation was established in Washington, on 2.9 million acres. Some of that land was later allotted to white settlers, and the reservation had slightly more than 1 million acres in the late twentieth century. Toward the century's close, the Colville were living very much like their non-Indian neighbors and making their living primarily by raising cattle, farming, and logging.

See also Okanagan; Salishan language family.

Comanche: Tribe

CULTURE AREA: Southwestern Plains
LANGUAGE GROUP: Shoshonean
PRIMARY LOCATION: Oklahoma
POPULATION SIZE: 11,322 (1990 U.S. Census)

The Comanche tribe arose as an offshoot of the Shoshone tribe. They call themselves the Nemena, "the real people." The name Comanche has been said to come from the Ute word *komanticia* ("an enemy," or "one who fights all the time"). The Comanches ruled much of the southwestern Plains until the middle of the nineteenth century and did "fight all the time" to maintain their ascendancy. They were also called the Paducah (or Padouca, a Sioux name) by the French and the Americans, who mistakenly thought that they were an Apache tribe that had once inhabited the region. The Comanche lands once made up much of modern Texas, New Mexico, Oklahoma, Kansas, and Colorado. Today, most Comanches live on Oklahoma reservation lands.

Tribal History. Tribal legends suggest that the Comanches and the Shoshones split into separate tribes because of disagreements about the fair division of game or in the aftermath of a disastrous disease epidemic. The pre-1700 tribal split led the Comanches into the southwestern Plains and kept the Shoshones in the Wyoming and Montana mountains. The Comanches soon controlled 24,000 square miles and defeated all those who contested their control. This success was attributable to their being one of the first tribes who had horses and to their superb military horsemanship.

The Kiowas and the Comanches, at first bitter enemies, became military allies in the eighteenth century. The close alliance continued until the pacification of the Plains tribes placed them all on reservations. The main enemies of the Comanches were the Apaches, the Navajos, the Osages, the Pawnees, and the Utes. The Comanches ranged far into Texas and Mexico in raids seeking horses and other plunder.

Traditional Lifeways. The Comanche tribe was divided into thirteen autonomous bands that often cooperated in war but had no political consensus, no tribal chief, and no tribal council. Most numerous was the Penateka band (the Honey Eaters or Wasps). Other prominent Comanche bands were the Quahadi (the Antelopes), the Nokoni (the Wanderers), the Kutsueka (the Buffalo Eaters), and the Yamparika (the Yamp, or potato, Eaters). The Comanche tribal organization was so loose that any warrior could enter or leave a band at will. In battle, a war chief was in charge of all of a band's warriors. In time of peace, however, he had no power, and the tribespeople were autonomous, although they often listened to the advice of peace chiefs and of a council of elders.

Comanche men did not often marry until they were well-established warriors (usually at about age twenty-five). They were polygamous, especially as to marrying women who were the sisters or the widows of their brothers. Men could marry as many women as they were able to support, although most had only one wife. Each wife was given a separate dwelling, wherever polygamy occurred, but extended families shared most homemaking activities. Divorce was simple and favored the Comanche man. Female adultery was punished by beatings or nose-clipping. Children were loved and doted upon by all Comanches.

The Comanche religion is not thoroughly documented. Their main deities were a Creator (the Great Spirit), the Sun, the Earth, and the Moon. Comanches revered the boisterous trickster spirit Coyote; hence, they did not eat coyotes or dogs. The young Comanche men, like those of most Plains tribes, went on vision quests to achieve their adult names and to obtain their medicine power. It was believed by the Comanches that all "the real people" who died went on to an afterlife unless they had been scalped, died in the dark, or had been strangled.

Funerals included dressing the deceased in the finest clothing they owned, painting their faces, and interring them in caves or in shallow graves along with their finest possessions. Before 1850, a warrior's favorite wife was often killed to accompany him to the afterlife. During mourning, both family and friends gashed clothing and bodies, burned the dwellings of the deceased, and destroyed horses and other wealth in their honor. Afterward, the names of the deceased were never again mentioned by any tribe member.

Comanche bands had men's secret societies, many ritual dances, and many other medicine ceremonies. They were so secretive about these ceremonies, however, that very little is known about Comanche ritual, compared with those of many other tribes. The Sun Dance—very important to most other Plains Indian tribes—was not celebrated by the Comanches until the late nineteenth century.

Comanches lived in well-designed, finely decorated buffalo-hide tipis, made by women, and moved when new campgrounds were sought (sometimes because of the need for fresh forage for their horse herds). The buffalo provided most Comanche needs, including food. Comanches were nomad hunter-gatherers who neither farmed nor fished. Their plant foods, such as potatoes, nuts, and various fruits, were all

Comanche tribal chairman James Cox (left) signing a peace treaty with Ute leaders in July, 1977, that signified the ending of two hundred years of intertribal disputes. (AP/Wide World Photos)

gathered by women's foraging expeditions. In contrast, the Comanches were expert horse breeders, fine horse trainers, and excellent primitive veterinarians. Their horse herds were tremendous and contained exceptionally fine animals.

Comanche men's personal adornment included painting their faces and the heads and tails of their mounts before battle. Buffalo-hide shirts, leggings, and boots, as well as very elaborate headdresses, were also worn. Long hair was desired by all Comanche men, and they acquired it both via natural hair growth and interwoven horse hair. Prior to the use of firearms, Comanche weapons were buffalo-hide battle shields so strong that arrows and bullets did not easily pierce them, long war lances, heavy war clubs, and bows and arrows. The chief decorations of all Comanche weapons were feathers, bear teeth, and scalps of enemies. War was the main occupation of Comanche men, providing them with sport, horses, and other plunder. The Comanches were viewed as exceptionally fierce warriors.

Comanche cooking consisted mostly of the roasting of meat on sticks over open fires and of boiling it, with other foods, in skin pouches into which hot stones were dropped. Comanche eating utensils were very simple. Their weapons and shields, on the other hand, were very well-crafted and attractively adorned. Comanche bows, arrows, and lances were most often made of the very tough wood called bois d'arc (Osage orange) by the French explorers of North America.

Movement to Reservations. In the 1850's, the Penatekas were the first Comanche group to move to a reservation. After the Medicine Lodge Treaty and the Battle of the Washita, in the 1860's, most Comanche bands moved onto reservations. Comanche resistance ended in 1875, when Quanah Parker and his Quahadi band, the last Comanche warrior holdouts, surrendered. Slowly changing their ways but retaining their heritage, the Comanches have acclimatized themselves to mainstream American life. The 1930's passage of the Oklahoma Indian Welfare Act remedied some tribal grievances, and a Kiowa-Comanche-Apache Business Committee aimed at improving the lot of the three tribes. In the 1960's the Comanche Business Council began to seek to improve Comanche life. Today's Comanches have opened businesses, entered the general workforce and many professions, and are well represented in the American armed forces. At the same time they continue to fight to keep tribal traditions alive both in their homes and in the schools where their children are taught. —*Sanford S. Singer*

See also Buffalo Hump; Horses; Isatai; Parker, Quanah; Plains; Ten Bears.

BIBLIOGRAPHY

American Indian Publishers. *Dictionary of Indian Tribes of the Americas*. Newport Beach, Calif.: Author, 1980.

Hagan, William T. *United States-Comanche Relations: The Reservation Years*. New Haven, Conn.: Yale University Press, 1976.

Richardson, Rupert N. *The Comanche Barrier to South Plains Settlement.* Glendale, Calif.: Arthur H. Clark, 1933.

Wallace, Ernest, and E. Adamson Hoebel. *The Comanches: Lords of the South Plains.* Norman: University of Oklahoma Press, 1952.

Comcomly (c. 1765, Northwest Coast, U.S.—1830, Northwest Coast, U.S.): Tribal leader

TRIBAL AFFILIATION: Chinook

SIGNIFICANCE: Comcomly aided white exploration of the Northwest Coast

A Chinook leader, Comcomly assisted Meriwether Lewis and William Clark as they traveled to the mouth of the Columbia River in 1805. In 1811, he aided John Jacob Astor's fur traders, who had been shipwrecked while traveling on the *Tonquin.* The following year, he welcomed Astor's minions, the Overland Astorians, who established the Astoria trading post at the mouth of the Astoria River. To secure relations with the traders, he offered his daughter in marriage to Duncan M'Dougal, leader of the Astorians' expedition.

During the War of 1812, Comcomly extended military support to the Americans. The following year, when the Americans abandoned their post, he aided the British who moved into the region.

An extraordinarily wealthy man, Comcomly relished extravagant displays. During visits to Vancouver, he was accompanied by three hundred slaves, who carpeted his path from ship to town with beaver and otter furs.

After his death from smallpox in 1830, his skull was stolen by a white trader, who then sold it in Edinburgh.

See also Chinook.

Comox: Tribe

CULTURE AREA: Northwest Coast

LANGUAGE GROUP: Central Salish

PRIMARY LOCATION: South of Johnstone Strait and west of Discovery Portage, British Columbia and Washington

POPULATION SIZE: 800 in Canada (Statistics Canada, based on 1991 census)

Prior to European American contact, the Comox were divided into the Island and Mainland groups, living in split-cedar gable-roofed houses, located for exploiting the Strait of Georgia and numerous streams of their territory. Their main source of food was fishing, supplemented by the hunting of deer, black and grizzly bear, mountain sheep, and goats. Smaller animals were caught with traps and snares. Most bird species were hunted, primarily for feathers and plumage. Women gathered seeds, berries, nuts, tubers, roots, and cambium.

By 1792, the British and Spanish had entered the Strait of Georgia, trading metal tools and beads for food. Maritime fur trade was active until the demise of the sea otter. Epidemics reduced native populations and brought some demographic shifting. Roman Catholics opened missions in the 1860's, denouncing the Winter Dance, potlatching, and other of the traditional ways, forcing people into a wage economy. Today

the descendants of the Comox live primarily in British Columbia. There are three groups, the Homalco, Klahoose, and Sliammon.

Conquering Bear (?—Aug. 19, 1854, Wyo.): Tribal chief

ALSO KNOWN AS: Mahtoiowa, Whirling Bear

TRIBAL AFFILIATION: Brule Sioux

SIGNIFICANCE: Conquering Bear was killed while attempting to accommodate whites; his death precipitated war in the northern Plains

Conquering Bear's band of Sioux lived along the North Platte River, which was part of the Oregon Trail. When a party of Mormons passed through the region in August, 1854, a cow wandered onto Conquering Bear's land. Its Mormon owner fled to nearby Fort Laramie, reporting that Indians had stolen his livestock. Meantime, High Forehead, a visiting Miniconjou Sioux, slaughtered the cow. Conquering Bear, who in 1851 had signed the Treaty of Fort Laramie pledging peace along the Oregon Trail, traveled to the fort offering restitution. The fort commander, however, dispatched a newly commissioned and eager West Point lieutenant, John Grattan, to arrest High Forehead.

Even after cavalrymen murdered one of his men, Conquering Bear restrained his warriors. Grattan, however, ordered his men to attack, and Conquering Bear was killed. Conquering Bear's warriors retaliated, killing all but one of Grattan's detachment. Subsequently, on September 3, 1855, General William S. Harney and his forces attacked a Sioux camp. Thus began the wars of the northern Plains.

See also Bozeman Trail wars; Crazy Snake; Spotted Tail.

Coos: Tribe

CULTURE AREA: Northwest Coast

LANGUAGE GROUP: Coos

PRIMARY LOCATION: Coos Bay, Oregon

POPULATION SIZE: 216 (1990 U.S. Census)

The Coos tribe is a small estuarine community living in the Coos Bay area of southwestern Oregon. The words "Coos," "Coosan," and "Kusan" are of uncertain origins but might have originated with a word in their native tongue, Kusan, described as a dialect of the Macro-Penutian language spoken by several tribes of possible Yakonan stock in southern Oregon and northern California.

The Kusan culture, made up primarily of the Miluk and Hanis communities, lived exclusively around Coos Bay, Oregon, and upriver along its tributaries. They were part of a family of peoples composed of four related groups who shared territories covering parts of present-day Coos County. The name the people use for themselves, even today, is Miluk-Hanis. The Coos, Kusan, or Coosan peoples, as they are collectively known, were actually four communities who spoke related dialects of a source tongue and who shared an estuarine environment.

Western Coos County, from Ten Mile Lake to the north to the south bank of the Coquille River, and from two miles offshore inland to the crest of the Coast Range Mountains, was home to the Kusan peoples. The Melukitz lived on the far south and west sides of Coos Bay. The Naseemi lived on the banks of the Coquille River to the south. The Miluk occupied the north shore of the Coquille and ranged up the headlands of Cape Arago from Coos Head to the place on the bay now known as Tar Heel Point. The Hanis resided on the south side of the bay and up the estuary, from just south of the town of Empire to the downtown area of present-day North Bend.

These four branches of the Kusan family lived peaceably together in an unbelievably rich ecosystem. As a unit they are often grouped with several other cultural units to the north, usually categorized by language affiliation or genetic stock, such as their Yakonan-speaking ancestors, who remain as the Alsea, Kuitish, Siuslaw, Umpqua, and Yaquina. To the south are the distantly related language groups and cultures of the Klamath Basin Culture Area. The Kusan say they are not necessarily related to the riverine peoples to the north and south.

Indirect contacts with whites came in 1828. It is estimated that there were about two thousand people living around Coos Bay at that time. White settlement of the bay area commenced in the late 1840's. The Kusans did not fight; they tried to make treaties but were rapidly overwhelmed.

They joined with the Lower Umpqua and the Siuslaw to form the Confederated Tribes of the Coos, Lower Umpqua, and Siuslaw Indians in 1855. About that time they were forced to move to a reservation on the Siletz River. They did not return for many years to their homeland, which was taken over by American settlers during their absence. The confederation endures today and is recognized as an Indian nation by the United States government.

See also Coos language; Northwest Coast; Siuslaw; Umpqua; Yakonan language family.

Coos language

Culture area: Northwest Coast
Tribes affected: Kusan peoples
The Coos language is spoken by the Coosan, or Kusan, peoples, who traditionally occupied the lands around Coos Bay, on the southwestern Oregon coast. Remnants of the original tribe still live in the area and have a small reserve in Empire, Oregon. The language of the Kusan is commonly classified as a part of the Macro-Penutian language phylum, spoken by a number of tribes of possibly related Yakonan stock in the Columbia River basin, along the Oregon coast, in Northern California, and elsewhere to the south.

The Kusan peoples consist of four bands which are known to have spoken distinct yet related dialects. On the other hand many Coos tribal citizens believe themselves and their language to be unrelated to, or only distantly related to, the languages of their immediate or distant neighbors. Eastward and inland, the speakers of Athapaskan and Siouan languages dominated. North of the Columbia River, speakers of the Salish language were in the majority. Regional trade languages such as Chinook jargon also developed across the Columbia Plateau in response to the need for commerce between diverse groups of unrelated stock. At the time of first contact with whites in the early 1800's, Coos informants used Chinook jargon to communicate with the explorers.

Isolates of Coos were spoken by the Melukitz, the Naseemi, the Miluk, and the Hanis bands of the Kusan peoples. Other isolates of the Macro-Penutian language family are thought by scholars to have been spoken by the Nez Perce, Kuitish, Alsea, Siuslaw, Umpqua, and Yaquina to the north of Coos territory and by the Klamath, Modoc, Maidu, Mayas and others far to the south. Some scholars have argued that there is evidence to support the theory that speakers of these languages may have migrated to the Pacific Northwest from Central America or southern Mexico; perhaps, it has been suggested, they originally came to the Americas from the South Pacific. The dominant theory, however, is still that they migrated across the Bering land bridge. There is evidence to suggest that Macro-Penutian speakers migrated into the coastal areas and river basins from the north. Tribal stories suggest that the peoples who spoke the Coos language were created in, and have always resided in, the territories they occupy today. Thus the origins of the Coos language are uncertain.

The language of the Coos Bay peoples gives evidence of its origins in the sea. It is rich in myths, legends, and stories reflective of the rich maritime, estuarine, and riverine environments they occupied. Today it is, for the most part, lost. The last original speakers died out in the 1920's. The Kusan language died with the last native speaker, Martha Johnson, in 1972.

What remains today was recorded and remarked upon by Leo J. Fractenberg, and later by Melville Jacobs, around the time the last of the Coos speakers and informants were dying out. They made a number of recordings of the language and wrote about their findings in linguistic and textual analyses still regarded by scholars as definitive.

See also Coos; Northwest Coast; Siuslaw; Umpqua; Yakonan language family.

Copalis: Tribe

Culture area: Northwest Coast
Language group: Salishan
Primary location: Grays Harbor, Washington
Traditionally the Copalis, a relatively small group, lived in an area nearly surrounded by water. Division of labor was based on age, sex, status, and ability. The importance of fish and marine products was reflected in various rituals, technology, status, and the First Salmon Ceremony. Inland areas were hunted for bear, deer, and elk; smaller animals were taken by traps and snares for food, skin, and by-products. Rights of usufruct applied to whaling and clamming beaches, berry patches, barnacle stacks, and timber areas. Low tides provided a variety of foods. Numerous food plants were utilized, particularly camas.

Though earlier naval expeditions had probably visited the Copalis, first documentation was by Meriwether Lewis and

William Clark in the years 1805-1806, who estimated the population to be two hundred, in a total of ten dwellings. By 1811, fur trappers and traders were in the area, but the opening of Fort Vancouver in 1825 by Hudson's Bay Company brought considerable socioeconomic change—including a major epidemic of malaria. Missionaries, loggers, and settlers in the Quinault and Lower Chalis area sustained deculturation.

See also Quinault.

Copan: Archaeological site
DATE: 160-822
LOCATION: Western Honduras
CULTURE AFFECTED: Maya

Copan was the second largest Mayan city of the Classic period (c. 120-800 C.E.). Located in Western Honduras in the Copan River valley, near the Guatemalan border, Copan was on the southeastern margin of the Mayan world. The city covered 75 acres (30 hectares) and housed twenty thousand people at its height. The area in which Copan is found has been continuously inhabited since around 1100 B.C.E., originally by foraging cultures and after 900 B.C.E. by farming cultures. Dates contained on monuments at the site fix the founding of the city as December 18, 159 C.E. The city was dominated by what is called the Acropolis, an artificial hill on which several temples, ball courts, and other structures were laid out on a north-south axis, a typical plan for Mayan cities. Most of the major structures seen today were built either in the reign of the king known as Smoke-Imix-God K (628-695 C.E.) or his successor, Eighteen-Rabbit (695-738); Mayan kings were typically named for the day on the Mayan calendar on which they were born.

The art and architecture of Copan are unusual among Mayan cities. While most Mayan stonework was done in limestone, which allows for flat, sunken relief sculpture, artists at Copan worked with a volcanic tuff called trachyte, a greenish, fine-grained stone which is relatively soft when first quarried but which hardens on exposure to air. This allowed for three-dimensional sculptures, especially evident in the many stelae, or tree stones, found at the site. Copan is also notable for the Temple of the Hieroglyphic Stairs, built by the king Smoke-Shell, who reigned from 749 to approximately 760. This temple contains sixty-three steps covered with more than two thousand hieroglyphic symbols; it is the longest pre-Columbian text known in the New World. These glyphs record the accessions and deaths of Copan's rulers. The most accurate solar calendar produced by the Mayas is also found at Copan, dating from about 700.

Copan was abandoned in the early ninth century. Several factors are thought to have contributed to the demise of the city, including overpopulation, the appropriation of the richest cropland for building sites, and the deforestation of the hillsides surrounding the city, with the accompanying effects of erosion. There is also evidence of increased rivalry and tension between the king and the lesser nobility toward the end of the city's history. The land surrounding Copan was so ravaged by overfarming and deforestation that only in the twentieth century has the area been extensively resettled.

Copan was discovered by Spanish explorers in the early sixteenth century; the Spaniard Diego Garcia de Palacios wrote about Copan in 1576. The site was reconstructed between 1936 and 1950 by a group jointly sponsored by the government of Honduras and the Carnegie Institute of Washington, D.C.

See also Chichén Itzá; Maya; Palenque; Tikal; Uxmal; Yaxchilan.

Copway, George (c. 1818, near the mouth of the Trent River, Ontario, Canada—c. 1863, near Pontiac, Mich.): Writer
ALSO KNOWN AS: Kahgegwagebow (Stands Fast)
TRIBAL AFFILIATION: Ojibwa
SIGNIFICANCE: Copway published a number of books on Ojibwa topics

George Copway spent his early years in a traditional Ojibwa environment until 1827, when his parents converted to Christianity. Copway attended Ebenezer Manual School in Jacksonville, Illinois, in 1838 and shortly thereafter married Elizabeth Howell. In the 1840's he served as a Methodist missionary to Ojibwas in Wisconsin and Minnesota. His first book was an autobiography, *The Life, History, and Travels of Kah-ge-ga-gah-bowh* (1847), later revised and reissued as *The Life, Letters and Speeches of Kah-ge-ga-gah-bowh, or G. Copway* (1850).

In 1850-1851, Copway represented Christian Indians at a world peace congress in Germany. He subsequently published a book based on his travels, *Running Sketches of Men and Places, in England, France, Germany, Belgium, and Scotland* (1851). For a few months in 1851, Copway also published a newspaper, *Copway's American Indian*. Copway's last book was a history of the Ojibwa; it was first published as *The Traditional History and Characteristic Sketches of the Ojibway Nation* (1850) and was later reissued as *Indian Life and Indian History, by an Indian Author* (1858). Copway was baptized Joseph-Antoine in the Catholic church on January 17, 1869, and died a few days later.

See also Journalism; Ojibwa.

Corn

TRIBES AFFECTED: Mesoamerican, Northeast, Plains, Southeast, and Southwest tribes
SIGNIFICANCE: North American corn was first domesticated in Mexico, and by the seventeenth century it was a staple across much of the North American continent

Corn, or maize (*Zea mays*), is currently grown worldwide, but the crop is indigenous to the Western Hemisphere. Only after European contact was maize propagated beyond the American continents. When the Europeans arrived in the Americas, domesticated maize was cultivated from the Canadian Great Lakes region to Argentina. Several varieties of corn were grown in different ecological zones in North and South America, ranging from sea level to high in the Andes and other mountains.

European explorers described maize agriculture among the Aztecs, the Mayas, and the Incas of Latin America and among North America Indians of the Southwest, the Plains, the Southeast, and the Northeast. Indeed, at different times during the early contact period, the survival of European settlers depended on corn and other foods provided by the indigenous peoples of these regions. In many of these corn-growing areas, the new settlers recorded aboriginal oral traditions which emphasized the cultural importance of corn. Such was the case among the Mayas of Central America and the Iroquois of upstate New York.

Archaeological Information. Studies concerning the prehistoric origin, domestication, and use of corn rely upon archaeological investigations. Perhaps as a result of the contact-period accounts of the primacy of corn agriculture, archaeologists of the early 1900's often overemphasized the importance of corn to prehistoric peoples. Generally, it was suggested that prehistoric cultures that possessed traits such as settled villages or impressive architecture (which indicated complicated social organization) depended for their subsistence primarily upon corn agriculture. By the 1990's it was recognized that corn was one of several species that were important for New World agriculturalists and that, in addition, not all complex societies depended on corn for their subsistence. It was also formerly believed that maize domestication was a rapid process which had immediate cultural impact. It is now apparent that the process of maize domestication took place over hundreds of years. Maize probably first served merely to supplement local wild plant foods and only later became an important resource. Gradual genetic changes among the maize plants accompanied these slow cultural adaptations. For example, corn cobs became larger, and the number and size of the kernels increased. These and other changes marked the process of domestication. Some maize cobs, kernels, and other remains can be definitely identified as either "wild" or "domesticated," whereas other plant remains fit somewhere on a continuum in between.

General theories concerning the speed of the development of New World agriculture are based on specific archaeological information concerning ancient subsistence. At some archaeological sites, corn agriculture is well documented by finds of maize plant remains, while at other locations lacking botanical data, researchers may rely on indirect evidence, such as the presence of agricultural implements. For example, ancient use of hoes, milling stones, and storage facilities may indicate a dependence on corn, but archaeologists exercise caution in their inferences, since these tools were also associated with other crops. For this reason, the strongest demonstration of ancient maize agriculture is the discovery of pieces of corn plants, such as stems, leaves, kernels, and cobs. Cobs often provide additional information (such as the corn variety), which contributes to data concerning its origin, domestication, growth, and use. Smaller plant remains, such as pollen or phytoliths (tiny silica bodies within the plant) can also provide evidence for the presence of corn agriculture.

Botanical remains are best preserved under stable environmental conditions which discourage rotting, such as dry heat, cold, or water inundation. They are also more likely to be preserved when burned to a carbonized state. For these reasons, many plant remains left at sites by past peoples are not preserved in the archaeological record. In addition, the preservation of botanical remains does not ensure that they will be carefully and scientifically excavated by professional archaeologists. Unfortunately, site looting and destruction is a major problem throughout North and Central America.

Corn Domestication. Archaeological sites that provide important evidence concerning the earliest domestication of corn have been found in the Tehuacán Valley, Puebla, Mexico. The Tehuacán archaeological-botanical project was directed by Richard S. MacNeish, who devoted decades to the search for evidence of early corn domestication. MacNeish excavated the dry caves in the Tehuacán Valley because they would have provided shelter for ancient habitation, and he anticipated good preservation of any botanical remains. The Tehuacán sites date from approximately eleven thousand years ago to the time of the Spanish conquest, and maize pollen and wild maize cobs were excavated from levels dated to about 7000-5000 B.C.E. Cultivated maize was dated to about 5000-3500 B.C.E. This early evidence of corn agriculture is also helpful for determining the ancestral grasses of *Zea mays*. Botanists have argued that corn developed from a wild grass called teosinte, although this has not been definitively demonstrated.

In the 1980's, results from bone chemistry analyses contributed to the archaeological understanding of the Tehuacán Valley. Stable carbon isotope tests of Tehuacán human skeletal remains demonstrated that a chemically distinct group of plants, which included maize, composed 90 percent of the ancient diet from 4500 B.C.E. onward.

Based on the available evidence, it seems that North American maize originated in central Mexico. It may have appeared in the southwestern United States by approximately three thousand years ago. The seasonally occupied sites of the corn-growing Chochise may date to approximately 1200 B.C.E. in southern New Mexico. These people obtained corn (the Chapalote variety of *Zea mays*) and their knowledge of corn agriculture from people in northern Mexico. The Southwest cultures farmed in harsh, unpredictable climatic conditions with the use of highly developed agricultural techniques, ranging from planting strategies to the use of irrigation.

A second variety of corn (Maiz de Ocho, also known as New England flint corn) was introduced later into the Southwest. The earliest use of Maiz de Ocho in this region may date to 1000 B.C.E., but this date is controversial. Generally accepted Maiz de Ocho dates are considerably later. This corn variety was more productive than the earlier Chapalote, and this variety diffused eastward across the continent. Maize agriculture on the Plains dates to approximately 800-900 C.E., while for the Southeast there are a few dates as early as

A Hopi girl preparing corn meal (1909 photograph). (Library of Congress)

200 C.E. Agriculture did not provide a substantial contribution to the Southeast diet until 800-1000 and, in some areas, such as the Lower Mississippi, not until as late as 1200. By this time, corn was being grown in regions as diverse as southeast Colorado and upstate New York. Indeed, by 1300, maize agriculture was vital to the Iroquoian economy.

Despite its utility, successful corn agriculture has distinct requirements. Generally, corn plants need adequate moisture and approximately 120 frost-free days to mature. A healthy crop also requires some weeding and care of the developing plants. Maize growing rapidly exhausts the soil's nitrogen stores, and these must be replenished through planting other crops (such as beans, which contribute nitrogen), using fertilizers, or allowing the soil to rest fallow. Corn lacks an amino acid (lysine), essential for humans, and a diet based only on corn is inadequate. Many groups ate beans as well, which provided the missing lysine and resulted in a balanced, healthy diet. —*Susan J. Wurtzburg*

See also Agriculture; Beans; Corn Woman; Food preparation and cooking; Green Corn Dance; Squash; Subsistence.

BIBLIOGRAPHY

Cohen, Mark N., and George J. Armelagos, eds. *Paleopathology at the Origins of Agriculture*. New York: Academic Press, 1984.

Creel, Darrell, and Austin Long. "Radiocarbon Dating of Corn." *American Antiquity* 51, no. 4 (1986): 826-837.

Ford, Richard I., ed. *Prehistoric Food Production in North America*. Anthropological Papers 75. Ann Arbor: Museum of Anthropology, University of Michigan, 1985.

Fritz, Gayle J. "Multiple Pathways to Farming in Precontact Eastern North-America." *Journal of World Prehistory* 4, no. 4 (December, 1990): 387-435.

MacNeish, Richard S. "A Summary of the Subsistence." In *Prehistory of the Tehuacan Valley*, vol. 1, edited by Douglas S. Byers. Austin: University of Texas Press, 1967.

Watson, Patty Jo, and Mary C. Kennedy. "The Development of Horticulture in the Eastern Woodlands of North America: Women's Role." In *Engendering Archaeology: Women and Prehistory*, edited by Joan M. Gero and Margaret W. Conkey. Oxford, England: Basil Blackwell, 1991.

Yarnell, Richard A., and M. Jean Black. "Temporal Trends Indicated by a Survey of Archaic and Woodland Plant Food Remains from Southeastern North America." *Southeastern Archaeology* 4, no. 2 (1985): 93-106.

Corn Woman

TRIBES AFFECTED: Apache, Cherokee, Chickasaw, Chippewa, Choctaw, Creek, Iroquois Confederacy, Navajo, Pueblo, Seminole

SIGNIFICANCE: Corn Woman is important in terms of cosmology and religious practices in tribal cultures where maize is the key food source (Northeast, Southeast, Southwest)

The domestication of corn had moved north from Mexico to the Pueblo tribes of present-day New Mexico by 3500 B.C.E. and almost immediately became the preferred food plant in the region, superseding various inferior domesticated plants. Most tribes believed that corn was a gift from the gods, and this transmission was often recounted in folktale and song.

Therefore, it was logical that, especially in Keres (a number of the Pueblo bands, including the Acoma Pueblo and Laguna Pueblo, speak Keresan dialects) cosmogony, Corn Woman should serve as a sort of mother goddess—source of life and a staple of their diet.

The Keres people believed that in the time immemorial, Ts'its'tsi'nako (Thought-Woman, or Creating-Through-Thinking Woman) chanted into life Naotsete and Uretsete, her sister goddesses. In this matrilineal cosmogony, Naotsete served as the cacique, or internal chief, and Uretsete served as the hotchin, the war chief or outside chief. Naotsete and Uretsete carried baskets from which came all creatures, plants, and elements of the earth. Uretsete gave birth to twin boys, one of whom married Naotsete, and their issue became the Pueblo race. As time progressed, Uretsete became known as Corn Woman (*Iyatiku*), Mother Corn Woman (*Naiya Iyatiku*), or Earth Woman. Corn Woman is considered to be the mother of all people, gods, and animals. Some folk myths place Mother Corn Woman as a guardian at the gate of the spirit world.

See also Allen, Paula Gunn; Corn; Mother Earth.

Cornplanter (between 1732 and 1740, Conewaugus, N.Y.—Feb. 18, 1836, Cornplantertown, Pa.): War chief

ALSO KNOWN AS: Kayehtwanken (By What One Plants), John Abeel, John O'Bail

TRIBAL AFFILIATION: Seneca

SIGNIFICANCE: Cornplanter achieved prominence as an Iroquois war chief fighting for the British in the American Revolution; at subsequent treaty conferences he emphasized the need for peaceful coexistence between Indians and the United States

Cornplanter, the son of a Seneca woman and a Dutch trader, John Abeel (or O'Bail), was born at Conewaugus on the Genesee River sometime between 1732 and 1740. Little is known of his childhood except for his recollections of being teased because of his light skin.

Along with Red Jacket, he argued for neutrality in the American Revolution, but when his view did not prevail, he joined the British, participating in the Wyoming, Cherry Valley, and Newtown campaigns (1777-1778). During the attack on Canajoharie (1780), he met his father and refused to take him prisoner.

Emerging from the Revolution as a major Seneca war chief, he decided the wisest course for the Senecas was to establish peaceful coexistence with the United States. He was present at the treaty negotiations at Fort Stanwix (1784) and Fort Harmar (1789), which resulted in the loss of Seneca lands to the Americans. He later complained to U.S. officials about the tactics used to exact Seneca concessions. Despite strong opposition from Red Jacket's more conservative faction, he maintained this pro-U.S. policy and mediated with other Indian nations to promote friendship with the Americans. His assis-

Cornplanter became a major Seneca leader after the American Revolution, advising peace with whites. (Library of Congress)

tance at the Treaty of Fort Harmar allowed Pennsylvania to acquire the Erie Triangle, and he was given fifteen hundred acres in gratitude. He visited Philadelphia in 1789 to voice complaints before the Pennsylvania Assembly about white incursions on Indian land and remained to meet President George Washington. Cornplanter requested technical assistance for his people, and Washington recommended the Quakers, who established a model farm and school for the Senecas. Thus began an association that would last two centuries.

The land promised by Pennsylvania was patented to Cornplanter in 1796, and many Senecas in the Allegany region lived on his grant pending settlement of reservation boundaries in New York. Among those with him was his half-brother, the prophet Handsome Lake, whose visions were recorded by resident Quakers.

The land was deeded to Cornplanter as an individual and therefore lacked reservation status. When agents tried to collect taxes, he appealed to Pennsylvania, and in 1822 the land was declared tax exempt as long as it was held by Cornplanter or his descendants. Following his death in 1836, the land was partitioned among his heirs. In 1871, Pennsylvania erected the first monument to an Indian in the U.S. in recognition of his friendship and aid.

Cornplanter's descendants continued to live on the land grant until the early 1960's, when most of it was flooded by the backwaters of Kinzua Dam. The descendants organized to fight the dam but lost because of a lack of federal protection.

Their association continued into the 1990's, with descendants gathering from throughout the United States for an annual celebration of their Cornplanter heritage.

See also Brant, Joseph; Fort Stanwix, Treaty of; Handsome Lake; Red Jacket; Seneca.

Cornstalk (c. 1720, western Pa.—Nov. 10, 1777, Point Pleasant, W.Va.): War chief

ALSO KNOWN AS: Wynepuechsika

TRIBAL AFFILIATION: Shawnee

SIGNIFICANCE: Cornstalk opposed white settlers in the Ohio Valley and intermittently warred against them from the 1750's to his death in 1777

Cornstalk was born about 1720 in western Pennsylvania. By the 1750's, he was a Shawnee war chief leading raids against the white settlements being established in Shawnee territory. His most significant battle was in October, 1774, at Point Pleasant, on the south bank of the Ohio River. Cornstalk led an attack to stop a planned invasion of Shawnee territory by the Virginia militia. Although Cornstalk was defeated, he was able to make a peace treaty with the British governor of Virginia.

When the American Revolution began in 1775, Cornstalk said he desired Shawnee neutrality, but this was only a diversionary tactic. In 1776, he attempted to form an Indian alliance to drive all whites back across the Appalachians. Despite eloquent appeals, he was unsuccessful, and neutrality again became his policy. In November, 1777, Cornstalk and his son went to Fort Randolph at Point Pleasant to discuss the rapidly worsening relations between Shawnees and whites. Cornstalk and his son were taken hostage. On November 10, they were murdered by a band of militia men.

See also Lord Dunmore's War; Shawnee; Tecumseh; Tecumseh's Rebellion; Tippecanoe, Battle of.

Costanoan: Tribe

CULTURE AREA: California

LANGUAGE GROUP: Costanoan

PRIMARY LOCATION: San Francisco Bay to Monterey Bay, California

POPULATION SIZE: 1,023 (1990 U.S. Census)

Historically, the Costanoan lived in approximately fifty politically autonomous tribelets or nations, each with a permanent village. Their culture was based on patrilineal clans that were divided into bear and deer moieties. Acorns were the most important plant food, but numerous seeds, berries, and tubers were collected by season, and animals were trapped and hunted. Waterfowl and numerous bird species were hunted for food and feathers. Gathered insects were an important source of protein.

First European American contact was in 1602 by the Sebastián Vizcaino expedition. Groups later explored Costanoan territory between 1769 and 1776. The mission period, 1770-1835, brought many devastating changes—particularly a population decline from disease and a diminishing birth rate. The missions discouraged traditional social and religious rituals. Later, secularization of the missions and the proliferation of settlers further disrupted the Costanoan culture, which by 1935 brought the language to extinction. By 1970, Costanoan descendants had united into a corporate unity, known as the Ohlone Indian Tribe. These people have never been compensated for the loss of their lands during the Gold Rush.

See also Acorns; California.

Cotton

Tribes affected: Pima and tribes of Mexico, Central America, South America

Significance: Cotton, a South American domesticate, spread to the American Southwest and was cultivated by the historic Pima for fiber and food

Cotton (*Gossypium herbaceum*) has a highly complex domestication history with independent domestications in both Africa and South America. All cotton in pre-Columbian America descended from that domesticated in coastal Peru sometime before 4,000 B.C.E. Cotton spread northward through Central America and Mexico, finally entering North America in the Southwest. People of the Hohokam archaeological tradition, centered in the Sonora Desert of Arizona and adjacent Mexico, were the first North Americans to use cotton, probably around 100 C.E. They used the fiber for spinning thread from which clothing, bags, and other items were woven; they also used the seed for extracting its nutritious oil. Cotton requires a considerable amount of water for successful growing, and its cultivation probably was a spur to the development of the sophisticated irrigation developed by the Hohokam. The Pima, the Sonoran Desert tribe widely believed descended from the Hohokam, were growing irrigated cotton when the Spanish first encountered them in the seventeenth century.

See also Food preparation and cooking; Hohokam; Pima; Weaving.

Council of Energy Resource Tribes (CERT)

Date: Established 1975

Tribes affected: Pantribal

Significance: CERT, founded by a group of tribal leaders, provides tribes with advice on developing and marketing the mineral and energy resources on their lands in ways that will maximize profit for, and control by, the tribes themselves

The Council of Energy Resource Tribes (CERT), with offices in Denver, Colorado, was organized in 1975 to gain an understanding of the natural resources controlled by the Native American tribes within the United States. Peter MacDonald, then chairperson of the Navajo Nation, was the first elected chair of the organization. It initially set out to inventory the natural resources of the various tribes in the western United States. It found that the tribes controlled one-third of the energy sources in coal and uranium as well as large supplies of petroleum, natural gas, and other essential resources. The next step was to integrate all aspects of reservation development.

The Council of Energy Resource Tribes undertook a series of studies that indicated that the U.S. Bureau of Indian Affairs (BIA) had based its development efforts on irrelevant and inaccurate assumptions. CERT indicated that it was imperative that American Indian tribes work harder to provide employment. Tribes and CERT had to leverage funds and services to obtain the financial resources necessary for balanced development. CERT recognized the desire to advance on the part of the tribes, whereas the BIA could not recognize this in tribal actions. CERT also saw that prosperity and the Indian ways of doing things were not mutually exclusive.

See also Resources.

Councils, tribal

Tribes affected: Pantribal

Significance: Tribal councils, established by the U.S. government as reservation-based decision-making bodies representing tribal members, were opposed by many native people

At one time each native tribe ruled with a form of government unique to its culture but usually based on a consensus process. As the tribes were conquered, they were deprived of their sovereignty and subjected to the rule of the U.S. government through the agents of the Bureau of Indian Affairs (BIA). In 1871, Congress ended treaty-making with the tribes, and the relationship of the government to the tribes became one of guardian to ward.

In 1934, Congress passed the Indian Reorganization Act (IRA), which has been the subject of heated debate ever since. Under the provisions of this act, any tribe, or the people of any reservation, could organize themselves as a business corporation, adopt a constitution and bylaws, and exercise certain forms of self-government.

Because the IRA did not recognize existing traditional forms of government, such as those provided by spiritual leaders and elders, many people boycotted the process of voting in these IRA-sanctioned governments. As a result, only a minority of tribal members voted to establish the tribal councils, which are structured after European American and hierarchical models.

The matters with which these councils could deal were strictly limited, and decisions and actions were subject to the approval of the BIA. In fact, the reservation superintendent, an agent of the secretary of interior, had full control over the property and financial affairs of the tribe and could veto anything the council did. Because of this, tribal councils were often labeled puppet governments of the BIA.

Various attempts have been made by tribal members to address this situation. In 1944, tribal leaders formed a pan-Indian organization called the National Congress of American Indians (NCAI). In 1961, several hundred native activists issued a "Declaration of Indian Purpose," which called for, among other things, the government's recognition of the rights of tribes. As tribes continue to assert their sovereignty, power has moved from the BIA to the individual tribal councils, which represent the needs of the people.

See also Indian Reorganization Act; National Council of American Indians; Sovereignty.

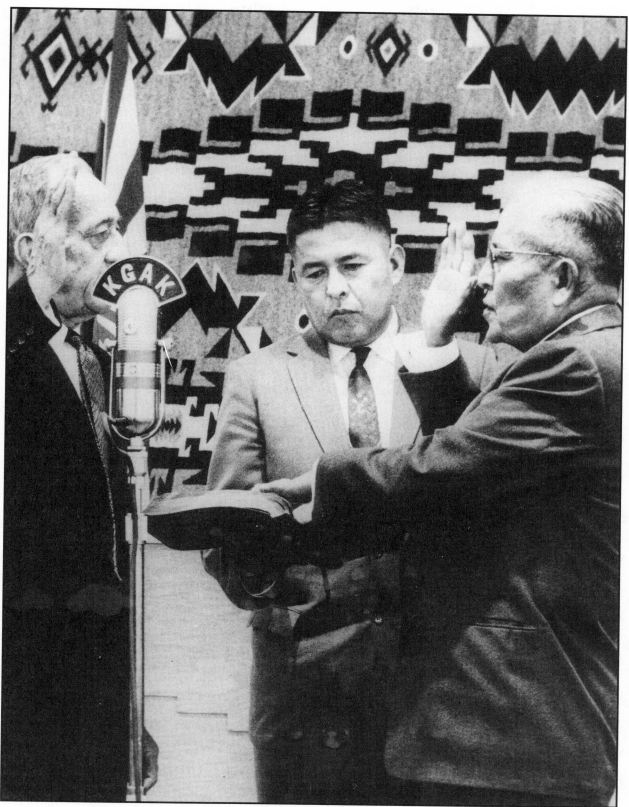

Paul Jones (right) being sworn in as chairman of the Navajo Tribal Council. (Gene Price, Museum of New Mexico)

Coup sticks and counting

Tribes affected: Primarily Plains tribes, including Arapaho, Assiniboine, Blackfoot, Cheyenne, Crow, Iowa, Kiowa, Omaha, Sioux

Significance: In warrior cultures, counting coup was a way to prove bravery and merit by touching the enemy; success was rewarded with both signs of honor and tribal status

The term "counting coup" comes from the French word *coup*, meaning "to strike a blow." In warrior cultures, bravery was the highest virtue. A way to prove bravery was to touch (count coup) the enemy, whether the enemy was living or dead. More than one warrior could count coup on the same enemy, but "first coup" had higher status than second, and second ranked higher than third. Touching could be done either with the hand or a special stick (a coup stick). Among the Cheyenne, a ceremonial striped stick was used. All acts of coup had to be witnessed.

Acts of coup earned tribal designation, marked by symbolic dress such as wearing a feather, special face paint markings, stripes painted on leggings or on one's horse, or, as among the Crow, wearing a fox tail on the back of one's moccasins. Such markings distinguished among the levels of bravery. First coup might entitle the warrior to wear an eagle feather, while third or fourth coup might earn only a buzzard feather. Groups such as the Kiowa and Crow based tribal ranking and chief status on accumulated acts of bravery including acts of counting coup.

See also Dress and adornment; Feathers and featherwork; Lances and spears; Military societies; Scalps and scalping; War bonnets; Warfare and conflict.

Courts, tribal

Tribes affected: Pantribal

Significance: All tribes had aboriginal mechanisms for resolving disputes; with the establishment of reservations, however, new courts were created by the U.S. Department of the Interior, and most of these courts have been replaced by tribal courts

Prior to European contact all American Indian tribes and bands had institutional mechanisms for settling disputes. The mechanisms varied from Eskimo song duels and Yurok mediation to Cheyenne and Pueblo councils. Under United States law, tribal governments have the right to retain or modify adjudication procedures unless Congress limits that right.

For example, in the nineteenth century the Cherokee legal system went through a series of changes from a clan- and council-based system to a system based on an Anglo-American model. In the late nineteenth century Congress expanded federal court jurisdiction in Cherokee territory and finally passed the Curtis Act (1898), which abolished Cherokee tribal courts.

Pueblo adjudicatory systems have been influenced by Spanish and U.S. institutions and policies but were never abolished by federal edict and continue to develop. For example, many Keresan pueblos have a council which decides cases. Many disputes are settled before a partial council or single official acting as a mediator. Important cases are decided by the full council; the presiding officer may act as both prosecutor and a judge. Litigants may be advised by kinsmen or ceremonial group members. In a modification of this system, Laguna Pueblo has a full-time judge while retaining the council as an appellate court.

In the mid-nineteenth century a number of tribes were confined to reservations, creating new problems of social order. In 1883 the Department of the Interior established Courts of Indian Offenses. The judges, tribal members appointed by reservation superintendents, enforced administrative rules established by the Department of the Interior. The superintendent had appellate power over the judges' decisions. In 1888 Congress implicitly recognized the legitimacy of these courts by appropriating funds for judges' salaries.

By 1900 Courts of Indian Offenses had been established on about two-thirds of the reservations. These courts were even established in some pueblos, where they competed with indigenous legal systems. Courts of Indian Offenses have an enduring legacy as a model for the procedures and codes of many contemporary tribal judicial systems.

In 1935 substantive law administered by the Courts of Indian Offenses was revised. Moreover, the Indian Reorganization Act (1934) made it easier for tribes to establish court systems less dominated by the Interior Department. Insufficient tribal economic growth slowed replacement of the Courts of Indian Offenses. By 1992, however, only twenty-two remained. By contrast, there were more than 150 tribal courts.

Tribal courts vary in size, procedure, and other matters. The Navajo Nation, for example, now has an independent judicial branch which processed more than eighty-five thousand cases in 1992. There are seven judicial districts and fourteen district court judges. The practice of law before these courts is regulated. Appeals may be taken to the high court. Appellate decisions of note are published. In addition, there are local "peacemaker" courts with 227 peacemakers who act generally as mediators.

See also Indian police and judges; Reservation system of the United States; Sovereignty.

Coushatta: Tribe

Culture area: Southeast
Language group: Muskogean
Primary location: Texas, Louisiana
Population size: 1,269 (1990 U.S. Census)

The origin of the Coushatta tribe is unknown. Variants on the tribal name include Koasati, Coosawanda, and Shati. Differing folklore traditions place them coming from the north as well as Mexico. The first contact with Europeans occurred in 1540, when Hernando de Soto found the tribe living on Pine Island in the Tennessee River in Alabama. During the eighteenth century, Coushatta villages were connected with one another and with white settlements. The relationships between Indians were usually peaceful, and villages often engaged in athletic competition. The English settlers changed the Coushatta economy by trading cloth, munitions, and alcohol—all new to the Indians—for animal pelts.

The Coushatta lived side-by-side with other Creek peoples. They shared many cultural traditions, including a religion revering "Isakita immissi" or the "Master of Life/Holder of Breath." The deity was worshiped as "resident of the sky" and linked to sun worship. Many religious rituals and taboos regulated eating and drinking, as the Creeks believed that the consumer would acquire the qualities of the food he ate. Women gathered food and fuel; men hunted with blowgun and bow and arrow and fished with nets and spears. The linking of the Creek people with one another fostered a flourishing trade of goods. Indian traders traveled, offering distant tribes items they could not obtain in their living area.

During the 1790's, the Coushattas retreated from white settlements into Spanish Louisiana. They flourished in Louisiana during the first half of the nineteenth century and pushed into Texas, where they suffered from disease and ultimately united with the Alabamas in one village. There they traded with the white communities and got along quite well. The land they settled had to be conducive to agriculture and on a navigable river. They built huts of wood with bark roofs. Their diet consisted of game, corn, and wild fruit.

Migration and white society had a negative effect on the social organization of the Coushatta. By the mid 1800's, the clan and town had little social meaning. Intermarriage between Coushattas and other tribes, whites, and African Americans was frowned upon but not uncommon. The family began to assume the traditional functions of the clan and town, including education and responsibility for children until they married.

In the twentieth century, the Coushatta are led by a chief chosen by a committee of medicine men and shamans. They also have a "war chief" who is the purveyor of justice in the community. The actual governance is carried on through an elected council. Many traditional religious rituals and practices have persisted to this day, though Christianity has now supplanted tribal religion. In 1990, approximately four hundred Coushattas lived in Louisiana and Texas on a 4,000-acre reservation; others lived in Alabama and Oklahoma. English is the primary language, although even as late as 1990 many of the older Coushattas spoke their native language. Most Coushattas in Texas and Oklahoma earn their living in either the timber or tourism industry.

See also Caddo.

Cowichan: Tribe

CULTURE AREA: Northwest Coast
LANGUAGE GROUP: Salishan
PRIMARY LOCATION: Vancouver Island, British Columbia
POPULATION SIZE: 9,360 (Statistics Canada, based on 1991 census)

The Cowichan (the Cowichan included the Pilalt and Sumass) inhabited six villages on the lower course of the Cowichan River, on Malahat, and one village on Saanich Inlet. Permanent dwellings were large rectangular post-and-lintel constructions of split and hewn cedar. Households cooperated in numerous ceremonies and for mutual protection. The Cowichan were dependent upon a wide variety of marine products, some of which was stored for winter consumption and trade. The harpoon was used for sea mammals. Hunting and trapping of land mammals was the responsibility of the men; women gathered a wide variety of food and utilitarian plants.

In 1775, the Bruno de Hezeta-Juan Francisco de la Bodega y Quadra expedition became the first European American group to have contact with the Cowichan, and they brought smallpox with them. Malaria, measles, influenza, dysentery, and typhoid followed. Fort Langley prevented attacks by the Cowichan upon the Upper Stalo Salish, but they continued to fight with the Clallam, Lummi, and Musqueam. In the 1860's, the Cowichan encroached upon Pentlatch territory to use the Qualicum fishery.

See also Salishan language family.

Cowlitz: Tribe

CULTURE AREA: Northwest Coast
LANGUAGE GROUP: Salishan
PRIMARY LOCATION: Lower and middle course of Cowlitz River, Washington
POPULATION SIZE: 773 (1990 U.S. Census)

The socially stratified Cowlitz were dependent upon the local streams where they located their permanent villages for fishing. Eulachon, when dried, was a valuable trade fish. Inland game was also fully exploited for food and needed byproducts. The Cowlitz harvested great amounts of camas, which stored well—as did numerous types of berries, tubers, and nuts. Canoes and rafts were utilized for water transport. Dwellings were of split hewn cedar and housed as many as ten families.

In 1812 the first fur traders, from Astoria, penetrated Cowlitz territory, and by 1833 the Hudson's Bay Company regularly used the Cowlitz Trail. The company established the Cowlitz Farm in 1839. The 1850 Treaty of Washington and the Oregon Donation Act of 1850 permitted European Americans to enter and exploit the region. The estimated Cowlitz population of a thousand declined to 105 by 1910.

The Cowlitz were not compensated for the loss of their lands until the 1960 and 1969 Indian Claims Commission hearings. The Cowlitz award was held in trust until 1988.

See also Salishan language family.

Crashing Thunder (c. 1865—?)

ALSO KNOWN AS: Sam Blowsnake, Big Winnebago, Hágaga
TRIBAL AFFILIATION: Winnebago
SIGNIFICANCE: Crashing Thunder's autobiography is filled with cultural information, personal detail, and psychological revelation

Crashing Thunder and his Winnebago relatives became known to generations of students. His life story—elicited, translated, and published (as *Crashing Thunder: The Autobiography of an American Indian*, 1926) by ethnologist Paul Radin— reveals the day-to-day lives and the fundamental beliefs of the Winnebago. When he was born, Crashing Thunder relates, his mother was told that he would not be an ordinary individual. This prediction came true in the sense that Crashing Thunder, who with great reluctance and after years of avoiding the task, wrote an important social history of his people, despite his and other tribe members' worries that such a record, however valuable to the tribe it might be, would certainly be misunderstood by whites and would lead to trouble.

In another sense, and fortunately for students of Indian culture, Crashing Thunder was ordinary and his life experiences typify those of many of his contemporaries. Reading his book, one learns what childhood, adolescence, and adulthood were like for a Winnebago of his time. His rich and varied life included some of the following experiences: the childhood and adolescent tradition of the vision quest, courtship and sexual experience, marriage, family life (including the murder of a brother), murder, alcoholism, storytelling, ceremonies, migrant work and trouble in the white world, and conversion to the Native American Church and its peyote rituals.

See also Mountain Wolf Woman; Winnebago.

Crazy Horse (c. 1842, Black Hills of S.Dak.—Sept. 5, 1877, Fort Robinson, Nebr.): Tribal chief

ALSO KNOWN AS: Tashunca-uitko

TRIBAL AFFILIATION: Sioux (Lakota or Teton group, Oglala band)

SIGNIFICANCE: Crazy Horse was instrumental in the U.S. Army's defeats at Rosebud and the Little Bighorn; his staunch opposition to white encroachment made him one of the most famous of all Indian leaders

Crazy Horse's parents were both Sioux. His father was an Oglala Sioux medicine man; his mother died when Crazy Horse was young. He was reared by his mother's sister. Crazy Horse was regarded as an unusual and strange boy. He seldom participated in the rambunctious play of other children; he presented a serious and thoughtful demeanor and preferred to stand quietly in the shadows around the adults. As a young boy he was called Curly and Tight-Haired Boy because of his soft, pale hair. At about age ten he started training to become a warrior. His successes led him to be honored by being renamed Horse Looking.

During fights with other Indians, Crazy Horse distinguished himself, and his name was changed to Crazy Horse. Accounts of the name change differ. Some say his father, also called Crazy Horse, gave his son his name. Others say he was given the name because of his repeatedly ramming his horse into the enemies' horses and knocking off the riders. He became a full-fledged member of raiding parties around 1858. He participated in many raids and fights and earned a reputation as a courageous, skilled, and cool warrior. Because of his outstanding abilities as a leader and as a warrior, Crazy Horse was made a chief.

Whites, feeling unprotected because of the Civil War, raised volunteer units and engaged in a series of conflicts with the Sioux and Cheyenne in the 1860's. In 1868, Red Cloud, a prominent Oglala Sioux chief, signed a treaty in which he pledged to stop fighting and accept government supervision in exchange for territory. Crazy Horse and other Indians refused to accept this treaty, however, and continued to live in this land. In the 1870's, the inevitable post-Civil War westward movement of the railroad and settlers, and reports of gold, led to encroachment into this unsettled territory. By summer, 1875, a gold rush was in progress.

The government tried to secure permission from the Indians for mining and mineral rights but was rebuffed. The government then ordered all non-agency Indians to report to the agencies, which most—including Crazy Horse—refused to do. In the spring of 1876, the army launched a campaign against these "hostiles." In major battles on June 17 and 25, 1876, the army was soundly defeated at the Rosebud River and the Little Bighorn. In both of these engagements, Crazy Horse acquitted himself brilliantly and became known to both Indians and whites as one of the best military tacticians and warriors in the Sioux Nation.

A reinforced army vigorously pursued these "hostiles" throughout the summer but with little success. As winter approached, some Indians wanted to stop fighting, but Crazy Horse would not. Finally, in November, 1876, the army soundly defeated the Cheyenne. The survivors were taken in by Crazy Horse's camp. The camp's numbers swelled to about three thousand, severely taxing its ability to provide adequate resources. The ensuing hardship, suffering, and pressure exerted by the army led the Indians first to splinter off into smaller groups and then eventually surrender.

In mid-April, 1877, small groups from Crazy Horse's camp arrived at the Spotted Tail Agency. On May 6, 1877, Crazy Horse and the rest of his camp, a two-mile-long procession of about nine hundred people and two thousand horses, marched into the Red Cloud Agency. With the capture of a few splinter bands shortly after, the whites' conquest of the Sioux was complete.

Crazy Horse favorably impressed the whites and was held in the highest esteem by the young braves at the reservation as a leader who brought honor and glory to the Sioux. As his stature and prestige increased, other chiefs became jealous and hostile toward him and spread malicious rumors about his rebelliousness. Crazy Horse became doubtful of the wisdom of his decision to surrender. Besides the intratribal rivalries, Crazy Horse was aware of the government's mistreatment of other tribes and suspicious of what might befall his tribe at the government's hands. Mistranslation further added to the confusion and uncertainty of Crazy Horse's intentions. All these factors culminated in the army's decision to arrest Crazy Horse and resettle him at a distant reservation. On September 5, 1877, after consultations with the army, but unaware of the army's intention, Crazy Horse rode into the Red Cloud Agency. He was arrested and led toward the guardhouse. A scuffle ensued. Crazy Horse received a mortal wound, most probably from a guard's bayonet, and died that night.

Robert A. Clark wrote in *The Killing of Chief Crazy Horse* (1988) that the death of Crazy Horse was a "sad tale of a brave and proud man's death, a death that symbolized the unworthy end of a unique culture. May the dignity of all men be held in greater value."

The esteem in which Crazy Horse is held by the Sioux is made evident by their commissioning a mountain memorial to Crazy Horse in the Black Hills. The sculpture of Crazy Horse on his horse, begun in 1948, will be more than 560 feet high and 640 feet long and will be the world's largest sculpture.

—Laurence Miller

See also Little Bighorn, Battle of the; Red Cloud; Rosebud Creek, Battle of; Sioux.

BIBLIOGRAPHY

Andrews, Ralph W. *Indian Leaders*. Seattle: Superior Publishing, 1971.

Friswold, Carroll. *The Killing of Chief Crazy Horse*. Lincoln: University of Nebraska Press, 1988.

Hyde, George E. *A Sioux Chronicle*. Norman: University of Oklahoma Press, 1956.

Lazarus, Edward. *Black Hills, White Justice*. New York: HarperCollins, 1991.

Utley, Robert M., and Wilcomb E. Washburn. *The American Heritage History of the Indian Wars*. New York: American Heritage, 1977.

Crazy Snake (1846, near Boley, Okla.—April 11, 1912, near Smithville, Okla.): Tribal chief

ALSO KNOWN AS: Chitto Harjo, Wilson Jones

TRIBAL AFFILIATION: Creek

SIGNIFICANCE: Leader of the traditionalist faction of the Creek Nation, Crazy Snake led an unsuccessful uprising to prevent the allotment of tribal lands in 1901

Crazy Snake rose to prominence in the late nineteenth and early twentieth centuries as leader of the traditionalist faction within the Creek Nation, making him the successor to Opothleyahola, Oktarharsars Harjo (Sands), and Isparhecher. Traditionalist Creeks, many of whom were full-bloods, sought to maintain the old tribal religion and lifestyle; in addition, they resisted assimilation and the settlement of whites on tribal lands. They distrusted tribal leaders, who were often of mixed blood and thus more acculturated. A vital aspect of traditional Creek life, namely the communal ownership of land, came under direct threat in the 1890's when Congress established the Dawes Commission to extend the policy of allotment (the division of tribal lands among individual Indians) to the Creeks and the rest of the Five Civilized Tribes.

In opposition to allotment, Crazy Snake and his followers (called "Snakes") organized a rival government in opposition to the recognized tribal authorities, who were reluctantly cooperating with the federal government. Crazy Snake's "government" called on the United States to keep its treaty obligations. It issued decrees forbidding the acceptance of allotments, and

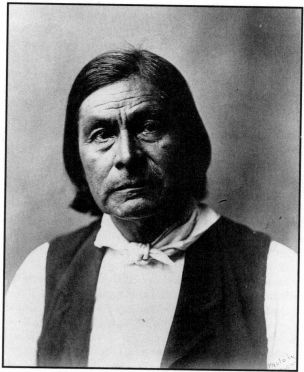

Crazy Snake, leader of an anti-allotment uprising among the Creeks in 1901. (Library of Congress)

organized its own tribal police (lighthorse) to enforce its policies. In 1901, this campaign of interference with allotment policy developed into a full-scale rebellion; Indians who had accepted allotments—as well as white settlers—were attacked. Crazy Snake and sixty-six of his followers were arrested and convicted, but were allowed to return home under suspended sentences. Thereafter, Crazy Snake generally found more peaceful ways—such as lobbying—to oppose allotment. He was also a vocal opponent of Oklahoma statehood.

In 1907, after Oklahoma became a state and the Creek government was dissolved, Crazy Snake became involved in a skirmish known as the Smoked Meat Rebellion, in which traditionalist Creeks were accused by whites of sheltering a thief. Fighting erupted, and Crazy Snake spent the rest of his life as a fugitive.

See also Allotment system; Creek; Isparhecher; Opothleyaholo.

Cree: Tribe

CULTURE AREA: Subarctic

LANGUAGE GROUP: Algonquian

PRIMARY LOCATION: Surrounding and to the east of Hudson Bay

POPULATION SIZE: 119,810 in Canada (Statistics Canada, based on 1991 census); 8,290 in U.S. (1990 U.S. Census)

The first European contact with the Cree occurred in 1611, but it was fully a hundred years before extensive contacts between the Hudson's Bay Company and the Cree created one of the most lucrative settler-Indian partnerships for a colonial economy in North America. The arrangement initially had advantages for the Cree as well. When the Hudson's Bay Company first established contacts and trading posts on the shores of Hudson Bay, they planted themselves in the center of Cree territory. The Cree dominated all contact with the white traders by controlling the waterways from the lands west of the bay, allowing only their allies the Assiniboine to have equal contact with the Europeans. The fame of the Cree comes from their essential role as a "middleman" in relations with Indians far to the west of Hudson Bay itself. According to Leonard Mason, the history of Cree-settler contact can be divided roughly into three periods: the period of the Cree initiating contact with settlers (1610-1690), the period of settlers initiating contact with the Cree (1690-1820), and Indian rehabilitation (1820-1940).

Traditional Lifeways. The traditional lands of the Cree lay between Hudson Bay and Lake Winnipeg—to the southeast, south, and southwest of Hudson Bay itself. The Crees' environmental location did not allow an extensive agricultural base to develop for the tribal subsistence, so the Cree were famed hunters, who also gathered berries from the harsh boreal landscape when they were available. The long winters in this region can be devastating, and failure to gather enough food during prime hunting seasons could lead to disaster during the snowy winter months. The Cree hunted caribou, moose, black bear, beaver, otter, mink, muskrat, fox, wolf, wolverine, geese, and duck.

The Cree people, related to the larger Algonquian cultural tradition, did not live in large settlements and often traveled in small bands, a situation that led to a separate identity for some of the Cree peoples. There are not strong clans or lineage traditions that unify a larger Cree identity. The Cree themselves recognize three large "divisions," corresponding roughly to the lands and ecological niches that they occupy: the "Swampy People" (maskekowak), inhabiting lands between Hudson Bay and Lake Winnipeg, the "Woods People" (saka-wiyiniwak), in the forested lands away from the shores, and the "Prairie People" (paskwa-wiyiniwak), who wandered farther east into the high Canadian prairie. Another division, known as the Tete de Boule Cree, who occupy lands in the lower St. Maurice River in Ottawa, were already separated from the others at the time of contact with white settlers. Some scholars simply differentiate between Woodlands and Prairie Cree, considering the "Swampy Cree" label to apply to the Woodlands group and implying that this is the major division between the two groups.

The Woodland/Swampy Cree are surrounded by the Beaver and Chipewyan tribes to the north and west, the Saulteaux to the south, and Hudson Bay itself to the east. The Cree social organization is rather simple, with no central authority or formal leadership patterns. They are reputed to remain a reserved people to this day, exercising social control through reputation (maintained through frequent gatherings to ex-

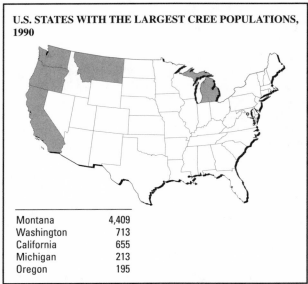

U.S. STATES WITH THE LARGEST CREE POPULATIONS, 1990

Montana	4,409
Washington	713
California	655
Michigan	213
Oregon	195

Source: 1990 U.S. Census.

change information and rumor) and the threat of conjuring and witchcraft. The separation of the Prairie Cree, from about 1790, transformed the canoe-based Cree culture of eastern Canada along the tributaries of the bay into a Plains culture based on hunting, warring, and buffalo.

In the movement of the Woodlands Cree up the rivers of Canada, they came into contact with the Blackfoot, who would transform Cree life. It is difficult to date this meeting with precision, but scholars suggest that by 1690, the initial contacts had been made. The Cree were able to take great advantage not only of their connections with the trapping interests of the Hudson's Bay Company but also of their alliance with the Blackfoot, to whom they supplied European weapons in the Blackfoot wars against the Snake. A second major change in the culture of the Plains Cree came after securing horses; new alliances were formed in an attempt to secure a steady supply of horses from southern tribes in the United States area. The securing of horses can possibly be dated to just before 1770. The importance of horses to the Plains Cree greatly increased with the expansion of European trading posts farther and farther up the various tributaries. This expansion reduced dependence on the canoe and increased reliance on horses. These inland trading posts also demanded more supplies from their Cree contacts. They needed food as well as furs, and the Cree began to supply it from hunting the buffalo. It has been suggested that beaver populations were also declining, putting pressure on trapping as an economic resource for the Cree.

With all this adoption of the Plains lifestyle and dependence on the buffalo, the decimation of the buffalo herds had a devastating impact on the Cree, since the buffalo herds first disappeared from their lands in Canada. The response of the Plains Cree was to solidify their territorial claims in the mid-1870's and to make war on the Blackfoot, their former allies, who still had access to the remaining herds. The defeat of the Prairie Cree made them dependent on relations with the Blackfoot. The traditional partners, and occasional adversaries, of the Cree were the Blackfoot, the Hidatsa, and their perennial allies, the Assiniboine.

Religion and Social Organization. Cree religious life is today dominated by the influence of Christian missionaries; however, some aspects of traditional belief remain. Religion does not consist of a dominant ideology in Cree life, except for important rituals that surround the killing of prey in hunting, widely reported in most discussions of Cree religion and ritual. There are varying forms of belief in a central "great spirit" (kitci manitu) as well as varying versions of a belief in a malevolent, evil spirit (matci manitu) who must occasionally be placated in order to prevent illness and other problems in social life. There are shamans who are practiced in various forms of witchcraft. One of the most prevalent features of Cree religious/social life is the "shaking tent." This is a tent reserved for ceremony and storytelling. The shaking tent is regularly a feature of larger Cree social gatherings.

The Cree traveled in small bands, and membership in these bands was fluid, changing with circumstances and environmental factors. Leadership was gained through prestige, particularly through success in warfare for the Plains Cree. There were warrior societies among the Cree, led by a warrior chief. The highest office was "chief," selected from among the warrior chiefs. As was the case in other Plains societies, however, peacemaking was considered one of the most honorable virtues of a Cree leader. The second manner of acquiring status was through generosity. Food gathered by the band was distributed to all, and a form of "Plains communalism" maintained a balance with those possessions that were considered to belong to an individual.

The Cree experienced, as did other Native North Americans, a series of devastating plagues that considerably reduced their numbers. There were serious smallpox outbreaks in 1780 and 1782, and one of the more extreme estimates from historians is that only one in fifty survived. The native peoples could not believe that illness could transfer from one person to another. Estimates of the Cree population in 1809 ranged around 5,000 individuals, increasing to 13,000 in 1860. Flu epidemics of 1908, 1909, and 1917 had a devastating impact on the Cree population. In 1924, census figures indicated a population of roughly 20,000. Present estimates of the Cree population vary widely, with some sources putting the population at 100,000 or more.

When the fur trapping economy began to break down in the nineteenth century because of a decreasing interest in the European markets, the economic incentive for settler contact with the Cree also broke down. The Cree had become economically dependent on their settler contacts, and the reduction in the fur trade had a devastating effect on Cree independence. By 1940 there was a situation of serious dependence on the Canadian government for continued subsistence.

—*Daniel Smith-Christopher*

See also Algonquian language family; Indian-white relations—Canadian; Shaking Tent Ceremony; Subarctic.

BIBLIOGRAPHY

Jenness, Diamond. "Hunting Bands of Eastern and Western Canada." In *The North American Indians: A Sourcebook*, edited by Roger Owen, James Deetz, and Anthony Fisher. New York: Macmillan, 1967.

Kupferer, Harriet J. "The Cree Indians of the Subarctic." In *Ancient Drums, Other Moccasins: Native North American Cultural Adaptation*. Englewood Cliffs, N.J.: Prentice Hall, 1988.

Mason, Leonard. *The Swampy Cree: A Study in Acculturation*. Anthropology Papers of the National Museum of Canada, Ottawa, 13. Ottawa: National Museum, Ottawa, Dept. of the Secretary of State, 1967.

Milloy, John S. *The Plains Cree: Trade, Diplomacy, and War, 1790-1870*. Studies in Native History 4. Winnipeg: University of Manitoba Press, 1988.

Creek: Tribe

CULTURE AREA: Southeast
LANGUAGE GROUP: Muskogean
PRIMARY LOCATION: Alabama, Oklahoma
POPULATION SIZE: 43,550 (1990 U.S. Census)

While tribal tradition held that the Creeks, or Muskogees, originally came from west of the Mississippi, they occupied large areas of Georgia and Alabama by the seventeenth century. The name "Creek" is of English origin and derived from Ochesee Creek, a tributary of the Ocmulgee River. (Ochesee was the name given the Muskogees by neighboring Indians.) English traders originally referred to the Muskogees as Ochesee Creeks but soon shortened the name to Creeks. The Creeks were not originally a single tribe, and not all Creeks spoke Muskogee. They were instead a collection of groups that included, among others, Muskogees, Alabamas, Hitchitis, Coushattas, Natchez, Yuchis, and even some Shawnees. Those living along the Alabama, Coosa, and Tallapoosa Rivers came to be regarded as Upper Creeks, while those along the Chattahoochee and Flint Rivers came to be known as Lower Creeks. Over time, the English (and later American) habit of regarding the Creeks as a single nation and dealing with them as such encouraged more of a sense of overall Creek identity. Few tribes, however, could match the ethnic and linguistic diversity of the Creeks.

Traditional Culture. Despite their diversity, the Creeks did share something of a common culture. At the time of contact with the English, the Creeks were an agricultural people whose major crop was corn. The green corn ceremony, or busk, was held in July or August. It marked the beginning of the new year and remained the ritualistic focal point of Creek culture.

The Creeks generally lived in towns centered on a square ground. The major towns of the Upper Creeks included Abihka, Atasi, Fus-hatchee, Hilibi, Kan-hatki, Kealedje, Kolomi, Okchai, Pakana, Tali, Tukabachee, Wiwohka, and Wokakai; Coweta, Eufala, Kashita, and Osachi were important

Lower Creek towns. Each town (or *talwa*) had its chief (or *micco*), as well as its military leader (*tastanagi*). There was no chief of all the Creeks, though a Creek National Council met annually to discuss matters of common concern. Loyalties to individual towns were strong, and individuals were more likely to think of themselves as Tukabachees or Cowetas than as Creeks.

The social structure in all the towns was based on clans. An individual was born into the clan of his or her mother, but marriage within the clan was strictly forbidden. Since clans transcended town boundaries, the clan system helped to keep the Creek towns united in a rather loose confederacy.

Warfare was an integral part of Creek society as it was through military exploits that males earned the reputations that brought status within the tribe. Traditional enemies included the Cherokees and the Choctaws. Warfare also played a symbolic role in Creek social organization: Towns (and clans) were considered to be either "red" or "white." White towns were considered to be more oriented toward peace, and red towns to war. Over time this distinction lost much of its meaning, but into the nineteenth century it was customary for civil matters to be discussed at councils in white towns, while military affairs were discussed in red towns.

European Impact. The Creeks first encountered English traders in the seventeenth century. Finding clothes, weapons, and other goods attractive, the Creeks became willing participants in trade, providing deerskins in return. Hunting parties ranged extensively, returning with the hides that allowed them to purchase the English goods that were increasingly deemed necessities. As long as English settlements did not threaten Creek hunting grounds, the trade appeared to benefit both sides.

The commerce in deerskins, however, changed Creek society. Not only did the Creeks become increasingly dependent on European manufactures, but white traders came to live among the Indians, often intermarrying with Creek women. This introduced a mixed-blood element into Creek society that often brought with it increasing acculturation to European ways. Traders also brought their slaves with them, introducing an African influence. Though there was some precedent for slavery in traditional Creek society, the institution took root more slowly among the Creeks than among some of the other southern tribes; Africans also intermarried with Creeks.

Creeks and European Americans. After the American Revolution, the Creeks felt increasing pressure from white settlers. In the first treaty made by the United States after ratification of the Constitution, Alexander McGillivray and other Creek chiefs ceded some of their lands in Georgia in 1790. As American influence became more intense, it became increasingly difficult to maintain the deerskin trade. Some Creeks looked to Britain for protection, while others believed it wiser to come to terms with the Americans. Increasingly, Creek society divided. Some of the more acculturated Creeks, often of mixed blood, sought a closer relationship with the United States and followed the advice of Indian agent Benjamin

Hawkins, who encouraged the Creeks to take up American-style agriculture and to put away tribal traditions such as the communal ownership of property. The McIntoshes of Coweta prospered by following such advice and became increasingly powerful. Many such Creeks came from Muskogee backgrounds and wanted to see the Creek National Council become a centralized government.

Others, however, resisted and sought to retain the old ways. Many of these were of non-Muskogee backgrounds. They were reluctant to abandon the deer-hunting economy and to see the autonomy of the towns reduced. Traditionalist Creeks were much affected by a religious revival that swept the Indian country in the early 1800's, calling for a return to old tribal ways as a means of restoring order to a disordered world. The traditionalists were also influenced by the pan-Indianism of Tecumseh, and the Shawnee leader (whose mother was a Creek) won many supporters when he visited Creek country in 1811.

The Creek War. The increasing divisions in Creek society led to bloodshed in 1812 when the traditionalists retaliated against the National Council's attempt to punish Creeks involved in attacks against settlers. A Creek civil war erupted, with Red Sticks (as the traditionalists were called) launching attacks on the towns of Creeks friendly to white settlers. In 1813, the war expanded to include the United States, which was itself at war with Britain. Despite early successes, notably at Fort Mims, an aroused United States inflicted a crushing defeat on the Red Sticks. In the Treaty of Fort Jackson (1814), Creek chiefs were forced to agree to the cession of roughly one-half the tribe's remaining lands. Some Red Sticks escaped into Florida, where they joined their Seminole kinsmen. There they kept up resistance until defeated in the First Seminole War (1817-1818).

Removal. The influx of settlers into former Creek lands spelled the end of the deer-hunting economy and made it increasingly difficult for Creeks to live as Indians. As whites eyed remaining tribal lands, some of the more acculturated leaders were receptive to suggestions that the Creeks move west. In 1825, William McIntosh signed a treaty ceding away all that was left of Creek lands in Georgia. His subsequent assassination was evidence that many Creeks disagreed. McIntosh's heirs and some others voluntarily departed for the Indian Territory (modern Oklahoma).

Though most Creeks remained in the South, President Andrew Jackson's removal policy proved inescapable. In 1832 a new treaty was signed that paved the way for removal. Though some traditionalists resisted in the spring of 1836, the bulk of the tribe left peacefully for the Indian Territory under Opothleyaholo's leadership. The Creeks' Trail of Tears was less dramatic than that of the Cherokees, in part because most of the Lower Creeks moved by water, but at least 10 percent of the tribe perished en route, and as many died in the first year in their new homeland.

Creeks in Indian Territory. Once in Oklahoma, the Creeks attempted to re-create the social order they had known in the

South. New towns were founded, often bearing the names of ones left behind, and sacred fires kindled from ashes brought from Alabama burned in the square grounds. Settling largely along the Canadian and Arkansas Rivers, the Creeks adjusted to their new surroundings as one of the Five Civilized Tribes of transplanted southern Indians. The Creeks were slower than the other tribes to organize a tribal government, however; not until 1867 was a constitution drafted and a national government created with its capital at Okmulgee.

By this time, internal division had reappeared. During the Civil War the more acculturated Creeks, led by the sons of William McIntosh, committed the tribe to an alliance with the Confederacy. The traditionalists, led by Opothleyaholo, were pro-Union. Another Creek civil war resulted, in which the pro-South faction gained the upper hand. The eventual Union victory brought an imposed treaty that cost the tribe half of its Oklahoma lands and required that the Creeks incorporate their former slaves within the tribe.

The life of the Oklahoma Creeks continued to be marked by division—one reason, perhaps, for the organization of the country's first tribal police force (the Creek Lighthorse) in 1877. Though the more acculturated Creeks generally controlled the nation's government, traditionalists periodically attempted to oust them, sometimes by force. The most serious conflict arose in the Green Peach War (1882), when Isparhecher and his followers fought with the tribal government. Around the end of the nineteenth century, Chitto Harjo (Crazy Snake) led a religious revival among traditionalists that sought to stem the tide of acculturation.

Twentieth Century Changes. By 1900, the Creeks were again coming under pressure from the outside. The Five Civilized Tribes had been exempted from the General Allotment Act (1877). The desirability of their land, however, and the assimilationist thrust of government policy led to passage of

the Curtis Act (1898), which provided legal authority to allot the lands of the Five Civilized Tribes and to dissolve their governments. In 1901 the Creeks agreed to allotment, with each individual receiving 160 acres. Though some traditionalists resisted by refusing to take up their allotments, they acted in vain. By 1936, fewer than 30 percent of Creeks still held their allotments. In preparation for Oklahoma statehood, the tribal governments of all Five Civilized Tribes were abolished on March 6, 1906.

Under the Oklahoma Indian Welfare Act (1936), Indians in the state were allowed to organize governments again and to hold land communally. Creeks initially responded to the act at the town level, and in 1939 three towns adopted constitutions. In 1970 Congress allowed the election of principal chiefs in the Five Civilized Tribes, and the Creeks adopted an updated constitution that restored tribal government with elected legislative, executive, and judicial branches. Resurgent population growth made the Creeks the country's tenth largest tribe by 1990.

The twentieth century also saw a revival among the descendants of the small number of Creeks who evaded removal in the 1830's. Though largely acculturated, several hundred individuals maintained a Creek identity in southern Alabama. After several decades of struggle, they received federal recognition as the Poarch Band of Creeks in 1984.

—*William C. Lowe*

See also Black Drink; Crazy Snake; Creek War; Isparhecher; McGillivray, Alexander; McIntosh, William; Muskogean language family; Opothleyaholo; Seminole.

BIBLIOGRAPHY

Green, Michael D. *The Politics of Indian Removal: Creek Government and Society in Crisis*. Lincoln: University of Nebraska Press, 1982. The best account of the removal era, bringing out the internal divisions within Creek society. Index and bibliography.

Hudson, Charles. *The Southeastern Indians*. Knoxville: University of Tennessee Press, 1976. Best overall account of the traditional cultures of the Five Civilized Tribes. Contains much information on the Creeks and provides a useful context for comparing them with neighboring tribes. Illustrations, comprehensive index.

Littlefield, Daniel F., Jr. *Africans and Creeks: From the Colonial Period to the Civil War*. Westport, Conn.: Greenwood Press, 1979. An excellent account of the role of African Americans in Creek society.

Martin, Joel W. *Sacred Revolt: The Muskogees' Struggle for a New World*. Boston: Beacon Press, 1991. Account of the Creek War that stresses the religious motivations of the Red Sticks. An outstanding account of the worldview of Creek traditionalists.

Owsley, Frank L., Jr. *Struggle for the Gulf Borderlands: The Creek War and the Battle of New Orleans, 1812-1815*. Gainesville: University Presses of Florida, 1981. The best narrative account of the Creek War. Stresses the international context. Good bibliography.

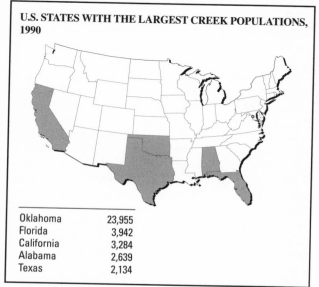

U.S. STATES WITH THE LARGEST CREEK POPULATIONS, 1990

Oklahoma	23,955
Florida	3,942
California	3,284
Alabama	2,639
Texas	2,134

Source: 1990 U.S. Census.

Paredes, J. Anthony, ed. *Indians of the Southeastern United States in the Late Twentieth Century*. Tuscaloosa: University of Alabama Press, 1992. A collection of essays that includes an account of the Poarch Creeks' successful struggle for federal recognition. Photographs.

Wright, James Leitch, Jr. *Creeks and Seminoles: The Destruction and Regeneration of the Muscogulge People*. Lincoln: University of Nebraska Press, 1986. Best overall history of these related tribes from European contact through removal. Emphasizes ethnic differences as the root of Creek divisiveness. Illustrations and a good bibliography.

Creek War

DATE: 1813-1814
PLACE: Alabama
TRIBES AFFECTED: Creek, Seminole
SIGNIFICANCE: The Creek War broke the military power of the Creeks and led to the loss of half of the tribe's land

In the years before 1813, the Creeks became divided into two major factions: those who sought to maintain friendly relations with the United States (and were more open to the adoption of American habits) and those known as Red Sticks. The latter sought to retain traditional ways of life and tribal lands and were much influenced by a religious revival that swept through Indian country in the early 1800's. This movement stressed a return to Native American ways and intertribal cooperation in resisting further white encroachments. The pan-Indian leader Tecumseh visited the Creeks in 1811, inspiring the Red Sticks and winning much support, especially among the Upper Creeks.

Bloodshed erupted between the rival factions in 1812 when the Creek National Council attempted to punish Creeks who had attacked settlers. The Red Sticks were also confident of British assistance when Britain and the United States went to war in May, 1812. When Peter McQueen's band of Red Sticks repulsed an attack by militiamen on July 27, 1813, at Burnt Corn Creek in present-day southern Alabama, the Creek internal conflict became the Creek War, though friendly Creeks under William McIntosh fought as allies of the United States, as did groups of Cherokees and Choctaws.

Under William Weatherford (Red Eagle), the hostile Creeks won a stunning victory at Fort Mims. The subsequent killing of the fort's white inhabitants and friendly Creek survivors, however, was widely regarded as a massacre and provoked a furious reaction. Creek country was soon invaded from the south, east, and north. The Upper Creek towns, which furnished the bulk of Red Stick support, bore the brunt of the fighting and consequent destruction. Andrew Jackson emerged as the dominant figure on the American side, and he won the decisive engagement of the war on March 27, 1814, at Horseshoe Bend (Tohopeka) on the Tallapoosa River. Eight hundred Red Sticks died.

Peace was made at Fort Jackson, Alabama. Instructed by the federal government to seek relatively modest territorial concessions and to protect the interests of friendly Creeks, Jackson demanded a much larger cession that included land held by friendly Creeks. In the Treaty of Fort Jackson (August 9, 1814), which officially ended the war, the Creeks parted with approximately half of their tribal lands. Friendly Creeks were allowed to retain one-square-mile plots in the ceded lands provided they actually lived on them. Settlement of Creek lands proceeded rapidly, making it increasingly difficult for Creeks to follow their traditional lifestyle. The prospect of removal would soon be upon them.

The treaty did not completely end the fighting. Some of the Red Sticks fled to Florida, where they joined their Seminole kinsmen. The latter were already resisting American encroachments in a conflict that would soon give rise to the First Seminole War (1817-1818). Red Sticks again faced Jackson in what was to them a continuation of the struggle begun in 1812.

See also Creek; Fort Mims, Battle of; Horseshoe Bend, Treaty of; McIntosh, William; McQueen, Peter; Menewa; Seminole Wars; Tecumseh.

Crow: Tribe

CULTURE AREA: Plains
LANGUAGE GROUP: Siouan
PRIMARY LOCATION: Montana
POPULATION SIZE: 8,588 (1990 U.S. Census)

The Crow tribe, of Siouan ancestry, split off from the agriculturalist Hidatsa tribe. Crows, who called themselves *Absaroka* (bird people, or children of the long-beaked bird), were hunter-gatherers who inhabited parts of Montana and Wyoming. The tribe was divided into three groups by yearly migration patterns. They were one of the tribes which cooperated with European settlers and the U.S. government (as army scouts, for example). This policy, and the accomplishments of astute Crow chiefs, led to preservation of some Crow ancestral lands as a Crow reservation. Modern Crows have been fairly successful in accommodating to contemporary American ways while retaining tribal values. Among their many achievements are the election of a Crow to the Montana State Senate and a Crow Fair, which creates income from tourism.

Tribal History. The Crow or Absaroka are a Hokan-Siouan tribe. It has been said that the name "Crow" (or Kite) came from misconceptions of French explorers and that the tribe was actually named for the sparrow hawk. The Absaroka arose between the mid-sixteenth and early seventeenth centuries, after two groups broke away from the Hidatsa tribe. Hidatsas were Indian agriculturalists who lived along the Missouri River. There are several Crow legends about the basis for the split. It is believed that the first Crows were Awatixa Hidatsas who became disenchanted with the lifestyle associated with farming and sought the excitement to be found in a society of nomad hunter-gatherers. Certainly this is what they became, nomads whose economy was based mostly on the buffalo. Later, after obtaining horses—probably by trade with the Shoshone—the Crow evolved into a mobile and powerful fighting force and became wide-ranging hunters.

The Crow originally inhabited the eastern part of the Rocky Mountains at the head of the Yellowstone and Missouri rivers. They were subdivided into three distinct groups. Mountain Crows (Acaraho), originally the Awatixa Hidatsa, settled in the Big Horn and Absaroka mountains. They hunted there most of the year but wintered in warmer areas south of today's Wyoming-Montana border. River Crows (Minisepere) were a second group of dissatisfied Hidatsas, whose migration pattern followed the Missouri River. The third group, an offshoot of the River Crows, "Kicked in the Belly" Crows (Erarapio), migrated through the Little Bighorn and Powder River valleys.

These three groups interacted peaceably and protected one another from encroachments of the Blackfoot, Shoshone, and Sioux to the north, south, and southeast, respectively. The Crow allied themselves with the Hidatsa and other nearby tribes, including the Mandan. These alliances were particularly important because the Crow tribe was not large (reportedly never exceeding sixteen thousand people) and their tribal land abounded with game, making it desirable to others.

In the 1820's, non-Indians began to arrive in Crow territory. Initially, most were traders who introduced Crows to metal tools, enhanced their use of rifles for hunting and war, and provided glass beads as well as other materials useful in Crow handicrafts. Non-Indians also brought European disease that decimated the Crow population. According to several sources, smallpox was the main factor that dropped the Crow population from sixteen thousand to under three thousand.

By 1851 various trading posts and forts had been built in Crow territory, and the expanding westward flood of American settlers began to force other tribes (especially the Sioux and Blackfoot) off their own lands. This situation put them in serious competition for Crow lands. The U.S. government brought the Plains tribes together at Fort Laramie in 1851 to define "Indian homelands." This action, probably aimed mostly at protecting American settlers from the results of Indian wars, resulted in defining the Crow country as a 38-million-acre area bounded on the east, north, south, and west by the Powder River, the Missouri and Musselshell rivers, the Wind River Mountains, and the Yellowstone River, respectively.

The generation of fixed boundaries of a Crow homeland represented the first loss of territory by the tribe. It was followed, in rapid succession, by the disappearance of most of their territory and by huge disruptions of every facet of Crow tribal life. All this occurred despite the friendliness of the Crows to American settlers and their service as army couriers and scouts. First, in 1868, the Crows, under chief Middle of the Land, were stripped of nearly 30 million acres of the homeland granted to them in 1851. They retained 8 million acres bounded on the south by the Montana-Wyoming border, on the east by longitude 107 degrees, and on both the west and the north by the Yellowstone River.

The 1868 treaty involved subjugating the Crow tribe in order to "prepare them for civilized life." It did this by placing them under the control of Indian agents, who were to

"help them to blend into American mainstream life." This blending—not desired by the Crow tribe—included establishment of schools to modernize them, churches to Christianize them, supplementation of their food supply, and an attempted precipitous conversion of hunter-gatherers into farmers.

Then, three successive steps—in 1882, 1891, and 1904—diminished the Crow reservation to its present 3 million acres, divided into individual farms and ranches. As time went by, the Crows were forced more and more into mainstream American culture. They resisted in a variety of ways, such as the introduction into their religion of the Shoshone Sun Dance, a ritual which enabled young Crow men to prove their bravery by bearing great pain (it replaced the earlier Crow Sun Dance).

The retention of the rites of their Tobacco Society, an important part of traditional Crow life, was also very influential here, as was the development of the Native American Church, which utilizes peyote in its ceremonies. In addition, the strength and solidarity of Crow family life, the retention and routine use of the Crow language, and the annual Crow Fair have helped to maintain Crow tribal identity. Always essential, throughout Crow interaction with mainstream American society, have been the achievements of a continuum of insightful Crow leaders; these statesmen include Eelapuash (Sore Belly), Medicine Crow, Plenty Coups, and Robert Yellowtail.

Traditional Lifeways. The Crow were subdivided into thirteen clans, described in detail in Robert H. Lowie's *The Crow Indians* (1956). Each of these tribal subgroups (large groups of closely related families) was headed by a man with a distinguished record in intertribal war. Members of all clans were found in the Acaraho, Minisepere, and Erarapio encampments.

Each encampment was governed by a council of chiefs, shamans, and tribal elders. Chiefs were individuals who attained this title by performing four specific deeds: leading successful war parties, counting coup by touching an enemy and escaping, taking an enemy's weapon from him, and cutting loose a horse from an enemy camp. One member of the tribal council, usually a chief, was elected head of each encampment. At all levels, chiefs lost their power if they stopped living up to Crow ideals.

The Crow men were divided into men's military societies such as Foxes, Lumpwood, Crazy Dogs, Big Dogs, and Ravens. Membership in the societies was open to any proven warrior. The societies, each having its own rules and customs, competed to recruit the most promising young men. Every spring, one military society was appointed as the tribal police force to keep order in Crow encampments, enforce discipline during important tribal activities such as the buffalo hunt, and keep war parties from setting out at inappropriate times.

Crows almost always married outside their own clans, sometimes by interclan wife-capturing (in which the wives-to-be were willing candidates). More often, wives were purchased from their families for a bride price. Most women were married by puberty. Marriage taboos forbade men and women to look at or talk to mothers-in-law or fathers-in-law, respectively. Other elaborate rules governed the behavior of other family members.

Fathers lavished attention on their sons, praising them for any good action. In addition, all adults lavished praise on youngsters for achievements in hunting, war, and general life (for example, boys returning from a first war party would be praised by all their relatives). Inappropriate actions, on the other hand, were handled by people called "joking relatives," who gently and jokingly ridiculed bad behavior. Such teasing discipline was much more effective than harsh treatment in a society in which cooperation was essential for tribal survival. Youngsters, in turn, treated all adults respectfully.

The most important tribal religious ceremonies were those of the Tobacco Society and the Sun Dance (later replaced by the Shoshone-Crow Sun Dance), which helped men to prove their bravery. The Tobacco Society ceremonies were held three times each year: at the spring planting of tobacco (the sole Crow crop), when the tobacco was harvested, and at initiations. The Sun Dance was held when needed; it was most often associated with acts of revenge or initiation into war. One religious hero of the Crow tribe was Old Man Coyote, the creator of the world, a smart, clever being who was the subject of many lively and educational Crow tales.

The Crow Indians lived in skin tipis. These skin houses were often 25 feet high and could accommodate forty people. They were made of as many as twenty buffalo skins, sewn together and supported by lodgepoles. The preparation of a new tipi was communal woman's work. It was carried out by a skilled woman, hired by the owner of the planned dwelling, and a group of her friends. Inside each tipi was a draft screen, painted with pictures that depicted important tribal events and the brave deeds of the tipi owners. At the rear of each tipi, directly opposite its door, was a place of honor for its owner or special guests.

When a Crow died, the body was taken out through a hole cut in one side of the tipi, rather than by the door; it was believed that if a body were taken out by the door, another tipi occupant would soon die. Dead bodies were placed on wooden scaffolds in their best clothing, where they remained until their decomposition was complete. At that time the remains were taken down and buried. Common Crow mourning practices included giving away property, cutting the hair, tearing clothing, and gashing the body. In some cases mourners cut off a finger joint.

The main food source of Crow Indians living on the plains was buffalo, which were hunted by driving them over cliffs, surrounding them on horseback and shooting them, or driving them into traps. Deer were another major meat source. Most meat was roasted over fires, cooked in the ashes of fires, or boiled in skin-lined pits. Some meat was mixed with berries and fat and dried to produce pemmican food reserves. Edible roots, berries, and fruit such as wild plums were har-

vested by women to supplement meat, which was the main Crow food.

Crows were exceptionally fine horsemen and possessed huge numbers of horses per capita. Many of these horses were obtained by theft from other tribes, and the Crows had the reputation of being exceptionally accomplished horse thieves. They were also, however, very successful horse breeders.

The tools and weapons of the Crow were of fine construction. Their bows were fabricated from hickory and/or ash and horn, when possible. Crow bow and arrow makers were very skilled, and all Crow artifacts, including buffalo horn cups and wooden bowls, were well made. Crow handicrafts such as clothing, arrow quivers, and various adornments were of very fine quality and were sought after. These adornments enhanced the appearance of a people who were usually relatively tall (many men were near 6 feet). Crow men rarely cut their hair, letting it grow very long and lavishing much attention on it. Hence, many traders called Crows "the long-haired Indians."

Clothing, blankets, and other items that modern society manufactures from cloth were made of animal skins. Preparation of the skins began by soaking them in water for several days. Then, loosened hair and scraps of flesh were scraped off, a paste of animal brains was added to soften the skins, and scraping was continued. Finally, the skins were tanned and used to make garments that were soft and flexible in any weather. Prior to the advent of European traders, skin objects were decorated with dyed porcupine quills and feathers. Later, glass beads replaced quills.

Contemporary Life. Contemporary Crow life, to a large extent, has been that of the reservation. In the 1880's, buffalo had become nearly extinct because of hide hunting. At this time, a Crow named Wraps His Tail (Sword Bearer) excited some Crows into revolt, but his death at the hands of Crow reservation police ended the movement.

The next forty years saw strong efforts by the Bureau of Indian Affairs to force the Crow tribe to enter modern life completely. Their program included attempting to force the Crows to remain on the reservation, to become Christians, to follow mainstream marriage and social customs, and to farm or ranch. At this time Crow children were forced to attend boarding school, which was intended to turn them into mainstream Americans. During this period (up to the end of World War II), Crows reacted by constructing a cultural base which preserved the core of their culture. In essence, Crows went their own way while acceding to many demands of the federal government. This action was complicated by a need to interact with the world outside the reservation, a world in which Crows were often treated with contempt.

Most Crows thus remained on the reservation whenever possible, where most social relationships were regulated by Crow tradition. For example, Crows often belonged to an Indian Christian church but married and interacted according to Crow custom. Ironically, the Crow tribe, which had gener-

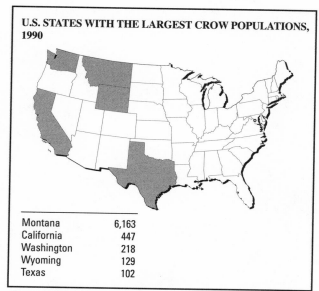

U.S. STATES WITH THE LARGEST CROW POPULATIONS, 1990

Montana	6,163
California	447
Washington	218
Wyoming	129
Texas	102

Source: 1990 U.S. Census.

ally interacted peacefully with the American government, was the least tractable Plains Indian tribe in parting with their traditions. Canny and pragmatic, they made the best of advantages of mainstream culture without losing sight of their Absaroka culture. This feat was not accomplished without mental anguish, and some Crows fell victim to depression and alcoholism.

By the 1940's the peyote religion of the Native American Church and the Crow-Shoshone Sun Dance were firmly in place in Crow life. The church provided an alternative to straight Christian worship. Combined with other shamanic rituals, the Sun Dance both provided Crow health care and enabled Crow young men to prove courage in a variant of the old way. In addition, the tribal customs of gift giving, respecting the family, and using "joking relatives" were applied to situations as disparate as winning an athletic event or having a young relative be graduated from high school or college.

In the political arena, Crows developed political and legal machinery to defend the reservation against further encroachment by whites. Primary among their leaders was Robert Yellowtail. In addition, in 1948 the Crow tribe adopted a reservation constitution based on their traditional tribal council but allowing every Crow adult to vote. The council elected officers, including a chairman, and established committees to solve tribal needs.

Abetted by a federal government policy more sensitive to American Indian needs, Crow leaders became ever more useful to the tribe. Successful legal action against the federal government, sale of the land used for Yellowtail Dam (named after Robert Yellowtail), and a recreation site on the Bighorn River, as well as royalties on coal discovered on the reservation, swelled the coffers of the tribe.

In the early 1990's a third of reservation residents were non-Indians, and 20 percent of Crows lived off the reservation.

Many contemporary Crows work for the tribal government, which has improved health care, education, and housing for tribe members with funds from the tribal treasury. They also teach at nearby colleges and other schools, work at many levels in local industry, and successfully own and run ranches and farms. The annual Crow Fair is a valuable tourist attraction. Robert Yellowtail died in 1988; however, others, including his son (Bill Yellowtail), have followed him. Bill Yellowtail has been a Montana State senator.   —*Sanford S. Singer*

See also Fort Laramie Treaty of 1851; Hidatsa; Plains; Siouan language family; Tobacco Society and Dance.

BIBLIOGRAPHY

Hayne, Coe Smith. *Red Men on the Bighorn*. Philadelphia: Judson Press, 1929. These vignettes on Crows describe aspects of Crow culture, the training of young men to embody Crow ideals, and aspects of the lives of some well-known Crows. This interesting reading expands understanding of the Crow and some of their problems between 1871 and the 1920's.

Hoxie, Frederick E. *The Crow*. In *Indians of North America*, edited by Frank W. Porter III. New York: Chelsea House, 1989. A brief but thorough book that describes many historical and cultural aspects of Crows. Major topics are the creation legend, tribe origins, the arrival of white people and its consequences, the reservation era, and Crows today. Fine illustrations give a sense of the Crows and show how their tribal lands diminished.

Lowie, Robert H. *The Crow Indians*. New York: Holt, Rinehart and Winston, 1956. This thorough, definitive work covers in depth tribal organization, life, artifacts, burial custom, military societies, religion, clans, rites and festivals, and many other topics.

Voget, Fred W. *The Shoshoni-Crow Sun Dance*. Norman: University of Oklahoma Press, 1984. Crow life, aspects of Crow history, and events (including reservation life and abandonment of the Crow Sun Dance) that led the Shoshone Sun Dance to become part of their lives are described. The book also identifies Crow efforts to retain their cultural identity.

Yellowtail, Thomas. *Yellowtail: Crow Medicine Man and Sun Dance Chief: An Autobiography*. Norman: University of Oklahoma Press, 1991. Via description of the life of Thomas Yellowtail, Crow history, Crow efforts to conserve traditions in modern times, and the Crow religion are illuminated.

Crow Dog (c. 1835—1920, Pine Ridge Reservation, S.Dak.): Warrior chief

ALSO KNOWN AS: Kangi Sunka
TRIBAL AFFILIATION: Brule Sioux
SIGNIFICANCE: Crow Dog was an important figure in the Ghost Dance phenomenon of 1890

Crow Dog was present when Crazy Horse was killed at Fort Robinson, Nebraska, in 1877; he helped prevent a retaliatory attack on soldiers at the fort. He was police chief at the Rosebud Reservation in 1879-1880, during which time he assassinated Spotted Tail.

Brule Sioux war chief Crow Dog, pictured circa 1900. (Library of Congress)

Crow Dog was born at Horse Stealing Creek, Montana Territory, into a family of esteemed warriors. Before submitting to reservation life, he made his reputation in battle. As the Sioux were confined on reservations following the Battle of the Little Bighorn, dissension rose between some of their leaders. On one occasion, Red Cloud accused Spotted Tail of pocketing the proceeds from a sale of tribal land. Crow Dog heard rumors that Spotted Tail was selling Lakota land to the railroads and building himself an enormous white-styled mansion with the proceeds. In mid-July of 1880, Spotted Tail was called before the general council by Crow Dog's White Horse Group, where he denied the charges. The council voted to retain him as head chief, but Crow Dog continued to assert the chief's complicity in various crimes against the people. Crow Dog carried out his own sentence on Spotted Tail, executing him on August 5, 1881. Blood money was paid in traditional Brule fashion for the crime. Crow Dog was convicted of murder in a Dakota Territory court, but he was later freed on order of the U.S. Supreme Court when it ruled that the territorial government had no jurisdiction over the crime (*Ex parte Crow Dog*, 1883).

Later, Crow Dog was one of the leaders in spreading the Ghost Dance among the Lakota; he had adopted the religion from Short Bull. Crow Dog vociferously opposed army occupation of South Dakota Indian reservations and was one of the last holdouts after the massacre at Wounded Knee during December of 1890. He spent the last years of his life in relative peace on the Rosebud Sioux reservation in South Dakota.

See also Ghost Dance; Spotted Tail.

Crowfoot (c. 1830, present-day Calgary, Alberta, Canada— April 25, 1890, Canada): Tribal chief

ALSO KNOWN AS: Isapo-Muxika, Astoxkomi (Shot Close)

TRIBAL AFFILIATION: Blackfoot

SIGNIFICANCE: Crowfoot was a skillful chief who led his people through the twenty-year transition from nomadic freedom to reservation life

Crowfoot, who was born a Blood Indian, became a Blackfoot by adoption when his widowed mother married a man from that tribe. Because the Blackfoot were a hunting and raiding people, buffalo and horses were important fixtures in their existence, and life revolved around the acquisition of both. Crowfoot matured and excelled in this environment, earning his place as chief because of his bravery in fighting and hunting.

As the white settlers advanced westward across the land, the ways of the Blackfoot suffered. Although Crowfoot was the leader of a particular Blackfoot tribe, the whites thought him to be the supreme leader of the entire Blackfeet Confederacy. Thus, he had great influence with the whites, particularly with the North West Mounted Police, who were organized in 1873 in the service of Queen Victoria.

Crowfoot signed a treaty in 1877 giving reservation lands to the Blackfeet Confederacy and ceding some fifty thousand acres to the whites. He also kept the Blackfoot out of the unsuccessful Riel Rebellion of 1885, maintaining his position as a trusted and peace-seeking leader. His overwhelming concern was the welfare of the Blackfoot people in the face of advancing white authority. Thus, he also led his tribe in the shift to agriculture as a primary means of subsistence.

See also Blackfoot and Blackfeet Confederacy; Riel Rebellions.

Cuello: Archaeological site

DATE: 1200 B.C.E.-250 C.E.

LOCATION: Belize

CULTURE AFFECTED: Maya

Cuello, in northern Belize, is the best documented agricultural village of the Preclassic period (1200 B.C.E. to 250 C.E.) in lowland Maya culture. Occupied for about fifteen centuries, it provides important information on the genesis of the brilliant Maya civilization. Cuello was excavated in the late 1970's and the 1980's by a team led by archaeologist Norman Hammond. It has provided some of the earliest radiocarbon dates for settled village life in the Maya lowlands. At first, these dates suggested that the earliest Maya pottery, called the Swasey complex, was being manufactured as early as 2000 B.C.E. This made Swasey ceramics some of the earliest in Mesoamerica. A reappraisal of the date series, however, indicated that this interpretation was erroneous. Swasey pottery, now dated to between 1200 and 900 B.C.E., appears almost a thousand years later than the earliest Mesoamerican ceramics (known from sites on the Pacific Coast of Chiapas, Mexico). It is still one of the first ceramic industries in the Maya lowlands.

The archaeological features at Cuello indicate the presence of a small farming village that, although it played a marginal role in the emergence of political and religious complexity in the Maya lowlands, is representative of a way of life shared by most early Maya people. The population of the site during the Early Preclassic Swasey phase (1200 to 900 B.C.E.) is estimated at three hundred to four hundred people. The subsistence economy was based on slash-and-burn agriculture and the cultivation of maize, beans, squash, and other cultigens.

The earliest pottery at Cuello, appearing during the Swasey phase, is characterized by monochrome vessels finished with a polished red or orange slip. Forms include squat jars, bottles, spouted vessels, and round plates. Swasey is followed in time by a phase called Bladen (800 to 600 B.C.E.). Bladen ceramics include the earliest human figurines and roller stamps, associated with increased ceremonial activity at the site. Among architectural remains was a low, limestone platform that has been interpreted as the foundation of an early temple ceremonial structure with rubble fill, coated on the exterior with lime plaster, dating to 600 B.C.E. There are some hints that the Middle Preclassic occupants of Cuello may have been participating in a larger cultural tradition that included Olmec peoples of the Gulf Coast of Mexico. The Lopez Mamom phase (600 to 400 B.C.E.) sees the appearance of spangle-shaped, claw-shaped, and bird-shaped pendants of blue-green jade in burials. This material was favored by the Olmecs at La Venta, and the presence of jade beads in child burials has been interpreted as evidence of inherited status, suggesting ranking and social differentiation at this early date.

The largest occupation of Cuello occurred during the Late Preclassic Cocos Chicanel phase (400 B.C.E. to 250 C.E.), at which time the village had a population of around twenty-six hundred people. This is relatively small when compared to contemporaneous occupations at sites such as El Mirador, Tikal, Nakbe, Cerros, Lamanai, and Komchen; Cuello must be considered as representative of the small villages that were located in territories away from major ceremonial centers. Nevertheless, Cuello has evidence for simple, uncarved limestone stelae that may have borne painted designs and are possible precursors to the elaborate historical monuments of the Early and Late Classic periods (250-900 C.E.).

Cuello's significance lies in the fact that, although not a major ceremonial center, it has provided detailed information on the nature of Maya village life during the Preclassic period. It also demonstrates that there was a marked degree of social complexity even in small Maya villages from the first millennium B.C.E. on.

See also Copan; La Venta; Maya; Palenque; Tikal.

Culture areas

TRIBES AFFECTED: Pantribal
SIGNIFICANCE: Ecological conditions determined tribal methods of material subsistence (food supply, type of shelter) as well as their main cultural patterns

No single method of assigning cultural boundaries between different groupings of Native Americans is fully adequate. Persuasive arguments exist for groupings that place primary emphasis, for example, on the most important language groupings (Algonquian, Athapaskan, Siouan, Tanoan, Muskogean, Caddoan, and Shoshonean). Because Native American groupings have undergone a series of displacements from region to region, however, their linguistic origins overlap, a situation which results in an equal amount of overlap in generalizations concerning original cultural traits.

Another mode of assigning culture areas draws on basic forms of technology—specifically on methods of producing household wares such as pottery and basketry. Here again one encounters a phenomenon of cultural overlap because of patterns of borrowing between tribal groupings.

To some degree, essential social indicators of culture can be transferred over time and space, making it difficult to draw boundaries between peoples of clearly distinct traditions. Such sociocultural factors include assignment of leadership, matriarchal versus patriarchal systems, degrees of formalization of kinship ties, and marriage patterns.

Considerations such as these make a division based on geographical/ecological factors the most manageable and, indeed, the most commonly adopted one in the general literature. Such a comparison of Indian culture areas necessarily involves discussion of material and cultural questions shared by all human societies. Among these cultural differences are food subsistence, lodging construction, common artifacts, group organization, and spiritual expression. Each of these elements of Indian life was influenced by the environmental conditions that existed in relatively distinct geographical zones.

Arctic and Subarctic. The northern continental zone running from the Arctic north to British Columbia and eastward to Hudson Bay, while not one culture area, was characterized by a common practice: Natives survived primarily by hunting and fishing. Because the northern Arctic zone is frozen most of the year, Eskimo populations that specialized in sea mammal hunting (especially the Aleuts) stayed isolated in areas where access to prey was assured. Central Inuit hunters in the interior of Alaska and the MacKenzie Territory, where kayak transportation was limited to a short summer season, reached their prey (usually caribou and moose) on toboggans or snowshoes.

Both Central Inuit and Athapaskan-speaking Dene peoples inhabited the less bountiful Subarctic zone that forms the interior land mass of northern Canada. Because of the limited density of animal populations, Subarctic hunters relied extensively on trapping devices spread over a vast network, according to the season. Limited food sources limited human population patterns as well, especially deep in the interior. Frequent displacement for subsistence meant that Subarctic tribes maintained semipermanent camps rather than substantial villages.

Like their Eskimo neighbors farther north, Subarctic Indians maintained a network of customs in common that, in good times, helped celebrate nature's bounty. One tribal meeting was the "potlatch," when food-gathering tasks were temporarily suspended and groups from afar could share shelter, gifts, and storytelling, either with distant kin or "friendly" neighbors.

Religious traditions in these northern areas were usually based on a belief in spiritual forces coming both from the sky and the earth, including living spirits in the form of animals or one's deceased kin.

Northwest Coast and Plateau. Indians in these areas lived more easily off nature's bounty, partially because the climate was less harsh, facilitating seasonal hunting of deer and bears. Abundant sealife near the coast of Washington and Oregon and easy hunting grounds inland made Northwest Indians such as the Wakashan and Chinook relatively "wealthy," in terms of both subsistence and displays of their "good fortune."

The Kwakiutl of the Wakashan showed their wealth through large houses of split logs. Their clothing and bodies were decorated with copper and ornate shell jewelry. Frequent public potlatches to commemorate social advancement (such as passage rites for youths and marriages) were paid for by the wealthiest families to attain recognition.

Farther inland was the Plateau, inhabited by tribes of two main linguistic groups: the Sahaptin (including Walla Walla and Nez Perce) and the Salish (Flathead and Wenatchi). In this region, freshwater salmon fishing could be combined with hunting. Plateau river communication networks were less extensive than those of the Northwest, limiting the scope of interaction, even between clans of similar tribal origin. When

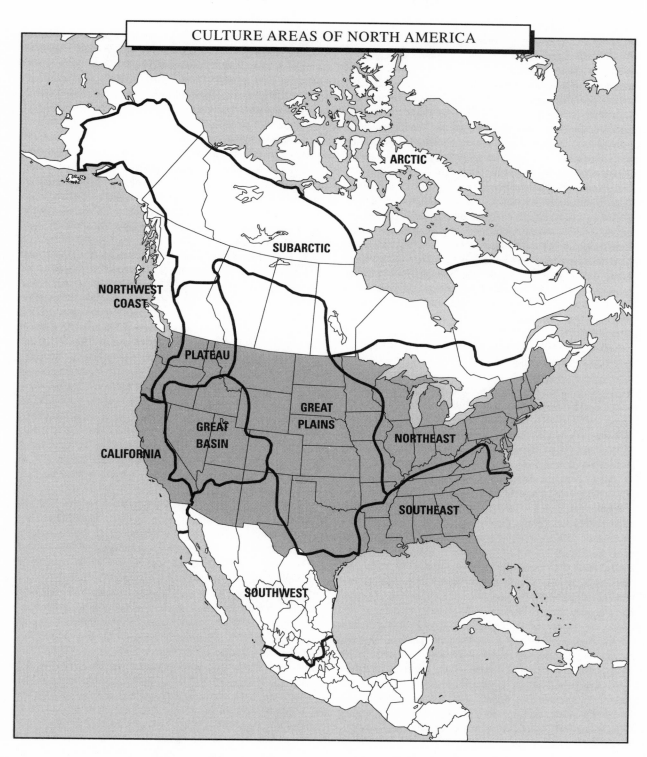

CULTURE AREAS OF NORTH AMERICA

horses were introduced from the Great Basin Shoshones, some tribes moved seasonally over the mountains into Idaho to hunt bison. Such groups abandoned their traditional pit house structures for portable hide-covered tipis.

California. The Western coast and inland area farther south were more diversified in language groupings, which broke down into the main Penutian and Hokan families (the former including Klamath-Modoc, Miwok, and Central Valley Yokut and Maidu; the latter including Washoe and Yana in the north and in the central eastern zone near Nevada).

Three cultural zones corresponded primarily to ecological subregions. In the northwest corner, dense forests, rugged topography, and the absence of a coastal plain set off isolated (both linguistically and culturally) inhabitants from the fertile core of Penutian-Hokan groups around San Francisco Bay and in the much milder ecological zone of the Central Valley. In this core zone, economic patterns, based on hunting, fishing, and the gathering of available vegetal food sources (including a universal staple, acorn meal), tended to lend similarities to tribal social and cultural patterns. One similarity was the relative lack of formal institutional structures defining tribal organization and authority. Chiefs tended to be heads of the most numerous family among a multitude of generally equal family subdivisions of each clan. One of two main forms of lodging predominated: either the "house pit" scraped out of rolling knolls, or the wickiup, a bark-thatched covering stretched around portable poles. Central California tribes were highly skilled in basketweaving, some (mainly Pomos and Patwins) producing wares sufficiently tightly woven to serve as water containers.

South of the Central Valley, increasing aridity affected not only food-gathering conditions; basic technology (reflected in lodgings and artisanal production, including modes of dress) never attained levels that could be compared with tribes in the central region. Notable degrees of west-east interaction occurred, particularly between the Luiseños of present-day San Diego and Riverside counties (themselves of Shoshone stock) and Nevadan tribes. These contacts were reflected not only in trade of goods, but also in some shared cultural values that set the inland (less than the coastal) southern zone off from the relatively more developed Central Valley region.

Southwest. Beyond California was the inland cultural area of the Southwest. Despite the ecological austerity of these vast expanses, nearly all Southwest Indians practiced some form of agriculture, supplemented by seasonally available wild plant foods. Most also developed technologically advanced cultures, as judged from the remains of their lodging and ceremonial sites (particularly the pueblos) and various artifacts, especially pottery and weaving.

Among the several Indian subgroupings in the Southwest are the Hopi, Navajo, and Zuni. Their life patterns, although not identical, exemplify the main lines of Southwest Indian culture. Characteristically, Indian villages in the Southwest were constructed in the compact stone and adobe pueblo form, usually located on higher ground or on mesas for purposes of defense. The limited circumstances of dry farming often meant that plantations were located some distance from the pueblo.

In addition to being a dwelling and defense unit, the pueblo was a microcosm for both political and religious life. Particularly among the Eastern Pueblos, different responsibilities, from practical work tasks to ceremonial leadership, were traditionally divided between two fully cooperative factions. Living in different sections of the village, each faction maintained a kiva, or religiously designated meeting place for its elders, and ceremonial dance (kachina) groups, or medicine men, organized in societies. When a particular "season" for representation of the pueblo's ceremonial, political, or administrative needs was recognized, all loyalty was due to the kiva of the designated faction, while others rested from their responsibilities.

Southwest Indian religion and ceremonies were frequently tied to the concept of an "earth mother navel" shrine located in a sacred place within each pueblo. Around this ultimate source of bounty for the members of each tight-knit pueblo community were arranged the symbols of life (seeds and their products). Such symbols, plus other symbols of nature (especially rain) were incorporated into each pueblo's ceremonial dances, according to the season.

Great Basin. In the area wedged between California and the Plateau to the west, and the Southwest and Great Plains to the east, Indian cultures tended to be rather dispersed. Areas of habitation remained highly dependent on the availability of water and vegetation to sustain limited village life. Although broad tribal groupings existed (including Ute, Paiute, and Shoshone), the main activities of Indian life, from food gathering through marital, social, and political alliances, tended to be conducted in smaller bands. Contacts between subtribal bands (the Ute, on both the Colorado and Utah sides of the Rockies, counted some dozen territorial bands) could be only periodic. This rather lower level of tribal cohesiveness relative to Plateau and Southwest Indians, for example, allowed quarreling families from one band to "transfer" over to a band to which they were not tied by kinship; even lines between the tribes (Ute and Paiute, for example) were not that definitely drawn.

Some shared features of cultural existence within and between Great Basin tribes countered this general trend. Although religious consciousness among Great Basin Indians never attained a high degree of ceremonial sophistication, certain symbolic rites, among them the Sun Dance, provided a common cultural symbol in most regions.

Plains. It was among the Plains Indians that the most dramatic subsistence struggle was played out, by tribes such as the Sioux, Cheyenne, Pawnee, and Comanche. Acquisition of the horse from the Spanish after about 1600 transformed the subsistence potential of the Plains, which became the buffalo-hunting domains of competing Indian tribes. Pursuit of the great native herds of buffalo on horseback, beginning in the 1600's, created a situation of Indian nomadism on the Plains. Buffalo hunting affected not only food supply, but also provided raw material for the organization of Plains tribes' movable lodgings and the production of multiple lightweight artifacts. The high degree of mobility of Plains Indians also contributed to another key cultural trait: their tendency to war with rivals over hunting access.

Among the Sioux, the Lakota were drawn into the Plains from the Eastern Prairie region after becoming expert horsemen, well before the French entered the upper Mississippi Valley. Soon their nomadic way of life on the Plains allowed them to subjugate sedentary groupings such as the Arikara and Mandan, who were forced to trade their agricultural goods with the Lakota. The characteristic warring urge of such Plains nomads resulted in serious intertribal disputes, the best known resulting in the reduction and forced relocation of the Pawnee people after multiple encounters with representatives of the Sioux Nation.

The simplicity of the material culture of the Plains Indians was to some degree offset by the complexity of some of their social and cultural patterns. A number of honorary societies, ranging from warrior groups through "headmen" societies (elders who had distinguished themselves earlier as warriors or leaders), provided means for identifying individuals of importance emerging from each family or clan within the tribe. Recognition was also given, among the women, to highly skillful beadworkers, who defined qualification for entry into their "guild" and excluded inferior workmanship from being used in ritual ceremonies.

Another specialized subgrouping, particularly among the Dakota peoples, was the Heyoka, consisting of people who were recognized as possessing some form of supernatural or visionary power. Although not specifically connected to Plains religious beliefs (frequently associated with Sun Dance ceremonies and related celebrations of thanks for bounty, physical endurance, and interclan alliances), Heyoka status implied the ability to communicate with spirits, either good or evil. In some Siouan tribes, such as the Omaha, Heyoka societies were evenly divided into specialized branches, the most notable being one reserved specifically for individuals presumed to have the power to cure diseases.

Northeast and Southeast. In the eastern third of the continent, a higher degree of sedentariness among various tribes prevailed, although this did not necessarily mean that agriculture was more developed. Plantations for food tended to be scattered in the heavily wooded Northeast, with hunting and trapping at least as important in most tribal economies. Another product of the forest, the paperlike bark of the birch tree, served multiple purposes, ranging from tipi-building material to the famous birchbark canoes used to fish or to travel through the extensive river and stream systems of the region.

In general, social organization among the tribes of the Northeast bore two major characteristics. Groups that were known as hunters (such as the Micmacs of New Brunswick and Maine) lived as nuclear families, paramount status being reserved for the hunter-head of closely related kin. Lodgings might be limited to a single family (typically a tipi) or a grouping of families under the single roof of an extended longhouse. In most cases, ascription of chieftainship was determined by a hierarchy that also depended on hunting skills.

A second characteristic of Northeast Woodlands Indian life revolved around political confederations involving several tribes. The best known of these was the Iroquois "Five Nations," but other groups, including the Algonquins and Hurons, formed federations for mutual security against common enemies.

Although the Southeast region of the United States can, like the Northeast, be described as heavily wooded, offering a combination of possibilities for hunting and agriculture, the Indian cultures of this area were substantially different. Some experts argue that there was less communality in cultural development in the Southeast, making distinctions, for example, between peoples who were clearly reliant on the ecology of the first "layer" of the broad coastal plain (called the "Flatwoods," blanketed by conifers and scrub oaks); those inhabiting the so-called Piedmont (further inland, with higher elevations and differing vegetation patterns); and those living in the Appalachian woodlands, with their extensive hardwood forests.

Some experts, noting communality in traits (such as a horticultural maize economy, nucleated villages, and matrilineal clan organization) between key Southeastern tribes such as the Creek, Choctaw, Cherokee, Natchez, and the Iroquois, found farther north, assign a southeastern origin to the Iroquois. A substantial number of differences marked by cultural specialists, however, suggest closer ties between coastal and inland dwellers in the Southeast (especially in linguistic links) than between Southeast Indians as a whole and any of their Northeast neighbors. A series of lesser, but culturally significant, traits justify treating Southeast Indians as a largely homogeneous entity, including modes of processing staple nuts, especially acorns; rectangular, gabled houses with mud wattle covering; an absence of leather footwear; characteristic nested twilled baskets; and varied use of tobacco.

Even among key Southeast tribes, however, parallel traditions (such as matrilineal kinship descent) could be offset by striking differences. The Natchez tribe alone, for example, had a class system dividing tribal nobles (deemed descendants of the Sun), from whom the chief, or "Great Sun" was chosen, and commoners, who could not even enter the presence of tribal aristocrats.

—*Byron D. Cannon*

See also Arctic; California; Great Basin; Northeast; Northwest Coast; Plains; Plateau; Southeast; Southwest; Subarctic.

BIBLIOGRAPHY

Catlin, George. *Letters and Notes on the Manners, Customs, and Conditions of North American Indians.* New York: 1841. A recognized classic, including personal observations of Indian ceremonial practices and daily life. Some editions include extremely valuable illustrations, which have gained international fame.

Driver, Harold E. *Indians of North America.* 2d ed. Chicago: University of Chicago Press, 1969. A widely cited textbook organized by subject area (for example, "Rank and Social Class," "Exchange and Trade") rather than geographical location.

Kehoe, Alice B. *North American Indians: A Comprehensive Account.* 2d ed. Englewood Cliffs, N.J.: Prentice-Hall, 1992. Like the Spencer and Jennings book (below), this textbook is divided by geographical region. Less detailed on local conditions of life, it contains useful summary texts within each chapter and a number of translations of original Indian texts.

Ross, Thomas E., and Tyrel Moore, eds. *A Cultural Geography of North American Indians*. Boulder, Colo.: Westview Press, 1987. Contains contributions by specialists dealing with several different geographical themes relating to culture, including "Spatial Awareness," "Land Ownership," and "Migration."

Spencer, Robert, Jesse D. Jennings, et al. *The Native Americans*. 2d ed. New York: Harper & Row, 1977. A very detailed text. Attention is given to diverse patterns of local division of labor, kinship, rites of passage, and so on.

Sturtevant, William, gen. ed. *Handbook of North American Indians*. Washington, D.C.: Smithsonian Institution Press, 1978-. The Smithsonian series is a projected twenty-volume set, with a volume either published or planned for each of the culture areas. The scholarship and coverage are both first rate. The set was initiated in 1978 with the volume on the Northeast, edited by Bruce Trigger, and nine volumes had been published by 1994.

Cupeño: Tribe

CULTURE AREA: California
LANGUAGE GROUP: Cupeño
PRIMARY LOCATION: San Jose de Valle valley, California
POPULATION SIZE: 371, including Agua Caliente (1990 U.S. Census)

The Cupeño were patrilocal and married outside their kin groups. With no direct access to the ocean, the Cupeño relied on acorns, seeds, berries, deer, quail, and other small animals. They occupied two politically autonomous villages, united by trade, marriage, rituals, and language. Clans were headed by men through inheritance; they maintained the clan's ceremonial dance house and paraphernalia. Ceremonies were concerned with mortuary rituals, world-renewal rites, and an eagle-killing ritual.

The Cupeño were first contacted by the Spanish in 1795, but no sustained contact was established until 1820 when *asistencias* were built by the Spaniards to graze their cattle. With control of their lands gone, the Cupeño were forced to work as serfs until eventually the "owners" of Cupeño lands wanted them removed in the late 1890's. Years of litigation and national protest prevented this, until the California Supreme Court removed the Cupeño to the Pala Reservation in Luiseño territory.

See also Luiseño.

Curly (c. 1859, along the Rosebud River, Mont.—May 22, 1923): Army scout

ALSO KNOWN AS: Ashishishe
TRIBAL AFFILIATION: Crow
SIGNIFICANCE: Curly served as scout for General George A. Custer at the Battle of the Little Bighorn; after Custer's defeat, he escaped and reported the annihilation of Custer's army, but questions later arose concerning his involvement in the battle

Curly was born in Crow country along the Rosebud River in Montana. There is little knowledge of the thin young brave with long black braids prior to his service as an Indian scout for the Seventh Cavalry. In April of 1876 Curly and several other young Crows were recruited for the famed Yellowstone expedition. Enlisted for their intimate knowledge of the region, their mission was to aid in the search for hostile tribes. Curly and five of his Crow scouts were assigned to General George Armstrong Custer's ill-fated detachment.

Like Custer's ominous battle, Curly has become embroiled in controversy. None of Custer's men escaped the Battle of the Little Bighorn; however, the Crow scouts did, including the seventeen-year-old Curly. He claimed to have remained with the battle until it appeared hopeless, then, tying his hair similar to the Sioux and wrapping himself in a fallen Sioux's blanket, rode away undetected. He journeyed to the fork of the Bighorn and Yellowstone Rivers where the *Far West*, an Army supply boat, waited. There he delivered the first news of Custer's terrible defeat.

The other Crow scouts tell a different story. They claim they were instructed before the battle began to remain in the rear; they watched from a distance as Custer led his troops to their death, and when the outcome seemed apparent, Curly rode to the supply boat while the rest rode home. Many historians, in search of the true story, sought Curly in his later years; unfortunately, his reluctance to talk and seeming inconsistencies only added to the debate. Curly died in 1923 and was buried in Montana at the National Cemetery on the Custer Battlefield.

See also Little Bighorn, Battle of the.

Curtis, Charles (Jan. 25, 1860, Topeka, Kans.—Feb. 8, 1936, Washington, D.C.): Politician

TRIBAL AFFILIATION: Kansa
SIGNIFICANCE: Curtis was the first American of Indian descent to serve in the United States Senate and the first to become vice president of the United States

Charles Curtis was born and spent much of his childhood in Topeka, Kansas. In 1881, Curtis established a law practice in Topeka. He soon won election to become the prosecuting attorney of Shawnee County, serving from 1885 to 1889. Curtis' first foray into national politics occurred in 1893, when he won election to the United States House of Representatives on the Republican ticket. Curtis served until 1907, when he was elected to the United States Senate. As the first Native American to serve in the Senate, Curtis took an active role in Indian matters, chairing the Committee on Indian Depredations. Curtis was a member of the United States Senate from 1907 to 1913, and again from 1915 to 1929. During that period, Curtis was the Republican whip, responsible for gathering and counting votes, from 1915 to 1924, but then he ascended to the position of Senate majority leader, considered to be the most powerful leadership role in the Senate, which he held from 1925 to 1929.

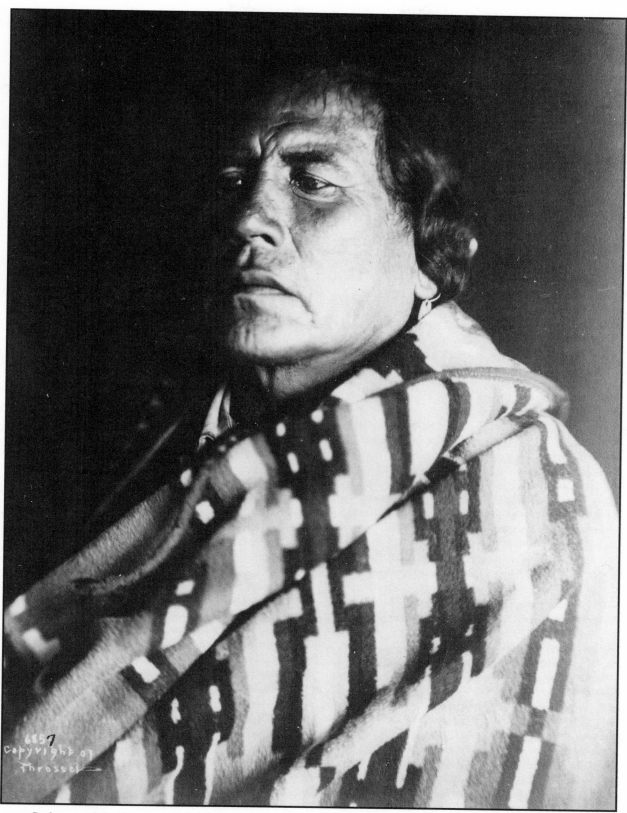

Curly, one of the Crow scouts for the army who survived the Battle of the Little Bighorn. (Library of Congress)

Curtis was elected vice president of the United States in 1928, serving under President Herbert Hoover from 1929 to 1933. After failing to win re-election, he resumed the practice of law in Washington, D.C., where he resided for the remainder of his life. Curtis died in Washington, D.C., on February 8, 1936. His remains are interred at the Topeka Cemetery in Topeka, Kansas.

BIBLIOGRAPHY

Seitz, Don Carlos. *From Kaw Teepee to Capitol: The Life Story of Charles Curtis, Indian, Who Has Risen to High Estate*. New York: Frederick A. Stokes, 1928.

Unrau, William E. *Mixed Bloods and Tribal Dissolution: Charles Curtis and the Quest for Indian Identity*. Lawrence: University Press of Kansas, 1989.

Charles Curtis, a Kansa, the first American Indian U.S. senator, was elected in 1907. (Library of Congress)

Dances and dancing

TRIBES AFFECTED: Pantribal

SIGNIFICANCE: Among American Indians, dancing has always played a highly significant role in religious ceremonies and other celebrations

When white explorers and settlers first came to North America, they were immediately impressed by the amount of dancing in which the native population engaged. Centuries later, some of the significance of tribal ceremonies has been lost, as more and more Indians have accepted white culture and religion. Nevertheless, dancing still plays an important part in American Indian life, whether it represents a true continuation of the original tribal cultures, a celebration of birth, death, or other rites of passage, or merely a performance for white tourists.

Historical Background. When European explorers and settlers first encountered the native population of what would later become the United States, they found a wide variety of cultures, all of them vastly different from the ones they had left behind. The American Indians had never developed a technological civilization, and the land was much less densely populated than that of Europe. The religious beliefs were like nothing the Europeans had ever encountered.

The first Europeans in North America had no understanding of the native languages they encountered. The usual view of the "red man" was as a savage—inherently inferior to the settlers and potentially dangerous. The two major activities of the Europeans were to conquer the natives and to try to bring to them the Christianity that was virtually universal in Europe at the time.

The result was a long series of wars, in which the Europeans were ultimately victorious. In the process, many native cultures were destroyed altogether, while others were forced to move west. By the late nineteenth century, the last of "Indian territory" had been conquered, and Indians lived on reservations, generally under very harsh conditions.

Gradually, many Indians who survived the early warfare became a part of white culture and accepted its religious beliefs (chiefly Christianity). In the late twentieth century, many Indians began to try to reclaim their ancient heritage, often moving beyond tribal lines and creating a pantribal movement that strove to preserve the Indian cultures from complete assimilation.

As a result of all these factors, it is very difficult to determine the significance of many tribal rituals as they exist today. Some Indians still retain their ancient beliefs and traditions despite centuries of domination. Others may hold on to a tradition for the sake of tradition itself, while at the same time going to Christian churches, speaking English as their primary language, and even living in large cities. For some, the old rituals, including dances, are little more than a way of attracting tourists.

Regardless of this confusion, all the following rituals will be discussed in the present tense, and it will be assumed that the dances still hold their original meaning to the participants.

Some of these dances are rarely performed nowadays, while others are making a resurgence as Indians try to regain their lost cultural identity.

Religious Significance. By the time Europeans were settling in the Americas, their own traditions had changed greatly since their days as small tribal groups. It is very likely that the Europeans had once had a culture in which dancing and music were integral to religion, but this had long become a thing of the past. Certain traditions suggested this past; singing is still an important part of many Christian ceremonies and probably always will be. Dances, however, had largely become stylized, social affairs, with no deep religious or cultural significance.

The American Indians, however, had never developed such a differentiation between religious and social climates. To them, the earth and all living creatures on it were possessed by spirits, and these spirits were understood, and to some extent controlled, by a great number of elaborate dances and songs. There were dances for hunting, fishing, rites of passage, rain, and success in warfare.

The many Indian tribes in North America have different religious rituals, including dances. Conditions in different parts of the continent vary, and different spirits must be appeased under different circumstances. The one aspect almost all of these people have in common is a close tie to the earth and the spirits that control it, although different tribes respond to this in different ways.

The Northwest. The Indians of the Pacific Northwest generally perform their dances singly. Both men and women are involved. The dancers are considered to be possessed by spirits, and the dances can become highly frenzied and emotional. The dances are accompanied by drumming and chanting.

An excellent example of Northwest dancing involves the Kwakiutl, who live along the coast of Oregon and Washington. The Kwakiutl have highly formalized dancing, during which various taboos are enforced and dancers are called only by ceremonial names. Even seating arrangements at the festivities are based on dancing societies rather than on families and clans.

The Kwakiutl have three mutually exclusive dancing societies, sometimes called "secret societies." Initiation into one of these societies is highly ritualized, and numbers are limited. The Shaman Society is concerned with violent and dangerous supernatural spirits. The most prestigious dancer is a cannibal/dancer, or Hamatsa. People in the Dluwulaxa Society are possessed by spirits of the sky. The Nutlam are possessed by their mythical ancestors, the wolves.

The Northwest Coast was never very heavily populated by Indians, and it was one of the last areas settled by European Americans. There are still many Indians who follow tradition as much as possible in the Northwest, but few live on reservations. There is a large American Indian population in big cities such as Seattle, Washington, and Portland, Oregon. Farther inland, where most of the land is mountainous and much is national park and national forest land, the traditions also continue.

The Southwest. The condition in the Southwest is quite different. This area was highly populated by a variety of Indian

Kwakiutl masked dancers, photographed in the early twentieth century. (American Museum of Natural History)

tribes, then taken over by the Spanish, the Mexicans, and finally the United States government. Climatic conditions vary widely. There are mountain ranges, coastal areas subject to regular flooding, and deserts in which water is the most important consideration for survival. This is the area where the greatest number of Indian reservations exist today and where the greatest proportion of Indians still practice their original rites.

It must be understood that most of the reservations were placed on land the white settlers did not want, and where the climate is harsh. Reservation Indians have both their own problems and their own advantages. There is great poverty, and the social problems that accompany poverty, frustration, and isolation are severe. On the other hand, these Indians are more closely in touch with their origins. The Southwest is probably the best place in the United States to find Indian ceremonies in a state very close to what they were before white people appeared on the scene.

An interesting example of the dancing ceremonies in the Southwest is the Kachina dances among the Zuni of New Mexico. The Kachinas are considered to be the spirits of children, lost long ago in the wilderness and transformed into gods who live under a mystic lake. The Kachinas wear masks and dance for rain. The dancers impersonating the Kachinas "become" rain gods and invoke the spirits who will provide the parched land with much-needed water.

The traditional cultures of the Southwest may be the hardest for white visitors to understand, because many reservations have made tourism a major economic factor. There are certainly many Indians there who still believe in the traditional religions; on the other hand, the great poverty in this area has led many to reenact ceremonies long extinct in order to please tourists.

The Southeast. The southeastern United States is probably the most easily endured climate in North America. While there are hurricanes and other natural disasters, for the most part the people live in a generally warm and hospitable climate, and food is abundant. Hunting is never easy, however, so the spirits must be evoked.

The southeastern tribes were among the first to be encountered by Europeans, a fact which has had two directly opposite results in terms of the study of these cultures. On one side, these Indians were not opposed to accepting white people as a new tribe moving into the area, and many tribal ceremonies were seen by the explorers in their original state. When Sir Walter Raleigh and his men first set foot on the North Carolina coast, wars between Indians and Europeans were a long way in the future. Therefore, some of the best early descriptions of Indian dances and other rituals exist from this area. On the other hand, when the wars did take place, they began on the East Coast. Some cultures were entirely destroyed, and others were forced to move from their home territory. In many cases, there is little but historical evidence on which to draw.

The Southeast Indians use rattles made from gourds and filled with peas, beans, or pebbles; flutes made of reed or cane; and drums made of clay, gourd, or wood, with stretched deerhides for skin, as accompaniments to their dances.

Indians of the Southeast generally dance in large groups, sometimes for many hours at a stretch, with groups of dancers replacing other groups as they grow tired. Masks are often worn, especially in hunting ceremonies, where animal masks are used. The dances are often named after animals.

The Northeast. The Indians of the Northeast also encountered Europeans very early, but the initial meetings were not nearly as friendly as they were farther south. In the Middle Atlantic and New England areas, conditions could be extremely harsh, and good land was not as plentiful as it was in the south. In addition, the northeastern Iroquois were held together by a confederation of six tribes and an alliance with others. Their chief rivals among Indians were the Algonquins, with whom they were often at war. In fact, during the French and Indian War, the Algonquins took the part of the French and the Iroquois that of the English.

White settlers rarely saw Indian ceremonies; in general, these ceremonies tended to be more social and political (and less religious) in nature than those of most North American Indians. Dancing seems to had less significance here than it did elsewhere. These civilizations are by no means completely gone. There are Indian reservations in New York, for example, where Iroquois live in longhouses and still maintain many of their ancient traditions. The British victory over the French in North America decimated the Algonquins, but there are still many Iroquois in the area.

As in most Indian cultures, many dances have animals as their subjects; the Iroquois, however, are celebrating the animals' lives rather than worshiping their spirits. Dancing involves men, women, and children and is not as clearly structured as it is in the cultures previously described. Since Iroquois dances generally take place inside the longhouses, they cannot be as elaborate or involve as many people as the dances held outside by more southerly tribes.

The Northern Plains. Dance is an integral part of the religious rites of the Indians of the northern Plains. These are performed by both men and women, in large groups, and are highly formalized. Colorful, elaborate costumes are worn. The Plains Indians are the Indians who have been stereotyped in westerns, with feathers, beads, fur, and facial and body paint.

A dance of particular interest is the Sun Dance, a celebration of the cyclical nature of life. The Sun Dance is of interest for several reasons. First, it is still very much in practice, although its nature has changed somewhat. Second, it has been elaborately described by Indians in the twentieth century, who saw it in its original form as children. Finally, the Sun Dance was one of the first Indian ceremonies to be banned by the U.S. government, because of its rather violent nature. This ban,

never completely successful, was lifted in 1933, after which the ceremony continued in a somewhat curtailed fashion.

In its original form, the Sun Dance is more than a dance. It is a ceremony formed around the building of a lodge. Frenzied singing and dancing accompany the erection of the lodge. After this, young men are initiated into the tribe and become warriors by having their breasts cut by a medicine man and a thong sewn through the cuts. The young men dance and attempt to remove the thongs. Grave injury sometimes results.

Such ceremonies have been curtailed in modern society. The Sun Dance is still practiced, but young men are not as prominently figured in it as they originally were, and the mutilation has been replaced by symbolic sacrifice.

The people now called the Sioux, actually a mixture of related tribes, are strongly dominated by males. Men have traditionally held the central place in dances, as in most other aspects of life. As elsewhere, however, some aspects of the modern world have changed the basic ceremonies. At the beginning of the Sun Dance ceremony, for example, the American flag is praised, and there may be Christian as well as Sioux prayers said.

The Southern Plains. The dances of the southern Plains groups are not far different from those of their northern neighbors in terms of symbolism and theme. One difference is a greater preponderance of war dances. The most important way in which the two areas differ in their ceremonies is in the degree of formality and the exclusiveness of a dance or ceremony to a particular tribe.

In the southern Plains, dances and pow-wows are as much social gatherings as religious rituals. Often, many tribes will participate. Nearly anyone can get up and join in the festivities, and although the costumes can be as elaborate as they are in the north, formalized dress is not required. Today, among the dancers dressed in beads and feathers, one may see others dressed in jeans and flannel shirts.

The southern Plains were the last area in the contiguous states to be taken formally from the Indians, and thus the most traditional ceremonies can often be seen here. Oklahoma, until it was opened to white settlement in 1889, was still considered Indian Territory. Oklahoma has one of the largest proportions of Indian population in the United States.   —*Marc Goldstein*

See also Buffalo Dance; Ghost Dance; Gourd Dance; Grass Dance; Music and song; Pow-wows and contemporary celebrations; Stomp Dance; Sun Dance; Tobacco Society and Dance; White Deerskin Dance.

BIBLIOGRAPHY

Bancroft-Hunt, Norman. *People of the Totem*. New York: G. P. Putnam's Sons, 1979. A description of Northwest American Indian culture, including a study of their history, ceremonies, and contemporary conditions.

Buttree, Julia M. *The Rhythm of the Red Man*. New York: A. S. Barnes, 1930. A description of Indian rituals, especially music and dance, including step-by-step instructions for a great number of dances and rituals followed by a variety of tribal groups.

Hamilton, Charles. *Cry of the Thunderbird: The American Indian's Own Story.* New ed. Norman: University of Oklahoma Press, 1972. A compilation of articles by American Indians about their culture, including memories of childhood, historical beginnings, and contemporary conditions.

Heth, Charlotte, ed. *Native American Dance: Ceremonies and Social Traditions.* Washington, D.C.: National Museum of the American Indian, Starwood Publishing, 1992. An illustrated guide to the dances of many American Indian tribes, with descriptions of specific dances as well as general discussions of dance practices by region.

Spencer, Robert F., Jesse D. Jennings, et al. *The Native Americans.* New York: Harper & Row, 1977. An encyclopedic discussion of American Indian culture, from prehistory to contemporary times.

Dancing Rabbit Creek, Treaty of

DATE: September 27, 1830

PLACE: Mississippi

TRIBE AFFECTED: Choctaw

SIGNIFICANCE: In the first treaty signed after passage of the Indian Removal Act, the experience of the Choctaws foreshadowed that of many tribes as they sold their lands in Mississippi and agreed to move west

The Choctaws originally occupied much of present-day Mississippi. The tribe prided itself on good relations with the United States and the fact that it had never fought against the United States. Instead Choctaws had fought as American allies in the Creek War (1813-1814) and War of 1812.

Nevertheless the Choctaws came under increasing pressure from American settlers as the area filled rapidly after the War of 1812. In treaties going back to 1801, the Choctaws had ceded land to facilitate settlement. Pressed by General Andrew Jackson, in 1820 the tribe agreed to the Treaty of Doak's Stand. Five million acres of land in western and west-central Mississippi were sold to the United States; in return, the Choctaws acquired thirteen million acres west of the Mississippi. The acquisition of western land clearly raised the prospect of removal, though few Choctaws chose to emigrate.

American pressure mounted, however, especially after Jackson's election to the presidency in 1828. Encouraged by his administration's stated goal of removing the tribes east of the Mississippi, in January, 1830, the Mississippi legislature voted to extend state jurisdiction over Choctaw lands, effectively ignoring tribal claims to the land. Feeling pressured and believing that American power was irresistible, Choctaw leaders agreed to negotiate. Terms proposed by Greenwood Le-Flore, recently elected principal chief of the tribe, were rejected as too expensive. The Choctaws then agreed to a new round of negotiations at Dancing Rabbit Creek.

There in September, 1813, chiefs LeFlore, Mushulatubbee, and Nitekechi and six thousand Choctaws met American commissioners John Eaton and John Coffee. The Americans had made elaborate preparations to feed and entertain the Choctaws and to create a festive air for the negotiations. Reluc-

tantly, the chiefs agreed to the terms requested: In return for a $20,000, twenty-year annuity and other financial considerations, the Choctaws would give up the remaining ten million acres of their land in Mississippi and move to their lands in present-day southeastern Oklahoma. Choctaws who wished to stay in Mississippi would receive one-square-mile allotments and U.S. citizenship, provided they registered within six months of the treaty's ratification and lived on their lands for five years. (Federal officials saw to it that relatively few Choctaws remained under this provision.)

Though a few hundred Choctaws had departed for Indian Territory in 1830 in hopes of locating the best land, removal of the bulk of the tribe began in 1831 and extended over a three-year period. Much hardship accompanied the Choctaw "Trail of Tears," especially in 1831, and about 15 percent of the tribe died during removal. The Choctaws were the first major tribe to be moved under the Indian Removal Act, and their experience established an important precedent that would be followed with other eastern tribes.

See also Choctaw; Creek War; Indian Removal Act; Indian-white relations—U.S., 1831-1870; Removal; Trail of Tears.

Danger Cave: Archaeological site

DATE: c. 9000 B.C.E.-c. 1400 C.E.

LOCATION: Western Utah

CULTURES AFFECTED: Desert or Western Archaic culture, recent Paiute

Danger Cave is one of a number of caves in the hills near Wendover, Utah, to have yielded archaeological data on prehistoric Indian life. Findings in the roughly 60-by-120-foot cave include human skeletal remains, animal and plant material, tools, clothing fragments, and basketry artifacts. The findings are distributed in five or six differentiated layers, some as deep as 13 feet. Radiocarbon dating shows rather wide gaps in time between layers, indicating sporadic occupation. The number and complexity of artifacts increases from the earliest to the latest layers, but some features are common to all—particularly the milling stones which, together with remains of seeds from types of plants still growing in the area, indicate that ground seeds were a dietary staple for all the hunter-gatherers who lived in the cave.

Stone spear or dart points are also found in all layers; interestingly, arrow points appear only in the most recent. Leather moccasins, as well as antelope hairs found in fecal remains, show that animal materials were used for both food and clothing. Basketry underwent a shift from twined (wrapped around upright twigs) to coiled forms. Ceramics appear only in recent layers. About two thousand years ago, the deposits in the cave almost completely blocked its entrance and reduced its use to the rocky overhang at the front. Pottery shards of the Shoshone type in the putative sixth layer suggest relatively recent camps of Paiute tribes. Other caves in the same area as Danger Cave (Hogup, Raven, and Juke Box caves) have yielded similar archaeological finds, substantiating the conclusions about the Western Archaic life inferred from Danger Cave: relatively small groups of thirty or forty persons, probably family-related, who eked out a thin living in difficult surroundings, devoting most of their time to food-finding, with little evidence of any important ceremonial tradition.

See also Archaic; Desert culture; Paleo-Indian; Prehistory—Great Basin.

Dating methods

TRIBES AFFECTED: Pantribal

SIGNIFICANCE: A variety of methods, both absolute and relative, are used by scholars to establish dates for archaeological sites and artifacts

Archaeological sites in the Americas are assigned ages based either on absolute dating methods, in which a date in calendar years is provided, or on relative dating methods, in which an age either relatively older or younger is provided. The main absolute dating methods used in the Americas, occupied since about 9500 B.C.E., include radiocarbon dating, obsidian hydration dating, and dendrochronology. The major relative dating techniques are stratigraphic analysis, seriation, and cross-dating.

Radiocarbon Dating. The invention of radiocarbon dating by Willard Libby in 1949 revolutionized archaeology by providing an absolute means for dating sites. The radiocarbon method is based on the knowledge that cosmic radiation entering the earth's atmosphere produces neutrons which react with nitrogen to produce carbon 14. Carbon 14 is unstable and subject to gradual radioactive decay. Living organisms maintain the same level of carbon 14 as that found in the atmosphere because of their intake of carbon dioxide. At death, however, the ratio of radioactive carbon 14 to stable carbon 12 decays at a constant and known rate. Half of the original carbon 14 disappears in 5,568 years, known as the "half-life" of carbon 14. Organic material, notably charcoal, wood, shell, bone, and hair, can be radiocarbon dated to seventy thousand years, provided there is sufficient carbon remaining.

Whenever a neutron leaves a carbon 14 nucleus, a radioactive (beta) particle is emitted. The amount of radioactivity remaining in the sample can be measured at a radiocarbon laboratory by counting the number of beta emissions per gram of carbon. The accelerator mass spectrometry (AMS) method allows radiocarbon dating of material containing between 0.3 and 0.002 gram of carbon, such as a single corn kernel. Something this small was not datable by the standard method, which requires at least 1 gram of carbon, retrievable from 10-20 grams of charcoal.

A laboratory radiocarbon date of 1,270 +/- 60 B.P. means radiocarbon years before present (B.P.), with present at 1950 C.E. The date is expressed as one standard deviation, meaning there is a 68 percent probability that the age of the dated specimen is between 1,210 and 1,330 years old. Doubling the standard deviation increases the accuracy of the date to 95 percent. Radiocarbon dates are corrected or "calibrated" because of minor fluctuations in carbon 14 in the atmosphere

from variations in cosmic radiation and the earth's magnetism by comparison with tree-ring dates. "Calibration curves" are published in the journal *Radiocarbon*.

Dendrochronology. Wooden artifacts, particularly house beams, are dated in California, British Columbia, Alaska, and Mexico by the tree-ring method, dendrochronology, developed by A. E. Douglass around 1913. Climatic variations cause minor fluctuations in the annual growth pattern on trees. Ages of prehistoric wood are assigned by comparing the patterning of the annual growth rings with an established tree-ring chart, extending 8,200 years, based on the California bristle-cone pine.

Obsidian Hydration. Obsidian hydration is used to date artifacts made of obsidian, a volcanic glass used to make blades and other items. A freshly made or reworked obsidian artifact absorbs water (or "hydrates") at a known rate, creating an obsidian hydration band that can be visually measured in microns with a microscope. Since the obsidian hydration rate is subject to local climatic variations, hydration sequences are established for particular locations. Sites in California, British Columbia, and Middle America, where obsidian was widely used in prehistory, have been dated by obsidian hydration.

Other Absolute Dating Methods. Correlation of prehistoric calendars, such as the Maya calendars that recorded and dated historical events on carved monuments, or "stelae," with the Christian calendar can date archaeological sites. Archaeomagnetic dating of clay from fire hearths measures the magnetism in the clay sample in comparison with records of fluctuations in the earth's magnetic field. Thermoluminescence provides an age range for pottery or other baked clay objects, which emit a visible light when heated in a laboratory and measured.

Stratigraphic Analysis and Cross-Dating. Stratigraphic analysis is the most common relative dating technique for prehistoric America. Since the layers of the earth were created by natural processes of wind, water, and erosion (termed "uniformitarian" processes), archaeologists follow the law of "superimposition," whereby artifacts in lower layers are considered older than those in upper layers. Artifacts, house floors, structures, or other features discovered in a particular level of a site during excavation are placed into the same category. The stylistic changes of artifacts observed in the different levels reflect stylistic changes over time. Cross-dating is a technique used to date sites of unknown age by comparing the styles of the artifacts with those from sites of known age. Once a chronological framework is established for a site or culture area, artifacts of unknown age are often dated by comparison.

Seriation. Seriation is a technique that is used to assign a relative age to artifacts, structures, or even entire sites without stratigraphic analysis, based on the assumption that styles change over time: A style is introduced, becomes popular or has a period of maximum frequency, and then wanes in popularity. Seriation is carried out by comparing the stylistic similarities and differences of the items under consideration. Artifacts collected from the surface of a site of unknown age are sorted into categories based on their similarities. An age is then assigned based on the relative frequencies of particular styles in comparison with a known sequence from another site or from comparison with sites showing the frequencies of stylistic change over time.

Other Relative Dating Methods. Early sites in glaciated regions may be dated by their location relative to glacial advances and retreats during the last Ice Age (Pleistocene), a technique known as Pleistocene geochronology. Pollen analysis, or palynology, dates sites by comparison of the vegetation identified from pollen in soil from a site with established pollen sequences. —*Heather McKillop*

See also Adena; Anasazi; Archaic; Clovis; Desert culture; Hopewell; Middens; Woodland.

BIBLIOGRAPHY

Deetz, James. *Invitation to Archaeology*. Garden City, N.Y.: Natural History Press, 1967.

Michels, Joseph W. *Dating Methods in Archaeology*. New York: Seminar Press, 1973.

Pearson, Gordon W. "How to Cope with Calibration." *Antiquity* 61 (1987): 98-103.

Stuiver, Minze, and Gordon W. Pearson. "High-Precision Calibration of Radiocarbon Time Scale, A.D. 1950-500 B.C." *Radiocarbon* 28 (1986): 805-838.

Taylor, R. E., and Clement W. Meighan, eds. *Chronologies in New World Archaeology*. New York: Academic Press, 1978.

Datsolalee (Nov. 1835, Carson Valley, Nev.—Dec. 6, 1925, Carson City, Nev.): Artist

ALSO KNOWN AS: Louisa Keyser; Dabuda (Wide Hips)
TRIBAL AFFILIATION: Washoe
SIGNIFICANCE: Datsolalee (Louisa Keyser) was an accomplished Washoe designer and basketmaker

Datsolalee was widely recognized in the art world for the beautiful design and weaving of her baskets. Basketry had long been a fine art among the Washoe, and she was recognized as its most accomplished practitioner. She was married twice (her first husband died), both times to Washoe men, and had two children by her first marriage, but it seemed to those who knew her that her primary concern was her work.

In 1895, Datsolalee first arranged to sell her baskets to the proprietor of a clothing store in Carson City. He was a basket collector as well, and he was delighted that she had kept the tradition alive; for many years, because of the outcome of a dispute with the Paiute, the Washoe were legally prohibited from making baskets. The store owner, Abram Cohn, actively found markets for her basketry and kept written records of the sales of her work. About forty of her baskets are considered major pieces; one sold for $10,000 in 1930.

It was said that Datsolalee often saw designs in her dreams before doing her weaving. Her technical expertise impresses weavers to this day. One of her most famous works (she entitled it "Myriads of Stars Shine over the Graves of Our Ancestors") took more than a year to weave and contains more than thirty-six stitches per inch. Her designs reflected both

Washoe tribal tradition and her own deep involvement with her art. She continued to work nearly until her death in 1925.

See also Arts and crafts—Great Basin; Baskets and basketry; Washoe.

Dawes Severalty Act. *See* General Allotment Act

Death and mortuary customs

TRIBES AFFECTED: Pantribal
SIGNIFICANCE: American Indians have a wide variety of religious traditions and thus a wide variety of practices regarding the disposition of the dead

Among the many American Indian tribes studied by modern anthropologists, there is a great variety of practices concerning death, dying, and the disposition of dead bodies. There is a virtually universal belief in the existence of a spirit separate from the body which can exist when the body is dead. Since these spirits are considered capable of harming the living, they are often feared. In many Indian cultures death is accepted stoically by individuals, but rituals are considered necessary to provide protection for the living.

Traditional Practices. Unfortunately, many Indian tribal traditions had become extinct before they could be studied by modern scholars, and some puzzling remains have been found. Generally, burial seems to have always been the most common way of disposing of dead bodies, though there is considerable evidence of cremation, as well. In the southwestern United States, mass graves have been found, sometimes consisting merely of piles of heads or headless bodies. In a few cases, burial sites have been found in which only the bones of hands are buried.

In more recent times, Indians have been known to bury their dead in coffins, with ceremonies not greatly different from those of Christians and Jews. There are, however, quite a number of exceptions. On the West Coast, for example, many tribes had the custom of leaving bodies lying in state above ground for as long as a week, after which the remains were buried or cremated. In the far north, among the Eskimos (Inuits), bodies have been left above the ground permanently, usually on a hill far from the village.

Many northern tribes, including the Athapaskans and the Tlingit, begin ceremonies with mourning and wailing and then proceed to have a potlatch, a joyous gathering of tribe members where gifts are exchanged and long, involved feasts take place. A few tribes, including the Mesquakie (Fox) and some Eskimos, traditionally believed that the departing spirit needed a guide and killed dogs for the purpose, which were buried with their former masters. Many tribes surrounded the body with possessions belonging to the deceased.

Beliefs in an Afterlife. Because American Indians have never been a single culture, beliefs vary considerably. There are certain ideas, however, which seem to be almost universal among North American Indians. One of the most common is the belief that the spirit, like the soul of Christian belief, is separate from the body and can leave the body. Many tribes believe that the spirit actually leaves the body during sleep and is capable of wandering in the land of the dead. During this time, the spirit can gain great knowledge of the afterworld and communicate with its ancestors. At death, the separation is final.

The postulated location of the land of the dead also varies. In some cases, it was considered to be very close to the land of the living; such places were dreaded and avoided. Much more often, however, the realm of spirits was placed far from the living lands—in the sky, under ground, beyond the sunset, or over the seas. As a general rule, this land was considered to be very much like the land of the living, with the spirits eating and drinking, hunting, and dancing.

The Current Situation. Many of the practices cited above are unacceptable in the modern world. Leaving a decaying body outside for a week at a time, for example, is considered a clear health hazard. In addition, the majority of modern Indians have accepted Christianity, at least in part. It is not unusual, especially in the more remote areas of the Arctic and Subarctic, for two death ceremonies to be held: one Christian, one traditional. Among the Athapaskans, for example, the body is generally buried in a Christian ceremony presided over by a minister and conducted in English. Afterward, the traditional potlatch is held, conducted in the native language.

—*Marc Goldstein*

See also Ethnophilosophy and worldview; Etowah; Feast of the Dead; Mounds and mound builders.

BIBLIOGRAPHY

Carmody, Denise Lardner, and John Tully Carmody. *Native American Religions: An Introduction*. New York: Paulist Press, 1993.

Ceram, C. W. *The First American: A Study of North American Archaeology*. Translated by Richard Winston and Clara Winston. New York: Harcourt Brace Jovanovich, 1971.

Oswalt, Wendell H. *This Land Was Theirs: A Study of North American Indians*. 4th ed. Mountain View, Calif.: Mayfield, 1988.

Spencer, Robert F., Jesse D. Jennings, et al. *The Native American*. 2d ed. New York: Harper & Row, 1977.

Wissler, Clark. *Indians of the United States*. Rev. ed. Garden City, N.Y.: Doubleday, 1966.

Declaration of First Nations

DATE: 1981

TRIBES AFFECTED: Canadian native peoples

SIGNIFICANCE: Increased activism beginning in the 1960's resulted in a statement of principles that has guided subsequent native political activities and land-claims negotiations in Canada

Though not without strains, Canadians generally regard their country's multiethnic heritage with pride. Multiculturalism is applauded in a variety of ways, but special recognition is accorded to the "founding nations" of Canada. Unfortunately for Native Canadians, the term "founding nation" is usually reserved for only two groups—the French and the English.

Public and government recognition that Canadian Indians as a group had suffered economically, socially, and educationally became widespread in the 1960's. In order to engage natives in a dialogue regarding the issues that most affected them, the federal government encouraged the development of both regional and national native political organizations. The National Indian Council, which was formed in 1961, represented treaty Indians, non-treaty Indians, non-status Indians, and Metis. In 1968 this group divided into the Canadian Metis Society, representing Metis and non-status Indians, and the National Indian Brotherhood as the organization of status Indians (both treaty and non-treaty).

Politicization grew, particularly following introduction by the government of its White Paper on Indian Affairs in 1969. In 1975, the various Dene bands sought Canadian recognition of the Subarctic Athapaskans as a distinct nation. The National Indian Brotherhood became highly involved in Canadian constitutional reform. The Declaration of First Nations, issued in 1981, was a concise statement of native sovereignty meant to influence the constitutional reform process. Following the Declaration of First Nations, the National Indian Brotherhood was dissolved and reconstituted as the Assembly of First Nations. They were ultimately successful in inserting language that affirmed "existing aboriginal and treaty rights," though not explicitly defined, into the Constitution Act of 1982.

Natives have continued to pursue the recognition of their cultures as distinct societies and as "founding nations" of Canada by defeating the Meech Lake Accord and by working for a form of native self-government apart from the provinces and the federal government.

See also Activism; Indian-white relations—Canadian; Meech Lake Accord; Sovereignty; White Paper of Canada.

Decora, Spoon (c. 1730-1816): Tribal leader

ALSO KNOWN AS: Choukeka

TRIBAL AFFILIATION: Winnebago

SIGNIFICANCE: Winnebago leader who played a leading role in negotiating the St. Louis Treaty of 1816

Also called Choukeka, Spoon Decora was one of the first of several Winnebago leaders to carry the name "Decora." He was born to a French trader, Joseph des Caris, and a Winnebago named Hopokaw. He married a daughter of Nawkaw and had six sons and five daughters with her. Decora took a leading role in the Winnebagos' conflicts with the Chippewas and, shortly before his death, in negotiating the St. Louis Treaty of 1816. He generally refrained from becoming involved in conflicts with whites. Spoon Decora's son, Konoka, became the Winnebagos' principal chief in 1816 following the death of the elder Decora.

Deer, Ada Elizabeth (b. Aug. 7, 1935, Keshena, Wis.):

Educator, activist, BIA commissioner

TRIBAL AFFILIATION: Menominee

SIGNIFICANCE: Ada Deer was appointed BIA commissioner by President Clinton in 1993

Born in Kenesha, Wisconsin, Ada Deer earned a bachelor's degree at the University of Wisconsin, Madison, in 1957 and a master's in social work at Columbia University in 1961. Her first interest after graduation was social work, including lecturing in the fields of social work and Native American studies at the University of Wisconsin's Madison campus.

Deer also became involved in political action and organizing, working as a lobbyist for the Menominees in Washington in the early 1970's. She chaired the Menominee Restoration Committee between 1973 and 1976; that group was primarily responsible for the restoring of federally recognized tribal status to the Menominees (the tribe had been "terminated" in 1954). During the late 1970's, she was a member of the American Indian Policy Review Commission. President Bill Clinton appointed her commissioner of the Bureau of Indian Affairs in 1993.

See also American Indian Policy Review Commission; Bureau of Indian Affairs (BIA).

Deer Dance
TRIBES AFFECTED: Pueblo tribes
SIGNIFICANCE: The Deer Dance was a winter ceremony called by hunters to ensure an increase in game and good luck in hunting

In Pueblo culture, all social and religious life revolves around the theme of achieving harmony with the gods of nature to ensure the prosperity of agriculture and hunting. The Deer Dance is performed to achieve harmony with the spirits of the deer to ensure daily survival. Like all game animal dances, the Deer Dance is believed to cause an increase in the deer population and also to enhance the skills of those who hunt them.

In the Pueblo calendrical cycle, agricultural ceremonies are held in the summer, while curing, warfare, and hunting ceremonies occur in the winter. The Deer Dance, along with other game animal dances, is performed in the winter months, when household supplies are at their lowest and families feel the need for spiritual assistance in gathering food. While the ceremony differs from pueblo to pueblo, reciprocity through gift-giving between humans and spirits is an inherent part of the dance. In the Deer Dance, the deer are enticed to the village with cornmeal and are fed; later the deer will feed the people.

See also Dances and dancing; Pueblo tribes, Eastern; Pueblo tribes, Western.

Deganawida (c. 1550—c.1600): Prophet
TRIBAL AFFILIATION: Huron
SIGNIFICANCE: Deganawida is said to have founded the Iroquois Confederacy

The story of Deganawida, founder of the Iroquois Confederacy, was not recorded until the nineteenth century. As a result, there are several extant versions that differ considerably. The only complete version in an Iroquois language was dictated by John Gibson in 1912 and published in original and translated forms in 1992.

The confederacy was most likely founded in the sixteenth century, although some archaeological evidence suggests the

fifteenth century. Its rituals were reported by Jacques Cartier when he visited Hochelaga (Montreal) in 1535. All versions of the story, and the archaeological data, agree that the time preceding Deganawida's birth was one of chronic warfare among the Iroquois tribes. According to legend, it was to address this conflict that the Creator sent Deganawida to deliver the Message of the Great Peace and Power and Law. Because of hostilities, his mother and maternal grandmother left their Huron village and were living along the northern shore of Lake Ontario, when it was revealed to them that the unborn child would have miraculous powers and undertake a divine mission.

Upon reaching adulthood, Deganawida traveled eastward in a stone canoe and converted a cannibal (in some versions this is Hiawatha) and met a Mohawk chief who agreed to work for the establishment of an Iroquois Confederacy. In recognition of this, Deganawida conferred upon him the title of Hiawatha, and together they set out to take the Good Message to other Iroquois chiefs. One by one, the Mohawk, Oneida, Seneca, Onondaga, and Cayuga leaders accepted it, and Deganawida conferred the other forty-nine chiefly titles upon them. The final holdout was the Onondaga Atotarho, who had caused the deaths of Hiawatha's wife and daughters. With the chiefs of the Five Nations present, Deganawida offered him the role of confederacy spokesman and established the central fire of the league at Onondaga. Atotarho accepted, and Hiawatha straightened his twisted mind and body.

The confederacy was portrayed as a longhouse stretching across Iroquoia, symbolizing a single family. The Senecas, the most populous of the tribes, guarded the western door and provided the league with its two war chiefs. Although only men could be named chiefs, the titles were vested in the matrilineages, because women first accepted the Good Message.

To represent the end of feuding, a Great Tree was uprooted and the weapons of war thrown into the hole. The four roots of the tree served to guide other nations to the confederacy, and provision was made for the adoption of new members. An eagle perched atop the tree warned of impending danger, five arrows bound together symbolized strength through unity, and a mat of white wampum represented peace and truth.

Although the focus of the confederacy has shifted over the centuries, its organization and rituals as set forth by Deganawida continue to exist in attenuated form in Canada and the United States. Having completed his mission, Deganawida is said to have disappeared, and his name does not appear on the Roll Call of Chiefs.

See also Atotarho; Hiawatha; Iroquois Confederacy.

Dekanisora (c. 1650, Onondaga, N.Y.—c. 1732, Albany, N.Y.): Orator, diplomat
TRIBAL AFFILIATION: Onondaga
SIGNIFICANCE: Dekanisora was the leading Iroquois orator of his era and a noted neutralist politician and diplomat in Iroquois dealings with the English and French in the Northeast

Respected and admired by both his own people and the French and English, Dekanisora masterfully played these two European powers in the Iroquois backyard off against each other. Devoted to the cause of neither imperial power but rather to the cause of the Onondagas and the Iroquois Confederacy, he forced both the English and the French to court him. In 1700, when his wife died accidentally, he was so overcome with grief that he resolved to mourn her indefinitely by giving up his activities as negotiator and statesman for the Iroquois confederacy and retiring as a recluse. So great was his influence that the English at Albany, New York, pleaded with him not to do so, but rather to attend peace talks in Montreal. It was highly unusual for English officials to ask an Iroquois politician to negotiate with the French; this request underscores the fact that the English believed their interests would be much better served by Dekanisora's diplomacy than that of another Iroquois negotiator.

Dekanisora played a leading role in engineering the major peace settlement of 1701 between the Iroquois, French, and French-allied tribes. He continued in this role of diplomat for the Iroquois confederacy until it became apparent that he was suffering memory loss associated with old age; he was replaced as chief orator of the Onondaga nation in 1721, but was still active as a sachem ("chief") of the Onondagas. Dekanisora most likely died in the early summer of 1732, as James Logan, negotiator for the Pennsylvania colonial government, mentioned soon after that the politician's son had taken his deceased father's place as an Iroquois representative to English colonial officials.

See also Indian-white relations—English colonial; Indian-white relations—French colonial; Iroquois Confederacy; Onondaga.

Delaware. *See* Lenni Lenape

Delaware Prophet (c. 1725—c. 1775): Indian prophet
ALSO KNOWN AS: Neolin (Enlightened One)
TRIBAL AFFILIATION: Lenni Lenape (Delaware)
SIGNIFICANCE: The Delaware Prophet, an important religious leader in the mid-eighteenth century, was known for his renunciation of "white ways"

While little is known of his early life, the Delaware Prophet came into prominence as an Indian prophet in the 1760's during Pontiac's efforts to unite tribes against the European invaders. The Delaware Prophet's requirements for salvation were twofold: (1) renounce all white influence, especially liquor, and avoid all trade; and (2) return to the traditional ways but without the evil practices of war dances and medicine-making. These laws were reportedly given to him by the Master of Life, whom he had met in heaven in a mystical experience. The Delaware Prophet also devised a prayer stick for his people.

Pontiac believed that his efforts were strengthened by his adherence to the Delaware Prophet's teachings. The Ottawa chief, most noted for the coordinated attack on English out-

posts in the Great Lakes area in the 1760's, captured eight British forts and forced the abandonment of a ninth. The Delaware Prophet predicted Pontiac's defeat of the whites. When Pontiac was ultimately defeated, the Delaware Prophet's position was greatly diminished; little is known of him after 1770.

See also Apes, William; Lenni Lenape; Pontiac; Pontiac's Conspiracy.

Delgadito (c. 1830, near Nazlini, N.Mex. Territory—c. 1870, near Chinle, N.Mex. Territory): Silversmith, medicine man
ALSO KNOWN AS: Atsidi Sani (Old Smith), Beshiltheeni (Knife Maker)
TRIBAL AFFILIATION: Navajo
SIGNIFICANCE: Delgadito was the first Navajo metalsmith; his pride in craftsmanship continues to influence Navajo smiths, and silverwork has become the single most important source of individual income to the tribe

Like his older brother, Barboncito, Delgadito was a medicine man and ceremonial singer of the Ma'iidee-shgiizhnii (Coyote Pass) clan at Canyon de Chelly. He learned silversmithing from a Mexican craftsman in the 1850's. Later he learned other metal techniques from an American blacksmith, and still later he taught the craft to other Navajos, thus establishing the silversmithing tradition among his people. His artistic talents did not keep him from participating in the Navajo War of 1863-1866. Delgadito and Barboncito supported Manuelito's efforts against the American army at Fort Defiance. When the "resettlement" policy was announced and eventually implemented by Colonel Christopher (Kit) Carson, Delgadito and Barboncito sent a third brother, El Sordo, as an envoy to negotiate a truce. He offered to construct hogans near Fort Wingate and settle there. El Sordo's proposal was rebuffed and he was told instead that all Navajo nation members were to "resettle" to Bosque Redondo. Delgadito resisted, but he and a large number of women and children were the first Navajos to be taken to the Bosque. On June 1, 1868, Delgadito was a signatory of the treaty allowing the Navajos to return to their ancient lands.

See also Barboncito; Manuelito; Navajo War.

Deloria, Ella Cara (Jan. 30, 1888, Yankton Sioux Reservation, S.Dak.—Feb. 12, 1971, Tripp, S.Dak.): Ethnographer, linguist, novelist
ALSO KNOWN AS: Anpetu Waste (Beautiful Day)
TRIBAL AFFILIATION: Yankton Sioux
SIGNIFICANCE: Ella Deloria collected and translated numerous traditional Sioux stories and beliefs; she was a leading authority on Sioux culture, and posthumously she was recognized as a novelist

When Ella Deloria was born in 1888 on the Yankton Sioux Reservation in South Dakota, the Sioux population was nearing its nadir. (The Wounded Knee Massacre in South Dakota occurred the following year.) Deloria's parents were determined that the Sioux culture would thrive in their household. Deloria's mother, Mary (Sully Bordeaux), reared the family in the tribal traditions and language even though she was only one-quarter Sioux. These Dakota views, along with Christian beliefs (Deloria's father was an Episcopalian minister), strongly influenced Deloria's life.

The year following her birth, Deloria's father transferred to St. Elizabeth's Church on the Standing Rock Sioux Reservation in South Dakota. There Deloria attended St. Elizabeth's School until 1902, when she transferred to All Saints Boarding School in Sioux Falls, South Dakota. Graduating in 1910, Deloria then studied at Oberlin College in Ohio, the University of Chicago, Illinois, and Columbia Teachers College in New York.

Awarded a bachelor's degree in 1915, Deloria returned to All Saints Boarding School to teach. Four years later, she moved to New York City to work for the Young Women's Christian Association (YWCA) as its health education secretary for native schools, a position that afforded Deloria exposure to several western reservations. In 1923, Haskell Indian School in Lawrence, Kansas, offered Deloria a teaching job in an experimental program designed to explore the spiritual aspects of physical education within native traditions.

Recognizing her work with native culture, Franz Boas, the preeminent American anthropologist of that time, recruited Deloria in 1927 to translate traditional Sioux stories. As an ethnographer and linguist, Deloria worked with Boas until his death in 1942.

With a mission to explain Dakota insights to non-natives, Deloria published several books. *Dakota Texts* (1932) contains a bilingual collection of traditional Sioux stories. In *Dakota Grammar* (1941), she collaborated with Boas to show Dakota

Writer Vine Deloria, Jr. (right) talking with Ojibwa activist Vernon Bellecourt. (AP/Wide World Photos)

linguistic rules. She explored native and non-native differences in an effort to dispel cultural misunderstandings in *Speaking of Indians* (1944). In her writings, Deloria stressed that native philosophy was rooted in complex patterns and that non-native educators should work with these traditional designs and not against them.

During the 1940's, Deloria was America's major authority on Sioux culture. To generate further public awareness, she traveled extensively to give lectures and to present pageants with Sioux songs and dances. In 1955, Deloria returned to St. Elizabeth's to be its director for three years. In the 1960's, Deloria worked on linguistic projects at the University of South Dakota in Vermillion, where she spent her final years.

Upon her death on February 12, 1971, Deloria left hundreds of pages of unpublished manuscripts. Seventeen years later, in 1988, her novel *Waterlily*, drafted during the early 1940's, was published. *Waterlily* focuses on women's roles in traditional native life. Even though Deloria was never formally trained as an anthropologist, her research on Sioux culture and her transcriptions of oral histories have recovered voices from a fading culture.

See also Siouan language family; Sioux.

Deloria, Vine, Jr. (b. Mar. 26, 1933, Martin, S.Dak.): Writer

TRIBAL AFFILIATION: Yankton or Standing Rock Sioux
SIGNIFICANCE: Vine Deloria, Jr., is the most prolific of Indian protest writers and an advocate of education for American Indians

After receiving his B.S. degree from Iowa State University, Deloria studied for a career as a minister, earning an M.Th. from the Lutheran School of Theology in Illinois. Then he earned a J.D. from the University of Colorado, which enabled him to serve as the executive director of the National Congress of American Indians. He taught political science and Native American studies at the University of Arizona, which he left to direct the Indian studies program at the University of Colorado.

Much of the power of Deloria's writing comes from his sharp-witted political satire, as manifested especially in two books on contemporary Indian life. His first book, *Custer Died for Your Sins: An Indian Manifesto* (1969), indicts the U.S. government's treatment of Indians and has served as a manifesto for Indian activists. In *We Talk, You Listen: New Tribes, New Turf* (1970), he pleads for a return to tribalism, by which he means a return to a balanced relationship among people, land, and religion. He has written much about political and legal issues concerning Indian-white relations, including *Behind the Trail of Broken Treaties: An Indian Declaration of Independence* (1974); *American Indians, American Justice* (1983); and *American Indian Policy in the Twentieth Century* (1985). Best-known of his books on Indian religion is *God Is Red* (1973), in which he argues that Indian religions that promote an ecologically sound relationship with the environment are more appropriate in contemporary America than

Christianity. He also edited *A Sender of Words: Essays in Memory of John G. Neihardt* (1984), a volume that contains essays on *Black Elk Speaks*.

See also Activism; American Indian studies programs and archives; National Congress of American Indians (NCAI); Wounded Knee occupation.

Delshay (c. 1835, present-day Ariz.—c. 1874, Ariz.): Tribal chief

TRIBAL AFFILIATION: Apache
SIGNIFICANCE: Delshay was murdered by a bounty hunter, and his head was publicly displayed as a warning to other Apaches who raided white settlements

Following their uprisings between 1861 and 1863, Apache bands continued raiding neighboring whites. In 1868, Chief Delshay agreed to peace and resettled his band at Camp McDowell on Arizona's Verde River. In 1871, after the Camp Grant Massacre, in which Eskiminzin's peaceful band of Aravaipa Apache were attacked after having been granted sanctuary, Delshay requested permission to move his band from the region.

Meanwhile, with settlers calling for military action, the U.S. army under General George Crook launched a massive campaign against the Apaches, winning decisive battles at Skull Cave, December 28, 1872, and Turret Peak, March 27, 1873. Delshay surrendered in April, 1873, and his band was relocated to Fort Apache on the White Mountain Reservation. Later he was granted permission to settle at Camp McDowell in return for promises that he cease hostilities. For a time, peace was maintained. After he was joined by Apache fugitives, however, Crook ordered Delshay's arrest. When he eluded capture for several months, a bounty was offered for his head; two rival claims were honored and the heads were displayed at Camp Verde and at the San Carlos Reservation.

See also Apache Wars; Cochise; Eskiminzin; Geronimo; Nakaidoklini; Victorio.

Demography

TRIBES AFFECTED: Pantribal
SIGNIFICANCE: After European contact, most Native American nations experienced dramatic population losses, but today they represent one of the fastest-growing segments of American society

When Europeans arrived on the shores of North America, they encountered an estimated 1.2 to 18 million people. They were the "original Americans," descendants of people who journeyed to North America thousands of years before Europeans. Over the millennia, Native Americans evolved hundreds of unique cultural traditions with their own worldviews, perhaps two hundred languages (of several distinct families), ecological adaptations to every environmental situation, and a range of forms of governance. Native North America, prior to the arrival of Europeans, represented one of the most ethnically diverse regions in the world. Tragically, much of this cultural mosaic was extinguished by massive population declines after

European contact. Yet Native Americans survived this demographic and cultural onslaught to represent one of the fastest-growing segments of American society today.

Prehistoric Demographic Trends. The colonization of the Americas by Paleo-Indians (an anthropological term for the ancestors of Native Americans) was one of the greatest demographic events in global history. There has been considerable controversy regarding the dates for early migrations to North America. Some scholars have suggested that the earliest migrations occurred as far back as fifty thousand years ago; some have said that migration may also have occurred as recently as three thousand years ago. A more generally agreed-upon time frame for the migrations, however, is between twenty-five thousand and twelve thousand years ago.

Although many Native Americans reject the hypothesis that their ancestors immigrated from greater Eurasia, archaeological evidence suggests that some first Americans may have entered the Western Hemisphere during the many glacial periods that exposed Beringia, the Bering Strait land bridge. Beringia periodically linked Siberia with the Americas, allowing animals and humans access to both continents. Others may have made the journey using boats, following a maritime route or traveling down a coastal corridor. In any event, these irregular waves of colonizers represented the last great global movement of people into unoccupied land—a migration hallmark in human history.

How many "first Americans" entered the Americas is unknown. Archaeologists note that the Late Wisconsin glacier's recession about fifteen thousand years ago allowed Native American people to migrate southward, eventually colonizing the remainder of the Americas. Prior to that time, the glacier largely prevented further immigration and colonization. What specific routes they took and how rapidly people dispersed across both continents are topics of considerable archaeological debate. There is firm evidence that by 9400 B.C.E. Native Americans had reached southern South America, indicating that Native Americans had dispersed widely across the "New World's" landscape. Despite hypotheses that argue for an accelerated population growth rate, it is likely that during this early colonization period, the Native American population's growth rates were slow to moderate, with cyclical rates of growth and decline. These population fluctuations reflected a complex array of changing social, demographic, and ecological conditions as local populations adapted to regional conditions.

In North America, Native American demographic distribution and redistribution paralleled closely the glacial retreat north, the trend toward regional and climatic aridity that altered local resources, and cultural innovations. The above factors, by 9000 B.C.E., eventually made possible the colonization of every available area on the North American continent. These hunter-gatherers and, later, the cultural traditions known as Archaic societies, developed a greater variety of lifeways, producing marked differences in population size, distribution, and vital events.

ESTIMATES OF PRE-CONTACT NORTH AMERICAN POPULATION	
Author and Date of Estimate	*Estimated Population*
Mooney, 1910	1,148,000 [1]
Rivet, 1924	1,000,000-1,148,000 [2]
Mooney, 1928	1,153,000
Kroeber, 1934	1,001,000
Wissler, 1934	750,000
Kroeber, 1939	900,000
Rosenblat, 1945	1,000,000
Steward, 1945	1,000,000
Rivet et al., 1952	1,316,000
Rosenblat, 1954	1,000,000
Aschmann, 1959	2,240,000
Driver, 1961	1,000,000-2,000,000
Dobyns, 1966	9,800,000-12,250,000
Driver, 1969	3,500,000
Ubelaker, 1976	2,171,000
Denevan, 1976	4,400,000
Hassan, 1981	1,120,000
Dobyns, 1983	18,000,000
Thornton, 1987	7,000,000
Ramenofsky, 1987	12,000,000
Ubelaker, 1988	1,894,000

1. Mooney's initial estimate was partially in response to Garrick Mallery's 1877 estimate.
2. Although Rivet gave a 1,000,000 population estimate for Native North America, his tribal population figures totaled 1,148,000, emulating Mooney's 1910 estimate.

Paleopathological evidence indicates that prehistoric Native American populations faced a number of health risks. Documented cases of malnutrition, anemia, tuberculosis, trachoma, trepanematoid infections, and degenerative conditions occurred in pre-Columbian North America. These afflictions, coupled with periodic trauma, accidents, and warfare, affected the demographic structure of regional populations.

A cultural innovation that had significant demographic consequences was the invention and diffusion of agriculture. Sometime before 3500 B.C.E. in Mesoamerica, maize, beans, and squash were domesticated. As this cultural knowledge spread northward, many Native American societies east of the Mississippi River, in the Southwest, and along the major waterways of the greater Midwest adopted agriculture. Demographically, agriculture promoted the development of larger populations, residing in sedentary villages or cities. Near present-day Alton, Illinois, along the Mississippi River, for example, was the urban center of Cahokia. At its height about 1100 C.E., Cahokia extended over 5 square miles and had a population of perhaps thirty thousand people. Although regional population concentrations arose across native North America, by 1300 C.E. many areas containing high population densities began to decline. The causes of the decline and social reorganization in some regions are open to debate. It is clear that in a number of regions, high population densities and size remained until the European encounter.

By the time of European contact, native North America demographically contained a variety of population sizes and densities, ranging from fewer than one person per 10 square miles in the Great Basin to the densely settled, resource-rich regions of the Pacific Northwest, Northeast, Southeast, and Southwest. These areas may have supported from five to more than one hundred people per 10 square miles. By the time Europeans arrived, Native Americans already had undergone a number of profound demographic events.

Historical Demographic Trends. The European colonization of North America launched a series of catastrophic events for Native American populations. Native American societies experienced tremendous population declines. Native American populations periodically experienced mortality increases, decreases in their fertility performance, forced migration, as well as a deterioration of their societal health status.

Of all the factors that affected post-contact Native American societies, the accelerated death rates from the introduction of European diseases remain prominent. Europeans brought smallpox, measles, cholera, and other infections that were foreign to Native American people. It has been estimated that ninety-three epidemics of Old World pathogens affected Native Americans from the sixteenth to the twentieth centuries. Old World diseases, combined with warfare, genocide, and the introduction of alcohol, forced migration and relocation, and the overall destruction of indigenous lifeways resulted in the demographic collapse of native North America. One Native American scholar called it the "American Indian Holocaust."

Within decades of European contact, Native American populations declined. The colonization of the Spanish, French, and, later, English set in motion significant population changes. Between 1500 and 1820, Native American populations residing east of the Mississippi River declined to approximately 6 percent of their at-contact size. In the southeastern region, for example, the estimated Native American population in 1685 was 199,400. By 1790 their population was approximately 55,900—a decline of 71.9 percent. Paralleling this demographic collapse, the ethnic diversity of indigenous societies residing east of the Mississippi River declined between 25 and 79 percent, as distinct Native American nations were driven to extinction or forced to amalgamate with other Native American nations.

In 1830, the remaining Native Americans in the East were forcibly removed to west of the Mississippi River under President Andrew Jackson's administration. Between 1828 and 1838, approximately 81,300 Native Americans were thus removed. For their relocation efforts, the U.S. government acquired 115,355,767 acres of Indian lands and resources. Furthermore, the Choctaw, Chickasaw, Cherokee, Seminole, and Muskogee lost between 15 and 50 percent of their population during the forced relocation. Other removed Native American

tribal nations suffered similar demographic losses. By about 1850, the estimated Native American population stood at 383,000.

As Native American populations declined, the European, African American, and Latino populations grew, occupying the available lands acquired from Native Americans. Aside from losing their land and resources, the increasing contact with non-Indians had other important demographic consequences. Since contact, Native Americans have experienced an increased genetic exchange with European and African populations. The rise of people with Native American-European or Native American-African ancestry, or of all three ancestries, may have had significant implications for tribal survival and demographic recovery. Some scholars suggest that depopulation and the following demographic recovery resulted in certain physical and genetic changes in those who survived the epidemic. The incorporation of Europeans, African Americans, or other Native Americans promoted further those phenotypic and genotypic processes.

As the American population of European descent surpassed twenty-three million by 1850, Native Americans west of the

| NATIVE AMERICAN POPULATION, 1800-1990 ||
Year	Population
1800 [1]	600,000*
1810	—
1820 [2]	471,417*
1830 [3]	312,930*
1840 [4]	383,000*
1850	400,764*
1860	339,421*
1870	313,721*
1880	306,543*
1890	273,607
1900	266,732
1910	291,014
1920	270,995
1930	362,380
1940	366,427
1950	377,273
1960	551,636
1970	827,273
1980	1,420,400
1990	1,959,000

Notes: Dash (—) indicates unavailable information. Asterisk (*) indicates a population estimate. Figures from 1850 to 1990 are U.S. Census figures (1850-1880 figures are estimates). Beginning in 1880, enumeration of Native Americans was affected by changing definitions, including shifting blood-quantum criteria and interpretations of the term "Indian."
1. Office of Indian Affairs estimate (1943).
2. Morse population estimate (1822).
3. Secretary of war estimate (1929).
4. Schoolcraft population estimate (1851-1857).

Mississippi River began to experience directly the brunt of colonization and settlement. Prior to that time, western Native American populations had experienced introduced infectious diseases, intermittent warfare with Europeans, and an erosion of their resources. The Mandan, for example, boasted an estimated at-contact population of possibly 15,000. After the 1837-1838 smallpox epidemic, their population collapsed to between 125 and 1,200 individuals, forcing them eventually to merge, culturally and biologically, with the Arikara and Hidatsa. Western indigenous nations, from 1850 through 1880, witnessed continued demographic upheaval. Their population changes during those decades were affected by the dramatic social and economic changes in U.S. society. The United States economy was industrializing, American society was becoming more urban, and the federal government desired a link between the east and west coasts as a completion to its nation-building. In addition, the United States experienced a dramatic influx of European immigrants. In three decades, from 1850 to 1880, the European population increased to 50,155,783. This prompted the federal government to alienate Native Americans from their remaining lands. To meet these economic and political demands, western lands and resources were needed. The continued demographic collapse of many Indian nations occurred under the guise of the nation's rhetoric of Manifest Destiny.

In an attempt to subdue the remaining indigenous populations and force them onto reservations, the U.S. government either negotiated a series of treaties or carried out military expeditions. The combined impact of war, disease, and the continued destruction of their lifeways resulted in further population decline. By the time Native Americans were relegated to reservations or rural communities in 1880, there were 306,543 Native Americans surviving in the coterminous United States.

The indigenous population of the United States reached its nadir in 1890. The 1890 U.S. Census recorded 248,253 Native Americans in the continental United States. Although most infectious diseases experienced during the pre-reservation era began to diminish, these acute infections were replaced with chronic diseases on reservations. Poor sanitation, poor nutrition, overcrowding, and severe cultural oppression resulted in the appearance of tuberculosis, trachoma, and intermittent measles and influenza outbreaks, as well as a rise in infant mortality. As these afflictions reached epidemic proportions, the Native American population between 1900 and 1920 remained rather static. Most Native Americans continued to live on reservations or rural areas, isolated from society. In 1920, only 6.2 percent of Native Americans resided in urban areas.

After 1930, however, Native Americans began to experience a tremendous growth rate. With the passage of the Indian Reorganization Act (1934), cultural oppression lessened, health and sanitation conditions improved, and social programs began to affect Native American demography positively. Native American populations grew because fertility increased, infant survivorship improved, and the death rate fell. The result was a young age-sex structure.

The advent of World War II witnessed a migratory shift away from reservations and rural communities. Attracted by service in the armed forces and urban job prospects, many Native Americans migrated to major cities. The outflow of Native American immigrants to urban centers initiated a demographic trend that continues to the present. The outmigration of Native Americans was stimulated further by the Bureau of Indian Affairs. In the mid-1950's, the federal government instituted a relocation program. The program assisted Native Americans through job training and support services in being placed in an urban center. In 1990, for the first time since indigenous people have been recorded by the U.S. Census Bureau, the census recorded that more Native Americans resided in urban than in rural areas. The Greater Los Angeles metropolitan area, for example, had 87,500 people of Native American descent, an increase of 5 percent over the previous decade.

Since the 1950's, the Native American population has grown tremendously. In 1960, there were 551,636 Native Americans. By 1970, there were 827,273 people who identified themselves as Native American. The 1980 U.S. Census witnessed a 71.1 percent increase. The reasons for this growth are complex and multifactorial. First, after the transfer of the Indian Health Service from the Bureau of Indian Affairs in 1955, Native American health improved dramatically, especially infant and child health care. Second, Native American fertility increased and mortality decreased, adding significantly to the population. Finally, more Americans are identifying themselves as having Native American ancestry.

Contemporary Demographic Trends. The Native American population of the United States is young and growing. As a result, the Native American population suffers from social problems in which demography plays an important role. Native American health status lags behind that of the United States' general population. Deaths by accidents, violence, suicide, tuberculosis, diabetes, and numerous other conditions exceed national averages. Unemployment, in both rural and urban areas, remains high, although the number of Native American-owned businesses increased by 64 percent between 1982 and 1987. Poverty also continues to plague Native American families. In the ten states with the most Native Americans, between 17 and 47 percent of Native American persons live in poverty. Finally, Native American people continue to report various risk factors associated with the above conditions. According to 1988 statistics, 31.1 percent of eighth-grade Native American children resided in single-parent households, 40.1 percent resided in households that earned less than $15,000 annually, and 18.6 percent spent more than three hours home alone every day. These factors conspire to promote continued poverty, low educational attainment, high unemployment, and ill health.

The 1990 census counted 1,878,000 Native Americans, an increase of more than 25 percent since 1980. Native American people reside in every state in the union, but the majority of the population is concentrated in the west. Also, a major portion of the population is concentrated in ten tribes.

AGE DISTRIBUTION OF AMERICAN INDIAN POPULATION, 1990

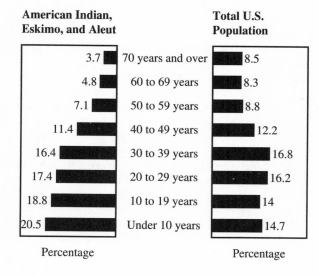

American Indian, Eskimo, and Aleut		Total U.S. Population
3.7	70 years and over	8.5
4.8	60 to 69 years	8.3
7.1	50 to 59 years	8.8
11.4	40 to 49 years	12.2
16.4	30 to 39 years	16.8
17.4	20 to 29 years	16.2
18.8	10 to 19 years	14
20.5	Under 10 years	14.7
Percentage		Percentage

Source: U.S. Bureau of the Census, *We, the First Americans.* Washington, D.C.: U.S. Government Printing Office, 1993.

The phenomenal growth rate among Native Americans exceeds the growth for African Americans and Americans of European descent but not the increase in the Latino or Asian populations. Today, Native Americans and Alaska Natives compose approximately 1 percent of the United States population but continue to represent a higher percentage of the country's cultural diversity.

Native Americans have undergone a number of significant population changes. Initially, their ancestors colonized a continent. Over time, these small groups of hunter-gatherers flourished, their population increased, and some societies constructed large, urban centers. After European contact, as the table "Native American Population, 1890-1990 indicates, the Native American population suffered a devastating demographic collapse that lasted for almost four hundred years. In spite of the demographic and cultural disruptions, economic and social problems, as well as continued ill health, the twentieth century Native American population made a remarkable recovery. All demographic indicators point to continued population growth into the future.   —*Gregory R. Campbell*

See also Beringia; Diseases, post-contact; Migrations; Relocation; Removal; Reservation system of the United States; Reserve system of Canada.

BIBLIOGRAPHY

Hodgkinson, Harold L. *The Demographics of American Indians: One Percent of the People, Fifty Percent of the Diversity.* Washington, D.C.: Center for Demographic Policy, Institute for Educational Leadership, 1990. A concise discussion of sociodemographics among North American Indians.

Reddy, Marlita A., ed. *Statistical Record of Native North Americans.* Detroit: Gale Research, 1993. A useful guide to Native American statistics.

Snipp, C. Matthew. *American Indians: The First of This Land.* New York: Russell Sage Foundation, 1989. A comprehensive analysis of Native American contemporary demography.

Stannard, David E. *American Holocaust.* New York: Oxford University Press, 1992. A discussion of Native American population decline in relation to European conquest and colonization.

Stuart, Paul. *Nations Within a Nation: Historical Statistics of American Indians.* New York: Greenwood Press, 1987. A work of compiled historical statistics about Native Americans.

Thornton, Russell. *American Indian Holocaust and Survival: A Population History Since 1492.* Norman: University of Oklahoma Press, 1987. Provides an overview of Native American population and recovery from European contact to 1980.

Verano, John W., and Douglas H. Ubelaker, eds. *Disease and Demography in the Americas.* Washington, D.C.: Smithsonian Institution Press, 1992. A collection of articles assessing the health and demography of pre-contact and post-contact Native American populations.

Department of Indian Affairs and Northern Development (DIAND)

DATE: Established 1967

TRIBES AFFECTED: Pantribal

SIGNIFICANCE: Since the Indian Act of 1868, Indian affairs have been handled by various Canadian government departments; DIAND officially took over this function in 1967

The Department of Indian Affairs and Northern Development in its present form was created as a separate entity within the Canadian government in 1967 by an act of Parliament. Before that time, Indian affairs and policy were overseen by a Department of Indian Affairs that was often part of a larger governmental unit with other responsibilities. The Indian Act of 1868 gave responsibility for Indian affairs to the secretary of state. In 1880, a revision of the 1876 Indian Act created a separate Department of Indian Affairs. The department was given the power to "depose" western Indian leaders in 1894; in 1895 it was given the power to rent out reserve lands to individual Indians regardless of whether the band approved. In 1936, Indian affairs became the responsibility of a branch of the Department of Mines and Resources. In 1959 the Indian Affairs branch was transferred to the Minister of Citizenship and Immigration. In 1965 the Department of Northern Affairs and Natural Resources took charge of Indian affairs.

As its name implies, the Department of Indian Affairs and Northern Development was established with a twofold purpose: to administer the Indian Act, including the provision of funds and services to the eligible Indian and Inuit populations, and to promote and manage development of the northern territories. DIAND is involved in providing or assisting with Indian education, housing, medical care, and economic assistance. DIAND generally is concerned with those bands recognized under the Indian Act; therefore, many thousands of Indian, Inuit, and Metis people—perhaps 75 percent of the population of these groups—receive no services from DIAND. The Indian and Inuit services section of DIAND is composed of a number of branches that report to a deputy minister and to the minister, who is a member of Parliament. There are also a number of regional and district offices; since 1988, the structure has been changing (many district offices have been closed) as First Nations themselves have assumed responsibility for delivering programs, with DIAND acting in an advisory capacity and providing technical support.

Historically, the Department of Indian Affairs long continued the paternalistic attitude established by the British; this began to change significantly only in the late 1960's. One controversy involved the Canadian government's proposed "White Paper," released in 1969, intended to provide a new framework for Indian-government relations. Many bands strongly opposed the White Paper's proposals, and the government withdrew it two years later. In 1973, the Office of Native Claims was established as a branch of DIAND to consider and negotiate native land claims. Since the 1970's, DIAND has been dealing with Indian concerns about environmental damage to their land base. DIAND has also been involved in negotiations concerning the establishment of a new native territory in the north, to be known as Nunavut. Nunavut will comprise most of the eastern Northwest Territories.

See also Fifteen Principles; Indian Act of 1876 (Canada); Indian Act of 1951 (Canada); Indian Act of 1989 (Canada); Indian-white relations—Canadian; Treaties and agreements in Canada; Voting rights—Canada.

Desert culture: Prehistoric and modern tradition
DATE: Since 8000 B.C.E.
LOCATION: Southwest, Great Basin
CULTURES AFFECTED: Paiute, Shoshone

The term "Desert culture" is used to refer to a widespread pattern of small, mobile, hunting and gathering populations adapted to dry environments of western North America. The Desert culture tradition begins around 7000 B.C.E. and continues into the historic period with peoples such as the Paiute of the Great Basin. In general, this term—coined by Jesse Jennings in the 1950's—has been replaced by more specific cultural phases in different geographical regions that emphasize regional and temporal variations as revealed by increasingly detailed archaeological data. The majority of these occur during a time referred to by archaeologists as the Archaic period.

As originally conceived, Desert culture referred to a lifestyle characterized by small social groups or band-level societies composed of extended families numbering, at most, twenty-five to thirty individuals. These groups moved across the landscape in annual cycles, taking advantage of a wide variety of different resources that varied with altitude, rainfall, soil conditions, and seasonal availability. Material possessions were limited to portable objects that were easily manufactured

as needed. Among these were baskets and milling stones, used in the transport and processing of plants and seeds, and chipped-stone projectile points. Vegetable foods were supplemented with hunting, primarily of small mammals, birds, and reptiles and mainly through the use of traps, snares, and simple weapons.

The earliest (and latest) manifestations of Desert culture occur in the Great Basin region. Danger Cave, in western Utah, yielded traces of slab milling stones, twined basketry, bone awls, and various small projectile points dating to between 8000 and 7000 B.C.E. Coiled basketry was found in later levels, accompanied by wooden darts, skewers, and pins, a variety of bone implements, and cordage made from hides and vegetable fibers.

One of the regional variants of the Desert culture is the Cochise tradition of the southwestern United States. Its earliest phase, Sulphur Spring, dates to about 7000 B.C.E. and is characterized by percussion-flaked projectile points together with simple manos and metates. It is followed by several thousand years of successive phases, known mostly from open sites, that provide evidence of gradual changes in both chipped- and ground-stone technology. At the site of Bat Cave (New Mexico), evidence for the use of maize appears in the context of a late Cochise tradition occupation.

The Desert culture, in its broadest conception, is the oldest and most persistent indigenous tradition in North America. This is probably attributable both to its simplicity and to its versatility in the face of environmental change. Desert culture represents the most flexible adaptation to a landscape in which natural food resources were varied and widely dispersed. Even during difficult climatic conditions, the Desert culture way of life permitted the survival of small populations as populations of large game hunters declined.

See also Archaic; Bat Cave; Danger Cave.

Determined Residents United for Mohawk Sovereignty (DRUMS)
DATE: Established 1974
TRIBE AFFECTED: Mohawk
SIGNIFICANCE: DRUMS opposed speakeasies and casinos on Mohawk reservations

Determined Residents United for Mohawk Sovereignty (DRUMS) was established at the Akwesasne Mohawk reservation in 1974. The Akwesasne Mohawk reservation (also called the Saint Regis Mohawk reserve) straddles the United States-Canadian border near Massena, New York, and Cornwall, Ontario. Beginning in the early 1970's, Akwesasne residents established DRUMS to combat increasing smuggling across the border. In the late 1970's and early 1980's, DRUMS's main focus turned to "speakeasies"—small, illegal drinking establishments that were contributing to an increasing number of traffic accidents on the reservation.

By June, 1989, DRUMS members were beginning to talk of blockading Route 37, the reservation's main highway, to keep away the clientele of several illegal casinos that had been constructed with smuggling profits. If the New York state police refused to close the gaming houses, many people believed civil disobedience to be their only option. DRUMS planned a blockade for June 9 but abandoned it in favor of a peaceful march. On July 20, two hundred FBI agents and New York state troopers raided seven casinos on the reservation, arresting thirteen people and seizing cash and financial records. DRUMS continued to oppose the casinos until May 1, 1990, when two Mohawk men, Mathew Pyke and "Junior" Edwards, were shot to death in firefights. After that, New York, Ontario, and Quebec police occupied the reservation, and the gaming houses were closed.

See also Gambling; Mohawk.

Diegueño: Tribe

CULTURE AREA: California
LANGUAGE GROUP: Hokan
PRIMARY LOCATION: Southern California
POPULATION SIZE: 2,276 (1990 U.S. Census)

The range of the Diegueño, a Southern California group, extended across deserts and mountain valleys. Actually, the term "Diegueño" is misleading, a throwback to Spanish colonial designations. The Tipai and Ipai together, peoples who were linguistically and culturally related, made up the Diegueño. Technically, the Diegueño were not a true tribe, but rather groups of autonomous bands or tribelets.

The Southern California climate was very warm in summer, but winters were mild. Dwellings varied according to the season: brush shelters in summer; frameworks of bent poles covered by thatch, bark, or pine slabs in winter. The tribelets usually were composed of a single clan; leadership was provided by a clan chief and his assistant. Shamans cured the sick, presided over ceremonies, and interpreted dreams.

To the Diegueño, as for many California native groups, the acorn was a major staff of life. Acorns were gathered, ground into meal, then baked or made into a kind of mush. Great care was taken to leach out the bitter tannic acid from the acorns.

The Tipai-Ipai/Diegueño were the first California Indians to experience repression under Spanish colonial rule, when Mission San Diego de Alcalá was founded in their territory in 1769. Early conversions to Christianity were probably genuine, but the Tipai-Ipai soon found that they had traded freedom for a kind of semi-serfdom as the Spanish tried to suppress native culture and religion in the name of civilization.

After a few years of repression, however, the Tipai-Ipai, now called Diegueño after the mission, staged a revolt in November, 1775. Led by a mission Indian named Francisco, eight hundred warriors stormed Mission San Diego, burning the buildings and killing three Spaniards. Superior Spanish weaponry eventually restored control over the Diegueño, and the mission was restored. By the 1990's, the Diegueño were scattered on fourteen reservations of varying size, from six to fifteen acres. Modern Diegueño call themselves "Kumeyaay," since the former term is associated with the colonial past.

See also Acorns; California.

Diseases, post-contact

TRIBES AFFECTED: Pantribal
SIGNIFICANCE: Within decades after contact with Europeans, Native American societies experienced rapid population declines; although the reasons for the demographic collapse of native North America are complex, a prominent factor in that decline was Old World infectious diseases, introduced by European explorers and settlers

After the arrival of Europeans, the estimated aboriginal population of native North America began to decline. The Spanish intrusion into the Southwest and Southeast, circa 1520, launched a series of lethal epidemics that infected various Native American people. The epidemiological conquest of native North America accelerated after the early seventeenth century with English and French colonization along the Atlantic seaboard. The dramatic population decline of indigenous people continued until the early twentieth century. By 1920, 270,995 Native Americans remained after the epidemiological onslaught of European colonization. They were the survivors of perhaps 1.2 million to 18 million Native Americans who inhabited North America at the time of the arrival of Europeans.

Increased mortality among Native Americans as a result of introduced European diseases is not attributable to a lack of sufficient immunological response to infections in general but to the fact that Native Americans had no prior exposure to these pathogens. The "new" pathogens therefore not only created a high degree of physiological stress but also engendered cultural stress. Epidemic episodes often resulted in a breakdown in the social system, elevating mortality levels.

Although it is recognized that European infectious diseases devastated many Native American societies, it also must be acknowledged that pre-contact native North America was not a disease-free paradise. Biological and archaeological evidence documents the fact that pre-contact Native American populations suffered from a number of afflictions. Malnutrition, anemia, and a variety of tuberculoid, trepanematoid, and other degenerative, chronic, and congenital conditions plagued indigenous populations. The general state of health, in combination with ecological and cultural factors, therefore, greatly affected the post-contact disease experience of Native American societies.

Sixteenth and Seventeenth Centuries. No Old World pathogen was more lethal than smallpox, which was unleashed in the Americas during the Spanish conquest. For four years, 1520-1524, the disease diffused across Central and North America. Whether smallpox reached pandemic proportions is debatable, but in populations with no prior exposure, mortality could be as high as 60 percent. The infected native populations experienced high death rates. Florida's Timucua population may have once had 772,000 people, but by 1524 the group was reduced to 361,000. Today the Timucua are no longer a distinct ethnic group.

Throughout the 1500's and into the next century, twenty-three European infectious diseases appeared in native North America (see table, "North American Epidemics and Regions

NORTH AMERICAN EPIDEMICS AND REGIONS AFFECTED, 1520-1696

Date of Onset	Epidemic	Regions Affected
1520	Smallpox	All regions
1531	Measles	Southwest
1545	Bubonic plague	Southwest
1559	Influenza	South Atlantic states, Gulf area, Southwest
1586	Typhus	South Atlantic states, Gulf area
1592	Smallpox	North Atlantic states, South Atlantic states, Old Northwest, Great Lakes states, Midwest east of Mississippi River, Southwest
1602	Smallpox	Southwest
1612	Bubonic plague	North Atlantic states, South Atlantic states, Gulf area, Southwest
1633	Measles	North Atlantic states
1637	Scarlet fever	North Atlantic states
1639	Smallpox	North Atlantic states, South Atlantic states, Old Northwest, Great Lakes states, Midwest east of Mississippi River
1646	Smallpox	Gulf area, Southwest
1647	Influenza	North Atlantic states
1649	Smallpox	North Atlantic states, South Atlantic states, Gulf area
1655	Smallpox	Gulf area
1658	Measles, diphtheria	North Atlantic states, Gulf area, Old Northwest, Great Lakes states, Midwest east of Mississippi River, Southwest
1662	Smallpox	North Atlantic states, Old Northwest, Great Lakes states, Midwest east of Mississippi River
1665	Smallpox	South Atlantic states, Old Northwest, Great Lakes states, Midwest east of Mississippi River
1669	Smallpox	North Atlantic states
1674	Smallpox	Gulf area, southern Plains
1675	Influenza	North Atlantic states
1677	Smallpox	North Atlantic states
1687	Smallpox	North Atlantic states
1692	Measles	North Atlantic states, Old Northwest, Great Lakes states, Midwest east of Mississippi River
1696	Smallpox, Influenza	South Atlantic states, Gulf area

Sources: Data are from Dobyns, Henry, F., *Their Number Became Thinned* (Knoxville, University of Tennessee Press, 1983); Thornton, Russell, *American Indian Holocaust and Survival: A Population History Since 1492* (Norman: University of Oklahoma Press, 1987).

Affected, 1520-1696"). In these various regions, Native American populations contracted diseases on the average of every 7.3 years. Smallpox, measles, influenza, and the bubonic plague affected Native American populations largely east of the Mississippi and in the Southwest. The Huron tribe, which possibly numbered up to thirty-five thousand people in the early 1600's, was reduced by 1640 to an estimated ten thousand people.

An American Indian afflicted with tuberculosis in 1915. (National Archives)

Seventeenth century Europeans generally viewed the decline of surrounding Native American populations as evidence of divine intervention. God would destroy "Godless savages," they thought, so that Christian civilization could prosper. Demographically, European populations grew and expanded geographically as declining indigenous populations relinquished their lands and resources. Those Native Americans that resisted white encroachment were vanquished through genocidal warfare or reduced to mission life.

Eighteenth Century. By the eighteenth century, the European population had reached an estimated 223,000 people. Although Europeans were not the demographic majority, epidemics continued to pave the way for further colonization. Throughout the Atlantic coastal region and into the interior westward, native populations were decimated through genocidal warfare and diseases. In the southeastern region of North America, for example, the estimated Native American population in 1685 was 199,400. By 1970, the population was reduced to approximately 55,900—a decline of 71.9 percent. By contrast, Europeans and African Americans in the region increased their population to 1,630,100 or 31.4 percent.

In sum, European expansion during the three first centuries of colonization produced a demographic collapse of Native American populations. Introduced European infectious diseases, combined with periodic genocidal warfare and the destruction of indigenous lifeways, reduced Native Americans to approximately 600,000. By contrast, the European population grew to 5,308,483.

Nineteenth and Twentieth Centuries. The nineteenth century represents the final century of Native American population decline as a result of epidemics. During this century, twenty-four epidemics affected Native American populations. Smallpox continued to appear every 7.9 years among some segment of the Native American population. Between the smallpox episodes, Native Americans contracted measles and cholera every 22.5 years. According to Henry Dobyns, an anthropologist and authority on Native American historical demography, more epidemics occurred during this century, with more frequency, than during any other.

One of the most devastating epidemics during this century was the 1837-1838 smallpox epidemic. The disease diffused across most of native North America, but the Northern Plains region was hit especially hard. It is estimated that seventeen thousand Native Americans on the northern Plains died before the epidemic subsided. Such acute infectious diseases continued to plague Native American communities into the early reservation period. Only then did these infections give way to the twentieth century epidemics of influenza, tuberculosis, and trachoma—chronic conditions that would infect Native Americans until the 1950's.

The post-contact epidemic history of Native North America can be described as one of continual population decline coupled with the destruction of numerous unique lifeways. Native Americans, however, during these tragic times, did not remain passive actors. Native American societies employed a number of cultural adaptations to respond to the onslaught of infectious diseases. Some societies modified their kin systems, fused with other tribal nations, or created new nations from various remnant tribes. Diseases were powerful agents of cultural and biological change.

The placement of Native Americans on reservations or in rural communities did not mark the end of epidemics. Acute infectious diseases have been replaced by "diseases of poverty." Many of these afflictions reach epidemic proportions in some Native American communities. Deaths from tuberculosis, type II diabetes mellitus, violence, suicide, accidents, and alcoholism exceed the national average. In addition, Native Americans now have to contend with another epidemic—the threat of human immunodeficiency virus (HIV) infection—a disease that has made its presence felt in some Native American communities. —*Gregory R. Campbell*

See also Alcoholism; Demography; Medicine and modes of curing, post-contact; Medicine and modes of curing, pre-contact.

BIBLIOGRAPHY

American Indian Culture and Research Journal 13 (1989). Special issue on contemporary issues in Native American health, edited by Gregory R. Campbell. A collection of articles that focus on issues revolving around American Indians' health in the later 1980's.

Campbell, Gregory R. "The Politics of Counting: Critical Reflections About the Depopulation Question of Native North America." In *Native Voices on the Columbian Quincentenary, 1492-1992*, edited by Donald A. Grinde. Los Angeles: American Indian Studies Center, University of California, 1994. An examination of the European manipulation of Native American population counts as justification for continued colonial expansion.

Dobyns, Henry F. *Their Number Became Thinned*. Knoxville: University of Tennessee Press, 1983. A comprehensive volume addressing the population dynamics of eastern North America.

Stannard, David E. *American Holocaust*. New York: Oxford University Press, 1992. A discussion of Native American population decline in relation to European conquest and colonization.

Thornton, Russell. *American Indian Holocaust and Survival: A Population History Since 1492*. Norman: University of Oklahoma Press, 1987. Provides an overview of Native American population and recovery from European contact to 1980.

Verano, John W., and Douglas H. Ubelaker, eds. *Disease and Demography in the Americas*. Washington, D.C.: Smithsonian Institution Press, 1992. A collection of articles assessing the health and demography of pre-contact and post-contact Native American populations.

Dodge, Henry Chee (Feb. 22, 1860, Fort Defiance, Ariz.—Jan. 7, 1947, Ganado, Ariz.): Interpreter and tribal chairman

ALSO KNOWN AS: Hastin Adiits'a'ii (Mr. Interpreter)

TRIBAL AFFILIATION: Navajo

SIGNIFICANCE: Dodge played a central role as an interpreter, businessman, and tribal chairman in more than half a century of dealings between the U.S. government and the Navajos

Henry Chee Dodge's father was a captured Mexican who was killed in the conflict between the Navajos and New Mexicans shortly after Henry's birth. His mother was Jemez (Pueblo) and Navajo, and since Navajos trace family lineage through the mother, he was considered a member of the Navajo Maii'deshgizhnii (Coyote Pass People) Clan. His family hid during the Navajo Wars, but they nevertheless went hungry—victims of the U.S. Army's scorched-earth policy. His mother left him with a family that had more food, but he was subsequently abandoned by them. An aunt then took charge of him at about the age of five, moving him first to Fort Sumner and then to Fort Defiance. She married a white man who adopted the child, and his contact with his stepfather as well as the soldiers helped him to develop a masterful command of English. This ability served him well throughout his life, despite his having had only a few months of formal schooling.

With the rare skill of speaking both Navajo and English, Dodge was employed as a teenager at the Fort Defiance Indian Agency. At twenty, he was promoted from clerk to official interpreter for the U.S. government, and he continued in that position for ten years. During this time he assisted Washington Matthews in collecting Navajo legends and chants. In 1884, Indian Agent Dennis Riordan appointed him "head chief" of the Navajos, and he escorted three medicine men to meet President Chester A. Arthur in Washington, D.C.

Dodge saved his wages, and at age thirty he entered into a partnership to operate the Round Rock Trading Post. He married Asdzaan Tsinnijinnie and settled at what is now Crystal, New Mexico, on the Arizona-New Mexico border, where he opened a store in his house. Dodge divorced his first wife because she was a gambler and then married two sisters with whom he had a total of four children. He stressed education, and sent his children to school in Salt Lake City.

In 1892, Dodge helped save an Indian agent from angry Navajos who objected to having their children sent to boarding schools. Dodge's trading post was attacked for three days as the agent barricaded himself inside.

In 1922, Dodge became a member of the Tribal Business Council and the tribe's first chairman the following year, serving until 1928. His son, Tom, became tribal chairman in 1932, and Ben—another son—served on the Tribal Council. Dodge went on to direct the tribal police force and was re-elected tribal chairman in 1942.

See also Navajo.

Dogrib: Tribe
CULTURE AREA: Subarctic
LANGUAGE GROUP: Northeastern Athapaskan
PRIMARY LOCATION: Northwest Territories, Canada
POPULATION SIZE: 2,845 (Statistics Canada, based on 1991 census)

The Dogrib, a tribe of the Athapaskan language group, get their name from a traditional legend according to which the first tribesmen came from the mating of a woman and a dog. Dogrib people have lived since the 1500's in the Northwest Territories of Canada, between Great Slave and Great Bear lakes along the Mackenzie River. Their earliest contact with Europeans dates to 1771, when French trappers encountered tribal members and began trading for furs and caribou hides. Epidemics began to take their toll, however, and the population began a rapid decline. By the 1880's, caribou herds began to decline and musk-ox robes became the main trade good. By this time, Catholic missionaries had entered the area, built mission schools, and converted most of the Dogrib to Christianity. In 1900, when the population had dipped below 1,000, tribal leaders signed a reservation treaty with Canadian authorities retaining control of much of their traditional homeland. A gold rush in the 1930's brought an influx of whites, who built the town of Yellowknife.

Traditionally, the tribe had divided into six regional bands. Each band had a leader who generally was the best hunter and the most generous gift-giver to the group. The Dogrib believed that human beings got their power from spirits inhabiting animals and trees—and that these spirits caused sickness, controlled the population of animals to be hunted, and dictated the weather. Illnesses could be cured by confession of sins and misbehavior in front of group leaders.

Many Dogrib practiced their traditional way of making a living until the 1960's. They hunted beaver and muskrat in the spring, caribou in the summer, and fished in the river until the October freeze-up. Winters were the hardest times because of the intense cold and dwindling supply of animals. Government assistance programs began in the 1960's, with health and medical services, a public housing program, schools, and a new highway. The population began to increase, although many Dogrib remained poor. Employment came mainly from these government programs, and after construction was completed the only jobs available were as fishing guides, or janitors and clerks in the assistance programs.

See also Athapaskan language family; Subarctic.

Dogs
TRIBES AFFECTED: Pantribal
SIGNIFICANCE: Dogs provided hunting assistance, food, and companionship among all Indian groups

The first dogs in America were domesticated from wolves in Asia and were brought to the Americas some time between forty thousand and fifteen thousand years ago. There were two major breeds of dog in native North America, one long-legged and the other short-legged. The former resembled a German shepherd in build, and the latter was similar to a beagle, though both were extremely variable in coloring and hair length. There is no evidence of selective breeding to keep breeds separate, and dogs with intermediate characteristics were common.

Both breeds of dog were used primarily as hunting aids, flushing game into the open or treeing it. Some dogs apparently were adept at forcing animals into the open by digging into their burrows, but it is unclear whether any tribes regularly trained dogs for hunting skills. Dogs also were used for hauling travois in the Great Plains, for pulling Inuit dogsleds, and as pets everywhere.

Dogs occasionally were eaten throughout North America, especially in times of food shortage. Some groups, such as the Iroquois, had annual feasts at which the eating of a dog was a central part of the activities. In Western Mexico, dogs were eaten more regularly, and the modern chihuahua is descended from a dog bred particularly for eating. These dogs are depicted in ceramic sculptures in prehistoric shaft tombs, especially in Colima, appearing either as plump animals (indicating bounty) or as gaunt, starving animals with jutting jaws and protruding ribs (representing famine).

See also Horses; Hunting and gathering; Transportation modes.

Dohasan (c. 1805—c. 1866, Indian Territory, present-day Okla.): War chief
ALSO KNOWN AS: Little Mountain, Little Bluff, Dahauson, Tohauson
TRIBAL AFFILIATION: Kiowa
SIGNIFICANCE: Dohasan forged an alliance between independent Kiowa bands, making the tribe a major power in the southern Plains in the 1840's

After the Kiowas were defeated in war by the Osage in 1833, Dohasan was chosen to replace the deposed chief, Adate. Dohasan quickly proved his worth by uniting the several bands of Kiowa into a cohesive and formidable tribe. He likewise negotiated peace with the Osage.

In the 1840's, as the Kiowas were devastated by cholera and smallpox and were increasingly threatened by white migration onto their lands, Dohasan led numerous raids against the white intruders. After army retaliation, Dohasan signed the Treaty of Fort Atkinson in 1853, by which the Kiowa were paid an annuity in exchange for promising to cease their raiding. Hostilities continued virtually unabated, however, until Dohasan agreed to the Little Arkansas Treaty of 1865, by which the Kiowas agreed to settle on a reservation in the Oklahoma panhandle in Indian Territory.

After his death in 1866, Dohasan was succeeded by Lone Wolf, the tribe's compromise choice, over the war leader Satanta and the peace faction's leader, Kicking Bird.

See also Fort Atkinson, Treaty of; Kicking Bird; Kiowa; Lone Wolf; Satanta.

Donnaconna (?—c. 1539, France): Principal chief
TRIBAL AFFILIATION: Huron
SIGNIFICANCE: Donnaconna was the first Indian leader of note to resist the French incursion into tribal territory in present-day Canada

When the French explorer Jacques Cartier erected a cross at the Iroquoian village of Stadacona (present-day Quebec City) in July, 1534, the village chief, Donnaconna, strenuously objected. Cartier forced him aboard his French ship on the banks of the St. Lawrence River adjacent to Stadacona; and after some negotiations, Cartier released him but took Donnaconna's two sons, Domagaya and Taignoagny, captive. They were taken to France to become interpreters for Cartier, whose plans included exploring further up the St. Lawrence River to the Iroquoian village of Hochelaga (now Montreal) and beyond.

Cartier returned from France the following year with Donnaconna's sons, feasted with the chief, and planned an expedition to Hochelaga with his two young interpreters. The boys, however, intrigued against Cartier in an attempt to prevent French penetration of the interior of the continent. Cartier ventured without them and relations between the French and Stadaconans worsened. Donnaconna told Cartier of the "kingdom of the Saguenay" along the river of that name in what is now eastern Quebec, where he would find "immense quantities of gold, rubies and other rich things." Donnaconna was trying to divert the explorer from the St. Lawrence Valley and from his nation's territory. Although Domagaya inadvertently saved the French crew of more than one hundred from death by scurvy through a white cedar bark cure, Cartier connived with Donnaconna's rival Agona to oust Donnaconna from his role as chief. Cartier seized the deposed leader, his two sons, and seven other Stadaconans. On May 6, 1536, Cartier left for France with these ten captives. None of them returned to their homeland; all but one died soon after arrival in France. Before his death, however, Donnaconna received an audience with King François I and told him of great gold and silver mines and spices such as nutmeg, cloves, and pepper, which existed in northern North America. Donnaconna probably concocted this fiction in order to be released and allowed to return home. The former chief also was interviewed by the monk and cosmologist André Thevet, who later wrote extensively about Donnaconna's homeland. When Cartier next ventured to Stadacona in 1541 without Donnaconna, his sons, or any of the other captives, the Stadaconans, including chief Agona, grew increasingly wary. War broke out between them and the French in 1542.

See also Huron; Indian-white relations—French colonial.

Dorset: Prehistoric tradition
DATE: 950 B.C.E.—1000 C.E.
LOCATION: Canada's eastern Arctic, southern Greenland
CULTURE AFFECTED: Inuit

The Dorset cultural tradition is said to have begun around 950 B.C.E. Pre-Dorset hunters were the earliest known occupants of the central and eastern Arctic, and they were living in the area by 3000 B.C.E. They established themselves there during a period of postglacial warming.

By 950 B.C.E., during another period of climatic warming, pre-Dorset culture had evolved into the distinctive Dorset tradition, centered at northern Foxe Basin and southern Baffin Island. Thereafter, from roughly 200 B.C.E. to 200 C.E.—the period of its maximal distribution—the Dorset tradition was marked by viable colonies scattered throughout the Arctic from Banks Island in the west, around Hudson Bay in the center, to Greenland, Labrador, and Newfoundland in the east. Dorset colonies in Newfoundland were planted farther south than Inuit have ever been discovered. By 1000 C.E., the Thule people, moving out of the western Arctic with superior technology, began occupying areas previously marked by the Dorset tradition. Anthropologists are unsure whether the Dorset were already in decline or whether the Thule merged with or simply displaced them.

Many Dorset cultural characteristics were continuations of pre-Dorset patterns; subsistence still rested heavily on hunting seal, walrus, and smaller whales along shorelines and ice floes, activities which were supplemented by organized drives to kill caribou as well as by fishing for salmon and trout. Accordingly, the Dorset tradition developed a distinctive and a wide range of hunting weapons: flaked chert harpoons, slotted bone and barbed harpoon heads, beveled slate lance points, fish spears, flaked chert snub-nosed scrapers, flaked chert bifaced knives, beveled slate flensing knives, burins, and snow knives for igloo building. Though lacking bows or floating drags for kayak hunting, the Dorset built hand-drawn sledges, used dogs for hunting or food, crafted blubber lamps, constructed several types of housing, were expert at grinding and polishing tools, and carved elaborate magico-religious art objects.

See also Arctic; Inuit; Prehistory—Arctic; Thule.

Dozier, Edward Pasqual (Apr. 23, 1916, Santa Clara Pueblo, N.Mex.—May 2, 1971, Tucson, Ariz.): Anthropologist
ALSO KNOWN AS: Awa Tside
TRIBAL AFFILIATION: Santa Clara Pueblo
SIGNIFICANCE: One of the first American Indian professors of anthropology, Edward P. Dozier published many important articles and books based on his research among Pueblo people and in the Philippines

Although American anthropologists have often studied Indian people, very few have been Indian themselves. Such an imbalance has meant that, within the educational system, the authorities on the history and cultural experiences of Indian people have tended to be outsiders to Indian communities. As an Indian, Edward Dozier is a major exception in the history of American anthropology.

Dozier grew up in Santa Clara Pueblo and learned to speak Tewa, Spanish, and English. As an adolescent in the 1930's, he worked as a research assistant for Elizabeth Sergeant, a journalist and ethnographer conducting research among the Pueblos.

Dozier applied his diverse linguistic and cultural experience to his academic studies in anthropology. In 1952, Dozier received a Ph.D. in anthropology from the University of California, Los Angeles. After conducting research in a community of Tewa people living among the Hopi in Arizona, Dozier went on to teach anthropology and linguistics at the University of Oregon, Northwestern University, and the University of Arizona. His books include *The Tewa of Arizona* (1954), *Hano: A Tewa Village in Arizona* (1966), *Mountain Arbiters: The Changing Life of a Philippine Hill People* (1966), and *The Pueblo Indians of North America* (1970).

Throughout his career, Edward Dozier attempted to further the interests of Indian people. At the University of Arizona, he established an American Indian studies program. Between 1957 and 1971, he served on the board of the Association on American Indian Affairs.

See also American Indian studies programs and archives; Pueblo tribes, Eastern.

Dragging Canoe (c. 1730, Running Water Village on the Tennessee River, Tenn.—Mar. 1, 1792, Running Water Village, Tenn.): Chief

ALSO KNOWN AS: Cheucunsene, Kunmesee, Tsungunsini

TRIBAL AFFILIATION: Cherokee

SIGNIFICANCE: Cherokee leader Dragging Canoe violently opposed white expansion into Indian land

Unlike his father, Chief Attakullakulla, the peace leader for the Cherokee who sought accommodation with whites, Dragging Canoe was opposed to any form of white encroachment on Cherokee lands. Angered by the 1775 agreement through which the Cherokee sold all of Kentucky and part of Tennessee, he prophesied that the Cherokee would eventually be banished to some distant land. Dragging Canoe led a dissident group who refused to sign the treaty.

While Attakullakulla and most Cherokee sided with the Americans during the revolutionary war, Dragging Canoe sided with the British, using British-supplied weaponry to attack settlers in Tennessee. Although betrayed by his cousin Nancy Ward, who warned settlers of pending attacks, his band inflicted several white casualties. When the Cherokee were driven from the region in 1782, Dragging Canoe established a new home near Chickamauga, Tennessee, from which he continued to attack white settlers. In retaliation, the Americans destroyed all Chickamauga villages. As the Cherokee continued signing away their land, Dragging Canoe maintained his policy of armed resistance. In 1782, he again led his people to a new settlement downriver, though in 1784, these new villages were also destroyed. Afterward, Dragging Canoe finally agreed to peace.

See also Cherokee; Indian-white relations—U.S., 1775-1830; Ward, Nancy.

Dress and adornment

TRIBES AFFECTED: Pantribal

SIGNIFICANCE: Designed for comfort, protection, and utility, American Indian clothing and decoration also often designated group affiliation, social role, and rank; it often conveyed—and still conveys—a spiritual message to both wearer and observers

European accounts of early contact vividly describe the wide variety of clothing worn by the original people of North America. Recorded in detail by skilled artists, varied styles of dress emphasized the uniqueness of each group.

Drawings showed Inuit (Eskimo) people of the far north dressed in two-layered outfits of caribou skin, one layer with fur turned out, the other with fur against the body. Sealskin mittens, moccasins, and parkas, all lined with fur, made an insulated cocoonlike outfit designed for survival in the bitterest of Arctic winters. The decorative touch to the male Eskimo's outfit was a carved ivory labret—a disk "buttoned" into his perforated lower lip. Its trade value was twenty-five caribou skins. A ruff of wolverine fur on the hooded parka and eye coverings with narrow slits to protect against the sun's glare on snow left no part of the body exposed to the elements.

In distinct contrast, the men of the Plateau west of the Rockies were shown wearing the simplest of outfits—nothing. Occasionally they wore sandals and a short robe of rabbit skins. Women of nomadic Plateau cultures wore no shirts, only simple apron-skirts and sandals woven of soft fibers. A woman would wear a basketlike hat to protect the forehead from the carrying strap of the basket slung over the back.

Similar modes of dress were seen among other peoples in similar climates. Between these extremes was a vast assortment of styles. Virtually every substance in nature was used in the making of clothing or ornamentation. Materials used ranged from buffalo wool spun on a spindle to the inner bark of cedar trees woven into fabric. It was the custom to use all parts of anything taken from its natural habitat. Furs, skins, feathers, shells, bones, teeth, and claws of animals, birds, and fish were the main materials for clothing or adornment. Fabrics were woven of grasses, tree bark, cotton, and other fibrous plants. Mosses, leaves, and downy plants such as milkweed were used for insulation. Plants were used for making natural dyes.

Clothing of Ancient Peoples. The early people of North America created clothing for comfort and utility. Clothing evolved to suit the climate and the physical, social, and cultural activities of the people. The Hohokam, Mogollon, and Anasazi, ancient peoples in the Southwest, wove clothing and blankets from cotton, animal fur, and feathers, and adorned themselves in turquoise jewelry. Rabbit fur and deerskin were punched with an awl and laced together with thongs. Women's aprons and sandals were made of yucca, a fibrous desert plant.

People of the Adena and Hopewell cultures, ancient Eastern Woodland cultures, fashioned clothing from deerskin, adding leggings and moccasins to the men's shirt and breechcloth. Women wore wraparound skirts and tunics of deerskin.

Two Aleut men (of Alaska's Aleutian Islands) dressed for hunting. (I. Dutcher, American Museum of Natural History)

Hopewell people wore copper breastplates, ornate feather cloaks, and headdresses. The Adena wore copper bracelets and rings, stone gorgets (armor for the throat), bone masks, pearl beads, and mica ornaments.

Decoration could be functional as well as attractive. A ceremonial feather cloak could serve as a sunshade or raincoat in a tropical climate. Gorgets protected the vulnerable throat. In later times, when clothing was tailored, fringe helped wet buckskin to dry quickly by wicking moisture away from the body. Beads and quillwork added strength to skins or fabric for longer wear.

Meanings Conveyed by Clothing. Artful adornment created by each group of American Indians expressed both spiritual style and beauty. Clothing and decorations carried meaning, symbolizing the beliefs, values, and intentions of the wearer. A warrior painting his body as he dressed for battle was visibly declaring his purpose and praying for a successful outcome.

Dress and adornment could indicate membership in a particular group, clan, or society, making it possible, even from a distance, to distinguish outsiders from those belonging to the group. In battle, this distinction could mean life or death. An outfit that indicated clan membership could guarantee food and shelter from other clan members for a traveler. Clothing often helped to identify social or familial bonds between people who had just met.

Plains People. Among the northern Plains people, clothing and items of adornment for both men and women were carefully planned, patiently made, finely decorated, and functional. In early times animal skins were used; the same designs were rendered later in trade cloth. Motion was expressed in swaying fringe, splashes of bright paint, jingling bells, and beads or elk teeth. The decorations recalled the swaying grasses of the Plains.

Clothing could be packed and transported easily when the nomadic Plains people traveled. The people's mobility helped promote a common style among various Plains groups. Gifts of clothing were exchanged during large seasonal gatherings. Garments worn in successful battles were often copied, both to honor the warrior and to acquire some of his powerful medicine.

The breechcloth, a single panel of plain buckskin or cloth held in place with a thong belt, was the everyday garment for the Native American man of the Plains. A coating of bear grease protected his skin from cold, insects, brush, and germs. For formal wear, the breechcloth was usually beaded or painted. Crow men preferred a two-part apron, with finely beaded floral designs, similar to those worn by Woodlands men. Leggings of elk hide or deer hide were practical for walking or riding through the brush or for sitting on the ground. The ever-present fringe was handy for making repairs or using as cords. If snagged on brush or stone, the fringe would break off, leaving the wearer free and the garment intact.

Men often wore tunic or poncho-style shirts with split sides. Under the shirt a belt held up the leggings and carried weapons, tools, and a pipe bag. In cold weather a decorated robe of buffalo hide or fur completed the outfit.

The war shirt, worn only for ceremony or battle, was richly decorated with fringe, beads or quills, ermine tails, scalps, and other medicine items. Painted with symbols of power, these shirts were believed to be protective for the wearer. When beaded and decorated, the war shirt could weigh as much as forty pounds—an acceptable burden because of its medicine power, which gave confidence and status to the wearer.

The southern Plains groups used rich, dark-green dyes, eagle feathers, eagle bone whistles, and medicine bags for decoration. In contrast, the northern peoples—Mandan, Crow, Blackfoot, and Sioux—created ornate shirts with beads and quillwork. When the long northern winter brought a hiatus to war, it provided time for tailoring, repairing, and decorating garments.

Other Regions. In the Southeast, as in most warm climates throughout the continent, the usual outfit for men was breech-cloth and moccasins. Algonquian men of the temperate Northeast coastal area spent the summer months in breechcloth and moccasins, and during cooler weather wore skin pants or leggings, skirts, and robes. Men shaved their heads except for a scalp lock, and war paint was worn for ceremonies. Crowns and cloaks of turkey feathers and necklaces made of prized wampum—purple clam shells and white conch shells—made elegant outfits. Women wore sliplike tailored dresses topped with cape-sleeves or the short poncho shirt. They sewed strings of valuable sacred wampum to their deerskin shirts, tied the strings around their waists and in their hair, and wore them as necklaces and bracelets. Leggings and moccasins completed the outfit.

Among the Iroquois of the Woodlands area, men wore deerskin kilts and leggings topped with shoulder sashes of woven fiber. In cooler weather skin shirts and moccasins were added. Women dressed in wrapped deerskin skirts, loose shirts, and moccasins. Elk teeth or cowrie shells adorned the shirts.

The ceremonial dress of the Zuni woman was a rectangle of black hand-loomed cloth trimmed in dark blue. She tied it over her right shoulder, wrapped a long woven sash around her waist, then covered her shoulders with a white robe.

The valuable Chilkat blanket marked the high point of Northwest weaving art. The Tlingit people made this blanket of goat's wool woven into a cedar bark core in boldly stylized images of clan animals using black, white, yellow, and the prized blue dye. Chilkat blankets originated with the coastal Tsimshian group and were worn by men and women in ceremonial dances.

A wealthy Hupa woman of northern California wore a fringed skirt covered with a full apron of shells. Dozens of

This Tolowa woman from Northern California wears an apron decorated with shells. (Library of Congress)

shell necklaces covered a sleeveless shirt. Shell hair ties and earrings completed the outfit.

Jewelry and Body Decoration. All peoples of North America used jewelry for decoration and nearly all to indicate status. The earliest jewelry was of shells, feathers, turquoise stones, and easily worked copper. In addition to the purple and white shell wampum in the eastern woodlands, the bear claw necklace was highly prized by warriors. The artisans of the Southwest worked with silver and turquoise to create distinctive jewelry—the Navajo "squash blossom" necklace and concha belt, the Hopi layered silver cutout bracelet, and the Zuni silver pins inlaid with stone and shell.

Face and body painting was done in most groups, sometimes for decoration, more often for ceremonies. Paint could also take the place of clothing in the summer. Red, black, and white were favored colors. Body piercing for adornment was common and included jewelry such as labrets in the lips, earrings for men and women, and rings, bones, or shells worn in the nose.

Tattooing was done with charcoal, needles, dyed thread or cactus spines, and burned shells. Various styles included: Subarctic (marks on the chin during girls' puberty rites), Haida (crests on arms, legs, chest, and back, especially for the highborn), West Coast people (bands on chin, cheek, or forehead for men or women, with wrist bands and lines on the chest for some women), Teton women (lip and facial tattoos), and Natchez women (across the nose). High ranking men and women wore intricate designs that often completely covered the body.

Hair Styles and Status. Hair was a symbol of strength, individuality, and spirituality. In some groups, women wore their hair long and men wore their hair short. In others this custom was reversed. There was great diversity even among the same people. Styles varied from hair that was never cut (sometimes touching the ground), worn straight or braided, to shaved head with only a small scalplock left on top. Men of the Subarctic tucked their long hair under a turban. Some Plains men wore as many as eight long braids. Aztec commoners kept their long hair uncovered, and Creek men shaved the sides of their heads, leaving a center strip from forehead to the nape of the neck. Natchez men shaved one side of the head and wore their hair long on the other.

Women's hair styles included shoulder length with bangs for Western Apache, side buns of the "squash blossom" style for Hopi maidens, a middle part with two long braids for Jicarilla Apache, braids woven with ribbons and wrapped around the head for Aztec commoners, several braids for Natchez women, a topknot with ribbons for Creek, and hair brought up and forward in bonnet shape (creating a natural sun visor) for Seminole women.

In complex societies with various status levels, hair and headdressings designated a person's role or rank. More valuable materials and more ornate designs denoted higher status. The Aztecs defined four levels: commoner men and women wore their hair long and uncovered, chiefs wore leather head-bands with multi-colored tassels or gold and turquoise crowns, warriors had large feather headdresses, and the priestly wore elaborate outfits with headdresses representing gods and goddesses.

Effects of European Contact. European contact influenced the clothing of almost every group, in style, fabric type and color, and adornment. Earlier garments of natural colored fiber, fur, and hides were replaced with wool and other red or blue fabrics richly decorated with beads or quillwork. Additions or ribbonwork and appliqué to basic styles were most elegantly done by East Coast people, especially Iroquois of the north and Seminole of the south. Satin dresses took the place of coarse woven fiber outfits. Western Apache women adopted the European full skirt of bright calico topped with a belted hip-length blouse.

Zuni men replaced their short cotton kilts with European-style loose white cotton shirts worn over white pants. Leather concho belts with silver disks and hard-soled sandals set a style eventually copied by Europeans. In the North, caribou and buffalo robes were replaced with woolen coats or the hooded "capote"—a cloak made from the colorful Hudson's Bay Company trade blanket. —*Gale M. Thompson*

See also Appliqué and ribbonwork; Beads and beadwork; Blankets; Cotton; Feathers and featherwork; Headdresses; Hides and hidework; Masks; Moccasins; Quillwork; Shells and shellwork; Tattoos and tattooing; War bonnets.

BIBLIOGRAPHY

Billard, Jules B., et al. *The World of the American Indian.* Washington, D.C.: National Geographic Society, 1974. More than 440 illustrations, maps of culture areas, poems and chants, tribal location supplement with keys to back-pocket maps, index, and acknowledgments.

Brown, Joseph Epes. *The North American Indians: A Selection of Photographs by Edward S. Curtis.* New York: Aperture, 1972. Images selected from thousands of photographs in the Curtis collection. Features people of many groups west of the Mississippi River, with excellent examples of clothing and headdresses. Songs, quotations from well-known traditional people of North America, historians, and anthropologists, captions and detailed notes on photographs.

Mails, Thomas E. *Mystic Warriors of the Plains.* Garden City, N.Y.: Doubleday, 1972. An in-depth study of Plains people: social customs and religion, arts and crafts, clothing, warriors' regalia and weapons, buffalo and horse. Hundreds of drawings by the author, including a diagram of the buffalo showing uses for every part of the animal.

Maxwell, James A., et al. *America's Fascinating Indian Heritage.* Pleasantville, N.Y.: Reader's Digest, 1978. Comprehensive account of all culture areas, prehistory (including Mesoamerican), cultural, political, and social issues of early twentieth century, paintings, color photographs, and drawings, descriptions of ceremonies, list of museums, historic villages, and archaeological sites.

Sturtevant, William, gen. ed. *Handbook of North American Indians.* Washington, D.C.: Smithsonian Institution Press,

Drumming at a 1990 pow-wow in Madison, Wisconsin. (James L. Shaffer)

1978-. Nine volumes of this projected twenty-volume set had been published by 1994. The scholarship and thoroughness of the Smithsonian volumes are exemplary, and they include considerable information on (and illustrations of) modes of dress.

Underhill, Ruth M. *Red Man's America: A History of Indians in the United States.* Chicago: University of Chicago Press, 1953. Surveys origins, history, social customs, material culture, religion, and mythology. Written from the perspective of the first peoples of North America.

Drums

TRIBES AFFECTED: Pantribal

SIGNIFICANCE: Drums and other percussion instruments are an almost universal part of Indian music; they are also used in nonmusical tribal ceremonies and have served as a means of communication

Drums are used for a variety of purposes in almost every American Indian culture. Most often drumming accompanies singing, although the singers do not necessarily follow the rhythm of the drums.

Drums come in a variety of types. The hand drum is carried by an individual and can be played while dancing. The most common material for this type of drum is hollowed wood, but woven baskets and hollowed gourds are often used as well. There are also large drums around which several people sit and play together. Water drums are made from hollow logs and are partially filled with water. The water greatly increases resonance, and such drums can be heard for miles.

Drums are often decorated elaborately. Much of American Indian singing has religious significance, and the proper gods and spirits must be evoked. One way of doing this is to paint the proper pictures on the body of the drum. Drumsticks are sometimes given much more significance than they have been accorded in European cultures. For some ceremonies, drumsticks are decorated according to their particular ceremonial meaning, and the possession of such sticks may be a sign of prestige. Apart from the more common types of drums, in some area poles or planks may also be beaten. Elsewhere, stretched hides, without any attached drum body, are used.

As well as providing musical accompaniment, drums were used as a form of long-distance communication. A sort of "Morse code" system was used, and it was different for every tribe. Since the signals produced were kept as secrets within a particular tribe, drumming can be seen as a very secure form of communication.

See also Dances and dancing; Music and song; Pow-wows and contemporary celebrations.

Dull Knife (c. 1810—c. 1883): Chief

ALSO KNOWN AS: Wahiev, Morning Star, Tamela Pashme
TRIBAL AFFILIATION: Northern Cheyenne
SIGNIFICANCE: Dull Knife, with Little Wolf, led the 1,500-mile journey of the Cheyenne from their exile in Indian Territory to their northern home in Montana

As a soldier chief, Dull Knife had a reputation for never sending anyone ahead of him, and he often counted the first coup. Dull Knife and Little Wolf are both noted in connection with an incident in 1856 at the Upper Platte Bridge, according to historian Stan Hoig the first significant conflict between Cheyennes and U.S. troops.

Prior to the killing of Black Kettle and his people in 1864, Dull Knife had been a noted warrior and respected chief who chose peace. He fought alongside Sioux and Northern Arapahos in many of the major engagements of the northern Plains. During the War for the Bozeman Trail (or Red Cloud's War), 1866-1868, and the Fetterman Fight of December, 1866, he allied with the Sioux leaders Crazy Horse, Gall, and Hump. Dull Knife's participation in negotiations at Fort Laramie, however, and his subsequent signature on an agreement to allow a fort in the Powder River country may have permanently affected his role as a leader. In May, 1868, Dull Knife was one of the signers of the Fort Laramie Treaty. In November of 1873, Dull Knife and Little Wolf led a delegation of Cheyenne and Arapaho chiefs in negotiations with the commissioner of Indian affairs in Washington, D.C. The leaders explained that they had never given up their homelands and that they did not want to move south to Indian Territory. The differing interpretations of the treaty arrangements provided another four years of freedom for the Cheyenne people, but the Battle of the Little Bighorn in 1876 changed that. Following the defeat of George Armstrong Custer, the government was determined to move the Sioux and Cheyenne peoples to Indian Territory.

At dawn on November 25, 1876, eleven hundred cavalrymen under Colonel R. S. Mackenzie attacked the village of Dull Knife and Little Wolf in a canyon of the Bighorn Mountains. Forty Cheyennes died. As deadly was the destruction of tipis, clothing, and the entire supply of winter food—burned by the soldiers. When the temperature dropped to thirty below zero that same night, more lives were lost. The Cheyenne who surrendered were sent to Indian Territory. Of the one thousand people sent to the Darlington Agency in August, 1877, six hundred became ill in the first two months, and forty-three died. After several failed attempts to convince the authorities that they should be returned to their Montana homeland, Dull Knife—with Little Wolf and about 350 people—set out for Montana in September, 1878. The group included 92 men, 120 women, and 141 children. After six weeks of flight, the group split, part following the leadership of Little Wolf, who wanted to continue north to the Tongue River, and part following Dull Knife, who wanted to seek shelter with Red Cloud. Dull Knife did not know that the Red Cloud Agency had been moved.

During a blizzard in October, Dull Knife's 149 Cheyenne people were surrounded by troops from Fort Robinson; they surrendered and initially were lodged at the fort until the Indian bureau could determine their disposition. On January 3, 1879, the bureau determined that the Cheyenne people should be returned to Indian Territory. When Dull Knife said his people would rather fight than go back, the doors to the barracks they were housed in were chained shut. Food and firewood were denied in an effort to freeze and starve them into submission. On January 9, after six days without provisions, the Cheyenne people broke from the barracks building. In the first moments of gunfire, those jumping from the windows were shot, but the confusion allowed some to escape. Even so, in that first half-mile to freedom, more than half of the Cheyenne fighting men were killed. On January 21, the so-called Cheyenne Outbreak ended with one last battle at Antelope Creek. Of the 149 people who had fled the prison barracks, 64 had been killed in the fighting and 78 were recaptured. Dull Knife was one of the seven who escaped. He was captured later when he went to the Red Cloud Agency for help. He was later returned to the Northern Cheyenne reservation secured by Little Wolf in the Rosebud Valley. The Northern Cheyenne were officially granted the Tongue River Reservation in Montana in 1884, the year following Dull Knife's death.

Dull Knife had one son, the warrior Bull Hump. Dull Knife Memorial College in Lame Deer, Montana, recognizes the Cheyenne leader's encouragement to acquire an education to learn a new way of life.   —*Tonya Huber*

See also Bozeman Trail wars; Fort Laramie Treaty of 1868; Little Bighorn, Battle of the; Little Wolf.

BIBLIOGRAPHY

Bouc, Ken. "Indian Wars, 1874-1880." *Fort Robinson Illustrated* 64, no. 1 (1986): 22-37.

Dockstader, Frederick J. *Great North American Indians: Profiles in Life and Leadership.* New York: Van Nostrand Reinhold, 1977.

Grinnell, George Bird. *The Cheyenne Indians: Their History and Ways of Life.* 2 vols. New Haven, Conn.: Yale University Press, 1923. Reprint. Lincoln: University of Nebraska Press, 1972.

_____. *The Fighting Cheyennes.* New York: Charles Scribner's Sons, 1915.

Hoebel, E. Adamson. *The Cheyennes: Indians of the Great Plains.* New York: Holt, Rinehart and Winston, 1978.

Hoig, Stan. *The Peace Chiefs of the Cheyennes.* Norman: University of Oklahoma Press, 1980.

Sandoz, Mari. *Cheyenne Autumn.* New York: McGraw-Hill, 1953.

Utley, Robert M. *The Indian Frontier of the American West, 1846-1890.* Albuquerque: University of New Mexico Press, 1984.

Waldman, Carl. *Who Was Who in Native American History: Indians and Non-Indians from Early Contacts Through 1900.* New York: Facts on File, 1990.

Duwamish: Tribe

CULTURE AREA: Northwest Coast
LANGUAGE GROUP: Salishan (Nisqually)
PRIMARY LOCATION: Seattle
POPULATION SIZE: 201 (1990 U.S. Census)

The Duwamish were divided into five different territorial groups. Though they were a maritime people and fish was a staple, they also depended on vegetable foods and land animals. Numerous types of waterfowl were caught, and tidal foods were abundant, particularly shellfish. Traditional forms of wealth were dentalia, slaves, canoes, blankets of dog and mountain goat wool, fur robes, and clamshell disk beads.

The first European-American contact with the Duwamish was in 1792, when George Vancouver explored Puget Sound. John Work of the Hudson's Bay Company explored the region in 1824. In 1833, the company established Fort Nisqually as a trading post, which brought many changes through increased trade. In 1854 and 1855 the Treaties of Medicine Creek and Point No Point reserved land for some tribes. By the 1880's, the Indian Shaker Church had spread through the area.

The final Judge George Bolt decision in 1979 denied the nonreservation Duwamish their fishing rights. In 1988, a petition for recognition by the Duwamish and other landless tribes of western Washington was drawn up and was still in litigation in the early 1990's.

See also Salishan language family.

Earthlodge

TRIBES AFFECTED: Plains tribes

SIGNIFICANCE: Earthlodges were among the earliest forms of shelter devised by cultures living on the Plains

Earthlodges are circular dome-shaped structures roofed by earth and entered by a covered passageway. Earthlodges appeared around 700 C.E., housing the earliest farm cultures on the Plains. Semi-nomadic villagers constructed earthlodges in three areas of the Plains. In the Dakotas the Mandan, Hidatsa, and later the Arikara erected villages along the Missouri River. The Pawnee built earthlodge villages in the central Plains of Kansas and Nebraska. To the northeast the Omaha, Oto, and Ponca also constructed earthlodges.

Earthlodge

All these people built their lodges in similar fashion. Four or more central posts—usually cottonwood—were set in the ground and were connected by cross beams. A slanted sidewall of smaller posts marked the circumference. A wheel of roof rafters radiated from the central smoke hole and extended to the central posts. The walls and roof were covered alternately with layers of willow branches, grass thatching, a shingling of sod, and a final coat of wet earth that dried like plaster. The average earthlodge was 11 to 13 feet in height and 40 to 50 feet in diameter. Earthlodges lasted from seven to ten years and were the property of the women, who provided much of the labor in building.

Inside arrangements included a sacred area, platform beds along the wall, food platforms, a fencelike wooden fire screen, storage (cache) pits, and often a horse corral. The fireplace was in the center of the earthlodge, and an opening in the roof vented smoke. In the Upper Missouri a bullboat was inverted over the hole to shut out moisture and regulate downdrafts. When the people went on large summer buffalo hunts they utilized tipis; however, their primary residence was the earthlodge.

See also Architecture—Plains; Pit house; Tipi.

Eastman, Charles Alexander (Feb. 19, 1858, near Redwood Falls, Minn.—Jan. 8, 1939, Detroit, Mich.): Author, physician

ALSO KNOWN AS: Ohiyesa (The Winner)

TRIBAL AFFILIATION: Santee Sioux

SIGNIFICANCE: Through his many publications and participation in Indian-related activities, Eastman became a leading advocate of Indian reform during the early twentieth century

Charles Eastman was born at a time when the Santee Sioux were facing the hardships of reservation life. He later became recognized as the most highly educated Indian in the United States and devoted his entire career to helping Indians adjust to the dominant white society.

Eastman's mother, who died giving birth to him, was the mixed-blood daughter of Captain Seth Eastman, noted artist; his father belonged to the Wahpeton band of the Santee Sioux. Eastman received the name Ohiyesa to represent symbolically a victory by his band over another in a lacrosse game. After the ill-fated Santee Sioux uprising in Minnesota in August, 1862, Eastman was among those who fled to Canada. He believed his father, Many Lightnings, had been killed during the uprising.

Eastman's paternal grandmother and uncle reared him in the traditional ways of a Sioux boy. He became a skilled hunter and anxiously awaited his initiation as a warrior. His traditional upbringing abruptly ended in 1872 when his father appeared in Canada to reclaim him. Many Lightnings had been imprisoned for his actions in the Sioux uprising and became a Christian while in confinement. After his release, he established a home at Flandreau, Dakota Territory. Many Lightnings convinced Eastman to return with him to Flandreau and later to adopt an English name and to begin his formal education in white schools.

For the next seventeen years, Eastman attended several schools. In 1887, he received his B.S. degree from Dartmouth College, and in 1890, he obtained his medical degree from Boston University. The Indian Rights Association and the Lake Mohonk Conference of Friends of the Indian, two powerful reform groups, praised his accomplishments and used him as a model for other Indians. Eastman was now thirty-two years old and ready to begin a career dedicated to helping Indian people.

Eastman's adult years paralleled an important period of federal Indian policies—from the Dawes Severalty Act of 1887 to the Indian New Deal of the 1930's. During that time, he held several federal jobs and became a nationally known author, lecturer, and reformer.

Eastman served as government physician at Pine Ridge Academy, South Dakota, 1890-1893, witnessing the Ghost Dance and the Wounded Knee tragedy; administrator at Carlisle Indian School, Pennsylvania, 1899; government physician at Crow Creek, South Dakota, 1900-1903; head of the revision of the Sioux allotment rolls, 1903-1909; and Indian inspector, 1923-1925. Eastman frequently clashed with his white superiors during his employment with the federal government. For example, white Indian agents often felt threatened by an educated Indian and suspected him of undermining their authority.

Eastman's nongovernment jobs included establishing a brief medical practice in St. Paul, Minnesota, in 1893; serving as the Indian secretary of the International Committee of the

YMCA, 1894-1898; and representing the Santee Sioux claims in Washington, D.C., for many years.

Eastman became a prolific writer, authoring eleven books and numerous articles. Elaine Goodale Eastman, his wife, who was also a writer and reformer, helped him with his work. His writings focused on autobiography, Indian history and culture, and Indian-white relations. For example, *Indian Boyhood* (1902) and *From the Deep Woods to Civilization* (1916) covered his life, and *The Soul of the Indian* (1911) and *The Indian Today* (1915) concerned the latter subjects. His books received good reviews, sold well, and were translated into several foreign editions. Although Eastman tended to be somewhat romantic in his writings, he wrote about Indians from his perspective as an Indian—a unique situation in the early twentieth century. He was also in demand as a lecturer.

As a reformer, Eastman helped to organize and later served as president of the Society of American Indians, a pan-Indian organization formed in 1911. He worked hard to protect Indians from injustices and to improve reservation conditions. He initially supported the Dawes Act, but later, like many other reformers, began criticizing its elimination of Indian-owned lands. Eastman called for improved health and educational

Charles Eastman, a Sioux physician and writer, devoted his life to helping Indians and advocating reform. (Library of Congress)

programs on reservations; disapproved of the use of peyote by Indians; supported the Indian Citizenship Act of 1924, believing that suffrage would help Indians to achieve equality; and condemned the Bureau of Indian Affairs for not doing its job. As an acculturated Indian, Eastman most likely supported the acculturation approaches of the Indian New Deal, which allowed Indians to be Indians and still operate in the dominant society.

Eastman spent his last years separated from his wife. He purchased a cabin in Canada in the late 1920's and continued to lecture and do research. In 1933, the Indian Council Fire, a pan-Indian organization, honored Eastman as their first recipient of an annual award that recognized his many achievements in improving Indian and white relations.

Charles Eastman believed that Indians did not have to discard their Indianness to survive in the dominant society. He developed, as did many Indians, a special syncretism, or blending of cultures, which allowed him to operate in two different worlds. —*Raymond Wilson*

See also Education, post-contact; Indian-white relations—U.S., 1871-1933; Medicine and modes of curing, post-contact; Minnesota Uprising; Peyote and peyote religion; Wounded Knee Massacre.

BIBLIOGRAPHY

Eastman, Charles Alexander [Ohiyesa]. *From the Deep Woods to Civilization: Chapters in the Autobiography of an Indian.* 1916. Reprint. Lincoln: University of Nebraska Press, 1977.

_____. *Indian Boyhood.* New York: McClure, Phillips, 1902. Reprint. New York: Dover, 1971.

_____. *The Indian Today: The Past and Future of the First American.* Garden City, N.Y.: Doubleday, 1915.

_____. *The Soul of the Indian: An Interpretation.* 1911. Reprint. New York: Johnson Reprint, 1971.

Wilson, Raymond. *Ohiyesa: Charles Eastman, Santee Sioux.* Urbana: University of Illinois Press, 1983.

Education, post-contact

TRIBES AFFECTED: Pantribal

SIGNIFICANCE: Since 1568, three major groups—Christian missionaries, the federal government, and public school systems—have assumed responsibility for educating American Indians under policies that often have devastated tribal well-being

As more and more European settlers entered that part of the Americas now known as the United States, education was seen as a way of assimilating young Native Americans into the dominant white culture. The history of Europeanized Indian education over four centuries tells a story of cultural genocide.

Missionary Activity and Paternalism, 1568-1870. The first school specifically founded for the education of Indian youth in the New World was established by the Jesuits in Havana, Florida, in 1568. For the next three hundred years, Catholic and Protestant religious groups dominated non-Indian attempts to educate Indians. In 1617, King James asked

Anglican clergy to collect money for building "churches and schools for ye education of ye children of these Barbarians in Virginia." One of the earliest of these religious schools was founded by the Reverend John Eliot in 1631 in Roxbury, Massachusetts. He developed a plan to bring Indians together in small, self-governing "Indian prayer towns" where they could be instructed in Christian ethics and arts. In order to become accepted by the Puritans in these prayer towns, Indians had to give up their old way of life completely, including long hair for men and short hair for women.

Another example of colonial religious schools was Moor's Charity School, founded in 1755 by Eleazar Wheelock, a Congregationalist minister. This Connecticut school concerned itself with the academic training of Indian youngsters and included reading, writing, arithmetic, English, Greek, and Latin in its curriculum. The school operated until 1769 and enrolled as many as 150 Indian youth.

A common method of providing educational assistance during this period was by treaty stipulation. From the first treaty in 1778 until 1871, when treaty making with the Indians ended, the United States entered into almost four hundred treaties, of which 120 had educational provisions. The terms usually called for teachers, material, and equipment for educational purposes.

The first specific appropriation by Congress for Indian education was the Act of March 30, 1802, which allowed $15,000 per year "to promote civilization among the aborigines." The money went mostly to missionary groups. In 1819, Congress established a civilization fund, which lasted until 1873, to provide financial support to religious groups and other interested individuals who were willing to live among and teach Indians. The Act of March 3, 1819, which established this fund, also gave the president complete authority over Indian education and remained the basic authorization for the educational activities carried out by the government on behalf of Indian people.

Manual labor schools had their beginnings during the period when the tribes were being moved out of the East and Northeast. Usually these were located in Indian country or at a site convenient to several tribes and, for that reason, were agreeable to the Indians. They also drew support from the government, which believed that it was a waste of effort to provide only academic training. The first manual labor school, the Choctaw Academy, was organized in 1837 by Colonel Richard Johnson in Scott County, Kentucky. This school, and others that came later, offered religious, academic, and practical instruction. Six hours were spent daily in the classroom and six at work on farm and shop detail. By 1840, the U.S. government was operating six manual labor schools with eight hundred students and eighty-seven boarding schools with about twenty-nine hundred students.

Several Indian tribes, with the help of missionaries and educators, built and supported their own schools. The Mohawks did this as early as 1712 under the influence of the Reverend Thomas Barkley, an Anglican missionary. This school, with one temporary suspension, operated until the end of the American Revolution. The Choctaws and Cherokees, before their removal from their original homelands, had instituted common schools, supported with funds obtained from the United States for land cessions. After the removal of these tribes to lands west of the Mississippi, the Cherokees, in 1841, and the Choctaws, in 1842, reestablished their schools. (A number of states had not yet provided for a system of common schools in 1842.) The Cherokee system, by 1852, included twenty-one elementary schools and two academies. The enrollment in that year was given as 1,100. The Choctaws had nine schools, of which seven experimented with teaching reading and writing to adults. Teachers were brought from the East to be in charge of advanced academic work, and the course of study included music, astronomy, Latin, botany, algebra, and elocution. Within ten years, however, the majority of their teachers had changed from eastern-educated missionaries to locally trained teachers. The Chickasaw, Creek, and Seminole tribes, also members of the "Five Civilized Tribes," followed the example of the Cherokees and Choctaws within a few years and established school systems. In all cases, the schools were tribally supported, and they operated without federal supervision until 1906, when the tribal governments of these five tribes were destroyed by an act of Congress.

In 1851, the period of reservation settlement began and did not end until the 1930's. Schools established on reservations were designed to devalue the traditional culture and religion of Indian people. One of the most significant ways of undermining Indian culture was the government's attempt to suppress native language. In 1880, the Indian Bureau issued regulations that "all instruction must be in English" in both mission and government schools under threat of loss of government funding. In 1885, some teachers and administrators, recognizing the small utility of standard educational training and methods, suggested that special materials be created for Indian children. No special textbooks were developed, however, until well into the twentieth century.

Government Control and Dependence, 1870-1923. In 1865, under President Ulysses S. Grant, Indian boarding schools had their birth. After studying conditions among some of the western tribes, a congressional committee suggested that "boarding schools remote from Indian communities" would be most successful in solving the "Indian problem." Grant, believing that the only solution lay in "the civilization" of Indians into white culture, supported the move. In 1878, the boarding school system was launched when the Carlisle Indian School in Carlisle, Pennsylvania, was founded by General Richard Henry Pratt. Pratt, alarmed at the "gross injustices to both races [Indians and blacks]" which he had observed, believed that true equality could come to the Indians only if they learned to feel at home in the white world, where they deserved both "the opportunities and . . . safeguards of our Declaration and Constitution." At Carlisle, which enrolled children from the midwestern and western tribes, students were required to speak, read, and write English and to assume the

MAJOR EVENTS IN POST-CONTACT EDUCATION

1568   Jesuits establish a school at Havana, Florida.

1617   King James asks Anglican clergy to collect money for the erecting of "churches and schools for ye education of ye children of Barbarians of Virginia."

1631   The Reverend John Eliot establishes a school in Roxbury, Mass.

1636   Harvard College is founded in part to provide education for Indian youth.

1755   Eleazar Wheelock founds Moor's Charity School in Connecticut.

1775   The Continental Congress makes a conciliatory gesture toward Indians by appropriating $500 to educate Indians at Dartmouth College.

1802   In the Act of March 30, Congress appropriates $15,000 per year to "promote civilization among the aborigines."

1819   In the Act of March 3, Congress establishes a fund to provide financial support to individuals and religious groups who are willing to live among and teach Indians.

1832   The position of commissioner of Indian affairs is created.

1837   Choctaw Academy, the first manual labor school, is organized by Colonel Richard Johnson in Scott County, Kentucky.

1867   A Peace Commission appointed by President Grant calls for assimilation and specifically for the extinguishing of Indian languages.

1879   The establishment of the U.S. Indian Training and Industrial School at Carlisle, Pennsylvania, begins era of large off-reservation boarding schools.

1884   Haskell Institute is established at Lawrence, Kansas.

1900   All direct government funding of missionary schools is ended.

1924   Passage of the Indian Citizenship Act makes all Indians citizens of the United States.

1924   The Committee of One Hundred Citizens recommends better facilities and better-trained personnel for teaching Indian students.

1928   The Meriam Report criticizes government policies and services for Indians; it calls for dramatic reforms.

1931   John Collier becomes commissioner of Indian affairs and immediately seeks to implement the recommendations of the Meriam Report.

1934   The Indian Reorganization Act and the Johnson-O'Malley Act are passed.

1953   Six termination bills are passed; according to the bills, states are to assume the responsibility for the education of all Indian children in public schools.

1959   The Center for Indian Education is established at Arizona State University.

1967-   The National Study of American Indian Education is carried out at the University of Chicago; results are
1971   summarized in *To Live on This Earth*.

1968   The first tribally controlled college, Navajo Community College, is founded.

1969   A Special Senate Subcommittee on Indian Education produces a report entitled *Indian Education: A National Tragedy, a National Challenge*.

1971   The Coalition of Indian Controlled School Boards is formed.

1972   The Indian Education Act is passed.

1989   Twenty-four tribally controlled colleges exist in ten states.

Sioux boys upon arrival at the Carlisle Indian School in 1879. Soon they would be wearing European-style clothing and hair styles. (National Archives)

clothing and customs of white people. They were taught skills which would later help them become employed in trades such as blacksmithing, carpentry, tailoring, and farming. Girls were taught domestic skills. After completing school, students were placed with white families for three years; they worked in exchange for their upkeep. The families were paid fifty dollars a year to cover costs of clothing and health care. This practice came to be called the Carlisle Outing, which Pratt proclaimed to be the "right arm" of the school.

Forts no longer needed by the army were converted into boarding schools. Between 1889 and 1892, twelve such boarding schools were established. Little attention was paid to tribal differences in language and customs. It was assumed—rightly—that if children could be taken at a young enough age and moved far enough away from the influences of family and tribe, the odds against their ever again becoming a part of their original environment were remote. Children as young as five years old were sent to the boarding schools. The shock, fear, and loneliness which these children faced upon being uprooted from everything familiar and known can only be imagined. Pratt, operating under the noblest of intentions, had unwittingly contributed to one of the saddest chapters in Indian history.

By 1887, Congress was appropriating more than a million dollars a year for Indian education. About half the appropriations went to missionaries who were contracted to educate Indians. Feuding between Protestants and Catholics, however,

aggravated because the Catholics were much more successful in establishing schools, led the Protestants to support funding only government-run schools. With the appointment in 1889 of General Thomas J. Morgan, a Baptist minister, as commissioner of Indian affairs, the Republicans made a systematic effort to stop government funding of all missionary schools. By 1900 all direct funding to these schools was ended. Tribes continued to receive a portion of the dollars which the federal government had previously provided the churches for funding of the mission schools. Some tribes maintained these schools in spite of the reduced resources; most used the funds for other needs.

Moves to Reform Indian Education, 1924-1944. As the new century began, the continued inability of boarding schools and English-only education to transform Indians into white people led to disillusionment and lowered expectations for Indian education. Increasingly, Indians were viewed in the same light as blacks at that time: as a permanent underclass for whom an inferior, nonacademic, vocational education was appropriate and adequate.

At the same time, because of the staggering loss of land and the inefficiency of education, the total Indian situation was growing progressively worse. In 1902, the Bureau of Indian Affairs (BIA) was operating twenty-five boarding schools in fifteen states for 9,736 students. By 1912, there were more Indian children in public schools than in government schools. As government schools lost ground, efforts to increase Indian enrollment in public day schools did not include examining the ability of these schools to meet Indian needs.

In 1924, a "Committee of One Hundred Citizens" was called together by the secretary of the interior to discuss how Indian education could be improved. The committee recommended better school facilities, better trained personnel, an increase in the number of Indian students in public schools, and high school and college scholarships. These recommendations helped establish reservation day schools up to the sixth grade and reservation boarding schools up to the eighth grade.

In 1928, a government-sponsored study (the Meriam Report) claimed that the Bureau of Indian Affairs was providing poor-quality services to Indians; it particularly pointed to the shocking conditions found in boarding schools. The committee recommended that elementary children not be sent to BIA boarding schools at all. Shortly after publication of the study, John Collier, one of the BIA's leading critics, became commissioner of Indian affairs and immediately sought to implement the recommendations of the Meriam Report. The Johnson-O'Malley Act (1934) allowed the federal government to pay states for educating Indians in public schools.

The Termination Era, 1945-1970. In the 1950's, under President Dwight Eisenhower, six "termination" bills were passed. They were intended to end all federal involvement with the Indians, leaving policy issues in health, education, and welfare up to the states. Conditions improved little as states, for the most part, failed to provide adequate services in any of these arenas. Another program aimed at "relocation" helped Indians move from reservations to cities, where, presumably, educational and employment opportunities were better. Indian children in cities showed improved academic achievement, but many felt displaced and unhappy.

Between 1967 and 1971, Robert J. Havighurst of the University of Chicago directed a research project entitled the National Study of American Indian Education. Their recommendations called for greatly increased Indian participation in goal setting and in implementation of programs. During this same period, a report compiled by a Senate subcommittee on Indian education revealed that Indian school dropout rates were twice the national average, that Indian students lagged two to three years behind white students in school achievement, that only 1 percent had Indian teachers, that one-fourth of teachers of Indian students preferred not to teach them, and that "Indian children more than any other minority group believed themselves to be 'below average' in intelligence."

During this time, Indian educators had become increasingly active, and, by the end of the decade, the National Indian Education Association had been formed. In 1968 the first tribally controlled college, Navajo Community College, was founded, and in 1971 the Coalition of Indian Controlled School Boards was established.

The Move Toward Self-Determination Since 1970. The Senate report on the plight of Indians led to the passage of the Indian Education Act in 1972. This act provided for special programs benefiting Indian children in reservation schools as

well as those attending urban public schools. It was amended in 1975 to require that Indian parents be involved in the planning of these programs. The amended version also encouraged the establishment of community-run schools and stressed culturally relevant and bilingual curricular materials. The Office of Education, after a two-year study, recommended that tribal history, culture, and languages be emphasized, using students' own tongue as the language of instruction. During 1977, President Jimmy Carter created the new post of assistant secretary of the interior for Indian affairs and named a member of the Blackfoot tribe, Forrest J. Gerrard, to the position.

In spite of efforts to improve educational opportunities for Indians, in the last decade of the twentieth century Indian students still struggled for visibility in the education market. High-school dropout rates for Indian students continued to be the highest for all minority groups, with fewer than 50 percent completing a high school education. Some reservation schools reported a yearly teacher turnover rate of 90 percent. In 1990, bachelor's degrees earned by Indians comprised less than 0.5 percent of all degrees conferred. Doctorates earned by Indians between 1980 and 1990 actually dropped, from 130 to 102.

In the 1990's, two urban public school districts with relatively large Indian populations began to experiment with schools that focus on Indian culture along with traditional academic curricula. The American Indian Magnet School at Mounds Park All-Nations School in the St. Paul, Minnesota,

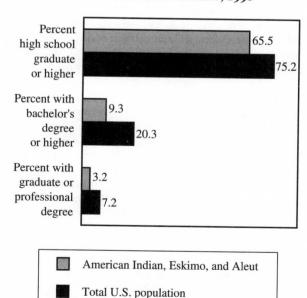

EDUCATIONAL ATTAINMENT, 1990

Percent high school graduate or higher: 65.5 / 75.2

Percent with bachelor's degree or higher: 9.3 / 20.3

Percent with graduate or professional degree: 3.2 / 7.2

☐ American Indian, Eskimo, and Aleut

■ Total U.S. population

Source: U.S. Bureau of the Census, *We, the First Americans.* Washington, D.C.: U.S. Government Printing Office, 1993.

Note: Graph gives percentage of persons twenty-five years old and older with a high school diploma or higher degree.

public school system declared the goal of "placing education into culture instead of continuing the practice of placing culture into education." Three centuries of national educational policy must take at least partial responsibility for the tragic decline of tribal cultures in the United States, but perhaps it will also take the lead in providing a vehicle for the land's original citizens to assume their rightful place in American society. —*Dorothy Engan-Barker, assisted by Bette Blaisdell*

See also American Indian Higher Education Consortium (AIHEC); American Indian studies programs and archives; Carlisle Indian School; Children; Dozier, Edward Pasqual; Indian Child Welfare Act; Meriam Report.

BIBLIOGRAPHY

Cahn, Edgar S., and David W. Hearne. *Our Brother's Keeper: The Indian in White America*. New York: New American Library, 1975. A collection of writings and pictures compiled by the Citizens' Advocate Center in Washington, D.C.; chronicles the plight of American Indians and actions of the Bureau of Indian Affairs.

Collier, John. *Indians of the Americas*. New York: W. W. Norton, 1947. The author, a former U.S. commissioner of Indian affairs, writes about four centuries of Western European impact on American Indian cultures.

Embree, Edwin R. *Indians of the Americas*. 1934. Reprint. New York: Collier Books, 1970. Embree, writing in opposition to the trend that sought to "integrate" the Indian, revived world interest in the unique lifestyles of North, Central, and South American tribes; focuses on customs, manners, and mysteries of their religion.

Fey, Harold, and D'Arcy McNickle. *Indians and Other Americans: Two Ways of Life Meet*. Rev. ed. New York: Harper & Row, 1970. History of the European influence on the culture of the American Indian; includes first-person accounts by Indians from diverse tribes who shared common experiences regarding attempts by whites to "civilize" them.

Fischbacher, Theodore. *A Study of the Role of the Federal Government in the Education of the American Indian*. San Francisco: R & E Research Associates, 1974. Chronological account of the role of the federal government in the education of American Indians living within the territory of the United States as disclosed in the government's official records.

Fuchs, Estelle, and Robert Havighurst. "Boarding Schools." In *To Live on This Earth*. Garden City, N.Y.: Doubleday, 1972. Summarizes events leading up to and including the establishment of Indian boarding schools, including a discussion of those still operating in the 1960's.

Josephy, Alvin M., Jr. *Red Power: The American Indian's Fight for Freedom*. New York: American Heritage Press, 1971. A collection of excerpts from speeches, articles, studies, and other documents providing a documentary history of the critical decade of the 1960's.

Pratt, Richard H. *Battlefield and Classroom: Four Decades with the American Indian, 1867-1904*. Edited by Robert M. Utley. New Haven, Conn.: Yale University Press, 1964. The memoirs of General Richard Henry Pratt, chronicling his work in the establishment of Indian boarding schools; includes photographs from the period.

U.S. Bureau of the Census. *Statistical Abstract of the United States, 1993*. 113th ed. Washington, D.C.: Government Printing Office, 1993.

U.S. Congress. Senate. Committee on Labor and Public Welfare. Special Subcommittee on Indian Education. *Indian Education: A National Tragedy, a National Challenge*. Washington, D.C.: Government Printing Office, 1969.

Education, pre-contact

TRIBES AFFECTED: Pantribal

SIGNIFICANCE: Pre-contact education did not anticipate great changes in existing lifestyles and therefore centered on the maintenance and preservation of the tribe's culture and way of life

Education or socialization of the young is an important concern in all societies, including American Indian societies in the pre-contact period. With the exception of the "high cultures" of Peru and Mexico, however, education did not occur in formal schools. Instead, education of the young was a shared function of families and communities. Owing to the diversity across native cultures, the content of such education varied. In general, both sex and age differences were observed.

Learning Role Skills. One focus of education was the learning of skills necessary for adult roles. Such skills were learned through imitation, often involving play activities, as well as through direct instruction. Among those peoples who subsisted by hunting and gathering, fathers and other older male relatives taught boys the skills of the hunter. Among these same peoples, mothers and other older female relatives served as teachers of girls in gathering plant foods as well as processing and preparing both game and plant foods. Among native peoples who subsisted by farming, fathers and male relatives served as primary teachers of boys, while mothers and female relatives served as primary teachers of girls. Similarly, children received much instruction from adults in learning such skills as weaving, pottery making, tanning, tool making, and the decorative arts. These, too, were differentiated according to gender.

Moral Education. Another major focus of education was the learning of attitudes and values appropriate to the culture. In addition to role modeling, direct instruction was involved. The advent of puberty, with a girl's first menses, was generally marked with advice and instruction on the girl's new status and responsibilities. Older female relatives, and sometimes a shaman and older male relatives, played a part in this. In those native societies that had sodalities, initiates were instructed in the character requirements as well as in the songs, prayers, and powers associated with them.

A major device in instilling proper attitudes and values in children was storytelling. There were not only stories of the sacred, traditions, and events but also stories of culture heroes. The latter, in particular, played a major part in moral education. The storytellers were most often older members of the family or community who were highly regarded for their storytelling skills.

Discipline Strategies. American Indians were noted for their love and mild treatment of children. Discipline was generally marked by an absence of corporal punishment. Instead, children were most often teased and cajoled into proper behavior by their parents and elders. In some of the matrilineal societies, much of the responsibility for discipline was taken on by the mother's brother. Cultural "frighteners" were also known but were not usually flagrantly used.

A Dakota (Sioux) Example. Being primarily a hunting and gathering people, the Dakota had no need for an extensive program beyond that of basic survival and limited arts and crafts. Since they were seasonally nomadic, it was not practical to amass personal possessions and unnecessary items. Consequently, they did not develop their craftsmanship as extensively as did more agrarian cultures. When there was leisure, the women did magnificent quill work, and this was taught to the younger females along with their domestic responsibilities.

In the early years, the Dakota lived in small villages, sometimes as small as an extended family. These villages were extremely independent and required great responsibility and self-discipline from their members. Only the very young child had no responsibilities. There were numerous chores to be done. Among the social responsibilities were preparing for the hunt, gathering roots and berries, harvesting wild rice, making maple sugar, preparing hides, and arranging and preparing for social events. The young were gradually brought into these work roles.

Although education may have been simplified, it was not insignificant or trivial. The Dakota were sustained by a highly efficient ecosystem that had a cyclical chain of events that not only provided subsistence but also brought meaning and identity. They regulated their hunting and trapping to maintain a balance of nature. The young men were thus taught to respect living animals and not to allow them to depopulate.

Education, or the passing on of knowledge, was accomplished in a variety of forms. One of these was ritual. Rituals were performed in order to recall events and certain natural laws. If the ritual was performed exactly as instructed, and the meaning was clearly explained, then whenever the ritual was performed, learning was reinforced. Another form of learning was storytelling. Many stories and legends were passed down as soon as a young child could understand the spoken word. Stories contained moral lessons, humor, and stimulating anecdotes.

There was also much to be learned through experience. The younger males would accompany the older men on hunts and be allowed to witness warfare from a distance. Young females would start their training even earlier, accompanying the older women when they picked berries and gathered roots.

One of the most important learning experiences for the Dakota youth was the vision quest. When a vision was received, it was a monumental event. One could not easily claim a vision, because the vision had to be confirmed through a careful evaluation by the council of elders. Once confirmed, the vision gave a young man (the vision quest was typically a male experience) direction and purpose. The young person might not clearly understand the vision, but during his lifetime, he would seek its meaning.

Probably the single most important learning experience for young Dakotas was the sessions with elders. During these sessions the elders presented their experiences through the years. They would relate how their own foolishness had caused them much grief and misery in the past. In talking about their mistakes, the elders were teaching the young people the things they should avoid doing. This left the avenue clear for the youths to pursue their own visions and goals armed with wisdom about what not to do. When asked for advice or direction, elders used stories and examples that would help youths make their own decisions. This allowed young people to accomplish on their own the things they felt they should pursue. In this sense, the Dakota did not limit creativity or initiative in educating their young.

—Donna Hess and Elden Lawrence

See also Children; Clowns; Games and contests; Gender relations and roles; Joking relations; Menses and menstruation; Puberty and initiation rites; Rites of passage; Toys.

BIBLIOGRAPHY

Deloria, Ella C. *Speaking of Indians*. Vermillion, S.Dak.: Dakota Press, 1979.

Driver, Harold E. *Indians of North America*. Chicago: University of Chicago Press, 1961.

Eastman, Charles A. *Indian Boyhood*. New York: McClure, Phillips, 1902. Reprint. New York: Dover, 1971.

Hodge, William. *The First Americans: Then and Now*. New York: Holt, Rinehart & Winston, 1981.

Hungry Wolf, Beverly. *The Ways of My Grandmothers*. New York: Quill, 1982.

Kupferer, Harriet J. *Ancient Drums, Other Moccasins: Native American Cultural Adaptations*. Englewood Cliffs, N.J.: Prentice Hall, 1988.

Pond, Samuel W. *The Dakota or Sioux in Minnesota as They Were in 1834*. St. Paul: Minnesota Historical Society Press, 1986.

Powers, Marla N. *Oglala Women*. Chicago: University of Chicago Press, 1986.

Sandoz, Mari. *These Were the Sioux*. New York: Hastings House, 1961.

Wissler, Clark. *The American Indian*. New York: Oxford University Press, 1950.

Effigy mounds: Archaeological sites

DATE: 400-1200
LOCATION: Illinois, Iowa, Ohio, Michigan, Wisconsin
CULTURE AFFECTED: Oneota

Low, earthen mounds in the shape of animals, geometric forms, and other forms are among the most distinguishing features of the Woodland culture of the midwestern United

States. Effigy mounds are known primarily from southern Wisconsin, southeastern Minnesota, northeastern Iowa, and northern Illinois. Many have been preserved in state parks. Unfortunately, the majority have been destroyed by plowing, looting, and construction activities.

Effigy mounds were constructed by mounding earth into large, low shapes. They occur mainly in groups with conical and linear mounds. The majority of mounds reported have eroded and indistinct shapes; however, others clearly represent life forms. Among the animals represented are bears, deer, felines, wolves, foxes, buffalos, and turtles, as well as eagles, swallows, and geese. Only two or three have been reported in human form. The effigies can be quite large. At Mendota, Wisconsin, one bird effigy was 6 feet tall and had a wingspan of 624 feet. In general, the mounds are no more than 2 to 5 feet high. The majority of these mounds appear to have been burial grounds. Examples have been found to contain primary or secondary bundle burials, the latter containing as many as thirty individuals, as well as cremations. These burials are usually situated in key parts of the effigies, such as the head, the position of the heart, or (in bird effigies) between the head and tail. Offerings included with the dead include pottery vessels, copper, stone axes, and tobacco pipes of various materials.

The dates for effigy mound construction are not precisely known. Artifacts found associated with burials in effigy mounds include late Middle Woodland pottery in the form of conical or round-bottomed containers decorated with techniques such as cord-marking, fingernail impressions, dentate stamping, and punctuations. These suggest that the features are roughly contemporaneous with the late Hopewell culture of southern Ohio around 200-700 C.E. There is also evidence, however, for a spread of Mississippian populations from the American Bottom in central Illinois to areas of northwestern Illinois and southern Wisconsin around 800-1000, or the early Late Woodland period, and many of the mounds may have been built around that time.

Effigy Mounds National Monument, in McGregor, Iowa, is one location where these mounds have been preserved and restored. Among the examples at this site are bird and bear effigies. The largest concentrations of effigy mounds are in southern Wisconsin, near Madison and in Sauk and Waukesha counties, where many have been preserved in parks or other public areas.

The largest and most famous effigy is the Great Serpent Mound in southern Ohio. Winding along the top of a prominent ridge, it represents an undulating snake with a tightly coiled tail; the snake appears to be holding an oval object in its mouth. The mound, including coils, is 1,330 feet long. Great Serpent Mound, unlike most effigy mounds, did not contain burials. Its age is Early to Middle Woodland (circa 200 to 400), making it several hundred years earlier than the Wisconsin mounds.

See also Adena; Hopewell; Mounds and mound builders; Oneota; Serpent mounds.

Elderly

Tribes affected: Pantribal

Significance: Native definitions of old age are predicated on tribal custom rather than chronological age; in general, the elderly are treated with respect, although attitudes vary by tribe

American Indians and Alaska Natives constitute less than 1 percent of all Americans sixty-five years of age and older. The exact number of older people among Native American populations has been difficult to determine, but 1980 census data placed the number at that time at about seventy-five thousand. About 30 percent of the aged Indian population live on reservations, and perhaps another 25 percent live in rural areas.

Traditional Views. The concept of aging is quite different in many native cultures from that of European American society. Birthdays were only introduced on reservations one hundred years ago, and while birthdays are celebrated, one's chronological age is not an operative factor in defining who that person is. Among native people, grandparenting or physical disability would qualify a person as elderly, whereas reaching the age of sixty would be meaningless. In most traditional Indian tribal cultures, there was no concept equivalent to the modern idea of retirement. Older people remained active as long as they were able.

Each tribal culture and society had different attitudes toward the elderly. In some societies, when they became physically unable to care for themselves, the elderly "gave themselves back to the spirit world" by starvation or exposure to extremes of weather. At times they were assisted in this by family members. In other societies, they were "rulers of the house" and simply died of old age.

Despite the trend in many native cultures toward a quick death once productivity was impossible, elderly native people generally enjoyed high esteem because of their age and experience, very often serving in tribal positions of leadership. If capable of performing minimal, even symbolic labors, old people were treated with respect. Only at the extreme, where they became too incapacitated to function, were they either abandoned or likely to dispose of themselves.

Contemporary Issues. American Indian elders are not well-served by a definition of aging set by a chronological measure. Because native people often measure age by productive capability and social role rather than by chronology, under Title VI of the Older Americans Act, Indian tribes are permitted to define, based on their own criteria, who will be considered an older Indian and therefore will be eligible to receive Title VI services. Studies by the National Council on American Indians indicate that American Indians living on reservations at age forty-five show the same age characteristics that other Americans do at sixty-five—a reminder that many racial and ethnic groups experience premature aging under the stress of harsh living conditions.

Disruptive changes have altered much about Indian life. Many Native American senior citizens were sent away to

Indian boarding schools as children, separated forcibly from their families. At many of these institutions the children were made to feel inferior and were ridiculed when they spoke their language or showed respect for their Indian heritage.

Today, the prestige associated with old age has persisted among Native Americans, and Native American elders are still, on the whole, treated with respect and honor. Retirement has also become more accepted, and because of high rates of unemployment among native people generally, it is not uncommon for elderly people to help support younger family members with their old-age benefits.

Many elderly Indian people living in urban areas were part of a large American Indian federal relocation project following World War II. This population has now reached retirement age and many have no intention of moving back to the reservation. Many American Indian elders living in cities are deprived of social contact with each other and with younger members of their tribes. Unlike other ethnic groups, city-living American Indians have not congregated in neighborhoods. Some studies also indicate that the popular image of older American Indians living in multigenerational, extended family households is greatly exaggerated in the context of an urban setting. Many native cultures, however, do maintain a tradition of communal sharing among family members and a sense of family responsibility for the care of the elderly. The fact that the elderly represent the repositories of traditional knowledge is widely recognized and is a major factor associated with their good treatment and high status. —*Lucy Ganje*

See also Education, pre-contact; Kinship and social organization; Oral literatures.

El Tajín: Archaeological site

DATE: 300-1100
LOCATION: Veracruz, Mexico
CULTURE AFFECTED: Totonac

The site of El Tajín, located in the tropical lowlands near Papantla, in northern Veracruz, Mexico, is one of the most important centers of Classic and Early Postclassic period civilization in the Gulf Coast region. With its principal occupation dating from between 600 and 1100 C.E., El Tajín served as an important center of commerce and a focus for ceremonial activities based on the Mesoamerican calendar, ritual ball games, and human sacrifice. The site is currently revered by the Totonac Indians.

El Tajín was probably within the sphere of Teotihuacán influence during the Early Classic period (300 to 600 C.E.), but it rapidly expanded during the Late Classic (600 to 900) to control a tribute state in northern Veracruz and the adjoining state of Puebla. The final occupation of El Tajín, from 900 to 1100, corresponds in time to the expansion of Toltec civilization.

The architecture of El Tajín is characterized by the use of the talud/tablero style of vertical panels atop sloping walls, ornamental niches and "flying" cornices, corbelled vaults, roof combs, and sculptured relief panels. It is unique for the extensive use of asphalt and poured concrete. Among the most impressive structures at El Tajín is the Pyramid of the Niches, erected around 600. Rising in six terraces, with a broad central stairway, the facade of this building is inset with a total of 365 niches that corresponded to days in the solar year. It was originally painted in red, black, and blue, and was probably utilized for calendric rituals associated with agriculture and kingship.

Buildings at El Tajín were decorated with low relief sculpture, carved on flat panels and cylindrical columns. The style is baroque, with many double-outlined scrolls. Reliefs depict the activities of various rulers at the site, shown together with subordinates in the performance of ceremonies, sacrifices, and the ritual ball game. Bar-and-dot numerals were used, as were name glyphs. Images of death are ubiquitous, with stylized representations of skulls and vertebral columns. Sculpted relief panels in the sanctuary on top of the Pyramid of the Niches show costumed individuals and cacao plants. Another structure, the Building of the Columns, has relief sculptures on cylindrical columns portraying sacrificial rituals during the reign of a leader named "13 Rabbit." In the South Ball Court there is a depiction of the heart sacrifice of a costumed ball player by knife-wielding opponents.

El Tajín was an important center for the development and practice of the ritual ball game, played in a special court with large rubber balls. Eleven such courts have been found, more than at any other site in Mesoamerica. Artifacts of Classic period civilization at El Tajín include a variety of objects associated with the ritual ball game, known as *yugos*, *palmas*, and *hachas*. *Yugos*, or yokes, are heavy replicas in stone of U-shaped wooden objects that were worn around the waist. They are usually decorated with elaborate carving representing human faces together with snakes, toads, and other mythical beasts. *Palmas*, also called palmate stones, were long, paddle-shaped objects that may represent elongated devices attached to the fronts of the players' yokes. *Hachas*, or axes, were not cutting tools but thin, life-sized silhouettes of human heads and skulls. The precise function of these objects remains unknown, although some are perforated in a way that would have allowed for their attachment to a costume.

El Tajín is situated in ideal territory for the cultivation of cacao, rubber, and other lowland products. Given its proximity to the coast, it may also have served as a major center for trade in valued marine shells, used in large quantities by craftsmen and priests at Teotihuacán, north of Mexico City. The importance of this center may have been linked to its role in interregional trade; the Gulf Coast region was of special importance for the *pochteca*, or elite Aztec merchant class.

The traditional interpretation of El Tajín is as an ancestral center of Totonac culture. Given the site's abandonment centuries prior to the first Spanish records, however, connections between Classic period inhabitants and modern Totonac peoples remain to be clearly demonstrated.

See also Ball game and courts; Maya; Pochteca; Teotihuacán; Veracruz.

Emerald Mound: Archaeological site

DATE: 1300-1600
LOCATION: Stanton, Mississippi
CULTURE AFFECTED: Natchez

The Emerald (Selzertown) Mound site is located on Fairchild's Creek in the hardwood-covered lœssial hills of southwestern Mississippi about six miles east of the Mississippi River, one mile north of Stanton Station, and nine miles northeast of Natchez. It was the last major ceremonial seat of the prehistoric Natchez Indians immediately before European contact.

The site consists of six confirmed mounds and a nearby area bearing a light scatter of pottery. The mounds sit on top of an artificially widened ridge crest. Dirt was added to the upper slopes of the ridge, forming a steep-sided, flat-topped platform measuring 435 by 770 feet at the base, 345 by 640 feet at the summit, and between 27 and 35 feet high. The summit plateau covers 5 acres.

Mounds lined the edges of the massive platform, two small ones along each side and a large one on each end (west and east). Only the two largest structures survive today. The western mound stands 30 feet high and has basal dimensions of 160 by 190 feet. It seems to have originally been a truncated pyramid with a ramp leading up its eastern face. The mutilated eastern mound is only 5 feet high, and its original shape is not clear. The other four mounds were small low rises, largely obliterated during the early nineteenth century.

Emerald was occupied from circa 1300 to 1600 C.E., or during the late Anna or early Foster through the Emerald phases of the Late Mississippian period. The earliest occupants lived on the ridge crest and built houses framed by posts set in wall trenches. Earthwork construction started a short time later. First, an earthen embankment was put up around the ridge nose, followed by infilling behind the embankment and general mantling that raised the artificial apron to the level of the exposed ridge crest. All this construction was completed during the Foster phase. Finally, mounds were erected atop the platform during the Emerald phase.

The Emerald Mound site resembles the nearby Anna site, located on the Mississippi River bluff, and is believed to have succeeded Anna as the primary center of the late prehistoric and protohistoric Natchez Indians. Some authorities identify Emerald as the home of the arrogant Quigualtam, chief of a powerful native province, who upon being summoned to worship and serve the conquistador, Hernando de Soto, challenged the Spaniard to dry up the Mississippi River as proof that he was a god or else face a mortal's fate if he tried to confront Quigualtam. Whether the home of Quigualtam is Emerald or somewhere farther north, as other authorities maintain, Emerald was the most politically, socially, and ceremonially prominent site in the Natchez locality during the fifteenth and sixteenth centuries. Prominence subsequently shifted south to the Fatherland site, the Grand Village of the historic Natchez Indians; by the seventeenth century, Emerald was abandoned or used as a minor campground on the outskirts of Natchez tribal territory and political authority.

See also Architecture—Southeast; Mississippian; Mounds and mound builders; Prehistory—Southeast.

Employment and unemployment

TRIBES AFFECTED: Pantribal
SIGNIFICANCE: Before contact with Europeans, the labor of American Indians served group or tribal purposes; employment and unemployment patterns in the twentieth century reflected the profound disruption of Indian life that occurred following contact

In the pre-contact period, Indians had extensive trading networks throughout Canada, the United States, and Central and South America. Agricultural goods, manufactured items such as jewelry, pottery, and tanned hides, and natural resources such as seashells were bartered or sold.

Traditional Labor. Labor was required to sustain this extensive trade network, but little is known about how the labor systems were organized. Tribal groups in the Mississippi River area, the southwestern United States, and Central and South America had highly specialized labor forces in which both men and women participated. Division of labor was determined in part by gender, talent, and social position. These societies were organized hierarchically and sometimes incorporated slaves (captives from other tribes), who performed undesirable labor.

Much of North America and Canada was inhabited by nomadic hunting and gathering societies and semisedentary agriculturalists. In these societies, division of labor was based primarily on gender and was less complex, with most tribal members working toward the common goal of providing food, shelter, and clothing for survival. In these subsistence economies, there was little opportunity for members to specialize in any one area, such as art or medicine. Such cultures stressed sharing and egalitarianism as a way to ensure the well-being of the people. Everyone worked for the common good.

Arrival of Europeans. European migration to North America was primarily motivated by economic interests. The first phase of European-Indian relations revolved around the fur trade, which required the incorporation of Indian labor. The early period of the fur trade is marked by relative equality among Europeans and native people. Indian men and women labored to supply processed hides and pelts for the fur trade. In return for their labor, Indians were paid with European trade goods—metal pots, needles, knives, guns, and a variety of domestic goods. During this period, those Indian people who obtained European trade goods would redistribute them among tribal members, thus maintaining the tribal ideal of generosity and sharing. The trade goods changed the work patterns of both Indian men and women. Guns and traps permitted more men to hunt and kill more game, and, in turn, women were required to tan more hides for trade. Indian labor during this period was still directed toward the good of the tribe, but increasingly tribal welfare depended on sources outside the tribe.

The fur trade was an important source of labor for American Indians, but the fur trade period ended as animal populations

An Ojibwa language teacher at Bay Mills Community College, a tribally controlled college in Michigan. (Raymond P. Malace)

decreased and as European fashion changed. The decline in the fur trade coincides with the emergence of the United States and marks a period of change in the economic position of Indians. Indians were no longer needed as laborers in the new economy. The European American population was rapidly increasing and there was an increased desire for land. Indians became a hindrance in this emerging economic system. The relative lack of demand for Indian labor, coupled with the high demand for Indian land, caused the U.S. government to remove Indians from areas coveted by European Americans and resettle them on poor lands.

The reservation system was firmly in place by the late nineteenth century, and it caused considerable change in the work patterns of tribal groups. For the most part, hunting and fishing were no longer possible on the restricted land base, and traditional agricultural practices were not viable or were discouraged. The reservation system afforded little opportunity for Indian people to provide adequately for their families and it is directly linked to contemporary reservation poverty.

During the early reservation period, some Indian men worked for federal agents as freight haulers, policemen, and laborers. Indian women sometimes sold pottery, beadwork, baskets, or other small items. Income from these sources was small. Government policy largely confined Indian people to their reservations, so they were unable to sell their labor for wages off the reservations. Federal Indian policy, most notably the General Allotment Act (1887), reduced the Indian land base and subdivided the land among many heirs so that productive use of reservation lands became nearly impossible. High Indian unemployment rates caused gradual loosening of federal policies of confinement to reservations, and by the early twentieth century Indians commonly worked in off-reservation jobs such as laborers on farms and ranches, and in mines. The 1930 census indicates that 80 percent of Indian men were working for wages, mostly in agricultural jobs. Most of this work was unskilled, seasonal, and off-reservation.

The 1930's. In the 1930's, federal Indian policy sought to address the problem of high unemployment and poor economic opportunity on the reservations. A 1928 study, *The Problem of Indian Administration*, commonly known as the Meriam Report, criticized federal Indian policy that intentionally removed Indian control over lands and resources and contributed to the widespread poverty and unemployment that characterized reservations. Partly in response to this study, the Indian Reorganization Act was passed in 1934. This intended to enable tribes to consolidate severely checkerboarded reser-

This Hupa man works in the timber industry in Northern California. (Ben Klaffke)

vation lands, take out low-interest loans to establish economic ventures on reservations, and encourage farming and ranching opportunities on reservations. The Great Depression prevented any significant business development on reservations; however, a fair number of Indian people benefited through various New Deal programs, particularly the Indian Division of the Civilian Conservation Corps, which employed and trained more than eighty-five thousand Indians in nine years. During the same period, the Bureau of Indian Affairs organized a division to place Indians in off-reservation jobs.

Changes in the Mid-twentieth Century. Thousands of Indians joined the wage labor force during World War II (1939-1945). Many Indian men and women joined the armed services or moved to urban areas to work in war industries. After the war, many Indian people remained in urban centers, while those who returned to reservations began to focus on reservation economic development and employment. Reservations remained poor and unemployment high, however. Few jobs came to the reservations, tribes had difficulty securing loans, reservation laws made business investments difficult, and many reservations were distant from markets. Additionally, off-reservation seasonal farming jobs became scarce with increasing technology. As a result, large-scale Indian urban migration continued after World War II and was encouraged by the federal policy of the 1950's known as relocation. Through the relocation program, Indians were removed to urban areas where jobs could be found. They received job

training and housing assistance. The lack of any meaningful jobs on reservations, coupled with federal Indian policy, contributed to unprecedented Indian migration to urban areas from 1950 to 1980. By the 1980 census, more than half the Indian population resided in urban areas. Indians continue to move to cities because of poor economic opportunities on reservations. Urban Indians experience higher employment rates and per capita incomes than reservation Indians. They remain poor, however, with per capita income slightly ahead of urban African Americans and well behind urban whites, and unemployment rates more than double those of the urban white population.

The federal government abandoned relocation programs in the late 1960's and turned its attention to revitalizing reservation economies. Concurrently, tribal governments were strengthened and tribes began pursuing economic development initiatives independent of the federal government. Success has been mixed, and reservations still have high unemployment and poverty rates.

Modern Labor Force Participation. On the majority of reservations, the largest single source of jobs is government, either tribal or federal. Despite many sincere efforts, there has been little economic investment or growth on reservations, primarily due to lack of resources, capital, location, and a skilled labor force. Few businesses locate on reservations, and unemployment rates are in the 80 to 90 percent range on some reservations. Census figures on labor force calculate only those who are employed or are actively seeking employment. According to the 1990 census, 62 percent of Indians sixteen years and older were in the labor force (69 percent of the males and 55 percent of the females). Many of the jobs held, however, were seasonal or part-time. A larger number of American Indians than the total population were employed in service

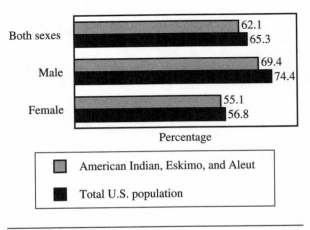

LABOR FORCE PARTICIPATION BY SEX, 1990

Both sexes: 62.1 / 65.3
Male: 69.4 / 74.4
Female: 55.1 / 56.8

Percentage

▨ American Indian, Eskimo, and Aleut

■ Total U.S. population

Source: U.S. Bureau of the Census, *We, the First Americans*. Washington, D.C.: U.S. Government Printing Office, 1993.

Note: Graph gives percentage of employed persons sixteen years old and older.

AMERICAN INDIAN EMPLOYMENT BY OCCUPATION, 1990

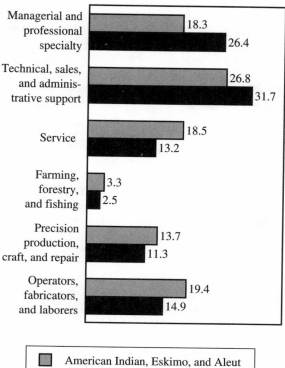

Managerial and professional specialty
18.3
26.4

Technical, sales, and administrative support
26.8
31.7

Service
18.5
13.2

Farming, forestry, and fishing
3.3
2.5

Precision production, craft, and repair
13.7
11.3

Operators, fabricators, and laborers
19.4
14.9

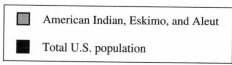

American Indian, Eskimo, and Aleut

Total U.S. population

Source: U.S. Bureau of the Census, *We, the First Americans.* Washington, D.C.: U.S. Government Printing Office, 1993.

Note: Graph gives percentage of employed persons sixteen years old and older.

jobs: farming, fishing, forestry, construction, or manufacturing. Fewer Indians, as compared to the total population, were employed in managerial or professional specialty occupations. In 1990, the median income of Indian workers was considerably less than that of the total population, and 31 percent of American Indians were living below the poverty level, compared with 10 percent of all American families. According to the 1990 census, 51 percent of the reservation population was living in poverty.

American Indian labor force participation on reservations continues to be low because of a lack of economic opportunities. The Indian population is young and lacks jobs experience. More significant, however, is the education deficit among Indians. Only 56 percent of American Indians graduate from high school, compared to 69 percent of the white population. Urban areas offer more job opportunities, but male Indian labor is largely confined to manual occupations, which are subject to fluctuation because of economic downturns, weather, and other factors. Female Indians are employed primarily in low-skilled, nonmanual service jobs both on and off the reservation.

During the 1980's, some tribal governments managed to attract businesses and increase employment opportunities, but overall, success was limited. Indian gaming, sometimes referred to as "the new buffalo," is being explored by many tribes as both a source of income for the tribe and as a way to provide jobs. The gaming operations have brought jobs to many reservations, but these tend to be low-wage service positions such as cashiers and waitresses. Tribal governments look to gaming as a way to strengthen reservation infrastructures and improve the lives of the people while they search for other means to address the dual need for Indian employment and real economic development on the reservations.

Indian participation in the labor force has increased as Indians have moved off reservations; however, even in urban settings, Indian unemployment remains high. Job opportunities on the reservations are scarce. Tribal governments are increasingly asserting their sovereign status and distancing themselves from the federal government in hopes of creating viable economic institutions that will bring job opportunities to the reservations. Federal law continues to frustrate these efforts.

—Carole A. Barrett

See also Agriculture; Indian Reorganization Act; Meriam Report; Ranching; Relocation; Reservation system of the United States; Reserve system of Canada; Urban Indians.

BIBLIOGRAPHY

Ambler, Marjane. *Breaking the Iron Bonds: Indian Control of Energy Development.* Lawrence: University Press of Kansas, 1990. Ambler provides a historic analysis of problems, paternalistic government policy, and exploitation which have prevented economic development on Indian lands. She focuses on the potential for energy development on reservations as a source of economic revitalization for tribes.

Biolsi, Thomas. *Organizing the Lakota: The Political Economy of the New Deal on the Pine Ridge and Rosebud Reservations.* Tucson: University of Arizona Press, 1992. Examines what happened to the political and economic life of the Lakota people when the Indian Reorganization Act was implemented on two western reservations. The reform agenda of the IRA was not really designed to transfer power to tribal governments; as a result, tribes continue to be hamstrung in attempts to develop economically or politically apart from the federal government.

Cornell, Stephen. *The Return of the Native: American Indian Political Resurgence.* New York: Oxford University Press, 1988. Cornell's book does not focus directly on Indian economic issues; rather it takes a broad look at the complexity of Indian-white relations in the United States. Economics is a strand woven into this tapestry. This broader view permits one to see clearly some of the reasons reservation economic development has been so bleak to this point and why it is so vital for the continuation of tribal governments.

Lawson, Michael. *Dammed Indians*. Norman: University of Oklahoma Press, 1982. Explores the devastating economic impact of dams along the Missouri River to Sioux reservations. In the 1950's a series of dams upset reservation economies and caused long-lasting economic and cultural hardships.

Meriam, Lewis, et al. *The Problem of Indian Administration*. Baltimore: The Johns Hopkins University Press, 1928. This seminal work appraises the failings of the federal government to give Indian people a true voice in their governance and destiny. It explores in depth the poor economic conditions on reservations in the 1920's and the reasons for them. Much of the analysis is still meaningful.

Erdrich, Louise (b. June 7, 1954, Little Falls, Minn.): Writer

TRIBAL AFFILIATION: Turtle Mountain Chippewa (Ojibwa)

SIGNIFICANCE: One of the most widely acclaimed Native American writers of fiction and poetry, Louise Erdrich tells of intertwining relationships and histories among an extended family of twentieth century Chippewas

The fragmented narratives and multiple voices in Louise Erdrich's writing have often been linked to the work of William Faulkner. They have also been praised as apt techniques for representing the disruptions and continuities experienced in modern Chippewa lives.

Louise Erdrich's novels draw upon her Chippewa heritage and her own family's experiences. (Michael Dorris, Harper & Row)

Erdrich's writing draws on her experiences growing up in a large family in Wahpeton, North Dakota. Her grandfather was the tribal chair of the Turtle Mountain Reservation, and her parents worked at the Wahpeton Indian School. Erdrich's literary sophistication was achieved through studies at Dartmouth College, where she received her B.A. degree in 1976, and at The Johns Hopkins University, where she received an M.A. in 1979. Erdrich became a nationally renowned writer with the publication of her first novel, *Love Medicine* (1984, rev. 1993). The characters who so captured the attention of her readers later reappeared in *The Beet Queen* (1986), *Tracks* (1988), and *The Bingo Palace* (1994). Erdrich has also published numerous short stories and two volumes of poetry, *Jacklight* (1984) and *Baptism of Desire* (1989).

Erdrich credits her husband, Michael Dorris, an anthropologist and fiction writer, with greatly influencing her writing. In 1991, Erdrich and Dorris published a jointly authored novel, *The Crown of Columbus*. Erdrich has won numerous awards, including the National Book Critics Circle Award in 1985.

See also Ojibwa.

Erie: Tribe

CULTURE AREA: Northeast

LANGUAGE GROUP: Iroquoian

PRIMARY LOCATION: South shore of Lake Erie

The Erie were a powerful sedentary tribe closely related to the Hurons, occupying lands south of Lake Erie down to the Ohio River in the early seventeenth century. With an economy based on horticulture, the women produced the crops of corn, beans, squash, and sunflowers, while men hunted and fished, thereby creating a varied and stable diet. Consequently, the Erie people numbered as many as fourteen thousand in the early seventeenth century, living in palisaded villages. They were matrilineal and matrilocal. Known as excellent warriors, they frequently clashed with the Iroquois tribes to their east, particularly the Senecas, over hunting grounds. The Erie had only limited contact with Europeans, mainly French missionaries who called them "the Cat (*chat*) Nation" because of their customary dress style of animal skin robes complete with tails. (The name "Erie" came from the Huron term for "it is long-tailed.")

In 1651, the Erie Nation was attacked and destroyed by the Iroquois, although the victors adopted more Erie people into their families than they killed. The Erie did not survive this attack as a distinct group, and their language became extinct as their descendants were forced to speak Iroquois languages. The Iroquois were successful at destroying the Erie Nation not because of superior numbers of warriors or greater skill in battle, but rather because of the firearms they had acquired from the Dutch. The Erie did not have access to such weapons. After having engulfed these people, the Iroquois claimed Erie territory as their ancestral hunting grounds.

See also Beaver Wars; Huron; Iroquoian language family; Iroquois Confederacy; Neutral; Tobacco.

Eskiminzin (c. 1825, Gila region, present-day Ariz.—1890, San Carlos Agency, Ariz.): Chief
ALSO KNOWN AS: Big Mouth, Hackibanzin
TRIBAL AFFILIATION: Apache
SIGNIFICANCE: Although a proponent of peace, Eskiminzin was victimized by white settlers seeking retaliation for Apache raids

Born a Pinal Apache, Eskiminzin married an Aravaipa Apache, eventually becoming the Aravaipa principal chief. During the Apache wars, Eskiminzin's people were peaceful agave farmers. Seeking asylum, in 1871 Eskiminzin led his people to Camp Grant near Tucson, where Lieutenant Royal Whitman allowed them to settle rather than forcing their relocation to a reservation.

In retaliation for Apache raids in March and April, 1871, Tucson settlers assaulted Eskiminzin's band. In what became known as the Camp Grant Massacre, 150 Apache, including eight members of Eskiminzin's family, were murdered. After the raiders were tried and acquitted, Apache hostility escalated. Thereafter, Eskiminzin was arrested on several occasions; each time he escaped or was released after brief incarcerations. In 1886, at the cessation of hostilities, he traveled to Washington, D.C., for negotiations. He was again arrested in 1888 and was imprisoned in Florida and Alabama; returning home in 1888, he died shortly thereafter. Although he counseled peace, Eskiminzin frequently was a scapegoat for white anger—a convenient target, though an innocent one.

See also Apache Wars; Cochise; Geronimo; Victorio.

Eskimo. *See* **Inuit**

Eskimo-Aleut language family

CULTURE AREAS: Arctic, Subarctic
TRIBES AFFECTED: Aleut, Inuit (Eskimo)

The Eskimo-Aleut family of languages is spoken by people along the coasts of the Atlantic, Pacific, and Arctic oceans, from Alaska to Greenland. While there were probably still at least thirty thousand people who considered themselves Eskimos or Aleuts well into the twentieth century, the original language and culture began a rapid process of extinction as soon as modern technology made it possible for people of European ancestry to bring modern civilization to the natives.

Since none of these languages had a written form, and since little archaeological evidence survives, it is impossible to date clearly the migration over the Bering Strait (or Bering land bridge) that brought these people to North America. There is, however, firm linguistic evidence that this language group is related to languages spoken in Siberia. Estimates for when the original language, called Eskaleut, broke into its two branches vary from about three thousand to six thousand years ago.

Some time between eight hundred and eighteen hundred years ago, the Eskimo branch split into two varieties. Yupik is the branch spoken on the Pacific Coast and in south mainland Alaska. Inupik is spoken north of the Yukon River in Alaska and the Yukon, in the Northwest Territories, and in Greenland.

While the Inupik branch covers a huge territory, surprisingly few differences in dialect have arisen. It is possible for an Alaskan Eskimo to communicate with relative ease with one living in Greenland. While the reason for this situation is impossible to prove, as European contact with the tribes is very recent, a major factor may be that Eskimos have a tendency to be migratory, following game according to local abundance or scarcity and moving with the seasons. Thus, the various tribes may have intermixed in previous centuries.

There is some archaeological evidence that in the distant past, the Eskimos occupied a much larger territory than they do now, inhabiting lands far inland. The interior of the Subarctic, however, has been dominated by the Athapaskans for many centuries. The two cultures and languages are apparently unrelated, and even the physical appearance of the two groups is widely different.

See also Aleut; Arctic; Inuit.

Esselen: Tribe

CULTURE AREA: California
LANGUAGE GROUP: Esselen
PRIMARY LOCATION: Monterey County, California

Not only were the Esselen one of the smallest of the California Indian tribes, they were also probably the first to disappear ethnographically. Because no identifiable Esselen could be located by anthropologists even in the nineteenth century, nobody knows what name they may have had for themselves. "Esselen" or variant spellings appeared in Spanish records referring to a village in the area that is now modern Monterey County, and scholars adopted it for the tribe in the absence of any other information.

The Spanish explorer Sebastián Vizcaíno entered Monterey Bay in 1602 and observed many Indians, some of whom may have been Esselen. Actual European contact, however, did not begin until 1769, when the Spanish expedition led by Gaspar de Portolá passed through Esselen territory. The population at that time has been the subject of widely divergent estimates, but 750 is a probable compromise figure. In 1770, Spanish missionaries established Mission San Carlos, originally on Monterey Bay but later moved to the mouth of the Carmel River. From that mission, which served as the headquarters of Junípero Serra and Fermín Francisco de Lasuén, the padres recruited Esselens for conversion to Christianity and Spanish culture. Mission Soledad, founded in 1791 on the Salinas River, also included some Esselen among its converts. Mission life did not agree with the Esselen, and by the early nineteenth century their numbers had dropped precipitously. By the time of the secularization of the missions around 1834, both San Carlos and Soledad were nearly abandoned because of the near extinction of both Esselen and non-Esselen populations. No significant features of Esselen culture and very few Esselen people survived the mission experience. By 1928, when the federal government undertook to enroll all California Indians, only one person claimed Esselen ancestry, and that was a one-quarter link of questionable authenticity.

Since anthropologists and other scholars have had essentially no informants on which to base their research, the little knowledge of Esselen culture has been obtained from a few scattered records of the Spanish missionaries, members of other tribes who could recall a few Esselen words and cultural features, and the archaeological record. Although some Esselen lived along the Pacific coast and utilized fish and abalone for subsistence, most inhabited the mountainous regions of southwestern Monterey County and relied on acorns and other plants. Since they lacked bows and arrows, hunting was not possible, but the Esselen snared skunks, rabbits, lizards, and dogs. Some rock art, a few burial sites of cremated remains, some chipped-stone artifacts, and a large number of bedrock mortars have been found. The relative paucity of artifacts has led one archaeologist to suggest that the alleged Esselen sites were only visited periodically by Indians of other tribes and to question whether an actual Esselen tribe ever existed. The only evidence of distinct Esselen culture is linguistic and is mostly from indirect secondary sources.

See also California; Indian-white relations—Spanish colonial.

Ethnophilosophy and worldview

Tribes affected: Pantribal

Significance: Despite the diversity among indigenous American cultures—their environments, beliefs, and adaptations—the underlying philosophy of these cultures is a respect for the natural world and their place within it

Around the world and throughout history, indigenous peoples have developed belief systems that shape their lifestyles to their natural environment in order to enhance their survival within it. Such has been the case among the indigenous peoples of North America.

Definitions. The ethnophilosophy, or worldview, of any culture is a description of how that culture explains the structure and workings of the world in which it lives. It is based on experience, observation, and intellectual inquiry. In many cultures, this worldview is relatively distinct from other aspects of its ideology. One of these other aspects that is especially important is religion, which might be defined as the description of a group or individual's relationship with that world, a behavioral guide that relies to some extent on emotional appeal. Myths are a link between philosophy and religion.

The distinction between worldview and religious influence, however, is much less clear-cut in North American native cultures. This blending has been both a strength and a weakness for the indigenous American peoples since Europeans came to their lands. The extent to which these closely tied phenomena shape the daily lives and activities of indigenous peoples has been unrecognized or disregarded by the dominant, immigrant culture.

Recurrent Themes. As cultures and individuals, most North American natives consider their lives to be constant expressions of their abiding respect for the natural world and their place in it. Although there are many different belief systems and rituals among the groups, there are several recurrent themes that appear across the spectrum of differences. These are the acceptance of visions and dreams as legitimate realities, brotherhood with particular plants or animals, the necessity for maintaining balance in all aspects of life, and the sanctity of the circle. These motifs appear repeatedly in art and decoration, music, dance, and many rituals. Reverent, constant attention to these themes is an integral experience of daily life.

In many Native American cultures, dreams and visions are welcomed, even sought, as sources of wisdom. There are rituals to prepare seekers for a vision experience. Spending a period of time in a sweatlodge is often part of the preparation. Fasting and solitude are also common practices. In some cultures, the use of hallucinogens facilitates the vision experience. Sometimes, though, these experiences are spontaneous. Whatever information is gained is considered reality, though perhaps reality in metaphor. It is wisdom.

Wisdom is always a gift. There are always sacred and unknowable "great mysteries." Their existence is recognized and appreciated as part of the bond that ties people to life. It is not only foolish but also disrespectful to ask too much about the great mysteries. Although shamans and members of secret religious societies might have more insight than the average tribe member into the ultimate and unknowable, even they are barred, by reverence for its infinite sanctity, from too much direct inquiry: All that they are to know will be revealed to them.

Usually during one of these dream or vision experiences some animal or mythical being communicates with the participant. Its message is shared with the tribe and may become part of the myth system for that tribe. Imagery from the dream or vision may be used later by their artists who make masks or who paint pottery. It may be woven into the pattern of a blanket or basket or may become part of a costume worn during a ceremonial dance.

Native Americans accept their place in the natural world as being a part of creation rather than being separate from it. They share equal status with other parts of creation, both living and nonliving.

Plants, Animals, and Mother Earth. Because of Native Americans' traditional reliance on the abundance of the land, certain plants and animals have always been accorded special status. Corn, squash, beans, rice, and tobacco were traditional crops. Buffalo, caribou, deer, fish, and whales were common sources of game food. Wolves, eagles, bears, and snakes are important symbols of wisdom and strength. Cedar trees, which provided Northwest Coast Indians with material for their homes, boats, clothing, and containers for storage and cooking, are revered in that region. In many indigenous cultures, when a person needs to kill something to use it, he apologizes to it first or explains to it the necessity for its death. Although North American natives' lives were particularly dependent on these living things, they recognized the worth of all forms of life and took care not to harm them if possible. Nonliving parts of the natural world were also valued.

The earth as mother is a major theme both in myth and in daily life. All life comes from and is dependent upon Mother Earth. Several groups believe that they emerged as a people from the earth. Some believe that future generations are developing within the mother now and will emerge from the mother as long as humankind exists. Many believe that after death their spirits will return to their source within Mother Earth. Crops emerge from the earth and are nourished by Her. Animals are sustained by the plants that the earth supports. Therefore, the only way to regard Mother Earth is with gratitude and reverence.

Certain mountains or rock formations, caves, or rivers, as well as the ocean, are considered sacred to those who live near them. These sites may be revered because the natives believe that their ancestors originated there or because their ancestors are buried there. It may be that the tribe believes that its future lies there—that the coming generations will need those places for their lives. Therefore, it is the responsibility of those currently living to take care of the site both physically, by not scarring or polluting it and spiritually, by regarding it with respect.

On a somewhat smaller scale, certain gems and minerals have particular symbolic importance. Solid forms may be fashioned into amulets or may be used in rituals; clay and various pigments, for example, are used for ceremonial body paint. Even a plain-looking small stone can carry a prayer if it is handled reverently.

Life in Balance. Balance in the natural world and in individual lives is seen as crucial for survival. In their relationship with the environment, Native Americans see it as their responsibility not to disturb natural balances. They must not take more resources than they need for their survival or take more than the environment can bear to give. They must treat with respect all that is taken from their surroundings.

Balance must also be maintained in relationships within their communities. Political systems have varied widely among groups. In pre-contact days, some North American tribal leaders were monarchs, and their subjects lived within strict caste systems. Other groups enjoyed relative democracy, their governments involving representatives in voting councils. The model for the United States' government was influenced by the Iroquois' Confederacy of Six Nations, which is one of the oldest continuously functioning systems of governance in the world.

Personal lives must be kept in balance by respectful attitudes, ethical behavior, and avoidance of excess in order to maintain physical and mental health. When a person is suffering because he or she is out of balance, a healer or shaman may be able to help find the cause. The sufferer may not even remember a seemingly minor transgression committed several years before, or a child may be suffering because one of his or her parents unknowingly did something before the child was even conceived. Whatever the cause, once the source of the problem is recognized, the healer or shaman performs ceremonies and offers advice to help the sufferer regain the balance necessary for good health.

All creation is bound by a sacred circle, and since the indigenous people live within it, they must take care not to break it by either carelessness or intentionally destructive behavior. The circle expresses itself repeatedly throughout the natural world—in the rounded vault of the sky, in the cycle of the seasons, in the shape of the sun and moon, and in the nests of birds and the webs of spiders. The circular pattern is reiterated in the shape of many tribes' houses, in the hoops of games, in the choreography of dances, and in the form of religious structures.

While these motifs are prominent in nearly all indigenous cultures of North America, many of the ways in which they are honored might not seem obvious. Factors as basic as the name by which a tribe knows itself and its environment, as major as the education of its children, and as seemingly insignificant as the proper way to move about in the home are all matters related to the philosophy of respect for the worlds among which the various American indigenous cultures live.

Tribal Names and Traditions. Most tribes credit mythical figures or their ancestors with having provided tribal names. Because of the sacred source for these names, tribal membership offers spiritual as well as social identity. Frequently a tribe is named for its location or for some trait of its community. For example, the Pimas' indigenous name is Akimel O'odham, which means "River People," and their Papago neighbors, the Tohono O'odham, are the "Desert People." Many tribes are known in their native tongues simply as "the People." Among them are the Dine (Navajo) of the American Southwest, the Nimipu (Nez Perce) of eastern Washington state, the Kaigini (Haida) of the Pacific coast, and the Maklaks (Klamath) of the mountainous California-Oregon border region. A few variations on this are Ani-yun-wiya (Cherokee), or "Real People"; Kaigwu (Kiowa), or "Main People"; Anishinabe (Chippewa), "First Men"; and Tsististas (Cheyenne), "Beautiful People."

In every tribe, Indian children are given instruction in the proper way to behave and are introduced to their origins through stories and myths told by parents and relatives or by tribal storytellers. Children are discouraged from asking too many questions. Instead, they are advised over the years to listen to stories several times. As the children grow up in this oral tradition, they come to understand the metaphors and realities that are the bridges connecting their people's history, philosophy, religion, and traditions. Everything the children learn must be relevant to their lives; it is vital for the physical, spiritual, and social survival of the children individually and for the tribe as a whole. The oral tradition continues to be a sacred responsibility for both the teller and the listener.

Among some tribes, even the way people move about within the group or inside their homes or religious structures is an expression of respect. Children are taught not to cross between the fire and their elders so that they are not deprived of any heat or light. In some tribes, the pattern of movement in the homes is always in a clockwise direction, the way that the sun moves across the sky. Participants in nearly all religious and political meetings gather in a circle.

Sentimentalization Versus Reality. It is important to realize that one should not become carried away with oversentimentalizing the worldviews and practices of Native Americans. (This type of sentimentalizing was prominent in the eighteenth century, with the European concept of the "noble savage.") Certain tribal hunting techniques, as well as some tribes' capturing and selling of slaves and cruelty in warfare, attest the side of Indian life that sentimentalists do not consider.

Before they had horses to use in their hunting expeditions, the method that several tribes used to slay buffalo was to herd and stampede them into running off cliffs. Although it was customary for the hunters to apologize to the dying and dead, the number of animals lost was in excess of what their tribes could use, and many carcasses remained at the foot of the cliffs to become carrion.

Taking slaves was a common practice for tribes in many parts of the continent. Often these slaves were captured from other tribes during raids for that purpose. Sometimes non-natives were enslaved, including African Americans taken by the Cherokee. Comanches took Spaniards as slaves. In the Pacific Northwest, a large portion of the Chinook economy was the slave trading that they did up and down the coast. The Ute captured people for other tribes to use for slaves, trading them for horses. Several tribes in the Southeast captured other natives for the English and Spanish to use on their ships and in the Caribbean colonies.

Human sacrifice and cannibalism were not unknown. Most tribes that practiced human sacrifice used prisoners who had been captured in conflicts. Those who were not suitable for slaves or sacrificial purposes, or who would not make good wives, were often tortured before they were killed. The Pawnee sacrificed captured females—or one of their own, if necessary—as part of a ritual to ensure an ample harvest. Most cases of cannibalism involved using the victims' hearts to gain the enemies' valor and strength.

The potlatch, the celebration among British Columbian and Pacific Northwest natives that has been seen as a symbol of generosity and a ceremony of sharing the host's wealth among the guests, was not always an altruistic event. The Kwakiutl, for example, also used it as a political tool to humiliate their enemies and to gain power over them.

Immigrant Philosophy Conflict. Throughout their history with European immigrants, Native Americans have suffered near annihilation—physical, cultural, and spiritual—because of the ethnophilosophical differences between the two groups.

When Europeans began arriving on the shores of North America, they brought with them a philosophy that was radically different from that of the natives they encountered. The newcomers did not see themselves as being an integral part of their natural environment, participants in it who had to obey its laws. They saw themselves as separated from it by their level of civilization—by how far they believed they had risen above the brutality and unpredictability of the natural world and by

how well they had managed to exploit its resources. The essential difference in worldview was, and continues to be, a source of conflict that has been disastrous to Native American communities across the continent. —*Marcella T. Joy*

See also Children; Education, pre-contact; Medicine and modes of curing, post-contact; Mother Earth; Oral literatures; Religion; Religious specialists; Sacred narratives; Symbolism in art; Visions and vision quests; Warfare and conflict.

BIBLIOGRAPHY

Beck, Peggy V., and Anna L. Walters. *The Sacred: Ways of Knowledge, Sources of Life*. Tsaile, Ariz.: Navajo Community College Press, 1977. Discusses several North American cultures while concentrating on southwestern peoples. Many photographs and maps. Extensive bibliography and film lists.

French, Lawrence. *Psychological Change and the American Indian: An Ethnohistorical Analysis*. New York: Garland, 1987. Academic, theoretical approach. Well organized and well documented. Focuses on educational policies with discussion of pre- and post-contact attitudes among Cherokee, Athapaskan/Apache, and Plains Sioux.

Highwater, Jamake. *The Primal Mind*. New York: Harper & Row, 1981. Philosophy in elegant, simple language. The author's views are based on academic studies and on life experience in both Blackfeet (Blood) and non-native cultures. Extensive bibliography.

Inter Press Service, comp. *Story Earth: Native Voices on the Environment*. San Francisco: Mercury House, 1993. Essays by the world's indigenous peoples, including American Indians, compiled by a global newswire. Introduction by the prime minister of Norway. Interesting non-American editorial perspectives.

McLuhan, T. C., comp. *Touch the Earth: A Self-Portrait of Indian Existence*. New York: Simon & Schuster, 1971. Native Americans' quotations from the last three hundred years. Many photographs. Insightful and visually beautiful. Well documented; includes suggested readings.

Nerburn, Kent, and Louise Mengelkoch, eds. *Native American Wisdom*. San Rafael, Calif.: New World Library, 1991. Short quotes from numerous Native Americans, past and present, discussing ways that philosophical concepts are expressed in daily life.

Ridington, Robin. *Trail to Heaven: Knowledge and Narrative in a Northern Native Community*. Iowa City: University of Iowa Press, 1988. Anthropological study of the philosophy, social life, and customs of the Beaver Indians in British Columbia. Some photographs and a long reference list.

Suzuki, David, and Peter Knudtson. *Wisdom of the Elders: Honoring Sacred Native Visions of Nature*. New York: Bantam Books, 1992. Views of indigenous peoples from around the world, including North America. Scholarly but readable. Several epigraphs by scientists from many disciplines, theologians, and social scientists. Romanticized non-native assumptions are examined. Well documented.

Vecsey, Christopher. *Imagine Ourselves Richly: Mythic Narratives of North American Indians*. New York: Crossroad,

1988. A broad-ranging anthology. The introduction includes academic discussion of sources and functions of myths in general and of their value to Native Americans specifically.

Wall, Steve, and Harvey Arden. *Wisdomkeepers: Meetings with Native American Spiritual Elders.* Hillsboro, Oreg.: Beyond Words, 1990. Long quotations from interviews with several American Indians. Not an academic work but informative and insightful. Moving text and photographs.

Etowah: Archaeological site

DATE: 700-1650

LOCATION: Etowah River Valley, near Cartersville and Atlanta, Georgia

CULTURES AFFECTED: Mound builders, protohistoric Creek, historic Cherokee

Etowah Mounds and village site, the largest Indian settlement in the Etowah Valley, occupied between 700 and 1650 C.E., was a political, religious, and trade center for several thousand people of the Mississippian or mound builder culture. Influences from the Adena and Hopewell periods are evident along with possible Mesoamerican influence.

The 50-acre site along the Etowah River was fortified on the remaining three sides by a stockade and moat. The village contained two large plazas surrounded by seven mounds, where several hundred burial sites were uncovered by archaeologists. Laborers constructed these mounds by carrying hundreds of thousands of basketfuls of earth from nearby pits. Three ceremonial mounds, the largest 63 feet high and covering 2.9 acres, were topped with richly decorated temples or houses for chief priests. Artifacts found in burials under these summit temples include elaborate ceremonial outfits and ritual paraphernalia used by priests. Burials around the mound bases contained masks, ornaments, pearl and shell necklaces, baskets, and stone tools. One mound reveals a number of building periods, marked by varying layers of clay, possibly indicating the beginning of a new ceremonial cycle when the old temple was destroyed and a new one built.

Etowah is important for its elaborate religious art similar to that of the higher culture of Mexico. Designs on items of shell, stone, tortoise shell, and copper reveal a preoccupation with death in images of human sacrifice and symbols of skulls and bones. Such death-related symbols suggest a connection with the Southern Cult or Death Cult; this shared religion supported trade relationships and prevented warfare among other centers throughout the Southeast. A gathering place for large festivals and a major craft center, Etowah was gateway from the Middle Mississippi subregion to the Southern Appalachian. Trade between these areas was facilitated by an extensive network of rivers which flowed toward the Gulf of Mexico.

Mound builders had a rigid caste system of royalty, nobles, honored men, and commoners, with priests living atop the mounds and commoners living in thatched-roof huts around the plazas. Chief priests controlled religious life by presiding over festivals and mortuary rites, and they directed daily life by overseeing food distribution. Sandy soil, fertilized every few years by flooding, produced an abundance of corn, beans, and pumpkins. Hunting and gathering added to the plentiful food supply, allowing time for development of a rich social and religious life.

In 1965 Etowah was designated a National Historic Landmark. Outstanding artifacts, the largest found in the history of southeastern archaeology, are two mortuary figures, male and female. Carved of white marble and bearing traces of original paint, 2 feet high and approximately 125 pounds each, they are thought to be memorials to deceased chiefs or priests.

In 1817, the Reverend Elias Cornelius was guided to the Etowah site by Cherokee chiefs who were uncertain about its significance. Archaeological research in the late 1920's and mid-1950's revealed the flourishing culture of these mound builders.

See also Adena; Cahokia; Death and mortuary customs; Hopewell; Mounds and mound builders; Moundville; Southern Cult.

Fallen Timbers, Battle of

DATE: August 20, 1794

PLACE: Lucas County, Ohio

TRIBES AFFECTED: Huron (Wyandot), Lenni Lenape, Miami, Ojibwa, Ottawa, Potawatomi, Shawnee

SIGNIFICANCE: Anthony Wayne's destruction of pan-Indian resistance in the Maumee Valley region of Ohio and Indiana marked the beginning of intensive white settlement in the Old Northwest

During the early 1790's a confederation centered along the Maumee River Valley between modern Fort Wayne, Indiana, and Toledo, Ohio, conducted one of the most vigorous resistances to American territorial expansion in the country's history. Under the nominal leadership of the Miami war chief Little Turtle (Michikinakoua), the tribes most associated with him were the Shawnee (led by Blue Jacket or Wyeapiersenwah) and the Lenni Lenape (led by Buckongahelas). Their villages were mostly near The Glaize (modern Defiance, Ohio). The confederacy had support from the Ottawa, Potawatomi, and Ojibwa to their north and associated themselves with the Cherokee and Creeks to the south.

Little Turtle's warriors inflicted two critical defeats on United States military incursions into their territory. Brigadier General Josiah Harmar led an expedition to Fort Miami that was badly mauled in two engagements by a pan-Indian force (October, 1791). When the next American expedition, commanded by the Northwest Territory's governor, Major General Arthur St. Clair, encamped at the headwaters of the Wabash River (modern Fort Recovery, Ohio), Little Turtle led a dawn surprise attack (November 4, 1791) that constitutes the most disastrous defeat of the U.S. Army at the hands of Indians in the entire history of the Indian Wars (1790-1890).

Indian resistance was never totally unified, however, and the intensity of devotion to the cause decreased as the distance from the Maumee Valley increased. Accommodationist Indian leaders urged the concession of white settlements north of the Ohio River that the Maumee confederacy would not allow.

In 1794, Major General Anthony Wayne brought the third American expedition northward. Even though the British had built Fort Miami at the Maumee rapids (at present-day Maumee, Ohio) and Alexander McKee, a British Indian Department agent, promised redcoat support, Little Turtle and others began to have doubts. Concurrently, intertribal rivalries emerged, especially between Ojibwa and Maumee warriors. McKee urged an attack on one of Wayne's outposts, Fort Recovery, located at the site of St. Clair's defeat, and, despite

Forces under Anthony Wayne defeated a weakened Indian confederacy once led by Little Turtle at the Battle of Fallen Timbers. (Library of Congress)

Little Turtle's opposition, the assault took place and was repulsed (June 30, 1794). Wayne's methodical advance left the Indians no easy ambush point, and they were forced to engage the Americans a few miles west of Fort Miami among wind-downed trees. By this time Little Turtle's authority was eroded, many warriors had deserted, and Blue Jacket had become the nominal commander. The resulting Battle of Fallen Timbers was a rout of the few remaining Indians. As Little Turtle suspected, the British in Fort Miami failed to support their allies.

Wayne subsequently destroyed the Indian villages of the Maumee Valley and established Fort Wayne at its headwaters. The next year the Indians conceded American settlement north of the Ohio at the Treaty of Fort Greenville. Little Turtle and many other veterans of this campaign became accommodationists, and their opposition to fighting the Americans was a key factor in Native American disunity during Tecumseh's Rebellion (1809-1811) and the War of 1812.

See also Brant, Joseph; Fort Greenville, Treaty of; Fort Stanwix, Treaty of; Little Turtle; Wabash, Battle of the.

BIBLIOGRAPHY

Carter, Harvey Lewis. *The Life and Times of Little Turtle: First Sagamore of the Wabash.* Urbana: University of Illinois Press, 1987.

Eid, Leroy V. "American Indian Military Leadership: St. Clair's 1791 Defeat." *Journal of Military History* 57 (January, 1993): 71-88.

False Face Ceremony

TRIBES AFFECTED: Iroquois tribes

SIGNIFICANCE: During the False Face Ceremony, certain tribal members don special masks which they believe give them the power to cure disease

The False Face Ceremony refers both to the rite performed by members of the False Face Society during the Midwinter Ceremony and to individual healing practices during which members of the society control sickness with the power of the spirit in the mask and the blowing or rubbing of ashes on the patient's body. At midwinter, the society comes to the longhouse to enable people to fulfill particular dreams or to renew dreams during a ritual called the Doorkeeper's Dance.

The False Face Society uses wooden masks with deepset eyes; large, bent noses; arched eyebrows; and wrinkles. The mouths vary, but they are most often "*O*"-shaped or spoon-shaped (a horizontal figure-eight shape). Often spiny protrusions are carved on the mask. The original "Great False Face" comes from an origin story and is depicted as a hunchback with a bent nose. His name links him to the legend of the test of moving a mountain, in which he engaged with Hawenio, or Creator. The Great False Face is the great trickster figure, although tricksters occur in Iroquois legends with many names and manifestations.

Hawenio, recognizing that Shagodyoweh-gowah (one of the names for the Great False Face) has tremendous power, tells the Great False Face that his job is to rid the earth of disease. Shagodyoweh-gowah agrees that if humans will make portrait masks of him, call him "grandfather" or "great one" (gowa), make tobacco offerings, and feed him cornmeal mush, he will give the humans the power to cure disease by blowing hot ashes. Shagodyoweh-gowah travels the world using a great white pine as a cane, without which he would lose his balance. His movement is mimicked during the Doorkeeper's Dance.

See also Iroquois Confederacy; Masks; Midwinter Ceremony; Tricksters.

BIBLIOGRAPHY

Doueihi, A. "Trickster: On Inhabiting the Space Between Discourse and Story." *Soundings: An Interdisciplinary Journal* 67, no. 3 (1984): 283-311.

Fenton, William N. *The False Faces of the Iroquois.* Norman: University of Oklahoma Press, 1987.

Feast of the Dead

TRIBES AFFECTED: Algonquin, Huron, Iroquois

SIGNIFICANCE: The Feast of the Dead provided an outlet for mourning the dead and promoted tribal unity

The Feast of the Dead was a Native American religious ceremony that provided several villages a chance to gather together, reestablish friendships, and collectively mourn their dead. Though the Feast of the Dead is frequently referred to as an Algonquin ceremony, it was also practiced by Huron and Iroquois nations.

Every few years, tribal councils gathered and announced the date and location for a Feast of the Dead. The bodies of the dead were disinterred from their temporary burial sites to be reburied in a common grave. Family members exhumed the bodies and prepared them for the ceremony. They removed the flesh, which was burned, and wrapped the remains in beaver robes. Each village then traveled to the placed selected by the councils. At the site, a large pit was dug. The inside was lined with beaver robes. The bones of the dead and the goods that had been buried with them were suspended from a platform. In turn, each family threw their deceased and grave goods into the pit, which was covered with mats, bark, and logs.

When the Northeastern Indian nations broke up and moved west or north, it became increasingly difficult to gather tribes for a Feast of the Dead. The Mohawk and Seneca tribes continued to practice a variation of the ceremony into the twentieth century.

See also Algonquin; Death and mortuary customs; Feasts; Huron; Iroquois Confederacy.

Feasts

TRIBES AFFECTED: Pantribal

SIGNIFICANCE: American Indians traditionally celebrated special occasions with special meals; feasts as part of sacred ceremonies usually included specified dishes and practices, while secular feasts usually had greater flexibility

Native Americans, in common with most peoples around the world, celebrated special occasions with communal meals, generally rendered as "feasts" in English. Some feasts formed part of seasonal sacred ceremonies, others accompanied meetings of secular voluntary societies, and still others commemorated family events, such as the visit of a dignitary, a success in diplomacy or war, the naming of a child, or the completion of a house. In general, feasts that were part of a sacred ceremony were more formalized in their structure and might include fixed prayers or practices, while the more secular feasts followed less rigid guidelines of expected behavior and courtesy.

Common Features. Regardless of the type of feast, there were certain common features. Unlike European and Asian feasts, American Indian feasts tended not to be elaborate affairs, and they were presented with the same implements that would be used in everyday eating. While the meals often included ingredients and dishes that might appear at any meal, feasts usually featured choice ingredients and a wider diversity of foods than other meals.

The sponsor was expected to provide food for a feast, and kin often would be called upon to assist; their assistance would be repaid later when they were sponsoring feasts and needed assistance. Family feasts were sponsored by the family as a communal unit, although a head of the household usually was conceived as the sponsor. In many tribes, this would be a man, but some of the matrilineal tribes considered a woman to head the family, and she would serve as sponsor. Feasts accompanying the meetings of secular societies usually were sponsored by a person or persons who were seeking membership in the society or by the person at whose house the meeting was to be held. Feasts accompanying sacred ceremonies would be sponsored by the tribe as a whole or by its chief as its representative. The sponsor had to take special care that no foods were included that would be taboo for any of the diners.

Typically, food was prepared by female members of the sponsoring group and was then ladled out by them from a communal pot onto each diner's bowl or plate. Small family feasts usually would be served by the female head of household. Under certain conditions, particularly if a feast was to honor a prominent person, the sponsor and his immediate kin might abstain from eating during the feast, appointing another guest to do the serving. Details of manners varied from tribe to tribe, but the male head of household, chief, or religious leader usually would signal the beginning of the feast by lifting up a bit of the food, sometimes presenting it to the four cardinal points, then dropping it to the ground or into the fire. This thanksgiving offering to the gods was performed in silence.

Many feasts were part of the ceremonies surrounding the beginning of the season when an important food became available. Among the Nootka of the Northwest Coast, for example, salmon captured during their fall spawning runs were dried for use throughout the year, and this staple was recognized as critical to survival. The first catch of salmon, regardless of who caught them, would be presented to the chief, who would sprinkle them with goose down while greeting the fish with a formalized welcome. Women, except those menstruating, would be designated to prepare the salmon, and everyone

(except menstruating women) would partake of the food. Bones and innards from this feast would be returned to the water, ensuring that future generations of salmon would be plentiful and well-formed.

Agriculturalists also held feasts within harvest festivals. Many Eastern tribes, such as the Cherokee, held a four- or eight-day ceremony, often called the "Green Corn Dance," at the time of the earliest corn harvest. This ceremony included social dances, the rekindling of fire, the forgiving of transgressions, and a feast centered on the new corn. Ceremonies serving similar purposes were conducted by Pueblo agriculturalists at harvest time.

Memorial Feasts. Other sacred ceremonies focused on the dead. Many tribes maintained that a feast should be held in honor of a recently deceased person at a fixed number of days after that person's death. For most of the Plains tribes, the feast was held after four days, while the Iroquois waited ten days; some groups waited several months. These feasts typically were family-sponsored.

Other tribes held special memorial feasts for all the dead of the tribe at a certain date or season. The Huron, for example, held the Feast of the Dead in autumn, at which time they disinterred their dead from the previous year, reverently stripped the remaining flesh from the bones, dressed them in the best of clothes, and laid them to their final rest in a communal burial pit. This was accompanied by a feast in the evening, sponsored by the entire community and dedicated to the well-being and memory of the dead. The Inuit and most Northwest Coast tribes also held communal feasts for their dead in the winter, when the dead were conceived to return for the feast, enjoying the food that was given them by placing it on the ground or passing it through the fire.

Calendric Festivals, Societies, and Guests. Other feasts were part of calendric festivals, such as the myriad religious ceremonies held by the Hopi. Major ceremonies lasted eight days, while minor ceremonies lasted only four days; given the number of ceremonies per year, fully one-quarter of the year could be taken up with ceremonies. To share the burden of sponsorship, different villages would sponsor different ceremonies each year, and participants would travel to that village. The feasts that were part of these ceremonies, then, served the practical purpose of feeding visitors and others whose ritual obligations kept them from regular eating arrangements. These feasts were viewed as a secular part of the overall ceremonies, and women and others not permitted to participate in the sacred kiva rituals were welcomed at the feasts.

The meetings of volunteer societies, especially in the Plains, were characterized by a feast following the other activities. These feasts followed different protocols, depending on the tribe and the society. Sometimes food was brought ready-cooked to the meeting, kept warm, and ladled out to members; in other cases it was prepared during or after the meeting. Two common threads, however, united these feasts. First, there was no public invitation, since only members were expected to attend and a herald notified them individually. Second, each person brought his or her own bowl, and they were served from a communal pot or pots.

Feasts held by families to commemorate special events were the most variable. Unlike feasts held with ceremonies or institutional activities, they seldom had a rigorous, prescribed structure. Instead, they were flexible, permitting the sponsoring family to adjust according to circumstances.

Among the best-known early Indian feasts are those honoring guests, since these were the ones that early European writers were most likely to have witnessed and recorded. Europeans, even those inclined to disparage Indian culture, universally were impressed by Indian hospitality. Time and again, accounts noted that even in times of famine or personal tragedy, the arrival of a significant visitor was celebrated with a feast of the best foods available. Alvár Nuñez Cabeza de Vaca, the early sixteenth century Spanish traveler who entered North America through Florida and left it through the Southwest and West Mexico, described dozens of feasts at which nearly starving Indians marshaled their scant resources to honor him. Other writers echoed this experience, one that had been shared by thousands of Indian visitors before the coming of the Europeans.

The Royal Feast. Feasts in native North America were communal affairs, to be shared by members of the tribe, a voluntary society, or family. Farther south, in Mexico, an additional type of feast also existed: the royal feast. This meal was sumptuous, often involving extravagant numbers of dishes unavailable to commoners and served only to the Aztec emperor. As described in native and European books, the emperor would have up to three hundred different dishes prepared for his dinner. The emperor ate alone, separated even from his retainers (servants) by a gilded door, so that he would not be seen in the act of eating. He would sample the various dishes, passing one or another on to a retainer on the other side of the screen, as a special favor. Leftovers were eaten by guards. This type of feast, aggrandizing a single individual and setting that person apart from others, was entirely alien to North American Indian practices, where feasts were an act of community.

Functions. Feasts served many functions in traditional Native America. They filled the bellies of those involved, which was significant in terms of ceremonies at which large numbers of visitors were present. In a broader sense, these feasts permitted those experiencing bad years to share in the good fortune of those with abundant food; over a lifetime, every community would experience good years and bad years, and the generosity of one year would be repaid subsequently. In addition, feasts gave people an opportunity to demonstrate their common bond, since food sharing is a universal human symbol of oneness. For many ceremonies, the entire community or tribe feasts together and demonstrates its commonality; in other ceremonies, it is only a voluntary society of perhaps only a single family, but the principle is the same. Ceremonies for the dead, at which the living eat the food and the dead share symbolically, bond the dead with the living members of the

tribe. Other ceremonies unite the spirits and the people in the sharing of food. —*Russell Barber*

See also Feast of the Dead; Food preparation and cooking; Green Corn Dance; Potlatch.

BIBLIOGRAPHY

Beck, Mary Giraudo. *Potlatch: Native Ceremony and Myth on the Northwest Coast.* Anchorage: Alaska Northwest Books, 1993. A very readable book treating major ceremonies, including feasts, of the Northwest Coast tribes. Emphasizes the cultural context of feasting.

Benitez, Ana M. de *Pre-Hispanic Cooking—Cocina Prehispánica.* Mexico City: Ediciones Euroamericanas, 1974. An excellent distillation of information on Aztec foodways, drawing on the Florentine Codex and other primary sources. Bilingual in Spanish and English.

Highwater, Jamake. *Ritual of the Wind: North American Indian Ceremonies, Music, and Dance.* New York: Viking Press, 1977. A widely available compilation of several ceremonies from different tribes. Little detail on feasts as such, but information of the ceremony of which they are part.

Kimball, Yeffe, and Jean Anderson. *The Art of American Indian Cooking.* Garden City, N.Y.: Doubleday, 1965. The most widely available of American Indian cookbooks. The introduction provides a historic (though somewhat romantic) context for the recipes, which are divided by culture area.

Root, Waverly, and Richard de Rochemont. *Eating in America: A History.* New York: William Morrow, 1976. A general history of food and cooking in North America, devoting four chapters to Native American foods and cooking.

Swanton, John R. *The Indians of the Southeastern United States.* Bulletin of the Smithsonian Institution, Bureau of American Ethnology 137. Grosse Point, Mich.: Scholarly Press, 1969. This classic and massive work contains detailed descriptions of the tribes of the Southeast, including considerable information on feasts and food. Includes some extended quotations from early accounts describing feasts.

Waugh, Frederick W. *Iroquois Foods and Food Preparation.* Memoir of the Canada Department of Mines, Geological Survey 86 (Anthropological Series 12). 1916. Reprint. Ottawa: National Museums of Canada, National Museum of Man, 1973. Perhaps the best work of its kind, this monograph summarizes food, food preparation, feasts, and related subjects for the Iroquois tribes in great detail.

Feathers and featherwork

TRIBES AFFECTED: Pantribal

SIGNIFICANCE: Indian tribes used feathers for decorative and symbolic purposes

Feathers obtained from native birds were an important natural material used by North American Indians for both decorative and symbolic purposes. Although not believed to possess inherent power, feathers could be used to represent spiritual powers and actual achievements of the wearers.

Among the items of spiritual significance that were decorated with feathers were the calumet, or peace pipe, the prayer stick, and the wand. The calumet shaft was often heavily decorated with feathers and even the skins and heads of birds. The feathers on the shaft might be painted red when war was planned.

By far the most valued and significant feathers used were those of the eagle. Indians preferred the feathers of the less common golden eagle found in the western mountains, and birds were sometimes raised from eaglets and then plucked at maturity. Another way to acquire eagle feathers required a hunter to conceal himself in a covered pit near a baited noose and overpower the snared eagle attracted to the food. This was a courageous act, as the eagle was taken alive. Feathers would also be obtained through trade. Eagle feathers were especially important in constructing war bonnets and as "exploit feathers." A white feather with a black tip was preferred. Among the Dakota Sioux, each of these exploit feathers had a particular meaning depending on how it was shaped or painted. A red spot painted on top represented the killing of an enemy; if the feather was cut off at the top it meant that the enemy's throat had been cut. The number of notches in a feather indicated if a warrior had been second, third, or fourth in counting coup on an enemy. If the edges were cut, he may have been fifth. A split feather served as a medal of honor, indicating the warrior had been wounded in battle. Eagle feathers were also considered best for feathering arrows.

Other bird species used for various purposes included the wild turkey, hawk, woodpecker, meadowlark, quail, chaparral cock (or roadrunner), duck, bluejay, and blackbird. Some California tribes were reputed to have used the scalps of certain small birds as a form of currency. Feathers of the roadrunner, called "Medicine Bird" by the Plains tribes, were believed to bring good luck if hung within the lodge. Roadrunner feathers were also fashioned into whistles for use in the Medicine Dance.

Woodland Indians of the eastern United States used turkey, crane, and heron feathers to fashion their headdresses. Other tribes made caps of overlapping circles of small feathers, sometimes topped by a single eagle feather. Sometimes feathers of small birds were prepared and used for decoration in the same manner as porcupine quills.

Elaborate feather robes were constructed by eastern tribes, and also by some tribes in the west. Both feathers and skins of birds were used, the skins sometimes being cut into strips and interwoven to form the garment. Elaborate figures or patterns were often created in these feather robes.

Heavy depredations by American and European fashion designers in the late nineteenth century threatened many native bird species, and by the early twentieth century, laws such as the Lacey Act of 1900 were passed to protect native birds. In 1916, the Migratory Bird Treaty, also aimed at protecting birds from extensive predation, was signed between the United States and Great Britain (for Canada), and other treaties with nations such as Mexico followed. Although allowances were made for American Indians, this has sometimes caused difficulty for those who wished to continue to use certain feathers for decorative and symbolic purposes.

See also Beads and beadwork; Dress and adornment; Headdresses; Quillwork; War bonnets.

Federally recognized tribes

Tribes affected: Pantribal
Significance: Federal recognition of tribes is an issue with both political and economic ramifications

The term "federally recognized tribe" is a U.S. government designation for an American Indian tribe that has official relations with the United States. These relations have been established in various ways through the years—through treaties (treaty making ended in the late nineteenth century), executive orders, court decrees, and acts of Congress, and through meeting the requirements set forth by the Federal Acknowledgment Program. Federal recognition is both a political and economic issue, as recognized tribes are eligible for federal services that unrecognized tribes cannot receive, such as education, housing, and health benefits.

The Federal Acknowledgment Program (a Bureau of Indian Affairs program) was created in 1978. The Federal Acknowledgment program established criteria and procedures through which unrecognized tribes could attempt to attain recognized status. The creation of a federal recognition process was hailed a victory by some American Indians, but others countered that the requirements are unnecessarily complex, even unfulfillable. Among the criteria is proof of continuous existence as a tribe; the tribe also must have a governing body, be governed by a constitution or similar document, and have membership criteria and a roll of current members.

In the 1950's a government policy known as termination successfully urged many tribes to disband; subsequently, some terminated tribes have attempted to regain recognized tribal status; the regaining of tribal status by the Menominees was the first major success. (Terminated tribes are not eligible for recognition through the Federal Acknowledgment Program.) In 1991 there were 510 federally recognized tribes; in mid-1994 the number had grown to 543. Some of these groups are very small; for example, there are some two hundred Alaskan village groups.

See also Indian Reorganization Act; Termination policy; Tribe.

Fernandeño: Tribe

Culture area: Southern California
Language group: Hokan
Primary location: Northern San Diego County, Southern Orange County

The Fernandeño are among the small California tribal groupings that once occupied the area of modern-day Los Angeles county, specifically the northern valley areas or present San Fernando Valley. Today they live slightly to the south. Their near neighbors, the Gabrielino, also had villages on the islands of Catalina, Santa Barbara, San Nicolas, and San Clemente. The name "Fernandeño," like the Gabrielino, derives from the people who surrounded the San Fernando Mission, one of the early Catholic missionary stations founded in the Southern California region. Fernandeño speak a dialect, also called Fernandeño, of the Gabrielino language, which is part of the Shoshonean division of the Uto-Aztecan linguistic division.

Little is known of either Gabrielino or Fernandeño life because of the decimation of their traditional lifestyle and ideologies before trained recorders were available to record aspects of their life. It is known that their homes were domed, circular huts with thatched roofs, and reports indicate that some of these dwellings were large enough to hold fifty people.

The noted anthropologist of the California native groups, Alfred Kroeber estimated that the Fernandeño and Gabrielino combined totaled approximately five thousand in 1770. California Indians generally are not to be understood as "tribes," but rather "tribal groups" of perhaps a hundred persons at most, usually not all of them permanent members, which surrounded a centrally recognized permanent village. The Fernandeño shared many common cultural traits with other village communities up and down the California coast, including a simple artistry in basket weaving, simple agriculture, and architecture. As with other Southern California native peoples in the region's near-tropical climate, the Fernandeño typically dressed very lightly.

Today, most of the Fernandeño live in the southern Orange County and northern San Diego County areas. There are no reservations. As with the Gabrielino, Fernandeño religious expressions were focused largely on the cult of the god Chingichngish, who was also recognized among related peoples such as the Luiseño and the Serrano. There was a fully developed shamanism, whose members were rain-makers, finders of lost objects, and healers (as well as instigators) of illness.

See also California; Hokan language group.

BIBLIOGRAPHY

Bean, Lowell John, and Charles Smith. "The Gabrielino (and Fernandeño)." In *Southwest*, edited by Alfonso Ortiz. Vol. 9 in *Handbook of North American Indians*, edited by William Sturtevant. Washington, D.C.: Smithsonian Institution Press, 1978.

Kroeber, Alfred. "The Indians of California." In *The North American Indians: A Sourcebook*, edited by Roger Owen, James Deetz, and Anthony Fisher. New York: Macmillan, 1967.

Miller, Bruce W. *The Gabrielino*. Los Osos, Calif.: Sand River Press, 1991.

Fifteen Principles

DATE: 1983; reaffirmed in 1985

TRIBES AFFECTED: Abenaki, Algonquin, Cree, Huron, Inuit, Micmac, Mohawk, Montagnais, Naskapi

SIGNIFICANCE: Efforts toward Canadian federal constitutional reform prompted the Quebec provincial government to formulate an administrative and legal policy regarding the Indian and Inuit residents of the province

In the midst of federal constitutional negotiations, the province of Quebec established a legal framework to guide its relationships with the Inuit and Indian residents of Quebec. Known as the Fifteen Principles, the policy statement affirmed that the province of Quebec accepted native claims to self-determination with respect to culture, education, language, and economic development. It further acknowledged that natives are entitled to certain aboriginal rights and land claims (left to be determined by future negotiations). Finally, the Fifteen Principles recognized that those aboriginal rights applied equally to men and women.

The Fifteen Principles were adopted, in large part, to bolster the claim by the ruling Parti Québécois that Quebec is a distinct and sovereign nation either within or apart from Canada. If this was to be the case, Quebec could not argue, as it had previously, that the federal government bore sole responsibility for natives living within the borders of Quebec. In fact, it was Quebec's earlier insistence that the federal government must absorb all the costs of native administration that led to the 1939 Supreme Court decision that for legal purposes Inuit were to be regarded as Indians as specified in the British North America Act. By adopting the Fifteen Principles, Quebec attempted to place itself on equal footing with the Canadian government.

See also Indian Act of 1876 (Canada); Indian Act of 1951 (Canada); Indian Act of 1989 (Canada); Indian-white relations—Canadian; Meech Lake Accord; Proclamation of 1763; Treaties and agreements in Canada.

Fire and firemaking

TRIBES AFFECTED: Pantribal

SIGNIFICANCE: Fire was the Indian's most versatile tool; it cooked food, provided the focal point for religious ceremonies, and altered the environment

The origins of human use of fire go so far back in prehistoric time that no one can say exactly when it began. It seems probable that when the ancestors of the North American Indians crossed the land bridge between Siberia and Alaska they brought fire with them.

The Indians are known to have used several methods of making fire. The Indians of Alaska used stones to generate sparks, in the fashion of the flint stone. Much more widespread, however, was firemaking by wood friction. A hearth of wood, with pits in it, was placed on the ground and held firmly in place by the knees of the fire maker; he or she had already prepared some very dry vegetable material, shaved or rubbed to act as tinder. A "drill"—a stick that is rotated rapidly with the hands with one end set in one of the pits of the hearth—was used. The drill-stick shed fine material onto the hearth, and the friction generated by rapid movement produced enough heat to make the material on the hearth smolder; it could then be blown into life and the tinder touched to it. Rapid rotation of the drill could also be produced by looping a string around it and tying both ends to a bow; the bow was moved back and forth.

The possession of fire made many Indian practices possible. It made it possible to bake the pottery that was so widely used for containers; it made it possible to brew a variety of drinks; it made it possible to bake foods and to boil water. Fire made it possible to keep warm in the colder months that all Indians experienced. Fire made it possible to cook the meat that Indians obtained by hunting wild animals. Fire was essential for cooking the beans, squash, and corn that were central to the Indian diet.

Fire was also central to the religion of many tribes. Religious ceremonies nearly always took place around a fire. Fire was a cleansing and purifying agent. Keeping a fire going was a religious duty; when the Indians wanted to mark the end of a cycle, they put out the old fires and started a new one. Tribal deliberations took place around the council fire.

Most important of all, fire was the tool that Indians used to shape the natural environment to meet their needs. When they cleared a plot of land of trees to create a field in which to plant crops, they burned the vegetation. In so doing they not only disposed of unwanted plant material but also added lime and potash to the soil to make it more fruitful.

It was common practice, widely noted by the first Europeans to come to America, for the Indians to burn the woods each year. This was done to eliminate underbrush and make it easier to move about in the woods. It served another purpose: It drove game animals into groups so they could more easily be hunted. Many of the trees that are associated with Indians of the forest grow only in areas that have been burned over; the birch is the most widely known of these, but pitch pines also grow best in burned-over areas. Without fire, many of the cultural practices commonly associated with American Indian societies would have been impossible.

See also Feasts; Food preparation and cooking; Paleo-Indian; Powhatan Wars.

Fish and fishing

Tribes affected: Pantribal
Significance: Fish were a dietary mainstay in northern and northwestern North America and a significant part of the diet in most other regions of the continent

With the exception of a few tribes, such as the Hopi, for whom fish are taboo, all Indians utilized fish for food. Fish were captured by an impressive array of technology, including hooks and lines, gorges (double-pointed spikes on lines, swallowed by fish), harpoons, bows and arrows, leisters (spears with grabbing hooks alongside their points), fish traps, and nets. Hooks, gorges, and traps sometimes were baited. Nets were set, thrown, or dipped; weirs (fencelike fish traps) sometimes incorporated set nets. In some places, vegetable poisons were thrown into pools to bring stunned or killed fish to the surface. When spawning fish were dense, they might be clubbed out of the water or simply grabbed with the hands. All these techniques were widespread in North America. Men most frequently did the fishing, though women often collected fish after they had been poisoned.

Shellfish were collected by different methods. Most mollusks were collected by hand or by digging, work that usually was considered to be like plant gathering and was done by women. Lobsters, crabs, and other crustaceans usually were captured in nets or traps by men. Although shell heaps left from such gathering sometimes are extensive, few tribes relied on shellfish heavily.

The degree of reliance on finfish varied around North America. The greatest reliance was in the Pacific Northwest, where salmon runs provided vast quantities of food that was preserved for use through the year. In this culture area, the salmon run was a critical annual event surrounded by religious and social ritual to ensure success. Less intensive river and ocean fishing secured a variety of other fish, including the olachen, a fatty fish used for candles. The Inuit of the Arctic also used a considerable amount of fish, though sea mammals provided the greater part of their diet. Tribes of the northern forests of Canada used large quantities of lake fish seasonally, when mammals were less available. Fish were important to tribes of the Atlantic coast, the interior woodlands, and California, but they did not assume the importance they did in the aforementioned areas. Fish were relatively unimportant in the Plains and the arid Southwest and West.

Most fish come together in great numbers during seasonal spawning, and maximum advantage of their abundance can be taken only if their flesh can be preserved. In the far north, this can be accomplished by freezing, but elsewhere the technology must be more complicated. Placing fish on racks over low fires dries the meat and impregnates it with chemicals from the smoke. These chemicals flavor the meat and inhibit the growth of microorganisms, and fish can be preserved for several months by this method. Such drying-smoking racks are known archaeologically from as early as 6000 B.C.E. in New York's Hudson Valley. There is no evidence that any Indian tribe used salt to preserve fish or other meat.

See also Hunting and gathering; Salmon; Water and water rights; Weirs and traps.

Flat Mouth (1774, Leech Lake, Minn.—1860, Leech Lake, Minn.): Chief

Also known as: Guelle Plat, Wide Mouth, Eshkebugecoshe
Tribal affiliation: Ojibwa (Chippewa)
Significance: Flat Mouth was a principal chief during the struggles for control of the upper Mississippi Valley region

Flat Mouth succeeded his infamous shaman father, Wasonaunequa, who, as village chief of the Leech Lake Chippewas, attained his position by poisoning his enemies. As a young man, Flat Mouth traveled extensively, living for a time among various tribes, including the Cree and Assiniboine.

With Hole-in-the-Day, Noka, and Curling Hair, Flat Mouth led Chippewa warriors against the Sioux, who were battling for domination of land surrounding the Mississippi headwaters.

Apparently influenced by Tecumseh's brother, the Shawnee Prophet, Tenskwatawa, Flat Mouth denounced poison as a means for eliminating rivals. Despite Tenskwatawa's influ-

A Yurok (California) fisherman, photographed circa 1920 by Edward S. Curtis. (Library of Congress)

ence, however, Flat Mouth refused aid to Tecumseh during his pan-Indian rebellion in 1809-1811, choosing instead to remain friendly to white Americans. Similarly, Flat Mouth spurned British entreaties to attack Americans during the War of 1812, occasionally aiding Americans during the war. Flat Mouth's Chippewas were among the few Indian tribes to resist relocation, remaining on tribal lands.

See also Hole-in-the-Day; Tecumseh; Tenskwatawa.

Flathead: Tribe

Culture area: Plateau
Language group: Salishan
Primary location: Montana, Northern Idaho
Population size: 4,455 ("Salish," 1990 U.S. Census)

The Flathead, or Inland Salish, are related to the Shuswap, Thompson, Wenatchi, Columbia, Okanagan, Sanpoil, Colville, Kalispel, Spokane, and Coeur d'Alene. They live in northern Idaho, eastern Washington State, and Montana. Today, the Flathead share their reservation with the Kutenai, around Flathead Lake near Dixon, Montana. A Flathead Indian museum is maintained in St. Ignatius, Montana, and a traditional pow-wow of the Flathead/Kutenai tribes is held in early July every year. They are united by their common use of the "Inland Salish" dialect, as differentiated from the dialect of the Coastal Salish peoples.

The name "Flathead" is a misnomer, apparently deriving from Europeans' descriptions of people holding their hands on either side of their faces, a sign-language gesture that was misunderstood by the settlers. The name has nothing to do with a tradition of "flattening heads" of children which was practiced among other western coastal peoples. The people themselves prefer "Salish."

Around 2000 b.c.e., internal migrations of native peoples forced some Salish to the area of Bitterroot Valley, which is considered to be the tribal homeland. Around 1700 c.e., the Salish language dialects became a kind of *lingua franca* of the West Coast, since there were Native Americans who could be found as far away as present-day Montana who could understand them.

The Inland Salish are to be sharply differentiated in their culture development from their coastal cousins. The Inland Salish developed into a Plains people, hunting buffalo, and were largely nomadic in the summer as they engaged in hunting and fishing. While the Flathead remained in the Rocky Mountains, they fished the many tributaries of the Columbia River, but they shifted to buffalo hunting as they moved eastward. The women traditionally prepared food and made clothing while the men hunted, guarded camp, and made weapons. As with other Plains-dwelling native nations, the domestication and use of the horse revolutionized Inland Salish life, allowing far more wide-ranging travel for food. The Flathead got most of their horses, according to Flathead tradition, from trade with the Shoshone. For dwellings, the Flathead used the traditional Salish "longhouse" structures until they adopted a tipi-like structure later in their Plains development. Unlike other Plains tribes, they never used skins around the conical pole frame, but spread vegetation and bark around it and then partially buried the base.

Constant wars with the Blackfoot forced the Flathead/Inland Salish people to flee to various locales. Peace was established between the Blackfoot and the Flathead through an intermediary, Pierre Jean de Smet, a Jesuit missionary who lived with the Flathead between 1840 and 1846.

Tribal ceremonies and religious life were generally simple among this group. The Flathead consider themselves to be the descendants of Coyote, whom they believe to be responsible for the creation of human beings. There was a belief in countless numbers of spirits, and supernatural powers were consulted to ward off the evil effects of others' power and the evil spirits of animals. There were dances and prayers directed to the sun and moon, largely for success in hunting and for general success in life. Power was demonstrated by wealth and luck, and men often carried a pouch containing symbols of their various powers. Shamanism was practiced as a healing and supernatural art. An interesting aspect of Flathead oral tradition was the arrival of "Shining Shirt," possibly an Iroquois, who acted as a prophetic figure announcing the coming of the "black robes" (the Jesuits). Other Iroquois followed, and it is possibly from their influence that Catholic Christianity was established among the Flathead.

Historic estimates of the population of the Inland Salish people vary from four thousand to fifteen thousand; they were decimated by smallpox epidemics between 1760 and 1781. In 1805, the Flathead chief Three Eagles encountered Meriwether Lewis and William Clark, who immortalized the Flathead people in their journals. Although relations with the settlers were always friendly, by the 1850's both war with the Blackfoot and the settlers' diseases had reduced their numbers to fewer than five hundred. Today, estimates of the Flathead vary from three thousand to five thousand, counting those who live away from the reservations.

The Flathead people first requested missionary educational support in 1841; the earliest respondents were the Jesuits, who formed mission schools that had wide-ranging and extensive influence on Native American life. In 1891, Chief Charlot sold the traditional Bitterroot land, and the Flathead people were moved to the reservation lands that they now share with the Kutenai.
                                                    —*Daniel L. Smith-Christopher*
See also Salish; Salishan language family.

Bibliography

Bigart, Robert. "Patterns of Cultural Change in a Salish Flathead Community." *Human Organization* 30 (Fall, 1971): 229-237.

Fahey, John. *The Flathead Indians*. Norman: University of Oklahoma Press, 1974. "The Flathead." In *Northwest Coast*, edited by Wayne Suttles. Vol. 7 in *Handbook of North American Indians*, edited by William Sturtevant. Washington, D.C.: Smithsonian Institution Press, 1978.

Johnson, Olga Wedemeyer. *Flathead and Kootenay*. Glendale, Calif.: Arthur Clarke, 1969.

A Flathead camp on the Jocko River in the late nineteenth century. (Library of Congress)

Ruby, Robert, and John Brown. *A Guide to the Indian Tribes of the Pacific Northwest.* Rev. ed. Norman: University of Oklahoma Press, 1992.

Waldman, Carl. "The Flathead." In *Encyclopedia of Native American Tribes.* New York: Facts on File, 1988.

Flutes

TRIBES AFFECTED: Pantribal

SIGNIFICANCE: Flutes were played in many American Indian cultures, usually by shamans and participants in ceremonies.

Flutes, rattles, and hand drums are the oldest and most widespread musical instruments in the New World, and they were probably derived from Old World paleolithic prototypes. The flute and similar wind instruments such as pan-pipes and ocarinas were commonly revered by shamans and curers as sacred instruments for contacting the spirit world, in many cases literally manifesting the "voice" of the spirits.

Though flutes were widespread throughout the Americas, the majority of archaeological specimens have been recovered from preserved deposits in the western and southwestern United States, Mexico, and South America. Flutes could be constructed of any appropriate material, including wood, reed, bone, and ceramic. Most versions were simple hollow tubes with four or five finger holes to control pitch.

Major cults centered on the playing of flutes arose in several locales throughout the Americas and flute players are commonly depicted in paintings, ceramics, and jewelry from South America, western Mexico, and the American Southwest. Flute players figure prominently in several Native American myths and legends. In South America, reed flutes up to 6 feet in length, called *queñas*, were played during male initiation ceremonies, and several pre-Columbian deities, such as Tezcatlipoca, the Aztec god of darkness, deception, and shamanic power, were commonly depicted as flute players.

A particularly strong version of a flute cult appeared in the American Southwest around 500 C.E. The central character in this cult is a figure identified by modern Hopi as "Kokopelli," a mythological hump-backed figure, sometimes depicted as an insect or ithyphallic male and commonly recognizable by his playing of the flute. Masked representations of Kokopelli appear in modern Hopi ceremonials, and a seasonal dance called the Flute Ceremony is specifically devoted to the playing and honoring of large wooden flutes. Flute playing was traditionally restricted to male shamans and ceremonial participants.

See also Dances and dancing; Drums; Music and song.

The most perfect Folsom point found at the site near Bison Quarry (Folsom, New Mexico). (T. L. Bierwert, American Museum of Natural History)

Folsom: Archaeological site and prehistoric tradition
DATE: 9000-7500 B.C.E.
LOCATION: Folsom, New Mexico (site); North America (tradition)
CULTURE AFFECTED: Folsom

Folsom is the name of the prehistoric site near Folsom, New Mexico, where the antiquity of people in the Americas was finally accepted by the scientific community in 1926. Folsom also is the name of the Paleo-Indian tradition associated with the distinctive Folsom projectile point. The Folsom discovery marked a significant turning point or "paradigm shift" in American archaeology in 1926: The presence of people in the Americas at the same time as Ice-Age or Pleistocene animals that are now extinct was accepted with the discovery of a Folsom "fluted" point embedded in the ribs of an extinct species of bison, *Bison antiquus*. The site's investigators, Jess Figgins, director of the Colorado Museum of Natural History, and Harold Cook, a geologist, telegraphed leading scientists in North America asking them to view and validate the find in the ground, which effected immediate acceptance. Since 1926, the occurrence of Folsom fluted points across North and Middle America has been regarded as part of the Folsom Paleo-Indian tradition, dated between 9000 and 7500 B.C.E.

Folsom fluted points are distinctive stone tools manufactured by flaking two sides of a narrow blade struck from a stone tool, normally chert. The point has a channel or flute removed from each side at the base. In contrast to the earlier Clovis points, the Folsom points are smaller, but the flute extends virtually the entire length of the point.

The subsistence for Folsom Paleo-Indians was based on hunting the now extinct bison, as discovered at the Folsom site. Excavations at the Olsen-Chubbock site in Colorado by Joe Ben Wheat uncovered a kill site where about 157 bison had been stampeded into a dry gulley and trampled to death. Seventy-five percent of the animals were butchered, which Wheat estimates provided meat for a hundred people for one month. Other bison-kill sites are located at Lindenmeier, Colorado, excavated by Frank Roberts in the 1930's; Casper, Wyoming, excavated by George Frison; and the Jones-Miller site in Colorado, excavated by Dennis Stanford.

Despite poor preservation of plant or animal remains from Paleo-Indian times, remains at other sites indicate that the diet included other animals. At Debert, Nova Scotia, George MacDonald suggested reliance on caribou (*Rangifer*), which has been substantiated by caribou bones at other sites in northeastern North America, notably at the Udora site by Peter Storck and Arthur Spiess and at the Sandy Ridge site by Lawrence Jackson and Heather McKillop in Ontario, Canada, and at the Holcombe site in Michigan by Charles Cleland. As the large Pleistocene animals became extinct, the Folsom Paleo-Indians adapted their hunting strategies to small animals and began to gather plants during what archaeologists refer to as the Archaic tradition in North America.

See also Archaic; Clovis; Lehner; Paleo-Indian; Plano.

Food preparation and cooking

TRIBES AFFECTED: Pantribal
SIGNIFICANCE: Cooking techniques among indigenous North American peoples varied according to whether a tribe was mobile or sedentary and whether it used pottery

Most foods in traditional North American Indian cuisines were eaten cooked. While a few, such as animal livers and berries, commonly were eaten raw, the rest were transformed through techniques constrained by the available ingredients, technology, and energy sources.

The greatest constraints surrounded heat for cooking. Much of North America had plentiful wood supplies, though parts of the arid West and the Arctic were deficient. Wood typically was burned in an open fire, with food or cooking vessels suspended over it or buried in its coals. Flat rocks could be used as griddles. Sometimes, especially in the East, the fire was made in a pit and covered with dirt, forming a slow-cooking earth oven (aboveground ovens were not used anywhere). The masonry bread oven of the Pueblos was introduced by the Spanish. While ceramic pots could be exposed to fire, skin and bark vessels would burn up. Tribes who made only the latter had to heat liquids in them by adding hot stones, never obtaining more than a low simmer.

These factors meant that the more mobile tribes, most of whom made little or no pottery, were quite limited in their cooking techniques, especially if they lived in an area with limited fuel. The Washoe, for example, prepared most of their food by simmering ground seeds and tubers, often mixed with greens, meat, berries, or whatever was available. Other foods were wrapped in leaves and roasted in the coals.

Sedentary tribes usually made pottery, and they could exploit full boiling. The Wampanoag, for example, ate primarily stews and gruels, based on cornmeal with various additions. Biscuits were made on rock griddles, and dumplings were made from leaf-wrapped dough. Meat often was roasted on racks above a fire, while vegetables usually were roasted in the coals.

Desert agriculturalists of the Southwest had a special problem: dense populations with limited fuel. There, the Pima developed sautéing as an adjunct to boiling, baking, and roasting. Sautéing is quick and conserves fuel, but it requires a fat that will not burn easily, as will most animal fats. The Pima grew cotton and extracted oil from its seeds, using it for sautéing and seasoning. The Pueblo peoples had no cotton from which to extract oil, but they developed other fuel-saving practices. Stews and soups, the most common meals, were cooked in large pots for an entire extended family, then ladled into individual serving bowls. Some dishes, like paper-thin piki bread, cooked almost immediately.

Without refrigeration, storing food became a major challenge, and drying was most commonly used. Some foodstuffs, such as beans and corn, dry easily and well, while others pose

This Sarsi (northern Plains) woman preparing a meal in the nineteenth century is combining traditional techniques with European American tools. (Library of Congress)

greater difficulties. Fish and meat require a smoky fire to produce a nonperishable product, and the resultant taste became a flavoring for other dishes. Indeed, eating large chunks of meat was unusual, and most tribes used meats to complement the plant seasonings collected and cultivated. Pemmican, a tasty mixture of dried meat, berries, and fat, was widely used in the East.

Every tribe had distinctive rules surrounding cooking and eating. Some foods were taboo, while others were relished. Certain foods might be eaten politely only with the hands, while others required the use of spoons or leaf scoops. Many tribes offered a prayer before eating. These and other social conventions made eating an event with cultural, as well as nutritional, significance.

See also Agriculture; Buffalo; Corn; Feasts; Fire and firemaking; Hunting and gathering; Pemmican; Pottery; Subsistence.

Foreman, Stephen (Oct. 22, 1807, Rome, Ga.—Dec. 8, 1881, Park Hill, Indian Territory): Minister, educator

TRIBAL AFFILIATION: Cherokee

SIGNIFICANCE: A fully ordained Presbyterian minister, Foreman served as a spiritual and political leader to the Cherokee

Foreman was one of twelve children of a Scottish trader and a Cherokee woman. When he was a boy, his family moved to Tennessee, where young Foreman attended a missionary school. When his father died, Foreman was sponsored by the Congregational minister Samuel Worcester at New Echota, Georgia. He also attended the College of Richmond, Virginia, and Princeton Theological Seminary, where he was ordained in 1835. Afterward he returned to live among the Cherokee and immediately became embroiled in the Cherokee resistance to removal. For a time he was imprisoned for his antiremoval activities. In 1841, he led one of the last Cherokee detachments on the Trail of Tears, continuing his ministry in Oklahoma.

With Worcester, Foreman translated the Bible into Cherokee using the syllabary created by Sequoyah. He also served as associate editor of the Cherokee newspaper, the *Cherokee Phoenix*. In 1841, Foreman organized a public school system for Cherokee children and in 1844 was elected to the Cherokee Supreme Court. From 1847 through 1855, he served as executive councilor of the Cherokee tribe. During the Civil War, Foreman lived in Texas, where he continued proselytizing, returning to Indian Territory at war's end. There he purchased the former home of Cherokee leader Elias Boudinot and established a church, where he preached until his death.

See also Cherokee; Indian Removal Act; Removal; Syllabaries.

Fort Atkinson, Treaty of

DATE: 1853

PLACE: Southwestern Kansas

TRIBES AFFECTED: Apache, Comanche, Kiowa

SIGNIFICANCE: This treaty was an attempt to establish peace among southern Plains tribes in order to ease white passage westward and facilitate the building of a transcontinental railroad through Indian lands

Personally negotiated by Thomas Fitzpatrick, a white trader and Indian agent of the Upper Platte Agency, the Treaty of Fort Atkinson was one of a series of U.S.-Indian treaties signed during the 1850's to open passage to America's Far West while promoting the Christianization and civilization of the Plains Indians. Fitzpatrick previously had helped to bring the Sioux and seven other Plains tribes together to sign the Treaty of Fort Laramie with the United States in 1851. The signatories to the Fort Atkinson Treaty agreed to establish peace among the affected Indian tribes, as well as between Indians and whites. It sanctioned the passage of whites through Indian lands, and acknowledged U.S. rights to establish military roads and posts thereon. It also provided for annuities to be paid by the United States (for a ten-year term) to the affected Indians.

See also Apache; Apache Tribe of Oklahoma; Comanche; Fort Laramie Treaty of 1851; Gadsden Purchase; Indian-white relations—U.S., 1831-1870; Sioux uprisings.

Fort Greenville, Treaty of

DATE: 1795

PLACE: Region between the Great Lakes and the Ohio River

TRIBES AFFECTED: Tribes of the Old Northwest

SIGNIFICANCE: The Treaty of Fort Greenville, combined with Jay's Treaty, served as an important benchmark in the tripartite Anglo-American-Indian struggle for control of the region between the Great Lakes and the Ohio River

During the twenty years following the end of the American Revolution in 1783, the question of which power—American Indians, the United States, or England—would control the region between the Ohio River and the Great Lakes constituted one of the greatest challenges confronting the new government of the United States.

Historical Background. According to the terms of the Treaty of Paris (signed on September 3, 1783), Great Britain agreed to remove its commercial and military presence from the region between the Great Lakes and the Ohio River, a region then called the Old Northwest. Notwithstanding this commitment, however, the British delayed in implementing this treaty provision. Several factors accounted for this delay, but one of the most significant was the conviction of many influential Britons that the region north of the Ohio was too strategic to surrender to the Americans. Instead, they believed that Britain should attempt to maintain at least an indirect presence in the area, thereby placing Great Britain in an advantageous position should the loosely confederated United States politically disintegrate. It was in this context that the British considered the possibility of sponsoring the creation of a British satellite or buffer state spanning the territory between the Ohio River and the Great Lakes and consisting of a confederation of Indian tribes. Thus, in the hope of promoting such an entity (there were also other reasons), London opted to maintain its commercial and military presence south of the Great Lakes. Indeed, not only did the British continue their presence at Michilimackinac, Detroit, Fort Niagara, Oswego, and other locations on American soil, but also, in 1786, British authorities issued a directive to hold or, if necessary, recapture these sites should the United States attempt to seize them.

Simultaneously, beginning in 1785, British agents actively attempted to promote the establishment of a pro-British confederation among the tribes. For their part, the Indians were extremely dissatisfied with Congress' policy toward the tribes and the northwest region generally. The Indians thought that the treaties of Forts Stanwix, McIntosh, and Finney, which had been concluded between several of the tribes and the United States government, were unfair to Indian interests. Indeed, many of the original signatory tribes had subsequently repudiated these treaties. Those tribes which had not been parties to these treaties naturally refused to abide by their terms. The treaties, however, provided the context for an infusion of American frontiersmen into the lands north of the Ohio River. The small military force which Congress had raised from the states was clearly insufficient either to prevent the frontiersmen from intruding into Indian territory or to overawe the tribes into abiding by the treaties—to say nothing about convincing them to make additional territorial concessions. Consequently, the British agents sent to promote the establishment of the Indian confederation north of the Ohio under British protection met with a receptive audience.

Finally, in 1788, the Chippewa, Delaware (Lenni Lenape), Iroquois, Miami, Ottawa, Potawatomi, Shawnee, and Wyandot (Huron) tribes formed a confederation and repudiated the treaties of Forts Stanwix, McIntosh, and Finney, agreed not to cede any additional land to the United States without the consent of the entire confederation, and demanded U.S. recognition of an Indian state between the Ohio River and the Great Lakes. This development, combined with the continued British military and commercial presence on U.S. territory south of the Great Lakes, provided London with a strong bargaining position as the United States and Great Britain opened regular diplomatic relations. Great Britain's new ambassador to the United States arrived in Philadelphia in October, 1791, with instructions from his government to agree to the evacuation of the British presence south of the Great Lakes only if the United States agreed to abide by the British interpretation of the terms of the Treaty of Paris and accepted the establishment of the Indian state, de facto under British protection, between the Ohio River and the Great Lakes.

The Washington Administration totally rejected the British stance as a violation of U.S. territorial integrity and sovereignty. With only a small military force, the administration attempted to negotiate a new treaty with the Indians. In the negotiations, held at Fort Harmer in January, 1789, the territorial governor, Arthur St. Clair, capitalized on dissension among the tribes and succeeded in concluding a treaty that, while providing some compensation to the Indians, reaffirmed the boundaries established under the terms of the treaties of Forts McIntosh and Finney. By the autumn of 1789, however,

war had erupted along the frontier as a result of continued Indian resentment of U.S. policy generally and the Treaty of Fort Harmer specifically, as well as the continued provocations from the American frontiersmen in Indian country.

Military Operations, 1790-1794. Yielding to pressure from the westerners, the Washington Administration dispatched a series of military expeditions into the wilderness north of the Ohio River. The first two of these expeditions, in October, 1790, and August-November, 1791, under the successive leadership of Josiah Harmer and Arthur St. Clair, designed to overawe the Indians and assert U.S. control over the region, yielded disastrous results. Harmer's October, 1790, expedition resulted only in the destruction of a few Miami villages along the Maumee River and the death of a small number of Indians at the cost of 75 regulars and 108 militiamen killed and another 31 wounded. Similarly, St. Clair's late summer and autumn 1791 expedition resulted in a second disastrous defeat with 623 soldiers killed and 258 wounded. Indeed, St. Clair's defeat was considered an especially significant setback in asserting U.S. sovereignty over the region north of the Ohio. Conversely, the Indians were euphoric with success and, encouraged by British expression of support for the Indian Confederation, intensified warfare against the American frontiersmen while demanding U.S. recognition of their confederation.

In the autumn of 1793, the new U.S. military commander in the Ohio Valley, Major General Anthony Wayne, initiated a new offensive against the Indians. Throughout the winter and spring of 1794, Wayne carefully launched a limited operation into Indian country. He methodically constructed a series of forts to serve both as a line of defense and as a base for a new offensive against the tribes. Moreover, his emphasis on training and his focus on troop discipline, combined with his perseverance during the harsh winter, impressed the Indians.

Meanwhile, throughout the winter, as Wayne consolidated his position, the British reinforced their policy in the Northwest. In February, 1794, the British governor in Canada told the Indians that when war between the United States and the tribes came, Britain would support the Indian attempt to regain full control over their lands. Simultaneously, the British began construction of a new post, Fort Miami, on U.S. soil along the Maumee River. The new fort was intended to solidify the British position in Indian country further as well as to provide an advance defense for the British presence at Detroit. These developments convinced the Indians that London would support them against General Wayne's army. Hence, confident of future success, the tribes assembled approximately two thousand warriors outside Fort Miami.

On June 30 and July 1, 1794, the Indians attacked Wayne's forces but were repulsed and withdrew into the wilderness along the Maumee River. On July 28, Wayne, now reinforced (bringing his total force to about thirty-five hundred men), advanced into Indian country. Although he reached the Maumee River on August 8, he delayed in assaulting the Indians until he had secured his lines of communications and established a forward base (Fort Defiance). Finally, on August 20, after a series of deceptive initiatives, Wayne surprised and defeated the Indians at the Battle of Fallen Timbers. Following the battle, the defeated Indians retreated to Fort Miami, whereupon the British refused to provide any refuge or assistance. Realizing that they had been betrayed by the British, the disillusioned Indians retired to the forest.

The Treaties. The dramatic change in the British policy toward the Indians reflected a larger transformation in British policy toward the United States. During the spring of 1794, the British government moved toward a rapprochement with the Americans; during the summer of 1794, negotiations were opened in Britain between the U.S. representative, John Jay, and British officials. It was in the context of this change in the complexion of Anglo-American relations that the British decided to abandon the Indians rather then precipitate a crisis on the Maumee River which could, in turn, lead to the collapse of Anglo-American negotiations before they had begun and possibly provoke a war between the two powers. Eventually, on November 19, 1794, the negotiators concluded a new treaty, Jay's Treaty, which resolved the outstanding Anglo-American disputes stemming from the 1783 Treaty of Paris. Under the terms of Jay's Treaty, London, among other things, agreed finally to evacuate the British posts on U.S. soil.

Deprived of British support, the demoralized Indians entered into new negotiations with General Wayne from a position of weakness. On August 3, 1795, Wayne and chiefs representing the Delaware, Miami, Shawnee, and Wyandot Indians and the United States delineated a demarcation separating Indian lands from those open to settlement. The line ran along the Cuyahoga River, across the portage to the Tuscarawas River, westward to Fort Recovery, and finally southward to the Ohio River across from its confluence with the Kentucky River. Hence, the U.S. government opened for settlement all of the future state of Ohio, except the north-central and northwest portions of the state, as well as opening the extreme southeastern corner of the present-day state of Indiana. In addition, the U.S. government reserved a series of specific sites within Indian country primarily for commercial and/or military purposes. Thus, as a result of the Treaty of Fort Greenville and Jay's Treaty, a new balance between the Americans and the Indians was struck along the northwestern frontier. Almost immediately, however, pressure began to mount which soon challenged the supposed permanence of the Fort Greenville Treaty line, and the stage was set for the next phase in American westward expansion at the expense of the Indians.

—*Howard M. Hensel*

See also Fallen Timbers, Battle of; Fort Stanwix, Treaty of; Indian-white relations—U.S., 1775-1830; Northwest Ordinance.

BIBLIOGRAPHY

Bemis, Samuel Flagg. *Jay's Treaty.* Rev. ed. New Haven, Conn.: Yale University Press, 1962.

Billington, Ray Allen. *Westward Expansion.* New York: Macmillan, 1949.

Kohn, Richard H. *Eagle and Sword.* New York: Free Press, 1975.

Philbrick, Francis S. *The Rise of the West, 1754-1830.* New York: Harper & Row, 1965.

Prucha, Francis Paul. *The Sword of the Republic.* New York: Macmillan, 1969.

Fort Laramie Treaty of 1851

DATE: September 1-20, 1851

PLACE: Fort Laramie, Wyoming

TRIBES AFFECTED: Arapaho, Cheyenne, Crow, Shoshone, Sioux

SIGNIFICANCE: In an unprecedented effort to promote peace during early western expansion, a treaty council was convened at Fort Laramie whereby ten thousand Indians of various nations gathered at one time to sign a peace treaty with representatives of the U.S. government

During the mid-nineteenth century the continuing rush of covered wagon immigrants across the Plains of the United States began to have an unsettling effect on American Indian tribes living there. Wild game was driven out and grasslands were being cropped close by the immigrants' cattle and horses. U.S. government policy provided some reimbursement to Indians for losses of game, grass, and land caused by the continuing influx of white settlers. In 1847, Thomas Fitzpatrick was appointed the first U.S. government representative to the various nomad tribes of the High Plains. Aware of the mounting losses and the potential for Indian uprisings against the settlers, Fitzpatrick campaigned long and hard for congressional funding to help alleviate growing tensions.

In February, 1851, Congress appropriated $100,000 for the purpose of holding a treaty council with the tribes of the High Plains. D. D. Mitchell, superintendent of Indian affairs at St. Louis, and Fitzpatrick were designated commissioners for the government. They selected Fort Laramie as the meeting location and September 1, 1851, as the meeting date. Word was sent throughout the Plains of the impending treaty council. By September 1, the first arrivals included the Sioux, Cheyennes, and Arapahos. Later arriving participants included the Snakes (Shoshones), and Crows.

Because of the vast number of participants—more than ten thousand Indians and 270 soldiers—it became apparent that the forage available for Indian and soldier ponies and horses was insufficient. The council grounds were therefore moved about 36 miles south, to Horse Creek.

On September 8, the treaty council officially began. The assembly was unprecedented. Each Indian nation approached the council with its own unique song or demonstration, dress, equipment, and mannerisms. Superintendent Mitchell proclaimed that all nations would smoke the pipe of peace together. The proposed treaty asked for unmolested passage for settlers over the roads leading to the West. It included rights for the government to build military posts for immigrants' protection. The treaty also defined the limits of territory for each tribe and asked for a lasting peace between the various nations. Each nation was to select a representative, a chief who would have control over and be responsible for his nation. In return, the government would provide each Indian nation an annuity of $50,000 for fifty years, the sum to be expended for goods, merchandise and provisions.

After much discussion and conferencing, the treaty was signed on September 17 by the U.S. commissioners and all the attending chiefs. Adding to the festivities, on September 20, a delayed caravan of wagons arrived at the treaty council with $50,000 worth of goods and merchandise. These goods were summarily distributed to all the nations represented, and feelings of good will permeated the gathering. To further the sense of lasting peace, Fitzpatrick later took a delegation of eleven chiefs with him to Washington, D.C., where they visited with President Millard Fillmore in the White House.   —*John L. Farbo*

See also Fort Laramie Treaty of 1868; Indian-white relations—U.S., 1831-1870.

BIBLIOGRAPHY

Hafen, LeRoy, and Francis Young. *Fort Laramie and the Pageant of the West, 1834-1890*. Glendale, Calif.: Arthur H. Clark, 1938.

Hedren, Paul L. *Fort Laramie in 1876*. Lincoln: University of Nebraska Press, 1988.

Ellis, Richard N. *The Western American Indian*. Lincoln: University of Nebraska Press, 1972.

Fort Laramie Treaty of 1868

DATE: April 29-November 5, 1868

PLACE: Laramie fork of the North Platte River in modern Wyoming

TRIBE AFFECTED: Sioux

SIGNIFICANCE: This treaty was meant to provide a lasting peace through mutual concessions involving territorial rights and peaceful behavior; the treaty ultimately failed

By mid-1800's the vast area of land claimed by the Sioux Nation was subjected to inexorable pressures from America's westward expansion, which accelerated after the end of the Civil War in 1865. Pioneers, settlers, farmers, gold prospectors, railroads, and the army all encroached on Sioux territory. Inevitably, armed conflict between whites and Indians occurred. Attempts to arrive at a peaceful solution and compromise, such as the treaties of 1851, 1865, and 1866, provided only short-lived respites.

On July 20, 1867, after vigorous debate over whether to subdue the Indians militarily and punish them or reach a peaceful accord with them, both houses of Congress approved a bill which authorized a government commission to make peace with the Plains tribes. The commission was directed by Congress to establish peace, remove if possible the causes of war, safeguard frontier settlements and the rights-of-way for the transcontinental railroads, and establish reservations for the Plains Indians with adequate arable land so they could become self-sufficient farmers.

Terms of the Treaty. The peace commission, headed by Commissioner of Indian Affairs Nathaniel Taylor, worked its way west, meeting various tribes of Sioux and listening to their demands. In April, 1868, the commission convened at Fort Laramie with a draft treaty that met many of these demands. Article 2 established the Great Sioux Reservation, which gave to the Sioux all of present-day South Dakota west of the Missouri River, including the sacred Black Hills, "for the absolute and undisturbed use and occupancy of the Sioux." Article 16 established the Powder River Country to the north and west of the Great Sioux Reservation as "unceded Indian territory," where whites were not permitted to go unless given permission by the Sioux. Article 11 gave the Sioux hunting rights along the Republican River and above the Platte River in Nebraska and Wyoming for "so long as the buffalo may range thereon in such numbers as to justify the chase." Other articles promised that all Sioux who resided within the Great Sioux Reservation would be provided with food for the next four years (until they learned to become farmers). The reservation was promised schools, mills, blacksmiths, doctors, and teachers and an agent to administer the various programs and maintain order. Additionally, no chief could unilaterally sign away treaty rights, as any sale of land had to be approved by three-fourths of all adult Sioux males.

In return, the United States asked for peace and asked that the Sioux make their permanent residence within the boundaries of the reservation. The Sioux relinquished the right to occupy any lands outside the reservation permanently, including the unceded territory. The Sioux were not to oppose the building of railroads on the plains and were not to attack settlers and their wagon trains or take white prisoners. Additionally, provisions would be distributed by the government not at the western end of the reservation, near traditional hunting grounds and where the Sioux customarily traded with whites, but at agencies established along the Missouri River in the eastern part of the reservation, in order to reorient Sioux life to these agencies.

Failure of the Treaty. Red Cloud was the final Sioux chief to sign the treaty, on November 5, 1868, only after the government abandoned its forts along the Bozeman Trail in Sioux territory. The treaty was rejected, however, by the influential and powerful Sioux chiefs Crazy Horse and Sitting Bull, who remained in the unceded territory and refused to live on the reservation.

In the end, this treaty proved no more effective in maintaining the peace and Sioux way of life than previous ones had been. Violations of Sioux territory by white emigrants and the army, the discovery of gold in the Black Hills (and the taking of the Black Hills by the government in 1877 without compensation), problems administering the reservation, and the refusal of Crazy Horse and Sitting Bull to live on the reservation despite government threats of war undermined any hope that the treaty's terms would be honored and observed. By 1880 the Sioux had been either killed or defeated and were confined to the reservation.   —*Laurence Miller*

See also Black Hills; Crazy Horse; Fort Laramie Treaty of 1851; Red Cloud; Sitting Bull.

The 1813 victory of Creek Red Sticks at Fort Mims, reported by whites as a massacre, soon brought white revenge against the Creeks. (Library of Congress)

Fort Mims, Battle of

Date: August 30, 1813

Place: Alabama

Tribe affected: Creek

Significance: Though William Weatherford's Creeks won a major victory at Fort Mims, reports of a massacre there led to a rapid mobilization of state and federal forces that eventually overwhelmed the Creeks

Tensions within the Creek (Muskogee) Nation and between some Creeks and European Americans reached the boiling point in 1813. Fighting was already raging between the Creek Red Sticks, who favored maintaining the traditional Creek values and lifestyle and who opposed further encroachments on Creek land, and friendly Creeks who were more receptive to the assimilationist policies being pushed by the United States government and whose leaders had adopted many aspects of American life, including plantation slavery.

On July 27, 1813, a force of territorial militia unsuccessfully attacked a band of Red Sticks at Burnt Corn Creek, a tributary of the Alabama River. The Creek War now began, though it was only the Red Stick faction of Creeks that waged war with the United States. Encouraged by their initial success, the Red Sticks determined to attack Fort Mims. William Weatherford (Red Eagle), a mixed-blood traditionalist of considerable ability, gathered a force of about 750 warriors and moved toward the fort.

Fort Mims was located near the Alabama River about 40 miles north of Mobile and was defended by a garrison of about 120 militia commanded by Major Daniel Beasley. The fort also became a haven for approximately 275 to 300 whites and friendly Creeks plus about a hundred slaves.

Doubting that the Red Sticks would attack a fort, Beasley was lax in maintaining security. On August 29, two slaves reported a large number of hostile Indians nearby. When scouts failed to find any, Beasley ordered the slaves whipped for giving a false alarm. The fort's defenses were unmanned the next day when Weatherford launched his attack at noon, catching the fort's garrison and inhabitants at lunch. Red

Sticks rushed into the fort's open entrance. Others began firing into the fort through rifle ports in the walls. The battle raged for several hours before the buildings inside the walls were set on fire. A few militiamen and others managed to escape into the surrounding woods. Most of the whites and friendly Creeks who survived the battle were killed, some by torture. Most of the slaves who survived the battle were taken away as prisoners.

Whites regarded the Fort Mims fight as a massacre, and the numbers reported to have been killed rapidly swelled. No fort of its size had ever been taken by Indians, and something akin to panic seized the southern frontier.

Fort Mims proved to be a costly victory for the Creeks, however; around a hundred Red Sticks were killed, and the reports of a massacre roused neighboring white settlers to seek revenge. Georgia and Tennessee mobilized their militias for service against the Creeks, and the federal government diverted some of its scarce military resources from the war it was fighting against England for service against the Creeks. The tide soon turned against the Red Sticks, and all Creeks suffered as a result of their eventual defeat.

See also Creek; Creek War; McQueen, Peter; Weatherford, William.

Fort Stanwix, Treaty of

DATE: October 12-23, 1784
PLACE: Stanwix, New York
TRIBES AFFECTED: Cayuga, Mohawk, Oneida, Onondaga, Seneca, Tuscarora
SIGNIFICANCE: The treaty ended formal hostilities between members of the Six Nations confederacy and the United States; in exchange for peace, the Iroquois ceded specific lands to the new nation

The American negotiators came to Fort Stanwix with specific demands for a treaty settlement. They wanted the Six Nations to return all "white and black" prisoners captured during the American Revolution. The Americans were also to reconfirm the Oneida and Tuscarora nations' right to the land the tribes then claimed. Both nations had allied themselves with the Americans during the war. American negotiators also demanded a new boundary settlement with the Six Nations. This new settlement would supersede an earlier agreement between the Iroquois and the British in 1768, an agreement also reached at Fort Stanwix. In exchange for the return of prisoners and the land cession, the Americans agreed to order specific goods for the Iroquois. These demands allowed American negotiators to present a unified front.

For their part, the Iroquois were anything but united when they met the American negotiators. They came to Stanwix under the assumption they had maintained sovereignty over their lands. Unfortunately for the Iroquois representatives, the Treaty of Paris (1783) had ignored Iroquois claims to their land. The American Revolution had also divided the people of the longhouse. The war produced separate factions supporting the British and Americans. Though the war had ended, these factions harbored grievances against each other for actions that occurred during the war. In addition to the factional fighting there was a generational struggle between warriors and sachems. As the Mohawk war chief Aaron Hill noted, the warriors had come to dominate Iroquois politics. Only one sachem, in fact, signed the Fort Stanwix Treaty. Nevertheless, sachems were still politically important in Iroquois politics, and they later voiced their displeasure with the conference. The Six Nations did not present a unified front to the Americans.

Delegates to the treaty signed the official treaty on October 22, 1784. The next day Pennsylvania delegates secured their own territorial cession from Iroquois representatives. Pennsylvania officials forced Iroquois representatives to cede much of the northwestern area of present-day Pennsylvania to the state. The Iroquois received $5,000 in continental scrip for the purchase. The Six Nations council refused to ratify the cessions made by their representatives. Council members offered a smaller land grant to pay for the presents their representatives had taken but refused the treaty in principle. American officials refused the sachem's counteroffer and acted as if the Stanwix agreement was a fait accompli. The treaty is a clear illustration of how Americans used European constructs to secure their territorial objectives. They coerced the Six Nations into the agreement even though some Americans raised constitutional questions regarding New York's actions.

Even before the Fort Stanwix agreement, a British representative had purchased a tract of land for the Mohawks in southern Ontario. The Stanwix treaty provided an impetus for other Iroquois to leave their traditional homeland and resettle in Canada. As for the Tuscaroras and Oneidas, New York officials never defended their lands from speculators. In 1785 New York officials began a process that eventually extinguished Oneida title to their lands in New York.

See also Indian-white relations—U.S., 1775-1830; Iroquois Confederacy.

Fort Wayne, Treaty of

DATE: September 30, 1809
PLACE: Indiana
TRIBES AFFECTED: Lenni Lenape, Miami, Potawatomi
SIGNIFICANCE: Negotiated by William Henry Harrison and repudiated by Tecumseh, the leader of a pan-Indian movement, this treaty precipitated a chain of events that culminated in the Battle of Tippecanoe

On September 30, 1809, Governor of the Indiana Territory William Henry Harrison met with leaders of the Delaware (Lenni Lenape), Miami, and Potawatomi in the fort built by General "Mad Anthony" Wayne. They signed the Treaty of Fort Wayne, which exchanged 2.5 million acres of Indian land southeast of the Wabash River for goods worth about $7,000 and an annuity of $1,750. Later that year, a separate treaty with the Kickapoo and Wea added half a million acres. While the exchange rate of two cents per acre was higher than usual for such treaties, it was still an unfair exchange. The treaty culminated a process begun in 1795 with the Treaty of Fort Green-ville, which had ceded a meager 6 square miles of Miami land to the United States government. In the ensuing period, more than fifteen treaties had been signed, most of them negotiated by Harrison, relinquishing control of Indian lands. While Harrison was able to maintain friendly relations with the major tribal leaders, the loss of native lands had started a counter-movement.

Led by the Shawnee prophet Tenskwatawa, a pan-Indian movement developed based on opposition to the cession of Indian lands and to the tribal leaders who had negotiated the treaties. Tenskwatawa, his brother Tecumseh, and their followers, refused to recognize the validity of the treaties on the ground that the land belonged to all Indian peoples so the chiefs had no authority to sign the lands away. To show defiance of the treaties, Tenskwatawa established new Indian towns at Greenville from 1806 to 1808 in defiance of the Treaty of Greenville. From 1808 to 1811, he established Prophetstown at Tippecanoe to show that his movement did not honor the Treaty of Fort Wayne.

As Harrison continued his plans to open the recently acquired lands, Tecumseh assumed the role of war chief and took command of the nativist movement. He warned Harrison to keep surveyors and settlers out of the territory. So threatening was his presence that for two years, virtually no settlement occurred. In order to break the stalemate, Harrison led troops on Prophetstown in 1811 while Tecumseh was farther south trying to gain allies among the Creek, Choctaw, and Cherokee. The ensuing Battle of Tippecanoe efficiently removed Tecumseh's followers from the immediate area. It was also, however, the opening action of a war that would last until 1815 and would see Tecumseh ally his forces with the British in the War of 1812.

See also Fort Greenville, Treaty of; Indian-white relations—U.S., 1775-1830; Land claims; Tecumseh's Rebellion; Tenskwatawa; Tippecanoe, Battle of.

Fox: Tribe

Culture area: Northeast
Language group: Algonquian
Primary location: Iowa, Kansas, Nebraska, Oklahoma
Population size: 4,517 ("Sac and Fox," 1990 U.S. Census)

The Fox are generally thought to have originated in southern Michigan. They belong to the Algonquian family and are closely related to the Sauk (or Sac), Kickapoo, and perhaps the Mascouten. The designation "Fox" was given them by French explorers; the group's name for themselves was Mesquakie (in other transliterations, "Meshwakihug" or "Meshwakie"). Another name for the tribe is Outagami, which they were called by other tribal groups.

Mesquakie means "the people of the red earth" and may signify either the soil coloring of their primal homeland or a mythological belief (that they were created from the "red earth"). When the French called them the Reynards (Foxes, or Red Foxes), they were probably confusing a clan designation for the name of the entire people. Since the eighteenth century, the Fox have been closely identified with the Sauk people; the two groups are often regarded as a single entity by the U.S. government (as in census figures). The Fox have a long and tragic history, an economic life combining features of both the Eastern Woodlands and the Great Plains, a rich social and cultural heritage, and a contemporary existence characterized by survival and revival.

Prehistory and French Contact. William T. Hagan has described the history of the Fox as "a case study of the results of the clash of two civilizations." The Fox encounter with Western culture—as embodied successively in the French, the British, and the Americans—was inherently tragic. Near genocide was followed by their displacement from their ancestral homeland in the Midwest. By the dawn of the twentieth century the Fox had declined in numbers (from about twenty-five hundred in 1650 to only 264 in 1867) and were scattered among a tribal farm in Iowa and governmental reservations in Kansas, Nebraska, and Oklahoma.

Oral tradition suggests that prior to the arrival of Europeans the Fox had been eased westward from their lands in central Michigan because of pressure from the Chippewas. Resettled in southern Wisconsin and northern Illinois, the Fox were primarily located along the Wolf River, with a territory extended from Lake Superior to the Chicago River and from Lake Superior to the Chicago River and from Lake Michigan to the Mississippi. A western Great Lakes nation, they were known as "People of the Calumet" because of the sacred pipes they employed in their tobacco ceremonies.

Initial contact with Europeans was made when French traders, explorers, and missionaries visited Fox country in the early seventeenth century. Confusion commenced immediately, the French misnaming the tribe *Renards*. Conflict quickly ensued from major disagreements between the French and the Fox, resulting in an unusual chapter in American colonial history, the Fox being one of the few North American tribes to oppose the French actively. Several reasons for this anomaly have been offered. The Fox disapproved of the French policy of facilitating the fur trade by repressing even legitimate disputes between tribes. When the French extended the fur trade to their enemies, the Dakota, they protested. To the Fox, French trade goods and prices were inferior to those preferred by the British through their former enemies, the Iroquois, who now sought an alliance. Tribes hostile to the Fox fanned the fires of disagreement. Open warfare was almost inevitable.

The French-Fox War (1712-1737) was occasioned by the Fox demand that French traders pay a transit toll when plying the Fox River in Wisconsin. This the French refused to do, retaliating by arming the traditional enemies of the Fox, the Dakota and the Ojibwa. For a quarter of a century furious combat transpired. A brave and warlike people, the Fox were nevertheless vastly outnumbered. Many scholars believe they continued to wage war even though they realized that the French had adopted a deliberate policy of genocide. The

U.S. STATES WITH THE LARGEST SAUK AND FOX POPULATIONS, 1990

Oklahoma	1,833
Iowa	986
California	312
Kansas	237
Missouri	104

Source: 1990 U.S. Census.

French hoped to annihilate their adversaries through war and disease. Some French officials even suggested the total elimination of the Fox people through their deportation to the West Indies to work as slaves in the sugar colonies. Peace was restored only in 1737 when the French, weary of war, offered a general pardon to the Fox. A permanent legacy of distrust had been generated.

From 1750 to the Reservation Era. Fox survival had been facilitated through a close alliance with the Sauk. By the mid-eighteenth century the Fox and the Sauk were regarded by outsiders as a single people. The "Dual Tribes" moved westward and southward, inhabiting lands along the Mississippi River by the 1760's, modifying their Eastern Woodlands lifestyle with elements of the Siouan culture of the Great Plains. The disappearance of French rule with the signing of the Treaty of Paris (1763) and the advent of British hegemony did little to dissipate Fox distrust of Europeans.

The actions of the American government confirmed the Fox's fears. Not signatories to the Treaty of Fort Greenville (1795), the Fox and the Sauk resisted white settlement; they were active in Little Turtle's War (1790-1794) and in Tecumseh's Rebellion (1809-1811). Certain leaders, however, argued for "peace and accommodation," accepting, in 1804, an annual annuity from the United States government in return for the legal cession of Fox lands east of the Mississippi. Many Fox were angered and fearful after the British failure in the War of 1812. Chief Black Hawk, a Sauk warrior, argued for armed resistance. In the last Indian War in the Old Northwest Territory, Black Hawk's War (1832-1833), the Sauk and their Fox allies were routed. Most of Black Hawk's army was killed, and Black Hawk himself was captured by the U.S. Army and exhibited as a "trophy" during a tour through the East. Removal of the Sauk and Fox to lands west of the Mississippi River was now a foregone conclusion.

As a consequence of the Treaty of Chicago (1833), the Fox and their allies were removed to Iowa. This arrangement was not satisfactory for a number of reasons. The steady press of American settlers was a threat. Illegal seizure of the Fox lead mines near Dubuque, which had provided a revenue in excess of $4,000 annually from sales to traders, provoked outrage. There was a steady erosion of the traditional Fox way of life. By 1842 the Fox and the Sauk had migrated to Kansas. Reservation life led to serious disputes between the Fox and the Sauk. Disagreements centered on the distribution of annuity payments, fears of removal to Oklahoma, apparent government favoritism toward the Sauk, the inability to make a good living on the reservation (poor land, limited hunting opportunities), and the gradual loss of a separate Fox identity. The spread of epidemic disease was the "last straw." By the 1850's many of the Fox wanted to return to Iowa. In 1856 an act of the Iowa state legislature legalized the residence of the Fox within that jurisdiction. The following year five members of the tribal council purchased land in Tama County, the original 80 acres eventually becoming 3,000. As a nonreservation community, the Iowa Fox settlement avoided both assimilation and federal restrictions. The settlement survived through the twentieth century. By the 1990's the Fox people had been divided three ways: Some of them lived on the tribally owned lands in Iowa, some on reservations in Kansas and Nebraska, and the remainder in Oklahoma with the Sauk.

Economic Life. The Fox were unique among Algonquian peoples in that they were economically at home in both the Great Lakes and the Great Plains regions. In the course of their long history, the Fox adapted well to both areas.

Originally, the Fox inhabited the Great Lakes region, living in Michigan and later in southern Wisconsin and northern Illinois. The opportunities afforded by the Eastern Woodlands were fully exploited. Though the climate was harsh, the Fox prospered. Fishing was practiced; hunting was profitable. The marshlands provided a sky filled with waterfowl. On the eastern Plains were buffalo. In the primeval forests a wide variety of game flourished, including deer and moose, both of which were used for hides and meat. Trapping for furs began in earnest after contact with the Europeans. Food gathering supplied the Fox diet with nuts, berries, honey, tubers, herbs, fruits, and especially the "wild rice" (named "wild oats" by Americans) so common in the Midwest wetlands. Food producing occurred along rivers near Fox villages, the women raising corn, beans, squash, pumpkins, and melons. Tobacco was cultivated for ceremonial purposes. The forests of beech, birch, conifers, elms, oaks, and chestnuts offered materials for canoes, snowshoes, containers, writing materials, daily implements, and house construction. Maple sugar was harvested in winter. Surface metals (and copper) were mined for trading purposes.

Later in their history the Fox adjusted well to the economic opportunities of the Great Plains. This shift in lifestyle was stimulated by a variety of factors. Pressure from the Chippewas forced the Fox to flee Michigan for Wisconsin and Illinois. Contact with the Siouan peoples familiarized them with the possibilities of the prairie habitat. The arrival of Europeans supplied them with horses, firearms, and markets. Perhaps the most striking change was the adoption of the Great Buffalo Hunt. While the Fox continued their earlier seasonal economic cycle of food gathering and food producing, they significantly increased their dependance on the hunt.

A virtual exodus took place after the planting of crops in April and May, as Fox hunters went west of the Iowa-Missouri watershed seeking buffalo. During the long, dry summer they searched for bison herds. Prior to the extensive use of rifles, the hunters would surround the herd, start a grassfire, panic the buffalo, have a skilled bowman shoot the lead animal, and then start the "kill." Robert Cavalier Sieur de La Salle, the seventeenth century French explorer, reported that it was not unusual for two hundred buffalo to be taken in a single day. Women accompanying the hunters would strip, clean, pack, and dry the meat while tanning the hides. By August and the advent of harvest time, the hunters would return to their permanent villages with meat for the winter and hides to trade for ammunition. A smaller winter hunt was not unknown. By 1806 the Fox were reckoned the best hunters in the Mississippi and Missouri valleys, and American pioneer Meriwether Lewis estimated the value of their annual fur sales to be $10,000. By then the Fox had become part of the American economy, relying on traders for credit and a wide variety of consumer items (knives, blankets, arms, ammunition, tobacco, and various luxuries).

The end of the traditional Fox economy was evident by the start of the nineteenth century. In 1804 chiefs accepted an annual annuity of $400 from the United States government in exchange for surrender of the ancestral lands east of the Mississippi. Large numbers of whites were settling Fox territories. By 1820 the golden age of the Great Buffalo Hunt was over. Forced removal to Iowa in the 1830's doomed the traditional Fox way of life.

Social, Political, and Religious Life. The Fox have a rich and diverse heritage involving complex familial, tribal, and religious organizations. The fundamental social unit of Fox society was the family. Sometimes polygamous, often monogamous, the immediate family was composed of husband and wife (in plural marriages the additional wives were often sisters) and children. Courtship occurred around age twenty, with marriage resting on the consent of the bride (and her parents) to the suitor's proposal. Remarriage following death or divorce was permitted, although marital fidelity was strictly enforced. Initially the bride and groom would reside in the home of her parents, but following the birth of the first child (in the "birthing house") the new family would move to its own dwelling. Often there was a summer lodge (for farming and hunting) and a more permanent winter home (aligned along an east-west axis), conical in appearance, built around a central hearth. Families normally varied in size from five to more than thirty members.

Families, in turn, were organized into exogamous patrilineal clans. Anthropologists have identified eight (some claim fourteen) clans including Bear, Wolf, Swan, Partridge, Thunder, Elk, Black Bear, and Fox (from which the French apparently misnamed the tribe). The clan was a cohesive group, certain honors being hereditary within each extended family (as the office of peace chief). An institution called the moiety, also practiced among other Native American groups, helped lessen clan rivalries. Across kinship lines the Fox tribe was divided into two moieties (or societies), the White and the Black. Created by random division, these associations were utilized for games, ceremonies, and even warfare. This arrangement provided fellowship and friendship without distinction as to bloodline or office and was a solidifying force in tribal life.

The life of the individual Fox was regulated and supported by the family, the clan, the moiety, and the entire tribe. Children were prized highly and were reared with considerable affection and attention; corporal punishment was rare. By the age of six or seven, boys were imitating the hunting ways of the males and girls were assisting in farming and homemaking with the women. Puberty was a major event for both genders. Following her initial menstruation, the girl was sent to a separate lodge for ten days to reflect on her new status as a young woman. Boys at puberty were to experience the "vision," preceded by fasting and followed by a heroic deed. By the age of nineteen or twenty, both boys and girls were expected to be integrated fully into the adult life of the tribe.

The tribe had various types of leaders. One was the office of peace chief (often hereditary within the Bear clan), a male who was respected as an administrator, president at the tribal council, and person of wisdom, experience, and sound judgment. Another was the office of war chief (usually elected from warriors who had proved themselves repeatedly in combat), who, in times of danger, had near-dictatorial power and who was entrusted with leading the tribe to victory. A third office was ceremonial chief or shaman, a position depending on both heredity and demonstrated charismatic gifts. Though the shaman had no exclusive monopoly on spiritual functions, he was a major contact person with the supernatural. Temporary raiding chiefs were selected, men who, following fasting and a vision, would gather a band of warriors for a specific mission. Following the venture, the band dissolved. Lesser chiefs sat with the paramount chiefs in the tribal council, which decided matters of war and peace, the selection of hunting grounds, and diplomatic relations with other tribes and with Europeans.

The religious life of the Fox centered on a reverence for nature and its powers. The universe was divided into two portions: the Powers of the Sky (or the Upper Region, ruled by the Great Manitou) and the Powers of the Earth (the Lower Region, ruled by lesser spirits). The Lower Region was organized along the four points of the compass, the east (ruled by the sun), the north (ruled by the Creator), the west (the land of departed spirits), and the south (the region of the god of thunder). A powerful animism invested the earth, the sky, the waters, the forests, and all creatures with intelligent souls which could either help or hinder human activity. The Midewi-win, or Grand Medicine Society, was a secret group who believed themselves able to enlist the support of the spirit world for the tribe.

Religious rituals occurred in harmony with the change of seasons (as the Green Corn Feast at the onset of the harvest) and the various stages of life, as puberty and death. Funeral customs were intended to guarantee the happiness of the deceased person's spirit, burial being either in the earth (seated, or even seated on top of a dead foe, for a warrior) or on a scaffold. Gifts were buried; sometimes sacrificial animals (such as a dog) were also buried to serve as companions in the afterlife.

Contemporary Life. The United States Census of 1990 reported 4,517 Sauk and Fox Indians. Since the nineteenth century, the Fox have been divided into three groups: Some live in reservations in the Plains states (130 lived in Kansas and Nebraska in the 1970's), some live in Oklahoma (1,000 lived on the Oklahoma reservation in the 1970's), and the remainder live in Iowa. Since the 1820's there has been, for most Fox, little marked separation from the Sauk people. Those in Iowa have the most clear-cut identity. The wisdom of Fox tribal elders was demonstrated in the 1850's when they purchased 80 (later 3,000) acres near Tama, Iowa. They won recognition by the state legislature as to the legitimacy of their residence, thus freeing themselves from the restrictions accompanying reservation life. They prospered in Iowa, and by the end of World War II there were 653 Fox living on the tribal farms. Some commuted to urban jobs, while others managed land rentals (to white farms). In Iowa, family, clan, and tribal life continues, with nearly all Fox speaking the ancestral language (one-third speak it exclusively, the rest being bilingual). While some have accepted Christianity, the majority belong to medicine societies and practice the ancestral faith (with some adhering to the Native American Church). Though only a remnant of the once proud Fox, or Mesquakie, Nation, the Iowa tribal community demonstrates the power of the people to survive and gives evidence of a revived hope for the twenty-first century.

—*C. George Fry*

See also Algonquian language family; Black Hawk; Black Hawk War; Sauk; Tecumseh's Rebellion.

BIBLIOGRAPHY

Callendar, Charles. "Fox." In *Northeast*, edited by Bruce G. Trigger. Vol. 15 in *Handbook of North American Indians*, edited by William Sturtevant. Washington, D.C.: Smithsonian Institution Press, 1978. A definitive eleven-page essay, complete with illustrations and notes, which surveys the history, beliefs, and social life of the Fox.

Gearing, Frederick O. *The Face of the Fox*. Chicago: Aldine, 1970. A concise (158-page) volume that combines a readable text with reliable information. A good first book on the Fox.

Hagan, William T. *The Sac and Fox Indians*. Norman: University of Oklahoma Press, 1958. This 290-page study is a meticulous survey of Fox history since 1804.

Josephy, Alvin M., Jr. *The Indian Heritage of America*. New York: Alfred A. Knopf, 1968. Provides information on the Fox and their allies and adversaries.

Lambert, Joseph I. "The Black Hawk War: A Military Analysis." *Journal of the Illinois Historical Society* 32 (December, 1939): 442-473. A stunning piece of original research reviewing tactics and strategy employed in the last Indian War east of the Mississippi River.

McTaggart, Fred. *Wolf That I Am: In Search of the Red Earth People*. Boston: Houghton Mifflin, 1976. In brief compass (195 pages), with an excellent bibliography, this sympathetic study of the Fox proves to be reliable and enjoyable reading.

Owen, Mary Alicia. *Folklore of the Musquakie Indians of North America*. London: D. Nutt, 1904. Though dated, this short survey (147 pages), with revealing illustrations, has value as a turn-of-the-century view of the Fox.

Stout, David Bond, Erminie Wheeler-Voegelin, and Emily J. Blasingham. *Indians of Eastern Missouri, Western Illinois, and Southern Wisconsin, from the Proto-Historic Period to 1804*. New York: Garland, 1974. A vintage study of the Fox and their neighbors from the Stone Age to the era of Lewis and Clark in 319 pages. Plates, maps.

Tax, Sol. "The Social Organization of the Fox Indians." In *Social Anthropology of North American Tribes*, edited by Fred Eggan. Chicago: University of Chicago Press, 1937. A Depression-era analysis of Fox life showing the conflict of traditional and modern ways. Though dated, it still has merit.

United States. Indian Claims Commission. *An Anthropological Report on the Sac, Fox, and Iowa Indians*. 3 vols. New York: Garland, 1974. A classic study in 381 pages (with maps) based on field observations of Fox folkways.

Francis, Josiah (?—c. 1818, St. Marks River, Fla.): Leader, shaman

ALSO KNOWN AS: Francis the Prophet, Hayo, Hillis, Hillishago

TRIBAL AFFILIATION: Creek, Seminole

SIGNIFICANCE: Josiah Francis traveled the Mississippi Valley with Tecumseh, seeking allies for Tecumseh's rebellion

Although Francis' ancestry was an unknown mix of Indian and white, his affiliation was with the Red Stick Creeks and with the Seminoles. Francis' daughter was Milly Francis, best known for saving the life of a Georgia militiaman, George McKinnon (also known as Duncan McKrimm), whom Francis was about to order executed during the First Seminole War.

When Tecumseh attempted to recruit the Creeks for his pan-Indian alliance, most of the Creek White Sticks from the lower Creek villages were unresponsive. The traditional Creek warriors, the Red Sticks, including Francis, joined Tecumseh. In 1811, Francis traveled with Tecumseh throughout the Mississippi Valley, recruiting tribes for the new confederacy.

In the Creek War of 1813-1814, Francis fought against General Andrew Jackson, who referred to him as the "prophet." In 1814, Jackson forced the defeated Creeks to sign the Treaty of Fort Jackson, by which the Creeks lost twenty-three million acres of their land. Afterward, many Creeks, including Francis, settled among the Florida Seminoles. In 1815, Francis journeyed to England to solicit aid for Indians against the Americans. He participated in the First Seminole War in 1817-1818 and was captured in 1818, after being lured onto a gunboat in the St. Marks River. There Jackson ordered his execution.

See also Creek War; Foreman, Stephen; Horseshoe Bend, Treaty of; Seminole Wars; Tecumseh.

Francis, Milly Hayo (c. 1802, Fla.—c. 1848, near present-day Muskogee, Okla.): Peacemaker

TRIBAL AFFILIATION: Creek, Seminole
SIGNIFICANCE: In an incident reminiscent of the legend of Pocahontas and John Smith, Milly Francis is known for having intervened to save the life of a white soldier

Milly Francis was the daughter of the Seminole prophet Josiah Francis, who traveled throughout the Mississippi Valley seeking allies for Tecumseh's pantribal rebellion. According to legend, Josiah Francis, during the First Seminole War (1817), ordered the death of Georgia militiaman George McKinnon. After he was tied to a stake in preparation for burning, Milly Francis intervened, begging for McKinnon's release, claiming she would also die if he burned. After Josiah Francis relented, McKinnon lived with the tribe. He was eventually sold to the Spanish as a slave.

When a band of starving women and children, including Milly Francis, appeared at an army post after Josiah Francis' death, newly escaped McKinnon spared her life. Legend holds he offered her marriage, which she refused, believing he only asked out of a sense of obligation.

After relocating to Indian Territory, in 1844 Milly Francis was granted a pension by the U.S. government in gratitude for her actions during the First Seminole War. She died fours years later without having received any of the funds.

See also Francis, Josiah; Seminole Wars.

Fremont: Prehistoric tradition

DATE: 650-1250
LOCATION: Western Colorado plateau, eastern Great Basin
CULTURE AFFECTED: Paleo-Indian

The Fremont culture, named for the Fremont River in south central Utah, was first defined in 1931 by Harvard University anthropologist Noel Morss. Geographically, Fremont remains extend from the eastern Great Basin to the western Colorado Plateau. Although material traces go back much further, archaeologists estimate the main Fremont period to have been between 650 and 1250 C.E.

Some theories have tied the visibly less-developed Fremont to the better-known Anasazi because the last stages of both cultures, which were roughly contemporary, seem to have involved spatial retreats—the Anasazi into the Pueblo area, and the Fremont into the Southern Paiute, Ute, and Shoshone areas of the eastern Great Basin. Similarities in geometric designs on pottery are noted among remains left by both groups in both regions. Other archaeological evidence, however, suggests such major differences (beyond the obviously more substantial buildings and ceremonial sites left by the Anasazi) that Morss's separate classification has remained largely unchallenged.

A main characteristic of Fremont sites is that, although some general cultural links show similarities between groups, local diversites are notable. Similarities have been traced through a unique single-rod-and-bundle method of basket-making. Another distinctly Fremont artifact is the moccasin made from a single piece of deer or mountain sheep hocks. Although local variations are found in construction methods associated with both these artifacts, one area of Fremont archaeology shows a nearly universal practice: the use of a characteristic gray clay to fashion coil pottery forms. Although objects made by Fremont groups, and the designs used to decorate them, are not essentially different from those found in neighboring cultures, the material used is unique. Within the extensive Fremont zone, distinctions are made on the basis of proportions of granular rock added to the gray clay, or degrees of temper in the final baking. Subgroups have been labeled "Snake Valley Gray," "Sevier Gray," "Emery Gray," "Uinta Gray," and "Great Salt Lake Gray."

In terms of decorative style, Fremont artists used a unique trapezoidal shape reproduced in large numbers in small clay figurines with characteristic hair "bobs" and ornate necklaces. The same stylized human shape appears in the famous canyon petroglyphs at various sites in the Fremont Zone, particularly in the Colorado Plateau region.

Because some important differences exist between remains left by groupings on the Colorado Plateau and those inhabiting the Great Basin, there has been a tendency to refer to two general zones of Fremont archaeology: the Fremont proper and the Sevier-Fremont. Two key examples help explain this division. Stone not being as available in the Great Basin zone, most building remains (although nearly identical in form and function) were made of mud bricks. Trapezoidal baked clay and small stone-etched objects are far more common in the Sevier-Fremont zone, whereas petroglyphs predominate in the eastern Fremont.

See also Anasazi; Archaic; Prehistory—Great Basin; Prehistory—Plateau.

French and Indian Wars

DATE: 1689-1763
PLACE: Eastern United States, Canada
TRIBES AFFECTED: Tribes of the Northeast
SIGNIFICANCE: The defeat of the French meant that the trans-Appalachian West would be open to English settlement, resulting in the removal of Native Americans to lands west of the Mississippi within sixty years

The French and Indian Wars (also called the Colonial Wars and the Great War for Empire) were the American expression of a global struggle between Britain and France for dynastic supremacy, territorial expansion, and commercial concessions. Sometimes called the "Second Hundred Years' War," this contest was not finally resolved until the defeat of Napoleon at Waterloo (1815). These wars were waged on five continents and the seven seas, and their North American aspects immediately affected Native Americans.

The French and Indian Wars were composed of three preliminary phases and one final episode. (The fourth and final war, lasting from 1754 to 1763, is sometimes referred to as the "French and Indian War.") King William's War (or the War of the League of Augsburg, 1689-1697) commenced on Hudson Bay and spread to northern New England and westward along the Hudson Valley. Competition for the fur trade, territory, and the loyalty of Indian tribes fueled this furious war, which concluded with the Treaty of Ryswick (1697). Queen Anne's War (or the War of the Spanish Succession, 1702-1713) began with Britain's effort to prevent Bourbon rule in Spain as well as in France. Unresolved issues ignited warfare in North America from the Maritime Provinces and Newfoundland through New England to the Carolinas. In the Treaty of Utrecht (1713), France surrendered Newfoundland, Acadia, and the Hudson Bay to Britain, though ill-defined boundaries would occasion the next war. King George's War (or the War of the Austrian Succession, 1740-1748) began in central Europe with the invasion of Austrian Silesia by Prussia. Not at all decisive in North America, it ended with the Treaty of Aix-la-Chapelle (1748); conditions in the Colonies were essentially restored to their prewar state.

The fourth and final French and Indian War (in Europe, the Seven Years' War, 1756-1763; in America, the Nine Years' War, starting two years earlier than elsewhere) was occasioned not only by the legacy of violence between the tribes allied with the French and the British but also by European conflict for sovereignty, trade, and land in the North American interior. By 1749 the governor general of New France had forbidden English settlement in the Ohio Valley. A Virginia force under Colonel George Washington attempted, unsuccessfully, to secure the forks of the Ohio River in the spring of 1754. The initial four years of this war were inconclusive until, by 1757, the British rallied under the leadership of Prime Minister William Pitt and capitalized on their superior maritime, military, and mercantile power. The climax came on September 13, 1759, with the fall of Quebec. In the Treaty of Paris (1763), France relinquished all her political, economic, military, and territorial power in North America.

The significance for Native Americans was beyond calculation. With the defeat of France, many tribes lost a powerful defender. To placate the Indians, the British appointed Sir William Johnson as commissioner for the north (1755), in the Treaty of Easton (1758) renounced settlement west of the Appalachians, and, on June 8, 1763, proposed an "Appalachian Divide" between the settlers and the Indians, closing the West to European occupation. Former French possessions were organized as Quebec, East Florida and West Florida, with the trans-Appalachian West to be "Indian Country" under the crown's protection. These actions alienated colonials from their homeland, helping to prepare the way for the American Revolution.

See also Indian-white relations—English colonial; Indian-white relations—French colonial; Iroquois Confederacy.

Friends of the Indian organizations

DATE: 1879-1900's

TRIBES AFFECTED: Pantribal

SIGNIFICANCE: A variety of humanitarian Christian associations sought to reform federal Indian policy by supporting legislation aimed at abolishing "Indianness" and substituting American ideals of individualism, ownership, and Christianity

Friends of the Indian organizations were formed in the last two decades of nineteenth century by mainly eastern Christian humanitarians who were determined to influence federal Indian policy. Members of these organizations were convinced of the superiority of Christian civilization and were determined to do away with Indianness and tribal traditions; their goal was to turn individual Indians into patriotic American citizens.

The friends of the Indian groups supported allotment in order to break up tribal land ownership and force individual ownership; they sought to end tribal jurisdiction and bring Indians as individual citizens before the law. They supported vocational education for Indian children, particularly boarding schools, and they were generally intolerant of Indian culture or spiritual expression and worked to outlaw Sun Dances, vision questing, giveaways, plural marriages, and so on. These well-intentioned Christian men and women sought to influence and direct Indian policy by engaging in intense lobbying efforts with federal officials and by educating the general public through newsletters, pamphlets, and speakers. These reformers and their supporters were convinced of the righteousness of their cause and greatly affected federal Indian policy well into the twentieth century.

Beginning in 1883 these groups came together annually for the Lake Mohonk Conference of the Friends of the Indian in New Paltz, New York, to coordinate their efforts. General harmony and a good working relationship existed among the various groups because they shared a common religious outlook that they were doing God's will by guiding Indians from savagery to civilization. The most significant and far-reaching areas affected by these organizations were the federal Indian education system and the General Allotment Act (Dawes Act) of 1887. One of the most prominent groups, the Indian Rights Association, continues to exist; however, it now supports tribalism and tribal self-determination.

See also General Allotment Act; Indian Citizenship Act; Indian Rights Association; Indian-white relations—U.S., 1871-1933.

Gabrielino: Tribe

CULTURE AREA: California
LANGUAGE GROUP: Shoshonean
PRIMARY LOCATION: Northern San Diego County, southern Orange County
POPULATION SIZE: 634 (1990 U.S. Census)

The Gabrielinos are among the small California tribal groupings that once occupied the land where modern-day Los Angeles is located. The name "Gabrielino" derives from the fact that the people once lived around the San Gabriel Mission, one of the early Catholic missionary stations founded in the Southern California region. (This is also the case with the name "Fernandeño" for those peoples once surrounding the San Fernando Mission in the present San Fernando Valley, just northwest of urban Los Angeles.) The Gabrielinos are thus closely affiliated with the Fernandeños as part of the Shoshonean branch of the Uto-Aztecan linguistic division.

Anthropologist Alfred Kroeber's estimate for the Gabrielino population in 1770 was approximately five thousand, including the Fernandeños as well. California Indians generally are not to be understood as "tribes" but rather as small "tribal groups" of a hundred persons at most (groups were usually not permanent) that surrounded a centrally recognized permanent village. The Gabrielinos shared many common cultural traits with other village communities up and down the California coast, including a style of basket weaving, simple agriculture, and architecture. As with other Southern Californian natives in this near-tropical climate, the Gabrielinos typically dressed very lightly, if at all.

The Gabrielinos are among the few native peoples of the Los Angeles region. The Gabrielinos are divided in modern California along extended family lines. Unlike many other California groups, who have accepted the usefulness of the nontraditional office of "chief," the Gabrielinos recognize no central leader. Rival factions among the Gabrielinos have created problems in settling cultural questions and in being able to deal with issues of heritage, such as finding archaeological sites and approving construction projects. A representative of one family or faction may approve a project, thereby creating a great protest from those who do not recognize the authority of the Gabrielinos working on the project. There are even conflicts over the number of Gabrielinos because of the same factionalism and an inability to agree on who is and is not Gabrielino. Today, most Gabrielinos live in the southern Orange County and northern San Diego County areas. There is no Gabrielino reservation.

See also California; Fernandeño; Indian-white relations—Spanish colonial.

BIBLIOGRAPHY

Kroeber, Alfred. "The Indians of California." In *The North American Indians: A Sourcebook*, edited by Roger Owen, James Deetz, and Anthony Fisher. New York: Macmillan, 1967.

Miller, Bruce W. *The Gabrielino*. Los Osos, Calif.: Sand River Press, 1991.

Gadsden Purchase

DATE: December 30, 1853; ratified June 29, 1854
PLACE: Southern Arizona, New Mexico
TRIBES AFFECTED: Chiricahua Apache, Tohono O'odham
SIGNIFICANCE: The Gadsden Purchase resolved boundary disputes between the United States and Mexico resulting from the Mexican War but ignored consultation with affected Indians

James Gadsden was a South Carolina railroad promoter turned diplomat. On behalf of President James Buchanan, he negotiated America's purchase of 45,535 square miles of territory from Mexico for the payment of fifteen million dollars (reduced later to ten million). A block of land nearly the size of New York State, the Gadsden Purchase lies south of the Gila River, forming part of present-day Arizona and New Mexico. The treaty embodying the purchase was signed on December 30, 1853, and ratified on June 29, 1854, settling boundary questions between the United States and Mexico left unresolved by the Treaty of Guadalupe Hidalgo at the end of the Mexican War in 1848.

The purchase was prompted by American politicians eager to build a transcontinental railroad through the Southwest. Neither the Mexican nor American governments consulted with the Tohono O'odhams (Papagos) and Chiricahua Apaches who lived in the area, and these Indians subsequently ignored boundaries that were not theirs.

See also Apache; Guadalupe Hidalgo, Treaty of; Tohono O'odham.

Gall (c. 1840, near Moreau River in present-day S.Dak.— Dec. 5, 1894, Oak Creek, S.Dak.): Warrior

ALSO KNOWN AS: Pizi, Man Who Goes in the Middle, Red Walker
TRIBAL AFFILIATION: Hunkpapa Lakota (Sioux)
SIGNIFICANCE: Gall was a noted warrior and military tactician in the wars for the Bozeman Trail and the Black Hills; he was the principal Indian military strategist at the Little Bighorn

Gall was born about 1840 along the Moreau River in Dakota Territory. His father died when Gall was a young boy, and he was reared by his widowed mother and relatives. Sitting Bull took him as a younger brother, and for many years these two were close allies. He was most commonly called Pizi. According to family legend, as a child he tried to eat the gall of an animal. He was also known as Red Walker because as a child his father once dressed him entirely in vermillion clothing. Gall was also known as Man Who Goes in the Middle, and although the origin of this name is unclear, it probably refers to a battle exploit.

Gall rose to prominence in the 1860's and 1870's as a noted leader in the wars for the Bozeman Trail and the Black Hills. These battles were fought in present-day Montana, Wyoming, and South Dakota. He allied closely with Sitting Bull and was committed to resisting government attempts to confine the Lakota people to the Great Sioux Reservation after the 1868 Treaty of Fort Laramie.

Gall, a leader at the Battle of the Little Bighorn, later advocated acceptance of the reservation system. (National Archives)

Gall's greatest fame came from his participation in the Battle of the Little Bighorn on June 25, 1876. Major Marcus Reno's command was the first to approach the Indian village, and they attacked the Hunkpapa camp. Gall's two wives and three children were killed in this foray, and Gall later said, "It made my heart bad." Gall led the counterattack that drove Reno from the village, and then he joined Crazy Horse in repelling Colonel George Armstrong Custer's forces. Gall gained great notoriety in the American press for his military prowess at the Battle of the Little Bighorn, and a newspaper labeled him "the worst Indian living."

After Indian defeats following the Battle of the Little Bighorn, Gall accompanied Sitting Bull to Canada in 1877. Hungry and destitute, he reluctantly returned to the United States in 1881 with about three hundred people and surrendered at Poplar Agency in present-day eastern Montana. Gall was relocated to the Standing Rock Agency in North Dakota. There he was befriended by Indian agent James McLaughlin, who urged him to denounce Sitting Bull for his uncompromising attitude toward the reservation system. The early reservation period was difficult for the Lakota people, and Gall believed that it was best to compromise with the government officials; Sitting Bull did not. Gall became a favorite of Agent McLaughlin's, and in 1889 was appointed a judge of the court of Indian Offenses and a spokesman in the negotiations that brought about the breakup of the Great Sioux Reservation.

During his last years, Gall was an envoy to Washington, D.C., on behalf of his band. He became a strong proponent of education, and he enjoyed considerable prestige among whites. He took no part in the Ghost Dance religion when it spread to Standing Rock; some years before he had become a staunch Episcopalian. Gall's relationship with the United States government was not well received by other Indians, especially those who fought with him years earlier. This rejection was clear when Kicking Bear did a pictographic drawing of the Battle of the Little Bighorn in 1898 and left a blank space where Gall should have been. Gall died at Oak Creek, South Dakota, on December 5, 1894.

See also Black Hills; Bozeman Trail wars; Fort Laramie Treaty of 1868; Little Bighorn, Battle of the; Sitting Bull.

Gambling

TRIBES AFFECTED: Pantribal

SIGNIFICANCE: Gambling facilities have brought needed income to some native peoples, but some tribe members protest its presence on reservations

During the late twentieth century, commercial gambling became a major source of income on Indian reservations across the United States. While many Native American cultures practiced forms of gambling as a form of sport (such as the Iroquois peachstone game), there was no prior large-scale experience with gambling as a commercial enterprise. The arrival of gaming has brought dividends to some native peoples, but it has brought controversy culminating in firefights and death to others.

Development of Gambling. The history of reservation gambling begins in 1979, when the Seminoles became the first Indian tribe to enter the bingo industry. By early 1985, seventy-five to eighty of the federally recognized Indian tribes in the United States were conducting some sort of organized game of chance. By the fall of 1988, the Congressional Research Service estimated that more than one hundred Indian tribes participated in some form of gambling, which grossed about $255 million a year. In October of 1988, Congress passed the Indian Gaming Regulatory Act, which officially

MINNESOTA TRIBAL GAMBLING REVENUES, 1991	
Revenue Source	*Amount*
Video	$99.3 million
Blackjack	$28.5 million
Bingo and pull-tabs	$11.0 million
Concessions and other sources	$4.2 million
Total	$143.0 million

Source: U.S. Congress, *Implementation of the Indian Gaming Regulatory Act.* Washington, D.C.: U.S. Government Printing Office, 1992.

Note: Includes revenue generated by Sioux (Bois Forte, Leech Lake, Lower, Prairie Island, and Shakopee) and Mille Lacs Chippewa.

allowed legalized gambling on reservations. The act also established the National Indian Gaming Commission to oversee gaming activities. By 1991, 150 native reservations recognized by non-Indian governmental bodies had some form of gambling. According to the U.S. Department of the Interior, gross revenue from such operations passed $1 billion that year.

Individual prizes in some reservation bingo games were reported to be as high as $100,000, while bingo stakes in surrounding areas under state jurisdiction were sometimes limited to one hundred dollars. Marion Blank Horn, principal deputy solicitor of the Department of the Interior, described the fertile ground gambling enterprises had found in Indian country:

> The reasons for growth in gambling on Indian land are readily apparent. The Indian tribal governments see an opportunity for income that can make a substantial improvement in the tribe's [economic] conditions. The lack of any state regulation results in a competitive advantage over gambling regulated by the states. These advantages include no state-imposed limits on the size of pots or prizes, no restrictions by the states on days or hours of operations, no costs for licenses or compliance with state requirements, and no state taxes on gambling operations.

By the early 1990's, gambling had provided a small galaxy of material benefits for some formerly impoverished native peoples. A half-hour's drive from Minnesota's Twin Cities, blackjack players crowded forty-one tables, while 450 other players stared into video slot machines inside the tipi-shaped Little Six Casino, operated by the 103 members of the Shakopee Mdewakanton Sioux. By 1991, each member of the tribe was getting monthly dividend checks averaging two thousand dollars as shareholders in the casino. In addition to monthly dividends, members became eligible for homes (if they lacked them), guaranteed jobs (if they were unemployed), and full college scholarships. The tribe had taken out health insurance policies for everyone on the reservation and established day care for children of working parents. The largest casino to open by mid-1991 was the three-million-dollar Sycuan Gaming Center on the Sycuan Indian Reservation near El Cajon, a suburb of San Diego, California.

Death at Akwesasne. While gambling has brought benefits to some Native American communities, it brought violence to the Akwesasne Mohawks of St. Regis in upstate New York. As many as seven casinos had opened illegally along the reservation's main highway; the area became a crossroads for the illicit smuggling of drugs, including cocaine, and tax-free liquor and cigarettes.

Tension escalated after early protests against gambling in the late 1980's (including the vandalizing of one casino and the burning of another) were met by brutal attempts by gambling supporters to repress this resistance. Residents blockaded the reservation to keep the casinos' customers out, prompting the violent destruction of the same blockades by gambling supporters in late April, 1990. By that time, violence had spiraled into brutal beatings of antigambling activists, drive-by shootings, and night-long firefights that culminated in two Mohawk deaths during the early morning of May 1, 1990. Intervention of several police agencies from the United States and Canada followed the two deaths; outside police presence continued for years afterward. —*Bruce E. Johansen*

See also Determined Residents United for Mohawk Sovereignty (DRUMS); Games and contests; Trade; Urban Indians.

BIBLIOGRAPHY

Hornung, Rick. *One Nation Under the Gun: Inside the Mohawk Civil War*. New York: Pantheon Books, 1991.

Johansen, Bruce E. *Life and Death in Mohawk Country*. Golden, Colo.: North American Press, 1993.

New York State Legislature. Assembly. Standing Committee on Governmental Operations. *Public Hearing on the Crisis at Akwesasne (Day II)*. Vol 2 in *In the Matter of a Public Hearing into the Crisis at Akwesasne*. Albany, N.Y.: Stenotype Systems, 1990.

U.S. Congress. Senate. Select Committee on Indian Affairs. Murphy, M. Maureen. *Gambling on Indian Reservations and Land*. Washington, D.C.: Government Printing Office, 1985.

Walke, Roger. *Gambling on Indian Reservations*. Washington, D.C.: Congressional Research Service, Library of Congress, 1989.

Games and contests

TRIBES AFFECTED: Pantribal

SIGNIFICANCE: Games reflected the importance of athleticism to most Indian tribes, provided entertainment, and helped develop skills for work, hunting, and war

American Indians traditionally participated in a variety of games and contests. Children tended to mimic adult activities to ready themselves for work and war, while men tested themselves in preparation for hunting and warfare, developing their skills and endurance. Both men and women found entertainment in playing games, including games of chance.

Athletic games involved wrestling, throwing spears, shooting arrows, kicking sticks or balls, running, and many other activities. These games tested the strength, stamina, and courage required for survival in the Americas. Pre-Columbian Native Americans played forms of field hockey, ice hockey, soccer, and football, and they developed canoes, sleds, snowshoes, kayaks, toboggans, stilts, swings, and rubber balls. Many Native American games involved teams playing against each other, in contrast to the more individualistic sports of pre-contact Europeans. Unlike the spectator sports of today, there was more total participation, and participation was more important than winning, even though betting on outcomes was universally common.

Games also had a religious aspect, and their history and rules were often bound up in the traditional beliefs of the tribes. According to Stewart Culin, who did an extensive study of Indian games, they were played to drive away sickness, produce rain, and fertilize crops

Races and Ball Games. Different tribes had various forms of foot races. In pre-Columbian America, hunters literally ran

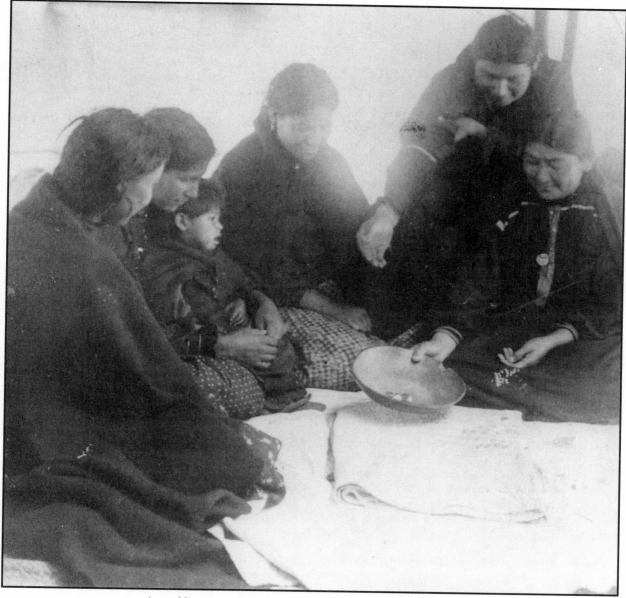

A gambling game known as kose-kaw-nuch. (Library of Congress)

down deer and other game, while communication within and among tribes took place using swift couriers. Inca runners ran thousands of miles, uniting their empire. Pueblo Indians would get up at dawn and run to their cornfields located miles away. Various forms of races were held to develop the endurance of runners, including shuttle relay races, kick-stick, and kickball races. In 1980, the Pueblo Indians celebrated the tercentennial of the Pueblo Revolt of 1680 by reenacting the part played by the runners who spread the word of the rebellion.

Plains tribes played a form of dodge ball in which the batter tossed and batted a rawhide ball. Fielders would try to catch the ball and then throw it at the batter, who would try to dodge out of the way. Football games were played across the continent, even by Inuits (Eskimos). Inuits also did a blanket toss, spreading a blanket like a trampoline and throwing participants as high as fifteen or twenty feet in the air. Various forms of kickball were played, including what was known in the 1980's as hackeysack. In the Southeast, ball games were used to earn hunting privileges, to settle disputes, or to determine who were the best warriors.

The Choctaw played a game called *kabocca* with a wooden ball about the size of a golf ball. As many as seven hundred players on one team would try to move the ball toward one or another of the goalposts, which were as much as a mile apart, using sticks with cup-shaped ends to catch and throw the ball.

Games could be very rough and could last several days—scores could run into the hundreds. The Iroquois called kabocca the "little brother of war." This game, now known as lacrosse, was uniquely American.

Shinny is a form of hockey that was played throughout North America. The ice version was played by both sexes, but the field version was played mainly by women. Doubleball was a variation of shinny that used two baseball-sized balls that were tied together with a half-foot leather strap. A player carried the double ball or threw it with a hooked stick.

Some tribes played games involving throwing or shooting arrows, either at circular targets drawn on the ground or through rolling hoops. Crow Indians still practice an arrow-throwing game involving throwing arrows at a circular target drawn on the ground.

Various forms of bowling were practiced. The Cherokee pitched stones at clay pins. Another Cherokee game involved rolling or sliding a disk-shaped stone while contestants simultaneously threw poles to land where they guessed the stone would stop. In the Southwest, corncob targets were knocked down with wooden balls.

Gambling Games. Gambling games were popular. Stick games that involved guessing which hand held a hidden marker were widespread. Crow Indians played the stick game with teams, and each team had supporters that dressed similarly and sang as the game was played to give their players power and to confound the opposing team. The Menominee would shake dice-like objects in a bowl and then throw them out. Other tribes would place an object in one of several moccasins, with the object of correctly guessing the moccasin hiding the object.

Children's Games. Children participated in a variety of games. Girls would put up miniature dwellings and play "house," while boys hunted small game to feed their "families." Northwest Coast children played games such as fish trap, a form of tag in which the "fishers" simulated a net while the "fish" tried to avoid getting caught.

Famous Athletes. While traditionally any recognition given outstanding Indian athletes was fleeting at best, in the twentieth century Indians have participated in non-Indian athletic events, and there have been a number of Olympic-class Indian athletes. Billy Mills (Sioux) won the gold medal for the ten-thousand-meter race at the 1964 Olympics, and in the process he beat the United States Olympic record of Louis Tewanima (Hopi), who had won the silver medal in the same event in 1912. The greatest Indian athlete was Jim Thorpe (Sauk and Fox). According to an Associated Press poll in 1950, he was considered the greatest athlete of the half-century. He won the gold medal for the pentathlon and decathlon in the 1912 Olympics and went on to play professional football and baseball. An American Indian Athletic Hall of Fame was established in 1972 at Haskell Indian Junior College to honor Indian athletes. —*Jon Reyhner*

See also Ball game and courts; Children; Gambling; Hand games; Lacrosse; Thorpe, Jim.

BIBLIOGRAPHY

Culin, Stewart. *Games of the North American Indians*. New York: Dover, 1975. First published in the twenty-fourth *Annual Report of the Bureau of American Ethnology* (1902-1903), this is the most extensive study of Indian games available. It includes detailed drawings of the various implements used in the games.

Grueninger, Robert W. "Physical Education." In *Teaching American Indian Students*, edited by Jon Reyhner. Norman: University of Oklahoma Press, 1992. Describes a variety of Indian games appropriate for schools.

Macfarlan, Allan, and Paulette Macfarlan. *Handbook of American Indian Games*. Illustrated by Paulette Macfarlan. New York: Dover, 1958. Describes various Indian games; intended to teach children how to play the games.

Nabokov, Peter. *Indian Running: Native American History and Tradition*. Santa Fe, N.Mex.: Ancient City Press, 1987. Describes the races held as part of the tercentennial commemoration of the Pueblo Revolt of 1680. In addition, discusses the history and accomplishments of Indian runners.

Oxendine, Joseph B. *American Indian Sports Heritage*. Champaign, Ill.: Human Kinetics Books, 1988. Comprehensive history and description of Indian games along with short biographies of Indian sports figures.

Schoor, Gene, with Henry Gilfond. *The Jim Thorpe Story: America's Greatest Athlete*. New York: Julian Messner, 1951. A biography of one of the most famous athletes of the twentieth century.

Ganado Mucho (c. 1809, near Klagetoh, Ariz.—1893, near Klagetoh, Ariz.): Headman

ALSO KNOWN AS: Tótsohnii Hastiin (Man of the Big Water)

TRIBAL AFFILIATION: Navajo

SIGNIFICANCE: Ganado Mucho was a Navajo leader during the tribe's difficult transition to reservation life

Ganado Mucho, which means "many cattle," was born into the Tótsohnii (Big Water) Clan of the Navajo, or Diné ("the people"). His father was a Hopi captured by the Navajos. A successful cattle grower and sheepman all his adult life, he worked with other Navajo headmen such as Manuelito to keep the peace with whites. He cooperated with United States Indian agents to return livestock stolen from New Mexicans. In February, 1861, he attended a council with Colonel Edward R. S. Canby to sign a treaty of peace along with other Navajo headmen. Unfortunately, the outbreak of the Civil War forced the abandonment of Fort Defiance and ended any chance for the treaty's success.

Soon it became impossible to meet the peacekeeping demands of the United States government while at the same time protecting his people from raids initiated by other Indians and Mexicans. Kit Carson's scorched-earth campaign was the final straw, and Ganado Mucho moved his people near the Grand Canyon. Eventually, he was forced to surrender to avoid starvation. On the journey to the government's desolate resettlement camp at Fort Sumner (Bosque Redondo), Mexicans kidnapped two of Ganado's daughters. After he arrived there in July of 1866, his son was killed by Comanche raiders. Ganado escaped the following year, but hunger again forced his return.

In 1868, he and seventeen other traditional leaders signed a peace treaty allowing the Navajo to return home. At the treaty council he stated:

> Let us go home to our mountains. Let us see our flocks feeding in the valley, and let us ride again where we can smell the sage and know of hidden hogans by the smell of piñon smoke. . . . We have learned not to kill and not to steal from the flocks of others. Here we have nothing. Our children grow up in ugliness and death. Let us go home.

He was appointed a subchief for the western side of the reservation by the Indian agent and settled near what was to become the reservation town of Ganado. The transition to reservation life without raiding was difficult. In 1878, Ganado Mucho helped kill an estimated forty Navajo "witches" who continued to raid white cattlemen.

See also Long Walk; Navajo.

Garakontie, Daniel (c. 1600, Onondaga, N.Y.—c. 1676, Onondaga, N.Y.): Diplomat, orator

ALSO KNOWN AS: Harakontie
TRIBAL AFFILIATION: Onondaga
SIGNIFICANCE: Garakontie was a highly skilled negotiator between the Onondaga (and other Five Nations Iroquois) and the French in New France

Not much is known of Garakontie's early life. He was first noted in European records for attempting to prevent war between the Iroquois and the French, and for sheltering Jesuits in Iroquois towns from attack by anti-French forces. He enjoyed warm personal relationships with several French Jesuit missionaries. Garakontie engineered a truce between the Iroquois and the French in 1661 and attempted in 1665 and 1666 to do the same. There were strong anti-French factions arrayed against him within the Iroquois tribes, which often foiled his efforts.

Following the 1667 French-Iroquois peace, Garakontie greatly encouraged the work of Jesuit missionaries in Iroquoia, although not until 1669 did he express his wish to be baptized. Political alignments clearly preceded his religious convictions. He was baptized in 1670 in the cathedral at Quebec City. The colonial governor, Daniel de Rémy de Courcelle, who served as his godfather, hosted a feast for the attending Indians following the ceremony. Garakontie remained devoted to his adopted faith, learned to read and write, and on a visit to New Netherlands, scolded Protestant Dutchmen who criticized his theological convictions.

Garakontie did not always enjoy popularity and support among his own people; many of them denounced him for accepting Christianity and for allying closely with the French. He was not, however, a mere tool of the French. Garakontie believed that his people could learn some useful things from the French, and that Iroquois interests would be best served in most cases by siding with the French rather than with the Dutch or the English in Albany. This cost him dearly at times, but he was at all times highly respected among his own people, and his oratory, political skills, and honesty were unquestioned.

See also Beaver Wars; Indian-white relations—Dutch colonial; Indian-white relations—English colonial; Indian-white relations—French colonial; Iroquois Confederacy; Onondaga.

Garra, Antonio (c. 1800, Southern Calif.—Dec., 1852, Southern Calif.): Chief, shaman

TRIBAL AFFILIATION: Cupeño
SIGNIFICANCE: Leader of the Garra Uprising, Antonio Garra attempted to halt white migration into California

As chief of the Cupeño Indians living in Southern California at the headwaters of the San Louis Rey River, Garra opposed white expansion into California. As migration into the California region of white miners and ranchers as well as of Mexicans and Mormons intensified during the Gold Rush era, Garra sought to organize a united Indian revolt. Claiming that he could transform his enemies' bullets into water, Garra and his Cahuilla, Chemehuevi, Cocopa, Kamia, Luiseño, Mojave, and Quechan supporters raided ranchers and sheepherders. Garra's son, also named Antonio Garra, fought with his father during the Garra Uprising.

Several other California bands elected to remain neutral, however, and some, including the Luiseños under Manuelito Cota, actively aided whites. The influential Cahuilla, Juan Antonio, was courted by both Indians and whites. Electing to assist white settlers, Antonio captured Garra in 1851, thereby ending the Garra Uprising. Antonio released Garra to the California militia, who convened a court martial that tried and hanged him.

See also Antonio, Juan; Cupeño.

Garry, Spokane (1811, near the junction of the Latah Creek and Spokane River, Wash.—Jan. 14, 1892, Indian Canyon, near Spokane, Wash.): Chief

TRIBAL AFFILIATION: Spokane (Salish)
SIGNIFICANCE: Spokane Garry both led his tribe in battle against whites and sought to Christianize his people

Spokane Garry went to a Hudson's Bay Company school in Canada (1825-1830). On returning home, he built a tule mat church and commenced teaching English, agriculture, and the Christian religion. As a pacifist, he opposed the Hudson's Bay Company policy of encouraging chiefs to flog Indians who committed crimes. He also restrained the Spokanes from joining the Yakimas and other Plateau groups in warfare against the whites during the Yakima War of 1855-1856. Yet because of the absence of treaties, increasing Spokane grievances against white incursion, and the military expedition by Colonel Edward Steptoe, Spokane Garry was forced to join other Indian warriors in the 1858 Battle of Four Lakes, losing to Colonel George Wright. He continued, however, to encourage the Spokanes to negotiate treaties to avoid violence in relation to what he believed was inevitable domination by whites.

He became disillusioned with Calvinistic revivalists Cushing Eells and Elkanah Walker and their establishment of Tshimakain Mission (1838), which increased religious factionalism. Eventually he gave up his teaching and preaching and joined the Spokane in hunting bison on the Plains. In middle age he was considered wealthy, having many horses and a productive farm. He was known for his abilities as a skillful negotiator.

See also Spokane.

Gender relations and roles

TRIBES AFFECTED: Pantribal

SIGNIFICANCE: Gender roles are culturally defined entities that serve to structure social organization; Indian societies were marked by variation in the types of gender categories present and in their manifestation over time

Gender is typically regarded as a cultural or social construction, in contrast to the biologically defined sexual division between male and female. The creation of gender is an active process that may involve more than simply two-gender categories and that may vary through time among different cultures.

Engendering Native Americans. Much of our understanding of North American Indians and their history and prehistory is "degendered"; that is, it is a tale of interactions among sexless cultures rather than among gendered individuals. Even those accounts of Native Americans which incorporate gender commonly only include male roles, for as Alice Kehoe ("The Muted Class," in Cheryl Claassen's *Exploring Gender Through Archaeology*, 1992) explains: "Dominant groups dominate discourse. Subordinated groups whose discourse differs from the dominant mode may not be heard." Typical of androcentric (male-oriented) writing is Claude Lévi-Strauss's statement: "The entire village left the next day in about 30 canoes, leaving us alone with the women and children in the abandoned houses" (remarked upon in Alison Wylie's "Gender Theory and the Archaeological Record," in Joan M. Gero and Margaret W. Conkey's *Engendering Archaeology*, 1991). The implication is that women and children are unimportant and do not contribute to village society. Such male-centered research creates obvious problems for an adequate understanding of human interactions and behavior, which involve both men and women.

Accounts of American Indian prehistory manifest similar problems. Generally, prehistories demonstrate cultural differences through archaeological studies of material culture, typically pottery or stone tools. Elizabeth Graham ("Women and Gender in Maya Prehistory," in Dale Walde and Noreen D. Willows' *The Archaeology of Gender*, 1991) succinctly explains: "Pots and lithics [stone tools] seem to move of their own accord across ancient landscapes, and tools are dropped here and there by faceless, sexless beings defined mainly in terms of the space in which they move, or the energy they expend." Such reconstructions of the past may demonstrate differences in manufacturing styles among groups but generally do not advance understanding of the interactions among the men and women who composed these groups.

Typical androcentric studies concerning Native Americans generally include such erroneous assumptions as the following: Gender roles and relationships are irrelevant for the understanding of other cultures, only two gender roles are found in other cultures, gender relationships among Native American societies correspond directly to those found among European groups, gender arrangements are unchanging through time, women's activities are defined in accordance to their reproductive capabilities, and women are passive and their work is of little value (whereas men are active and their work is socially important). For some American Indian groups, a few of these assumptions may be correct, while for others they may be completely inaccurate. The point is, these broad generalizations are often applied to Native Americans with little attempt to verify their truth.

Since the 1970's, but more intensely during the 1980's and 1990's, feminist studies have had an impact on the fields of anthropology, archaeology, history, Native American studies, and other fields which typically ignored gender among Indians. Some of this feminist-inspired research has a political component and is explicitly directed toward the empowerment of certain groups, such as women, American Indians, and gay populations. Not all is politically motivated, however, and not all is even concerned with women. The unifying theme underlying gender research is a theoretical outlook which views gender relationships as the fundamental structural component to social organization, much as the "man-land" relationship was typically seen as fundamental to cultural ecology. Gender studies also may stress social diversity by emphasizing the presence of multiple "voices" or "narratives" within a group.

Generally, gender research concerning American Indians includes three types of study: the investigation of women's behavior and history, the identification of more than two gender categories and their activities and history, and the development of theories to explain the identified gender relationships.

Investigation of Women's Behavior and History. This aspect of gender research includes many types of research, among them studies of famous women, women as gatherers and horticulturalists, women as tool-makers, and women in the colonial period. Studies of famous women represent attempts to balance a male-dominated history by showing the contributions of important women. Toward this goal, researchers have written biographies of well-known Indian women and of women anthropologists, archaeologists, and other scholars who have worked with Native Americans or Native American concerns.

Increased attention directed toward women's roles has focused research on their gathering activities. Studies have demonstrated that this anthropologically undervalued occupation can generate a large proportion of the household's daily diet. Previously, it had sometimes been assumed that male hunting contributed the major portion of the diet, based primarily on data from male-focused ethnographies. Other assumptions concerning women's collecting behavior have been similarly corrected. Previously, it had been assumed that women's biological functions (the bearing and rearing of children) limited their ability to roam far from home to obtain plants or raw materials. Among some cultures, however, gathering women, whether working as a cooperative group or on their own, do not remain consistently close to their home or camp, nor do these women always take their children with them on excursions. In fact, once women have given birth, varying strategies of child care are possible, and children may be looked after by other mothers (who can nurse the infant), other women, siblings, fathers, mother's brother and family, or other members of the group.

Based on the ethnographic data concerning women as gatherers and horticulturalists (practicing nonmechanized farming), there is an obvious linkage between women, plants, and crop domestication. Generally, studies of prehistoric North American Indians assume that the women gathered plants and that the men hunted animals. Hunting by males was regarded in the literature as an innovative and active event, whereas gathering was depicted as routine, passive behavior. An undervaluing of female roles appears to explain why descriptions of the development of horticulture commonly involve a process whereby "plants virtually domesticate themselves," rendering human (likely women's) actions or abilities unnecessary (according to Patty Jo Watson and Mary C. Kennedy in "The Development of Horticulture," in Gero and Conkey's *Engendering Archaeology*).

In addition to studies concerning women's contributions to household subsistence, some researchers have examined women's tool-manufacturing abilities. In the past, archaeologists and ethnographers typically emphasized "*man* the toolmaker." The role of women in tool manufacturing was commonly ignored, downplayed, or denied. Archaeologists and members of the public are commonly interested in aesthetically appealing, elaborate stone pieces which display complex flaking patterns; these items are typically identified as male hunting tools (such as arrowheads or spear points, termed "projectile points" by archaeologists). Of less interest are skinning, scraping, and food-preparing tools (such as knives), usually associated with women. In most cases, however, researchers have not conducted edge-wear analyses (microscopic examinations of stone tool edges), which demonstrate whether the items were used for piercing (point) or slicing (knife) functions, or on what material these actions were performed. Typically, the projectile-point identification is applied in excavated contexts ranging from open woodlands to domestic campsites, despite the fact that open areas might be more likely locations for points, while campsites are the more likely locations for knives and scraping implements. Joan M. Gero ("Genderlithics: Women's Roles in Stone Tool Production," in *Engendering Archaeology*) suggests that based on two assumptions—that "females comprised approximately half of all

prehistoric populations" and that "these women carried out production activities at prehistoric sites"—then surely "women can be expected to be most visible and active in precisely the contexts that archaeologists are most likely to excavate: on house floors, at base camps, and in village sites, where women would congregate to carry out their work."

In addition to the fact that women's roles as stone-tool users or manufacturers typically vanish in archaeological reconstructions, their roles in ceramic production may also be over- or understated. Anthropologists often indicate whether women or men are the "potters" among the society studied, but in many cases, this category is meaningless for traditional kinship-oriented groups. If the entire household participates in ceramic manufacturing, through the gathering of clay, water, fuel, fire-tending, decorating, and so on, then the actual shaping of the clay may not be the most important part of the process, although this role may be the only one which is recorded by the investigator.

Generally, discussions of North American prehistory assume that Indian women were the prehistoric potters if the historically documented communities had women potters. It has been ironically remarked by anthropologists with an interest in gender that women suddenly "appear" in the archaeologies of regions with the advent of ceramic manufacturing, much as men earlier "appeared" with the use of stone tools.

Despite dissatisfaction with such simplistically applied assumptions, it must be admitted that the identification of prehistoric gender-correlated activities is not an easy process. Even in cases for which historic documents exist, observers may provide only a partial account of events. For example, sixteenth century writings describing the involvement of Aztec women in weaving and cooking may not mention other roles, such as healing or marketing, shown in accompanying illustrations.

Scholars and Native Americans have worked to demonstrate women's participation in areas in which their influence is commonly denied. These include prestigious wealth-generating occupations (among Hopi, Iroquois, Ojibwa, and Tlingit), religion (among Blackfoot, Cree, and Kiowa-Apache), trade (Hidatsa and Mandan), and warfare (Cheyenne, Crow, and Pawnee).

A high proportion of the research concerning women's roles in American Indian societies has been directed toward the demonstration of changes which occurred with the encroachment of the European social and mercantile system. For example, many studies have concentrated on how changing trading priorities may have affected gender relationships. Research on Plains (such as Lakota Sioux), and Northeast (such as Ojibwa and Cree) cultures suggests that the European fur trade added value to the traditional production of prepared skins. Theoretically, a hunter (typically a man during the contact period for these groups) could obtain an infinite number of skins, but each skin had to be prepared (typically, the women's occupation at that time and place) before it could be exchanged with Europeans. As pelts increased in value, there was increased pressure for a man to create relationships with more women who could treat the animal skins. This could be achieved through polygynous unions (marriage to more than one wife). In this manner, women became producers within a system controlled by men, rather than being the producers and organizers of their own economic enterprises. It has been suggested that this situation probably resulted in decreased power for the women of these groups. Other effects of Indian-European contact have also been investigated. Several studies, for example, have examined the influence of missionization on traditional gender roles.

Identification of More than Two Gender Categories. Descriptions of American Indians have often ignored common culturally accepted changes in gender typical of many Native American groups. Relatively recent emphasis on the understanding of diversity has led to a greater study and recognition of gender transformations among American Indians. Patricia C. Albers' research, as described in "From Illusion to Illumination: Anthropological Studies of American Indian Women," in Sandra Morgen's *Gender and Anthropology* (1989), indicates that as many as 113 American Indian groups recognized transformative gender statuses and that among these, male transvestism (biologically male individuals who took on the cultural roles typical of women) predominated. There is abundant literature discussing the *berdaches* (typically defined as males who dress and behave as women) in the historic period. Within many Native American cultures, berdaches constituted a culturally accepted component of society. They were found across North America and have been identified during the historic period in the Arctic (Aleut, Pacific Inuit, Baffinland Inuit, and Quebec Inuit), the Subarctic (Hare and Ingalik), the Great Basin (Eastern Shoshone, Kawaiisu, and Paiute), California (Chumash, Salinan, Tolowa, Wiyot, and Yokuts), the Southwest (Karankawa and Navajo), the Great Plains (Lakota Sioux), the Northeast (Delaware, Illinois, Miami, possibly Tuscarora and Winnebago), and the Southeast (Timucua and Natchez).

Traditionally, anthropologists discussed the berdache phenomenon in the context of cultural relativism (the concept that cultures must be evaluated based on their own values, and not on those of outside groups), specifically as an example of how notions of normal and abnormal behavior are culturally defined within individual societies. Studies of berdaches from the 1970's onward have instead tended to discuss transformative behavior within its specific social context and to include women gender transformers (women behaving as men) in addition to identifying other gender categories.

Research has confirmed the expectation that gender varies culturally and that many Indian groups had roles for female gender transformers. Among them were the Atsina (or Gros Ventres), Canadian Blackfoot, Cherokee, Cheyenne, Kutenai, Lakota Sioux, Navajo, Ottawa, Piegan, and Tlingit. There are, or were, various gender categories within different cultural groups, and each of these has (or had) varying roles and social status. In some cases, individuals determined their own genders, while among other groups, parents or other adults could change the gender of a child. For example, among the historic period Inuit, girls were often dressed as boys if the parents had desired a son or if they wished the child to take on the name and characteristics of a deceased male.

Theories to Explain Gender. American Indian studies have concentrated more on the identification and description of different gender categories than on the explanation of these categories' creation or function. Theoretical works generally focus on the discussion of two gender categories—heterosexual men and heterosexual women—and often examine their relative status and power through time (typically precolonial versus colonial), using the variables of occupation or marital relationship. Activities do provide a strong indication of the demarcated gender role within the society (traditionally discussed under "divisions of labor"), although there are always exceptions. Among some groups, individuals could adopt the behavior of the opposite sex without changing their gender, whereas among other groups, such behavior was interpreted as a change in gender.

It has been suggested that in cases where women contributed noticeably to the household's subsistence (as among the Hopi and Iroquois), women had greater status than in societies where women contributed less to the daily diet. Many of the societies with socially valued women also granted women claims to the resources they generated, to the land, or to their homes.

Marital rights are also examined as an indicator of the relative freedom of women and men. Among some societies (as among Blackfoot, Hopi, Iroquois, and Ojibwa), women played an active role in the selection of a spouse and were able to divorce their husbands. Broadly, it seems that women have more freedom in marital matters when descent is traced through the women's line (matrilineal descent).

Improvement in women's social status generally is correlated with a number of factors. It is related to their economic contribution (such as their ability to contribute to the daily diet); it is also related to their control over basic resources (such as homes or land) and to the yields from these resources (such as crops). Additionally, it is related to their influence on the heredity of their offspring through matrilineal descent patterns. Societies having all these attributes (Hopi society, for example) tend to be marked by the presence of powerful, independent women.

Colonization resulted in many changes in the relationships between Indian women and men. In some cases, such as with the nomadic buffalo-hunting groups of the Plains, the European mercantile system seemed to decrease the status of women. In other cases, such as among the horticultural Iroquois, the European trading system may have advanced the status of women. During the later prehistoric and early historic period, Iroquois women controlled horticultural production (most importantly, corn) in the fields surrounding their villages. With the arrival of Europeans, Iroquois men became fur traders, and as prey became scarcer in the vicinity of their settlements, they ventured farther afield in search of fur-bearing animals. These extended absences from villages, both in fur trading and in raiding, meant that women assumed greater control of village organization and resources. For nomadic Plains groups, this male involvement in buffalo hunting (for hides and meat) did not translate into increased female status, since women were eliminated from the cooperative buffalo hunts and, as Albers notes, "became workers in a highly specialized production process over which men had ultimate control. As a result, the means of wealth accumulation and prestige were increasingly in the hands of men."

The most important result of gender research is that it has increased awareness of the variation among Native American populations. It is now recognized that anthropological descriptions which fail to take gender into account are incomplete at best, often misleading, and sometimes completely inaccurate. New perspectives on gender have had a profound impact on the understanding of society and culture in general and of Native Americans in particular.   —*Susan J. Wurtzburg*

See also Adoption; Children; Education, pre-contact; Marriage and divorce; Menses and menstruation; Puberty and initiation rites; Women; Women of All Red Nations (WARN).

BIBLIOGRAPHY

Allen, Paula Gunn. *The Sacred Hoop: Recovering the Feminine in American Indian Traditions*. Reprint, with a new preface. Boston: Beacon Press, 1992. Gunn's Laguna Pueblo and Sioux heritage influences her essays concerning Native American women, including gay women. Comprehensive index, no illustrations.

————. ed. *Spider Woman's Granddaughters: Traditional Tales and Contemporary Writing by Native American Women*. New York: Fawcett Columbine, 1989. Anthology of fictional and traditional prose. Brief authors' biographies and suggestions for further reading.

Bataille, Gretchen M., and Kathleen Mullen Sands. *American Indian Women: Telling Their Lives*. Lincoln: University of Nebraska Press, 1984. Essays concerning Native American autobiography. Comprehensive index and useful bibliography.

Bowker, Ardy. *Sisters in the Blood: The Education of Women in Native America*. Newton, Mass.: WEEA, 1993. Informative analyses based on interviews with 991 northern Plains women. Index, no illustrations.

Claassen, Cheryl, ed. *Exploring Gender Through Archaeology: Selected Papers from the 1991 Boone Conference*. Madison, Wis.: Prehistory Press, 1992. Anthology of papers by archaeologists providing research on gender issues. No index.

Gacs, Ute, et al., eds. *Women Anthropologists: Selected Biographies*. Urbana: University of Illinois Press, 1989. Biographical data concerning women anthropologists, many of whom wrote about Native Americans.

Gero, Joan M., and Margaret W. Conkey, eds. *Engendering Archaeology: Women and Prehistory*. Oxford: Basil Blackwell, 1991. Anthology of articles by specialists, most dealing with North America. Good theoretical introduction. Comprehensive index, charts, drawings, maps, and photographs.

Morgen, Sandra, ed. *Gender and Anthropology: Critical Reviews for Research and Teaching*. Washington, D.C.: American Anthropological Association, 1989. An anthology of articles focusing on the synthesis of research and teaching methods, including lesson plans and film suggestions. Contains useful review of research concerning American Indian women by Patricia C. Albers. No comprehensive index.

Spector, Janet D. *What This Awl Means: Feminist Archaeology at a Wahpeton Dakota Village*. St. Paul: Minnesota Historical Society Press, 1993. An innovative archaeologist's search for evidence and understanding of Dakota women. Index, charts, maps, illustrations and photographs.

Walde, Dale, and Noreen D. Willows, eds. *The Archaeology of Gender: Proceedings of the Twenty-second Annual Chacmool Conference*. Calgary, Canada: University of Calgary Archaeological Association, 1991. Selection of papers, most of which concern prehistory or history of Native Americans. No index.

General, Alexander (c. 1889, Six Nations Reserve, Ontario, Canada—1965): Tribal chief, activist, ritualist

ALSO KNOWN AS: Deskahe, Shao-hyowa (Great Sky)
TRIBAL AFFILIATION: Cayuga, Oneida
SIGNIFICANCE: General worked with anthropologists to promote understanding of traditional Iroquois beliefs and the cause of Iroquois nationalism

Alexander General was born on the Six Nations Reserve near Brantford, Ontario, in 1889 and given the name Shao-hyowa, or "Great Sky." Previously a faithkeeper, in 1917 he became the principal speaker for the Upper Cayuga Turtle Moiety at the Sour Springs longhouse. He was elevated to a confederacy chieftainship in 1925 and received the title Deskahe.

Strongly opposed to Canada's imposition of an elected council on the Six Nations in 1924, he traveled to England in 1930 to argue unsuccessfully for Iroquois sovereignty in Canada. He was instrumental in the organization of the Indian Defense League and the Mohawk Workers, early nationalist movements. Through various jobs in nearby cities he learned English and earned enough to establish himself as a successful farmer. For three decades, he worked closely with anthropologists in interpreting Iroquois ritual and ideology, emphasizing the close ties between the confederacy and the longhouse. He is best known for his collaboration with Frank Speck on *The Midwinter Rites of the Cayuga Longhouse* (1949), but he also worked with many other scholars.

See also Cayuga; Handsome Lake; Iroquois Confederacy; Oneida.

General Allotment Act

DATE: February 8, 1887
TRIBES AFFECTED: Pantribal
SIGNIFICANCE: The General Allotment Act (Dawes Act) established allotment as the focus of federal Indian policy, leading to a drastic reduction in the amount of land held by Native Americans

During the 1880's, there was much discussion in Congress of the need to reform federal Indian policy. To many self-styled "friends of the Indian," the only hope for the Indians was to free them from the perceived negative effects of tribal culture and reservation life and assimilate them into mainstream American society. Senator Henry Dawes of Massachusetts led a group in Congress that pressed for allotment—dividing tribal lands among individual Indians—as the means of "civilizing" Native Americans by making farmers of them. In this way, it was argued, they would become individual citizens like other Americans and prosper through individual initiative.

In early 1887, Congress passed the General Allotment Act (also known as the Dawes Act or Dawes Severalty Act). Under its provisions, the president was given authority to order the allotment of reservation land in severalty—in other words, among individual tribal members. Heads of families would receive 160 acres, persons over eighteen and orphans 80 acres, and other single persons 40 acres. Once a reservation's lands were allotted, the government could purchase land deemed surplus and make it available for white settlement. The act required that the government hold title to allotments for a twenty-five-year trust period, during which time the land could not be sold. An Indian receiving an allotment became an American citizen. Initially, the Five Civilized Tribes of Indian Territory and the Iroquois tribes of New York were exempted from the act.

The act contained no timetable for implementation, and at first it was implemented carefully. Pressure from assimilationists and land-hungry whites led to changes in allotment policy that made it easier for Indians to sell or lease their lands, with the result that much land passed into non-Indian hands. By the time the Indian Reorganization Act of 1934 ended the allotment policy, 86 million acres (out of 138 million) had passed from Indian control.

See also Allotment system; Burke Act; Indian Reorganization Act; Indian-white relations—U.S., 1871-1933; Meriam Report; Reservation system of the United States.

Geronimo (c. 1827, near Clifton, Ariz.—Feb. 17, 1909, Fort Sill, Okla.): Shaman, tribal leader

ALSO KNOWN AS: Goyathlay (One Who Yawns)

TRIBAL AFFILIATION: Chiricahua Apache

SIGNIFICANCE: Geronimo led one of the most successful Indian resistances to white domination in U.S. history

Geronimo's Apache name was Goyathlay (also spelled Goyahkla), or "One Who Yawns," a name that seems unfitting for a man of his energy and spirit. During one battle, Goyathlay so distinguished himself as a warrior that he stood out amid the confusion on the battlefield. Mexican soldiers, probably calling on Saint Jerome out of fear, nicknamed him Geronimo. Going by Western calendars, Geronimo placed his date of birth in June of 1829, but there is evidence that his birth actually occurred earlier in the 1820's (1827 is often given, but it may have been as early as 1823). His birthplace, a place that as an Apache he would not be mistaken about, was near the upper Gila River in Arizona. Apache children held special attachments to their birthplace; whenever they passed it they would roll on the ground in the four directions.

Geronimo was a member of the Chiricahua band of Apaches, named for the mountain range that was a part of their home. The Chiricahua had several notable leaders, among them Cochise, Mangas Coloradus, and Victorio. By 1881 all were dead, but Geronimo would continue to hold out for five more years despite overwhelming odds.

For most of his youth, Geronimo was untouched by the hostility that existed between the Spanish and some bands of Apache. Conquistadors would conduct slave-catching expeditions, and at one time the Mexican state of Sonora offered one hundred dollars for Apache scalps. The Apaches retaliated. Geronimo was admitted to the council of warriors at the early age of seventeen, going out on raids of Mexican ranches and pack trains with his brother-in-law, Juh. Obtaining his maturity early allowed him to marry his first love, Alope, a fragile young woman with whom he had three children. He would go on to have nine wives and several more children during his life.

When relations with the Mexican state of Chihuahua improved, the Apaches began going there to trade. During the summer of 1850, on a peaceful trading excursion, Geronimo returned to the Apache camp to find his mother, wife, and three small children among those slain by a general and his troops from Sonora. It was the greatest personal tragedy Geronimo would face and perhaps the greatest influence on his future life and career as a warrior. He would hold a deep-rooted hatred of Mexicans for the rest of his life.

The lure of the West and post-Civil War peace drew many settlers into native territory, where they found populations such as the Apaches ready to die in defense of their homelands. Early in his career, Geronimo's raids (some say vengeance for the killing of his family) were conducted in Mexico and were paid little attention by the United States. With more government restrictions, removal of tribes from desired locations onto wastelands, placement of hostile tribes onto the same reservations, and inadequate rations, Geronimo moved his warfare into Arizona. As he would later say, "My people were suffering much."

From the 1850's until his final surrender in 1886, Geronimo would go through what seemed to be an unending series of government agents, army officers, bloody battles, raids, captures, escapes, surrenders, and more escapes. He was never a chief in a hereditary sense, but rather a shaman, a medicine man to whom chiefs would turn for the wisdom that came to him in sudden visions. Geronimo's first glimpse into his power came at the loss of his family. He sat alone, crying, when he heard a voice call his name. "Goyathlay," it said four times, "no guns can ever kill you. I will take the bullets from the guns of the Mexicans, so they will have nothing but powder. And I will guide your arrows." Almost fifty years later an artist, Elbridge Ayer Burbank, was sent to Fort Sill to paint a portrait of Geronimo. Burbank was astonished when one day the kind, old Indian showed him the number of bullet holes in

Chiricahua Apache leader Geronimo in 1887, the year after his surrender to Nelson A. Miles. (National Archives)

his body. "Bullets cannot kill me," Geronimo told the artist.

The army in Arizona was becoming frustrated with Geronimo's elusiveness. Some officers blamed the terrain, calling it the most difficult in North America. The Apaches were a part of the land. They became legendary for their ability to make themselves invisible in a field or disappear into the landscape after conducting a raid. A general named Nelson A. Miles was appointed to restore calm by doing what no other commander had been able to do—remove Geronimo from the picture.

Miles secretly hoped to become president of the United States some day. He had an excellent reputation as an Indian fighter, partly because of his skill and partly because of his ability to take credit for himself. Miles had little respect for Apaches, thinking of them as ignorant, vicious savages. He would later write about Geronimo, though, that "every movement indicated power, energy, and determination. In everything he did he had a purpose."

Geronimo was naturally suspicious, a trait that had been reinforced by betrayals by Mexico and the United States. What most people underestimated was Geronimo's deep devotion to freedom. Some never understood that it was his love for the nomadic Apache way of life, more than fear or suspicion, that drove him into flight after flight.

Geronimo had a keen economic sense. On more than one occasion, he was able to negotiate good terms of surrender for his people (often not honored), and later he garnered financial proceeds for himself by charging fifty cents to print his name on the bows he made and selling photographs of himself for one dollar. He also loved to gamble. He would bet on anything from horse racing to marksmanship, shouting enthusiastically when he won.

On September 4, 1886, Geronimo made his last surrender to General Miles, who used deceitful tactics to win confidence. Miles promised that upon his surrender, Geronimo would be reunited with his wife and children, who had already been removed to Florida. It was not until 1887, when public opinion began to sway in favor of the Apaches, that Geronimo would see his family again. They were moved to Mount Vernon Barracks in Alabama and from there to what would be their final destination, Fort Sill in Oklahoma.

At Fort Sill, when he would become nervous from the long hours of inactivity, Geronimo would lie on his bed and, in a rich, deep voice, sing songs such as "I fly upon a cloud/ Toward the sky, far, far, far. . . ." In a newspaper interview before his death, he said, "I want to go back to my old home before I die. Tired of fight and want to rest. Want to go back to the mountains again." Geronimo had spent most of his life fighting with great skill and courage for causes most Americans admire—his homeland and his freedom. He conducted raids and killed people, but the number of his victims was almost certainly exaggerated (the governor of Sonora, for example, claimed that in the last five months of Geronimo's career, with the aid of sixteen warriors, he managed to slaughter some five to six hundred Mexicans).

Those who had the pleasure of meeting him would remark on what a loving husband and father he was or note how energetic and kind he appeared. Geronimo died on February 17, 1909, and was buried in the Apache cemetery at Fort Sill, Oklahoma. He never returned to the mountains he loved.

—*Kimberly Manning*

See also Apache; Apache Wars; Cochise; Guadalupe Hidalgo, Treaty of; Mangas Coloradus; Naiche.

BIBLIOGRAPHY

Adams, Alexander B. *Geronimo: A Biography*. New York: G. P. Putnam's Sons, 1971.

Bigelow, John. *On the Bloody Trail of Geronimo*. Los Angeles: Westernlore Press, 1968.

Davis, Britton. *The Truth About Geronimo*. Edited by M. M. Quaife. 1929. Reprint. New Haven, Conn.: Yale University Press, 1963.

Debo, Angie. *Geronimo: The Man, His Time, His Place*. Norman: University of Oklahoma Press, 1976.

Weems, John Edward. *Death Song: The Last of the Indian Wars*. Garden City, N.Y.: Doubleday, 1976.

Wood, Leonard. *Chasing Geronimo: The Journal of Leonard Wood, May-September 1886*. Edited by Jack C. Lane. Albuquerque: University of New Mexico Press, 1970.

Ghost Dance

DATE: Established 1890

TRIBES AFFECTED: Pantribal

SIGNIFICANCE: The Ghost Dance was one of many religious rituals and movements that arose in the wake of European contact in response to permanent changes in traditional lifeways for native peoples

The Ghost Dance began in 1890 as a result of the visions of a Paiute Indian from Nevada called Wovoka. As a result of his visions, Wovoka began delivering a series of prophetic messages that described a future which would restore Native Americans to their life as it had been before contact with the European American settlers and would drive away or destroy the settlers on Native American traditional lands.

Crisis Movements. The Ghost Dance movement is usually described by scholars as an "apocalyptic" or "prophetic"-type movement (borrowing descriptive terms from the study of biblical history). Such movements usually involve someone describing bizarre or frightening visions of a catastrophic change in world events, and these movements are often found among populations who are experiencing severe crisis. These crises can be natural (earthquakes, massive fires, volcanoes) but are more typically associated with political/military conquest by a foreign people who seem strange and overwhelmingly powerful. Such a description clearly fits the experience of Native American tribes who found their lifestyle severely disrupted by the newly arrived settlers. The old way of life, with its familiar routines, was disrupted forever, and the old ways were seen as a "golden age" to which many people wished to return.

Ghost Dance as a Crisis Movement. In the case of the Ghost Dance of 1890, the movement and its widespread popularity are usually attributed to the disastrous disruption of the traditional life of the indigenous populations of North America that came in the wake of European settlement beginning in the sixteenth century. White encroachment had disastrous effects on the native peoples in the West in the nineteenth century. Although the Ghost Dance movement became widespread in 1889-1890, Wovoka had begun having his revelatory visions and experiences in 1887. Also known as John (Jack) Wilson, Wovoka's most influential and serious supernatural experience was, as he himself described it, a visit to the spirit world on the occasion of the total eclipse of the sun on January 1, 1889.

The precise content of the visions of Wovoka and the teachings and implications which he derived from these visions are difficult to describe with confidence, since virtually all existing reports are second- and third-person contacts. The classic source is James Mooney's government-supported study, "The Ghost Dance Religion and the Sioux Outbreak of 1890," published in 1896. This study was conducted within memory of the events described. Mooney, as a white government official, had to interview sources and interpret his reports as best he

could. The major difficulty with this procedure is that the Ghost Dance movement was typically hostile toward white settlers' presence, and one must suspect that reports collected by Mooney would have been delivered in a more conciliatory tone than discussions among Native Americans themselves.

The United States government's interest in the Ghost Dance movement was a direct result of the fact that the message of Wovoka had a very rapid impact that quickly crossed tribal lines. The movement was deeply implicated in the historic massacre of Chief Big Foot's band at Wounded Knee in Pine Ridge, South Dakota. The Ghost Dance was interpreted in different ways in different tribal contexts; it took a relatively militant turn among the Lakota (Sioux) who were active in the movement.

Representatives from many other tribes were sent to hear of Wovoka's revelations, and through these messengers the movement spread widely among the Sioux, the Northern Cheyenne, and the Northern Arapaho. It was also influential on related movements, such as that based on the visionary experiences of John Slocum, a member of the Coast Salish tribe whose own prophetic experiences led to the founding of the Indian Shaker Church.

Wovoka's Visions. Included among the visions of Wovoka, and related by him to his followers and representatives of other tribes, were such basic ideas as the resurrection of tribal members who had died, the restoration of game animals, a flood which would destroy only the white settlers, the necessity and importance of the performance of a dance ritual (the Ghost Dance itself), and a time that is coming which would be free of suffering and disease. Of these major ideas, the primary focus seemed to be on the ideas of resurrection and the restoration of important elements of the old ways, as well as the performance of the dance itself. Related developments of the Ghost Dance movement were certain ethical precepts and, at least among the Sioux, the creation and wearing of distinctive "ghost shirts," which identified adherents to the movement and were used in the performance of the ritual dancing itself.

In Indian descriptions of the Ghost Dance precepts to white researchers such as Mooney, the motif of the destruction of whites was muted, and many interviewees stressed that the visions of Wovoka actually taught a peaceful coexistence with the white settlers. It is certainly possible that ideas varied, depending on the views and experiences of the tribes appropriating the basic message of Wovoka.

Roots of the Ghost Dance. An interesting summary of the Ghost Dance movement that emphasizes the important role of Wovoka himself is provided by Thomas Overholt, who compares Wovoka with certain prophets of the Bible such as Jeremiah. Overholt also suggests that the Ghost Dance of 1890 was preceded by, and possibly influenced by, similar visionary/apocalyptic movements, such as the Ghost Dance of 1870 (which also occurred among the Paiutes, initiated by a visionary named Wodziwob) and the Southern Okanagan Prophet Dance around 1800.

Attempts to trace a prehistory of the Ghost Dance of 1890, however, must also reckon with the very high probability of some influence from the Old Testament biblical prophets through early contact with European missionary teachers. Wovoka himself, for example, did have some contact with missionaries, as reported by Mooney. Yet it is also true that such visionary movements were not uncommon among western American tribes from the beginning of the nineteenth century.

As predicted dates for the cosmic events described by Wovoka came and passed, the initial fervor of the Ghost Dance and Wovoka's teachings in general began to dissipate. Among some tribes, however, the focus shifted from apocalyptic expectations of events to a longer-term stress on daily ethics. In short, the movement became partially institutionalized, which is not uncommon for religious groups whose roots lie in visionary experiences. —*Daniel L. Smith-Christopher*

See also Dances and dancing; Indian-white relations—U.S., 1871-1933; Sioux; Wounded Knee Massacre; Wovoka.

BIBLIOGRAPHY

Bailey, Paul. *Wovoka: The Indian Messiah*. Los Angeles: Westernlore Press, 1957.

Mooney, James. "The Ghost Dance Religion and the Sioux Outbreak of 1890." In *Annual Report of the Bureau of American Ethnology*. Vol 14. Washington, D.C.: Government Printing Office, 1896. Reprint. Chicago: University of Chicago Press, 1965.

Overholt, Thomas. *Channels of Prophecy: The Social Dynamics of Prophetic Activity*. Minneapolis: Fortress Press, 1989.

Wilson, Bryan R. *Magic and the Millennium*. New York: Harper & Row, 1973.

Gifts and gift giving

TRIBES AFFECTED: Pantribal

SIGNIFICANCE: Gift exchange was an essential mode of strategic interaction with other tribes and with the colonial powers

Gift giving was a central feature of exchange customs common to North American Indians. Treaties, trade, and other interactions demanded the distribution of various gifts among the parties. These presents symbolized the social bonds between the participants. Indians presented gifts to make and sustain alliances and to demonstrate continued control to the colonial powers. They used this gift giving to symbolize, sustain, and equalize human relationships. Presents were also given to create and alter social relationships. Other functions of gift giving were to establish an identity, to maintain peaceful interactions, to provide a basis for genuine friendships, to foster an egalitarian social order, and to create an economic order based on the redistribution of wealth.

The European powers were forced to comply with a gift-giving political economy in order to obtain commercial advantages. They presented gifts to guarantee loyalty from tribes and chiefs, to buy service from Indian leaders, to counter influence from rival colonial governments, and to foster trade. In addition, European gift giving served to create kinship ties to important chiefs and to signify respect for Indians.

There were many varieties of items in the gift-exchange economy. Among these items were artifacts such as looms, baskets, textiles, leather goods, and clothing. Plants, animals, shells, skins, food, and medicines were also offered as gifts. In addition, rituals could produce presents of songs, stories, or healing ceremonies. After European contact, commodities such as manufactured goods, rum, brandy, and other products were introduced into the gift-exchange economy.

Gift giving was supplanted by European-style commerce. Gift giving had always been in conflict with commercial economic activity. The Europeans first participated reluctantly in gift exchange to receive commercial advantage. Over time, however, Native Americans were drawn away from gift exchanges and toward commercial exchanges. This resulted in much destruction of their culture. For example, subsistence hunting was replaced with the near extinction of species because of the commercial desire for certain pelts in the fur trade. This commercial activity also countered the community-forming function of gift exchange by bringing Indians into conflict through commercial competition.

See also Money; Potlatch; Trade; Wampum.

Gilcrease, William Thomas (Feb. 8, 1890, Robeline, La.—May 6, 1962, Tulsa, Okla.): Art collector, oilman, civic leader

TRIBAL AFFILIATION: Creek

SIGNIFICANCE: Gilcrease devoted his life to American Indian art and history, gathering a large collection of artifacts, documents, and artwork

Born into the Creek Nation in Louisiana, Thomas Gilcrease moved with his family to Indian Territory as a young boy. Each member of his family received 160 acres of tribally allotted land before Oklahoma was granted statehood. Gilcrease's Indian land allotment was located south of modern Glenpool, Oklahoma's first major oil-producing field. He attended Bacone Indian College at Muskogee by using royalty money. He later transferred to Emporia State College, Emporia, Kansas. Gilcrease, however, was mostly self-educated; his early formal education consisted primarily of intermittent attendance at rural schools in Louisiana and Indian Territory.

In 1922, he organized the Gilcrease Oil Company, later moving to San Antonio, Texas. He had a long-term fascination with learning about, understanding, and collecting Native American art, artifacts, and literature. In the process of satisfying his interest in Native Americans, he also developed a preoccupation with the general collecting of historical Americana.

In 1942, he established the Tulsa-based Gilcrease Foundation, whose corporate charter was "to maintain an art gallery, museum, and library devoted to the preservation for public use and enjoyment the artistic, cultural and historical records of the American Indian." In 1949, a museum was opened and, in 1958, deeded in its totality to Tulsa, Oklahoma. Thomas Gilcrease devoted most of his adult life to his love of art and Indian people. Today the Gilcrease Museum is one of the world's largest repositories of Western art, artifacts, and book collections devoted to North American indigenous peoples.

See also American Indian studies programs and archives.

Gitksan: Tribe

CULTURE AREA: Northwest coast
LANGUAGE GROUP: Tsimshian
PRIMARY LOCATION: British Columbia, Canada
POPULATION SIZE: 4,560 (Statistics Canada, based on 1991 census)

The Gitksan are a tribal group of western-central British Columbia, closely related in language and culture to the Tsimshian, their neighbors to the west. They originally occupied the Skeena River valley; since 1900, however, some have moved into parts of the adjacent Nass river system to the northwest, where they have intermarried with some members of the Nishga, another group closely related to the Tsimshian.

The Gitksan possess many of the same general cultural features of other Northwest Coast groups. They rely on predictable and abundant salmon runs, fish for ocean species such as halibut and cod, and collect shellfish, including several species of clams. The Gitksan also traditionally hunted elk, blacktail deer, beaver, fox and several types of sea mammals (primarily seal).

In general, Gitksan social organization resembles that of other west-central coastal groups. Traditionally they traced descent through the female side (matrilineal descent), but married couples were obligated to reside in or near the house of the groom's parents (patrilocality). Cross-culturally, this is an unusual pattern. Some anthropologists have speculated that the Gitksan, along with other Northwest Coast groups, may have been exclusively matrilineal/matrilocal in the past, but because through time so much wealth and property was being accumulated by males, cultural evolution favored a shift to institutions sanctioning male control over residence and the eventual transference of property through the male line.

On October 23, 1984, the Gitksan, along with other native groups of central-western Canada, filed a land claim for a little more than 35,000 square miles of central British Columbia. In 1991, the Canadian Government decided against the Gitksan. These same groups, along with the Gitksan, subsequently filed an appeal. The Gitksan have also filed for what has been termed "community-based self government." This, in principle, is similar to the autonomy achieved by such groups as the Navajo (Diné) of the southwestern United States. If successful, the Gitksan would have more control over their local economic, political, and social circumstances.

See also Northwest Coast; Tsimshian.

Godfroy, Francis (c. 1788—c. 1840): War chief

TRIBAL AFFILIATION: Miami
SIGNIFICANCE: Godfroy was an ally of Tecumseh during Tecumseh's Rebellion and fought on the side of the British in the War of 1812

Francis Godfroy was born of a French father (Jacques Godfroy) and a Miami mother. He grew up near the present-day site of Fort Wayne, Indiana. He won renown as a war chief and as an ally of Tecumseh in Tecumseh's 1809-1811 attempt to stop white immigration into the Old Northwest. Godfroy was a large, stout man. Late in his life he weighed more than four hundred pounds.

Godfroy allied with the British during the War of 1812, and at one point he commanded a Miami force of three hundred men that routed troops sent against Miamis under the command of William Henry Harrison. With the defeat of the British, Godfroy accommodated the American advance as he moved to the site of his father's former trading post on the Wabash River and became a prosperous trader. He also benefited from grants of cash and land as he signed away much of the Miamis' homelands to the United States.

See also Tecumseh; Tecumseh's Rebellion.

Gold and goldworking

TRIBE AFFECTED: Aztec
SIGNIFICANCE: Using a variety of techniques, Aztec goldworkers produced jewelry, ornaments, and implements of great beauty

Before the Spanish conquest of Mexico in the sixteenth century, Aztec goldsmiths produced gold jewelry and implements of extraordinary beauty. Archaeological evidence suggests that goldworking was introduced from South America into Central America and Mexico relatively late; the Toltec culture was working gold around 900 C.E. Goldworking was not widespread in the pre-Columbian cultures of Mexico; the occasional gold pieces found in Mayan sites, for example, appear to have been the result of trade rather than local manufacture. Aztec goldworkers used gold nuggets or dust, or so-called virgin gold, for their artistry; there is no evidence for the smelting of gold ore in pre-Columbian cultures.

Goldworking was a highly valued skill among the Aztecs. It was a specialized task at the time of the Spanish conquest, with goldsmiths being divided into those who hammered or beat gold and those who cast it in molds; within these divisions, there were many categories of artisans, depending on the kind of work they produced. Gold was used by the Aztecs as a means of tallying tribute obligations; gold also had religious connotations. In the Aztec language, Nahuatl, the word for gold was *teocuitlatl*, or "excrement of the gods." Aztec goldworkers had their own patron god, Xipe Totec; anyone guilty of stealing gold was flayed alive to propitiate this deity.

The first pre-Columbian Mexican goldwork involved shaping nuggets by grinding and hammering them. Later it was discovered that gold dust and grains could be formed into ingots of workable size by fusing them, using a blowpipe to quicken the flame; Aztec drawings show goldworkers using blowpipes. Cold-hammering of gold nuggets or ingots into sheets eventually makes the gold springy and unworkable, but pre-Columbian smiths learned that heating the beaten gold returns its malleability. The process of alternately hammering and heating gold is called annealing, and it was widely used in Mesoamerica to produce not only gold but also various alloys of copper.

Aztec goldworkers also used the "lost-wax" method of working with gold. In this technique, a goldworker first makes a wax model of the desired piece, which is then covered with clay; the wax form is covered with powdered charcoal so that it will release smoothly from the clay mold. Vents are left in the clay to allow the wax to drain from the mold when it is heated. Molten gold is then poured into a vent, and after cooling the mold is broken apart. The lost-wax technique allows for the production of intricate and finely wrought gold jewelry or ornamentation. In addition, Aztec goldworkers learned to solder intricate pieces together using gold alloyed with copper or silver.

No archaeological evidence has yet been able to date precisely the emergence of the various skills in pre-Columbian goldworking. Similarly, no goldworking shop has been discovered or excavated. Detailed descriptions of Aztec goldworking are contained in Spanish historical records, however, along with extensive inventories of golden objects seized by the conquerors. The Spanish were astonished by the volume and value of Aztec gold, much of which they melted down into ingots or reformed into Spanish coins. Yet enough goldwork remains intact from the pre-Columbian and early contact period to testify to the great skill of Aztec goldworkers.

See also Aztec; Dress and adornment; Metalwork; Ornaments; Turquoise.

Gorman, R. C. (b. July 26, 1933, Chinle, Ariz.): Artist
TRIBAL AFFILIATION: Navajo
SIGNIFICANCE: One of the most commercially successful Indian painters, Gorman altered the non-Indian standard of Indian art; he was the first Indian artist to own a gallery

Rudolph Carl Gorman, or R. C. Gorman, has been called the "Picasso of Indian artists," "the Reservation Dali," and "the Vargas of Indian art," but he began life in a hogan during the Depression and herded sheep in Canyon de Chelly. At the private Ganado High School, volunteer teacher Jenny Lind influenced his drawing. After four years in the Navy, he won a scholarship from the Navajo tribe to study at Mexico City College in 1958. The muralists of Mexico profoundly shaped his art. In 1962, he moved to San Francisco and then, in 1968, to Taos, New Mexico, opening his Navajo Gallery. His unconventional paintings rapidly changed the Indian art market starting in 1965.

Apolitical images of strong, large women strolling or sitting, often with a child or pottery, drawn with a single line, are his hallmark. He carried these images into lithographs in 1966, posters in 1975, etchings in 1976, silk-screening, bronze sculpture, and ceramics in 1977, cast paper and glass etching in 1985—while continuing to draw and paint with charcoal and pastels. His work enjoys worldwide sales, and he has established a scholarship fund for Indians. Honors include the first one-man show for an Indian both in Taos and at the Heye Foundation, honorary doctorate degrees, and the Harvard Humanitarian Award in Fine Arts in 1986.

See also Art and artists, contemporary; Navajo.

Gosiute: Tribe
CULTURE AREA: Great Basin
LANGUAGE GROUP: Shoshone
PRIMARY LOCATION: Near Deep Creek, the Great Salt Lake, and Skull Valley, Utah
POPULATION SIZE: 282 ("Goshute Shoshone," 1990 U.S. Census), 416 (1994 Gosiute tribal record)

Historically, the Gosiute (or "Goshute") were a mixed tribe of both Shoshone and Ute heritage; though they spoke Shoshone and were a splinter group of that tribe, Gosiutes often intermarried with Utes. Gosiutes roamed the vast area between Ruby Valley, Nevada, and the Utah Wasatch Mountain Range. Their date of arrival in the area has yet to be established.

Because they resided in a barren, desert region of Utah and Nevada, it is believed that the early Mormon settlers of Utah were the first whites to visit the Gosiutes. The ensuing years, however, witnessed many gold miners passing through Gosiute territory on the overland route to California. During the 1860's, the Pony Express route also crossed Gosiute lands and overland mail stations were erected on that tribe's territory. After the White Pine War of 1875, many Nevada Gosiutes relocated permanently to Deep Creek Utah.

The Gosiute, or "desert people," had only a loose tribal association and two isolated settlements. An 1866 Indian agent described them as "peaceable and loyal." In the rare instances when they fought, it was usually to defend themselves. This peaceful, gathering tribe was more concerned with survival than with war. Gosiutes often roamed in small groups, scouring the desert for meager amounts of food. Men hunted small game, primarily jackrabbits, while women gathered edible plants and fruit. Pine nuts proved to be a favorite food source, and the yearly expedition to gather them was a major event. For cultural activities, Gosiutes participated in the Bear Dance and the Round Dance.

Early in the twentieth century, part of the tribe located on the Skull Valley Reservation in Juab and Tooele counties (Utah), while the other part moved to the Deep Creek Reservation in White Pine County, Nevada. President William Howard Taft allocated the Skull Valley region in 1912 by executive order; two years later, another such order created the Deep Creek Reservation. The tribe adopted and approved its constitution in November of 1940. By the 1990's, less than half of the tribe's members resided on the reservations, since their remote locations provide only low-paying, unstable employment opportunities.

See also Great Basin; Shoshone; Ute.

Gourd Dance
TRIBE AFFECTED: Kiowa
SIGNIFICANCE: Part of a four-day ceremony honoring a Kiowa victory in a major battle

In 1838, the Kiowa defeated the Arapaho and other enemies in a major battle along the Missouri River in Montana. Skunkberry bushes full of red berries covered the battleground. A warrior who became lost after the victory wandered around for days, seeking his people's encampment. Then he heard music coming from a red wolf, who taught him to dance to a beautiful tune accompanied by a gourd rattle. The wolf told him to take the song back to his people and teach them the dance.

The warrior returned, and in celebration of the victory and the return of the lost comrade, a Gourd Dance Society formed and shook red-painted gourds covered with representations of skunkberry bushes while dancing the dance of the red wolf. Only males performed the dance, which featured the dancers, a drummer, a whip man to keep the dancers moving, and a director who set the pace. Skunkberries were a symbol of endurance and bravery, and the Gourd Dance became part of a four-day festival until it was banned by reservation authorities in 1890. In 1955, the Kiowa brought back the dance as part of a newly established Gourd Day celebration taking place on the Fourth of July.

See also Dances and dancing; Kiowa.

Grass, John (c. 1837—May 10, 1918, Standing Rock Reservation, N.Dak.): Tribal leader, diplomat
ALSO KNOWN AS: Pezi (Grass Field), Mato Watakpe (Charging Bear)
TRIBAL AFFILIATION: Teton Sioux
SIGNIFICANCE: John Grass was a diplomat and political leader of the Sioux in their long struggle against the United States
John Grass's English name came from the Dakota "Pezi," meaning "field of grass"; he also was sometimes called Mato Watakpe (Charging Bear). He was a son of Grass, a Sioux leader of the early nineteenth century. He spoke a number of Dakota dialects as well as English, so he was one of few people in the Dakotas who could communicate with nearly everyone else.

In an attempt to break Sitting Bull's influence over the Sioux, Indian Agent Major James ("White Hair") McLaughlin set up Grass, Gall, and other Sioux as rival chiefs to Sitting Bull after the latter had surrendered in 1881. Over the objections of Sitting Bull, Grass signed an agreement in 1889 which broke up the Great Sioux Reservation. He probably was bowing to threats by McLaughlin that the U.S. government would take the land with or without Sioux consent. Even after the land was signed over, the government reduced the food allotments on northern Plains reservations, intensifying the poverty and suffering that helped increase tensions just before the massacre at Wounded Knee in 1890.

For more than three decades, Grass served as head judge in the Court of Indian Offenses of the Standing Rock Reservation. He died at Standing Rock in 1918.

See also Sioux; Sitting Bull.

Grass Dance

TRIBES AFFECTED: Arapaho, Arikara, Assiniboine, Blackfeet, Crow, Gros Ventre, Hidatsa, Iowa, Kansa, Lakota, Menominee, Ojibwa, Omaha, Pawnee, Ponca
SIGNIFICANCE: The Grass Dance is a men's competitive dance believed to give the participants the power to heal burns
The Grass Dance is a men's competitive dance. It may have originated with the Pawnee dance known as the *iruska*. Iruska means "the fire inside of all things." The Pawnee man Crow Feather was given this ceremony of fire-handling and dancing, which confers on participants the power to heal burns. In modern times, the Grass Dance is a part of the dance competition at pow-wows along the summer circuit in the United States. Grass dancers wear grass tied to their costumes. During the dance there is a considerable amount of athletic jumping, bending, and stomping. Dancers perform either individually or in pairs.

Grass Dance societies typically have a number of officers: a leader, a pipe keeper, whip bearers, food servers, drummers, and singers. The Grass Dance has developed a large repertory of drumming and singing sequences. There are music groups among some tribes that specialize in Grass Dance songs. The Grass Dance is regarded not only as a competitive event but also as a celebratory occasion.

See also Dances and dancing; Plains; Pow-wows and contemporary celebrations.

Grass house

TRIBES AFFECTED: Primarily California, Great Basin, and Southwest tribes
SIGNIFICANCE: The grass house was consturcted by covering a pole framework with layers of grass that formed both the walls and roof
There were basically two types of grass house: the conical beehive and the larger, elongated house, which could accommodate several extended families. In wet areas, grass houses were essentially dwellings set on exposed bearing poles several meters off the ground, with a ladder entrance. The beehive structure was formed by running straight or bowed poles to a vertical support center pole or simply by tying the slanted poles together at the apex. The longhouse was also constructed with vertical and horizontal poles.

The grass covering was applied in one of several ways. Most commonly, long grass was bunched, with the top third folded over a horizontal cane or thin wood pole, and tied with grass to the longer outside length; grass was added until the course was completed. The next course would overlap or shingle the lower row, providing, when finished, effective water-shedding. This layering continued to the long, longitudinal ridge pole, where the opposing topmost rows were tied together. Some grass house coverings were better secured by stitching external horizontal willow or cane rods to the internal frame. Because of accumulated smoke residue and general deterioration, grass houses would be rethatched every three to five years, using the original frame.

See also Architecture—California; Architecture—Great Basin; Architecture—Southwest; Wickiup.

Great Basin: Culture area

LANGUAGE GROUPS: Hokan, Numic (Shoshonean)
TRIBES: Bannock, Gosiute, Kawaiisu, Mono (Monache), Numaga (Northern Paiute), Panamint, Paviotso (Northern Paiute), Shoshone, Ute, Washoe
The Great Basin, an area relatively high in altitude, includes all of Nevada and Utah, most of western Colorado, and por-

tions of Idaho, Wyoming, southern Oregon, southeastern California, northern Arizona, and New Mexico. It is a "basin" between two large mountain ranges. Much of the region is steppe or semidesert, but true desert exists in southern Nevada and western Utah. The Great Basin covers an area of some 400,000 square miles, with internal river and stream drainage created by north-south mountain ranges that vary in elevation from 6,000 to 12,000 feet. Nomadic hunting and gathering people successfully inhabited the Great Basin for at least ten thousand years, and their ways of life remained relatively unchanged until European American incursion.

Language. All native speakers within the Great Basin, except the Hokan-speaking Washoe, are members of one of three Numic languages (western, central, or southern Numic), a division of the Uto-Aztecan language family of northern Mexico. The term "Shoshonean" is commonly used in referring to Numic-speaking groups of the Great Basin.

Technology and Subsistence. Depending on elevation and time of the year, vegetation types in the Great Basin vary greatly, with many plants of economic significance (such as creosote, various sagebrush, rice grass, and wheatgrass) found at lower elevations. In the higher elevations, the major seed tree is the piñon, which provided a so-called iron ration—its nuts and seeds are nutritious and store well.

The main food-obtaining activities of these highly mobile desert culture groups were hunting, gathering, and gleaning, strategies that required a relatively simple but effective multi-purpose technology. Their annual subsistence round (annual migration pattern for exploiting various food sources) was based on obtaining the plant and animal resources that occurred at various elevations in different locations at regular times of the year. The major source of calorie intake was plants, which made up 70 to 80 percent of the diet of Basin peoples. In early spring, lettuce, spinach, wild potatoes, onions, rhubarb, and numerous rhizomes and shoots were collected. In late summer, a variety of seeds, berries, and medicines were collected, often while deer hunting. Seeds from mustard, salt brush, rabbitbrush, sand grass, and other plants were stored for winter. After a killing frost, women gathered tules.

The men hunted deer, antelope, elk, mountain sheep, rabbits, hares, gophers, lizards, snakes, mice, sage hens, and rats. Even insects, such as crickets, locusts, ants, and grasshoppers (which are 74 percent protein), were collected in great amounts. In some areas, larvae would accumulate in large mounds on beaches, and these were dried and stored in baskets or grass-lined pits for winter consumption.

Hunting was often done by individuals (rather than groups) using sinew-backed bows; in these instances the ability to stalk was more important than marksmanship. Rabbits and insects, however, were hunted in large collective drives that forced game into bush barriers, where they were killed. On occasion, secondary harvesting became necessary, as when seeds were taken from stores by rats or squirrels. Seeds could be collected from human feces and then roasted and ground into food.

Some areas of the Great Basin had lakes that were fished in late May and early June for large sucker and trout, using various technologies including torch-fishing, wide-mouth baskets,

Northern Paiute (Paviotso) women gathering barley in baskets; basketry was highly refined among Great Basin groups. (R. H. Lowie, American Museum of Natural History)

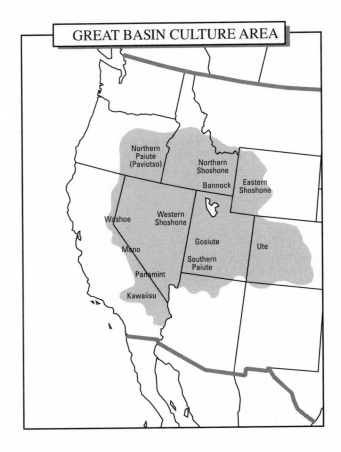

GREAT BASIN CULTURE AREA

harpoons, and drag and dip nets. After removing the roe from some species, the fish were split and air-dried for future use.

Social Systems. In the absence of complex technology, the maintenance of a highly mobile and flexible social structure was critical as a "tool" in effectively exploiting the environment. The principal sociopolitical group in the Great Basin was the mobile and flexible extended family, or kin clique, which was self-sufficient and remained fairly isolated throughout the year. Families were nonlineal and bilateral-based. Similar in some ways to the Plateau Indians, groups were essentially egalitarian, and decisions were based on consensus of opinion. Leadership was frequently temporary, based on one's skill, though more sedentary groupings had a headman, a "talker," who kept his group informed of the condition and occurrence of food resources. This person encouraged cooperation and group tranquillity by resolving interpersonal conflicts.

Polygyny was not common, and it was usually sororal polygyny. The levirate and sororate were recognized, usually to intensify kin unions. There was some cross-cousin marriage. A significant division of labor by gender and age increased the group's adaptive efficiency and tended to reduce conflict.

Belief Systems. Great Basin religion, not as complex as those of most other culture areas, was basically individualistic, though at certain times of the year the people were concerned

with collective rituals to ensure world renewal, availability and redistribution of resources, and sociopolitical tranquillity. The dominant religious practitioner was the shaman, either male or female, who had acquired a tutelary spirit and power for curing, hunting, gambling, and other concerns through dreaming or the vision quest. Curing shamans were concerned primarily with treating illness, which was considered the result of taboo violation, a ghost, or spirit or object intrusion by a sorcerer. Shamans were skilled in ventriloquism and legerdemain, possessed songs, and had an impressive array of sacred items. Usually people did not seek power, as power was feared; its possession was considered dangerous, since it could impose considerable strain on the individual and could bring on accusations of sorcery.

A primary individual religious concern was the avoidance and placation of ghosts and theriomorphic forms that inhabited an area if a person's burial was hastened or improperly conducted, or if any number of moral transgressions were committed by the living. The afterlife was considered an enjoyable place, one of bountiful resources, dancing, games, and gambling.

—*John Alan Ross*

See also Architecture—Great Basin; Arts and crafts—Great Basin; Hokan language family; Hunting and gathering; Prehistory—Great Basin.

Bibliography

Arkush, Brooke S. "The Great Basin Culture Area." In *Native North Americans: An Ethnographic Approach*, edited by Daniel L. Boxberger. Dubuque, Iowa: Kendall/Hunt, 1990.

D'Azevedo, Warren L., ed. *Great Basin*. Vol. 11 in *Handbook of North American Indians*. Washington, D.C.: Smithsonian Institution Press, 1990.

Fowler, Catherine S. "Subsistence." In *Great Basin*, edited by Warren L. D'Azevedo. Vol. 11 in *Handbook of North American Indians*. Washington, D.C.: Smtihsonian Institution Press, 1986.

Steward, Julian H. *Basin-Plateau Aboriginal Sociopolitical Groups*. Bureau of American Ethnology Bulletin 120. Reprint. Salt Lake City: University of Utah Press, 1970.

Stewart, Omer C. "The Basin." In *The Native Americans*, edited by Robert F. Spencer, Jesse D. Jennings, et al. New York: Harper & Row, 1965.

_____. "Culture Element Distributions: XIV, Northern Paiute." *University of California Anthrolopolgical Records* 4 no. 3 (1941): 361-446.

_____. "Culture Element Distributions: XVII, Ute-Southern Paiute." *University of California Anthrolopolgical Records* 6, no. 4 (1942): 231-355.

Great Sun (?—c. 1730): Tribal leader

Tribal affiliation: Natchez

Significance: The Great Sun who is known to history was the leader of the Natchez Revolt of 1729

Among the Natchez, "Great Sun" was the hereditary title bestowed upon the tribe's principal chief. The Great Sun who was the head of the tribe in the early eighteenth century had to face the problems that resulted when the French began to settle along the lower Mississippi River. He was the brother of Tattooed Serpent and the son of Tattooed Arm.

The Great Sun's family was strongly pro-French, but when Tattooed Serpent died, the anti-French faction began to gain influence. Trouble ensued when the governor of Louisiana demanded the Great Sun's village site for a plantation; the Great Sun refused, and the governor demanded payment in the form of crops. On November 30, 1729, Natchez warriors attacked French settlements along the Mississippi and inflicted more than five hundred casualties. French and Choctaw forces soon recaptured the main French fort (Fort Rosalie), and the captured Great Sun agreed to a peace. He escaped, however, and fought against French forces again in 1730. Again overpowered, he surrendered and was probably executed, perhaps in New Orleans. In the aftermath of the revolt, the tribal identity of the Natchez was destroyed.

See also Natchez; Natchez Revolt; Prehistory—Southeast.

Green Corn Dance

TRIBES AFFECTED: Cherokee, Creek (Muskogee), Seminole, others in Southeast culture area
SIGNIFICANCE: This was the principal dance performed in the most important harvest ceremony of the southeastern tribes

Dance is a central component of Native American ceremonial life. Nowhere is this more evident than in the Eastern Woodland Green Corn Rite. Ritual dance is an important feature of this ceremony, which takes place in July or August at the final corn harvest. The Green Corn Dance is a necessary part of the planting of the corn. Great spiritual benefit is believed to derive from the performance, which occurs in the newly cleaned and sanctified town square. The square contains the sacred fire, which binds the community to their deceased and to their deity. Into the newly kindled fire, such items as new corn, tea leaves, meat, and medicine are offered.

As it is presently performed in the Southeast, the dance has four stages, each of which is divided into various movements. Music includes the sounds of stone-filled gourd rattles as well as singing. Men and women, in their finest attire, dance separately but simultaneously around a high pole adorned with green boughs that provide shade for the musicians seated on benches below.

First the men begin to dance. A leader followed by a column of ten to twenty men carrying guns circles counterclockwise in an area a few hundred yards from the town square. The leader sings and plays a rattle while the other men shoot their guns at various times. The first man in the column shoots first, then the second, and so on until the last man, who shoots twice. By shaking his rattle, the leader thus directs the shots. The rifle shots are supposedly symbolic of the sound of thunder. This men's part of the dance takes place in the morning. At about noon participants break to eat food that the women have provided.

The women dance in a single line and side by side in the main square. They are directed by a woman leader who uses leg rattles to keep time. This second stage of the dance performance symbolizes the fertilization of corn. Men come to the central square and combine with the women's column, led by the men's dance leader. All the men and women then commence to circle counterclockwise. After this portion of the dance, the whole community takes part in a feast.

In the evening, the third stage of the dance begins. The men and the women are again separate, as in the beginning. The men carry guns and circle counterclockwise around the women. This movement continues until the sun sets. The fourth stage is done the next night, accompanied by animal sacrifices.

At the conclusion of the Green Corn Ceremony, the individual, the family, the clan, and the nation are all renewed for another year.

See also Cherokee; Corn; Corn Woman; Creek; Dances and dancing; Southeast.

Gros Ventre. *See* Atsina

Guadalupe Hidalgo, Treaty of

DATE: February 2, 1848
PLACE: Southwest
TRIBES AFFECTED: All tribes in the areas of present-day California, Nevada, and Utah, and much of Arizona, Colorado, and New Mexico
SIGNIFICANCE: This treaty ended the Mexican-American War; in it, Mexico ceded to the United States about half its national territory, and the ramifications for native peoples in the ceded territory were profound

The Mexican-American War and the treaty that ended it were largely the result of Manifest Destiny, the theory used to justify American acquisition of both Indian and Mexican territory. President James K. Polk, a leading advocate of Manifest Destiny, was the most important figure in the Mexican-American War and the peace negotiations that followed. In Mexico chronic instability caused by the struggle between the various political parties and leaders made waging war and negotiating peace difficult and made preserving the peace impossible.

Tension between the United States and Mexico had been increasing in the years preceding the war. Mexico was aware of, and feared, the Polk Administration's desire to annex New Mexico and California. The United States was pressing claims against Mexico, and the Texas boundary dispute was becoming more critical. After fighting broke out in the disputed area along the Rio Grande, the United States declared war. Attempts to negotiate peace before and during the war were unsuccessful. Mexico saw no advantage in it, and the United States hoped to occupy more territory.

As a result of its military success, the United States was able to make acquisition of New Mexico and California a condition of peace. Polk chose Nicholas P. Trist as peace commissioner in April, 1847, and gave him a draft of a treaty which called for the cession of Alta and Baja California and New

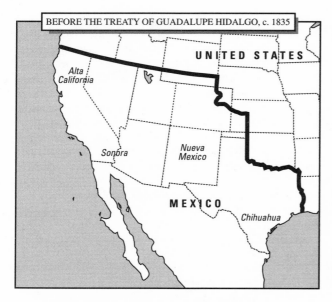

BEFORE THE TREATY OF GUADALUPE HIDALGO, c. 1835

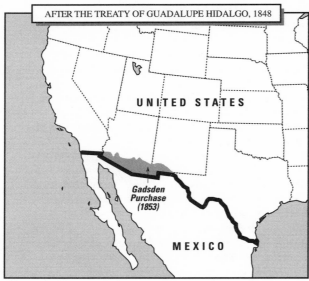

AFTER THE TREATY OF GUADALUPE HIDALGO, 1848

treaty was signed on February 2, 1848, in Guadalupe Hidalgo, and ratification was exchanged on May 30, 1848, in Mexico City.

Although Articles IX and X guaranteed the political and property rights of Mexican citizens and Indians in the territory transferred to the United States, the Indians of California did not receive citizenship, nor were their property rights protected. As a result of violence and other factors such as disease, the Indian population declined by 100,000 within two decades. In New Mexico Territory the Indians were placed under federal protection and denied citizenship, but they did not lose their lands. Citizenship was granted to the Indians in 1869, and reservations were later created.

See also Indian-white relations—U.S., 1831-1870; Land claims; Voting rights—United States.

Guale: Tribe

CULTURE AREA: Southeast
LANGUAGE GROUP: Muskogean
PRIMARY LOCATION: Georgia coast

These maritime and river-oriented people were divided into northern, central, and southern groups occupying numerous permanent villages connected by language, marriage, and trade. They had a diversified subsistence base that included horticulture, hunting, gathering, and fishing.

First contact with European Americans (with a Spanish colony) occurred in 1526. Soon the Spanish drove the French from Florida and began to occupy Guale territory. By 1597, French Jesuits were active among these people; they created a Guale grammar. The Franciscans had established a mission in 1573, but by 1597 all but one missionary had been killed. In retaliation, the governor of Florida had many Guale villages and granaries burned and destroyed, thereby bringing the Guale under Spanish control by 1601. Guale opposition to missionization continued, however, resulting in many of the Guale moving inland or to the islands of San Pedro in 1686. Facing continual conflict, the Guale fled to the Creek, who had united for the 1715 Yamasee War, among whom they lived in two missions near St. Augustine.

Guardian spirits

TRIBES AFFECTED: Pantribal
SIGNIFICANCE: According to a belief held by many American Indian cultures, an individual may obtain contact with the supernatural world by seeking a guardian spirit to serve as a personal guide and protector

For many American Indians, the concept of a guardian spirit was most commonly associated with the natural world through the visible representation of animals or birds, such as the bear, wolf, or eagle. The particular association of a guardian spirit with a certain animal was the result of either ancestral ties (most typical of the Northwest Indians), the personal vision quest (common among Plains Indian tribes), inheritance (more typical of the Indians of the Southwest and Mexico), or, least often, transference or purchase.

Mexico, the right of transit across the Isthmus of Tehuantepec, the Rio Grande as the Texas border, and a payment to Mexico of $15 million plus the assumption of claims of United States citizens against Mexico.

Opposition quickly developed in both Mexico and the United States to the proposed treaty. Mexico did not want an imposed peace, and the United States envisioned better terms. When Trist negotiated a peace unacceptable to Polk, the president recalled Trist. Trist remained in Mexico, however, and finally negotiated a modified treaty that Mexico accepted because of financial problems and fear of additional losses if war continued. The possibility of a successful revolution in Mexico added urgency to the peace process.

The United States dropped its demand for transit across the isthmus and agreed to stop Indian raids across the border. The

In the Northwest the guardian spirit of the clan is represented in the totem. The clan members obtain protection from the clan totem at the puberty ceremony. The totem can also become a guardian spirit offering personal as well as communal protection. Totem poles depict the guardian spirit of the ancestral father and other figures from the natural and supernatural world.

Guardian spirits may also be obtained through a vision quest ritual in which the individual seeks a vision of the guardian spirit in a secluded place. At its appearance, the guardian spirit gives the individual some kind of special capacity and a medicine bundle to be used in hunting rituals. The vision quest is usually preceded by fasting, a sweatlodge experience and bathing, and a preparatory ascetic style of living. The spirit generally appears as an animal, but not in form and shape identical to a natural animal. An individual may cause the guardian spirit to depart if any taboos are violated, and not everyone who seeks a guardian spirit through the vision quest receives one. The vision quest is still practiced today, although not for hunting purposes in the way it was practiced prior to European contact.

Guardian spirits had the most significance among the hunting tribes because they helped in providing game during the hunt. It was taboo to eat the animal represented by the guardian spirit. Agricultural tribes of the Southwest and Mexico relied more on a variety of spirits for assistance in regard to fertility cycles and typically did not seek a personal guardian spirit, believing that one had already been received at birth. Boys more often than girls sought a guardian spirit, and obtaining a guardian spirit was often done as a puberty rite directly relating to future hunting success.

An American Indian's relationship to his or her guardian spirit is personal and intimate, expressed physically by wearing the fur, claws, or feathers of the spirit and symbolically by incorporating the animal's name into his or her own. The shaman or medicine man was often believed to be able to change into his guardian spirit.

See also Bundles, sacred; Peyote and peyote religion; Puberty and initiation rites; Religion; Religious specialists; Sand painting; Sun Dance; Totems; Visions and vision quests.

Guns

TRIBES AFFECTED: Pantribal

SIGNIFICANCE: Guns obtained from Europeans altered patterns of intertribal warfare and Indian-white warfare as well as traditional native economies

The introduction of guns by European traders and settlers powerfully reshaped American Indian patterns of warfare, intertribal politics, and economic life. Early seventeenth century muskets had a much greater effective range than traditional bows, and they inflicted more lethal wounds. Warriors armed with bows were easily defeated by smaller numbers of Europeans armed with guns. As Indians along the Atlantic coast learned of the effectiveness of the unfamiliar weapons in war and in hunting, they eagerly traded furs, the native commodity Europeans chiefly sought, to obtain them.

Tribes situated along the coast became middlemen in the exchange of European goods for furs from tribes in the interior. As tribes trapped out the beaver or other animals in their own territories, they made war on less well-armed neighbors to take possession of their hunting grounds, so that guns and the accompanying fur trade created an entirely new and more deadly source of intertribal warfare. The mid-seventeenth century destruction of the Huron Confederacy by the better-armed Iroquois is the best-known example. The trade in furs and skins for guns and other European goods disrupted the traditional subsistence economies of Indian peoples, making them dependent on the Europeans, but no one could risk ignoring the new weapons. Guns spread steadily into the interior, reaching the Great Plains in the early nineteenth century. Armed with guns, Indians became a far greater military threat to Europeans.

See also Beaver Wars; Bows, arrows, and quivers; Tomahawks; Warfare and conflict; Weapons.

Hagler (c. 1690, S.C.—Aug. 30, 1763, S.C.): Tribal chief
ALSO KNOWN AS: Haiglar
TRIBAL AFFILIATION: Catawba
SIGNIFICANCE: Hagler was the most significant of the eighteenth century Catawba chiefs; he established peace with the white colonists and unified his people

From the time of first contact with the English, the Catawba Indians conferred the title of king on their chiefs. No date is established for Hagler's birth, but it is known that he was murdered August 30, 1763, by Shawnee warriors. It is assumed that, following the death of chief Young Warrior in 1749, Hagler became leader of the Catawbas. Though Catawba chiefs were elected and served with a tribal council, both Young Warrior and Hagler were absolute in their rule.

The Catawbas and other tribes warred constantly during the first half of the sixteenth century. This constant conflict was considered a threat by whites, and in 1750 Governor DeWitt Clinton of New York called for a meeting of Indian nations in Albany, New York. Hagler and five headmen sailed from Charles Town on May 23, 1751, and arrived in New York on May 30. The negotiations in New York were successful, and the Catawbas returned to the South believing a permanent peace was at hand. Their optimism was short-lived, however: Within two years, tribes from the north were making forays into Catawba territory, taking property and attacking people.

The Cherokees also continued to attack the Catawbas. By 1759, Hagler expressed solidarity with the white people against the Cherokees. He and forty other Catawbas served in the "Indian Corps" of an army commanded by Captain Quentin Kennedy and fought in the second Battle of Etchoe. It is clear that it was the alliance forged by Hagler with white South Carolinians that enabled the Catawbas to survive.

The greatest enemy of the Catawbas, though, was smallpox. Warriors brought the disease to the tribe when they returned from Fort Duquesne. Hagler survived by having his own encampment separate from the tribe. He was able to keep the tribe together, and by 1787 the Catawbas were the only organized Indian tribe in South Carolina.

Hagler was very much opposed to alcohol and the harm it seemed to be doing to his people. In 1754 he attended a "treaty"—a time to list grievances between whites and Indians. There, he told the white state authorities that they were to blame for the illness and crime among his people by making and selling strong drink to them. This speech has been referred to as "the first temperance lecture in the Carolinas." Though an absolute ruler, Hagler was concerned for the welfare of his people—even demanding that the white community provide food for them. He also had a keen sense of justice, as evidenced by the return of stolen property and his punishment of Catawbas for crimes against the whites.

In 1760 the Catawbas, ravaged by smallpox, were moved to Pine Tree Hill. Hagler and his headmen negotiated a treaty which provided a 15-square-mile tract of land for the Catawbas. A fort was built for security, and the friendship with whites continued.

In 1763, Hagler was returning home to Twelve Mile Creek with a slave when he was shot six times by a party of seven Shawnee. The slave escaped and told the story. Following the murder, the Catawbas were so taken with grief and enmity that they perpetrated atrocities against the Shawnee. One of the murderers was captured with a group of Shawnees. He was hacked to death; the others were beaten senseless with hickory switches and then given over to the young Catawba boys for target practice. The scalps were presented to the South Carolina governor, who told the warriors to give them to their Catawba boys so they would be brave men. He told the party, "We loved King Hagler because he was a friend to the English and we are glad that the man that killed him was killed by the Catawbas." Hagler was buried with his personal possessions, including a silver-mounted rifle, gold, and other items of value. His grave was robbed less than a month after his death.

See also Catawba.

Haisla: Tribe
CULTURE AREA: Northwest Coast
LANGUAGE GROUP: Wakashan
PRIMARY LOCATION: Gardner Canal, British Columbia coast
POPULATION SIZE: 955 (Statistics Canada, based on 1991 census)

The technology of the Haisla and their annual migration pattern reflected their dependence upon fish. Women gathered shellfish and various types of berries and fruits. The basic social units were five matrilineal exogamous clans, each with territorial rights; they formed alliances for ceremonial purposes. Haisla society was ranked into nobles, commoners, and slaves. Numerous ceremonies existed; the potlatch was important for redistribution of traditional wealth and recognition of status change.

Contact was made by Juan Zayas in 1792, and again the following year by Joseph Whidbey of the George Vancouver expedition. Hudson's Bay Company established a fur-trading post at Fort McLoughlin in 1833 near Dean Channel. Breakdown of traditional culture began to occur after the arrival of Christian missionaries in 1833. Government banning of potlatches and dancing societies brought further breakdown of Haisla culture. In 1916, the Haisla had fourteen reserves with 1,432 allotted acres. By the mid-twentieth century, many Haisla were working in the fishing and logging industries, but by the 1970's, a shift had occurred, and working in aluminum smelting had become the primary source of income.

See also Northwest Coast.

Hako
TRIBES AFFECTED: Plains tribes, especially Pawnee
SIGNIFICANCE: The hako ceremony symbolizes the transferral of life forces from generation to generation

The word *hako*, which means "pipe" in the Wichita language, has been applied to a number of Indian ceremonies that center on the use of feather-ornamented hollow shafts of wood. In some general but not fully accurate descriptions, hako is deemed to be synonymous with the easily recognized calumet, or pipe ceremony, popularly associated with the "peace pipe." In the early twentieth century writings of American ethnologist Alice C. Fletcher, however, who is still recognized as the first authority on hako, the much broader cultural symbolism suggested by the Pawnee term *hakkwpirus*, or "beating [in association with] a breathing mouth of wood," is apparent.

Early Observations. Feather-decorated pipe ceremonies that could be considered prototypes of what Fletcher and her associates studied under the general label of hako were first observed, but not fully understood, in the last quarter of the seventeenth century by the French Jesuit Jacques Marquette among the Illinois tribes. Similar traditions appeared in ceremonies practiced by Algonquian and Siouan peoples. Very little was known about the specialized symbolic content of hako, however, until Fletcher carried out and published, in 1906, what remains the most extensive fieldwork on the subject. The ceremonies she described reflected the traditions of Plains Indians in particular.

Fletcher must have encountered a high degree of secrecy among the Omahas, where she first observed hako ceremonies during the 1880's. After failing over a number of years in her efforts to learn the meaning behind the Omaha ceremonies, she turned to the Pawnees, where a Chawi tribal holy man, Tahirussawichi, gave her essential explanations and some ceremonial texts. The latter were eventually translated with the assistance of her main Pawnee assistant, James Murie.

Meanings of the Ceremony. Before considering the hako ceremony itself, a description of the central "breathing mouth of wood" and accompanying ritual objects is essential. Usually the wood used (two pieces) consisted of stems three or four feet in length with burned-out piths to allow the passage of breath. One stem was painted blue to represent the sky. A long red groove symbolizing life stood for the path that would be symbolized in several phases of the ceremony. Ceremonial wood was always decorated with feathers on the forward tip to "carry" communications associated with hako. As in more general Indian belief systems, the brown eagle in particular is believed to have the power to soar to the domain of higher powers in the sky. Other forces were represented in the attachment of the breast, neck, and mandibles of a duck to the downward (earthward-pointing) end of the hollowed stem. The duck symbolized daily familiarity with all elements affecting life: land, water, and sky. A second white eagle-feathered stem, called *Rahaktakaru* (to contrast it with *Rahakatittu*, the "breathing mouth of wood with dark moving feathers"), was painted green for the earth. Its position in the hako ceremony was always different from its brown-feathered counterpart. The unconsecrated nature of the white eagle, and thus Rahaktakaru's association with the male father, warrior, and defender, kept it separate from two other symbolic elements of hako, namely the mother and the children. The former, the giver of fruit and abundance, was represented by an ear of white corn (*atira*, or mother breathing forth life), with a blue-painted tip (the sky, dwelling place of the powers) from which four blue-painted strips, or "paths," allowed powers to descend to join the red (life) grooves of the Rahakatittu.

Unlike many Indian ceremonies, hako was not associated with a particular seasonal activity, such as planting, harvesting or hunting. As a ceremony celebrating life, it could occur at any time when signs of life were stirring, either in mating (spring), nesting (summer), or flocking (fall), but not during winter dormancy. In a hako ceremony there is always a symbolic position reserved for participants representing the "parents" and a second reserved for the "children." The latter are traditionally from a group that is distinct from the host, or parent group. This element underlines the universality of the union of otherwise distinct groups in that all benefit from the cycle of life.

Journey of Mother Corn. Hako ceremonies symbolize a journey taken by Mother Corn leading from the place of origin in the group or tribe of the fathers to a destination in the group or tribe of the children. The importance of the "breathing mouth of wood" bearing the power of the brown eagle feathers is that it allows Mother Corn to attain the blue-domed abode of the powers before redescending to the ceremonial lodge. When the journey is concluded, Mother Corn will seek out the son, who is considered the paramount representative of the children. Successful conclusion of Mother Corn's passage symbolizes assurance of safe passage of life's bounty from one generation to another.

The songs accompanying the ceremony describe various stages in the arrival and reception of Mother Corn in the village, and then in the lodge of the son. After a song proclaiming her arrival, the tribe's chief stands at the doorway to the ceremonial lodge holding Mother Corn. He is flanked by the Ku'rahus (spiritual "headman") and his assistant, holding the brown eagle-feathered stem and the white eagle-feathered stem, respectively. As the son receives the bounty represented by Mother Corn, the central power image is the stem bearing the brown eagle feathers. Fletcher's 1906 description of the meaning of the stem's power is poignant: "*Kawas* [the brown eagle] has the right to make the nest and seek help from *Tira'wa* [the heavens] for the children." A following stanza describes kawas' flight inside the receiving lodge itself, the flapping of its sacred feathers driving out evil influences before a nest is made.

Overall the ceremony is intended to ask for the gift of children and sustenance for the next generation, as well as for a firm bond between the parent and child. It also can symbolize the wish for peace and prosperity between those bearing the sacred objects and those who receive them. Hence, hako is associated with a ceremony of peace between tribes, one representing the fathers, the other the children.

It is important to note that, although there is always a point in the hako ceremony for the offering of smoke to Tira'wa, and therefore the use of a ceremonial calumet, this aspect is not as important as the "true" symbol of the pipe in the ceremony, which is tied to the two "breathing mouths of wood" bearing the eagle feathers.

—*Byron D. Cannon*

See also Calumets and pipe bags; Corn Woman; Feathers and featherwork; Murie, James; Pawnee.

BIBLIOGRAPHY

Driver, Harold E. *Indians of North America*. 2d ed., rev. Chicago: University of Chicago Press, 1969. A general guide that can be used to compare forms of symbolism that place Hako in a broader cultural context.

Fletcher, Alice C. *The Hako: A Pawnee Ceremony*. Twenty-second Annual Report to the Secretary of the Smithsonian Institution. Washington, D.C.: Bureau of American Ethnology, 1904. This original work remains the most extensive description of Hako.

_____. "A Pawnee Ritual Used When Changing a Man's Name." *American Anthropologist*, n.s. 1 (1899): 82-97. Shows ways in which Hako symbolism extends to other realms.

Murie, James. *The Ceremonies of the Pawnee*. Smithsonian Institution Contributions to Anthropology 27. Washington, D.C.: Smithsonian Institution Press, 1979. General coverage, by Fletcher's primary assistant, of rituals that occur among the same tribes that practiced the "model" hako ceremony.

Half-King (c. 1700, near Buffalo, N.Y.—Oct. 4, 1754, Harrisburg, Pa.): Tribal chief

ALSO KNOWN AS: Tanacharison

TRIBAL AFFILIATION: Oneida

SIGNIFICANCE: Half-King joined the British forces during the French and Indian War

Half-King, or Tanacharison, was one of a number of Iroquois who lived in the Ohio Valley area during the eighteenth century. Some of these Iroquois, who were often called "Mingos" by the whites, had been delegated power from the Iroquois Grand Council to conduct diplomacy with local tribes. The whites called such delegates "half-kings," so the designation was more a title than a personal name.

Tanacharison, born a Catawba, was captured at an early age and reared as a Seneca near the eastern shore of Lake Erie. Tanacharison was a valued ally of the British in the French and Indian War, and held councils with several officials, including Conrad Weiser, George Croghan, and a young George Washington, who was serving in his first combat situation. Tanacharison fought as an ally of Washington in the Battle of Great Meadows (1754), the opening salvo of the final British war with the French in North America, which ended in 1763. As a result of this battle, in which Tanacharison killed at least one French officer, Washington surrendered Fort Necessity to the French.

Tanacharison later moved to Aughwick (now Harrisburg), Pennsylvania, where he died of pneumonia in 1754.

See also Indian-white relations—English colonial; Indian-white relations—French colonial; Oneida.

Hamatsa

TRIBES AFFECTED: Kwakiutl

SIGNIFICANCE: The Hamatsa, or Cannibal Dance, is intended to inspire fear and awe in the audience

The Hamatsa, a dance performed by the Kwakiutl of British Columbia, Canada, is used primarily to induct novice shamans into the Hamatsa Society. Their membership in this society assures them of higher status as community healers. The Hamatsa dance is also occasionally performed at ceremonial potlatches.

The Hamatsa or "cannibal," is the central figure of the dance. Before each performance, a fire is lit in a large ceremonial plank house. After the fire has burned down to coals and the proper mood has been established, the dance begins. Through repetitive arm gestures, shuffling of the feet from side to side, exaggerated and contorted facial expressions, and manipulations of the eyes, the Hamatsa dancer attempts to instill a sense of fear and awe in the audience. The skill of a Hamatsa dancer is measured by the reactions of people in the audience. If they seem uneasy and spellbound, the dance is considered successful.

The dance roughly follows the story of a "wild" or "unkept" cannibal who lives in the forest and occasionally comes near villages to devour unsuspecting children. It is interesting to note that although most Kwakiutl dances require the use of masks, they are not typically employed by Hamatsa dancers because so much of the effect of the dance relies on the improvisational use of facial contortions. To embellish the role of a wildman, the dancer's face must be visible.

Researchers who have worked with the Kwakiutl have speculated about the underlying functions of the dance. Some have suggested that it reaffirms a basic symbolic separation between things that are well-ordered, such as village life, and things that represent disorder, such as the forest. Thus, the Hamatsa theme might reinforce cultural values for village and societal togetherness, and at the same time point to what can happen if those values are neglected.

See also Kwakiutl.

Han: Tribe

CULTURE AREA: Subarctic

LANGUAGE GROUP: Athapaskan

PRIMARY LOCATION: Yukon River, both sides of U.S./Canadian border

POPULATION SIZE: 495 (Statistics Canada, based on 1991 census)

The three autonomous, wealth-oriented, matrilineal Han clans subsisted primarily upon fishing, supplementing their diet by hunting, trapping, and a limited amount of gathering. They lived in riverine villages, in semi-subterranean dwellings, and in domed skin houses when hunting and traveling; on water they used birchbark canoes and moose-skin boats.

At the time of their first contact with European Americans and the establishment of Fort Yukon in 1847, the Han were already influenced by European trade goods. The purchase of Alaska in 1869 by the United States brought white trapper-traders and gold miners who, through trade, diminished Han dependency upon traditional hunting and fishing subsistence by encouraging trapping and a cash economy, therefore making the Han dependent upon European American material culture. From 1919 to 1925, the Han suffered from epidemics of mumps, influenza, and measles.

Today many Han live in the Indian village at Eagle; they are seasonally employed in road construction, trapping, government positions, and firefighting. Few traditional skills remain, though some beading, birchbark baskets, and snowshoes are manufactured, mostly for sale. The Han are now predominantly Episcopalians.

See also Athapaskan language family.

Hancock (fl. early 1700's): Tribal chief

ALSO KNOWN AS: King Hancock
TRIBAL AFFILIATION: Tuscarora
SIGNIFICANCE: Hancock led his tribe in North Carolina's bloody Tuscarora War against white settlers

Little is known about Hancock except that, in 1711, he ordered his tribe to retaliate for the abusive treatment of his people at the hands of the English colonists in the Carolina colony. The tribe was located primarily in eastern North Carolina, in the rich and fertile lands along the Roanoke, Tar, Pamlico, and Neuse rivers. Population estimates put their numbers at about five thousand during Hancock's reign.

Throughout the first two decades of the eighteenth century, the Tuscaroras were abused by English settlers in the Carolinas. Slave traders raided their settlements and settlers took their most fertile lands away from them. The colonists' most incendiary act occurred in 1711, when more than four hundred Swiss colonists under the command of the opportunistic Baron Christoph Von Graffenried drove a number of families off a large tract of Indian land. Hancock ordered retaliatory raids throughout eastern North Carolina, which led to Von Graffenreid's capture and the death of the colony's surveyor-general, John Lawson, author of the famous narrative *A New Voyage to Carolina* (1709). The raids escalated so that the war involved the Coree, Pamlico, and Machapunga tribes as well as the Tuscarora. Nearly 140 settlers, mostly Swiss, died in the initial attacks.

In 1712, North and South Carolina sent a combined force under the leadership of Colonel John Barnwell against Hancock, destroying his main village of Cotechney. Hancock finally agreed to a peace plan, which was quickly broken by the colonists. Tuscarora raids began again. Hancock fled to Virginia with a considerable supply of booty but was captured by a band of Tuscaroras who remained allied to the whites. The chief was turned over to colony officials and executed.

In 1713, Colonel James Moore of South Carolina, with one thousand Indian allies, attacked the remaining Tuscarora force and quickly overcame them. To finance the campaign, Moore ordered all Tuscarora prisoners, about four hundred, to be sold into slavery. Survivors fled north and joined their Iroquoian brethren in New York. The Tuscaroras were formally accepted as the sixth Iroquois nation in 1722.

See also Indian-white relations—English colonial; Tuscarora.

Hand games

TRIBES AFFECTED: Pantribal
SIGNIFICANCE: Hand games were an important source of entertainment; they were used by shamans to dramatize their magic and by storytellers to illustrate important events

Native Americans played a wide variety of hand games, primarily for entertainment and for developing and displaying skill and dexterity. Hand games were frequently the basis of different games of chance and even gambling, and both genders and all ages participated. Children were encouraged in hand games at an early age, to help them develop hand-eye coordination. The more common hand games were jackstraws, stick games, basket dice, tops, ball juggling, four stick, tip cat, hidden ball/object, pebble games, ring and pin, shell game, whirling game with hemp, dice games, and cat's cradle.

Shamans used special hand games that involved legerdemain (sleight of hand), to demonstrate the user's religious power during curing rituals or prophesying. Skilled shamans could make game objects "speak" using ventriloquism, implying that the game had its own power or spirit. These special hand game objects were "fed" and sung to by their owners. Elders and skilled storytellers employed certain hand games to illustrate or dramatize events in creation stories or mythological accounts. Gifted hand game players frequently acquired status, and during winter confinement they would be called upon for entertainment.

See also Children; Games and contests.

Handsome Lake (c. 1735, Canawaugus Village on the Genessee River near Avon, N.Y.—Aug. 10, 1815, Onondaga, N.Y.): Religious leader

ALSO KNOWN AS: Kaniatario, Ganeodiyo
TRIBAL AFFILIATION: Seneca
SIGNIFICANCE: Handsome Lake was the founder of the Longhouse religion, widely practiced among the Iroquois

Handsome Lake was the Seneca (Iroquois) prophet whose visions became the basis for the Longhouse religion, or the *Gaiwiio*, the Good Word. This Seneca traditional religious movement is still practiced in Canada, New York, and Oklahoma, where the Seneca people are concentrated. Handsome Lake was born at the Seneca village, Canawaugus, near Avon, New York. He was a recognized Seneca chief. His first vision occurred in 1799.

In June, 1799, Handsome Lake was seriously ill and fell unconscious. He reported having a vision during this state. In this vision he saw three men holding berry bushes, who then offered berries to Handsome Lake. The berries had a healing effect, and as he recovered, he began to talk with the men. It was understood that there was one man missing, a fourth whom Handsome Lake later identified with the Great Spirit, who would come again at a later time. During his conversations with the three men, Handsome Lake heard them condemn alcoholism, pronounce a death sentence on a witch, and condemn witchcraft generally. Handsome Lake himself was told not to drink anymore. Furthermore, he was given to understand that his sins were not unforgivable and that he was to teach his people the proper way to live.

Handsome Lake had many such visions after the initial one, and over more than sixteen years of activity, a code of teachings was gathered and became a part of Seneca oral tradition. The code, which sounds very similar to apocalyptic biblical visions such as those found in the books of Daniel and Revelation, includes descriptions of heaven and hell. It involves a conversation between Handsome Lake and a being who describes what Handsome Lake is seeing and verifies its important message. Among the more significant of the visions of Handsome Lake are his reports of punishments in hell for specific sins, such as stinginess, alcoholism, witchcraft, promiscuity, wife-beating, gambling, and quarrelsome family relations. Each of these sins was associated with a particularly graphic punishment in hell.

The religious visions of Handsome Lake were the basis for a nearly complete transformation in the religion and practice of the Seneca. By the Civil War (1861), nearly all Seneca considered themselves members of either a Christian church or the Longhouse religion, and many considered active participation in both to be acceptable. The Longhouse religion of Handsome Lake was similar to other prophetic movements, such as Wovoka's and John Slocum's.

See also Longhouse religion; Slocum, John; Wovoka.

BIBLIOGRAPHY

Handsome Lake. *The Code of Handsome Lake.* Edited by Arthur C. Parker. Albany: University of the State of New York, 1913.

Wallace, Anthony F. C. *Death and Rebirth of the Seneca.* New York: Alfred A. Knopf, 1973.

_____, ed. "Halliday Jackson's Journal to the Seneca Indians, 1798-1800." Part 1. *Pennsylvania History* 19, no. 2 (1952): 117-147.

_____, ed. "Halliday Jackson's Journal to the Seneca Indians, 1798-1800." Part 2. *Pennsylvania History* 19, no. 3 (1952): 325-349.

Hare: Tribe

CULTURE AREA: Subarctic
LANGUAGE GROUP: Athapaskan
PRIMARY LOCATION: Northwestern Canada
POPULATION SIZE: 1,180 (Statistics Canada, based on 1991 census)

The Hare, or Kawchittine, Indians inhabited a large portion of northwestern Canada. The Hare were unique in that they depended almost entirely on the snowshoe hare for subsistence. Though a few other large animals and fish were consumed, there were not enough caribou and moose in the area they occupied to support the tribe. Because of the limited amount of game available to them, Hare Indians regularly suffered periods of starvation until as recently as 1920. They were required to travel great distances in search of food. Their relatively small population of 700-800 people covered more than 45,000 square miles of very diversified territory.

Hare Indians hunted large game with bows and arrows as well as with spears. Trout and whitefish were captured with nets and hooks; snowshoe hare were captured in snares. Food was smoked, dried, or frozen for winter storage. The Hare used birchbark and spruce canoes for water transportation, and snowshoes for winter travel. Women dragged toboggans to transport food and family possessions. Snowshoe hare skins were woven into blankets and capes. Caribou skins were used for pants, shirts, and mittens. Families lived in tipis covered with moss for insulation.

Hare Indians placed a high value on sharing and believed in the importance of dreams. Dreams were thought to predict their future and help them make important life decisions. Medicine men were said to receive their powers from spirits, whom they called to summon game and identify the proper native medicine to use on the ill.

Though the Hare traded with local Indian tribes who visited Europeans, direct contact between Hare and non-Indians did not occur until the late 1800's. They quickly became involved in the fur trade in order to obtain western wares. "Trading chiefs" emerged within the tribe to lead expeditions to local forts. Epidemic diseases devastated the Hare several times during the nineteenth century. In 1921, they agreed to give up their lands to the Canadian government in exchange for medical and educational services. In the mid-1940's, fur prices declined, forcing many Hare into wage labor jobs in the local oil refinery. Native practices disappeared as the population became more urbanized. It is difficult to determine population figures for the Hare Indians today, as many have intermarried with other Indian groups. Many Hare descendants now consider themselves Slave (Slavey) or Bearlake Indians. There are several Hare Indians at Fort Good Hope and Colville Lake, but population figures represent several Indian tribes.

See also Athapaskan language family; Hudson's Bay Company; Slave; Subarctic.

Harjo, Joy (b. May 9, 1951, Tulsa, Okla.): Poet

TRIBAL AFFILIATION: Creek
SIGNIFICANCE: Joy Harjo has published poetry, written screenplays, lectured, and taught in creative writing programs; she is also a jazz musician and artist

After study at the Institute of American Indian Arts in Santa Fe, New Mexico, Joy Harjo finished a B.A. degree at the University of New Mexico and an M.F.A. at the University of Iowa. Teaching positions include the Institute of American Indian Arts, University of Colorado, University of Arizona, and University of New Mexico. She is active in the National Association for Third World Writers; honors include fellowships from the National Endowment for the Arts and the Arizona Commission on the Arts. She has two children, Phil and Rainy Dawn.

Harjo's poetry has won many honors. *In Mad Love and War* (1990) received the William Carlos Williams Award of the Poetry Society of America, the Delmore Schwartz Memorial Poetry Prize, and the PEN Oakland Josephine Miles Award.

Earlier works also received praise: *She Had Some Horses* (1983) and *What Moon Drove Me to This?* (1979). In 1989 she collaborated with Stephen Strom, writing text to accompany photographs in *Secrets from the Center of the World*. Harjo's creative work is infused with sensitivity to suffering and a strong belief in the power of generosity and love to overcome distrust and enmity. She honors those she deems warriors in battles against discrimination, poverty, cruelty, and destructiveness. Her poetry embraces the natural world and draws images, often dreamlike, from the iconography of native traditions.

Harper, Elijah (b. Mar. 3, 1949, Red Sucker Lake, Manitoba, Canada): Politician
TRIBAL AFFILIATION: Cree
SIGNIFICANCE: Harper, the only native member of the Manitoba Legislative Assembly, blocked the adoption of the Meech Lake Accord in June, 1990, because it failed to mention native peoples

Elijah Harper was born on the Red Sucker Lake Reserve in Manitoba, Canada, on March 3, 1949, and educated at the University of Manitoba. From 1975 to 1977 he served as an analyst and legislative assistant to the minister of northern affairs. He served as Chief of the Red Sucker Lake Reserve from 1978 until his election to the Manitoba Legislative Assembly in 1981 as its sole native member, representing the northern riding (district) of Rupertsland. Reelected as a New Democratic Party candidate in 1986, 1988, and 1990, he served as minister of native affairs from 1986 to 1988.

Harper became a national hero to Canada's native peoples by delaying consideration of the Meech Lake Accord in the Assembly, thus blocking its adoption as Canada's constitution in 1990. Holding an eagle feather for spiritual strength, he quietly refused the necessary unanimous consent required for introduction of the accord because it made no mention of aboriginal peoples. He was awarded the Stanley Knowles Humanitarian Award in 1991 and was elected to the House of Commons as a member of the Liberal Party in 1993.

See also Cree; Department of Indian Affairs and Northern Development (DIAND); Indian Act of 1989 (Canada); Indian-white relations—Canadian; Meech Lake Accord.

Harris, LaDonna (b. Feb. 15, 1931, Temple, Okla.): Activist
TRIBAL AFFILIATION: Comanche
SIGNIFICANCE: Harris has been an outspoken leader in the fight for native rights and an advocate of native self-determination

LaDonna Harris was born to a Comanche mother and an Irish American father. Reared by her grandparents, she spoke only Comanche until she started school. The mother of three, her husband is Fred Harris, former United States senator from Oklahoma.

Harris has been a leader in the fight for the rights of underrepresented people and for social reform, serving as one of the first members of the National Women's Political Caucus in the 1970's. During the 1972 takeover of the Bureau of Indian Affairs building by the American Indian Movement (AIM) in Washington, D.C., Harris supported AIM by staying a night with the demonstrators. She actively protested the U.S. government policy of terminating Indian tribes and tribal lands and has been instrumental in forming coalitions involving native people and organizations, such as Oklahomans for Indian Opportunity.

Harris founded Americans for Indian Opportunity (AIO) in 1970 in Washington, D.C., and serves as executive director of AIO, which promotes economic self-sufficiency for indigenous people and supports self-determination projects for native people at the local, national, and international levels. She has been appointed to various national boards, including that of the National Organization for Women.

See also Activism; American Indian Movement (AIM).

Havasupai: Tribe
CULTURE AREA: Southwest
LANGUAGE GROUP: Yuman
PRIMARY LOCATION: Northern Arizona
POPULATION SIZE: 547 (1990 U.S. Census)

The Havasupai ("People of the Blue-Green Water") live in the village of Supai, located in a side canyon of the Grand Canyon of the Colorado River. They are related to the Hualapai tribe now located in Peach Springs, Arizona, and they have a long history of trading with the Hopis to the east and having their storehouses raided by the Apaches to the south. The Havasupai are noted for their basketry.

For at least six centuries they have lived in the summer at the bottom of a narrow side canyon growing corn, melons, and other crops on small farms watered by a large spring just above their village. In winter they ranged out along the south rim of the Grand Canyon hunting deer and other animals as far south as the present-day locations of Williams and Flagstaff, Arizona.

The United States government officially restricted them to a tiny reservation in Havasu Canyon in 1882, and during the 1920's white ranchers forced them off their winter hunting grounds on the surrounding plateau. The cliff-shaded canyon was an inhospitable place in the winter, lacking firewood and subject to flash floods. Three hundred people were crowded onto about 518 acres. The Bureau of Indian Affairs closed their small elementary school in 1955, forcing all students to attend boarding schools, and started a formal program of relocation the following year.

In the 1970's under the new government policy of Indian self-determination, things began to improve for the Havasupai. On January 3, 1975, Public Law 93-620 was signed by President Gerald Ford, giving back some of the plateau to the Havasupai. In the same year they took over the management of their elementary school.

As of 1995, students still needed to go to Bureau of Indian Affairs boarding schools in California or Arizona to attend high school. The village had electricity and telephone service, but by choice there was still no road to the village. Supai in

1995 was accessible only by helicopter, walking, or riding a mule or horse down an 8-mile trail. While the Havasupai still practiced a small amount of irrigation farming, the economy was based on running a campground, motel, store, and restaurant for tourists visiting the scenic waterfalls a few miles from the village.

See also Southwest; Yuman language family.

Hayes, Ira Hamilton (Jan. 12, 1923, Bapchule, near Sacaton, Ariz.—Jan. 24, 1955, Bapchule, Ariz.): U.S. Marine

TRIBAL AFFILIATION: Pima

SIGNIFICANCE: Hayes was one of the men photographed raising the flag of the United States on Iwo Jima during World War II

Ira Hayes was born in the small village of Bapchule, near Phoenix, Arizona. His parents were members of the Presbyterian church at Bapchule, where Ira spent his childhood and youth, and he also had friends in the local Catholic church.

Before he was twenty years old, Ira joined the Marines, and he was soon sent to serve in the Pacific theater during World War II. The turning point in Hayes's life occurred when he was discovered to be one of the servicemen in the famous photograph recording the flag-raising on Iwo Jima Island.

After the war and his discharge from military service, Hayes was in demand as a speaker (or token presence) at patriotic gatherings and in the media. He knew that he was being exploited as a patriotic icon even as the Pima people and other Indians were suffering discriminatory treatment, and he spoke out against mistreatment of Indians whenever he could. As a single individual, however, he could not accomplish much. With limited education, it was difficult for Hayes to find work, and he struggled throughout his life with alcoholism. His last job was picking cotton at three dollars per hundred pounds. Shortly after his thirty-second birthday, he was found dead of exposure in a field not far from his birthplace.

See also Pima.

Ira Hayes as a paratrooper in the Marines in 1943. (National Archives)

RR AMERICAN INDIANS

LIST OF ENTRIES BY CATEGORY

ARCHAEOLOGICAL SITES

Awatovi
Aztalan
Bat Cave
Cahokia
Canyon de Chelly
Chaco Canyon
Chichén Itzá
Copan
Cuello
Danger Cave
El Tajín
Emerald Mound
Etowah
Key Marco
Koster
La Venta
Lehner
Mesa Verde
Middens
Midland
Mitla
Monte Albán
Oaxaca
Ozette
Palenque
Poverty Point
San Lorenzo
Snaketown
Spiro
Tenochtitlán
Teotihuacán
Tikal
Tres Zapotes
Tula
Uxmal
Veracruz
Yaxchilan

ART AND ARCHITECTURE

Adobe
Appliqué and ribbonwork
Architecture—Arctic
Architecture—California
Architecture—Great Basin
Architecture—Northeast
Architecture—Northwest
   Coast
Architecture—Plains
Architecture—Plateau
Architecture—Southeast
Architecture—Southwest
Architecture—Subarctic
Art and artists, contemporary
Arts and crafts—Arctic
Arts and crafts—California
Arts and crafts—Great Basin
Arts and crafts—Northeast
Arts and crafts—Northwest
   Coast
Arts and crafts—Plains
Arts and crafts—Plateau
Arts and crafts—Southeast
Arts and crafts—Southwest
Arts and crafts—Subarctic
Beads and beadwork
Chickee
Earthlodge
Grass house
Hogan
Igloo
Lean-to
Longhouse
Mosaic and inlay
Paints and painting
Petroglyphs
Pit house
Plank house
Pueblo
Quillwork
Sculpture
Shells and shellwork
Symbolism in art
Tipi
Totem poles
Turquoise
Wattle and daub
Wickiup
Wigwam

BELIEFS AND RELIGION

Bundles, sacred
Corn Woman
Ethnophilosophy and
   worldview
Guardian spirits
Kachinas
Kivas
Kuksu rituals and society
Longhouse religion
Manibozho
Maru Cult
Medicine bundles
Medicine wheels
Mother Earth
Native American Church
Peyote and peyote religion
Praying Indians
Quetzalcóatl
Religion
Religious specialists
Sacred narratives
Sacred, the
Sand painting
Shaker Church
Totems
Tricksters
Visions and vision quests
Windigo
Witchcraft and sorcery

CEREMONIES, DANCES, AND FESTIVALS

Bladder Festival
Booger Dance
Buffalo Dance
Chantways
Dances and dancing
Death and mortuary
   customs
Deer Dance
False Face Ceremony
Feast of the Dead
Feasts
Ghost Dance
Gourd Dance
Grass Dance
Green Corn Dance
Hako
Hamatsa
Husk Face Society
Midewiwin
Midwinter Ceremony
Morning Star Ceremony
Okeepa
Potlatch
Pow-wows and contemporary
   celebrations
Puberty and initiation rites
Rite of Consolation
Rites of passage
Shaking Tent Ceremony
Shalako
Snake Dance
Spirit Dancing
Stomp Dance
Sun Dance
Tobacco Society and Dance
White Deerskin Dance

CONTEMPORARY LIFE AND ISSUES

Activism
African American—American
   Indian Relations
Alcoholism
American Indian studies
   programs and archives
Amerind
Art and artists, contemporary
Certificate of Degree of
   Indian Blood
Civil rights and citizenship
Councils, tribal
Courts, tribal
Diseases, post-contact
Education, post-contact
Employment and
   unemployment
Federally recognized tribes
Gambling
Guns
Indian police and judges
Land claims
Medicine and modes of
   curing, post-contact
Pan-Indianism
Pow-wows and contemporary
   celebrations
Ranching
Relocation
Reservation system of the
   United States
Reserve system of Canada
Resources
Stereotypes

Suicide
Tribe
Urban Indians

Voting rights—Canada
Voting rights—United States
Water and water rights

White Paper of Canada
Winnebago Uprising
Wolf Mountains, Battle of
Wounded Knee Massacre

Wounded Knee occupation
Yakima War
Yamasee War

CULTURE AREAS

Arctic
California
Great Basin
Northeast
Northwest Coast

Plains
Plateau
Southeast
Southwest
Subarctic

DRESS AND ADORNMENT

Beads and beadwork
Dress and adornment
Feathers and featherwork
Headdresses
Moccasins

Ornaments
Quillwork
Shells and shellwork
War bonnets

HISTORICAL EVENTS

Acoma, Battle of
Adobe Walls, Battles of
Alcatraz Island occupation
Apache Wars
Articles of Agreement
Bacon's Rebellion
Bannock War
Bear River Campaign
Beaver Wars
Black Hawk War
Bozeman Trail wars
Cayuse War
Cherokee Tobacco case
Cherokee War
Creek War
Declaration of First Nations
Fallen Timbers, Battle of
Fifteen Principles
Fort Mims, Battle of
French and Indian Wars
Gadsden Purchase
Kickapoo Resistance
Kickapoo uprisings
King Philip's War
Little Bighorn, Battle of the
Lone Wolf v. Hitchcock
Long Walk
Longest Walk
Lord Dunmore's War
Manhattan
Meech Lake Accord
Meriam Report
Minnesota Uprising
Modoc War

Natchez Revolt
Navajo War
Nez Perce War
Northwest Ordinance
Pavonia Massacre
Paxton Riots
Peach Wars
Pequot War
Pima uprisings
Pine Ridge shootout
Pontiac's Conspiracy
Powhatan Wars
Proclamation of 1763
Public Law 280
Pueblo (Popé's) Revolt
Red River War
Riel Rebellions
Rosebud Creek, Battle of
Sand Creek Massacre
Saybrook, Battle of
Seminole Wars
Sioux uprisings
Snake War
Tecumseh's Rebellion
Termination policy
Texas Rangers
Thames, Battle of the
Tippecanoe, Battle of
Trail of Broken Treaties
Trail of Tears
Wabash, Battle of the
Wagon Box Battle
Walla Walla Council
Washita River, Battle of the

INDIAN-WHITE RELATIONS

American Indian
Captivity and captivity
  narratives
Indian
Indian Territory
Indian-white relations—
  Canadian
Indian-white relations—
  Dutch colonial
Indian-white relations—
  English colonial
Indian-white relations—
  French colonial
Indian-white relations—
  Norse
Indian-white relations—
  Russian colonial
Indian-white relations—
  Spanish colonial
Indian-white relations—
  Swedish colonial

Indian-white relations—
  U.S., 1775-1830
Indian-white relations—
  U.S., 1831-1870
Indian-white relations—
  U.S., 1871-1933
Indian-white relations—
  U.S., 1934-1995
Journalism
Keetoowah Society
Missions and missionaries
Native American
Oregon Trail
Patents
Railroads
Removal
Santa Fe Trail
Sovereignty
Trading posts
Wild west shows

LANGUAGES

Algonquian language family
Atakapa language family
Athapaskan language family
Beothuk language
Caddoan language family
Chitimacha language
Coos language
Eskimo-Aleut language
  family
Hokan language family
Iroquoian language family
Karankawa language
Keresan language family
Kiowa-Tanoan language
  family
Kutenai language

Language families
Muskogean language family
Na-Dene language family
Penutian language family
Salishan language family
Sign language
Siouan language family
Syllabaries
Timucua language
Tonkawa language
Tunica language
Uto-Aztecan language family
Wakashan language family
Yakonan language family
Yuman language family
Zuni language

LEGISLATION

Alaska Native Claims
  Settlement Act
American Indian Civil
  Rights Act
American Indian Religious
  Freedom Act

Burke Act
General Allotment Act
Indian Act of 1876 (Canada)
Indian Act of 1951 (Canada)
Indian Act of 1989 (Canada)
Indian Child Welfare Act

Indian Citizenship Act
Indian Education Acts
Indian Removal Act
Indian Reorganization Act
Indian Self-Determination and
    Education Assistance Act

Navajo Rehabilitation Act
Navajo-Hopi Land Settlement
    Act
Oklahoma Indian Welfare Act
Trade and Intercourse Acts

ORGANIZATIONS

Alaska Native Brotherhood
    and Alaska Native
    Sisterhood
All-Pueblo Council
American Indian Defense
    Association (AIDA)
American Indian Higher
    Education Consortium
    (AIHEC)
American Indian Movement
    (AIM)
American Indian Policy
    Review Commission
Bureau of Indian Affairs
    (BIA)
Carlisle Indian School
Council of Energy Resource
    Tribes (CERT)
Department of Indian Affairs
    and Northern Develop-
    ment (DIAND)
Determined Residents United
    for Mohawk Sovereignty
    (DRUMS)
Friends of the Indian
    organizations

Hudson's Bay Company
Indian Arts and Crafts Board
    (IACB)
Indian Claims Commission
    (ICC)
Indian Rights Association
Institute of American Indian
    Arts (IAIA)
International Indian Treaty
    Council (IITC)
Keeler Commission
National Congress of
    American Indians (NCAI)
National Council of American
    Indians
National Indian Association
National Indian Youth Council
    (NIYC)
Native American Church
Native American Rights Fund
    (NARF)
Society of American Indians
    (SAI)
Women of All Red Nations
    (WARN)

PERSONAGES

Adair, John L.
Adario
Alford, Thomas Wildcat
Allen, Paula Gunn
American Horse
Annawan
Antonio, Juan
Apes, William
Arapoosh
Arpeika
Asah, Spencer
Atotarho
Auchiah, James
Awa Tsireh
Bad Heart Bull, Amos
Banks, Dennis
Barboncito
Bear Hunter

Bear's Heart, James
Big Bear
Big Bow
Big Foot
Big Tree
Big Warrior
Black Elk
Black Hawk
Black Kettle
Blacksnake
Bloody Knife
Blue Eagle, Acee
Bonnin, Gertrude Simmons
Boudinot, Elias
Boudinot, Elias Cornelius
Bowl
Bowlegs, Billy
Brant, Joseph

Brant, Molly
Bronson, Ruth Muskrat
Bruce, Louis R.
Buffalo Hump
Bull Bear
Bushyhead, Dennis Wolf
Campbell, Ben Nighthorse
Canonchet
Canonicus
Captain Jack
Catahecassa
Charlot
Chisholm, Jesse
Cloud, Henry Roe
Cochise
Colorow
Comcomly
Conquering Bear
Copway, George
Cornplanter
Cornstalk
Crashing Thunder
Crazy Horse
Crazy Snake
Crow Dog
Crowfoot
Curly
Curtis, Charles
Datsolalee
Decora, Spoon
Deer, Ada Elizabeth
Deganawida
Dekanisora
Delaware Prophet
Delgadito
Deloria, Ella Cara
Deloria, Vine, Jr.
Delshay
Dodge, Henry Chee
Dohasan
Donnaconna
Dozier, Edward Pasqual
Dragging Canoe
Dull Knife
Eastman, Charles Alexander
Erdrich, Louise
Eskiminzin
Flat Mouth
Foreman, Stephen
Francis, Josiah
Francis, Milly Hayo
Gall
Ganado Mucho
Garakontie, Daniel
Garra, Antonio
Garry, Spokane

General, Alexander
Geronimo
Gilcrease, William Thomas
Godfroy, Francis
Gorman, R. C.
Grass, John
Great Sun
Hagler
Half-King
Hancock
Handsome Lake
Harjo, Joy
Harper, Elijah
Harris, LaDonna
Hayes, Ira Hamilton
Heat-Moon, William Least
Hewitt, John N. B.
Hiawatha
Hogan, Linda
Hokeah, Jack
Hole-in-the-Day
Hollow Horn Bear
Hooker Jim
Hopocan
Howe, Oscar
Howling Wolf
Hump
Hunt, George
Ignacio
Inkpaduta
Irateba
Isatai
Ishi
Isparhecher
Johnson, Emily Pauline
Jones, Peter
Joseph the Younger
Journeycake, Charles
Kamiakin
Katlian
Kennekuk
Keokuk
Kicking Bear
Kicking Bird
Klah, Hosteen
Konkapot, John
La Flesche, Francis
La Flesche, Susan
La Flesche, Susette or Josette
Lame Deer
Lawyer
Lean Bear
Left Hand the First
Left Hand the Second
Little Crow
Little Priest

PREHISTORIC CULTURE

TRADITIONAL LIFEWAYS

Iowa	Molala	Potawatomi	Tohono O'odham
Iroquois Confederacy	Moneton	Powhatan Confederacy	Tolowa
Juaneño	Montagnais	Pueblo tribes, Eastern	Toltec
Kalapuya	Montauk Confederacy	Pueblo tribes, Western	Tonkawa
Kalispel	Mountain	Puyallup	Tsetsaut
Kamia	Muckleshoot	Quapaw	Tsimshian
Kansa	Multnomah	Quechan	Tubatulabal
Karankawa	Nabedache	Quileute	Tunica
Karok	Nanticoke	Quinault	Tuscarora
Kaska	Narragansett	Salinan	Tuskegee
Kawaiisu	Naskapi	Salish	Tutchone
Kichai	Natchez	Samish	Tutelo
Kickapoo	Nauset	Sanpoil-Nespelem	Tututni
Kiowa	Navajo	Sarsi	Twana
Klamath	Neutral	Sauk	Tyigh
Klikitat	Nez Perce	Sekani	Umatilla
Koyukon	Niantic	Semiahmoo	Umpqua
Kutchin	Nipissing	Seminole	Ute
Kutenai	Nipmuck	Seneca	Waccamaw
Kwakiutl	Nisqually	Seri	Waco
Lake	Nooksack	Serrano	Walapai
Lenni Lenape	Nootka	Shasta	Walla Walla
Lillooet	Nottaway	Shawnee	Wampanoag
Luiseño	Ocaneechi	Shinnecock	Wanapam
Lumbee	Ofo	Shoshone	Wappinger
Lummi	Ojibwa	Shuswap	Wappo
Mahican	Okanagan	Siletz	Wasco
Maidu	Olmec	Sioux	Washoe
Makah	Omaha	Siuslaw	Wenatchi
Maliseet	Oneida	Skagit	Wichita
Manahoac	Onondaga	Slave	Winnebago
Mandan	Osage	Snohomish	Wintun
Massachusett	Oto	Snoqualmie	Wishram
Mattaponi	Ottawa	Sooke	Wiyot
Mattole	Paiute, Northern	Spokane	Yahi
Maya	Paiute, Southern	Squamish	Yakima
Menominee	Palouse	Suquamish	Yamasee
Methow	Pamlico	Susquehannock	Yana
Metis	Passamaquoddy	Swallah	Yaqui
Miami	Patwin	Tahltan	Yaquina
Micmac	Pawnee	Tanaina	Yavapai
Missouri	Pennacook	Tanana	Yazoo
Miwok	Penobscot	Tenino	Yellowknife
Mixtec	Pequot	Thompson	Yokuts
Mobile	Petun	Tillamook	Yuchi
Modoc	Pima	Timucua	Yuki
Mohawk	Pomo	Tiou	Yurok
Mohegan	Ponca	Tlingit	Zapotec
Mojave	Poospatuck	Tohome	